Corporate Responsibility Coalitions

This book is an indispensable guide to the role played by business-led coalitions in generating and disseminating socially responsible business practices. Written by two seminal figures in the field, it provides a comprehensive overview of what these coalitions have, and have not, achieved in aligning markets with the broader goals of social and environmental sustainability. It points to what needs to happen next if we are to get from here to there. Highly recommended for all who care about these issues – and everyone should!
John Ruggie, Berthold Beitz Professor in Human Rights and International Affairs, Harvard Kennedy School of Government

I learned new things from this interesting and thorough review. Corporate responsibility coalitions are globally important: this book covers comprehensively the past, the present, and the challenges for their future.
Sir Mark Moody-Stuart, Chairman, Global Compact Foundation

Corporate Responsibility Coalitions both captures the richness and diversity of a unique social movement as well as offering an exciting future vision of what more these coalitions could do. Anyone interested in the role that business can play to help tackle global problems will study carefully the agenda for action.
Dame Julia Cleverdon DCVO, CBE, Vice President, Business in the Community, UK

David Grayson and Jane Nelson's *Corporate Responsibility Coalitions* lifts up a much-overlooked aspect of business coalitions as a critical feature of the evolving role of business in society. While providing a rich history of the development of these coalitions and in-depth case examples, the book's real value lies in its analysis of what is driving these coalitions at this point in time, and the potential they have in resetting corporate responsibility in the era ahead. *Corporate Responsibility Coalitions* opens up some new thinking about the role of business, and coalitions' collective opportunity to co-create shared innovation just in time to provide the business community with a potent instrument for building sustainable business.
Bradley Googins, Former Director, Boston College Center for Corporate Citizenship; Senior Visiting Fellow, Deusto University, Business School Bilbao, Spain

Corporate responsibility coalitions play a vital role in helping businesses like ours accelerate the pace of change and engage our employees in sustainability. Responsible business is not just a moral imperative; it is essential to be a part of the solution, and core business engagement is fundamental to retain our license to operate.
Francesco Vanni d'Archirafi, CEO, Citi Transaction Services

Corporate Responsibility Coalitions is an important and necessary read for those who lead, practice, teach, and influence corporate behavior. David Grayson and Jane Nelson tell a story that too few know: the story of corporate-led coalitions and the role they played and continue to play in redefining the role of business in society. It is a story of social innovation at its best. Our future depends on understanding the complex relationships and breakthrough interactions that allowed the environmental and social gains over the last 30 years to be realized. Understanding these powerful coalitions and learning as much as we can from them will be essential in creating a more just and sustainable world.
Cheryl Y. Kiser, Executive Director, The Lewis Institute & Babson Social Innovation Lab, Office of the President, Babson College

Two of the most experienced practitioners in the field have compiled a 40-year survey of business-led coalitions – now numbering some 110 – that promote corporate social responsibility. With a panoramic overview of the field, covering the past, surveying the present, and setting an agenda for the future, this comprehensive volume makes the case for collective business action and a "coalition methodology" as an effective means for tackling some of the world's most challenging problems. In-depth profiles of 12 of these coalitions document impact and lessons learned as well as potential paths forward. An invaluable resource for anyone interested in the collaborative aspects of CSR.
Steve Lydenberg, Founding Director, Initiative for Responsible Investment, Harvard Kennedy School of Government

This is a challenging book. It reveals companies voluntarily cooperating to promote sustainability and ethical behavior. It thus throws out a challenge to our simple economic models, which treat companies as myopic profit maximizers. This "counterfactual" study deserves debate amongst economists everywhere.
David Pitt-Watson, Founder and Former Chair, Hermes Equity Ownership Service

Jane Nelson and David Grayson have been part of the vanguard of corporate social responsibility for decades. In this book they explore collective business action and wrestle with critical questions of leadership, governance, and resource mobilization. We should all applaud their extraordinary thought leadership and contribution to this field.
Michele Kahane, Professor of Professional Practice, Milano School of International Affairs, Management and Urban Policy

CORPORATE RESPONSIBILITY COALITIONS

THE PAST, PRESENT, AND FUTURE OF ALLIANCES FOR SUSTAINABLE CAPITALISM

David Grayson and **Jane Nelson**

Greenleaf
PUBLISHING

Published in the USA by
Stanford University Press
Stanford, California

Library of Congress Cataloging-in-Publication Data

Grayson, David, 1955- author.
    Corporate responsibility coalitions : the past, present, and future of alliances for sustainable capitalism / David Grayson and Jane Nelson.
        pages cm
    Includes index.
    "Published simultaneously in the UK by Greenleaf Publishing Limited"--Title page verso.
    Includes bibliographical references and index.
    ISBN 978-0-8047-8524-2 (cloth : alk. paper)
    1. Social responsibility of business. 2. Coalitions. I. Nelson, Jane, 1960- author. II. Title.
    HD60.G72 2013
    658.4'08--dc23

                                    2012043673
ISBN 978-0-8047-8710-9 (electronic)

Published simultaneously in the UK by
Greenleaf Publishing Limited
Aizlewood's Mill
Nursery Street
Sheffield S3 8GG
www.greenleaf-publishing.com

British Library Cataloguing in Publication Data:
    A catalogue record for this book is available from the British Library.
        ISBN-13: 978-1-906093-81-5 (hardback)
        ISBN-13: 978-1-907643-56-9 (electronic)
Cover by LaliAbril.com

Printed in Great Britain on acid-free paper by
CPI Group (UK) Ltd, Croydon, CR0 4YY

Time present and time past
Are both perhaps present in time future,
And time future contained in time past.
T.S. Eliot, *Burnt Norton*

Dedicated to the memory of our good friend and colleague,
outstanding social entrepreneur and visionary
Robert Davies
(1951–2007)
Founding CEO, The International Business Leaders Forum
Former Deputy CEO, Business in the Community
Friend, Mentor and Adviser to many

Contents

PART III. The Future:
The leadership challenge for corporate responsibility coalitions... 151

PROFILES OF LEADING CORPORATE RESPONSIBILITY COALITIONS AND *SUI GENERIS* ORGANIZATIONS

Figures, tables and boxes

Figures

Tables

Boxes

Abbreviations

A4S	Accounting for Sustainability
ABCN	Australian Business and Community Network
ADEC	Asociación de Empresarios Cristianos
AED	Asociación Empresarial para el Desarrollo
BAA	Business Action in Africa
BBLF	Bulgarian Business Leaders Forum
BCCCC	Center for Corporate Citizenship at Boston College
BCLC	Business Civic Leadership Center
BCSD	Business Council for Sustainable Development
BiE	Business in the Environment
BITC	Business in the Community
BLF	Business Leaders Forum
BRIC	Brazil, Russia, India, China
BSR	Business for Social Responsibility
CBCC	Council for Better Corporate Citizenship
CBLF	China Business Leaders Forum
CBCSD	China Business Council for Sustainable Development
CCCD	Centrum für Corporate Citizenship Deutschland
CCI	corporate community involvement
CECODES	Consejo Empresarial Colombiano Para el Desarrollo Sostenible
CECP	Committee Encouraging Corporate Philanthropy
CEDICE	Centro de Divulgación del Conocimiento Económico para la Libertad
CEIBS	China Europe International Business School
CEMEFI	Centro Mexicano para la Filantropia
CERES	Consorcio Ecuatoriano Para La Responsabilidad Social
CGI	Clinton Global Initiative
CRB	Center for Responsible Business
CSR	corporate social responsibility
CTI	China Training Institute
Defra	Department for Environment, Food and Rural Affairs (UK)
DFID	Department for International Development
EABIS	The Academy for Business in Society
ECRC	Egyptian Corporate Responsibility Center
EP	Equator Principles

EPA	Environmental Protection Agency
ESG	environmental, social and governance
EUROSIF	European Social Investment Forum
FAO	Food and Agriculture Organization
FDA	Food and Drug Administration
FTA	Foreign Trade Association
GIZ	Gesellschaft für Internationale Zusammenarbeit
GMOs	genetically modified organisms
GPN	Global Partner Network
GRI	Global Reporting Initiative
GTZ	Gesellschaft für Technische Zusammenarbeit
IBL	Indonesia Business Links
IBLF	International Business Leaders Forum
ICC	International Chamber of Commerce
ICCA	International Council of Chemical Associations
ICMM	International Council on Mining and Metals
ICTI	International Council of Toy Industries
IDG	Initiative for Global Development
IIRC	International Integrated Reporting Council
ILO	International Labour Organization
IMS	Institut du Mécénat de Solidarité
INCR	Investor Network on Climate Risk
IPIECA	International Petroleum Industry Environmental Conservation Association
JUCCCE	Joint U.S. China Collaboration on Clean Energy
MF	Media CSR Forum
MIST	Mexico, Indonesia, South Korea and Turkey
NEPAD	New Partnership for Africa's Development
OECD	Organisation for Economic Co-operation and Development
ORSE	Observatoire sur la Responsabilité Sociétale des Entreprises
PBSP	Philippine Business for Social Progress
PNBE	Pensamento Nacional das Bases Empresariais
PRI	Principles for Responsible Investment
PRME	Principles for Responsible Management Education
RBF	Responsible Business Forum
RDA	Regional Development Agency
SASAC	State-owned Assets Supervision and Administration Commission
SMEs	small and medium enterprises
SSE	Sustainable Stock Exchanges
UNDP	United Nations Development Programme
UNGC	United Nations Global Compact
USAID	U.S. Agency for International Development
WBCSD	World Business Council for Sustainable Development
WEC	World Environment Center
WEF	World Economic Forum
WHO	World Health Organization
WTO	World Trade Organization
YBI	Youth Business International

Preface

Over the past three decades, thousands of companies around the world have participated in the creation and expansion of a variety of business-led corporate responsibility coalitions with the explicit aim of promoting, implementing and scaling more responsible and sustainable business practices. During this period, we have both had the privilege of working with and in some of these corporate responsibility coalitions. This book is our effort to tell their story: how and why they were created, their current characteristics, diversity and impact, and our views on how they can continue to play a leadership role in an increasingly complex and challenging world.

Although we both currently lead academic-based corporate responsibility initiatives, we are primarily practitioners. We both worked in the corporate sector at the beginning of our careers, David at Procter & Gamble and Jane at Citi, in addition to us both having undertaken a variety of executive, advisory and governance roles in a number of the business-led corporate responsibility coalitions profiled in this book.

David was joint Managing Director of Business in the Community (BITC) for several years and subsequently of the BITC Business Strategy Group. He was responsible for several BITC thought-leadership projects including Directions for the Nineties (1991) and Work in Society (1993–95). He participated in the Charleston meeting to create the International Business Leaders Forum (IBLF) in 1990, chaired the Anglo-Hungarian Enterprise Initiative after the fall of Communism, and was involved in several of the IBLF's other early East European initiatives. He was rapporteur for a series of roundtables on small and medium-sized enterprises (SMEs) and corporate social responsibility (CSR) as part of the European Union's Multi-stakeholder Forum on CSR in 2003–04, and for almost a decade he chaired the UK Small Business Consortium, which was established by BITC and Scottish Business in the Community in partnership with the Institute of Directors, the British Chambers of Commerce and other small business organizations to promote responsible business practices among smaller firms. He is co-author with Adrian Hodges of *Everybody's Business: Managing Risks and Opportunities in Today's Global Society* and *Corporate Social Opportunity* and has contributed to several other books on responsible business and corporate sustainability. He has chaired or served on the boards of several public–private–community partnerships and from 2006 to 2011 chaired Housing 21, one of Europe's largest social enterprises. He has been active in the Academy for Business in Society (EABIS) since its establishment in 2002 and chaired the EABIS annual colloquium in 2008, the first and only time it was held in the UK. He is a frequent visitor to China and in 2011 was invited by China Mobile to develop a business school teaching case on the company's mobile health initiatives in rural China.

Jane worked with the World Business Council for Sustainable Development (WBCSD) from 1991 to 1993, at the time of the Rio Earth Summit, undertaking research on business and sustainable development in Africa, Latin America and Eastern Europe and on the role of the financial sector in promoting sustainable development. She joined the IBLF in 1993 and, as IBLF's Policy and Research Director and later its Director of Business Leadership and Strategy, was responsible for a number of thought-leadership projects over a period of more than 15 years. In 2001, she worked with the United Nations Global Compact in the executive office of the UN Secretary-General, writing a report for the UN General Assembly on partnerships between the UN and the private sector. She has continued to work with the United Nations, moderating a number of UN Private Sector Focal Points conferences, serving on the advisory council for the UN Development Programme's Growing Inclusive Markets Initiative, and in 2011 supporting a project led by the UN Global Compact and Unilever to develop a platform to promote more transformative partnerships between the UN and business. She has also served in a formal advisory capacity and on task forces for a number of other business-led coalitions, such as the World Economic Forum, The Copenhagen Centre, the Initiative for Global Development, the Global Business Coalition on Health, Instituto Ethos in Brazil, Business Fights Poverty and the International Council on Mining and Metals, and on award judging panels for the Committee Encouraging Corporate Philanthropy and the Business Civic Leadership Center at the United States Chamber of Commerce. She was one of the track leaders for the Clinton Global Initiative (CGI) annual gathering in New York and serves on CGI's advisory council, and on the Board of Directors of the World Environment Center, FSG and the International Council of Toy Industries CARE Foundation. She is a Senior Associate at the Cambridge Programme for Sustainability Leadership and a Senior Fellow at the Brookings Institution and has co-authored four books and more than 70 publications on the role of business in society as well as five of the World Economic Forum's Global Corporate Citizenship reports.

During the last three decades, we have worked with and for some remarkable business leaders, visionary campaigners and front-line community activists. Many of these people were together in October 2007 in the Wesleyan Chapel in London's East End for a memorial service to Robert Davies who had died, tragically young at 56, two months earlier. Davies was the founding CEO for the first 17 years of the International Business Leaders Forum, established by HRH The Prince of Wales and a group of business leaders in 1990; prior to that, he was deputy CEO of Business in the Community in the UK. Robert was a social entrepreneur. He made things happen. He rarely had time to consolidate his thoughts and big ideas into more than a blog or a well-delivered speech (usually with just a few scrawled notes).[1] His sudden death from cancer meant that his personal and institutional knowledge about a remarkable phase in world history – how international business responded to the collapse of Communism, the rapid process of economic liberalization and privatization, and the consequent new era of globalization – was lost. As friends and colleagues of Robert, we both recognized the importance of capturing and codifying knowledge of collective business action, before more key players' experiences were lost and at the very least before the early coalition leaders have moved on or retired. This was, and remains, one of our core motivations for collaborating on the book.

We also felt that the story of the pioneering business-led corporate responsibility coalitions has not been widely told beyond those active in the field. Corporate responsibility and sustainability have now become much better-known concepts around the globe, even if practice has been and remains patchy and insufficient. The growth of awareness is due to a number of factors, including employee pressures, activist campaigns in response to corporate scandals, the rise of socially responsible investment, the vision of individual business leaders, government incentives and the ideas of influential thought leaders and books. One relatively unchronicled actor has been business-led corporate responsibility coalitions such as Business for Social Responsibility, Business in the Community, CSR Europe, Instituto Ethos, the International Business Leaders Forum, Maala, the National Business Initiative in South Africa, Philippine Business for Social Progress, the World Business Council for Sustainable Development and World Environment Center. A few of these coalitions have been the subject of individual case studies, but most of them have not been tracked and the coalitions as a whole have not been analyzed. Indeed, remarkably little has been written about these coalitions and their history, activities, governance, funding, impact and role in the future.

This book is a modest contribution to remedying this gap and lack of institutional memory. After four years as no more than a half-promise to each other, and with only occasional emails and telephone calls with snippets of ideas and data, we have finally pulled our materials and memories together. More importantly, we have talked to the men and women across the world who have made this fascinating social movement happen.

We set out to answer a number of questions: why did these coalitions start and grow? What have been their impacts? Where are they heading now? Where should they be going? What is the future? We believe it is particularly timely to do this now. In a period of austerity in many parts of the world, business and public-sector funders of the coalitions must decide whether funding these coalitions should be a priority in future. Conversely, the world is facing a series of dramatic sustainability threats and uncertainties – what, cumulatively, some have described as "the perfect storm,"[2] or "the great disruption,"[3] or the "resource revolution."[4] Or the rise of the "VUCA" world – Volatile, Uncertain, Complex and Ambiguous.[5] Almost every government at the national and local level, in addition to global governance institutions, is facing a common challenge: how to restore and increase economic growth and job creation in a manner that is more inclusive, equitable and socially cohesive, while at the same time more environmentally efficient and sustainable.

If these complex and interdependent challenges are to be met, there will have to be a great deal more business involvement. Action by individual corporations will be necessary, but not sufficient. Even the world's largest global corporations, with thousands of subsidiaries, millions of employees and billions of consumers along their value chains, cannot on their own tackle the market failures and governance gaps that impede more inclusive and smart economic growth. There is also a need for far more collective action among companies, within and across business sectors, and more collaborative action between different sectors of society (business, public and civil) both nationally and internationally. Business-led corporate responsibility coalitions with, in some cases, three or even four decades of convening experience, could play an important future role in this process, if they are fit for purpose.

In the context of this story, neither of us can claim the detachment or intellectual rigor of a traditional academic. Inevitably, we bring the weaknesses (as well as, we hope, the insights) of being participants in the narrative we are seeking to tell. Based on our own experiences as well as interviews and discussions with practitioners and academic colleagues from a variety of disciplines and the findings of a global survey of the coalitions themselves, we have attempted to assess their collective impact and outline some of the criticisms against them in Chapter 11. However, the book is not intended to be an analytically rigorous evaluation of the coalitions, either individually or collectively, but rather an attempt to document who they are, what they do, how they do it, and what their role might be in future. Besides, a full evaluation would require a counterfactual analysis of what the world would be like without them, posing burden-of-proof issues for those who dismiss the coalitions for one reason or another. Having said that, we recognize our own optimistic biases and enthusiasm for collective business action. We are therefore enormously grateful to both academic and practitioner colleagues for their generous time and help in enabling this study to move from our respective "guilt lists of uncompleted work" to a publication and in challenging our thinking to help minimize its shortcomings (see Acknowledgments). Remaining errors and inadequacies are, of course, our responsibility.

Our three core messages are that:

- Coalitions have been an important factor in the spread of corporate responsibility

- Coalitions have conceived, created and continued to drive collaborative business action: initially mobilizing business action in the community; then around responsible business practices; and now collaborative action which meets broader business and societal needs

- Properly resourced and organized, coalitions and the coalitions methodology could play an even greater role in future

We finished writing the first draft of this book with David in Beijing and Jane in Rio de Janeiro for the Rio + 20 Earth Summit emailing revisions and suggestions to each other, even as we experienced some of the corporate responsibility coalitions in action. Our study expanded from the generalist national and international corporate responsibility coalitions to include the growing number of more specialized, industry-sector and issue-specific organizations. It also evolved from primarily a historical study into one that is also forward-looking. We are conscious that in the course of writing the book numerous new business-led coalitions and multi-stakeholder initiatives have emerged with the shared goal of leveraging private-sector skills and resources in tackling social, environmental and governance challenges. Indeed, hardly a week goes by without one of us receiving an email about the creation of another new coalition. Despite our best intentions to provide a comprehensive overview of this constantly emerging and multifaceted landscape, we had to draw the line and have focused primarily on the long-standing more generalist business-led corporate responsibility coalitions that have had a track record of trial and error, and of achievement. The leaders of these coalitions have encouraged us to be candid and to be challenging in our recommendations for the future, and we have tried to meet this challenge.

Our goal was to write a book that will not only provide a historical perspective but will also be useful for business-led corporate responsibility coalitions themselves. We hope that it will be relevant to key supporters and potential partners of such coalitions in companies, governments, international development agencies, foundations, non-governmental organizations, academic institutions and think-tanks. And, as teachers, we aim to inspire a future generation of leaders to be more aware of the role of business as a partner in driving more inclusive, green and responsible growth, and to help them develop new types of leadership skills so that they can be effective in finding multi-stakeholder solutions to complex and systemic challenges. We hope we have achieved at least some of our goals and are grateful to all those who have been part of our inspiring and fulfilling corporate responsibility journey. We look forward to the next stage.

David Grayson
Director
Doughty Centre for Corporate Responsibility
Cranfield School of Management

Jane Nelson
Director
Corporate Social Responsibility Initiative
Harvard Kennedy School

Acknowledgments

During the course of the book we have undertaken two stages of peer review. First a Delphi Panel process tested initial ideas and conclusions, which involved us approaching over 40 academic and practitioner experts and resulted in over 20 substantive responses and interviews. For their help in this first stage, we especially want to thank: Professor Kenneth Amaeshi, Mallen Baker, Peter Brew, Tom Dodd, John Elkington, Professor Brad Googins, Richard Hamilton, John Heaslip, Adrian Hodges, Professor Michele Kahane, Professor Daniel Kinderman, Peter Lacy, Jens Erik Lund, Brendan May, Celia Moore, Mads Øvlisen, Chris Pinney, Noel Purcell, Coro Strandberg, David Vidal, Dr. Wayne Visser, Toby Webb and Dr. Simon Zadek.

Second, we undertook a peer review of the full book manuscript by four of our academic colleagues: Professor Kenneth Amaeshi, Nadine Exter, Professor Daniel Kinderman and Dr. Palie Smart. Catherine Carruthers at Business in the Community and Marli Porth at Harvard Kennedy School also read and commented on the manuscript. We are immensely grateful for these reviews and the insights and improvements they enabled.

We are also especially grateful to Chris Coulter and Lakshmi Sivagnanasundaram at GlobeScan, who helped us survey over 50 of the business-led coalitions, and to the busy coalition leaders who found the time to complete the survey. We would like to thank Charlotte Wolf of ArcelorMittal and Joseph Matthews of ArcelorMittal Liberia, the current chair of the Corporate Responsibility Forum for Liberia, for supporting the online survey conducted by GlobeScan exclusively for this book. This support has ensured that we could obtain detailed and contemporary insights from the current leaders of corporate responsibility coalitions across the globe, which have enriched our analysis and conclusions.

We are particularly grateful to authors who have written the original drafts of exemplar coalitions' Profiles or case-profiles: Mallen Baker, Amelio Porfilio, Zi Jia, Peter Brew, Ros Tennyson, Heiko Spitzeck, Talia Aharoni, Rajiv Maher, Dr. Christian Toennesen, Terry Yosie and Lloyd Timberlake, and to current and former staff and stakeholders of these coalitions who commented on drafts and who are acknowledged at the beginning of each relevant profile.

Specialists have kindly helped us with material for particular sections of the book. We thank Brook Avory (BSR), Amy Bao (BSR), Professor Henri-Claude de Bettignies (CEIBS),

Rolf Dietmar (GIZ), Paul French (Ethical Corporation), Yin Gefei (WTO Tribune/GoldenBee China), Professor David Gosset (CEIBS), Dr. Peiyuan Guo (Syn Tao), Peter Lacy (Accenture), Adam Lane (BSR), Sam Lee (EABIS), Peggy Liu (JUCCCE), Steve McCoy Thompson (BSR), Jan Noterdaeme (CSR Europe), Bill Valentino (BNU), Chengo Wang (BSR), Li Wenbo (CDP) and Oliver Yang (formerly Shanghai American Chamber of Commerce) for their insights on the corporate responsibility coalitions and China. Our thanks to Ron Ainsbury, Baroness Jean Coussins and Mark Leverton for their help with the section on the alcohol sectoral coalitions and initiatives; and John Swannick for material on EABIS.

We would also like to thank the Greenleaf team, especially John Stuart, publisher, Dean Bargh, production manager, and Monica Allen, copy-editor. They have shown much-appreciated understanding and commendable restraint when our diaries and travel schedules tested deadlines (and surely their patience too!).

In our respective Centers, we would like to thank Professor John Ruggie, Scott Leland, Marli Porth, Jennifer Nash, Minoo Ghoreishi and Beth Jenkins at the CSR Initiative, Kennedy School of Government, Harvard; and Mattia Anesa, Nadine Exter, Thea Hughes, Rajiv Maher, Melody McLaren and Dr. Palie Smart at the Doughty Centre for Corporate Responsibility, Cranfield School of Management.

We also want to thank our family and friends who have had to put up with us being even more distracted and work-focused than usual. In particular, Jane wants to thank Tony and Libby Nelson, Michèle Flournoy and Scott Gould, Patrick and Jules Forth, Graham and Liz Light, Dena Skran and David Duncombe, Ira Jackson and the Riker and Massie families for all their friendship and support in helping her to feel "at home" whether in London, Boston, Hong Kong, Sydney or Washington DC. David wants to thank his mum – 90 years young – for being a continuing source of love and inspiration and patiently waiting while David disappeared for hours on end to "just do a bit more on the book"; Adrian Hodges for his continuing friendship and professional insights; and Pawel Zabielski, whose friendship, calmness and persistent good humor is always a tonic.

Introduction

The 1992 Rio Earth Summit was a defining moment in the emergence of new models of global governance, civic engagement and business leadership. As presidents and prime ministers from most of the United Nations' member states descended on the large steel and concrete edifice on the outskirts of Rio de Janeiro that housed the official UN Conference on the Environment and Development, back in the heart of the city the appropriately named Flamengo Park was ablaze with the bright colors, posters, tents, music and loudspeakers of several thousand youth, faith leaders, farmers, indigenous peoples' groups, and environmental, labor and human rights activists. The Rio Earth Summit was one of the first UN conferences to welcome so many diverse non-governmental actors to its deliberations, and they answered the invitation in the thousands – an environmental "Woodstock" alongside the official intergovernmental process.

Positioned between these two faces of the Summit was a small handful of chief executive officers (CEOs) leading some of the planet's largest corporations. Several of these business leaders ran companies with annual revenues comparable to the gross domestic product of many participating UN member states. Hitherto there had been little in common between their own business agendas and the primary issues under discussion at the conference: the environment and development. These business leaders were at the Earth Summit to try to bridge this gap under the auspices of a newly created business-led coalition, the Business Council for Sustainable Development, and the more established International Chamber of Commerce. They were there to offer concrete proposals on how private-sector resources, capabilities, technologies and innovation could be part of the solution to tackling environmental degradation and creating social value while at the same time delivering economic growth and shareholder value. Many of the non-governmental organizations (NGOs) and public officials at the 1992 conference treated the presence of these business leaders with either deep mistrust or indifference.

Fast-forward two decades. At the Rio + 20 Conference in June 2012, an estimated 2,700 business people converged on Rio. Some were participants in their country's official delegations. Business and Industry was one of the nine Major Groups identified by the UN to provide input for the first time into the official inter-governmental process. Business leaders from almost every industry sector and country also participated in numerous side events, such as the Corporate Sustainability Forum and Business Day events that offered some 150 different sessions and workshops covering the entire gamut of the conference's seven priority themes: jobs, energy, cities, food, water, oceans, and disaster management and resilience. Private-sector participants publicly announced over 200 voluntary commitments to take practical action in many of these areas.

In addition to several thousand individual business people and companies, there were at least 80 business-led coalitions actively engaged in the various dialogues and commitments. Two-thirds of these coalitions didn't even exist at the time of the original Rio Earth Summit. The World Business Council for Sustainable Development (created from a merger after the 1992 Summit) could now claim a membership of some 200 companies with combined annual revenues of US$7 trillion and a network of some 60 local and regional CEO-led business coalitions.[6] The UN Global Compact could point to almost 8,000 corporate members, over two-thirds of them from developing countries, and local networks in some 100 countries.[7] Over 20 of these local networks participated in Rio + 20. The Brazilian network alone mobilized a commitment by the CEOs of over 200 Brazilian companies to endorse *Business Contributions to a Green and Inclusive Economy*, laying out ten practical commitments to be achieved by each company.

There were meetings convened by participants of the UN Principles for Responsible Investment, a network of over 1,000 investment institutions with combined assets of US$30 trillion under management; signatory deans and academics from the Principles for Responsible Management Education, a global network of more than 300 business schools and universities; signatories to the Women's Economic Empowerment Principles, a platform for action endorsed by over 400 corporate chief executives worldwide; and members of a wide array of issue- and industry-specific leadership groups, such as the Sustainable Stock Exchanges Initiative, the International Council on Mining and Metals, the Sustainable Agriculture Initiative Platform, the CEO Water Mandate, the Corporate Leaders Network for Climate Action and the Green Industry Platform, to name just a few.[8]

While deep distrust of business and its motives still existed among some major NGOs and public officials at Rio + 20, for many of them the business community was there as a partner in the joint goal of working toward more inclusive, green and responsible models of economic growth and development. Many of the business participants knew their NGO counterparts as well as they knew their private-sector peers. In a number of cases, they were advocating for exactly the same public-policy reforms and financing incentives, and jointly criticizing the lack of government leadership in driving toward a more sustainable economic model.

Today, few public officials or NGOs would disagree that the private sector will have a substantial influence on determining whether the 9 billion people who will be living on the planet by 2050 can experience lives of a reasonable quality without destroying the ecosystem on which the survival of humankind depends. For some, this influence is still considered to be largely negative; they argue that business needs to be more heavily regulated in order to dramatically improve its environmental, social and governance (ESG) performance.[9] For others, voluntary business innovation, technology, resources and leadership are seen as an essential and necessary part of the solution, albeit one that still needs to be unleashed through better public policy and by government and capital market incentives.

Most leading business people recognize that both views have merit. They know that one of the greatest business leadership challenges of the 21st century will be to simultaneously manage and mitigate their ESG risks and costs *and* to harness their capabilities to deliver market-based solutions that create shareholder value while at the same time driving towards a more inclusive, green and responsible global economy. They also recognize that embedding good ESG risk management and performance and developing innovative new products, services and business models through their own individual operations and value chains is going to be vitally necessary – though insufficient on its own.

The most visionary leaders in the corporate sector know that another critical leadership challenge will be to drive the large-scale and systemic change that is going to be necessary to get onto a more sustainable pathway by 2050. They know this will require building fundamentally new models of transformative partnerships and complex multi-stakeholder platforms with their competitors and peers, as well as with governments and civil society. And they have no illusions that they need to meet this long-term challenge while also facing growing competition from around the world and ongoing demands from investors and consumers to deliver excellent short-term performance.

This book traces some of the social and institutional innovations that have occurred over the past few decades to bring leaders in the business community to this point of sustainability leadership. It recognizes that the changes have been driven by a mix of individual champions, companies and coalitions. While acknowledging throughout the vital leadership role of individual champions and companies, as well as the enabling role of governments, investors, foundations, academic institutions and NGOs, our focus is on coalitions: the *collective action* that groups of companies are taking to move forward the corporate responsibility and sustainability agenda. There is extensive literature on corporate responsibility within individual companies and on public–private partnerships, but far less has been written about the collective business-to-business coalitions that have emerged over the past two decades. This books aims to address the gap.

The book focuses specifically on business-led corporate responsibility coalitions that have been established with the explicit and, in most cases, dedicated goal of mobilizing business resources to directly tackle one or more environmental, social or governance challenges. We have defined these business-led coalitions as:

> Independent, non-profit membership organizations that are composed mainly or exclusively of for-profit businesses; that have a board of directors composed predominantly or only of business people; that are core-funded primarily or totally from business; and whose dedicated purpose is to promote responsible business practice.

At this writing, it is estimated that there are more than 110 national and international generalist business-led corporate responsibility coalitions, of which at least 30 are widely acknowledged as well-established and influential. Several hundred more coalitions are industry- and issue-specific. Many traditional business organizations such as representative chambers of commerce and trade and industry associations have also established dedicated units focused on corporate responsibility and sustainability issues. There are also a growing number of multi-stakeholder initiatives such as the UN Global Compact and its national chapters, and the Global Reporting Initiative, which has played an essential role in building the field for more rigorous and transparent reporting on ESG performance. The World Economic Forum deserves and receives special recognition for the vital leadership role it has played – and continues to play – in convening business leaders, policy-makers and social entrepreneurs to address a wide range of environmental, social and governance challenges. In less than a decade, the Clinton Global Initiative has also established a reputation for catalyzing practical business leadership through a similar multi-stakeholder platform.

Although we recognize the crucial leadership role of these and other multi-stakeholder platforms, they are not the principal focus of this book given their broader membership and remit. Nor are business corporate responsibility networks that are based at academic institutions, research-based consultancies or think-tanks and are not governed as independent entities. We readily acknowledge that these are fine dividing lines. Our examples of the business-led corporate responsibility coalitions will illustrate that most of them are partnering with, funded by or undertaking joint advocacy through networks that have active government or civil-society participation. As we look to the future, we argue that multi-stakeholder platforms, more traditional business associations and academic institutions will have an increasingly crucial role to play in embedding and scaling responsible business practices and sustainability, in addition to growth in industry- and issue-specific business-led coalitions. That said, our primary focus is on the more generalist business-led corporate responsibility coalitions that have helped to build the field over the past four decades.

We encourage readers to visit www.doughtycentre.info/coalitions and, in the spirit of Wikipedia, to suggest additions and amendments to the list of corporate responsibility coalitions, multi-stakeholder initiatives, units of business representative organizations and others.

Structure of the book

The book is divided into four parts.

In Part I, we explore the past. We focus on the emergence of new models of collective corporate action over the past four decades. After a brief overview of the rise of the corporate responsibility movement, which has been covered extensively elsewhere, we focus on exploring how business-led coalitions have emerged. The book outlines three main stages in the evolution of these coalitions:

- 1970–1989: the emergence of a small pioneering group of what we have termed the **corporate social activists,** largely responding to socioeconomic, political or environmental crises in particular countries. Most of them still exist in some form today, although they have evolved and renewed themselves over the four decades

- 1990–2000: the emergence and rapid growth in influence and reach of what we have termed the **global field-builders,** initially focused on raising awareness of the business case for corporate responsibility and helping companies to embed responsible business practices into their core business operations and value chains

- 2001–2011: the rise of what we have termed the **industry and issue specialists**. Some of the more generalist business-led coalitions started to focus more specifically on collective corporate action around particular industry sectors and issues. At the same time, we also saw the emergence of more business-led coalitions and multi-stakeholder initiatives that were fully dedicated to addressing a particular economic, environmental, social or governance issue or driving responsible business practices throughout a particular industry sector

Part I concludes with a brief discussion of the global trends, as well as the individual champions, companies and foundations that have driven the growth in business-led corporate responsibility coalitions.

Part II focuses on the present. First, we map the **current state of play of business-led coalitions** and their increasing number, diversity and complexity in terms of how and where they operate, exploring both the growth of coalitions in emerging markets, with a focus on China, and the growth in industry- and issue-specific diversity.

Second, we look at how coalitions are part of a **broader ecosystem** or architecture for corporate responsibility, which also includes governments and intergovernmental institutions, multi-stakeholder/multi-sectoral corporate responsibility initiatives, corporate responsibility consultancies, business school and university corporate responsibility centers, traditional and social media, NGOs tracking business behavior as well as more NGOs wanting to partner with or advise business, and corporate responsibility and sustainability initiatives within business representative organizations, such as chambers of commerce, federations of employers and industry and trade associations.

Third, we analyze the **key roles that coalitions have played** and are currently playing to raise awareness of corporate responsibility and sustainability, help embed responsible business practices within individual company operations and value chains, and build the field more generally. Despite the variety of governance, funding and operational approaches taken by these coalitions, most of them undertake some combination of the following leadership roles in order to achieve their goals: raising awareness and making the "business case"; identifying and disseminating good practices; advising and building the capacity of companies; brokering partnerships; implementing on-the-ground programs; setting standards and spreading norms; and promoting a public-policy agenda.

Fourth, we outline **how coalitions are organizing themselves** in terms of governance, funding and management. We examine the range of issues that different coalitions now cover and how coalitions are networking among themselves.

We then assess the **impact of business-led corporate responsibility coalitions** over the past few decades. We analyze their impact in three main areas that we consider crucial:

- Raising awareness of the societal need and the business case for responsible business practices and sustainability

- Embedding corporate responsibility into core business practices

- Scaling corporate responsibility

We review how effective the coalitions have been in raising awareness of the business case for corporate responsibility and sustainability and in helping individual companies to integrate better ESG risk management and innovation into their core business strategies, operations and value chains. We also examine how effective they have been in scaling corporate responsibility to more companies, regions and issues and at a more systemic level of transforming value chains, markets and public policy.

Given the complex and multi-dimensional nature of any social movement and field-building process, it is not possible to assign clear causality and we have not attempted to do so.

We offer our assessment based on a combination of personal engagement with many of the coalitions, surveys of more than 50 of the coalitions, extensive interviews, and a consultation process with 40 academic and practitioner experts in the field of corporate responsibility and sustainability. In particular, we worked with GlobeScan (www.GlobeScan.com) in early summer 2012 to run an exclusive online survey of the business-led coalitions. More than 50 coalitions responded, including all the international coalitions as well as many national ones. The full questionnaire is reproduced in Appendix 3.

We conclude Part II with a look at some of the strategic and operational criticisms that have been leveled against business-led corporate responsibility coalitions and some of the **lessons that have been learned** over the past few decades. We then suggest some strategic questions facing each coalition.

Part III looks to the future. In this we argue that **two core areas of concerted action are still needed.** Indeed, in the face of geo-political shifts, economic and financial challenges and growing natural resource uncertainty and scarcity, we argue that these two areas of action are more important than ever:

- **Ongoing and increased efforts to embed corporate responsibility into core business practices in thousands of individual companies and value chains around the world.** Drawing on research by Accenture, GlobeScan and others, we illustrate the ongoing "performance gap" that still exists even in most of the leading companies between what they have committed to do to achieve better ESG performance, risk management and innovation, and what they are actually doing. We also address the hundreds of thousands of other companies whose involvement and effort is still nascent, and look at how companies from emerging markets will implement and drive ESG performance

- **Dramatically increased collective efforts to drive more transformative, large-scale, system-level change in value chains, markets and public policy.** Work undertaken in the past few years by a number of the profiled coalitions points to the need for greater systemic impact if the world is to achieve more inclusive, green and responsible growth in the coming years. The World Business Council for Sustainable Development's *Vision 2050*, CSR Europe's *Enterprise 2020*, the International Business Leaders Forum's *Redefining Growth* platform, Business in the Community's *Visioning the Future*, BSR's *Accelerating Progress* framework, and Instituto Ethos's *Inclusive, Green and Responsible Economy* platform are all pointing in the same direction, as are recent studies by the G20, the World Bank Group, the Organisation for Economic Co-operation and Development (OECD), the United Nations and a variety of leading strategy consultants and think-tanks. Incremental, company-by-company or even government-by-government change is necessary but by no means sufficient. A new level and era of collective and multi-stakeholder action is needed

We explore some of the recent global developments and key trends unfolding. We propose ways in which business-led corporate responsibility coalitions can play an even greater role in embedding and scaling more sustainable business practices, business models, value chains, markets and public policies. In the new agendas of a number of the leading coalitions, we see the vision of a more sustainable model of capitalism emerging that is more inclusive, green and responsible than the model that has dominated previously. This more sustainable model delivers not only short-term performance and shareholder wealth creation but also long-term prosperity and shared value creation. We suggest that some coalitions or new combinations of coalitions could help to play a crucial leadership role in driving the following ten-step **Agenda for Action**:

1. Helping individual companies to overcome the "performance gap" and to embed responsible business policies and practices into the core of their corporate strategy, operations and value chains

2. Promoting pre-competitive collective action within specific industry sectors, geographies and value chains to drive scale and systemic impact

3. Convening companies to be part of more systemic and large-scale multi-sector collaboration between business, government and civil-society organizations

4. Spreading innovation from key emerging markets

5. Engaging with small and medium enterprises

6. Working with governments and advocating for progressive public-policy reforms

7. Improving the financial enabling environment

8. Partnering with business schools and universities

9. Raising public awareness and spreading the practice of sustainable consumption

10. Promoting a new vision for sustainable capitalism

However, we have identified a gap between the *potential* of the coalitions, and the greater role and impact the coalitions seek, and the *perceptions* of coalitions' capacities held by some of their stakeholders. This "potential–perception" gap suggests several scenarios for the future. We suggest how coalitions with the aspiration and the potential to grow could do so, and specify some of the tools that their boards and senior management teams could use to ensure they are fit for the future.

Our final recommendations are addressed to the coalitions themselves, especially those with the aspiration and potential to play a greater role; to current and future corporate members of the coalitions; to foundations, governments, development agencies and international institutions; and to business schools and centers of public policy in universities.

While some think the original model of general, business-led corporate responsibility coalitions may now have reached its peak in terms of market saturation, we see the "glass as half-full not half-empty" and that the essence of what such coalitions represent remains highly relevant and a valuable model for the way forward. In particular:

- Voluntary business commitment to higher ESG performance is more important than ever, and raising awareness, sharing best practice and how-to knowledge and providing focal points for communication, commitment and action are all key to helping individual companies aim towards corporate sustainability excellence

- Collaborative action both among businesses and between groups of businesses and other public-sector and civil-society partners is also more vital than ever in order to achieve the necessary scale and systemic impact

Indeed, as more businesses seek to achieve solutions to the challenging, complex and systemic issues that defy neat compartmentalization or answers delivered by just one sector, they will look to the coalitions that are able to adapt and innovate to help them, or they will create new hybrid coalitions. The lessons from the past four decades can help in either case. Just as the early pioneers of business-led corporate responsibility coalitions were perforce nimble and fleet of foot and lacked institutional baggage, so a new generation of more varied coalitions is emerging. Typically these will:

- Focus on outcome, and may be task- and time-limited

- Have greater industry-sector or issue specificity

- Collaborate with advocacy and delivery partners such as NGOs, academic institutions, governments at different levels and international institutions

The **fourth part** of the book provides **in-depth profiles** of what we consider to be some of the most strategic, effective and long-standing (all of them over 10 years old, several 30 to 40 years old) of the business-led corporate responsibility coalitions. The profiles flesh out the arguments of Parts I–III and provide more substantial examples of the coalitions in practice. We have attempted to provide some sense of each coalition's background, context and history, its core activities and how these have evolved since the coalition's establishment, its impact thus far, some lessons learned along the way, and prospects for the future. The coalitions profiled adhere to our stricter definition of those that are organizations *of* business, which are primarily governed, funded and led *by* business and which have a dedicated focus on corporate responsibility. They are: Business for Social Responsibility; Business in the Community, UK; CSR Europe; Instituto Ethos, Brazil; International Business Leaders Forum; Maala–Israel Business for Social Responsibility; National Business Initiative, South Africa; Philippine Business for Social Progress; World Business Council for Sustainable Development and the World Environment Center.

Additionally, we profile two *sui generis* organizations: the UN Global Compact, launched by the then UN Secretary-General Kofi Annan in 2000 and the World Economic Forum, especially its corporate citizenship work. While they do not fully meet our definition of a business-led corporate responsibility coalition (the former because of its multi-sectoral, multi-stakeholder governance, and the latter because of its much wider remit and activities), both the Global Compact and the World Economic Forum have become such a prominent part of the architecture promoting responsible business and involve so many companies and business people worldwide that their inclusion in the book is an important part of the story.

Box 1 **A word on definitions**

After a combined 50 years of working in the field of corporate responsibility and sustainability, we are both deeply conscious of the challenges of definitions and boundary-setting that bedevil this field. We have lost count of the number of times we have sat with academic or practitioner colleagues who are newcomers to the field and who call for a common definition that can be used universally across all industry sectors and national boundaries. Definitions are vital and language matters, but given varied starting points and legacies we don't believe there will be any common, universally accepted term any time soon, if ever.

In our teaching, we share the reports of six major energy companies with our students: the Shell *Sustainability Report*, the Chevron *Corporate Responsibility Report*, the Vattenfall *Corporate Social Responsibility Report*, the ExxonMobil *Corporate Citizenship Report*, the Total *Society and Environment Report*, and the Statoil integrated *Annual and Sustainability Report* (combining both its financial and sustainability performance). Despite the different terms used, a close analysis of each report shows that the main headings of the content inside the report are almost identical: same industry, same global trends, similar strategy and operating challenges, similar social, economic, environmental and governance risks and challenges, and similar opportunities to harness core capabilities, science and technologies to find solutions to these challenges. A similar exercise could be carried out with corporate reports of leading companies in almost any industry sector.

As such, we try not to get too caught up in the debate of "definition." We believe that many of the contributions and approaches offered over the past 20 years by a variety of thought leaders and practitioners, despite the different terms used, are all pointing in a similar direction even if they see different pathways for getting there. In particular, this direction recognizes:

- The private sector has a vital role to play in driving economic growth and inclusion, respecting human rights and social justice, and sustaining the natural environment on which human survival depends
- Companies can have by far their greatest impact on society (both positive and negative) through the way they manage and harness their core business strategies, operations and value chains. They can be most effective by identifying the economic, environmental, social and governance (ESG) risks and opportunities that are most material to their industry and business and by focusing on achieving performance excellence and greater accountability and transparency in these areas
- Any company that takes a strategic approach to these issues will focus first and foremost on how they relate to its core business, both from a compliance, cost and risk management/value protection perspective and from an innovation, opportunity and competitive/value-creation perspective
- In assessing their strategies for value protection and value creation, leading companies are explicit about and accountable for how they *protect* shared value for their shareholders and other stakeholders and how they *create* shared value for their shareholders and other stakeholders
- Most companies will continue to have philanthropic, community investment and employee volunteer programs; these should be aligned as closely as possible to core business interests and competences
- No matter how effective the world's largest companies are at integrating economic, environmental, social and governance performance into their value-protection and value-creation strategies, their positive impact will be limited by the value chains, markets and policy systems in which they operate. Thus pre-competitive cooperation with peers and competitors in the same value chain or industry sector, as well as multi-stakeholder engagement with governments, NGOs and other actors, is necessary to have large-scale and systemic impact
- Large-scale and systemic impact through collaboration is essential to achieving a more inclusive, green and responsible economy

➔

In short, the definitions of corporate responsibility and sustainability vary and the concept remains contested (from both free-market right and anti-business left). Despite this lack of a universally agreed definition, there can be little doubt that businesses around the world are faced with growing expectations from their stakeholders – whether regulators, investors, employees, customers, activists or the general public – to identify, manage and publicly account for the non-financial risks and opportunities that are most material to their company and industry. We particularly welcome the simplicity of the latest EU Commission definition that corporate responsibility is the responsibility that an enterprise has for its (social, environmental and economic) impacts.[10]

A vanguard of visionary companies is also proactively recognizing the potential to create both shareholder value and societal value by explicitly and strategically addressing particular socioeconomic and environmental challenges. The term **shared value** has become popular in recent years, following articles in *Harvard Business Review* by Michael Porter and Mark Kramer.[11] They define shared value as achieving business value by re-conceiving products and markets, redefining productivity in value chains and enhancing local clusters in a manner that solves a broader socioeconomic or environmental challenge or set of challenges. Among other terms, this proactive and strategic approach by business to explicitly aim for and measure against shareholder value and societal value has also been described as the **triple bottom line**,[12] **SVA²**,[13] **sustainable value**,[14] **corporate social opportunity**,[15] and **corporate social innovation**.[16]

Whether termed corporate responsibility (CR), corporate sustainability, creating shared value (CSV), corporate social responsibility (CSR), corporate social opportunity (CSO), corporate citizenship, triple bottom line or environmental, social and governance performance (ESG), the explicit management of non-financial risks and opportunities either to protect existing value for business and society or to create new shared value for business and society has become an increasingly strategic issue for many companies and the executives who lead them.

While acknowledging the different terms that many practitioners and thought leaders have coined, in this book we use the terms corporate responsibility, corporate social responsibility, responsible business practices, corporate sustainability and ESG somewhat interchangeably. In all cases we refer to companies harnessing their core business operations and capabilities, and recognize both the value protection/risk management and value creation/opportunity aspects of the term. At the broader system level we use the term "sustainable capitalism"[17] as a shorter way to describe the long-standing concept of "sustainable development"[18] and emerging calls for a more "inclusive, green and responsible economy."[19]

Part I
The Past
The emergence of new models of collective business leadership

Part I focuses on the past. Chapter 1 provides a brief overview of the rise of the corporate responsibility movement, which has been covered extensively elsewhere, and Chapter 2 gives a definition of business-led corporate responsibility coalitions. Chapter 3 focuses on three key stages in the evolution of these coalitions over the past four decades. Chapter 4 then highlights some of the global trends that have played a role in driving the growth of business-led corporate responsibility coalitions during this period and Chapter 5 reviews the role of individual champions, companies and foundations in supporting the creation and expansion of the coalitions.

1

The rise of the corporate responsibility movement

Corporate responsibility – in sum, the approaches that companies employ to embed environmental, social and governance (ESG) risks and opportunities into their core business strategies and operations with the aim of either protecting or creating shared value for business and society – is increasingly recognized as a fact of business life.

A 2010 Accenture study found that 93 % of more than 750 CEOs surveyed globally believed that sustainability is critical to their future business success, and 96 % said sustainability has to be embedded in business strategy and operations.[20] McKinsey, in its 2011 sustainability survey, reported that more than 70 % of over 3,200 company respondents from a range of industry sectors across the world said that sustainability is either a top three or priority item on the CEO's global agenda.[21] Also in 2011, KPMG found that 95 % of the world's 250 largest companies report on corporate responsibility, concluding that corporate reporting on ESG performance is now *de facto* law in some countries.[22] An academic study by Kolodinsky *et al.* in 2010 found that 90 % of Fortune 500 firms embraced corporate social responsibility as an essential element in their organizational goals.[23]

The underlying drivers of corporate responsibility over the past three decades have been well documented. The ESG performance of business has become a more important issue as the processes of economic liberalization, privatization, globalization and technological transformation have opened up markets around the world and expanded the reach, scope and influence of the private sector, especially that of multinational corporations, whose numbers, according to UNCTAD, have grown from circa 60,000 in 2000 to over 80,000 today. As David Rothkopf points out in *Power Inc.*, over the last few decades, the world's largest private-sector organizations have grown dramatically in resources, global reach and influence:[24]

> The world's largest company,[25] Wal-Mart Stores Inc., has revenues higher than the GDPs of all but 25 of the world's countries. Its employees (2.1 million) outnumber the populations of almost a hundred nations. The world's largest asset manager, a comparatively low-profile New York company called BlackRock, controls assets greater than the national reserves of any country on the planet.[26]

Simultaneously, the dramatic growth of information and communications technology and social media has enabled many more people around the world to learn about what is happening in previously remote locations or to become aware of issues that were known or noticed locally at best. It also means that these newly aware citizens can rapidly and effectively organize online campaigns against corporate behavior of which they disapprove. The continued growth of social media will only intensify the potential for viral campaigns against business misbehavior.

Corporate governance and ethics scandals and the global financial crisis have further undermined trust in business, especially in large corporations. As the Edelman Trust Barometer has tracked during 12 years of annual surveys, the corporate sector has a large, and growing, trust deficit to overcome in many countries.[27] It also has to meet a large gap in expectations. GlobeScan – an international center for objective survey research and strategic counsel – has, since 2000, tracked the gap between popular views about how business *should* behave on corporate social responsibility issues and perceptions of how business *is* behaving.[28] As Figure 1.1 illustrates, the private sector is failing to meet public expectations.

Figure 1.1 **Expectations versus performance gap**

Source: GlobeScan 2011

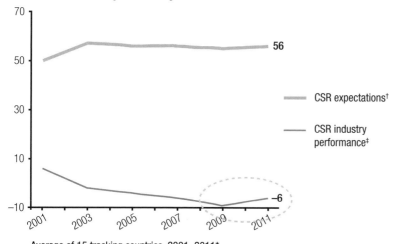

Large gap between expectations on CSR and industry CSR performance remains, as industry fails to meet public expectations

Average of 15 tracking countries, 2001–2011*

* Includes Australia, Brazil, China, France, Germany, Italy, Mexico, Nigeria, Russia, South Korea, Turkey, the UK and the USA

† Aggregate net expectations of up to 10 responsibilities of large companies (not all responsibilities were asked in each country each year)

‡ Aggregate net CSR performance ratings of 10 industries

The upper line is the aggregated figure of respondents expecting business to meet the basket of CR standards specified, and the lower line is the net aggregated figure of those respondents perceiving businesses to be meeting versus those not meeting these standards.

Underpinning all these trends has been growing evidence of climate change and natural resource depletion, and the role of business in exacerbating or addressing these challenges. The International Food Policy Research Institute has estimated that the demand for water will have increased by 30% by 2030 and that some two-thirds of watersheds will be stressed.[29] The UN's Food and Agriculture Organization estimates that food demand will have increased by 50% by 2030,[30] while the International Energy Association predicts that demand for energy will have also increased by 50% by the same period.[31]

As the McKinsey Global Institute noted in its seminal report of 2011, *The Resource Revolution*:

> The size of today's challenge should not be underestimated; nor should the obstacles to diffusing more resource-efficient technologies throughout the global economy. The next 20 years appear likely to be quite different from the resource-related shocks that have periodically erupted in history. Up to three billion more middle class consumers will emerge in the next 20 years compared with 1.8 billion today, driving up demand for a range of different resources. This soaring demand will occur at a time when finding new sources of supply and extracting them is becoming increasingly challenging and expensive, notwithstanding technological improvement in the main resource sectors. Compounding the challenge are stronger links between resources, which increase the risk that shortages and price changes in one resource can rapidly spread to others. The deterioration in the environment, itself driven by growth in resource consumption, also appears to be increasing the vulnerability of resource supply systems . . . Finally, concern is growing that a large share of the global population lacks access to basic needs such as energy, water, and food, not least due to the rapid diffusion of technologies such as mobile phones to low-income consumers, which has increased their political voice and demonstrated the potential to provide universal access to basic services.[32]

The combination of growing demand, increased resource scarcity, volatility and risk, and stronger links and feedback loops between certain critical resources (increasingly referred to as the energy–food–water nexus) is putting growing pressures on ecosystems, social systems, economic systems and political systems. This has led to consequent demands, including from business itself, for more concerted and systemic efforts to improve water, energy and food security, and to achieve sustainable development more broadly. Research by McKinsey and others has "established that both an increase in the supply of resources and a step change in the productivity of how resources are extracted, converted and used would be required to head off potential resource constraints over the next 20 years."[33] New models of corporate responsibility and sustainability will be essential to achieving this step change, alongside and within an enabling framework of better government policies.

At the same time, the economic and human costs of the global financial crisis, high levels of unemployment and growing inequality of opportunity in many nations have added further pressure on the private sector to help address broader socioeconomic issues. The International Labour Organization (ILO) *World of Work Report 2012* states that "more than 200 million workers will be unemployed in 2012," with some 50 million jobs having been lost since the financial crisis began in 2008.[34] According to the ILO's *Global Employment Trends 2012* report: "The world faces the 'urgent challenge' of creating 600 million productive jobs over the next decade to generate sustainable growth and maintain social cohesion."[35] The

ILO estimates that one out of every three workers in the world is classified as unemployed or poor, and argues that young people and the low-skilled are bearing the brunt of the jobs crisis. Young people are three times more likely to be unemployed than adults and over 75 million youth worldwide are looking for work. The ILO warns of a "scarred" generation of young workers facing a dangerous mix of high unemployment, increased inactivity and precarious work in developed countries, as well as persistently high working poverty in the developing world.[36] Growing inequality is also a problem in many countries. In the United States, the share of national income going to the upper 1% more than doubled from 1979 to 2012, from about 10% to about 23.5%.[37] According to the Economic Mobility Project of the Pew Charitable Trusts, only one-third of American families will surpass their parents in wealth and income and climb to a new rung on the economic ladder.[38] Similar patterns of high unemployment and declining equality of opportunity are being repeated elsewhere and they put increasing pressure on the private sector to play a more proactive role in working with governments to find solutions.

Another important driver of corporate responsibility over the past decade has been a growing focus on the responsibilities of business, especially large corporations, in relation to human rights. In 2005, following a series of well-documented cases of companies being responsible for or complicit in human rights abuses, the former UN Secretary-General, Kofi Annan, appointed Professor John Ruggie to serve as his Special Representative on Business and Human Rights. This was the first time in the history of the United Nations that such an appointment had been made to focus specifically on the role of the private sector. In 2008, after three years of extensive research and wide-ranging consultations around the world with governments, business associations, companies and civil-society organizations, Professor Ruggie proposed a framework to clarify the relevant actors' responsibilities in relation to human rights.

This framework, now referred to as the UN Framework on Business and Human Rights, and popularly called the "Protect, Respect, Remedy" Framework, was unanimously welcomed by the UN Human Rights Council. It rests on three pillars: the state duty to protect against human rights abuses by third parties, including business, through appropriate policies, regulation and adjudication; the corporate responsibility to respect human rights, which means to act with due diligence to avoid infringing on the rights of others and to address adverse impacts that occur; and greater access by victims to effective remedy, both judicial and non-judicial.[39]

The Special Representative's mandate was extended until 2011 to develop more operational guidance on how to implement the Framework, and in June 2011 the UN Guiding Principles were unanimously endorsed by the Human Rights Council. Professor Ruggie notes:

> we now have for the first time a common framework and set of normative standards with regard to business and human rights that have been unanimously endorsed by the Human Rights Council. This includes not only Western countries but also Brazil, China, India, Nigeria, Russia and every other of the 47 countries represented on the Council. The endorsement of the Guiding Principles was quite exceptional. It was the first time that the Human Rights Council or its predecessor had ever used the verb "endorse" in relation to a normative text that governments did not negotiate themselves. Furthermore, the "Corporate Responsibility to Respect Human Rights" component has been incorporated into the new OECD's Guidelines for Multinational Enterprises, which have

a complaints mechanism. It has been referenced by the International Finance Corporation, which affects access to capital. The International Organization for Standardization (ISO) recapitulates its core features in ISO 26000, and it has a whole industry of consultants behind it who are eager to help companies become certified that they operate in a socially responsible manner. The Guiding Principles are also included in the new European Union corporate responsibility strategy. All of this makes the Guiding Principles the most authoritative global standard in business and human rights.[40]

As a result of these developments and the growing global role and influence of the corporate sector, corporate responsibility is moving from the margins of corporate strategy and public policy to the mainstream. In some cases, this shift is being driven by changing societal expectations of business and by low trust in the private sector. In others, it is driven by companies themselves identifying new strategic risks and opportunities associated with fundamental shifts in economic, social, political, technical and environmental systems. For most industries and individual companies a combination of factors is usually at play. While very few companies have fully integrated these issues into mainstream strategy and planning, most of the world's largest corporations are now paying greater attention to what corporate responsibility means for their core business far beyond traditional philanthropy and compliance. It is increasingly clear that this trend is not a short-term fad, nor is it only a Western trend. While much of the early running on corporate responsibility was made by Western organizations, the first corporate responsibility coalitions were in Africa, Asia and South America, and in recent years there has been a growing exploration of the responsibilities and roles of business in societies around the world.

Debate about the role of business and how business people should behave has also been integral to each of the great religious and philosophical traditions. Islam teaches the importance of trading with integrity and *zakat* (giving back); Judaism teaches about *tzedek* – fairness and justice in transactions – and *tikkun olam* (repair the world); and Confucianism emphasizes the importance of all contributing to the "harmonious society." Christian doctrine inspired some of the great 19th-century Quaker businesses in Britain such as Cadbury and Rowntree. Today, there are more explicit connections between corporate responsibility theory and what the great religious, philosophical and spiritual traditions say about the role of business in society, in different parts of the world,[41] and hopefully a growing recognition of the opportunity to learn from each other's approaches.

Another key element of the emerging corporate responsibility movement has been efforts to put more rigor into measuring both the business benefits *and* the societal benefits of better environmental, social and economic performance. We have written elsewhere[42] of the importance of corporate responsibility for individual businesses and business collectively, as well as for governments and society (the public good). From a business perspective, properly conceived and well-executed responsible business can improve long-term value creation through:

1. Brand value and reputation

2. Employees and future workforce recruitment, retention and motivation

3. Operational effectiveness through better cost management, resource efficiency and productivity in the value chain

4. Enterprise and project-level risk management

5. Organizational growth

6. Business opportunity and competitiveness through the potential either to innovate and develop new products, services and markets or to enter new markets with existing products and services[43]

As well as being a driver for commercial risk management and innovation, corporate responsibility can also be a stimulus to social- and public-policy innovation, anticipating, obviating or complementing regulation, and as part of the redesign and delivery of "public goods."[44] It can also help to support national progress and sustainable development through a number of direct impacts and indirect multiplier effects. Research by the International Business Leaders Forum (IBLF) identified five potential contributions of companies that are focused on adding value for both shareholders and society. These are shown in Table 1.1.

In summary, the corporate responsibility movement has been gaining both momentum and traction over the past few decades. This trend is likely to continue as awareness grows among companies and other actors that business has both the opportunity and the responsibility to create new shared value and protect existing value through the way companies integrate social and environmental risks and opportunities into their core business. Although corporate philanthropy continues to have a role, as we have argued elsewhere, corporate responsibility is first and foremost about "how companies make their profits, not simply what they do with them afterwards."[45]

The evolving corporate responsibility movement has been driven by two broad sets of actors: those within the business community itself; as well as key stakeholders beyond the business community, such as governments, investors, NGOs, academic institutions and foundations. These actors are summarized in Figure 1.2.

Within the corporate sector, changes have been driven by a combination of:

- **Champions.** Individual chief executive officers, business unit directors and ESG professionals within companies and social entrepreneurs who have had the vision and the necessary leadership skills to mobilize their peers around a new way of perceiving the role of business in society and new ways of delivering practical business-led and market-based solutions to social, economic and environmental challenges

- **Companies.** Individual companies with supportive boards of directors, senior executive teams, ESG teams or employees that have been committed to embedding better ESG performance and new models of ESG innovation in the heart of their corporate strategy and day-to-day operations and as part of the way they manage their diverse value chains; and, in many cases, being willing and able to build non-traditional project-based partnerships with other companies, NGOs, academics and government entities to achieve this goal

- **Coalitions.** Groups of companies working together on a peer-to-peer collective basis, often in pre-competitive alliances, and, in a growing number of cases, with governments, NGOs and academics, to achieve large-scale transformation and more systemic change than any one company or project-based partnership could achieve on its own

Table 1.1 **The potential corporate contribution to national progress and sustainable development**

Source: J. Nelson, *Building Competitiveness and Communities: How World-Class Companies Are Creating Shareholder Value-Added and Societal Value-Added* (London: International Business Leaders Forum/United Nations Development Programme/World Bank Group, 1998)

Building and investing **economic capital** and strengthening economies	. . . by providing jobs; expanding local infrastructure, in terms of both physical assets and institutional development; transferring technology and international business standards; building supplier and distribution networks; releasing more disposable income into the economy and thereby fueling domestic consumption and additional growth opportunities; generating export revenues; taxes, royalties; and so on
Building and nurturing **human capital** and supporting human development	. . . by investing in the education, training, health and safety of people in the workplace; building cross-border teamwork and learning networks, thereby exposing local nationals to international contacts and practices; paying taxes for the government to spend on social services; investing in education, training, health and nutrition projects through social investment and philanthropy programs
Building and conserving **natural capital** and protecting the environment	. . . by introducing technologies and processes for cleaner production systems and by promoting energy and other natural resource efficiency; researching and developing environmentally sound products and services; promoting the concepts of product stewardship, life-cycle analysis and full-cost accounting; sharing international best practices in environmental management; training local technical specialists in this field; addressing environmental regulatory and fiscal policies with governments and civil society in an open and transparent manner
Building and legitimizing **political capital** and encouraging good governance	. . . both at the corporate level, by establishing, operating with and sharing internationally accepted good practices, especially in the areas of ethics and stakeholder accountability, and at the national or local level by helping governments increase the efficiency of public service delivery, eliminate bribery and corruption, and establish fair and transparent laws and regulations in areas such as private property rights, competition policy, foreign investment, employment, environmental protection and human rights
Building and promoting **social capital** and assisting social cohesion	. . . by helping to alleviate poverty and raise quality of life; building trust and mutual respect with host communities and other stakeholders through increased dialogue and participation in company activities; minimizing conflict resulting from the company's own activities and, where appropriate, helping to address conflict and disaster situations not resulting from the company's own activities; tackling crime; supporting social entrepreneurs and community-based capacity-building; helping young people and others who are excluded from mainstream society; encouraging cultural tolerance and diversity, in both the workplace and externally; and supporting arts and heritage projects

Figure 1.2 **Key actors driving the corporate responsibility movement**

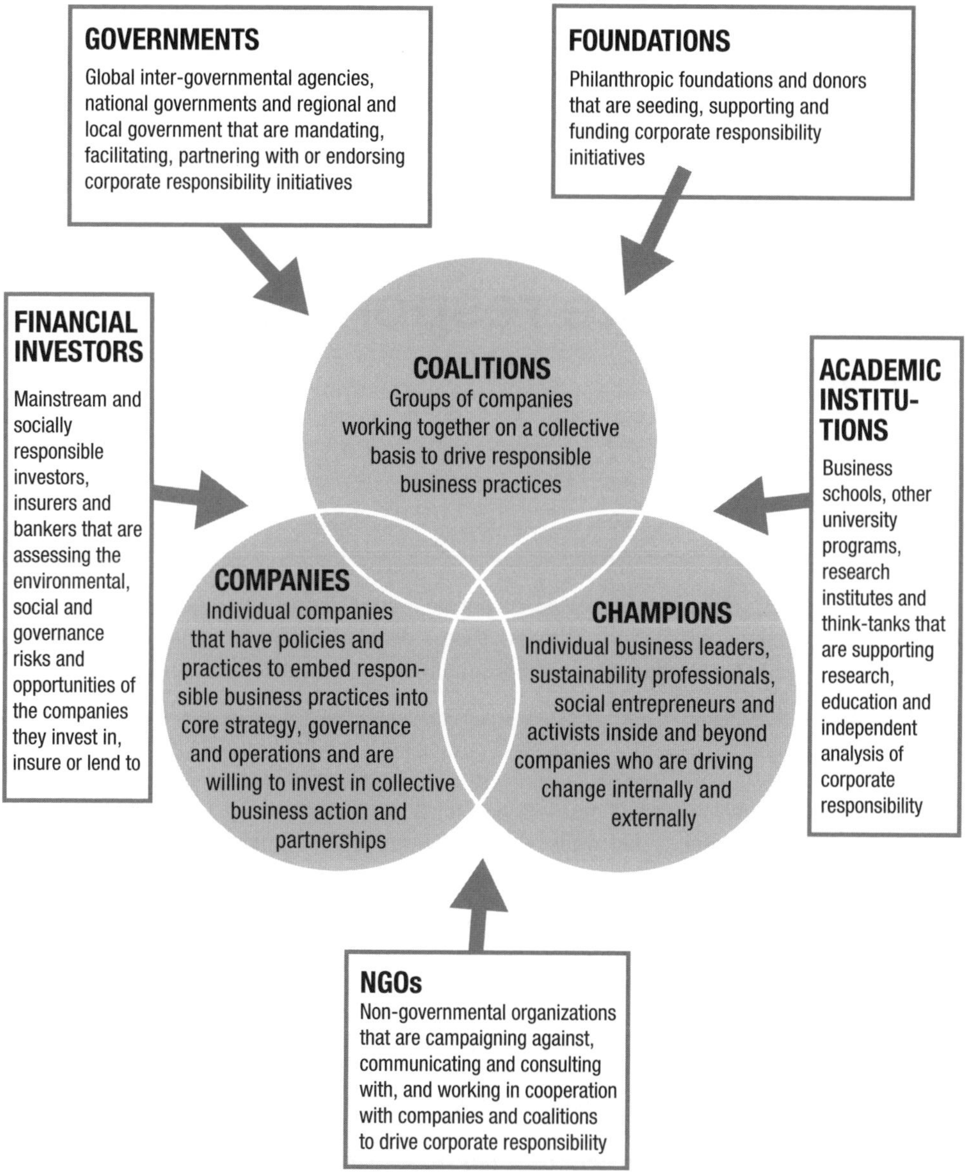

GOVERNMENTS

Global inter-governmental agencies, national governments and regional and local government that are mandating, facilitating, partnering with or endorsing corporate responsibility initiatives

FOUNDATIONS

Philanthropic foundations and donors that are seeding, supporting and funding corporate responsibility initiatives

FINANCIAL INVESTORS

Mainstream and socially responsible investors, insurers and bankers that are assessing the environmental, social and governance risks and opportunities of the companies they invest in, insure or lend to

ACADEMIC INSTITU-TIONS

Business schools, other university programs, research institutes and think-tanks that are supporting research, education and independent analysis of corporate responsibility

COALITIONS
Groups of companies working together on a collective basis to drive responsible business practices

COMPANIES
Individual companies that have policies and practices to embed responsible business practices into core strategy, governance and operations and are willing to invest in collective business action and partnerships

CHAMPIONS
Individual business leaders, sustainability professionals, social entrepreneurs and activists inside and beyond companies who are driving change internally and externally

NGOs
Non-governmental organizations that are campaigning against, communicating and consulting with, and working in cooperation with companies and coalitions to drive corporate responsibility

2
The definition of business-led corporate responsibility coalitions

Our focus is specifically on business-led corporate responsibility coalitions that have been established with the explicit and, in most cases, dedicated goal of mobilizing business resources to directly tackle one or more ESG challenges. As stated earlier, we define these business-led coalitions as:

> Independent, non-profit membership organizations that are composed mainly or exclusively of for-profit businesses; that have a board of directors composed predominantly or only of business people; that are core-funded primarily or totally from business; and whose dedicated purpose is to promote responsible business practice.

There has been considerable discussion of this definition and, therefore, of which organizations are defined as being within the scope of this book versus those excluded from the list of business-led corporate responsibility coalitions. Specifically:

- **Independent.** The definition excludes organizations that are part of a wider entity. Thus, for example, although they and the role they have played are referred to, the focus is not on corporate responsibility or corporate citizenship units of chambers of commerce or employers federations or trade associations or on corporate responsibility-related programs in public–private initiatives that have been established to address a wide range of issues above and beyond corporate responsibility

- **Non-profit.** Therefore, explicitly excluding private, for-profit organizations such as corporate responsibility-focused consulting firms

- **Composed mainly or exclusively of for-profit businesses.** Therefore excluding organizations with a significant non-profit or public-sector membership, or without a membership structure, or organizations made up of individuals[46]

- **Board of directors composed predominantly or only of business people.** Individuals currently in business should be in the majority and have governance responsibility – thus excluding organizations with multi-stakeholder boards where corporate leaders are not a majority,[47] or where ultimate executive authority rests outside the organization

- **Core-funded.** The definition distinguishes between core funding and program funding since a number of coalitions have significant program delivery and may, therefore, have significant public funding for this delivery role in one form or another

There are currently an estimated more than 110 such generalist business-led corporate responsibility coalitions operating on a national or international basis, with at least 30 of them regarded as well established and influential. The remainder are at various stages of development in terms of funding, business and societal influence, expertise, reach and scope.

Many traditional business organizations such as representative chambers of commerce, employers' federations and trade and industry associations have also established dedicated units or initiatives focused on encouraging their members to address corporate responsibility and sustainability issues. Some chambers and other business representative organizations have been instrumental in establishing independent, dedicated corporate responsibility organizations. The Sodalitas Foundation in Italy, for example, was created by Assolombarda, the largest territorial association of the Italian Industrial Union, on the occasion of its 50th anniversary in 1995. The Keidanren in Japan created the Council for Better Corporate Citizenship in 1989 (see Section 3.1). The Business Office for Sustainable Development in Vietnam is a non-profit entity under the auspices of the Vietnam Chamber of Commerce and Industry.

The same situation is occurring in a number of major global, regional and national trade associations. One example is the Foreign Trade Association (FTA), which was established in 1977 to represent the foreign trade interests of European retailers and importers. In 2003, recognizing the growing pressure its members faced to demonstrate their commitment to improving working conditions in global supply chains and the plethora of emerging standards in this area, the FTA created the Business Social Compliance Initiative. This initiative now engages more than 900 companies from a variety of sectors and sourcing countries and has influenced the governance structure and strategic priorities of the FTA itself.[48]

Another example is the Consumer Goods Forum, which was established in 2009 to bring together over 400 food and non-food retailers and manufacturers into a global joint trade and industry body. Although the Forum's mandate is wide-ranging, two of its five strategic priorities are sustainability, and safety and health. Among other activities, it has created the Global Social Compliance Initiative, the Global Protocol on Packaging Sustainability and the Global Food Safety Initiative, and made ambitious resolutions to achieve zero net deforestation through its members' own activities and in partnership with others by 2020 and to start phasing out the use of refrigerants that increase greenhouse gas emissions by 2015.[49]

Other trade and industry associations in sectors as diverse as textiles, toys, chemicals, agriculture, mining, oil and gas, and pharmaceuticals are developing similar sustainability initiatives and in some cases voluntary standards for their members to comply with. Although we illustrate examples from some of the leaders and suggest they have an increasingly important future role to play in mainstreaming corporate responsibility and sustainability among laggard companies, they are not the primary focus of this book given their much wider mandate and focus on advocating for business interests that go far beyond corporate responsibility.

In practice, it is a judgment call whether a particular coalition falls inside or outside these criteria and whether certain organizations meet all the criteria. In a number of cases adherence to the criteria has evolved and changed over time within a single coalition. Several of the main business-led coalitions profiled in depth in the last part of the book, for example, such as Maala in Israel and the World Environment Center, were initially started with foundation or donor funds but have evolved into business-led and funded membership entities. The in-depth examples of the business-led coalitions selected for profile will also illustrate that most are currently partnering with, funded by or undertaking joint advocacy through networks that have active government or civil-society participation.

It should be emphasized that no hierarchy of value is implied between business-led versus multi-stakeholder coalitions; between those leveraging significant public funds and those that have eschewed public funds; or between independent corporate responsibility coalitions and those that are part of business representative organizations, such as chambers of commerce and trade and industry federations, where the promotion of corporate responsibility is only one of numerous tasks. Indeed, as we discuss in Part III, in the future we believe that multi-stakeholder platforms, more traditional business associations and academic institutions will have an increasingly crucial role to play in terms of embedding and scaling responsible business practices and sustainability, in addition to a growing focus on industry- and issue-specific business-led coalitions. The primary focus here, however, is on the more generalist business-led corporate responsibility coalitions that have helped to build the field for corporate responsibility and sustainability over the past four decades.

The definition is designed to identify a specific and important subset of the range of collective initiatives to promote responsible business and to give some practical boundaries to the scope of the investigation. Much of the analysis and recommendations has relevance to all organizations promoting corporate responsibility and more sustainable markets and systems, and not just the independent business-led corporate responsibility coalitions focused on here.

3
The evolution of business-led corporate responsibility coalitions

This chapter outlines three main stages to date in the evolution of business-led corporate responsibility coalitions:

- 1970–1989 and the emergence of a small pioneering group of **corporate social activists.** These were business-led coalitions which were established primarily as a private-sector response to socioeconomic, political or environmental crises in particular countries. Most of them still exist in some form today, although they have all evolved and renewed themselves over the last four decades

- 1990–2000 and the emergence and rapid growth in influence and reach of a group of **global field-builders** and their national and regional affiliates. These are a small group of business-led coalitions which have supported the development of extensive networks of corporate responsibility coalitions around the world. During the decade from 1990 to 2000, they focused mostly on raising awareness of the business case for corporate responsibility and helping companies to embed responsible business practices into their core business operations and value chains (as opposed to addressing social and environmental issues mainly or solely through their philanthropic programs and community engagement activities)

- 2001–2011 and the rise of **industry and issue specialists.** Some of the existing more generalist business-led coalitions that had emerged in previous decades started to focus more specifically on collective corporate action around particular issues and industry sectors during this period. At the same time, the decade witnessed the emergence of a new generation of business-led coalitions and multi-stakeholder initiatives which were more targeted and dedicated to addressing a specific economic, environmental, social or governance issue or driving responsible business practices throughout a particular industry sector

3.1 **The corporate social activists (1970–1989): responding to social and political crises**

The coalitions formed in the 1970s and 1980s were in response to very specific national circumstances, often political, social or economic crises. These are the "pioneers." The first of the coalitions had no role models; rather, each was the product of a particular confluence of national circumstances coming together with some visionary business leaders prepared to take an initiative, and typically a social entrepreneur to make it happen.

p. 290

In the Philippines, **Philippine Business for Social Progress** (PBSP) (www.pbsp.org.ph) was established in 1970, during a period of national and economic unrest. Fifty Filipino businessmen pledged to set aside 1% of their companies' net income before taxes to pursue poverty reduction programs. These leaders were clear that the government alone was unlikely to be willing or able to tackle growing socioeconomic problems in the country and that failure to tackle them would create increasing problems for Philippine business and might ultimately lead to civil war, as excluded communities sought help from Communist regimes overseas.

p. 272

In South Africa, social inequalities, growing violent opposition to apartheid and increasing international isolation, especially after the Soweto Riots in 1976, led to the formation of the **Urban Foundation,** later subsumed within the **National Business Initiative** (NBI) (www. nbi.org.za). The Urban Foundation was established at the instigation of Harry Oppenheimer (1908–2000), the long-serving chairman of Anglo-American. As in the case of PBSP, the business leaders establishing the Urban Foundation acted in the belief that the government of the day would not address the socioeconomic or political problems that beset the country. Indeed, as a long-term opponent of the apartheid regime, Oppenheimer believed that the political system itself was fundamentally flawed.

p. 211

In the UK, **Business in the Community** (BITC) (www.bitc.org.uk) and **Scottish Business in the Community** (www.sbcscot.com) were formed on the initiative of a group of business leaders influenced by American urban renewal efforts in the 1970s. Their initiative was given added urgency by the UK's urban riots in 1981, which coincided with the establishment of BITC. The first significant activity of BITC was to support the replication of local enterprise agencies across the UK such as the Community of St. Helens Trust,[50] which had been initiated five years prior to BITC by Sir Alistair Pilkington of the Pilkington Glass company, who became the first Chairman of BITC in 1982. As Daniel Kinderman has argued in his doctoral thesis on the history of BITC,[51] and in a subsequent article,[52] unlike in South Africa with the Urban Foundation, a number of the original business founders of BITC were strong supporters of the newly elected Thatcher Government. This government had come to power in 1979 after a decade of increasing trade union militancy and economic decline, culminating in the "Winter of Discontent" with mass public-sector strikes, confirming the UK's image as "the sick man of Europe."[53] Kinderman argues[54] that while the initial instigation for BITC – an Anglo-American Conference in 1980[55] – had come from the previous Labour Government, a number of key early BITC supporters saw collective action by business to help arrest and reverse economic and social decline as an essential *quid pro quo* for the reduction of the role of the state that they and Margaret Thatcher and her supporters sought. BITC owed at least some of its early credibility to the enthusiastic endorsement from both the traditional

"One Nation Conservatives" and the more free-market wings of the Thatcher administration in the 1980s.

Jobs and Society Sweden (www.jobs-society.se) was established in 1985 at the instigation of the businessman and philanthropist Pehr Gyllenhammar. He commissioned Patrick Engellau to examine how to replicate the original BITC model of supporting local enterprise agencies, which involved large established businesses supporting social and economic regeneration through small business development.[56] Jobs and Society has continued to focus on helping small businesses and still acts as the umbrella for 90 Enterprise Agencies (Nyföretagar Centrum in Swedish), which cover 200 of Sweden's 290 municipalities.

Separately, **IMS–Entreprendre pour la Cité** (www.imsentreprendre.com) originally called Fondation du Mécénat Humanitaire, was set up in 1986 by the prominent French business leader Claude Bébéar, AXA's founder and the current Honorary Chairman of the Board of Directors, and a group of business leaders to engage French businesses with local communities, and especially to help the marginalized and socially excluded. Bébéar, a towering figure in French business life, was motivated by the idea that "the role of business is not just economic . . . each business must engage with the means at its disposal so that the city is doing better." Since the early 2000s, IMS has been promoting implementation of a Diversity in the Workplace charter, again inspired by Claude Bébéar.[57]

In Japan, the **Council for Better Corporate Citizenship** (CBCC)[58] was established by the Keidanren, the Japan Business Foundation, in 1989 as a separate non-profit membership organization. The background was the sharp appreciation of the yen following the 1985 Plaza agreement.[59] In response, many Japanese companies established factories in the United States. This strained relations between the American public and the Japanese-affiliated companies, which at that time did not know much about corporate citizenship, community relations and community investment, according to Hisako Komai, the CBCC's executive director. In response, the chairman of Sony Corporation, Akio Morita, took the initiative to found the CBCC to help Japanese companies to improve their relations with communities in the United States. From these community relations and corporate philanthropy roots, the practices of the CBCC have evolved to include stakeholder engagement and other activities under the umbrella of corporate social responsibility. The geographical focus has also changed from the United States to South-East Asia and China. The CBCC thus stands out as one of the business-led corporate responsibility coalitions that have always been international in their orientation.[60]

Meanwhile, two early corporate responsibility organizations were created in South America: **Asociación de Empresarios Cristianos** (ADEC) in Paraguay (www.adec.org.py) in 1981 and **Centro de Divulgación del Conocimiento Económico** (CEDICE) in Venezuela (www.cedice.org.ve) in 1984.[61] An association of Christian businessmen that *inter alia* promoted ethical business practices had earlier been formed in Costa Rica in 1961, **Asociación Empresarial para el Desarrollo** (AED; www.aedcr.com), and in 1988 Mexico's **Centro Mexicano para la Filantropia** (CEMEFI; www.cemefi.org) was founded, which later incorporated an interest in corporate citizenship.

Two decades after the creation of Philippine Business for Social Progress, these were the national, business-led corporate responsibility coalitions (see Fig. 3.1). Furthermore, at this stage, these organizations were focused on mobilizing business support for social improvement and were not involved in trying to influence either core business behavior in terms of business impacts in the workplace and marketplace or companies' own governance or ethical performance. As such, the focus was on corporate philanthropy and corporate community involvement (CCI) and, in some cases, policy advocacy, based on ideas of enlightened self-interest: that by social action businesses could help to tackle social exclusion, which would improve operating conditions for business in the long term.

Figure 3.1 **Business-led corporate responsibility coalitions by 1990**

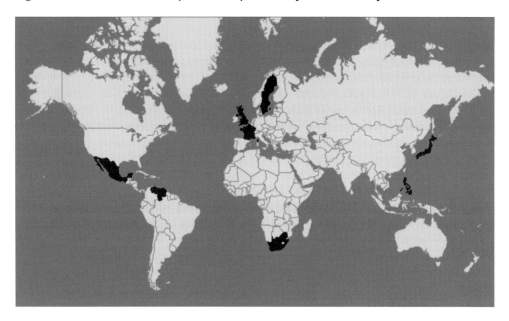

From the 1970s to the early 1990s, a few other business and society initiatives were established either by academic leaders or as the result of academic research.

One notable example of a global leadership coalition that had its origins in academic research and the academy, but which became an outstandingly successful independent leadership coalition in its own right, is the **World Economic Forum** (WEF; www.weforum. org). What was to become WEF was first conceived in January 1971 when a group of European business leaders met under the patronage of the European Commission and European industrial associations. Klaus Schwab, then Professor of Business Policy at the University of Geneva, chaired the gathering, which took place in Davos, Switzerland. Schwab then founded the European Management Forum as a non-profit organization based in Geneva. Schwab believed that the management of a modern enterprise must serve all stakeholders, acting as their trustee charged with achieving the long-term sustained growth and prosperity of the company. In 1973 at the organization's Annual Meeting in Davos, the stakeholder concept became the cornerstone of the Davos Manifesto, which articulated the fundamental principles of a corporation's social and environmental responsibility.[62] Since that time WEF has played a key leadership role in promoting concepts such as corporate governance, corporate philanthropy, corporate social responsibility, social entrepreneurship and global corporate citizenship, and in building multi-stakeholder alliances with strong business leadership to help tackle complex global challenges.[63] It has coordinated industry-wide collective action around social and environmental issues for several decades and from 2000

Profiles
p. 347

to 2010 it ran a workstream on corporate citizenship in partnership with a core group of its members' companies and the International Business Leaders Forum (and later Business for Social Responsibility and the CSR Initiative at Harvard Kennedy School). In 2008, WEF established the Global Agenda Councils, bringing together leaders from business and other sectors to look at strategic and systemic-level interventions in addressing over 80 key global challenges.[64] While WEF's multi-stakeholder governance structure and broader remit beyond corporate responsibility preclude it from inclusion in a strictly defined tally of business-led corporate responsibility coalitions, the attention it has given to global corporate citizenship, particularly since the anti-globalization protests at the Seattle World Trade Organization (WTO) Conference in 1999, has had a profound impact on business and on the work of the other coalitions.

Founded in 1974, through the United Nations Environment Programme (UNEP), the **World Environment Center** (WEC; www.wec.org) is another example of an entity that has become a primarily business-led, -governed and -funded organization which advances p. 318 sustainable development through the business practices of member companies and in partnership with governments, multilateral organizations, NGOs, universities and other stakeholders. WEC creates sustainable business solutions through individual projects in emerging markets, convenes leadership roundtables to shape strategic thinking across a range of sustainability topics and honors industry excellence through the annual awarding of its Gold Medal Award.

The **Center for Corporate Citizenship at Boston College** (BCCCC; bccorporatecitizenship. org) is another pioneer, originally established as the Center for Corporate Community Relations in 1985. For a quarter of a century, from its formation by its founder director the late Dr. Edmund Burke and subsequently under the leadership of Professor Bradley K. Googins, the Center played a major role as a convener and as an identifier and disseminator of good practice in corporate community relations. The Center promoted the concept of the company as a "neighbor of choice" earning a "license to operate" as well as being an employer and supplier of choice. It created a training program for corporate community involvement professionals, which has been certified since 1986. The Center developed *Standards of Excellence in Corporate Community Relations.* Through annual conferences from 1987 onwards, training courses, working with individual companies and its applied research, the Center became a global center of expertise on the theory and practice of corporate citizenship. In 2007, it consolidated more than 20 years' learning in a Corporate Citizenship Management Framework and companion Corporate Citizenship Assessment Tool, and in a book, *Beyond Good Company: Next Generation Corporate Citizenship*, written by the Center's Executive Director Bradley K. Googins along with Philip H. Mirvis and Steven A. Rochlin.[65] The Center was initially created as an autonomous and entrepreneurial start-up loosely affiliated to Boston College, housed in university accommodation adjacent to its campus. It became part of the Carroll School of Management within Boston College in 1995, and was ultimately controlled by the School of Management and University authorities. The business leadership of BCCCC was an international *advisory* board – it did not ultimately have governance responsibility – illustrated by the manner of a change of Center leadership imposed by the University in 2010 and the subsequent departure of several key staff from the Center. Hence, while the Center was a very significant influence on the evolution of corporate responsibility on both sides of the Atlantic and beyond, it is not defined as a business-led coalition because of its governance structure and status as part of an academic institution.

3.2 **The global field-builders (1991–2001): promoting and embedding responsible practices into core business**

The number of business-led corporate responsibility coalitions increased dramatically in the 1990s. This was driven by a combination of factors including:

- The collapse of Communism in Eastern and Central Europe in 1989, and the consequent opening up to the market economy. Organizations such as the **International Business Leaders Forum** (IBLF; www.iblf.org) and other private- and public-sector groups actively promoted democracy and the market economy and supported the establishment of business-led corporate responsibility coalitions in economies in transition, such as the **Polish Business Leaders Forum** and the **Hungarian Business Leaders Forum**. The IBLF subsequently extended its remit to other markets in transition around the globe beyond Eastern Europe, encouraging, among others, the establishment of **Indonesia Business Links** and **Vietnam Business Links**, and incubating Business Action for Africa in its early days

Profiles p. 246

- The growing awareness of the environmental challenges facing the world and the formation of the Business Council for Sustainable Development (BCSD) to provide a private-sector voice at the Rio Earth Summit in 1992 – subsequently the **World Business Council for Sustainable Development** (WBCSD; www.wbcsd.org) – which has gone on to affiliate with existing organizations or create new national affiliates in over 50 countries

Profiles p. 300

- The emergence of a generation of socially aware business entrepreneurs who established initiatives which became increasingly mainstreamed through larger companies and networks. In particular, the creation of **Business for Social Responsibility** (BSR; www.bsr.org) in the United States in 1992 by a group of entrepreneurs and its subsequent outreach work, for example, **Canadian BSR** in 1995, **Maala–Business for Social Responsibility**, Israel, in 1998 (www.maala.org.il) and in particular in Latin America after the establishment of **Forum Empresa** in 1997 (www.empresa.org) and the creation of **Instituto Ethos** in 1998

Profiles p. 194
Profiles p. 262
Profiles p. 235

- The growing recognition of the social and economic costs of exclusion and the challenge of improving employability among next-generation workers in Europe, which led to the creation of the European Business Network for Social Cohesion (now **CSR Europe**; www.csreurope.org) in 1995 at the instigation of the then EU Commission President Jacques Delors; and the subsequent work to create national affiliates in each member state where these did not already exist

Profiles p. 224

- Increased awareness by global policy-makers and business leaders that, to sustain the legitimacy of economic globalization and trade, there was a growing need for companies to adopt universally agreed principles in the areas of human rights, labor and the environment. This led to the creation of the **United Nations Global Compact** (UNGC; www.unglobalcompact.org) in 2000, following a speech made by former UN Secretary-General Kofi Annan to WEF at Davos in January 1999 calling on business

Profiles p. 328

leaders to form a "global compact" between business and the UN. The UNGC subsequently established or affiliated with local and national business-led networks around the world. The UNGC is not strictly a business-led coalition because it is housed in the United Nations and is governed by a variety of structures, which include a government-led donor committee and a multi-stakeholder board which includes a majority of business members, but is chaired by the UN Secretary-General, and it is funded by a combination of public-donor funds and the private sector. Similar to the World Economic Forum, however, the UNGC has played a highly influential role in building the field of corporate responsibility and driving collective business action around the globe, and as such is included in the profiles in this book

This phase can be called the era of "field-builders" as the IBLF, CSR Europe, BSR, the WBCSD and the UNGC created national and regional affiliates across the globe. Each of these significant coalitions is profiled in more detail at the end of the book.

3.2.1 International Business Leaders Forum

The International Business Leaders Forum (IBLF)[66] was created by Business in the Community in 1990 and was originally called International Business in the Community. It began as a vehicle to convene meetings of international business leaders under the banner of The Prince of Wales Business Leaders Forum. The first convening was in Charleston, South Carolina, arranged to coincide with an official visit to the United States by HRH The Prince of Wales, who served as President of the IBLF until 2010. The initial focus of the IBLF was on the newly democratic societies of Eastern Europe, although this quickly extended to other countries in transition to market economies and pluralism. To facilitate collective business engagement on the ground in practical initiatives, the IBLF encouraged the creation of a number of geographic and industry- or issue-specific coalitions – some of which stayed under its auspices while others were established independently or were subsequently floated off (see Table 3.1).

3.2.2 World Business Council for Sustainable Development

The origins of the World Business Council for Sustainable Development (WBCSD) lie in an invitation from Maurice Strong, then Secretary-General of the United Nations Conference on Environment and Development (UNCED), which would come to be better known as the Rio Earth Summit (1992), to the Swiss business entrepreneur Stephan Schmidheiny in 1990 to serve as his business adviser for the conference. Schmidheiny decided to establish a time-bound network of 48 business leaders, which he called the Business Council for Sustainable Development (BCSD). Alongside the global representative business organization, the International Chamber of Commerce, which had a long-standing relationship with the UN, the BCSD played a key role in preparing and participating in the Rio Earth Summit. It hosted consultations with hundreds of business leaders and companies around the world and produced a seminal report entitled *Changing Course*.[67] After the conference Schmidheiny agreed to continue the initiative. In 1995, the BCSD merged with the International Chamber of Commerce's World Industry Council for the Environment to form the World Business Council for Sustainable Development. Among other activities, the WBCSD established a network of business-led sustainability initiatives and now has affiliates which operate in more than 60 countries (see Table 3.1).

3.2.3 Business for Social Responsibility and Forum Empresa

Business for Social Responsibility (BSR), created in 1992, was the brainchild of a number of U.S. entrepreneurs who had also earlier established **The Social Venture Network**.[68] The initial focus for BSR included mobilizing business support for progressive public policies. It started to develop a global vision and outreach in 1994 with the appointment of a senior Levi Strauss executive, Bob Dunn, as President. While Levi Strauss had had a long track record for generous corporate philanthropy and community involvement, it had also been an early pioneer of accepting responsibility for the environmental, social and economic impacts of its core business activities – both in its own operations and through its supply chain. It had been one of the first American corporations to push through desegregation in the workplace and one of the first companies to take positive action on HIV/AIDS, encouraged by employees at its San Francisco headquarters. It had also been one of the first companies to develop a voluntary code of conduct for managing and improving working conditions along its global supply chain. Dunn brought this more rounded and comprehensive notion of corporate responsibility to BSR, which quickly developed significant programs to help member companies manage their impacts throughout rapidly outsourcing and globalizing supply chains.

In 1997 BSR was one of the founding members of Forum Empresa, established to help spread ideas of corporate responsibility across South and Central America. Bob Dunn, the philanthropist Peggy Dulaney and Oded Grajew, co-founder of Instituto Ethos in Brazil and a well-known businessman and entrepreneur, shared the vision of a network of business-led organizations that would promote corporate responsibility throughout the Americas. As a result of their initial dialogue, a group of 150 business and civic leaders from different regions within the Americas came together for a two-day conference in Miami in 1997 to share ideas and discuss a more responsible and sustainable role for the private sector throughout the hemisphere. This conference led to the formation of Forum Empresa. Its common goal would be to support companies operating in the region to become more commercially successful in ways that demonstrate respect for ethical values, people, communities and the environment. In doing so, it would also seek to promote greater cross-sector collaboration.[69]

BSR's current president, and former Empresa board member, Aron Cramer blogged that:

> Working with like-minded pioneers in Peru, El Salvador, and elsewhere in the region, Bob and Oded planted the seeds of a network that has grown to cover almost every country in the hemisphere. Indeed, EMPRESA has been actively involved in promoting sustainability in Cuba, embracing Inter-American solidarity more fully than many political figures have.[70]

Cramer also argues that "EMPRESA has served as an important conduit for Latin American voices to be heard in the Global Reporting Initiative (GRI), the UN Global Compact, and other international forums."[71]

For further information on the work of Forum Empresa see Chapter 10, Box 10.2 (page 131).

3.2.4 CSR Europe

CSR Europe[72] grew out of an initial idea from the then President of the European Commission, Jacques Delors, to engage business in helping to tackle social exclusion as the European Union made major adjustments; the EU sought to adjust internally to the impacts of enlargement and the creation of the European single market and externally to the rapid globalization of the world economy after 1990. Initially created as the European Business Network for Social Cohesion, CSR Europe was launched formally in 1996 and swiftly sought national affiliates; where these did not exist, it encouraged their creation (see Table 3.1).

3.2.5 United Nations Global Compact

At the end of the 1990s, a fifth global field-builder was established that has since surpassed all the others in its ability to attract corporate members from around the world and to build a global network of national business-led corporate responsibility coalitions: the UN Global Compact (UNGC). From the outset, while focused fully on engaging business for corporate responsibility, the UNGC was established as, and remains, a multi-stakeholder initiative. As such, strictly speaking, it is beyond the focus of this study with our emphasis on business-led coalitions. Nevertheless the UNGC is an important part of the story of the spread of corporate responsibility coalitions, and although *de jure* a UN corporate responsibility initiative, it might be described as *de facto* a "business-led UN corporate responsibility initiative."

The UNGC describes itself as "the world's largest corporate citizenship initiative," with about 8,000 signatory companies. CEOs are required to sign a written letter committing their company to implement the UNGC's Ten Principles in the areas of human rights, labor, the environment and anti-corruption. In addition, the UNGC claims a network of local business-led corporate responsibility coalitions in more than 100 countries, although these are in varying stages of establishment and activity.[73] In a number of cases, the national chapters of the UNGC are previously established corporate responsibility coalitions, but in many they have been created with the primary purpose of promoting the corporate responsibility goals and principles of the UNGC (see Table 3.1).

Particularly in countries lacking a well-established infrastructure of business-representative organizations and independent business leadership, the UNGC national chapter has sometimes provided a vehicle for peer-learning and mutual support. This was particularly important where the business sector lacked popular credibility and where there was a limited enabling environment: the UNGC offered a neutral, acceptable focal point.

Table 3.1 provides a sense of the important role that these five global field-builders have played in helping to spread the growth of business-led corporate responsibility coalitions around the world, especially over the past decade.

Table 3.1 **The global field-builders and their networks**

Field-builder	National coalitions that joined the network between 1991 and 2001	National coalitions that joined the network after 2001
International Business Leaders Forum (created 1990)	• Hungarian Business Leaders Forum • Czech Business Leaders Forum • St. Petersburg Partnership Initiative • Polish Business Leaders Forum • Bangladesh Partnership Forum • Indonesia Business Links • Youth Business Initiative International • Vietnam Business Links	• ENGAGE (Employee volunteering) • China Business Leaders Forum • Business Action for Africa • Serbia Business Leaders Forum • Croatia Business Leaders Forum
World Business Council for Sustainable Development (created in 1992)	Argentina, El Salvador, Philippines (Philippine Business for the Environment), USA, France, Malaysia, Thailand, Zimbabwe, Honduras, Mexico, Russia (Vernadsky Foundation), Australia, Brazil, Colombia, Croatia, Taiwan, Austria (respACT), Mongolia, New Zealand, UK, Algeria, Spain, Egypt, Korea, Peru, Portugal	Canada, Ecuador, India, Mozambique, Norway, Bolivia, Costa Rica, Guatemala, Hong Kong, Japan (Keidanren), Kazakhstan, Paraguay, Sri Lanka, Chile (Acción RSE), China, Germany, Panama, Turkey, Hungary, Nicaragua, Denmark, Pakistan, Uruguay, Curacao, Greece, United Arab Emirates, Vietnam, Indonesia, Israel (Maala), Belgium, Ukraine, Czech Republic, Poland
Business for Social Responsibility (created 1992) and Forum Empresa (created 1997) *(continued opposite)*	Partners that pre-date the creation of Forum Empresa: • Costa Rica: Asociación Empresarial para el Desarrollo (AED) (1961) • Paraguay: Asociación de Empresarios Cristianos (ADEC) (1981) • Venezuela: Centro de Divulgación del Conocimiento Económico (Cedice) (1984) • Argentina: Fundación del Tucumán (1985) • Mexico: Centro Mexicano para la Filantropia (CEMEFI) (1988) • USA: Business for Social Responsibility (BSR) (1992) • Peru: Perú 2021 and Business Council for Sustainable Development (BCSD) (1994) • Canada: Canadian Business for Social Responsibility (CBSR) (1995)	• Ecuador: Consorcio Ecuatoriano Para La Responsabilidad Social (CERES) • Panama: SumaRSE • Bolivia: Consejo Boliviano de la Responsabilidad Social Empresarial (COBORSE), • Honduras: Fundación Hondureña de Responsabilidad Social Empresarial (FUNDAHRSE) • Nicaragua: Unión Nicaragüense para la Responsabilidad Social Empresaria (UniRSE), BCSD • Uruguay: DERES

Field-builder	National coalitions that joined the network between 1991 and 2001	National coalitions that joined the network after 2001
Business for Social Responsibility (created 1992) and Forum Empresa (created 1997) *(from previous page)*	• Colombia: Consejo Empresarial Colombiano Para el Desarrollo Sostenible (CECODES) and Business Council for Sustainable Development (BCSD) (1997) New partners after Forum Empresa was created: • Brazil: Instituto Ethos • Chile: Acción RSE • El Salvador: Fundación Empresarial para la Acción Social (FUNDEMAS)	
CSR Europe (created 1995) *(continued over)*	National partners that pre-date the creation of CSR Europe: • United Kingdom: Business in the Community • Scotland: Scottish Business in the Community • France: IMS–Entreprendre pour la Cité • Czech Republic: Business Leaders Forum • Hungary: KÖVET, Association for Sustainable Economies • Italy: Sodalitas New partners after CSR Europe was created: • Norway: CSR Norway (known as Green Business Network Norway until 2010) • Croatia: Croatian Business Council for Sustainable Development • Belgium: Business & Society Belgium • Spain: Forética • Finland: Finnish Business & Society • France: Observatoire sur la Responsabilité Sociétale des Entreprises (ORSE) • Germany: econsense • Greece: Hellenic Network for Corporate Social Responsibility	• Portugal: RSE Portugal • Spain: Club de Excelencia en Sostenibilidad • Switzerland: Philias Foundation • Slovakia: Slovak Business Leaders Forum/Pontis Foundation • Sweden: CSR Sweden • Ukraine: Center for CSR Development • Austria: respACT (known after 2007 as: respACT: austrian business council for sustainable development) • Turkey: CSR Turkey • Romania: CSR Romania • Serbia: Business Leaders Forum Serbia

Field-builder	National coalitions that joined the network between 1991 and 2001	National coalitions that joined the network after 2001
CSR Europe (created 1995) *(from previous page)*	• Ireland: Business in the Community Ireland (BITCI) • Poland: Responsible Business Forum • Portugal: Grace • Italy: Impronta Etica	
United Nations Global Compact (created 2000)	India, Poland, Germany, Thailand	Ghana, Kenya, Zambia, Panama, Nordic countries, Turkey, Malawi, Mozambique, Brazil, Peru, Japan, Bulgaria, UK, Egypt, Argentina, France, Italy, Macedonia, Spain, Bolivia, Costa Rica, Dominican Republic, Pakistan, Singapore, Bosnia & Herzegovina, Lithuania, USA, Belarus, Gulf States, Morocco, Nigeria, Mexico, Indonesia, Austria, Cyprus, Hungary, Moldova, Netherlands, Switzerland, Ukraine, Ivory Coast, Senegal, South Africa, Chile, Korea, Sri Lanka, Vietnam, Croatia, Slovenia, Israel, Kosovo, Malaysia, Namibia, Sudan, Syria, Paraguay, Greece, Russia, Slovakia, Serbia, Colombia, Australia, Bangladesh, China, Armenia, Belgium, Georgia, Latvia, Mauritius, Portugal, Costa Rica, Montenegro, South-East Asia, Trinidad & Tobago, Uganda, Uruguay, Azerbaijan, Ecuador, Iran, Iraq

3.2.6 Other coalitions and hybrids that emerged in the 1990s

In New Zealand, social entrepreneur Dr. Grahame Craig was inspired by the British model of local enterprise agencies that had galvanized Sweden's Pehr Gyllenhammar to create Jobs and Society Sweden. Craig established the **Business in the Community Charitable Trust** in 1991 to provide a voluntary mentoring service to New Zealand small and medium enterprises (SMEs) under the banner of **Business Mentors New Zealand** (BMNZ). Since 1991, BMNZ has mentored over 50,000 SMEs including non-profit entities and works closely with New Zealand Trade and Enterprise and other government departments.[74]

From a left-of-center political tradition, the Danish government promoted the evolution of a distinctive Scandinavian interpretation of corporate responsibility in the mid- to late 1990s, beginning with an international conference in Copenhagen in 1997. This led to the creation in 1998 of **The Copenhagen Centre**, under the chairmanship of Danish business-man Mads Øvlisen, then chairman of Novo Nordisk, and the executive directorship initially of Jette Steen Knudsen and later of Jens Erik Lund. Supported by an international advisory board and with active business endorsement within Denmark, The Copenhagen Centre quickly established a name for thought leadership and new models of engagement between business and government to tackle social challenges. Some saw it as providing a useful alternative model of corporate responsibility to the then predominant "Anglo-American" variety represented by BITC, IBLF and BSR. The Centre hosted a number of international conferences and sponsored various studies on topics such as cross-sectoral partnerships, responsible competitiveness and SMEs, until an incoming Danish coalition government in 2007 abolished it and absorbed its mandate within a government department (and later, in the Danish Centre for CSR in the Danish Commerce and Companies Agency).[75] Although a multi-stakeholder rather than a business-led corporate responsibility coalition, The Copenhagen Centre worked closely with a number of the business-led coalitions – particularly CSR Europe and the IBLF.

While most of the business-led corporate responsibility coalitions created during the 1990s focused on helping their members to mainstream socially and environmentally responsible practices into their core business operations, the need to take a more rigorous and strategic approach to corporate philanthropy and corporate community investment was also recognized. This was especially the case in the United States, where philanthropic traditions remained strong within the corporate sector and in wider society. In November 1999, the **Committee Encouraging Corporate Philanthropy** (CECP) was launched in New York on the instigation of the actor-turned-businessman Paul Newman, and businessman-turned-philanthropist Peter L. Malkin. CECP involves more than 180 members, with membership at the CEO and chair level and day-to-day engagement undertaken by heads of corporate foundations and corporate citizenship functions. Members represent over 150 major corporations and approximately US$10 billion of annual corporate giving. CECP's initial mission was to lead the business community in raising the level and quality of corporate philanthropy. It offers members a proprietary online benchmarking tool, networking programs, research and opportunities for best-practice sharing. It positions itself as "the only international forum of business CEOs and chairpersons focused exclusively on corporate philanthropy."

Though it is primarily focused on one part of corporate responsibility, in recent years CECP has expanded its mandate to look more strategically at the overall contribution of business to addressing social and environmental challenges. It has commissioned reports on creating sustainable value written by strategy consultants McKinsey & Company and Accenture, and its annual award program and other activities increasingly support a more strategic direction, while still serving as a respected center of excellence on promoting more effective and high-impact corporate philanthropy. As the coalition states on its website: "CECP continues to inspire and challenge today's business leaders to find innovative ways to fulfill unmet social needs, to lead the way towards better alignment of business and social strategies, and to serve as business ambassadors."[76]

Around the same time that CECP was being created, **The Conference Board,** also based in New York and established in 1916 to serve as an independent source of economic and business knowledge for its largely corporate membership, formalized its interest in the broader social roles and responsibilities of modern business. The Conference Board recruited a former journalist, David Vidal, to head a new unit at the end of 1997, initially under the name Global Corporate Citizenship. Vidal quickly initiated an annual conference in New York on corporate citizenship trends, beginning in 1999 with the Leadership Conference on Global

Corporate Citizenship: "Values and the Business,"[77] and oversaw production of a steady flow of Conference Board briefing papers and guidance tools on the practice of corporate citizenship for member companies. Vidal scoured the world for good practice in corporate citizenship and created a platform to share global lessons with a predominantly U.S. audience that was still primarily focused on corporate philanthropy at the time. Global Corporate Citizenship was renamed the Center for Corporate Citizenship and Sustainability in 2006 and in 2010 it was again renamed and repositioned as the Center for Sustainability.[78] As well as an annual summit and a twice-yearly Directors Council on the Governance of Sustainability, the Center undertakes global, cross-functional research, hosts webcasts and produces a range of publications including "BRIC Market" – a periodic two-page letter with insight on sustainability news and developments in Brazil, India and China. We do not include The Conference Board Sustainability Center as a business-led corporate responsibility coalition because it is part of an organization with a wider remit but, again, mention its work and impact because it has influenced the thinking and practice of many corporations and business-led coalitions.

Thus by the millennium, geographic coverage of business-led corporate responsibility coalitions had extended dramatically compared to just ten years previously – see Figure 3.2 (and see Time-line in Appendix 1).

Figure 3.2 **Business-led corporate responsibility coalitions by 2000**

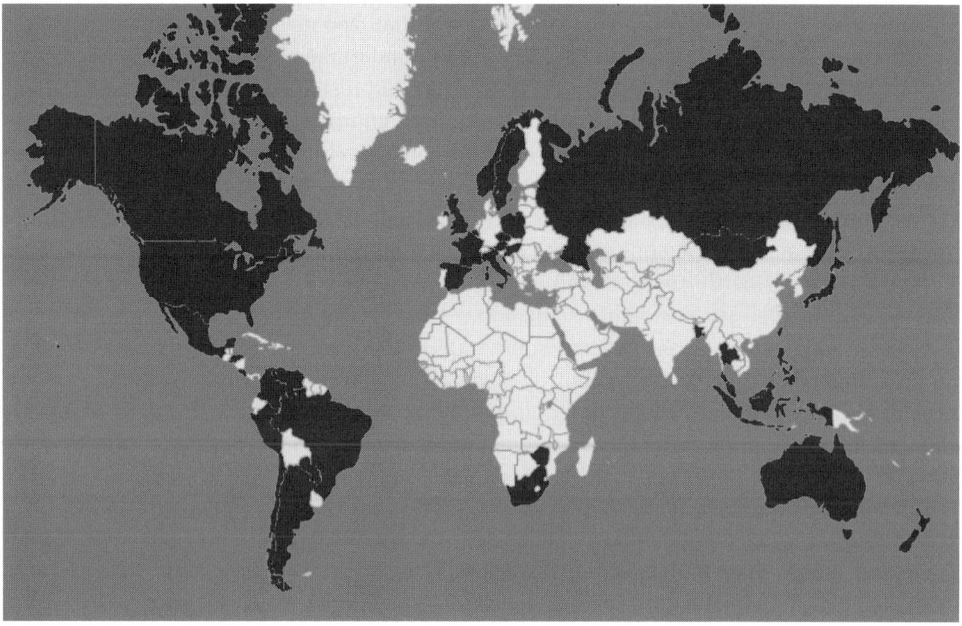

The focus of the growing number of coalitions also began to evolve. More began to switch the emphasis from corporate philanthropy and community involvement to the environmental, social and economic impacts of businesses themselves – how businesses behave in their core activities in the marketplace, the workplace and the environment, as well as in the community. For a number of the leading coalitions such as CSR Europe and BITC this occurred around the millennium, especially as their member companies expanded their operations into many more parts of the world. The IBLF, BSR and the WBCSD had all started with this broader focus from the outset, with a main emphasis on managing the social and environmental risks of core business activities, but over time a growing emphasis on the value-creation and social and environmental innovation agenda as well.

The shift to a more comprehensive approach focusing on how a company manages its core business was caused by a number of inter-related factors:

- **A series of public campaigns against the social and environmental performance of well-known corporations.** Several high-profile international NGOs engaged in media campaigns against business behavior. These included campaigns against Shell, over the disposal of a redundant North Sea oil installation, the Brent Spar, and over its operations in Nigeria; Nike, facing allegations that its suppliers' factories in Asia were sweatshops; BP, over allegations of complicity in the murder of activists in Colombia by contractor security forces; Monsanto, over its attempts to introduce genetically modified organisms in Europe; the "blood diamonds" controversy for De Beers and other companies in the diamond sector; Mars, Cadbury and Hershey facing child-labor allegations in cocoa plantations in West Africa; Chiquita, regarding rights of association for workers in its Caribbean suppliers' farms; and the collapse of the pharmaceuticals companies' court case against the South African Government over patent rights for HIV/AIDS medicines

- **Growing recognition of the lack of internal coherence and alignment.** There was also growing recognition by business leaders and business-led coalitions themselves that companies could not claim to be responsible if they were doing something pro-gressive through their community investment and philanthropy activities while hav-ing negative social or environmental impacts through their core business activities; for example, sponsoring community contributions to schools but failing to create learning organizations for their own employees, or claiming to be responsible due to sponsorship of environmental NGOs while being inveterate polluters in their own core operations. The need for coherence and consistency was articulated by one of the board members of Philippine Business for Social Progress in the mid-1990s:

  > [he] believes that PBSP's relationship with its members should not be based only on the 1% allocation for social development. He asks: What happens to the 99% of the company's earnings? If the 99% is spent on business practices that are inconsistent with development like wanton cutting of trees, polluting the environment, or selling the uncontrolled consumption of alcohol, then the 1% becomes "conscience money." PBSP's social development philosophy must permeate the whole com-pany. This is the only way true development can be achieved in the Philippines.[79]

- **A series of major corporate governance scandals.** The overall integrity, ethics and responsible business practices of large companies also came under the spotlight and met growing public anger following major corporate governance scandals in the United States and Europe, such as those involving Enron, WorldCom and Parmalat. The negative implications of these scandals for the corporate responsibility movement were exacerbated by the fact that several of these companies, notably Enron, and their CEOs had been lauded by many environmental and community-based organizations and had won awards for their "corporate responsibility"

- **Growing backlash against globalization.** There was a need for a corporate response to the anti-globalization protests, with their allegations of undue corporate power, which sprang up around the World Trade Organization meetings in Seattle, the World Economic Forum's annual meeting in Davos and elsewhere in the late 1990s. This growing public distrust of business was summed up by the Canadian journalist Naomi Klein in her best-selling polemic of 2000, *No Logo*,[80] as well as in earlier books, such as David Korten's *When Corporations Rule the World*.[81] It led many of the corporate responsibility coalitions to realize that they needed to focus on key business activities, corporate strategies and market trends, not only on corporate philanthropy and compliance

- **Business- and government-led commissions.** The growing focus on the broader societal impact of core business activities was also supported by initiatives of business leaders themselves, such as the Royal Society of Arts, Tomorrow's Company Inquiry in the UK and the Commission of Inquiry into a New Vision for Business, initiated by Tony Blair, then UK prime minister, and the late Anita Roddick from the Body Shop.[82] Other examples included several Blue Ribbon Commissions in the United States following the corporate governance scandals and WBCSD's *Global Scenarios* project

By 2000, there was a robust debate under way within and beyond the business community and in many parts of the world on the role of the private sector in society, focused on the impact and contributions of core business operations and value chains, which included but went far beyond corporate philanthropy and community engagement.

3.3 The industry and issue specialists (2001–2011): deepening and diversifying business solutions

The decade from 2001 to 2011 witnessed the ongoing global spread of generalist corporate responsibility coalitions to more countries and regions, but also the notable rise of the **industry and issue specialists.** Some of the existing more generalist business-led coalitions that had emerged in the previous decade started to focus more specifically on collective corporate action around particular industry sectors and issues during this period. At the same time, came the emergence of more business-led coalitions and multi-stakeholder initiatives that were fully dedicated to addressing a particular economic, environmental, social or governance issue or driving responsible business practices throughout a particular industry sector.

3.3.1 The continued spread of generalist coalitions to more countries and regions

The global spread of more generalist business-led corporate responsibility initiatives continued during this period, especially but not only in developing countries. As Table 3.1 in Section 3.2 demonstrates, the global field-builders – particularly the UNGC and the WBCSD – continued apace in adding national affiliates after the millennium. Further coalitions were initiated as business leaders, and social entrepreneurs sought to import successful coalition models from abroad and adapt them to their own locations. Some examples of the different ways in which engagement with and lessons from business-led coalitions in one country have led to a locally initiated and adapted coalition in another country include:

- Shalini Mahtani, a former investment banker from Hong Kong, organized a personal "internship" with Business in the Community in London, used the time to network actively with companies that had interests in Hong Kong and mainland China, and returned to her native Hong Kong to establish **Community Business Hong Kong** in 2003[83]

- Following a speaking tour to Australia by BITC's then-CEO Dame Julia Cleverdon, the **Australian Business and Community Network** (ABCN) was created in 2004 by a group of senior Australian business leaders whose vision was to inspire, challenge and engage businesses to have a greater positive impact in the community. The ABCN is now operating in most of the states and territories of Australia[84]

- Also in 2004, the **Arabia CSR Network** was launched, initially as an off-shoot of the Emirates Environmental Group, with the aim of working more closely with the corporate sector in the promotion of sustainable development in the United Arab Emirates. It runs workshops and seminars, including training on reporting against GRI guidelines and an awards program[85]

- The **Responsible Business Forum in Estonia** (Vastutustundliku Ettevõtluse Foorum) was established in 2006 as an independent, non-profit organization that grew out of a series of round-table dialogues organized by the Multistakeholder Forum initiative of the Open Estonia Foundation. It aims to further corporate responsibility in Estonian society through being the center of competence-building and communication on issues related to responsible business[86]

- One of the most recently established coalitions has been the **Corporate Responsibility Forum Liberia**. In this case, the global mining company ArcelorMittal has played a crucial role in partnership with the German government's international development agency Gesellschaft für Technische Zusammenarbeit (GTZ) (now Gesellschaft für Internationale Zusammenarbeit – GIZ) in incubating and launching the forum (see Box 3.1)

Box 3.1 **Corporate Responsibility Forum Liberia (CR Forum)**

Corporate Responsibility Forum Liberia is one of the youngest of the national business-led coalitions. It was formally established and launched in 2010.

Background

Liberia is Africa's oldest republic. The country declared its independence in 1847. A civil war started in December 1989, in which some 250,000 people were killed. The conflict left the country in ruins, with rampant corruption. Liberia is characterized by high unemployment and high poverty levels, with few job opportunities and low literacy and education levels. Infrastructure remains very basic. There is a general lack of respect for employee rights and labor standards, and a lack of information about them. The business community is small, with just a few international companies and no major indigenous private-sector employers. There is a lack of trust between employers and employees; bribery and corruption are widely perceived as major problems for economic development; and there are tensions over community rights and concession agreements for extractive-industry projects. Governance and regulatory enforcement remains weak.

Origins of the CR Forum

The CR Forum was the product of two parallel developments. ArcelorMittal (the world's largest integrated steel and mining company) was one of the first international companies to enter Liberia after the civil war and has been in Liberia since 2005. Following the merger of Arcelor and Mittal Steel, there was a renewed focus on corporate responsibility with the creation of a corporate department, the 2008 appointment of a global corporate responsibility manager, Charlotte Wolff, and a local manager in Liberia, Marcus Wleh. In parallel, the German international development agency GTZ's (now GIZ) Center for Cooperation with the Private Sector (CCPS) was interested in promoting collective business action to support development in Liberia and established a partnership with the CR Forum, based on a previous initiative in Ghana in 2006 to establish a CSR Forum there.

Joseph Mathews, then ArcelorMittal Liberia's CEO, convened business peers to discuss the creation of a forum to promote responsible business practices in Liberia. An exploratory meeting was held in September 2009 in Monrovia. The meeting established a steering group, and a formal launch, involving the Liberian President, Her Excellency Madam Ellen Johnson Sirleaf, took place in February 2010, with a call for private-sector business engagement and responsibility. The President declared:

> Government cannot, by itself, achieve the vision for Liberia that is enshrined in our poverty reduction strategy. We need the participation of the private sector – one that will bring in sustainable investment and promote good corporate citizenship.

GIZ has provided advisory and financial support – for example, the inaugural project, Capacity Building for Better Business in Liberia, and a series of practical workshops – and will link the Forum with other relevant GIZ initiatives in the region such as the Regional Natural Resources Governance in Fragile States of West Africa, in which Liberia is a focus country.[87]

Goals of the CR Forum

The CR Forum is a private-sector initiative that aims to promote responsible investment, good corporate citizenship and collective action for the sustainable development of Liberia with a focus on capacity-building and knowledge transfer among Forum members and the private sector.[88]

The future

There is a consensus on the need to develop a Code of Conduct to which CR Forum members will be asked to subscribe, covering anti-corruption, disclosure and business ethics, business and human rights, occupational health and safety, minimum wage, collective bargaining, and environmental, social and sustainability issues. Although corporate responsibility is relatively new in Liberia, it is resonating with large and small companies. As economic activity is picking up again, managers who have in the past had less time for CR Forum activities are taking steps towards this end.

So far, beyond the GIZ expertise, there has not been any tapping of significant international coalitions' experience, and CR Forum is now considering the possibilities of twinning with another coalition at a similar stage of development.[89]

Another trend during this period was the establishment of several business-led coalitions that focus explicitly on promoting the role of multinational corporations in driving more responsible and inclusive investment models to developing countries and partnering with companies and development agencies in these countries.

In 2003, for example, the **Initiative for Global Development** (IGD), was founded in the United States by a small group of retired business, civic and public-sector leaders. They were Bill Gates Sr., (a lawyer and philanthropist), Bill Ruckelshaus (a former corporate CEO, Director of the U.S. Environmental Protection Agency and one of the founder members of the WBCSD), Bill Clapp (a business entrepreneur and philanthropist), Dan Evans (a former U.S. Senator and State Governor), and John Shalikashvili (a former U.S. military general). The IGD was created to bring together business leaders to focus on large-scale poverty reduction in the developing world through strategic and catalytic investment in economic growth. With a current focus on Africa, the IGD convenes CEOs and senior executives to connect, share knowledge and take action to increase the volume and impact of commercial investment to drive both social and economic development. It has created the innovative **Frontier 100 network**, which brings together committed CEOs or business unit heads of companies operating in Africa that have at least $50 million in annual revenues. The network has hosted meetings in East, West and Southern Africa, in addition to the United States. It aims not only to catalyze new investments that are both profitable as well as socially and environmentally beneficial, but also to influence policy-makers in Africa and the United States to support market-driven solutions to development. In particular, the IGD has collaborated with other business-led and development agency coalitions to try to influence U.S. foreign policy to include both "aid and trade": that is, to maximize economic development and sustainable growth through foreign aid reform, trade for development, and investment in key sectors such as agriculture, power, inclusive financial services, consumer goods and information technology. To date the IGD has helped to catalyze more than $100 million in investment commitments to Africa, resulting in new employment opportunities, increased access to markets, and improved goods and services that help to serve low-income people.[90]

Another example of a business-led coalition focused on driving business investment combined with social and environmental innovation in emerging markets is **Business Action for Africa** (BAA). BAA was launched in 2005. Initially incubated by the IBLF, today BAA operates as an innovative network and online platform catalyzing collective business leadership and inclusive business models to support African development. It is primarily funded and governed by a small group of leading multinational companies with investments in Africa: AngloAmerican, British American Tobacco, the Coca-Cola Company, DeBeers, Diageo, SABMiller, Royal Dutch Shell, and Unilever; and it is also supported by the UK's Department for International Development (DFID), CDC (the UK's development finance institution), and the International Business Leaders Forum. Like IGD, BAA undertakes a combination of advocacy activities and shares best practices, as well as catalyzing specific investments and partnerships on the ground in Africa. It has been one of the most effective business-led coalitions in harnessing the potential and reach of social media, launching an interactive online community **Business Fights Poverty** in 2011. This online platform connects over 10,000 professionals from companies, development organizations, the international donor community and academia, all with a shared interest in scaling up market-based solutions, inclusive business models and collective business coalitions to drive more effective development outcomes. It offers a good example of the multiplier effect that social media can have in supporting the missions of business-led coalitions.[91]

3.3.2 The emergence of industry- and issue-specific coalitions

The other increasingly important feature of the last decade has been the expansion in the number and reach of industry- and issue-specific corporate responsibility coalitions. Some of these are business-led, while others are multi-stakeholder both in theory and in practice. The earliest of the sector-specific coalitions were among the first pioneer coalitions in the 1970s and 1980s, responding in large part to environmental crises and stakeholder challenges:

- The **International Petroleum Industry Environmental Conservation Association (IPIECA)** began in 1974, following the establishment of the United Nations Environment Programme. It is one of a few global associations involving both the upstream and the downstream oil and gas industries and is focused totally on working with the industry – both individual companies and national industry associations – to improve its environmental and social performance

- **Responsible Care** was initiated in 1985 by the Canadian Chemical Producers' Association in response to the Bhopal gas tragedy in India in 1984. It was subsequently adopted by the International Chemical Manufacturers Association and other national industry associations. Adherence to Responsible Care is now a requirement of membership of these associations (see Box 6.1 in Chapter 6, page 82)

There was a steady growth in industry- and issue-focused business-led coalitions in the 1990s and an intensification of this process since the millennium. Table 3.2 lists a small number of these initiatives and some further examples are provided in Parts II and III.

Table 3.2 **Growth in industry- and issue-focused business-led coalitions and multi-stakeholder initiatives**

	Single industry sector	**Single issue**
Business-led coalition	• IPIECA (global oil and gas industry association for environmental and social issues) (www.ipieca.org) 1974 • Responsible Care (www.icca-chem.org/en/Home/Responsible-care) 1985 • Portman Group (UK responsible drinking) (www.portmangroup.org.uk) 1989 • International Council on Mining & Metals (ICMM) (www.icmm.com) 2001 • Media CSR Forum (www.mediacsrforum.org) 2001 • Sustainable Agriculture Initiative (www.saiplatform.org) 2001 • The Global e-Sustainability Initiative (www.gesi.org) 2001 • International Council of Toy Industries (ICTI) CARE initiative (www.icti-care.org) 2004 • Electronic Industry Citizenship Coalition (www.eicc.info) 2008 • Consumer Goods Forum (consumer goods producers and retailers) (www.theconsumergoodsforum.com) 2009	• Global Business Coalition Against HIV/AIDS, Tuberculosis and Malaria (now the Global Business Coalition for Health, GBCHealth) (www.gbchealth.org) 2001 • Business Social Compliance Initiative www.bsci-int.org 2003 • Sustainable Packaging Coalition (www.sustainablepackaging.org) 2005 • Corporate Eco Forum (www.corporateecoforum.com) 2008 • Global Business Coalition for Education (www.gbceducation.net) 2012
Multi-stakeholder initiative *(continued over)*	• Voluntary Principles on Security and Human Rights (www.voluntaryprinciples.org) 2000 • Extractive Industries Transparency Initiative (EITI) (www.eiti.org) 2002 • Equator Principles (www.equator-principles.com) 2002 • Global Network Initiative (www.globalnetworkinitiative.org) 2008 • Sustainable Apparel Coalition (www.apparelcoalition.org) 2011	• Forest Stewardship Council (www.fsc.org) 1992 • Global Water Partnership (www.gwp.org) 1996 • Marine Stewardship Council (www.msc.org) 1997 • Global Reporting Initiative (www.globalreporting.org) 1997 • Ethical Trading Initiative (www.ethicaltrade.org) 1998 • International Cocoa Initiative (www.cocoainitiative.org) 2002 • Fair Labor Association (www.fairlabor.org) 1999 • Roundtable on Sustainable Palm Oil (www.rspo.org) 2003 • Sustainable Food Lab 2004 (www.sustainablefoodlab.org)

	Single industry sector	Single issue
Multi-stakeholder initiative *(from previous page)*		• Responsible Purchasing Network (www.responsiblepurchasing.org) 2005 • Roundtable on Responsible Soy Association (www.responsiblesoy.org) 2006 • CEO Water Mandate (www.ceowatermandate.org) 2007 • Better Cotton Initiative (bettercotton.org) 2009 • Sustainability Consortium (www.sustainabilityconsortium.org) 2009

Some of these industry- and issue-specific coalitions have also spread geographically around the world during the past decade to establish regional and national business-led coalitions. As such, they share some similar characteristics with the more generalist global field-builders that were profiled in the previous section. **GBCHealth** (formerly the Global Business Coalition Against HIV/AIDS, Tuberculosis and Malaria) is one example of an issue-specific business-led coalition that has initiated and supported a global network of national coalitions and also expanded its range of issues over time to respond to evolving member needs and global trends.

Originally incubated by the IBLF, the organization was established as an independent entity with strong UN support in 2001. With 17 founding member companies, it was initially dedicated to leveraging core business resources and expertise to tackle the scourge of HIV/AIDS. It helped to establish and networked with business coalitions on HIV/AIDS in over 20 countries, all of which played a vital role in raising awareness, overcoming stigma and mobilizing business resources to find practical solutions with governments and NGOs. In 2007, in response to the needs of its members, the model was expanded to include tuberculosis and malaria. In 2011, the organization expanded its mandate again, this time to include non-communicable diseases (such as diabetes), which have growing consequences in the workplace and communities in which business is conducted. Its name changed to reflect this expanded portfolio, to the Global Business Coalition on Health.

Today, GBCHealth has more than 200 member companies. It continues to mobilize collective business action around specific issues and countries, as well as sharing best practices for embedding better health programs within individual companies and value chains, and advocating for global health at the international level. GBCHealth's Collective Action initiatives include:

- The Global Fund Private Sector Delegation (PSD), in which GBCHealth is the entry point and coordinator for private-sector firms wanting to work with the Global Fund for AIDS, Tuberculosis and Malaria

- Healthy Women, Healthy Economies, focusing private-sector action on the health, well-being and opportunity of women and girls through four intervention areas that include health, education, economic empowerment, and rights and inclusion

- HIV-Free Generation/Kenya, bringing together the U.S. President's Emergency Plan for Aids Relief (PEPFAR) and corporate partners to focus on HIV prevention in Kenya

- The Corporate Alliance on Malaria in Africa (CAMA), concentrating on building country-level capacity for effective malaria control in sub-Saharan Africa

- The U.S. HIV Initiative, using social marketing, community interventions and advocacy from the private sector

- The China HIV/AIDS Media Partnership (CHAMP), which uses mass media and commercial marketing to raise awareness and reduce stigma around HIV/AIDS

These examples illustrate an interesting model for the future, where a business-led corporate responsibility coalition networks with other business-led initiatives in different industry sectors and geographies as well as with governments and NGOs to more effectively leverage the impact of the business community.

4

Global trends and motivations driving the growth of corporate responsibility coalitions

As outlined throughout the previous chapter, there have been a number of factors at work in the formation and growth of business-led corporate responsibility coalitions since the establishment of Philippine Business for Social Progress more than 40 years ago. These have ranged from specific political, social and governance drivers to broader underlying global trends, which have motivated business leaders to get more proactively engaged in such coalitions.

4.1 Specific political, social and governance drivers

Most of the earliest coalitions were in response to particular national crises. It was the end of the road for prevailing national orthodoxies: apartheid in South Africa, military dictatorship in the Philippines, and, in the UK, the collapse of the post-World War II political consensus in favour of central economic planning, nationalized industries and the welfare state known as "Butskellism."[92] In each case, small groups of visionary business leaders concluded that if they wanted change in their societies, they had to be part of the solution and make it happen. The traditional business representative organizations did not take up this mantle; rather, social entrepreneurs (including some academics who were also social entrepreneurs), supported by visionary corporate executives, created and led the early coalitions. The focus of most of these pioneer coalitions was largely inside-out, harnessing corporate resources and political connections to tackle broader societal challenges mainly through corporate community involvement and funding policy analysis and research.

In the second wave, the emergence of organizations with a remit to promote responsible practices as part of core business activities and to encourage the creation of other coalitions meant that a number of "mother ship" coalitions stimulated like-minded groups in different countries to replicate their work and concerns. The track record of the pioneers provided some reassurance that the concept could work. Like the earliest organizations, a few of the second-wave coalitions began as a response to corporate scandals or national crises. The focus of activities varied, with some concentrating on building the economic and social infrastructure for countries in transition to democracy and market economies, some on sustainable development, and others on social cohesion.

After the collapse of the old Communist regimes of Central and Eastern Europe, incoming governments and external donors saw corporate responsibility coalition-building as an integral part of the support program for building market economies: that is, part of the enabling environment for a properly functioning business sector. In some countries, it was also integral to efforts to build civil society.

More broadly, with more multinational companies operating in more countries and looking for proven models to help them establish local roots, increase their license to operate, build social capital and create a more benign environment in which to do business and bring expatriate staff to live, the coalitions model was seen as part of the societal infrastructure that needed to be created. Thus, increasing interest in corporate responsibility was part of a perceived "globalization package" for some business leaders; namely, if nation states were declining and multinational companies were growing more powerful, what was the responsibility of international business, and how could this best be discharged? In parallel, the reduced role of governments led a number of governments and intergovernmental institutions such as the European Union, the United Nations and the World Bank Group to encourage the creation of local and regional business-led coalitions.

Thus whereas the pioneers such as PBSP in the Philippines and the NBI in South Africa emerged as part of a reaction *against* the then governing structures of their respective countries, and BITC in the UK as part of the disillusioned reaction to post-war political and industrial consensus, the drivers of the second phase were different. In Eastern Europe, coalitions emerged as part of the architecture of newly democratic and market economies; in Western Europe, as a response to the perceived limitations of the traditional welfare state/social security net, to protect the most vulnerable citizens from the excesses of the new, globalizing economy; and in parts of Africa, Latin America and Asia, as part of the broader drive towards privatization, globalization and liberalization.

The continued global expansion and diversification – increasing numbers, more countries, extending remit and diversifying models of coalitions – that has occurred in the past decade and a half can be traced to intensifying globalization and the need to respond to the anti-globalization and anti-establishment backlash that has occurred in two key waves. First were the protests against big business of the late 1990s described earlier. More recently has been the Arab Spring, which spread rapidly in the Middle East against repressive regimes and crony capitalism, and the Occupy Wall Street movement, which spread to cities around the world protesting about the growing inequality between highly compensated financial and corporate executives and "the other 99%" of citizens, many of them from a middle class feeling under threat. The continued global expansion and diversification of business-led coalitions also reflects the increasing concerns about sustainable development and systemic challenges such as climate change and the energy–food–water nexus,[93] alongside the belief that business needs to take a more proactive lead in being part of the solution.

4.2 **Underlying global forces for change**

Behind the specific drivers outlined above were some underlying global forces for change, which might be summarized as revolutions of markets, technology, demographics and development, and values.[94] Together these factors provided the context for almost all of the coalitions to switch from a focus on philanthropy and corporate community engagement to corporate responsibility and sustainability more broadly. These factors are summarized in Table 4.1.

Table 4.1 **Global forces for change: from philanthropy and corporate community engagement to corporate responsibility and sustainability**

Source: Developed and expanded from D. Grayson and A. Hodges, *Everybody's Business: Managing Risks and Opportunities in Today's Global Society* (London: Dorling Kindersley/Financial Times, 2001).

Revolution of:	Involving:	Meaning:
Markets	• Collapse of Communism and planned economies • Privatization and liberalization • Businesses running previously state-controlled industries • Loss of state-owned enterprises that had provided welfare • Shift of transnational companies to multinationals to "global integrated enterprises"[95] • Global brands • Global supply chains and manufacturing shifts to low-cost economies	• More multicultural workplaces and marketplaces • Ubiquity of global brands means more reputational risk • Size and economic power of global businesses
Technology	• Computing power • Remote technology • Global connectivity • Rise of social media • Scientific breakthroughs (ahead of laws and ethics) • Ability to operate in remote parts of world and conditions previously not possible	• No hiding places: *The Naked Corporation*,[96] WikiLeaks etc.; accountability and transparency • Rise of citizens' journalism and online activism • Just-in-time supplies • Automation, customization, subcontracting, home-working • Businesses operating in remote, hostile conditions (e.g., deepwater) and exposing to indigenous peoples, virgin terrain

→

Revolution of:	Involving:	Meaning:
Demographics and development	• Population growth – urbanized, developing countries • 3 billion extra in market economy in 1990s versus previously in state-controlled economies • 2–3 billion more middle-class consumers by 2030 • Additional 2–3 billion people alive on planet • Climate change • Biodiversity loss • Environmental degradation	• Many more aspiring to middle-class lifestyles and consumption • Pressure on water and other resources • Moves to low-carbon economy • Perceived inequities and downsides of globalization • Inclusive markets and business at bottom (base) of pyramid (BOP) • Sustainable development: meeting the needs of the present without compromising the ability of future generations to meet their needs
Values	• Decline of deference • Questioning of authority and of traditional pillars of authority • Atomization of some societies – "Bowling alone"[97] • "Clash of civilizations"? • Rise of global tribes • Individualism	• Public distrust of corporations and institutions • Rise of activism, issue-based politics and "NGO police" • Ripple effect of "leadership companies" – in reporting, accountability, social investment • Companies facing diversity pressures in workplace and marketplace • More employees and consumers higher up Maslow's hierarchy of needs • From "trust me" to "tell me" to "show me'

4.3 **Motivations for companies to join the corporate responsibility coalitions**

Different arguments have been used to persuade companies to join the coalitions over time and in different parts of the world. These have included:

- If not tackled, social inequalities will harm business

- Corporate responsibility is part of the *quid pro quo* for less government

- Corporate responsibility is part of the "social license to operate" in certain markets

- Membership of a coalition demonstrates a company's public commitment to corporate responsibility

- Membership can help member companies to identify, codify, benchmark and share good practice in corporate responsibility

- Coalitions create platforms for dialogue with companies facing similar corporate responsibility challenges

- Active membership of a coalition creates leadership opportunities

- Companies can use coalition membership to convene other companies and other stakeholders to tackle an issue that the company wants to address, but is unable to do so alone

Some mixture of these arguments seems to have resonated with major companies as more of them have joined one or more of the coalitions and generally stayed in membership over the years. In a survey of the CEOs of UNGC signatory companies in 2010, Accenture found that 78% agreed that "Companies should engage in industry collaborations and multistakeholder partnerships to address development goals" (up from 56% in a similar survey in 2007). Furthermore, 64% of CEOs (compared to 43% in the 2007 survey) said their own companies were actually doing so.[98]

While social movement theory is more traditionally associated with society's disadvantaged and excluded members than with major businesses, a "resource mobilization" interpretation of social movement theory might also be applied to explain the attractions to individual businesses of creating or joining the collective force of the coalitions. Specifically, resource mobilization models argue that social movements need organizations because organizations bring five types of resources: material (money, physical capital); moral (solidarity, support for the movement's goals); social-organizational (organizational strategies, social networks, bloc recruitment); human (volunteers, staff, leaders); and cultural (prior activist experience, understanding of the issues, know-how).[99] A number of these factors are relevant in understanding the growth of the business-led coalitions over the past few decades.

The business-led corporate responsibility coalitions have also grown in number and diversity because of recognition by member companies and other stakeholders that they can play a number of roles that are harder for companies to fill on their own, or for other sectors such as governments or civil society to perform without business support. Examples include the following:

- Coalitions can identify good practice that works for business (i.e., practice not theory). Consultancies, NGOs and academics can do this as well, but may not be trusted to be as dispassionate (e.g., consultancies may be suspected of promoting their own pet solutions and intellectual capital). NGOs and academics may not be considered by business to be au fait with hard business realities

- Coalitions can provide neutral, safe space where businesses can discuss their sustainability challenges and experiment with possible solutions. Governments, NGOs and even academics will not generally find it as easy to win the confidence of business or to be able to create such safe spaces for honest conversations and experimentation

- Coalitions, as organizations of and for business, often find it easier to recruit business commitments and mobilize corporate resources – particularly when governments lack popular support or even a mandate to do so, and when politicians' motives are viewed suspiciously by business people

- Coalitions can float progressive and ambitious ideas about how to encourage more responsible business or more business engagement with challenging societal issues, on behalf of business and from business perspectives. They often have more freedom to do so than traditional business representative organizations such as chambers of commerce and employers' federations, which have more formal decision-making processes to go through and more diverse member interests to reconcile before public statements can be made or public advocacy positions taken

- Coalitions, particularly those that are operating at CEO and senior manager levels with their member companies, are able to convene senior business leaders with a speed and access that few governments, NGOs or multi-stakeholder initiatives could generally match, because of the depth of personal relationships, and the assumption that as business-led coalitions they will prioritize requests to member companies

- By definition, coalitions can provide governments and international institutions with insights about how these bodies can best work with business, which many non-business groups will not be able to do because of lack of first-hand knowledge of what it is like to run a business, although civil-society organizations can also help to provide broader legitimacy and public acceptance to such dialogues

5

The leadership role of individual champions, companies and foundations in building the coalitions

As this brief description of the beginnings and evolution of the business-led corporate responsibility coalitions has shown, there was no single driving force behind their creation and subsequent expansion. Some were encouraged by leaders of the governments or international institutions of the day. Others started as a reaction against the policies of governments. Some were started as part of the implicit *quid pro quo* for less government intervention. Others were inspired by left-of-center social democratic or socialist traditions of fraternity, or by religious teaching. In almost all cases, however, regardless of the original motivating factor or driver, nearly every effective business-led coalition owes its creation and its ongoing success to the leadership of **visionary individual champions** and **strategically led companies**. A number of them have also been seeded and sustained by funding and support from **foundations**, especially those that have invested in field-building activities to try to make entire systems work more effectively. The following sections look briefly at some examples.

5.1 The role of individual champions

Individual leaders from business and other sectors have played a crucial role in providing the political or financial support for the establishment of most of the business-led coalitions. Effective leaders and social entrepreneurs have also been important as first- and second-generation CEOs and managing directors of the most effective business-led coalitions. Indeed, where coalitions have faltered, invariably it has been due to challenges in a leadership transition, not unlike those associated with leadership transitions in other institutions – especially that between a founder chair, CEO or managing director and the next generation. Examples of individuals who founded or catalyzed well-known business-led coalitions and those who have managed and led them over the past few decades include the following.

5.1.1 The founders

Some coalitions have come into existence at the instigation of a government minister, a head of state or a significant business or civic leader with convening power. Examples include:

- HRH The Prince of Wales, who founded the International Business Leaders Forum and who has been President of several other business-led coalitions such as Business in the Community and Youth Business International, as well as championing a number of influential industry- and issue-based initiatives in recent years such as the Corporate Leaders Group on Climate Change and The Prince's Rainforests Project[100]

- Harry Oppenheimer (former Chairman, Anglo American Corporation), who founded the Urban Foundation in South Africa, which later became the National Business Initiative for Growth, Democracy and Development

- The Ayala family of the eponymous Ayala Group and Washington Sycip, the founder of SyCip Gorres Velayo & Co. (the Philippines' largest multidisciplinary professional services firm) who helped to create Philippine Business for Social Progress

- Sir Alastair Pilkington (former Chairman, Pilkington Glass) and Michael Heseltine (former British environment minister), who drove the creation of Business in the Community in the UK

- Pehr Gyllenhammar (former Chairman and CEO, Volvo), who founded Jobs and Society Sweden

- Claude Bébéar (founder of AXA Insurance), who established IMS–Entreprendre pour la Cité in France

- Stephan Schmidheiny (Swiss industrialist and entrepreneur), who founded the World Business Council for Sustainable Development

- Viscount Davignon (former European Union Commissioner and chairman of the Bilderberg Group), who founded CSR Europe

- Oded Grajew and Ricardo Young Silva (Brazilian business leaders and entrepreneurs), who co-founded Instituto Ethos with a group of their peers

- Akio Morita (founder of Sony), who initiated Japan's Council for Better Corporate Citizenship

Beyond founding or catalyzing specific business-led coalitions, most of these individual champions have also been important advocates and public spokespersons more broadly promoting the vital role that business plays in society. A number remain actively and publicly engaged with coalitions today.

5.1.2 **The corporate responsibility activists**

In chronicling the rise of the coalitions, it would be negligent to ignore the contribution of a number of individual corporate responsibility activists and practitioners who provided either managerial leadership or thought leadership in building business-led coalitions and in driving the corporate responsibility movement more broadly around the world.

An award-winning book, written in 2008 by Professor Sandra Waddock at Boston College, explored the role of 23 individual practitioners and thought leaders in the corporate responsibility and socially responsible investment communities, drawn primarily from Europe and the United States (see Box 5.1 for a list of these individuals). Entitled *The Difference Makers: How Social and Institutional Entrepreneurs Created the Corporate Responsibility Movement*, the book chronicles the personal stories of each individual alongside the development of a variety of new institutions that Waddock terms the "corporate responsibility infrastructure." Among these institutions, she includes business-led corporate responsibility coalitions, as well as independent research, monitoring and reporting initiatives, standard-setting and certification organizations, consultancies, responsible investment entities and university-based education programs.

Drawing on extensive interviews, Waddock describes "the difference makers" as:

> Remarkable people who have built the corporate responsibility infrastructure . . . [These] individuals were the pioneers, starting new organizations and institutions – often on a shoestring budget – to develop the social investment movement, corporate accountability standards, and codes of conduct and principles that aim to challenge the dominant credo that the maximization of shareholder wealth is the sole responsibility of the modern corporation. The difference makers are social and institutional entrepreneurs. Their stories clearly demonstrate that the ideas, insights, and leadership actions of one individual can effect change. Each of these people saw in his or her own unique and individual way that there were (and still are) significant problems with the responsibility of the corporation and how environmental, social, and governance issues are perceived in the boardrooms of the world. Each has done his or her part to change things.[101]

Of the 23 people profiled in *The Difference Makers*, a number of them directly founded or helped to catalyze the creation of a business-led or multi-sector corporate responsibility coalition.

The social and institutional entrepreneurs profiled in Waddock's book and their peers from elsewhere around the world could also accurately be described as "the travelers." These men and women criss-crossed the globe during the 1990s, talking about corporate responsibility and the activities of the existing coalitions, working with individual companies, advising emergent coalitions, mentoring new coalition-builders, and – often as prophets from other lands (cf. the biblical statement that "A prophet is not without honor save in his own country") – commanding media and business attention. Most of these travelers had at least a loose affiliation to one or more of the business-led coalitions profiled in this book.

At the risk of upsetting someone who might have accidentally been forgotten, we could list from among this group of travelers who helped to build some of the long-standing business-led corporate responsibility and sustainability coalitions and to promote their spread: the late Robert Davies, Peter Brew, Ros Tennyson and Adrian Hodges from the IBLF; Julia

Cleverdon, David Halley, Sue Adkins, Mallen Baker, Stephen O'Brien and Peter Davies from BITC; the late Edmund Burke, Brad Googins, Cheryl Kiser and Chris Pinney from the Center for Corporate Citizenship at Boston College; Bob Dunn, Arnold Hiatt and Aron Cramer from BSR; Jan Noterdaeme and Ann Vandenhende from CSR Europe; John Ruggie and Georg Kell from the UN Global Compact; Hugh Faulkner, Jan Olaf Willums, Björn Stigson, Margaret Flaherty and Marcel Engel from the WBCSD; Bob Massie, Allen White and Ernst Ligterinen of the Global Reporting Initiative; Judy Samuelson from the Aspen Business in Society program; Michele Kahane from the Ford Foundation's Corporate Community Involvement Initiative; David Vidal from The Conference Board; Theuns Eloff, André Fourie and Brian Whittaker from the National Business Initiative in South Africa; Talia Aharoni from Maala, Israel; and Charlie Moore from the Committee Encouraging Corporate Philanthropy.

Box 5.1 *The Difference Makers: How Social and Institutional Entrepreneurs Created the Corporate Responsibility Movement*

- Joan Bavaria, Trillium Asset Management; and Ceres
- Amy Domini, The Domini Social Equity Fund
- Robert Dunn, Fair Labor Association; and Business for Social Responsibility*
- John Elkington, SustainAbility
- Bradley Googins, Boston College Center for Corporate Citizenship
- David Grayson, Business in the Community*
- Laury Hammel, Business for Social Responsibility*
- Georg Kell, United Nations Global Compact*
- Peter Kinder, KLD Research & Analytics
- David Logan, Corporate Citizenship
- Steve Lydenberg, KLD Research & Analytics; and Institute for Responsible Investment
- Malcolm McIntosh, Corporate Citizenship, Warwick Business School
- Robert Massie, Ceres
- Jane Nelson, IBLF*
- James Post, academic
- John Ruggie, United Nations Global Compact*
- Judith Samuelson, Aspen Institute Business and Society program
- Timothy Smith, Interfaith Center on Corporate Responsibility
- Alice Tepper Marlin, founder of Council on Economic Priorities
- Steve Waddell, GAN-Net
- Allen White, Ceres; and Global Reporting Initiative
- Steven Young, Caux Round Table
- Simon Zadek, AccountAbility

* see Profiles

5.2 **The role of individual companies**

In almost all cases, coalitions were created by the combination of a visionary individual or group of individuals and supported by a small core group of companies that were willing to put sufficient funds and in-kind support on the table to help the fledgling organization get established and develop its value proposition to a broader group of corporate supporters. In some cases, the decision to provide corporate-level support came from the CEO or senior executive in the companies in question; in others, it was a chief sustainability officer or corporate responsibility director who channeled corporate resources to support the coalition. In many cases, it has been a combination of both.

It is difficult to estimate the enormous amount of senior executive "volunteer" time that goes into governing, supporting, coordinating and providing input and insights into the activities of most business-led coalitions. There can be no doubt however, that over and above the direct financial support provided by the core member companies, the indirect financial value, not to mention the strategic and intellectual value, of this contribution of time and talent is immense – and critical to the leadership voice and impact that the successful coalitions have been able to achieve.

The WBCSD has arguably developed, and institutionalized, the most effective combination of CEO-level governance and decision-making roles and operational-level working-group and coordination roles among its 200 or so corporate members. Companies sign up to the WBCSD at the chairperson or CEO level and a small group of CEOs serve as the organization's actively engaged Board of Directors. Each major work program of the WBCSD also requires the commitment of a minimum of two member-company CEOs before it can be launched. Every member CEO is also required to assign a liaison delegate to the WBCSD, usually the company's chief sustainability officer or head of environment or corporate responsibility. Liaison delegates work closely with the staff at the WBCSD to design and deliver its various programs and meet on a regular basis to learn from each other and influence the direction of the WBCSD's activities.

The UN Global Compact, with about 8,000 business members,[102] over two-thirds of them from developing countries, also has a core group of about 50 companies that it works with to drive its various working groups and projects. These constitute UNGC's LEAD network. Several CEOs from member companies also serve on UNGC's multi-stakeholder Board of Directors and many others get actively engaged at the country level.

The American political scientist Dr. Daniel Kinderman, who studies corporate responsibility coalitions, has analyzed the 1992 and 2007 memberships of corporate responsibility coalitions across Europe. He refers to the "big linkers" – companies that are members of multiple coalitions – and how this list (of a much expanded universe of European corporate responsibility coalitions) evolved from 1992 to 2007.[103] Table 5.1 shows the 15 firms with the highest network centrality in European corporate responsibility networks in 1992 and 2007. Analysis of the corporate memberships of a cross-section of 20 national coalitions (roughly equal numbers from the Americas, the Europe, Middle East and Africa region and Asia–Pacific) identified a small number of companies in membership of at least half of these coalitions: these were Coca-Cola, IBM, KPMG, Microsoft, Nestlé and PricewaterhouseCoopers (PwC).

In an ideal world, and to optimize their benefit from the coalitions and their added value to the coalitions in which they are members, "serial joiners" like these would be ensuring that their corporate representatives in each coalition are talking to each other and exchanging

Table 5.1 **Fifteen firms with highest membership of European corporate responsibility coalitions**

1992	2007
• KPMG	• KPMG
• BP	• Coca-Cola
• PricewaterhouseCoopers	• Johnson & Johnson
• British Gas	• Microsoft
• Barclays	• Orange/France Telecom
• ICI	• Deloitte
• IBM	• IBM
• Shell	• PricewaterhouseCoopers
• Grand Met/Diageo	• Ernst & Young
• American Express	• Danone
• 3M	• Vodafone
• Coca-Cola	• Shell
• Credit Suisse	• GlaxoSmithKline
• Axa	• Diageo
• DHL	• Citigroup

good-practice insights. Similarly, the "serial joiner" companies would be proactively managing their wish-lists from the coalitions in which they are members, in terms of work programs, profiling and the learning they are seeking from the coalitions. They would be making sure their representatives were consistently pushing this. Describing this ideal to company contacts usually gets wry smiles and sometimes "in your dreams!" or its equivalent. Clearly, where a chief sustainability officer or similar is personally holding his or her company's membership in several coalitions, there is a greater likelihood of this overview occurring. On the other hand, such concentration of engagement can make the company's institutional learning and utilization of the knowledge acquired very dependent on that individual.

One company that has consciously decided to be a "serial joiner" and to manage its memberships in a proactive way is IBM. The company explains its multiple memberships in terms of its societal contribution, setting an example to encourage other companies to join, and helping to familiarize local IBM management teams with the major corporate responsibility and sustainability issues in their country. Furthermore, as it currently holds the chair of CSR Europe, IBM expects the national IBM offices to be members of their local CSR Europe national partner organization. "It is," says Celia Moore, chair of CSR Europe, "part of extending the value of CSR Europe membership for IBM."[104]

IBM also provides an interesting example of evolving relations between corporate leaders in sustainability and the coalitions. It has quietly withdrawn from one of the leading coalitions where it did not feel it had found a niche or added value. In parallel, IBM has taken a lead in supporting another targeted collective action initiative, within the auspices of the World Environment Center to create an Innovations in Environmental Sustainability Council[105] with eight other companies that share its interest to collaborate on exploring mutual experiences in more specialized sustainability issues such as traceability, water and logistics. The aim is to get an eclectic wider set of insights from other sustainability leaders and more added-value from the coalitions in which the company is active.

5.3 **The role of foundations**

For some coalitions, the support of an independent philanthropic foundation has been a valuable catalyst in establishing the coalition and in helping it to invest in innovative new initiatives and to build new alliances. Examples include: Hungarian Business Links, which had early support from the Soros Open Society Foundation in Eastern Europe; Forum Empresa, supported by the Inter-American Foundation and Synergos Foundation; IARSE (Argentina), which benefited from the support of the AVINA Foundation and the Kellogg Foundation; and Maala, which was initially funded by the Kahanoff Foundation. Two long-standing foundations that have played an important role in helping to build the field of corporate responsibility and sustainability coalitions over the past few decades have been the Ford Foundation and the Rockefeller Foundation.

From 1995 to 2004, the Ford Foundation, through its **Corporate Community Involvement Initiative,** played a valuable field-building role in the United States and helped to strengthen a number of business-led corporate responsibility coalitions and networks.[106] Led by Michele Kahane, the initiative sought to more effectively leverage corporate resources in bringing economic opportunities to disadvantaged and underserved communities. During this period it made over US$45 million in grants and program-related investments to nearly 50 organizations. A number of them were fledgling business-led corporate responsibility coalitions. All of them were focused on developing market-based solutions and supporting more effective partnerships between companies and communities, and collective action by business to help low-income people improve their income and assets, while also benefiting business. The initiative demonstrated the crucial role that collective business action and market-based partnerships can play in addressing social challenges at scale. The lessons and some of the models developed as a result of the Ford Foundation's initiative have subsequently helped to inform collective business action both in the United States and globally.

Seed support from the Ford Foundation also enabled one of its former program officers, Judy Samuelson, who had worked with Michele Kahane in designing the Corporate Community Involvement Initiative, to create the **Business in Society Program at the Aspen Institute**. Although not included as one of our business-led coalitions, given its location within a policy think-tank, this program has also played a key role in leveraging collective business and investor action as a powerful force in tackling social issues and aligning business decisions with the public good.[107]

Since the mid-2000s, the Rockefeller Foundation has played a similar role in helping to build the field of impact investing, including the creation of a number of business or investor-led coalitions to promote more innovative financing to solve social and environmental challenges. Impact investments are investments made into companies, organizations and funds with the intention to generate measurable social and environmental impact alongside a financial return.[108] The Rockefeller Foundation hosted the initial dialogues and funded early research to demonstrate the enormous potential of impact investing. It is now working in partnership with other private foundations, commercial banks, investors and financial institutions to build the field of impact investing. This includes efforts to catalyze platforms for collective action, such as the **Global Impact Investing Network** (GIIN), the **Global Impact Investment Rating System** (GIIRS) and the **Aspen Network of Development Entrepreneurs** (ANDE); promote the concept and practice of impact investing in other regions of the world; support ongoing research and advocacy; and build industry-wide infrastructure and tools, such as measurement and rating tools.

Two new foundations that have been created since the millennium and that have played a major leadership role in helping to build the field for collective business action and multi-stakeholder partnerships to drive social change have been the Bill & Melinda Gates Foundation and the William J. Clinton Foundation. The Gates Foundation has focused its efforts on building multi-stakeholder initiatives and innovative new technologies and approaches to scale-up solutions for improving education (primarily in the United States), global health and global development. Although it hasn't focused on directly supporting business-led corporate responsibility coalitions *per se*, the foundation has engaged proactively with individual companies and business networks in key sectors such as information technology, healthcare, financial services and agriculture to help achieve its mission. The Clinton Foundation has supported a number of initiatives dedicated to mobilizing collective action by companies. Some of these are summarized in Box 5.2.

Box 5.2 **The Clinton Foundation and Clinton Global Initiative**

On leaving the White House in 2001, President Clinton established the William J. Clinton Foundation with the explicit mission of fostering partnerships among governments, businesses, NGOs and private citizens to deliver measurable results. The Foundation's initiatives work to strengthen health systems in developing countries; promote economic opportunity in Africa, Latin America, Haiti, and the United States; address the root causes of climate change; and fight childhood obesity in the United States. Several programs that began as part of the Foundation have grown into independent initiatives, including the Clinton Global Initiative, the Clinton Health Access Initiative and the Alliance for a Healthier Generation, while others remain within the Foundation itself.

The **Clinton Health Access Initiative** (CHAI), for example, has built partnerships between governments in selected countries and pharmaceutical companies, other private-sector actors and NGOs to find joint solutions to improve markets for medicines and diagnostics, lower the costs of treatments, expand access to life-saving technologies, increase access to effective malaria treatment, accelerate vaccine rollouts, and lower infant mortality. Among other results, by working collectively with business and government, CHAI programs have led to more than $1 billion in cost savings since 2007 for developing countries.

Likewise, the **Alliance for a Healthier Generation in the United States** has mobilized collective action by companies and schools to start tackling childhood obesity. Among a number of activities, it has achieved a collective voluntary agreement by some of the world's largest – and most competitive – beverage, snack food and dairy companies to address the calorie content of food and drinks available in schools. It also works with insurance companies, employers and provider organizations to reimburse for the cost of workplace obesity-prevention programs.

The following vignette briefly illustrates how the **Clinton Global Initiative** has harnessed collective business action and worked with business-led coalitions alongside other partners from government and civil society to drive social progress and transformation.

➔

The Clinton Global Initiative: from ideas to action

President Clinton started the Clinton Global Initiative (CGI) in September 2005 as an innovative platform to drive action-oriented partnerships between business, social entrepreneurs, impact investors, philanthropists, innovative community groups, non-governmental organizations and government leaders. Frustrated with too many well-intentioned conferences and events that did not lead to practical improvements for people's lives on the ground, the President had a vision for a network that would bring together individuals and institutions that have resources with creative innovators and ideas that need resources in order to develop practical solutions to global challenges. Individuals and institutions can become members of CGI. Many of the institutional members are companies, and CGI is committed to greater engagement with the business community in all its areas of activity. Every single member who attends a CGI event is asked to make a commitment. It can be a small personal commitment to help one child or one school or it can be a global collective action partnership between dozens of companies and other partners to tackle a complex systemic challenge; but it must be new, it must be specific, and it must be measurable.

The core role of the CGI team and the various networks and events that they coordinate is to help CGI's members to take real and meaningful action, and then to profile and celebrate the results of that action and to encourage many more individuals and institutions around the world to follow suit. In addition to an annual global meeting, CGI has also started a CGI America event and a CGI U network, which brings together remarkable university students from around the world. Between gatherings, the team at CGI coordinates a variety of ongoing action networks and regular dialogue with members to help them to identify and improve their commitments. Over the past few years, CGI has also become a vital platform for raising challenging and difficult issues with business and public-sector leaders. Violence against women and human trafficking have been two interrelated issues that the CGI has helped to put on the corporate agenda.

The CGI has also been a valuable platform for launching new collective action initiatives by business and other partners, such as the Global Impact Investing Network, the Haiti Action network, several projects supported by the Global Alliance for Improved Nutrition, Education (Plus) to improve education for refugees, the Palestinian Political Risk Insurance Project to attract more private investment to Palestine, and a variety of collective efforts between banks, foundations and insurance companies to improve access to financial services for the poor.

Less than a decade after its creation, CGI's members have reported making nearly 2,300 commitments totalling $73.1 billion and impacting an estimated 400 million lives around the globe. As it looks to the future, one of CGI's priorities will be to work with more companies around the world, both individually and collectively, to support further commitments and partnerships with each other and with governments and civil society that offer practical solutions to complex global challenges.

Having explored the past – the evolution of business-led corporate responsibility coalitions and new platforms for collective business action – in Part I, attention now turns to the present status of the field. Part II offers an overview of the different business-led coalitions that are now operating around the globe, exploring how they are networking with each other and with other actors in the broader corporate responsibility ecosystem, and then focusing on the key roles played by these coalitions and what their impact has been to date.

Part II
The Present
Assessing the impact of coalitions today

Part II focuses on the present, looking at the current characteristics, roles and impact of business-led corporate responsibility coalitions. Chapter 6 provides an overview of the number, diversity and global coverage of these coalitions, with a section focusing on the growing importance of collective business action in China and further information on the growth in industry- and issue-specific coalitions. Chapter 7 describes how coalitions are currently operating as part of a broader and increasingly complex and competitive ecosystem of actors dedicated to promoting responsible business practices. Chapter 8 outlines some of the key roles that business-led corporate responsibility coalitions currently play. Chapter 9 focuses on how they organize themselves and Chapter 10 illustrates examples of how they network among themselves. Part II concludes with Chapter 11, assessing the impact of these coalitions. It explores the impact of coalitions in two core areas: first, their effectiveness in raising awareness making both the business case and the public case for corporate responsibility, and their effectiveness at helping individual companies to embed responsible business practices into their core business strategies and operations; and, second, their effectiveness at achieving large-scale and systemic impact in spreading and institutionalizing corporate responsibility beyond the pioneers and leading companies. After summarizing some of the key criticisms of these coalitions, the chapter concludes with key lessons learned and some strategic questions for coalitions to consider for the future.

6

The number and diversity of corporate responsibility coalitions

The following section provides an overview of three main types of diversity that character-ize corporate responsibility coalitions today; their geographic spread and cultural diversity, with a section focused on the growing importance of collective business action in China; the growing number and diversity of industry- and issue-specific coalitions; and diversity in size and scope of operational focus.

6.1 Geographic and cultural diversity

A majority of countries around the world, including all those attending the G20 summits, now have some form of organization to promote corporate responsibility – whether this is business-led, part of a wider business representative organization, or a multi-stakeholder initiative. Around 70 countries have some form of business-led corporate responsibility coalition, including more than two-thirds of the world's 100 largest economies; this figure rises to at least 80% if multi-stakeholder corporate responsibility initiatives are included (see Table 6.1).

In addition, there are the international business-led corporate responsibility coalitions such as Business for Social Responsibility (BSR), CSR Europe, Forum Empresa, the Inter-national Business Leaders Forum (IBLF) and the World Business Council for Sustainable Development (WBCSD); the growing number of industry-specific and issue-specific coali-tions such as the Global Business Council on Health (GBCHealth) and Responsible Care; and the plethora of multi-stakeholder initiatives and sustainability/corporate responsibil-ity initiatives operating under the auspices of other organizations such as The Conference

Board, the Consumer Goods Forum, the International Chamber of Commerce, the World Economic Forum (WEF), business federations and trade associations, and business schools and think-tanks.

Table 6.1 **The world's 100 largest economies in 2011 and their corporate responsibility coalitions**

Source: Largest economies: IMF World Economic Outlook Oct 2011. Coalitions compiled from multiple sources including websites of CSR Europe, BITC's CSR360 Global Partner Network, WBCSD, IBLF, Forum Empresa, UNGC Local Partners Network; W. Visser and N. Tolhurst (eds.), *The World Guide to CSR* (Sheffield, UK: Greenleaf Publishing, 2010); authors' knowledge; and checked with expert panel. Inevitably, there is a churn of such organizations. Updates to this list are welcomed and will be posted at www.doughtycentre.info/coalitions website.

Rank	Country	Business-led corporate responsibility coalitions	Other corporate responsibility coalitions
1	United States	• Alliance for Business Leadership • Business for Social Responsibility • Business Council for Sustainable Development (BCSD) • Committee for Encouraging Corporate Philanthropy	• United Nations Global Compact (UNGC) national chapter • Boston College Center for Corporate Citizenship (BCCCC) • Aspen Institute Business and Society Program • Initiative for Global Development
2	People's Republic of China	• China Business Leaders Forum • BCSD	• UNGC national chapter • Golden Bee CSR Development Center
3	Japan	• BCSD • Council for Better Corporate Citizenship	• UNGC national chapter • Keidanren, Corporate Citizenship Initiative
4	Germany	• econsense • (also BCSD Germany)	• UNGC national chapter • UPJ Network for Corporate Citizenship and Corporate Social Responsibility • Centrum für Corporate Citizenship Deutschland (CCCD)
5	France	• IMS–Entreprendre pour la Cité • Observatoire sur la Responsabilité Sociétale des Entreprises (ORSE) • BCSD	• UNGC national chapter
6	United Kingdom	• Business in the Community • Scottish Business in the Community • BCSD	• UNGC national chapter • Centre for Tomorrow's Company
7	Brazil	• Forum Empresa • Instituto Ethos • BCSD	• UNGC national chapter
8	Italy	• Sodalitas • Impronta Etica	• UNGC national chapter
9	Canada	• Canadian BSR • BCSD	

Rank	Country	Business-led corporate responsibility coalitions	Other corporate responsibility coalitions
10	India	• BCSD	• UNGC national chapter • Business & Community Foundation • Confederation of Indian Industries CSR Initiative • Centre for Social Markets
11	Russia	• St. Petersburg Partnership Initiative • IBLF Russia • BCSD	• UNGC national chapter • Russian Union of Industrialists and Entrepreneurs
12	Spain	• Forética • Club de Excelencia en Sostenibilidad • Empresa y Sociedad • BCSD	• UNGC national chapter
13	Australia	• BCSD • Australian Business and Community Network	• UNGC national chapter
14	Mexico	• CEMEFI Centro Mexicano para la Filantropia • BCSD	• UNGC national chapter
15	South Korea	• BCSD	• UNGC national chapter • Business Institute for Sustainable Development of Korea Chamber of Commerce and Industry
16	Netherlands		• UNGC national chapter • MVO Netherlands
17	Turkey	• CSR Turkey • BCSD	• UNGC national chapter
18	Indonesia	• Indonesia Business Links • BCSD	• UNGC national chapter
19	Switzerland	• Philias Foundation	• UNGC national chapter
20	Poland	• Polish Business Leaders Forum • Responsible Business Forum	• UNGC national chapter
21	Belgium	• Business & Society Belgium	• UNGC national chapter
22	Sweden	• CSR Sweden • Jobs and Society	• UNGC Nordic chapter
23	Saudi Arabia		• Saudi Arabian Responsible Competitiveness Index (SARCI) • King Khalid Responsible Competitiveness Award (KKRCA)[109] • UNGC Gulf Region chapter
24	Republic of China (Taiwan)	• BCSD	

Rank	Country	Business-led corporate responsibility coalitions	Other corporate responsibility coalitions
25	Norway	• CSR Norway • BCSD	• UNGC Nordic chapter • Confederation of Norwegian Industries
26	Iran		• CSR Development Center in Iran • UNGC national chapter
27	Austria	• respACT–austrian business council for sustainable development (also affiliated with BCSD)	• UNGC national chapter
28	Argentina	• Fundación del Tucumán • BCSD	• UNGC national chapter • Fundación Compromiso, Empresa & Comunidad Department
29	South Africa	• National Business Initiative (NBI) (also affiliated to WBCSD and UNGC) • Business Leadership South Africa • New Partnership for Africa's Development (NEPAD) Business Foundation	• UNGC national chapter (run by NBI)
30	Thailand	• BCSD	• Thailand Business Coalition on AIDS • UNGC national chapter
31	Denmark	• BCSD	• The Danish Government Center for CSR • UNGC Nordic chapter
32	Greece	• Hellenic Network for Corporate Social Responsibility • BCSD	• UNGC national chapter • Hellenic Federation of Enterprises
33	United Arab Emirates	• BCSD	• Center for Responsible Business, Dubai Chamber of Commerce and Industry • Arabia CSR Network • UNGC Gulf Region chapter
34	Venezuela	• Cedice	• Venezuelan American Chamber of Commerce CSR Alliance
35	Colombia	• CECODES BCSD (affiliated to • BCSD)	• UNGC national chapter • Colombian Confederation of Chambers of Commerce
36	Finland	• Finnish Business & Society	• UNGC Nordic chapter
37	Malaysia	• BCSD	• UNGC national chapter
38	Portugal	• Grace • RSE Portugal • BCSD	• UNGC national chapter

→

Rank	Country	Business-led corporate responsibility coalitions	Other corporate responsibility coalitions
–	Hong Kong	• Hong Kong Business-Community Partnerships • BCSD	
39	Singapore		• UNGC national chapter
40	Egypt	• BCSD	• UNGC national chapter • Egyptian Corporate Responsibility Center (ECRC) • Junior Business Association
41	Nigeria		• UNGC national chapter
42	Israel	• Maala	• UNGC national chapter (Maala operated)
43	Ireland	• Business in the Community Ireland (BITCI)	
44	Chile	• Acción RSE • BCSD	• UNGC national chapter
45	Czech Republic	• Czech Business Leaders Forum	
46	Philippines	• Philippine Business for Social Progress (PBSP) • BCSD	
47	Pakistan	• BCSD	• UNGC national chapter • Pakistan Chambers of Commerce and Industry, CSR Standing Committee
48	Romania	• CSR Romania	
49	Algeria	• BCSD	
50	Peru	• Perú 2021 • BCSD	• UNGC national chapter
51	New Zealand	• BCSD	• Business In the Community Charitable Trust (Business Mentors)
52	Kazakhstan	• BCSD	
53	Ukraine	• Center for CSR Development	• UNGC national chapter
54	Kuwait		• UNGC Gulf Region chapter
55	Qatar		• UNGC Gulf Region chapter
56	Hungary	• Hungarian Business Leaders Forum • KÖVET, Association for Sustainable Economies • BCSD	• UNGC national chapter
57	Bangladesh	• Bangladesh Partnership Forum	• UNGC national chapter

Rank	Country	Business-led corporate responsibility coalitions	Other corporate responsibility coalitions
58	Vietnam	• Vietnam Business Links – now part of Chamber of Commerce and Industry • BCSD	• UNGC national chapter
59	Morocco		• UNGC national chapter
60	Slovakia	• Slovak Business Leaders Forum/ Pontis Foundation	
61	Angola		
62	Iraq		• UNGC national chapter
63	Libya		
64	Sudan		• UNGC national chapter
65	Ecuador	• CERES • BCSD	• UNGC national chapter
66	Croatia	• Croatia Business Leaders Forum • BCSD	• UNGC national chapter
67	Syria		• UNGC national chapter
68	Oman		• UNGC Gulf Region chapter
69	Belarus		
70	Luxembourg	• IMS	
71	Azerbaijan		• UNGC national chapter
72	Dominican Republic		• UNGC national chapter
73	Sri Lanka	• BCSD	• UNGC national chapter
74	Slovenia		• UNGC national chapter
75	Bulgaria	• Bulgaria Business Leaders Forum	• UNGC national chapter
76	Tunisia		• ACE
77	Guatemala	• BCSD	
78	Uruguay	• DERES • BCSD	• UNGC national chapter
79	Lebanon		• CSR Lebanon
80	Uzbekistan		
81	Serbia	• Business Leaders Forum Serbia	
82	Lithuania		• UNGC national chapter
83	Myanmar/Burma		
84	Costa Rica	• AED • BCSD	• UNGC national chapter
85	Kenya		• UNGC national chapter • Federation of Kenyan Employers

➜

Rank	Country	Business-led corporate responsibility coalitions	Other corporate responsibility coalitions
86	Ethiopia		
87	Yemen		
88	Panama	• SumaRSE • BCSD	• UNGC national chapter
89	Jordan		
90	Latvia		• UNGC national chapter
91	Cyprus		• UNGC national chapter
92	Tanzania		
93	Côte d'Ivoire		• UNGC national chapter
94	Cameroon		
95	El Salvador	• FUNDEMÁS • BCSD	
96	Bahrain		• UNGC Gulf Region chapter
97	Trinidad and Tobago		• UNGC national chapter
98	Estonia	• Responsible Business Forum in Estonia	• Responsible Business Forum in Estonia
99	Bolivia	• COBORSE • BCSD	• UNGC national chapter
100	Ghana		• UNGC national chapter

As different economies are at different stages of development, with varying sophistication in civil society, so are companies at different stages of corporate responsibility maturity. In some countries, with relatively few indigenous large companies and a small overall business community, it has probably made more sense to consolidate efforts to encourage responsible business behavior with other business activity, through organizations such as a chamber of commerce or an employers' federation. Thus, for example, in Saudi Arabia the Jeddah Chamber of Commerce and in the United Arab Emirates the Abu Dhabi Chamber of Commerce and the Dubai Chamber of Commerce and Industry have corporate responsibility initiatives or centers.

In other countries, stand-alone business-led coalitions have made little headway and the roles that elsewhere have been assumed by separate corporate responsibility coalitions have been taken on by existing, powerful business representative organizations. This has been the case in two major economies, India and, to a lesser extent, Japan, where respectively, the Confederation of Indian Industries and some of the larger chambers of commerce and Japan's Keidanren have had corporate responsibility initiatives for some time (see Section 3.1).

The case of Germany provides further support for Daniel Kinderman's thesis that corporate responsibility and corporate responsibility coalitions emerged and thrived earlier in deregulating economies such as the UK (see Section 3.1). In Germany, the post-war political consensus around the Erhard Social Market Economy model[110] with worker participation, tripartite structures for economic management (government, unions and management), a welfare safety net, and progressive environmental regulations meant less need and pressure for additional forms of business engagement or for business to assume additional responsibilities. Hence, one of the authors' discussions in the Federal Republic in the mid-1990s with leading German businesses revealed little corporate citizenship beyond arts sponsorship and a few company philanthropic foundations. However, in more recent times, a mix of globalization, international companies bringing their corporate responsibility practices to their German operations, and the growing recognition of sustainability as a core business issue and potential source of business opportunity has led to the emergence of a number of coalitions in Germany. These include: UPJ (www.upj.de), founded in 1996 and focused on community involvement, employee volunteering and helping small and medium enterprises (SMEs) to be involved in the community; econsense (www.econsense.de), created in 2000 and now involving 33 (mainly German-headquartered) major firms on all aspects of sustainable business practice; and most recently the WIE (Wirtschaft Initiative), a network of 14 major companies mobilized by the boutique corporate citizenship think-tank Centrum für Corporate Citizenship Deutschland (CCCD) (www.cccdeutschland.org/en) as a business initiative on civic engagement. Additionally, German organizations such as the federal government's international development agency GIZ (formerly GTZ) and the private Bertelsmann Foundation have been active in codifying and supporting initiatives to promote responsible business practices around the world and a number of German companies have engaged in effective large-scale partnerships with these organizations in developing countries.

In some countries, business-led coalitions have been less powerful than multi-stakeholder corporate responsibility coalitions. This is often where the state has played a more activist role, as in Singapore and the Gulf States. In Egypt, for example, the Egyptian Corporate Responsibility Center (ECRC) was established in 2004 as an initiative between the Ministry of Investment, the Egyptian Institute of Directors and the United Nations Development Programme (UNDP). It also serves as Egypt's national chapter of the UNGC.[111]

In some situations, a fragmented business community, separated by long distances or cool to the concept of business assuming government responsibilities for environmental and social impacts has meant that there have been only sporadic initiatives and no established peak body for corporate responsibility at a national level. This is the case in Australia, where initiatives have tended to focus on one or more of the major cities. The Australian Business and Community Network (ABCN) grew out of an initiative started in Sydney in 2004; ABCN now extends to the main cities in five states, but it remains focused on business and education links, principally through mentoring.[112] One of the more enduring organizations has been the small, non-profit organization, the St. James Ethics Centre, which has long had the promotion of corporate responsibility as one of its work programs. Among other activities, the Centre ran the Corporate Responsibility Index (CRI) in Australia under license from Business in the Community (BITC) in the UK from 2003 to 2010.[113] This contrasts with the Liberian example in Chapter 3 (Box 3.1), which described one of the youngest national corporate responsibility coalitions in the world, operating in one of the poorest countries, which has weak governance institutions and is also emerging from many years of conflict. If the Liberian Corporate Responsibility Forum prospers, it might show the potential for other post-conflict countries such as Myanmar/Burma and South Sudan, where tentative discussions about a responsible business initiative have started.

Business is not monolithic and has many different representative voices. It is not surprising, therefore, that having a single business-led corporate responsibility coalition that is widely recognized as the definitive voice on corporate responsibility in a country is only one model. In some countries, there may be several competing business-led corporate responsibility coalitions. Ad hoc groupings are also emerging more frequently. As this book was being completed, the entrepreneur Sir Richard Branson was teaming up with celebrity chef Jamie Oliver and the CEO of the sports goods company Puma, Jochen Zeitz, to launch a new movement "Screw Business as Usual" and a Branson book of the same title, aimed at serving as a catalyzer of innovative new business-led and market-based solutions to achieving sustainability.[114]

The flexibility and ability of the corporate responsibility coalition model to adapt to different national circumstances is exemplified with China. The Chinese "Renaissance" and re-emergence as a global economic powerhouse is one of the most dramatic global stories of the last three decades. China offers a useful example of a country with strong public institutions and active state control of economic actors that is aiming to ensure that sound environmental and social practices accompany the country's transition to a more market-based economy and its rapid economic growth both domestically and internationally.

6.1.1 Corporate responsibility coalitions and China

In the coming decade, a growing level of action and innovation in corporate responsibility is likely to come in the rapidly growing economies such as Brazil, India, Indonesia and Turkey. China will be especially important on account of its sheer size, but also because of the speed at which change occurs in China, the scale both of the sustainability challenges and of the country's ambitions, and because of the very particular role of the Communist Party of China (CPC).

Growing interest in corporate responsibility

Even casual visitors to China are fascinated by the complex interplay of managed capitalism, free market capitalism, Confucian and other philosophical traditions and the rapid urbanization and sophistication of a burgeoning Chinese middle class, and how all of this is influencing and being influenced by China's growing inter-connectivity with the rest of the world. Much of the early debate around corporate responsibility in China came from the growing number of foreign multinationals establishing themselves in the country in the 1990s. These companies introduced their international responsible business practices into their Chinese operations; through codes of conduct and supplier codes they started to specify requirements for health and safety, environmental standards and worker conditions for their Chinese suppliers.

Discussion ratcheted up after China's accession to the World Trade Organization in 2001 helped the country to assume the mantle of the "world's factory." A succession of product safety and other corporate scandals in China over the last decade have increased the interest of the Chinese authorities and the public in corporate responsibility. It is recognized that food contamination, shoddy construction practices (exposed after the 2008 Sichuan earthquake, for example), suicides in the electronics industry, intellectual property theft, and other cases of corporate *irresponsibility* have stoked domestic protests and damaged China's reputation internationally. As more Chinese companies internationalize through both expansion overseas and acquisitions, the image of "China Inc." becomes increasingly important.

Domestically, the rapid growth of Internet usage and social media in China, despite the restrictions imposed by the so-called "Great Firewall of China," is driving pressure for greater transparency and accountability – both for companies and for other organizations in China. It is estimated that there are now more than 500 million Internet users in China[115] – almost a quarter of all Internet users worldwide.[116] There are over 300 million users of *weibo*, a microblogging service (similar to Twitter), and "on Sina Weibo, China's most popular weibo service, over 250 million users send more than 86mln tweets a day."[117]

Official encouragement

Given these factors, the Chinese authorities have taken a number of steps to promote corporate responsibility, which is presented as an integral part of the official goal to achieve the "harmonious society," the very Confucian notion at the heart of government and CPC policy. The State-owned Assets Supervision and Administration Commission of the State Council (SASAC), the official agency that manages the state's holdings in the largest 118 state-owned enterprises (SOEs), published the SASAC CSR Guidelines in 2008. These specified that SOEs should "enhance their CSR awareness, actively fulfill social responsibility, and become model companies with legal compliance, integrity, energy efficiency, environmental protection and harmony."[118] The guidelines position CSR as a key component of the transformation of SOEs into modern corporate institutions and as a means for enhancing competitiveness.

Rolf Dietmar from Germany's GIZ office in Beijing, responsible for GIZ's China CSR Project, explains that a number of local governments in China – which often are responsible for a population and land-mass the equivalent of a mid- to large-sized European state – have also started to promote corporate responsibility:

> Besides institutions at central government level, numerous municipal governments have also launched CSR initiatives. Notable among these is the government of Pudong District in Shanghai, which has set up a differentiated CSR program which involves evaluating all the enterprises in its area of jurisdiction against a set of criteria. Depending on how companies perform, they are either rewarded with appropriate subsidies or required to come up with improvement measures. The Wenzhou municipal government and the Weihai and Yantai Economic Development Zones have all introduced similar evaluation systems.[119]

Official guidance has also been given on CSR for multinationals operating in China. The Shanghai and Shenzhen Stock Exchanges have issued guidelines on environmental, social and governance (ESG) reporting and have also developed a sustainability index (similar to the Dow Jones Sustainability Index). In Shanghai, all 100 companies that make the index each year are expected to publish their CSR activities.

More corporate responsibility reporters

As a result of the SASAC guidelines and other initiatives, there has been a rapid increase in the number of companies in China publishing CSR or sustainability reports. Estimates vary regarding the number of annual reports, but all recognize the leap forward in the number of reporters from 2008 to 2009, following the SASAC guidelines. At least 21 of these were based on the ISO 26000 criteria, while 164 of the reports published were based on the Global Reporting Initiative (GRI) guidelines[120] (see Fig. 6.1).

Figure 6.1 **Number of CSR reports published in China**

Source: China *WTO Tribune*, 2011

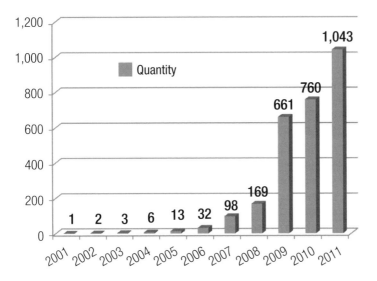

Chinese corporate responsibility initiatives

Growing official interest in corporate responsibility from SASAC, the Ministry of Commerce, the SME Bureau of the Ministry of Industry and Information Technology (responsible for improving the performance of China's more than 43 million SMEs), municipal authorities and others has encouraged a number of Chinese corporate responsibility organizations.

Among these is the **Golden Bee CSR Development Center**.[121] GoldenBee is an initiative of the *WTO Tribune* magazine, which was originally launched by China's Ministry of Commerce in 2003 to help Chinese businesses and policy-makers manage the consequences of WTO membership. The magazine found that it was increasingly covering CSR-related issues and was identifying the need for practical advice about embedding responsible business practices. As a result, *WTO Tribune* launched GoldenBee.

While it does not technically appear to meet the definition of a business-led corporate responsibility coalition, GoldenBee has many of the characteristics, and fulfills many of the roles, of such a coalition. It mobilizes business leadership around thematic programs of work related to responsible business practices; runs annual awards; has produced a sustainability assessment tool and a corporate responsibility reporting assessment tool; runs workshops, training and customized training (e.g., on implementation of ISO 26000); provides consultancy services; and conducts research and produces a range of publications in addition to what appears in *WTO Tribune* and on its portal *CSR China*: www.csr-china. net, which was initially financed by the Sino-German (GIZ-managed) CSR Project. It works closely with around 50 significant Chinese companies and has trained staff from over 1,000 firms. Funding comes from a mixture of corporate membership fees, corporate sponsorship of particular workstreams, international development institutions such as GIZ, and domestic sources. *WTO Tribune*/GoldenBee has worked with CSR Europe since 2005. As part of this collaboration, it is taking the CSR Europe *Enterprise 2020* program and adapting it to the Chinese context. The intention is to develop "common vision, common action, cross-border co-operation and shared value"[122] to achieve the sustainable enterprise of the future. *WTO Tribune*/GoldenBee has already become a significant Chinese-created and developed CSR initiative, with strong links to national and provincial governments, and to Chinese trade union and employer federations. This local credibility has been recognized by the German and Swedish governments providing financial support for GoldenBee activities. Indeed, the "Memorandum of Understanding on Corporate Social Responsibility Cooperation" signed by the Chinese Ministry of Commerce and the Swedish Ministry of Foreign Affairs is being implemented through GoldenBee, which is running the Sino-Swedish CSR Cooperation (www.csr.gov.cn).

Another indigenous Chinese organization with a growing interest in responsible business practices is the powerful **China Entrepreneur Club**, established in December 2006 by 31 influential Chinese entrepreneurs, economists and diplomats.[123] The club has produced an annual Top 100 companies' green ranking since 2010[124] and publishes the bimonthly *Green Herald*, founded in 2009.[125]

The growing industry-specific focus of corporate responsibility coalitions and initiatives seen in other parts of the world is already happening in China. To quote Rolf Dietmar again:

> The China National Textile and Apparel Council was the first industry association in China to publish its own guideline, CSC9000T, and to promote this internally within the association. In a further notable development, in December 2010 the China International Contractors Association adopted a guideline for implementing CSR in its member companies, of which there are over 1,300. These companies primarily handle overseas contracts, e.g., infrastructure projects such as bridges and roads in Africa. The guideline is currently being trialled in 29 pilot companies.[126]

Among other trade associations developing CSR initiatives are the Chinese Electronics Standardization Association (CESA), which has formed a CSR committee and produced CSR guidelines based on the ISO 26000 and SA8000 international standards;[127] the China Tea Marketing Association; and the Food Industry Association. Common to all these industry-sector initiatives is the goal of offering member firms assistance in accessing international markets by understanding and responding to those markets' sustainability requirements.

Some of the international chambers of commerce in China have CSR initiatives including the American Chamber (AmCham) in Shanghai and Beijing, and the EU–China Chambers in Beijing and particularly in Shanghai. The U.S. Chamber of Commerce has cooperated with the All China Federation of Industry and Commerce to hold a USA–China Forum on Corporate Social Responsibility Cooperation. Some China-based commentators dismiss many domestic trade associations as ineffectual and suggest there is little tradition of joining business representative organizations since they are not regarded as adding value. Nor, the same commentators argue, is there familiarity with the democratic and participatory nature of business representative organizations experienced in other parts of the world. Some China-based corporate responsibility experts also identify historic, and perhaps still current, sensitivities about disclosing confidential corporate information to foreign-controlled business organizations. Nevertheless, the early sectoral focus suggests some emerging elements of a "corporate responsibility architecture with Chinese characteristics." Meanwhile, several of the international corporate responsibility coalitions have initiated projects in China and even established offices in the country.

International corporate responsibility coalitions in China

The International Business Leaders Forum initiated and supported the Shanghai Business Leaders Project, which ran for several years in the 1990s. The IBLF subsequently supported the creation of the China Business Leaders Forum (CBLF), in association with the Renmin University of China. The CBLF was launched in March 2005 to provide a "safe haven" for leaders of Chinese and foreign companies and organizations to meet regularly, share good practice and to collectively develop a sustainable framework of corporate governance to be promoted across the wider business community. It has conducted more than 20 roundtables in Beijing and Shanghai. Discussion summaries and a collection of relevant international materials (adapted and translated into Chinese) are available at its bilingual website (www.cblf.org.cn). At the end of 2010, the IBLF and Renmin University launched the China Center for Corporate Sustainability to build on the established body of work and activities of the CBLF.[128]

In 2003 the China Business Council for Sustainable Development (CBCSD) was established, thanks to the joint efforts of China Enterprise Confederation (CEC) and the World Business Council for Sustainable Development, as well as long preparation by a number of well-known Chinese and international companies. The CBCSD is a coalition of leading Chinese and foreign enterprises. It is registered and operating in China as a national organization, established through the Ministry of Civil Affairs. The CBCSD seems to have been one of the more successful coalitions in engaging a significant number of large and influential Chinese firms including the Huafon Group, Jiangsu Shuangliang Group Co. Ltd. and Sinopec.[129]

Business for Social Responsibility has had an office in mainland China since 2005 (in Guangzhou) and in Beijing since 2007. Since 2004, BSR has operated the China Training Institute (CTI) "to help brand companies and their Chinese suppliers improve CSR (Corporate Social Responsibility) performance and overall competitiveness through a wide range of Training, Roundtables, Salons and Long-term Training Programs."[130] The CTI has the goal of improving workplace standards in China-based export factories. Its training program provides education, technical knowledge, skills and methodologies to factories owners, managers and supervisors seeking to improve working conditions and to comply with Chinese labor laws and buyer expectations. CTI partners with organizations in China to develop local capacity and to help organizations operate more sustainably. BSR China also undertakes consulting projects focusing on supply-chain management. Among current BSR China initiatives is strategic capacity-building of NGOs to enhance their ability to work with businesses both on strategic business–community partnerships and on core business issues. Funding for this particular program has come from the U.S. State Department, which for some may reinforce perceptions of BSR China as an "American" organization. Nevertheless, BSR has a rapidly growing presence and work program in China covering both industry- and issue-specific initiatives; and local corporate responsibility experts describe it as providing a valuable window onto international corporate responsibility good practices.

CSR Europe differs from BSR in terms of its engagement with China. Rather than establishing its own office, CSR Europe has chosen to support the activities of a Chinese partner: the aforementioned *WTO Tribune* and its associated GoldenBee initiative. In 2005, CSR Europe co-organized with *WTO Tribune* a Sino–European International Forum on CSR in Beijing. The outcome of the forum was a joint publication on CSR in China, aimed at supporting investors in China who were looking to combine performance requirements and sustainable development priorities. The conference has been organized each year since by *WTO Tribune*/GoldenBee China, still in association with CSR Europe (and with the Japanese Council for Better Corporate Citizenship), and the Sino–German CSR Project. On the occasion of the Sixth Conference in 2011, a new online platform for Chinese companies to enhance responsible competitiveness and contribute to global sustainable development was launched.

The UN Global Compact (UNGC) has been represented in China since the end of 2001. In 2009, the UNGC formally recognized the creation of the Global Compact Network China Center and contracted to house the Center's Secretariat with the Beijing Rongzhi Institute of Corporate Social Responsibility. The Secretariat is responsible for organizing and implementing the UNGC's various activities throughout China.[131] The Chinese chapter of the UNGC comes under the auspices of the Ministry of Foreign Affairs. A significant advance in official recognition of the UNGC in China came with the appointment to the global UNGC board of Mr. Fu Chengyu, Chairman of the Sinopec Group, the state-owned oil and gas refiner. As yet, however, the number of Chinese business signatories of the UNGC remains a tiny percentage of the total of Chinese enterprises.

Organized by Business in the Community (BITC), CSR360 Global Partner Network has recruited several Chinese members: the Center for International Business Ethics in Beijing, Sedex China and the Fuping Development Institute.[132] The Chinese Association of NGOs (CONGO), which operates under the Ministry of Commerce, has also applied to join in what might be perceived as a further discreet signal of official interest in learning from the work of corporate responsibility coalitions around the world.

Why China will be of growing importance to the coalitions

Projections vary as to exactly when China may again become the largest global economy, as it was for an estimated first 18 of the last 20 centuries.[133] Goldman Sachs predicted in 2011 that it would occur in 2027, while *The Economist* in 2010 suggested the date might be 2019.[134] That China is likely to become again the largest economy is justification on its own for why Chinese attitudes to corporate responsibility, and therefore to corporate responsibility coalitions, matter for any discussion about where the coalitions might be heading both within China and in the rest of the world, as Chinese companies and ways of working spread. Additionally, it is clear that many of the biggest sustainability challenges, and also the biggest opportunities, are in China. According to the World Bank, 16 of the world's 20 most polluted cities are in China.[135] It is anticipated that the percentage of China's population living in urban areas will grow from 27% in 1990 and 46% in 2010 to 70% by 2030.[136] Thus from 2010 to 2030, around 330 million Chinese will move from rural to urban areas – the equivalent of moving more than the entire population of the USA (314 million)[137] in 20 years. Rapid urbanization, the need for dramatic improvements in rural healthcare and the urgency around tackling pollution and resource depletion all create significant opportunities for coalitions to promote *sustainable innovation* and the pursuit of *shared value* to companies. Hence the advice of one corporate responsibility specialist: "If you want to impact sustainable development, be in China!" As for any other type of organization seeking to work in China, this requires a willingness to take the long view; to learn about Chinese culture, history and ways of interacting; and to respect the culture and traditions of China.

Critical success factors for coalitions in China

Any international coalition wishing to operate in China must choose the right Chinese partner and find and retain qualified staff who are effective interpreters between cultures. It is also essential to develop a distinctive set of service offerings or industry sectors to target. Securing long-term government sponsorship, retaining a critical mass of Chinese and international member companies and building a funding model that provides fair returns all round, while recycling Chinese funds in China, are all likely to be key to success.

Conversely, given the extent of current interest in sustainable development in China, the speed and scale of change in the country, the potential to implement to scale, and the number of businesses to engage, it must be anticipated that significant Chinese-headquartered coalitions will emerge – and they may grow quickly. Coalitions around the world will need to be geared up to learn from and adopt or adapt new approaches to helping embed corporate sustainability that have been created in China.

Supporting sustainable internationalization of Chinese business

Equally, there could be a valuable role for coalitions in other parts of the world, especially those operating in regions where there is already significant Chinese investment, to help mainland Chinese companies evaluate how to conduct business more sustainably as they expand operations into different markets. Just as American-headquartered companies, such as IBM, were among the founding members of BITC in the UK and later of CSR Europe, will Chinese companies join coalitions overseas? Will they, like companies from Japan and India before them, see local coalitions as one of the ways to build networks and enhance their understanding of how to do business in other parts of the world? China is forecast to invest $1–2 trillion abroad over the next ten years, from investments in industrialized economies to many emerging markets in Africa, Asia and Latin America.[138] Within five years, annual Chinese overseas direct investment is expected to exceed annual foreign direct investment in China.[139] Chinese companies expanding abroad either through acquisitions, strategic investment stakes or their own organic growth may need help to "unlearn" their domestic model of stakeholder engagement with its heavy emphasis on engaging the Communist Party of China and the layers of national through to municipal government. Instead, the corporate responsibility coalitions could potentially help these businesses understand that stakeholder engagement outside China needs to take more account of consumers, employees, NGOs, private investors and conventional and new media. Following government and CPC guidance may be a necessary but probably an insufficient requirement to ensure license to operate outside China.

One particularly important and sensitive region for Chinese companies is Africa. The United Nations Development Programme (UNDP), for example, has helped to create the

China–Africa Business Council (CABC) with the Ministry of Commerce and China International Center for Economic and Technical Exchanges. Non-state-owned businesses are the principal participants and beneficiaries of this new NGO.[140] There could be growing opportunities for existing and emergent corporate responsibility coalitions in Africa to help Chinese headquartered extractives and other firms to establish successfully and sustainably in Africa. One of the potential topics of the *WTO Tribune*/GoldenBee collaboration with CSR Europe going forward is about strategies for doing business at the base of the pyramid – something that could help both European and Chinese-headquartered companies in Africa, as well as in China and other parts of the world.

Equally, given that China has been able to move more people out of poverty more quickly in recent decades than any other nation in history, the insights and experiences of Chinese companies and organizations could help develop the corporate responsibility coalitions so that they are better placed to address the needs of fast-growing and rapidly changing businesses from emerging markets.

Reciprocity of interests and benefits

Encouraging greater interconnectedness and mutual learning and benefits between companies pursuing responsible business practices from China and the rest of the world could become an important aspect of the work of corporate responsibility coalitions around the world, as well as for those operating in China. This might be expressed visually in the matrix in Figure 6.2. It could be argued that activity so far has been in the lower half of the matrix, and while this is likely to remain the focus in the near future, over the next decade, attention will move more to the right half and extend to the upper half as more Chinese corporate responsibility organizations emerge and more Chinese companies internationalize.

Figure 6.2 **China and the coalitions**

In rest of world	• Engaging Chinese companies around world as they expand internationally • Taking learning back to home markets • Helping other corporate responsibility coalitions to understand how to work successfully with Chinese organizations	• Sharing distinctive Chinese responsible business practices which may emerge, e.g., in handling aging workforce, helping employees with eldercare responsibilities, and innovating products and services for older consumers
In China	• Supporting their multinational members and their supply-chains in China • Helping Chinese companies to internationalize	• Interpreting and disseminating international good practice for local conditions • Working with international companies to develop distinctive applications of their global corporate responsibility commitments to meet Chinese stakeholders' wants and needs
	International coalitions in China	**Chinese-headquartered corporate responsibility initiatives**

The re-emergence of China on the world stage as a major geo-political and economic leader is likely to influence the future shape and work of corporate responsibility coalitions far beyond China. While countries such as Brazil, India, Indonesia and Turkey are also growing in economic and geo-strategic importance, we do not anticipate that their attitudes to existing corporate responsibility coalitions will raise such substantial debates for the coalitions, because the concept of independent NGOs and representative organizations of and for business are already a feature of these societies. China, predicts Sinologist David Gosset, is set to be the "co-author of the 21st century world order" and it is simply now "too big and too important not to be discussed."[141]

6.2 **Growth in industry- and issue-specific diversity**

As outlined in Part I, alongside the growth of generalist, national and international corporate responsibility coalitions, there has been a marked increase over the past decade in coalitions that focus on addressing a specific issue or driving change within a specific industry sector. Some have been created by established trade associations in response to a particular crisis that affects the reputation and "license to operate" of companies throughout the industry. Responsible Care®, for example, was created by a number of chemical industry associations in the aftermath of the Bhopal gas leak disaster in India in 1984, and there have been several industry-specific initiatives established to improve safety and emergency-response practices in the energy sector since the BP deepwater well explosion in the Gulf of Mexico in 2010.

Other industry- and issue-specific coalitions have emerged because industry leaders have become concerned more generally that their own efforts to embrace responsible business practices could be undermined by the poor performance of industry peers. A number of anti-corruption and transparency, fair labor and sustainable agriculture accountability coalitions have been established with this motivation.

A few of the industry- and issue-specific coalitions have been created as small leadership groups ranging from 5 to 20 pioneering companies within a particular industry that want to "push the boundaries" on a set of social and environmental issues beyond what is possible through a larger representative business organization or even larger corporate responsibility coalition. The International Council on Mining and Metals, the Sustainable Agriculture Initiative Platform and the Sustainability Consortium are examples. Over time, these initiatives generally target industry-wide improvement and often promote the sharing of principles, standards and operational best practice.

Given the enormous diversity in their size and scope, their growing specificity and the constant evolution of these more targeted coalitions, it is difficult to ascertain exact numbers. If there are an estimated 110 or so generalist corporate responsibility coalitions, there are at least several thousand industry-specific and issue-specific coalitions focused on embedding and scaling responsible and sustainable business practices. Most of these can be categorized under the following four broad categories:

1. **Industry- and issue-specific coalitions incubated by or hosted within generalist corporate responsibility coalitions.** For example, the WBCSD has a long-standing program of industry-sector initiatives in the mobility, pulp and paper, and cement

sectors, each led by a core group of the major companies active in the relevant sector. BSR has established Industry Focus networks and Working Groups, focused on tackling a variety of clearly specified sustainability issues in over 15 different industries. The IBLF created the International Hotels Environment Initiative in 1993, now renamed the International Tourism Partnership, which has supported a number of industry-wide benchmarks and innovations in travel and tourism. All of the generalist corporate responsibility coalitions named above have also established issue-specific working groups among their members in areas such as water, climate change, education and health. The WEF also has an Industry Partners community, which consists of CEOs in some 20 industry sectors who meet on a regular basis within their industry sector to address strategic issues, including sustainability-related imperatives.

2. **Corporate responsibility initiatives incubated by or hosted within a broader trade and industry association.** A number of national and international trade and industry associations have established dedicated units and in a few cases independently governed initiatives aimed at using the association as a platform for promoting responsible business practices throughout the industry. Two of the most well-known examples of independently governed initiatives linked to trade associations are Responsible Care, which focuses on sustainability, product stewardship and safety in the chemical industry, and the International Council of Toy Industries (ICTI) CARE Foundation, which focuses on improving labor conditions for workers in the toy industry. The two examples are profiled in Box 6.1. These both offer useful models for of the potential of using representative business organizations and trade associations as a "scaling platform" for responsible business practices by making support for these corporate responsibility initiatives a part of the criteria for membership of major national industry associations.

3. **Independent, business-led coalitions dedicated to sustainability and corporate responsibility in a specific industry or issue.** A number of independently governed and funded industry- and issue-specific leadership groups have also been established over the past two decades. These have tended to be in challenging sectors where relatively small groups of leading companies have felt the need to create a dedicated organization focused solely on promoting responsible and sustainable business practices over and above what their representative trade and industry associations are able to do. Well-regarded examples include the International Council on Mining and Metals; the Electronics Industry Citizenship Coalition; Social Investment Forums in the United States, Europe and Asia; the Portman Group and Century Council within the alcoholic beverages sector (see Box 6.3); the International Petroleum Industry Environmental and Conservation Association; and the Equator Principles and Principles for Responsible Investment in the financial sector (see Box 6.2). Likewise, there are a number of emerging independent, cross-industry, business-led organizations that focus on a specific issue, such as the Global Business Coalition on Health created in 2001, the Corporate Leaders Group on Climate Change established in 2008, and the Global Business Coalition on Education, launched in 2012.

4. **Multi-stakeholder issue-specific coalitions with strong business leadership.** The fourth category, which is expanding in scope and scale, consists of coalitions that address a specific issue but are not solely or majority funded, governed or led by business, although they have a strong business membership and a markets-based approach to problem-solving. A growing number of global, national, regional and city-level multi-stakeholder coalitions exist in the areas of public health; improving working conditions in factories along global supply chains; improving accountability and responsibility in the development of oil, gas and mineral deposits; and promoting sustainability and inclusion in global food and agricultural supply chains. Their success relies on the active leadership and participation of the major corporations that drive these value chains, but they also need the engagement of non-business actors such as governments, donors and non-governmental organizations to build legitimacy and capability

Box 6.1 **Responsible Care® and ICTI CARE: scaling reach and impact through representative trade associations**

Industry leaders in the chemical and toy sectors have spearheaded two of the world's largest sector-specific coalitions by using their national and international trade associations as platforms to achieve scale and reach. The following brief overviews of the these two initiatives illustrate how other national and international trade and industry associations could play a more proactive and large-scale role in promoting responsible business practices among their member companies.

Responsible Care

Responsible Care is the chemical industry's global initiative that aims to improve health, safety and environmental performance; provide and encourage open and transparent communication with stakeholders; promote effective management of chemicals along the value chain; work towards the development and application of sustainable chemistry; and measure the industry's progress against these objectives. Responsible Care was founded in 1985 by the Canadian Chemical Producers' Association. Its global charter was launched in 2006 at the UN-led International Conference on Chemicals Management in Dubai. The International Council of Chemical Associations (ICCA) serves as the global guardian of Responsible Care and more than 50 national chemical manufacturing associations (with several thousand member companies) participate in the initiative. At the national level, member associations are responsible for the detailed implementation of Responsible Care by companies in their countries. Individual countries' programs are monitored and coordinated by the ICCA Responsible Care Leadership Group; Responsible Care is an essential part of ICCA's contribution to the UN's Strategic Approach to International Chemicals Management. Through the initiative, companies continue to work towards the vision they have committed to: that, by 2020, "All chemicals will be produced and used in ways that minimize risks for human health and the environment."

Responsible Care participant CEOs pledge to adhere to an enhanced, transparent and effective global governance process to ensure accountability in implementing initiative priorities. This governance process occurs through the ICCA and incorporates issues such as tracking and communicating performance commitments; defining and monitoring the implementation of obligations; support-ing national association governance; helping companies and associations achieve commitments; and establishing a global process for revoking, if necessary, the Responsible Care status of any participant that fails to meet its commitments.

Responsible Care promotes measurable performance of its objectives. National Responsible Care managers collect and report environment, health, safety, prod-uct stewardship and Responsible Care implementation data for their countries to the ICCA. Data is then shared with stakeholders in order to demonstrate progress in chemical management activities. Examples of progress extend across the globe.[142]

Responsible Care has fostered the development of the ICCA Global Product Strategy, which seeks to improve the industry's management of chemicals across the value chain. Responsible Care also enters into cooperative performance-based initiatives with government agencies and participates in community pro-jects such as the development of wildlife habitats and the creation of tailored programs for schools.

ICTI CARE

The International Council of Toy Industries' (ICTI) CARE (Caring, Awareness, Responsible, Ethical) Process aims to improve working conditions for approxi-mately 1.4 million toy-factory workers by eliminating sub-standard health, safety and labor practices in more than 2,500 factories. The ICTI CARE Process (ICP) was established by ICTI in 2006 "to enable the worldwide toy industry to assure consumers that its products are manufactured in safe and humane conditions by providing education and training for toy factory employees and enforcing a thor-ough and consistent monitoring program for toy factories." The ICP also partici-pates in the Global Social Compliance Programme, which focuses on achieving greater coherence and consistency between different supply-chain management initiatives.

The ICP aims to eliminate child labor, forced labor, indentured workers and other unethical hiring practices; advance transparency in toy-industry labor prac-tices, including wages and working hours; advocate for fire protection, security equipment and other safety-related standards; promote a minimum wage and fair work contracts; and serve as a recognized mechanism to certify ethical manu-facturing. Its main provision for doing so is a thorough and consistent auditing program for factories that are members of the ICP. Though its initial focus is in China, where 80% of the world's toy volume is manufactured, 31 countries are represented as members of the ICP.

The key to ICP's monitoring is the qualification, appointment and training of audit companies to carry out the audit process. By 2010, ICP-accredited auditors from eight approved auditing firms had conducted approximately 2,500 audits and issued nearly 1,200 Seals of Compliance. There was a 37.6% increase in the num-ber of compliant factories between 2009 and 2010, and 20% of audits reflected greater compliance in the payment of wages, including overtime pay. The ICP also added International Labour Organization Conventions about weekly rest, forced labor and equal pay for men and women to the ICTI Code of Business Practices;

→

phased in a new Wages and Working Hours Policy as part of its Continuous Improvement Process, towards which more than 90% of toy factory owners and managers agreed to work; and dropped 48 factories due to allegations of unethical behavior.

Employee education is another tool for the ICP. The program educates employees through on-site training, information cards, manuals and other presentations. ICP's help line, provided by the China Labor Support Network Occupational Health Consultation Services Co. Ltd., has resulted in more than 1,100 grievances being filed. Through a public–private partnership between the ICP and German development agency GIZ, a train-the-trainer program was launched in 2010; other NGO training partners have given in-factory presentations on sexual harassment and worker representation.[143]

Boxes 6.2 and 6.3 illustrate examples of different industry- and issue-specific coalitions in the diverse areas of sustainable finance and responsible alcohol use. These examples illustrate how leading companies in specific industry sectors have come together in pre-competitive coalitions to address strategic sustainability or corporate responsibility issues that represent either major risks or opportunities to their sector. A similar range and variety of business-led coalitions can be found in almost every industry sector today, the vast majority of which did not exist even ten years ago.

In the food and agriculture sector, for example, leading and often competing companies, ranging from commodity producers and traders to food processors and retailers, have joined forces with each other and in many cases with governments and NGOs to create alliances such as the Sustainable Agriculture Initiative platform, the Sustainable Food Lab, the New Vision for Agriculture, the Ethical Trading Initiative, the Consumer Goods Forum, the Sustainability Consortium, the Global Alliance for Improved Nutrition, and a variety of commodity roundtables to promote more sustainable production of commodities such as palm oil, soya, coffee, cocoa, beef and cotton.

Likewise in the energy and mining sectors, competitor companies have joined together in coalitions dedicated to addressing difficult issues such as respecting human rights, improving revenue transparency, tackling corruption and improving environmental practices. These include the International Petroleum Industry Environmental Conservation Association (IPIECA); the International Council on Mining and Metals (ICMM); the Partnering Against Corruption Initiative and the Responsible Mining Development Initiative, both convened by the World Economic Forum; the Extractive Industries Transparency Initiative; the Voluntary Principles on Security and Human Rights; the Diamond Development Initiative; the World Gold Council; the Responsible Jewellery Council; and a number of specific industry-wide environmental initiatives from biodiversity and water management to safety and hazardous waste management. Similar pre-competitive leadership initiatives have been created to promote more responsible and sustainable business practices in most industry sectors.

Box 6.2 **Industry-specific platforms to promote sustainability finance**

Over the past decade, there has been growing momentum within the financial sector itself and also engagement between leading corporations, corporate responsibility coalitions, financial-sector organizations and, increasingly, regulators and policy-makers to improve corporate sustainability performance and disclosure. This box profiles five coalitions led by the financial sector that aim to harness private investment and banking to achieve better corporate sustainability at scale. All five examples illustrate how leading investors, accounting firms, stock exchanges, corporations, intergovernmental agencies and, increasingly, regulators are cooperating through multi-stakeholder, but largely business-led, coalitions to achieve greater scale and systemic impact than any one actor could do alone, often in a shorter period of time than it would take for regulations to take effect. They offer interesting coalition models for other sectors.

Investor Network on Climate Risk (INCR)

The INCR partners with investors worldwide to advance the investment opportunities and reduce the material risks posed by sustainability challenges such as global climate change and water scarcity. When it was founded in 2003, the INCR had ten institutional investors managing US$600 billion; in 2012, it had 100 members managing nearly US$10 trillion in assets. Members include BlackRock, Deutsche Asset Management and TIAA-CREF, as well as public pension funds in California, Florida and New York. Examples of its success include spearheading the successful effort to petition the U.S. Securities & Exchange Commission and Canadian securities regulators to issue formal guidance on climate-change-related disclosure that companies must provide to investors in their financial filing and leading investor efforts with major oil and gas companies to strengthen risk oversight measures for deepwater oil drilling, natural gas hydraulic fracturing (fracking) and oil sands production. The INCR also hosted 500 financial leaders managing US$22 trillion in assets at the United Nations in 2010 to discuss investment opportunities and policy actions for mitigating global climate change and has persuaded dozens of Fortune 500 companies to improve their climate policies, practices and disclosure. The INCR is coordinated by Ceres, a non-profit organization that leads a national coalition of investors, environmental organizations and other public interest groups working with companies to address sustainability challenges such as global climate change and water scarcity.

Principles for Responsible Investment (PRI) Initiative

The UN-backed PRI Initiative is a network of international investors working together to put the six Principles for Responsible Investment into practice. The PRI were devised by the investment community in 2006 and reflect the view that, since environmental, social and governance (ESG) issues can affect the performance of investment portfolios, they therefore must be given appropriate consideration by investors in order for investors to fulfill their fiduciary (or equivalent) duty. The PRI provide a voluntary framework that includes (1) incorporating ESG issues into investment analysis and decision-making processes; (2) actively incorporating ESG issues into ownership policies and practices; (3) seeking appropriate

➔

disclosure on ESG issues by the entities in which a firm invests; (4) promoting acceptance and implementation of the PRI within the investment industry; (5) working within the investment community, particularly signatories to the PRI, to enhance the PRI's effectiveness; and (6) reporting on activities and progress towards implementing the PRI. The PRI Initiative was created to help investors to implement the principles. The Initiative has two UN partners, the UN Environment Programme Finance Initiative and the UN Global Compact, and supports investors by sharing best practice, facilitating collaboration and managing a variety of workstreams. As of April 2012, over 1,000 investment institutions had become signatories, with assets under management approximately US$30 trillion.

The Equator Principles

The Equator Principles (EP) coalition provides a voluntary and credit-risk management framework for its participating members to determine, assess and manage environmental and social risk in project finance transactions. The initiative was launched in June 2003 in Washington, DC, with ten banks as the founder signatories and with support from the International Finance Corporation (IFC). Based on the environmental and social standards of the IFC, the EP framework requires its signatories to voluntarily adhere to a set of environmental and social risk management criteria when financing projects in developing countries with capital costs above US$10 million. Revised in June 2006 to include a public reporting requirement and again in 2012 to include requirements for managing climate impacts and greater consideration of human rights,[144] the EP are supported by over 75 financial institutions in almost 30 countries, including most of the world's major banks as well as insurance companies, bilateral development agencies and export credit agencies. The banks that support the Principles are estimated to represent over 70% of total project finance debt in emerging markets. This offers a good illustration of how a relatively small number of major corporations can achieve scale in a short period of time by engaging in a pre-competitive corporate responsibility coalition. In order to actively engage the increasingly influential banks in China, Russia and India and other key emerging markets, an outreach working group has been formed. Other working groups led by participating banks cover issues such as stakeholder engagement, biodiversity, climate change and social risks.

The Prince of Wales Accounting for Sustainability Project (A4S)

The Prince of Wales Accounting for Sustainability Project (A4S) works with businesses, investors, the public sector, accounting bodies, NGOs and academics to develop practical guidance and tools for embedding sustainability into decision-making and reporting processes. A4S was set up by HRH The Prince of Wales in 2004; the output from the project's first phase formally launched in 2006. As of 2012, the project had involved the collaboration of more than 150 public- and private-sector organizations. Its four workstreams include (1) Integrated Thinking, to help organizations incorporate the value of all resources (including externalities and intangibles) in internal and external information and decision-making processes; (2) International Network, to expand the membership of the Accounting Bodies Network and develop an international network committed to raising awareness of the A4S forum principles, and also to explore the current practices and issues of integrating sustainability considerations into capital expenditure decision-making; (3) Engagement and Communication, to promote the application of connected, integrated reporting through workshops, the A4S website, and pilot studies and on an international basis; and (4) Integrated Reporting, to further the International Integrated Reporting Council (IIRC), which came out of A4S and the Global Reporting Initiative's work in 2009 on the need to integrate financial and sustainability reporting. The IIRC promotes Integrated Reporting, which aims to demonstrate the linkages between an organization's strategy, governance and financial performance and the social, environmental and economic context within which it operates. More than 80 companies were part of the IIRC's pilot program in the 2012 reporting cycle.

Sustainable Stock Exchanges (SSE) Initiative

The Sustainable Stock Exchanges (SSE) initiative is aimed at exploring how exchanges can work together with investors, regulators and companies to enhance corporate transparency, and ultimately performance, on ESG issues and encourage responsible long-term approaches to investment. The first meeting of the SSE was opened by Secretary-General Ban Ki-moon in New York City in 2009, hosted by the UNGC and co-organized by the UNGC, the UN Conference on Trade and Development, and the Principles for Responsible Investment; it featured approximately 100 leaders from institutional investors, stock exchanges and regulatory bodies. A similar convening followed in China in 2010. In 2011, as a result of its dialogues within the SSE initiative, Aviva Investors convened the Corporate Sustainability Reporting Coalition, which now includes over 40 organizations, primarily institutional investors, managing in excess of US$1.6 trillion. Members of this coalition urged all nations at Rio + 20 to commit to developing a Convention fostering the development of national measures requiring, on a comply or explain basis, the integration of material sustainability issues within the corporate reporting cycle of all listed and large private companies. At the Rio + 20 Corporate Sustainability Forum, five stock exchanges with over 4,600 listed companies (NASDAQ OMX, Brazil's BM&FBOVESPA, the Johannesburg Stock Exchange, the Istanbul Stock Exchange and the Egyptian Exchange) announced a public commitment to work with their listed companies, investors and regulators to improve the ESG disclosure and performance among companies listed on their stock exchanges. In addition, they committed to working with other exchanges through the World Federation of Exchanges to share lessons and best practices and spread this approach on a global basis.[145]

Box 6.3 Industry-wide platforms to promote responsible drinking

The alcoholic beverages industry provides a good example of industry- and issue-specific initiatives. Increasing societal concern about the misuse of alcohol and the consequent health and social problems has led to the formation of a number of national and international coalitions (which the alcohol industry describes as social aspects organizations [SAOs]), both to promote alcohol education and responsible drinking messages, and to establish and enforce collective self-regulation of the industry on matters such as advertising, marketing to young people and product strength.

The first such initiatives were STIVA (Stichting Verantwoord Alcoholgebruik), formed in the Netherlands in 1982, and the Industry Association for Responsible Alcohol Use, created in South Africa in 1986. The formation of the Portman Group in the UK in 1989 marked a turning point for the industry's initiatives. Until 2006, this coalition fulfilled both the public health education *and* a self-regulation role. In 2006, the public education function was spun off into a separate charity with a multi-stakeholder board, the Drinkaware Trust, leaving the Portman Group as a business-led coalition promoting responsible business practices specifically relevant to the alcoholic beverages industry. The Portman Group, unlike some of the analogous organizations it has inspired in other parts of the world, has engaged all the main alcoholic beverages players: producers of wines and spirits as well as brewers and retailers.

The Portman Group was the inspiration for the Century Council in the United States and similar groups in much of continental Europe. Thus, the European Forum for Responsible Drinking, which grew out of a loose grouping known a the Amsterdam Group in 1990, now has 14 national SAOs in membership, including the Portman Group, covering most major European alcoholic beverages markets. Only some of these SAOs, such as those in Denmark, Ireland and the Netherlands, are business-led corporate responsibility coalitions incorporating both public education and collective self-regulation; others are little more than industry lobbying groups. Critics dismiss these coalitions as smokescreens rather than genuine attempts to tackle the harmful use of alcohol.[146]

Table 6.2 **Alcohol coalitions**

Organization	Country	Year created
STIVA	Netherlands	1982
Portman Group	UK	1989
Entreprise & Prévention	France	1990
Arnoldus Group	Belgium	1992
Deutsche Initiative zur Forderung eines verantwortungsvollen Umgangs mit alkoholhaltigen Genussmitteln (DIFA)*	Germany	1992
Foreningen Gode Alkoholdninger (GODA)	Denmark	1993
The Sense Group	Malta	1997
Modus Foundation	Poland	1998

Organization	Country	Year created
Fundación Alcohol y Sociedad	Spain	2000
The Mature Enjoyment of Alcohol in Society (MEAS)	Ireland	2002
Forum PSR	Czech Republic	2003
HAFRAC	Hungary	2006
Forum PSR Slovakia	Slovakia	2010

* DIFA no longer in existence

Other prominent national or sub-national coalitions include Educ'Alcool in Quebec, Canada, which was the first alcoholic beverages-specific coalition to involve independent, non-industry members as well as industry representatives on its board. In Australia, Diageo took the lead in the creation of a multi-stakeholder initiative Drinkwise in 2004, modeled on the Educ'Alcool model.[147]

The International Center for Alcohol Policies formed in 1996 and based in Washington, DC, is a pan-industry initiative that acts as a think-tank and developer of best practices for the industry. It has done a lot of development work on both public education and collective self-regulation for the industry, especially in Africa and Latin America. In recent years, it has become much more active in helping countries to implement a focus on self-regulation, drunk-driving and non-commercial (illicit) alcohol problems.[148]

The Global Alcohol Producers Group was created by the industry in 2005 to promote dialogue with the World Health Organization on ways it can contribute to addressing harmful use of alcohol. It also represents industry viewpoints on alcohol policy and therefore also acts as a trade association.

These coalitions have helped to move the alcoholic beverages industry from being seen by many as a public health enemy to being treated as a genuine partner at least for some governments in tackling alcohol misuse. The Portman Group, for example, was the industry channel for negotiating the Responsibility Deal with the incoming UK coalition government in 2010–11 on alcohol and public health (see Box 7.1 in Chapter 7, page 95).[149] For a broader discussion of how coalitions could provide collective business input to responsibility deals, see Chapter 13.

Looking at the multiple reputational and performance challenges now facing other sectors such as pharmaceuticals and financial services, will more Portman Group/Century Council models of business-led sectoral corporate responsibility coalition be created for these other sectors? Or will one or more of the generalist corporate responsibility coalitions develop a sectoral specialty for such troubled industries? (See Part III.)

6.3 **Diversity in size and scope of coalitions**

The differences between business-led coalitions go much deeper than simply a division between generalist, international, national, industry- or issue-specific. Some are well resourced, with substantial staff teams and well-established programs, while some have only a few staff, precarious funding and fledgling programs. Some are corporate-CEO-led – others are corporate responsibility-practitioner-led; the business involvement in the work of the coalition (e.g., membership of the coalition's board) is either at the level of CEO/main board/country head of member companies or principally at corporate responsibility/corporate community involvement (CCI) manager level. Some of the coalitions are dominated by particular business sectors, whereas others have broad corporate involvement.

Some of the business-led coalitions are focused still on CCI and employee volunteering, while others have a much broader remit for responsible business. Some have evolved from the former into the latter. Some coalitions such as Philippine Business for Social Progress (until very recently) have successfully stuck to their CCI focus.[150] In some countries, significant business involvement in societal issues has focused on, or at least started with, one particular topic; as an example, tackling HIV/AIDS, as is the focus of the Thailand Business Coalition on AIDS, founded in 1993.[151] Still others grew from a focus on ethical sourcing or diversity (see Table 9.1 on page 123).

Similarly, there is considerable variety in the activities undertaken, and on what issues, among the coalitions. A 2009 survey[152] of coalitions in membership of the CSR360 Global Partner Network found that all 65 coalitions then affiliated as core partners worked on CSR strategy, with most also working on sustainable development, corporate community involvement and education/research (see Table 6.3). (The CSR360 Global Partner Network is discussed in more detail in Chapter 10.)

Table 6.3 **CSR360 Global Partner Network coalitions survey of topics covered, 2009**

Topic	Number of coalitions
Cause-related marketing	24
Community	58
CSR strategy	65
Diversity and equal opportunities	36
Education and research	58
Environment	45
Ethical supply-chain management	36
Human rights	29
Reporting	46
Sustainable development	60
Volunteering	44

The GlobeScan Coalitions Survey in 2012 (see Appendix 3), where respondents were primarily from the larger, more established, national and international generalist coalitions, asked respondent CEOs to rate the level of their organization's strategic focus in seven areas (Question 3A). Figure 6.3 shows their answers.[153]

Figure 6.3 **GlobeScan Coalitions Survey: strategic focus of organization**

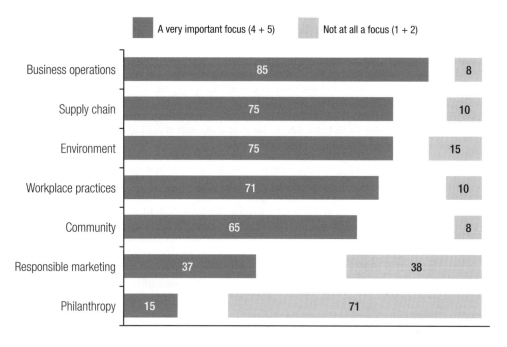

The CEOs responding to the survey generally do not expect their focus to change in the next five years.

Some corporate responsibility coalitions have chosen to prioritize certain sectors. Early on, BSR had an extractives industries specialty; it continues to focus on various sectors, which are now extended to include consumer products, financial services, food and beverage and agriculture, healthcare, ICT, manufacturing, media and entertainment, travel and tourism, and transport and logistics. Maala–Israel Business for Social Responsibility has had a financial services specialty, perhaps influenced by its first chairman who was CEO of the largest Israeli bank, and a high-tech specialty, reflecting the strength of Israel's high-tech companies. Some coalitions have a focus on business function (e.g., supply chain), issues (e.g., the IBLF was the first major coalition to highlight human rights as a business issue, and the WBCSD has had a long-term specialty around climate change); or corporate responsibility process (stakeholder engagement, board oversight of corporate responsibility, reporting etc.).

We are not suggesting that one model is inherently stronger or weaker than another. One size does not fit all circumstances. It is also clear that a particular coalition model may not remain optimal for a specific organization or for a particular market or society's evolution over time. The profile on GBCHealth in Chapter 3 illustrates such an evolution in response to its members' needs and global health trends. Likewise, the profile of Maala shows its evolution from an NGO started by a charismatic social entrepreneur, Talia Aharoni, into a corporate membership organization.

In practice, in many cases, why a particular model has flourished in one country but spectacularly failed elsewhere may have less to do with complex theories and much more to do with human factors such as:

- A charismatic individual attends a particular organization's conference abroad and returns to his or her home country inspired to replicate that organization (franchise X versus franchise Y)

- Personal chemistry – or the lack of it – between corporate responsibility champions and existing business representative organizations (part of an existing chamber of commerce or employers' federation versus an independent coalition)

- NGOs and the media target a particular corporate sector and in response leaders from that sector shape the work of the coalition

- Emergence of a well-connected activist credible with and capable of engaging top business leaders (CEO-led versus practitioner-led)

- An individual government minister or influential national or international figure with convening power lends their credibility and time to build a coalition versus some other priorities

In contrast to the 1990s, there is now far more activity, more diversity of approach and more cross-fertilization of insights and work between the coalitions.

7
Coalitions as part of a broader ecosystem promoting responsible business

Along with a greater number of corporate responsibility coalitions, there are many more other players reinforcing the messages of, but also now offering alternative services to, these coalitions. These include:

- Governments and intergovernmental institutions

- Multi-stakeholder/multi-sector corporate responsibility initiatives

- Corporate responsibility consultancies: both boutique consultancies and the sustainability practices of the major management consultancies, with many of these now having substantial thought-leadership/promotional activities

- Business school and university corporate responsibility centers

- More traditional and social media coverage raising awareness of sustainability and responsibility issues for business

- More NGOs tracking business behavior as well as more wanting to partner with or advise business

- More attention to corporate responsibility and sustainability among business representative organizations and trade associations

7.1 **Governments and intergovernmental institutions**

In addition to their vital role as regulators, governments can also influence voluntary corporate behavior in their capacity as major customers or purchasers of private-sector products and services, as investors through public-sector pension funds and the provision of public finance, as catalyzers through fiscal and other incentives, as convenors, and as partners in public–private partnerships.

Government support for corporate responsibility at the national level varies widely among different countries. In most cases, it consists of a variety of ad hoc and disconnected mechanisms led by different government departments, although there are rare examples of a coordinated national effort, such as the Danish Government's National Action Plan for Corporate Responsibility (see Box 7.1).

A World Bank study in 2004 identified four major ways in which the public sector can strengthen and spread the practice of corporate responsibility.[154] These can be summarized as:

- **Mandating.** Legislation and regulation from "command and control" and prescriptive regulations to principle-based and performance-based regulations

- **Facilitating.** Fiscal incentives such as tax breaks and subsidies, market mechanisms, government procurement, public pension-fund investments, catalytic financing, public certification and labeling programs, guidance and capacity-building initiatives that set non-mandatory goals and provide government-funded tools and training

- **Partnering.** Joint public–private ventures, collaborative multi-stakeholder platforms and cooperation

- **Endorsing.** Convening business leaders around key public issues, recognizing and rewarding good business performance and raising public awareness and sharing information about corporate responsibility

This framework was adapted by the Bertelsmann Foundation and the UN Global Compact in a study in 2010 under the four categories of awareness-raising, partnering, soft law and mandating.[155]

In a report released for the Rio + 20 Summit,[156] the World Bank offered a further framework for thinking about the role governments and others can play to influence and drive more inclusive and green growth as a pathway to sustainable development. The report focuses on three core types of intervention:

- **Incentivizing.** Providing effective market signals to drive inclusive and green growth

- **Informing and nudging.** Using information and framing to influence economic outcomes

- **Imposing.** Using rules and regulations

Government support for promoting more responsible and sustainable business practices at the regional and global level of intergovernmental institutions also varies widely, and is growing in both scope and scale. In addition to the UN Global Compact, numerous United

Nations programs, funds and specialized agencies now have initiatives dedicated to spreading responsible business standards or partnering with companies to solve global challenges. International financial institutions ranging from the World Bank Group to regional development banks are also establishing such initiatives, as are the bilateral development agencies of individual donor governments. Over the past few decades, the OECD and most regional intergovernmental organizations have created programs and in some cases standards and guidelines to promote responsible business practices and corporate sustainability, and both the G8 and the G20 have established a variety of active working groups and initiatives in partnership with business to tackle social and environmental challenges.

The European Union institutions have been particularly active in awareness-raising and capacity-building when it comes to promoting corporate responsibility and establishing business-led corporate responsibility coalitions. The EU Commission has issued a series of formal *Communications* on CSR (in 2002, 2006 and 2011);[157] convened a multi-stakeholder forum; and funded a series of promotional campaigns and training programs particularly aimed at SMEs. The EU rotating presidency has run a series of annual CSR conferences beginning with the Belgian Presidency CSR Conference in Brussels in 2001.[158] The European Parliament has tended to be more interventionist, with periodic calls for mandatory reporting by business of environmental and social impacts[159]. A small sample of other government interventions to drive corporate responsibility and collective business action at the national level are illustrated in Box 7.1.

Box 7.1 **Government initiatives to encourage responsible business**

Denmark

The Danish Action Plan for Corporate Social Responsibility was one of the first CSR action plans to be adopted by a national government. Launched in 2008, it promoted business-driven CSR and internationally recognized principles, such as the UN Global Compact and the Principles for Responsible Investment; it aimed to increase benefits to Danish companies from being at the global vanguard of CSR and put forth initiatives to ensure that Denmark and Danish businesses are generally associated with responsible growth. Building on the success of the 2008 plan, Denmark adopted a new CSR action plan for 2012–15 which focuses on continued respect for international principles (this time highlighting the UN Guiding Principles on Business and Human Rights and the OECD's guidelines on multinational enterprises); increasing responsible growth through partnerships; increasing transparency; and using the public sector to promote a framework for responsible growth. One important aspect of Danish legislation that has influenced international practice is the middle-way "report or explain why not" approach to corporate responsibility reporting.[160]

United Kingdom

The current British Government (in 2012) is experimenting with the concept of "responsibility deals." The concept was first floated by the British Conservative Party before the country's general election in 2010. Responsibility deals were described as:

➜

a mechanism to tackle overt and clear problems in British society in a collaborative way. Issues that they might address include business contributions to
tackling obesity, problem drinking, climate change, and reducing and recycling
waste . . . They are not designed to get industry and civil-society "input" or
"consent" into planned government activity, but rather about creating the right
kinds of frameworks for constructive and progressive activity from all sides,
with a bias against new government activity, except as a last resort. Responsibility Deals would be based on genuine collaboration throughout the process
from beginning to end. Using this mechanism, government, business and civil
society would jointly define the issue needing attention; agree which party is
best placed to do what; and move forward with defined responsibilities and
agreed goals and targets.

Participants in responsibility deals would be drawn from businesses and
business-representative bodies, NGOs and the voluntary sector, academic institutions, regulators, government bodies and investors. They would tackle important
societal issues by agreeing on a shared understanding of what the issue is, what
needs to be done and who will do what, and by when.[161] The first agreed responsibility deal, established in 2011, was with the alcoholic beverages industry and
the Department of Health.[162] The idea of responsibility deals is at an exploratory
stage and the early evidence is mixed as to their efficacy.

South Africa

South Africa's Black Economic Empowerment (BEE) policy is designed to advance
economic transformation and participation rates among the country's black
population and combines semi-mandatory and voluntary measures with incentive-
based structures. The Broad-Based Black Economic Empowerment Act of 2003
was meant to continue to address the country's inequalities and inequities stem-
ming from the apartheid years; among its many provisions, it grants the Minister
of Trade and Industry the power to publish transformation charters. Since the pas-
sage of the Act, several industry sectors have adopted such charters. The country's mining sector adopted a Mining Charter in May 2004 and aims to achieve
26% ownership of mining industry assets by "historically disadvantaged South
Africans" within ten years. The financial services sector adopted a ten-year Financial Services Charter in 2004, which included a goal of a minimum percentage of
black ownership of each financial institution by 2010. The information technology
(ICT) sector's charter focused on facilitating access to ICT in order to "bridge the
digital divide."

Colombia

The Green Markets (Mercados Verdes) program in Colombia was launched in 2002
as part of the National Strategic Plan for Green Markets (Plan Estratégico Nacional de Mercados Verdes). The program aims to create a national green market for
sustainable goods by boosting domestic demand for green products, strengthening organizational structures supporting the production of such products, and creating instruments to support the green products sector. The voluntary Colombian
Environmental Label (Sello Ambiental Colombiano) for environmentally friendly
products was introduced in 2005.

United States

Energy Star is a joint program of the U.S. Environmental Protection Agency (EPA) and the U.S. Department of Energy that promotes energy-efficient products and practices. Appliances and household products that have earned an Energy Star rating meet strict energy-efficiency guidelines set by the two agencies; in 2010, Americans saved nearly US$18 billion on utility bills through use of these efficient products. The program also rates the energy performance of commercial buildings so that businesses can measure their current energy performance, set goals, track savings and reward improvements. Under the Energy Star program, the EPA also offers tips, guidelines and other tools and resources for energy efficiency.

As the example of Corporate Responsibility Forum Liberia in Chapter 3 (Box 3.1) illustrates, bilateral development agencies and development finance institutions can also be valuable partners with individual companies in setting up coalitions and multi-stakeholder platforms in developing countries. The British Council, the UK Government's Department for International Development, Denmark's DANIDO, the Norwegian Ministry for Foreign Affairs, the Swedish, Dutch, Australian, Canadian, German, Japanese and United States bilateral development agencies, along with international institutions such as the United Nations Development Programme and the International Labour Organization have also been proactively supportive in funding and partnering with business-led corporate responsibility coalitions in a number of countries. There is potential for expansion of these activities by public donors to support coalitions in developing countries.

7.2 **Multi-stakeholder/multi-sector corporate responsibility initiatives**

As outlined in Part I the most recent wave of development in corporate responsibility coalitions since the millennium has been accompanied by an expansion in the number and impact of multi-sector initiatives seeking either to improve corporate responsibility and sustainability by changing business practices, or to increase the quality and extent of collective business engagement in tackling societal problems. Many of these operate at a global level and the American academic and social activist Steve Waddell has described these initiatives as "global action networks" and profiled a number of them in his book *Global Action Networks*.[163]

Some of the multi-sector initiatives have been started by governments or international institutions; some by NGOs; and some are the product of dialogues between NGOs and business (often occurring after critical NGO campaigns against specific businesses or business sectors). A few, such as the Sustainability Consortium, have been initiated by individual companies. The Sustainability Consortium was originally launched in 2009 with funding from and in partnership with Walmart to develop the standards to be used to rate the sustainable attributes of products. According to a GreenBiz article in 2009, "The world's largest retailer was careful at the time [of the launch of its own sustainability initiative] to say it didn't want to own the Consortium."[164] The Consortium is working to build the scientific platform that companies can use to assess the environmental impacts of consumer products throughout their life-cycle, and to develop tools to help companies find innovative ways to make products with fewer environmental impacts. Members include global companies such as the Coca-Cola Company, Dell, Disney, L'Oréal, Mars, Procter & Gamble, Tesco and Unilever; corporate responsibility coalitions such as BSR and Fundación Chile; trade associations such as the American Chemistry Council and the Forest Products Association of Canada; NGOs such as WWF and the Economic Development Foundation; the UK Department for Environment, Food and Rural Affairs (Defra); and academic partners. Management consultants McKinsey& Co. have provided executive and technical support.

Anything approaching a comprehensive listing of corporate responsibility-related multi-sector initiatives is hard to find. Box 7.2 lists some of those that are better-known. This is a fast-changing picture with initiatives waxing and waning in popularity and impact.

Box 7.2 Examples of multi-stakeholder initiatives

- **Business & Human Rights Resource Centre**
- **Carbon Disclosure Project**
- **Carbon Disclosure Standards Board**
- **Corporation 20/20**
- **EABIS–The Academy for Business in Society**
- **Ethical Trading Initiative**
- **EU Multi-stakeholder Forum on CSR**
- **Extractive Industries Transparency Initiative**
- **Food Security Coalition**
- **Forest Stewardship Council**
- **Global Fund to Fight AIDS, Tuberculosis and Malaria (often called The Global Fund or GFATM)**
- **Global Network Initiative**[165]
- **Global Partnership for the Prevention of Armed Conflict**
- **Global Reporting Initiative**
- **Institute for Human Rights and Business**
- **International Seafood Sustainability Foundation (ISSF)**
- **ISO 26000 process**
- **Kimberley Process for the certification of diamonds**
- **Marine Stewardship Council**
- **Microcredit Summit Campaign**
- **Publish What You Pay**
- **Roundtable on Sustainable Palm Oil**
- **Sustainability Accounting Standards Board**
- **Sustainable Food Lab**
- **Sustainability Consortium**
- **Transparency International**
- **UN Global Compact**
- **Voluntary Principles on Security and Human Rights**

7.3 **Corporate responsibility consultancies**

In recent years, the major consulting firms such as Accenture, Boston Consulting Group, Deloitte, Ernst & Young, KPMG, McKinsey & Company and PricewaterhouseCoopers have all developed a variety of sustainability and corporate responsibility consulting practices to work with their global corporate clients. KPMG, for example, hired the former UN chief for Climate Change, Yves de Boer, as a special adviser in its climate change practice. Several of these global practices have worked strategically with some of the major business-led coalitions (see Box 7.3). Similarly, advertising and communications agencies have developed specialist offerings: for example, Saatchi & Saatchi S, JWT Ethos, OgilvyEarth and Havas's Meaningful Brands project. There is also now a range of specialist sustainability consultancies working with companies on sustainability and global development issues such as AccountAbility, Article 13, Corporate Citizenship, Dalberg, Forum for the Future, FSG, Inspiris, Second Nature, SustainAbility and Volans, to name but a few based in the UK and USA. Specialist consultancies are by no means confined to the OECD countries. Since 2004, CSR Asia (www.csr-asia.com), with offices in Beijing, Hong Kong, Kuala Lumpur, Guangzhou and Singapore and with partnerships in Vietnam, Thailand and Bangladesh, and more recently CSR Middle East (www.csrmiddleeast.org) have been providing training, information, conferences and consultancy to companies in their respective regions. Consultancies were seen by some respondents to the GlobeScan Coalitions Survey (28%) as competitors to the coalitions for member companies' time and money. Interestingly, there does not appear to be a strong correlation between those seeing consultancies as competitors and those expecting to see an increase in their own consulting services for members over the next 5–10 years.

A noticeable feature, however, has been the way that some of the leading coalitions have tapped the growing expertise and dedicated resources of the major international management consultancies, particularly from McKinsey, PwC and Accenture. Sometimes, this *pro bono* help is to look at the strategy of the coalition itself. In other cases, management consultancies have supported the coalitions and *sui generis* organizations such as the WEF in the development of thought-leadership reports around responsible business (see Box 7.3).

Box 7.3 **Examples of coalitions working with consultancies**

Coalition	Consultancy	Project/report
WEF	Accenture	Sustainable Consumption
WEF	Accenture	Green Growth
WEF	Accenture	New Energy Architecture
WEF	McKinsey	Innovation Heat Map
WEF	McKinsey	More Credit with Fewer Crises: Responsibly Meeting the World's Growing Demand for Credit
WEF	McKinsey	International Partnership for Innovative Healthcare Delivery
WEF	PwC	Critical Mass Initiative[166]
WEF	PwC	Financing Sustainable Land Use Project
WBCSD	PwC	Sustainable Forest Finance Toolkit
WBCSD	PwC	Guide to Corporate Ecosystem Valuation
WBCSD	PwC, KPMG	Sustainable Consumption
WBCSD	PwC, Accenture	Vision 2050
WBCSD	McKinsey	New Waves of Agriculture

Overall, 57% of GlobeScan Survey respondents expect their coalition's consulting services to members to increase over the next 5–10 years; 26% to stay the same; 11% to decline; and 6% don't know (Appendix 3, Question 6Ad).

7.4 **Business school and university corporate responsibility centers**

In the last decade, a number of business schools and universities around the world have followed the example of early pioneers such as the Boston College Center for Corporate Citizenship (see Section 3.1) and have created dedicated corporate responsibility and sustainability centers, or developed a focus on corporate responsibility within a broader social innovation or social responsibility remit. Several have developed ad hoc or longer-term collaborations with one or more corporate responsibility coalitions. BSR, for example, works closely with the Center for Responsible Business at Haas School of Business, Berkeley, California.

Given their former careers, it is not surprising that both the centers run by the authors, the CSR Initiative at the Harvard Kennedy School and the Doughty Centre for Corporate Responsibility at the Cranfield School of Management, have developed links with coalitions. The Doughty Centre has worked particularly with Business in the Community. Several current or former BITC board members serve on the Centre's advisory council. Three ex-BITC chairmen have spoken at Doughty Centre organized events, and BITC executives and corporate members participated in the original stakeholder conference to help design the Centre's work program. The Centre designed and ran a training course for BITC member companies in change management for corporate responsibility and now licenses BITC to run this course. BITC has given the Doughty Centre access to the *Corporate Responsibility Index* leading to a number of joint studies and reports such as on the business case for responsible business,[167] and how companies go about organizing their board oversight and governance of corporate responsibility commitments.[168]

Likewise, the CSR Initiative at Harvard Kennedy School has cooperated with a number of leading corporate responsibility coalitions in research and policy outreach projects. For several years it has been the academic partner of a loose consortium composed of coalitions such as the WBCSD, the IBLF, Business Action for Africa, Business Call to Action, the Initiative for Global Development, the International Finance Corporation and the UN Global Compact to promote the role of business in supporting the Millennium Development Goals and to share good practices on inclusive business models and business partnerships with the development community. The consortium has hosted events in New York for several years linked to the UN General Assembly and the annual meeting of the Clinton Global Initiative. The CSR Initiative has also partnered with WEF, BSR and the IBLF on several research projects and publications presented at the WEF annual meeting in Davos, and with the UN Global Compact on a number of projects. One example has been an initiative led by UN Secretary-General Ban Ki-moon and Unilever CEO Paul Polman, supported by a group of multinational companies and UN agencies, to research best practices on UN–business partnerships and to design a new facility to support the development of more transformative and large-scale partnerships between UN agencies and companies.

These examples of collaboration suggest a number of mutual benefits for a corporate responsibility coalition and corporate responsibility center based in a university or business school from working together. The coalition can get access to Masters and Doctoral students, as well as to academic researchers, who can research topics of interest to the coalition. The coalition can also get independent analysis and thought leadership and external inputs for its conferences and other events. The academic center can gain enhanced access to companies and data (including, sometimes, the hard-to-obtain longitudinal data); exposure to experienced coalition staff who are used to working with member companies; and platforms to reach business audiences for their research and thought leadership – thereby increasing opportunities for the academic centers to obtain the much-prized "impact" on management practice.

One of the oldest academic-affiliated initiatives to promote corporate responsibility and business leadership for sustainability is the University of Cambridge Programme for Sustainability Leadership (CPSL), formerly the Cambridge Programme for Industry (CPI). CPSL is an institution now based within the University's School of Technology and was founded in 1989. HRH The Prince of Wales is its Patron and CPSL is a member of The Prince's Charities, a group of not-for-profit organizations of which His Royal Highness is President. HRH is actively involved in CPSL's work, and has founded two significant initiatives: The Prince of Wales's Business and Sustainability Programme (BSP) and The Prince of Wales's Corporate Leaders Group on Climate Change (CLG).

CPSL works with leaders across business, government and civil society, but predominantly in the corporate sector, to address urgent global challenges. It runs executive education programs on issues such as climate change, water scarcity and food security, as well as sector-specific and tailored events. Over 6,000 senior executives have taken part in seminars in Cambridge, Brussels, Cape Town, Melbourne and Atlanta, as well as in-company customized programs. Two Master's-level accredited programs offer participants the time to reflect on these issues, test new ideas back in the workplace, and build their credentials for creating organizational change. Building out of CPSL's alumni network, CPSL has, additionally, developed a series of business platforms that allow senior decision-makers to identify opportunities and overcome barriers to promote sustainability – between their organizations, across industry, and in the wider policy environment. These leadership groups focus around specific issues or sectors such as national-level action on climate change, insurance, natural capital, finance, investment, and professional services.

After nearly 25 years of catalyzing business action for change, CPSL's alumni and associates (the Cambridge Sustainability Network) bring together many of the most influential corporate sustainability leaders in the world who share an interest in and a commitment to creating a sustainable future. Today, the CPSL operates from offices in Cambridge, Brussels and Cape Town under the leadership of Polly Courtice, LVO.[169]

Individual academics have also created initiatives to work with business, notably Michael Porter of Harvard who co-founded the non-profit consultancy FSG and supported its latest project, the Shared Value Initiative.[170]

The business school world itself is facing major debates about continuing relevance and whether business schools are fit for purpose. Even some deans of business schools have questioned the relevance of their institution. The Dean of INSEAD, Dipak C. Jain, has observed that "what has gone wrong, is that business schools have put performance before purpose," and that in future, business schools' purpose should be "from success to significance,"[171] Roger Martin, the Dean of the Rotman School of Management, Canada, has written:

> For too long, MBA programmes have produced shallow, narrow and static thinkers – some of whom have gone on to vandalize, not enhance, our world. We need a better approach – an MBA that produces thinkers who are deep rather than shallow, broad rather than narrow and dynamic rather than static.[172]

Box 7.4 **Examples of business school and university centers**

***

Americas

- Boston College Center for Corporate Citizenship, USA
- Haas Business School Center for Responsible Business, Berkeley, USA
- CSR Initiative, Kennedy School of Government, Harvard, USA
- Center for Sustainable Global Enterprise, Cornell University's Johnson Graduate School of Management, USA
- William Davidson Institute, University of Michigan, USA
- IDEARSE Center for Corporate Sustainability and Responsibility Anahuac University, Mexico
- Vincular, Center for Corporate Social Responsibility at Catholic University of Valparaiso, Chile

Asia-Pacific

- Europe-China Center for Leadership and Responsibility (CEIBS), Shanghai, China
- Beijing Normal University Center for Social Responsibility, China
- The Centre for Social Impact, Melbourne, Perth and Sydney, Australia[173]
- The Ramon V. del Rosario, Sr. AIM Center for Corporate Responsibility, Asian Institute of Management, Philippines

Europe, Africa and the Middle East

- ALTIS, the "Postgraduate Institute Business and Society" of the Catholic University of the Sacred Heart of Milan, Italy
- University of Cambridge Programme for Sustainability Leadership, UK
- Centre for Responsible Leadership, University of Pretoria, South Africa
- College of Management Studies, Center for Corporate Responsibility, Israel
- CSR Initiative, Copenhagen Business School, Denmark
- Doughty Centre for Corporate Responsibility, Cranfield School of Management, UK
- INSEAD Centre for Social Innovation, France
- Lagos – endowment from Etisalat for a CSR Center, Nigeria
- Maastricht Centre for Social Innovation, Netherlands
- Nottingham University Business School, International Centre for CSR, UK
- Stockholm School of Economics, Sustainability Research Centre, Sweden

***

The former Dean of Erasmus Management School, Rotterdam, George Yip has argued that "most business schools need a new business model."[174] There are a number of organizations and initiatives trying to help business schools to rethink their purpose and *modus vivendi,* such as the Aspen Institute's Business and Society Program (www.aspeninstitute.org), the UN's Principles for Responsible Management Education (PRME) (www.unprme.org), a UN Global Compact for the world's business schools, and EABIS–The Academy of Business in Society (www.eabis.org) (see Box 7.5). A group of faculty from schools across the world initiated a Global Responsible Leadership Initiative, which, together with the PRME, has proposed a radical reframing of what should be the business school of the future: 50 + 20.[175] This argues for new approaches to what is researched, how it is researched and by whom. It also proposes a major redesign of the business school curriculum with more experiential learning and more input from experienced managers and business people.

Box 7.5 **EABIS–The Academy for Business in Society**

There are reputedly 13,000-plus business schools in the world today, producing millions of business graduates and executive course participants every year. INSEAD, one of Europe's largest schools, has 41,000 people on campus each year. These people are not just *tomorrow's* business leaders. With the shortening lag between MBA completion and appointment to C-suite roles and the proliferation of on-campus or in-company executive courses, these are increasingly *today's* business leaders.

One effective way of changing business thinking and practice is to embed sustainability in the mainstream research and curricula of business schools. That is the mission of EABIS–The Academy of Business in Society. It was founded in 2002, with the help of CSR Europe, as a compact between five global corporations and ten leading schools.

EABIS – initially with a European focus (the "E" stood for European) – has grown into the world's leading business–academic partnership, with 130 members in 26 countries across five continents. In 2012 as it celebrated its tenth anniversary, EABIS established operations in New York and Shanghai.

EABIS is the facilitator of an extensive research and education program focused on the key sustainability challenges facing business. The compact ensures business relevance allied to academic rigor and leading thinking given practical application. In essence, it is a membership organization that convenes and helps to design collaborative projects between individual or groups of companies and schools. The outputs are greater knowledge and potential solutions to problems that inform company actions and delivery of business education in management schools across the globe. The by-product is the creation of a platform for greater coherence in responses to sustainability challenges between and within business and a more extensive cross-disciplinary approach in schools, harnessing expertise in economics, finance, marketing, organizational behavior, innovation and so on.

EABIS does not claim to have transformed the business environment – not least as it still has to attract 12,900 or so business schools into its membership – but its survey of company CEOs and business school deans, conducted for its decennial reflection, does suggest solid progress. Over the next ten years, it is intended that rapidly accelerating membership and global activity will create real value through shared learning and practice for both companies and schools and act as a catalyst for more leading thinking between the two constituencies.[176]

7.5 **Media initiatives**

A number of traditional media companies have given increasing attention to corporate responsibility, sometimes in association with the corporate responsibility coalitions. The *Financial Times* newspaper has produced *Responsible Business* magazine and supplements with BITC and the IBLF since the early 1990s. More recently, the *Financial Times* has also partnered with BITC on the latter's annual Awards for Excellence and publication of the results of the BITC annual Corporate Responsibility Index benchmarking responsible business practices. Bloomberg, CNN, Fortune, Newsweek and a growing number of national and regional print, television and online media platforms are now offering comprehensive reporting on sustainability issues. There has also been growth in more specialist electronic media platforms dedicated to covering corporate responsibility and sustainability such as GreenBiz, EurActiv, Ethical Corporation, and Business Fights Poverty, and in corporate responsibility blogs such as those by Mallen Baker, Marc Gunther and Toby Webb. Media companies themselves have also developed coalitions to explore responsible business issues relevant to their own sector. One example is the UK Media CSR Forum (see Box 7.6).

Box 7.6 **UK Media CSR Forum**

The Media CSR Forum (MF hereafter) is a London-based partnership between major UK and European media companies, covering all strands of the media spectrum. It was founded by a group of media professionals who were frustrated with the lack of media-specific CSR understanding within the media industry and beyond. In particular, the founding members were perturbed by what they perceived to be the inflexibility and lack of media-sector relevance of the BITC benchmarking tool, the Corporate Responsibility Index, which was launched in 2001 (see BITC in Profiles).

Starting out as an informal group, Acona,[177] a boutique management consultancy, was appointed to provide secretariat services in 2003. Today MF is organized and run by Acona and has 19 of the largest European and UK media companies as members, including BBC, Sky, Channel 4, Guardian Media Group, Informa, ITV, News International, Pearson, Random House Group, Reed Elsevier, Turner Time Warner, United Business Media, Virgin Media and YELL.[178]

MF's collaborative work includes developing an understanding of the implications of CSR for media organizations, identifying areas for prioritization, sharing best practices, engaging with stakeholders, and running collaborative projects on key issues.

Christian Toennesen from Acona believes that there are four main advantages to sector collaboration around sustainability issues: a common view of corporate responsibility issues affecting a sector and a sense of materiality; information sharing – learning from each other; greater leverage – pooling resources to pay for projects; and bigger impact – a higher profile than any member could attract individually.

MF is designed for media companies to talk with each other about CSR issues that are pertinent to the media sector. Some of these are mainstream issues for any industry sector, such as reducing carbon emissions or increasing staff

volunteering, whereas others are specific to the media sector. These include the impact of content, diversity of output, editorial guidelines, accessibility, privacy, freedom of expression, creative independence, transparency of process, impartiality and balance, and media literacy.

The main activity of the MF is the quarterly meetings, which focus on topics related to responsibility and sustainability in the media sector and always include presentations from relevant stakeholders. Discussions are always carried out under the Chatham House Rule.[179] These have included the Big Bang Lab presenting the concept of cultural social responsibility as a means of preserving cultural heritage and improving media literacy; the consultancy Eco:metrics presenting a tool that allows companies to measure and compare the carbon emissions of media campaigns; the Oxford Internet Institute talking about digital engagement in the information society using evidence from its annual survey; the Institute for Public Policy Research and Linguistic Landscapes sharing the findings from their 2006 report *Warm Words*: an analysis of UK constructions and conceptions of climate change in the public domain; and WWF presenting its Media Manifesto published in Through the Looking Glass.[180]

Figure 7.1 **Mapping the landscape: CSR issues for the media sector, 2008**

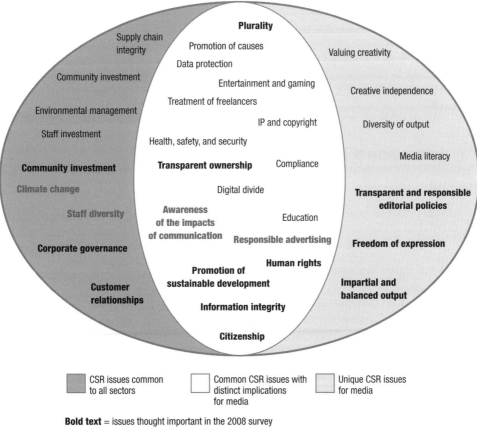

CSR issues common to all sectors

Common CSR issues with distinct implications for media

Unique CSR issues for media

Bold text = issues thought important in the 2008 survey
Gray text = new issues identified in 2008

In 2003, MF commissioned a "map" of the CSR issues that affect media companies, which was revised in 2008 and published as *Mapping the Landscape: CSR Issues for the Media Industry 2008*.[181] The report looked to identify the main CSR issues that the forum members, and media industry in general, face. This identified generic corporate responsibility issues, general corporate responsibility issues with media industry focus, and issues specific to the media sector (see Fig. 7.1).

As a platform that initiates open conversation between competing companies in the media industry about sustainable practices, MF has the potential to serve as a model for improving sustainability strategies in the media industry across the world. Inspired by MF, a Nordic Forum for media companies in Denmark, Finland, Norway and Sweden was launched in 2011. MF has also taken initial steps to establish a sister network in the United States, hosting an event in 2009 with the Carnegie Council in New York City.

Critical success factors include the fact that MF is industry-led: it reflects member-based priorities and helps share ideas, build connections and collaborate with other media companies. Additionally, MF is not trying to "sell" anything; all the research is published and meetings are for discussion, not pitching. It is genuinely a platform for collaboration and nothing else. Maintaining this relaxed and comfortable rapport is important to the effectiveness of the MF's activities .

Challenges include prioritization on strategy, ensuring relevance for all members, and getting consensus on projects. A further challenge is the turn-over of member companies' representatives and that these participants have a wide variety of levels of experience.[182]

7.6 **Increased NGO engagement**

The number, diversity, reach and influence of domestic and global NGOs have grown markedly over the past few decades. This process has been facilitated by the emergence of more open and democratic societies, economic liberalization, and unprecedented communications capacity and ability to organize via the Internet and social media. NGOs vary from millions of tiny community-based organizations staffed by volunteers and local citizens to a small but influential number of global networks with multi-million-dollar budgets and thousands of employees, such as the environmental organizations Greenpeace and WWF, development and humanitarian NGOs such as Oxfam, Save the Children, World Vision, CARE, Habitat for Humanity, and human rights NGOs such as Human Rights Watch and Amnesty International. Increasingly, they also include web-based NGO initiatives to track corporate power and promote transparency, such as Powerbase, which tracks "front groups funded by industry and industry-friendly experts and other corporate lobby groups,"[183] and SourceWatch, which "profiles the activities of front groups, PR spinners, industry-friendly experts, industry-funded organizations, and think tanks trying to manipulate public opinion on behalf of corporations or government."[184]

Along with their overall growth in scope and influence, NGOs have become increasingly important drivers and enablers of corporate responsibility and in some cases corporate responsibility coalitions. Their engagement with business varies widely. At the risk of over-simplifying a varied and complex set of relationships, as outlined in Table 7.1, the four broad categories of engagement between NGOs and companies aimed at driving corporate responsibility can be summarized as: confrontation, communication, consultation, and cooperation.

These different categories are not mutually exclusive. Often, the same NGO and company or industry sector will be engaged with each other in several different ways. Oxfam and WWF are just two examples that simultaneously run both campaigns against and engage in strategic partnerships with large companies and business coalitions:

- **Oxfam.** Many parts of Oxfam have created private-sector teams that are working in partnership with specific companies or corporate responsibility coalitions to improve the livelihoods and resilience of low-income households, producers and communities. Other parts of the global NGO network support campaigns and public protests against specific companies and industry sectors that are deemed to be exacerbating poverty through their business activities

- **WWF.** The global environmental organization is another example of an NGO that has combined campaigning against particular companies and industries with an increasing emphasis on partnering to promote environmental sustainability. In recent years WWF has identified about 100 major corporations, natural resource supply chains and industry sectors that it believes can have a large-scale and systemic impact on achieving more inclusive and green growth, and it has developed a highly sophisticated and market-based approach to supporting multi-stakeholder sustainability platforms focused on these game-changers

Table 7.1 **Examples of how NGOs engage with companies and business-led coalitions to influence corporate responsibility**

Source: Adapted from J. Nelson, *Expanding Opportunity and Access: Approaches That Harness Markets and the Private Sector to Create Business Value and Development Impact* (Cambridge, MA: CSR Initiative at Harvard Kennedy School, 2011); J. Nelson, *The Business of Peace* (London: International Business Leaders Forum/International Alert, 2000); J. Nelson, "The Operation of NGOs in a World of Corporate and Other Codes of Conduct," paper prepared for the 52nd Annual Conference, Rocky Mountain Mineral Law Institute, 2006[185]

Mode of engagement	Types of activity
CONFRONTATION Antagonistic relationships	• Lawsuits, litigation and other legally driven or supported actions • Media, online and other campaigns targeted at influencing the reputation of companies • Campaigns targeted at major investors or bankers encouraging them to disinvest from specific projects or companies • Examples include campaigns against: extractive companies for real and perceived environmental and human rights abuses; the introduction of genetically modified products by agribusiness and life sciences companies; pharmaceutical companies on access to essential drugs and intellectual property issues; banks for lending practices that are deemed to undermine development or to exploit the poor, etc.

→

Mode of engagement	Types of activity
COMMUNICATION One-way information flows	• Regular reporting or information availability from the companies or from specific projects • Site visits for NGOs and community leaders • Independent research studies by NGOs on specific projects, companies or industry sectors. There are several hundred NGO research reports on different industry sectors or individual companies relating to development, human rights and environmental issues. Some underpin campaigns, others are based on the cooperation and engagement of the company itself • NGO-led indexes, report cards and public benchmarking initiatives aimed at raising awareness of the comparative performance of companies within specific industry sectors or related to specific development challenges. Often managed in cooperation with the media and online platforms. Examples include the Access to Medicines Index and Carbon Disclosure Project
CONSULTATION Two-way dialogue and structured processes to reach agreement on crucial issues	• Community or project-level consultation structures. Many companies with a physical "footprint" in developing countries, especially in the extractive sector, have implemented such structures • Company stakeholder advisory committees or councils • Strategic, industry-wide or national consultation multi-stakeholder dialogue mechanisms
COOPERATION Formal agreements to work together in a mutually supportive manner	• Strategic philanthropy, volunteering community investment initiatives that harness core corporate competences and align with core business interests – often with a focus on local economic development and entrepreneurship, education and training, and health and environmental issues • Global trade union framework agreements • Companies and NGOs cooperating directly to build the capacity of low-income producers, consumers and employees or to help them to establish cooperatives and other ways of organizing collectively • NGOs partnering with companies on systemic value-chain initiatives • Companies and NGOs cooperating to raise public and consumer awareness and funds related to solving development challenges • Partnerships between NGOs and companies to jointly evaluate and monitor the development footprint of companies • Joint research projects, tools development, capacity-building or training focused on building more inclusive markets and inclusive business models • Cooperation between companies and NGOs to strengthen the NGOs' capacity to deliver key development outcomes through helping to strengthen the NGOs' management systems, technology platforms, marketing, communications and fund-raising capabilities etc. • Multi-stakeholder collaboration on more strategic issues, industry standards and public policy at a national, regional or industry-wide level

7.7 **More corporate responsibility initiatives within representative business organizations**

A further notable feature of recent years has been the development of corporate responsibility and sustainability initiatives and units within established business representative organizations such as chambers of commerce, confederations of industry, employers' federations and trade and industry associations (see Table 7.2).

As issues of corporate responsibility and sustainability have both matured and become more business-critical and, simultaneously, more of the issues and the solutions have become more sector-specific, it is hardly surprising that more trade associations and groups representing businesses in a particular industry have developed their own sustainability initiatives. This has potential advantages in terms of scaling the implementation of corporate responsibility, as these representative bodies often have hundreds or even thousands of members, whether nationally or within a specific industry sector. On the other hand, given

Table 7.2 **Examples of corporate responsibility activities of business representative and management organizations**

Organization	Activities
International Chamber of Commerce (ICC)	Established in 1919, the ICC is the world's largest representative business organization with hundreds of thousands of member companies and associations in over 120 countries. It has a long-standing history of engaging with the UN and other intergovernmental bodies on a range of social, environmental and governance issues of relevance to its members around the world. In addition, it has a variety of commissions and award programs specifically targeted at scaling up corporate responsibility performance. These include: the Commission on Corporate Responsibility and Anti-Corruption (which develops rules of conduct and best practice guidance); the Commission on Business in Society, (which has developed a Guide to Responsible Sourcing); the World Chambers annual competition (which includes a best CSR project since 2003); and a partnership with the IBLF and United Nations to make biannual awards for corporate leadership in inclusive business and sustainability projects. (www.iccwbo.org)
Business Civic Leadership Center, U.S. Chamber of Commerce	Although housed within the Chamber, the BCLC has its own active Board of Directors and is funded from a network of over 100 companies. At the same time it benefits from communication access to the Chamber's 3 million or so member companies in the United States and to AmCham networks overseas (a number of which also have active programs in corporate responsibility). BCLC implements its mission to "advance the positive role of business in society," both in the United States and globally, through four core programs: disaster recovery; U.S. community investment and engagement; environmental innovation; and global development. It works with member companies to share and implement best practices through activities such as research, toolkit development, conferences, high-profile awards, webinars, blogs and study visits. (www.uschamber.com)
Family Business Network International	Global summit 2011 (Singapore) launched "A sustainable future" pledge to "promote a business model that will sustain not only our own generation, but all those that follow us." The 2012 summit (London) held a plenary on sustainability in family-owned businesses and launched research on the subject (www.fbn-i.org)

→

Organization	Activities
Confederation of Indian Industries (CII)	Founded over 117 years ago, CII describes itself as "a non-government, not-for-profit, industry led and industry managed organization, playing a proactive role in India's development process."[186] It has a direct membership of over 7,000 organizations and indirect membership of over 90,000 companies through some 400 national and regional sector associations. The CII has long-standing corporate philanthropy programs. In recent decades it has partnered with WBCSD and others to promote eco-efficiency, environmental management and green technology, buildings and business models. It is also taking a more strategic approach to supporting integrated and inclusive development in India with a variety of programs that include: affirmative action, climate change, CSR and community development, disaster management, education, environment, public health, rural development, skills development, social development, special abilities and women's empowerment. The CII has partnerships with over 120 NGOs across India helping it and its members companies to carry forward development initiatives. (www.cii.in)
Responsible Business Charters of the Keidanren (Japanese Business Federation)	Created in 2002 by the amalgamation of two existing representative business organizations, the Keidanren has a membership of about 1,200 companies, 127 industrial associations and 47 regional economic organizations. As far back as 1991, its predecessor established an initial Charter of Corporate Behaviour[187] and a Global Environment Charter.[188] These have been updated over time and members are "urged to adhere" to them, although they are positioned as voluntary codes of conduct. They are also made freely available as a tool for other companies and business organizations to use around the world. (www.keidanren. org.jp/english)
Corporate Responsibility Program of the Confederation of Norwegian Industries (NHO)	NHO has been an active player in the field of corporate social responsibility at home and abroad since 1995. Over this period it has developed a number of guidance documents and tools for companies, supported by seminars and workshops. It is a regional partner of the WBCSD and a member of the UNGC, and it works actively with Norwegian companies, Innovation Norway and the Norwegian Ministry of Foreign Affairs to promote responsible and inclusive private-sector development in developing countries, including an initiative called Doing Responsible Business in Africa that has included research, study tours and workshops between Norwegian and African companies and investors. (www.nho.no)
Center for Responsible Business (CRB) at the Dubai Chamber of Commerce and Industry	The Dubai Chamber has over 135,000[189] members and in 2004 established a center dedicated to fostering corporate integrity and supporting companies operating in the region by promoting a culture of transparency, accountability and rule of law. Initially named the Dubai Ethics Resource Center, today the CRB has an active program of training, research, conferences and sharing good practices among local and foreign companies operating in the Gulf region. It is a member of a number of international corporate responsibility initiatives. (www.dubaichamber.com)
International Organisation of Employers (IOE)	Among other activities, the IOE has worked closely with Professor. John Ruggie on developing the UN Guiding Principles on Business and Human Rights and played a significant role in developing responsible business practice concerning the employment of those living with HIV/AIDS. (www.ioe-emp.org)

their remit to represent first and foremost the business interests of their members, there will be times when either these real or perceived "mainstream" business interests will be at odds with a more progressive social, environmental or governance agenda. Just as some NGOs continue to simultaneously campaign against and cooperate with business, many representative business organizations continue to simultaneously support innovate sustainability and corporate responsibility initiatives, while also lobbying against proposed policy reforms and regulations, which may further a social or environmental objective (such as healthcare reform or tougher environmental standards), but which the association believes will create a costly burden or undermine the competitiveness of its members.

Having said this, there is no doubt that as social, environmental and governance issues become more material to corporate competitiveness and risk management, traditional representative business organizations will become more active players in this arena. In some cases they will be allies and "force multipliers" for the business-led corporate responsibility coalitions. In others, the agendas may be at odds with each other.

8

The key roles of corporate responsibility coalitions

Given their diverse origins and contexts, not surprisingly the corporate responsibility coalitions play a variety of different roles. Most of them, however, undertake some combination of the following seven key roles:

- Raising awareness and making the "business case"
- Identifying and disseminating good practices
- Advising and building the capacity of companies
- Brokering partnerships
- Delivering on-the-ground programs
- Setting standards and spreading norms
- Promoting a public agenda

8.1 Raising awareness and making the 'business case'

Business leadership coalitions have often played a vital role in raising awareness among the wider business community of the "business case" for addressing environmental, economic and social issues in a more strategic manner. In many cases "making the business case" has involved coalitions undertaking two sets of necessary activities: first, identifying a particular social or environmental challenge and explaining why it represents a material risk or opportunity to a particular industry sector or to the business sector more broadly; and, second, providing specific examples or empirical data to back up this argument and to convince often busy and skeptical corporate executives and their investors why this challenge or set of challenges needs to be taken seriously by senior management.

From respecting human rights and improving labor standards along global supply chains to tackling corruption, addressing global health issues and improving environmental performance and eco-efficiency, it has usually been a small vanguard of individual corporate leaders who have joined forces to drive the agenda more broadly among their peer group. Over the past two decades in particular, these coalitions have helped to shift the focus of corporate responsibility from philanthropy and community investment to the way companies manage their core business operations and supply chains. The coalitions have often drawn on the experiences and case studies of their key member companies to demonstrate both the value protection/risk management and the value creation/social opportunity arguments for companies to improve the ESG performance of their mainstream business activities. A number of them have also cooperated with universities, think-tanks and strategic consulting firms to commission independent research on the links between better ESG performance and better financial or operational performance.

8.2 **Identifying and disseminating good practices**

Beyond putting corporate responsibility issues onto the mainstream business agenda, most coalitions also provide a platform for identifying and evaluating good practices, providing their members – and in some cases the broader business community as well as non-business stakeholders – with examples and data on what works and how to implement new governance, management and reporting practices. A number of coalitions support award programs to identify leadership case studies, share these lessons more widely and publicly recognize and create incentives for the leaders. Coalitions have the independence to Identify, Disseminate, Evaluate and then help companies Apply (IDEA) good practice in corporate responsibility. Coalitions also have independence to provide third-party validation and endorsement of responsible business practices. Some coalitions have also emerged as societal or media spokespeople for corporate responsibility.

One example is CentraRSE (Centro para la Acción de la Responsabilidad Social Empresarial). Founded in 2003 in Guatemala, CentraRSE has more than 100 member companies from 20 different productive sectors, representing 30% of the country's GDP. It helps to identify and disseminate good practice in corporate responsibility in Guatemala and throughout Central America through public awareness campaigns and programs, including the CentraRSE Awards, given to the best corporate responsibility practices in Guatemala and an annual National Summit. It has developed corporate responsibility indicators for Guatemala and through its membership of the Central American BSR Network (with El Salvador's FUNDEMAS, Honduras' FUNDAHRSE, Nicaragua's UniRSE and Costa Rica's AED), corporate responsibility indicators for Central America as a whole.[190]

Another example is the Hungarian Business Leaders Forum (HBLF). Founded in 1992 with support from IBLF, the forum has almost 100 members including local business executives, local representatives of international corporations and NGOs. HBLF works with its members to increase their awareness of corporate responsibility, support the integration of responsible business practices into business processes, encourage cooperation and networking, and help strengthen the country's capacity at all levels for effective corporate responsibility. It has also held master classes to help small and medium enterprises to learn from their colleagues in larger companies; offered a "manager-shadowing" program and a management-champion contest for students; and launched a women's business leadership program.

The development of reliable performance metrics and benchmarking tools has become an increasingly important goal for many individual companies as part of their efforts to identify and embed good practices into their core business operations, as well as their more traditional philanthropic and community engagement activities. A number of coalitions have helped to design, develop, test and then disseminate such tools. Some have focused on a specific social or environmental challenge, such as WBCSD's Greenhouse Gas Protocol and Global Water Tool, or IBLF's Guide to Human Rights Impact Assessment and Management. A few coalitions have aimed to provide a framework for companies to measure and report on their corporate responsibility performance more broadly, such as the Indicators for Corporate Responsibility developed by Instituto Ethos and Business in the Community's Corporate Responsibility Index and earlier Business in the Environment Index. Supported by *pro bono* assistance from Deloitte, the Committee to Encourage Corporate Philanthropy created the Global Corporate Giving Initiative, a tool that allows more efficient measurement and comparative analysis and benchmarking of corporate giving on a global scale through the establishment of a single, precise characterization of the types of financial and in-kind contributions and organizations that can be counted within corporate contributions programs.[191]

A number of coalitions have also undertaken research with member companies to identify and codify good practice through how-to guides and codes of business principles: for example, BITC's Responsible Marketplace Principles or Hong Kong Community Business's guides to community involvement. A number of the sector-specific coalitions such as the International Council on Mining and Metals (ICMM) and the International Petroleum Industry Environmental Conservation Association (IPIECA) have been especially active in best practice identification and dissemination. In the case of ICMM, all its members are required to implement ICMM's Sustainable Development Framework. This includes integrating a set of ten principles and seven supporting position statements into corporate policy, setting up transparent and accountable reporting practices, and providing a signed commitment by the company's chief executive officer.

Regular conferences organized by the coalitions for their member companies and others have also been a major dissemination channel – notably BSR's annual conference (held alternately on the east and west coasts of the United States every October or November) and Instituto Ethos's annual conference in June. Both are attended by some 1,000 practitioners and increasingly shared more broadly via social media. A growing number of coalitions are also offering webinars and other online dialogues to help their members to identify and share best practices.

8.3 **Advising and building the capacity of companies**

Coalitions can provide neutral "safe space" where business executives can come together to honestly discuss their sustainability challenges and experiment with possible solutions. Some of them offer benchmarking services to their members. This can provide endorsement for the leaders, helping them make the case with the skeptics within their own companies and with their external stakeholders and at the same time encourage and pressurize non-performers, giving their corporate responsibility teams and their stakeholders solid data against which to measure performance. By convening such dialogues, coalitions can help practitioners within companies to overcome the loneliness, uncertainty and, in some cases, professional risks associated with trying to implement corporate responsibility policies and practices during their early stages in a specific company, country or sector. A number of coalitions also offer their members some kind of advisory or consulting support or training programs and materials.

As its Profile shows, BSR has been particularly effective in developing a comprehensive suite of advisory and consulting services for its member companies over the past ten years. As BSR states: "We believe that the corporate responsibility field is moving from the 'why' to the 'how' of addressing global sustainability challenges. This shift requires a focus on service offerings and solutions that are practical, business-relevant, and built upon sustainability and industry expertise."[192] BSR has employed a growing number of people with specific industry or functional experience combined with consulting capabilities to offer fee-based advisory services to member companies in a variety of areas. These range from service offerings in functional areas such as corporate responsibility strategy and implementation, supply-chain management, stakeholder engagement, and reporting and communication to advisory services focused on how to address specific issues such as climate change and human right, to advisory services in particular countries such as China and Saudi Arabia.

Another example is respACT–austrian business council for sustainable development, which was formed in October 2007 from the merger of the Austrian Business Council for Sustainable Development (ABCSD) and respACT austria; its name is shorthand for "responsible action" and the coalition supports its member companies in implementing socially responsible actions into their core business activities. In 2009, respACT, together with the Research Institute for Managing Sustainability of the Vienna Business University, issued CSR guidelines *Success and Social Responsibility: A Guide to Future-Proofing Your Business* intended for use by any Austrian company regardless of size. It also runs the TRIGOS Award, honouring Austrian companies for exemplary CSR initiatives. To advise SMEs specifically, in 2010, the coalition launched "respACT goes regional," which includes networking activities, workshops and regional TRIGOS Awards. respACT austria is unique in being simultaneously the national partner of the UN Global Compact, the WBCSD Austrian member, the national platform for CSR Europe, and a member of CSR360 Global Partner Network.[193]

Experiential learning activities have been another way in which corporate responsibility coalitions have helped not only to make the business case and share good practices, but also to build the capacity and networks of their members to take action. One such tool used by some coalitions to build member company capacity (as well as to facilitate brokering of corporate help to good causes) has been Seeing is Believing visits where an already-engaged business leader leads a small group of less-experienced business leaders on a series of visits to study how individual and collective business action can help to tackle a societal ill. Seeing is Believing was pioneered in the UK by BITC, which then exported the technique to a number of other coalitions such as Empresa y Sociedad in Spain and the Australian Business and Community Network. Seeing is Believing involves a CEO already involved in community issues, hosting a small group of younger business leaders, identified by their companies or others as having top leadership potential, on visits to explore how business can help tackle social issues. The UK version, The Prince's Seeing is Believing program has run since 1990 and involves an annual report-back meeting with the Prince of Wales for participants on the program in the previous 12 months.[194] It now has more than 8,000 alumni. The IBLF also ran an international version called the Insight Programme, which worked in partnership with British Airways for a number of years to take both corporate and non-profit executives to visit partnership initiatives in other countries. This program in turn led to the establishment of a global network of partnership brokers and several certification programs for building cross-sector partnerships' skills and capacities.

8.4 **Brokering partnerships**

Several coalitions have played a crucial role acting as brokers and building trust between fiercely competitive companies, enabling them to come together in a common and pre-competitive space to address strategic environmental and social issues at greater scale and with greater systemic impact than could be achieved by the companies acting alone. Some of them have also provided a platform for dialogue and collaboration between groups of companies and other actors, such as governments and NGOs, to tackle complex and multi-dimensional challenges that span boundaries between the sectors and require actions by different "players," both individually and collectively, if problems are to be solved. Numerous coalitions have brokered specific project-based partnerships between individual businesses and non-profit or community-based organizations such as schools, charities, NGOs, small business development agencies, community and social entrepreneurs and communities or social causes. The coalitions have helped to play an intermediary role by matching the financial, managerial, technical or logistical needs of these non-profit organizations with the resources, skills and networks of their member companies. Brokering big business help for local enterprise agencies that helped small firms, skills development and community regeneration was how BITC and Scottish Business in the Community both started in 1982; this model was replicated by Jobs and Society in Sweden and New Zealand Business in the Community. The latter two organizations remain focused on this activity today.

In addition to brokering specific project-based partnerships, usually between an individual company and community partner, a few of the coalitions have also acted as crucial intermediaries in brokering more systemic and transformative partnerships between large numbers of companies within a specific industry sector, or between a number of companies and public-sector or civil-society organizations to address a specific challenge within a specific location. The WBCSD, for example, has developed a number of industry-specific initiatives. The sector project on Electricity Utilities, for example, brings together ten leading utilities from around the world to better understand sector challenges such as security, reliability, affordability, environmental impacts and basic access, and to explore policy needs and potential business solutions. The WBCSD Tire Industry Project is seeking to identify and address the potential health and environmental impacts of materials associated with tire-making and use. This project is chaired by the three largest tire manufacturers – Bridgestone (Japan), Goodyear (United States) and Michelin (France) – and includes a total of 11 companies representing approximately 70% of the world's tire-manufacturing capacity. The Cement Sustainability Initiative (CSI) involves 23 major cement producers with operations in more than 100 countries and who account for about one-third of the world's cement production. The CSI has focused on understanding, managing and minimizing the impacts of cement production and use by addressing a range of issues, including climate change, fuel use, employee health and safety, airborne emissions, concrete recycling and quarry management. Similarly, BSR leads or participates in 13 industry-focused working groups with members. These forums, including Better Coal, Future of Fuels, Clean Cargo, and Pharmaceutical Supply Chain, allow competing companies and their stakeholders to work together to reach solutions.

In addition to helping to convene, incubate and build cross-sector or business-to-business partnerships, a few coalitions have also focused on building skills and capacities for brokering such partnerships. Most notably, as outlined in its Profile, the IBLF has played a global leadership role in developing certification programs, training workshops, experiential learning journeys and practical toolkits dedicated to developing a global profession of "partnership brokers." It has worked not only with companies but also with the United Nations, governments and international NGOs to build both their institutional capacity and the skills of selected individuals to become more effective at building cross-sector partnerships for social progress and transformational change.

8.5 **Delivering on-the-ground programs**

In some cases, corporate members have used corporate responsibility coalitions as an implementing agency – in essence outsourcing certain corporate responsibility and community investment activities to a suitably trained team within the coalition. In such cases, the coalition can play a core role in conceiving, creating and managing corporate responsibility and community programs on behalf of member companies.

As the individual coalition profiles make clear, a number of the largest coalitions have been delivering on-the-ground programs on behalf of member companies or on behalf of governments, donor agencies and international institutions. Philippine Business for Social Progress, for example, is working with all these groups in the delivery of business support for schools and to help tackle the scourge of tuberculosis affecting the country. The National Business Initiative in South Africa has helped deliver social housing and education reforms, especially through the Business Trust, which operated from 1999 to 2011. During this time, the Business Trust combined the resources of business and government to accelerate the achievement of national objectives; these included creating jobs, building capacity and combating poverty in the early years of democracy. Work was undertaken to attract investment and improve market participation in the areas of tourism, business process outsourcing and community investment. The Trust aimed to help improve public services in the areas of education, infrastructure and public works.[195]

Another example is Youth Business International (YBI), which supports the development of youth business programs in countries around the world. YBI was originally established in 1999, and incubated by the IBLF to replicate the successful Prince's Youth Business Trust in the UK. In August 2008, it became an independent coalition focused on youth enterprise, mentoring and skills development. Today YBI is an international network of 38 programs that help disadvantaged young people to become entrepreneurs by providing mentoring and funds (www.youthbusiness.org).

8.6 **Setting standards and spreading norms**

In the absence of a more level playing field, even the most committed companies have recognized that they can only achieve so much environmental and social progress through their own company and value chain. Ideally, government regulations and legislation or market-based incentives should be the forces that create such a level playing field. This often does not happen because of a variety of market failures (such as lack of pricing signals and incentives) or governance gaps (ranging from public-finance shortfalls and administrative constraints to lack of political will and obstructive business lobbying). In some cases, business leadership coalitions have played a crucial role in bridging these governance gaps and market failures by developing voluntary standards and spreading norms. In a few cases, the adherence to certain social and environmental standards has become a requirement of membership, not only of a leadership coalition but even a few trade and industry associations (examples include the chemical industry's Responsible Care program and the toy industry's ICTI CARE process, described in Chapter 6, Box 6.1, page 82).

As outlined earlier, the member companies of the International Council on Mining and Metals (ICMM) are required to report publicly on their sustainable development performance on an annual basis, in line with standards set by the Global Reporting Initiative (GRI) and specifically the Mining and Metals Sector Supplement of the GRI, which the ICMM worked with the GRI to develop.[196]

The Bulgarian Business Leaders Forum (BBLF) is the business-led coalition association in Bulgaria promoting the values of corporate responsibility. Founded by 12 multinational companies in 1998, the BBLF now has over 220 members, both Bulgarian and international companies. The BBLF Business Ethics Standard has been accepted by over 1,500 companies.[197]

8.7 **Promoting a public agenda**

In addition to raising awareness, helping individual companies to embed corporate responsibility into their core business practices and spreading or scaling good practices by brokering partnerships or setting standards and spreading norms, some corporate responsibility coalitions have played an important role in putting sustainability issues more explicitly onto the public-policy agenda or onto the public agenda more broadly via the media and advocacy campaigns. Corporate responsibility coalitions often have greater flexibility and freedom to

publicly call for more progressive environmental and social business performance or public-policy positions than representative organizations such as chambers of commerce and
employers' federations, which have more formal decision-making processes to go through
and a wider diversity of members to engage before public statements can be made. At their
best, the coalitions have used real-time intelligence from business and from society to put
the right issues on the table in ways most likely to secure positive business engagement,
acting as what the writer Malcolm Gladwell has called the "mavens," connectors and sales-
people who spot new trends and promote new ideas.[198]

The WBCSD's origins are in public agenda-setting: its seminal report *Changing Course*
provided the agenda for business to participate for the first time in a UN conference – the
Rio Earth Summit of 1992. In 2012, the WBCSD returned to these agenda-setting origins by
publishing *Changing Pace* for the Rio + 20 Conference, which publicly called on governments
to take more proactive and progressive action in supporting an inclusive and green growth
agenda.[199]

The forerunners of the National Business Initiative (NBI), the Urban Foundation and the
Consultative Business Movement, helped to set the agenda for South Africa's largely peaceful transition to majority rule in 1994. The NBI has continued to work with government to
set the national development agenda through initiatives such as the Business Trust and the
National Energy Efficiency Policy.

Likewise, the forerunner to Instituto Ethos in Brazil, Pensamento Nacional das Bases
Empresariais (PNBE [National Thinking of the Entrepreneurial Class]), was instrumental
in the campaign to impeach President Fernando Collor de Mello in 1992. Ethos itself has
continued to provide agenda-setting thought leadership; for example, with its work on sustainable mega-cities, saving the Amazonian rainforests, and its recently launched a national
platform for Inclusive Green Growth, which by June 2012 had obtained public commitments
of support from over 200 Brazilian companies and the Brazilian government.

BITC's *Directions for the Nineties* report (1991) and Work in Society initiative (1993–94),
establishing how business could contribute to improving the UK's international competitiveness and social cohesion, were also calls to business action and government engagement.[200]
IBLF's *Business as Partners in Development* was a seminal publication influencing the policies and practices not just of many companies but also of the World Bank and other international institutions.[201]

More recently, WBCSD's *Vision 2050*, BITC's *Visioning the Future*, IBLF's *Inclusive,
Responsible and Smart Growth Programme*, CSR Europe's *Enterprise 2020* and BSR's *Accelerating Progress* frameworks all seek to engage member companies in exploring the business
consequences of political, economic, social, technological and environmental developments,
and encourage businesses to explore the strategic implications for their businesses. The individual profiles of some of the coalitions demonstrate these different roles in more detail.

Which roles a particular business-led corporate responsibility coalition may play will
depend on a variety of factors, including the coalition's financial and human resources;
national legitimacy with business, government and other stakeholders; their own interests and capacities and those of other players; and the state of understanding of corporate
responsibility among business and other parts of society in its country.

Typically, a corporate responsibility coalition may evolve from being an encourager and
a broker to play a broader range of roles including potentially agenda-setter, arbiter of good
practice, convenor and standards-setter. Some coalitions also evolve *out* of certain roles over

time – either generally or for particular aspects of responsible business. BSR, for example, makes it clear that once a topic is well-established with standards, the organization will move on and leave that topic to others, as it sees its role primarily as an agenda-setter.

This evolution may in some ways track the evolution described by Schwartz and Gibb for campaigning NGOs seeking to influence business behavior. In their book *When Good Companies Do Bad Things*, Peter Schwartz and Blair Gibb suggested five stages that NGOs may go through in first raising an issue with business and society through to becoming advisers and partners to business in finding solutions:

1. An activist NGO floats an issue as a problem

2. NGOs, usually in coalition, initiate a campaign to which public opinion responds

3. With enough public response, governmental or intergovernmental bodies become involved, and NGOs participate in drafting new laws, regulations or codes

4. NGOs become active monitors of legal/regulatory/code compliance

5. NGOs become resources for corporations in future policy decisions[202]

This evolution may also track how companies typically evolve in their attitudes to business and society issues, described variously as five stages of corporate responsibility or corporate citizenship maturity by a number of different academics[203] and practitioners such as Simon Zadek, Brad Googins and Phil Mirvis, Jean-François Rischard, and Jonathan Porritt and Chris Tuppen.[204]

Some companies are **in denial** that they have any responsibility for their environmental, social and economic impacts. Others choose simply to **comply** with legal requirements, which for companies doing business internationally may lead to inconsistencies in their approach in different parts of the world. A growing number of companies take a more proactive approach by seeking to **mitigate risks**. A small vanguard has moved beyond this in order also to **find business opportunities**, although they still also seek to mitigate risks. Arguably, for a company to take a more proactive solutions-oriented approach to sustainable development – in its capacity as a for-profit business – this is possible only if the company can find commercially attractive opportunities on a regular, systemic basis as a result of its commitment to sustainability. Some writers and business leaders envision a final stage where **leading companies** are willing to **champion,** to share competitive technologies and expertise, and to work in transformational partnerships with others, in order to respond to the scale of global challenges that humankind now faces (see Fig. 8.1).[205]

Figure 8.1 **Five stages of corporate responsibility maturity**

Stage 1   **Denier**

Stage 2   **Complier**

Stage 3   **Risk mitigator**

Stage 4   **Opportunity maximizer**

Stage 5   **Champion and transformer**

As the fulcrum of a coalition's membership shifts and more of the membership are at advanced stages of maturity, the types of activity and service that they need from the coalition changes. There is less need for basic information and education work about "what is corporate responsibility" and "why it matters to business" (the business case), or for community-engagement opportunities. Instead, at more advanced stages of maturity, member companies are more likely to be seeking thought leadership and the convening of groups around difficult common problems. This need and ability to evolve and adapt over time is well articulated by BSR in a publication to mark its 20th anniversary in 2012:

> The path ahead is fundamentally different than the one we have traveled. During BSR's first decade, our primary challenge was to raise awareness in the business community about the primary importance of sustainability. Throughout our second decade, much of our time has been devoted to integration: weaving social and environmental approaches into innovative business strategy and operations. While integration remains crucial, it has not gone far enough; we need to redouble our efforts. More substantial change depends on change not only inside individual companies, but also within entire systems. The era of the hermetically sealed, vertically integrated company is long gone. Every business, in every part of the world, operates within a web of systems: economic, cultural, political and natural. Every business relies on networks of suppliers, customers, and investors. In the decade ahead, the solutions we need to achieve our goals must be systemic. And while we have seen numerous collaborative efforts in recent years, even the most creative experiments and demonstration projects will not meet the scale of the challenge.[206]

9

How coalitions organize themselves

There is considerable variety in how coalitions organize themselves in terms of governance, staffing, funding models and membership, relationships with the "serial joiners" (companies that are members of a number of the coalitions); in the tools and techniques they use; and in how far they work with international consultancies.

9.1 **Governance**

The theory and practice of corporate governance has evolved substantially in the past 20 years, at least in some jurisdictions. Good corporate governance is self-evidently a central aspect of responsible business practice. This should include how companies ensure effective board oversight and governance of their commitments to corporate responsibility and sustainability.[207] Good governance is just as applicable to NGOs, including corporate responsibility coalitions. There is a separate study waiting to be done on the governance of coalitions and it has not been looked at in detail for this book. Anecdotal evidence and common sense suggests some variety, depending on national familiarity with corporate governance or its level of sophistication, and perhaps also depending on how far the coalition is the brainchild of a lone social entrepreneur – and whether that individual is still running the coalition or has moved on. As a coalition matures and where corporate members with high standards in their own corporate governance are participating in the coalition's board, the board will be active in setting the strategic direction of the coalition and overseeing the coalition's executive. Some boards are composed exclusively of member company representatives. Some also include occasional stakeholder voices from civil society and the public sector.

Among respondents to the GlobeScan Coalitions Leadership Survey (Appendix 3, Question 2A):

- 40% of coalitions have boards composed of CEOs/chairpersons and equivalent level

- 35% have boards composed largely of corporate responsibility functional-level representatives

- 21% have mixed boards: CEOs and people from other levels of companies and sectors

- 2% have heads of business units and people in other functions (corporate affairs, human resources [HR], etc.)

Among those with mixed membership, one model is to have a CEO of a member company as coalition chair, with other board members drawn from corporate responsibility directors or equivalents from other business functions such as external affairs or human resources. This tends to be the case in Latin American coalitions. Table 9.1 shows examples of coalitions with different governance models in relation to their focus.

Table 9.1 **Examples of coalition governance in relation to focus**

Focus	Board led by CEO/CEO-equivalent	Board led at operational-manager level
Responsible business overall	• WBCSD • BITC • IBLF • NBI, South Africa	• CSR Europe • econsense • Forética
Community involvement as primary focus	• Australian Business and Community Network • IMS, France • PBSP	• Fundación Compromiso Argentina • Instituto para o Desenvolvimento do Investimento Social (IDIS), Brazil

Note: CEO-led is defined as where CEOs or main board directors/country heads serve on the decision-making board that sets the overall direction of the coalition; speak, write, undertake representational meetings with governments, etc. on behalf of the coalition; and are able to articulate the coalition's broad purpose if challenged to do so by a journalist, etc.

9.2 **Staffing**

The number of staff working for individual coalitions varies substantially from one to several hundred (see Table 9.2).

Table 9.2 **Staff numbers of international coalitions and some national coalitions**

Source: Information accessed from websites and profiles, June 2012; WBCSD figure accessed from email exchange with WBCSD, August 2012; BSR and WEC data updated Oct 2012

BITC	BSR	CECP	CSR Europe	Forum Empresa	Instituto Ethos	NBI	PBSP	UNGC	WBCSD	WEC
370	100	9	24	3	55	27	300	c. 25	60	8*

* supplemented by a network of 50 additional persons (e.g., retired industry executives, consultants, former government officials) in various countries that are available on a project-specific basis as needed.

Note: Instituto Ethos also has seven staff working for its UniEthos, which offers courses for managers to aid the adoption of sustainability in the strategy, policies and practices of their companies.

Respondents to the GlobeScan Coalitions Leadership Survey (Appendix 3, Question 6Aa) generally expect staffing levels to increase over the next five to ten years.[208] As the corporate responsibility field matures, the backgrounds and previous experience of the coalitions' staff has broadened. A workshop in May 2012 for staff of BITC Ireland, for example, showed a mix of staff including those with:

- Senior management expertise from across a range of multinational companies and small and medium enterprises; some with 20–25 years' prior business experience

- Human resource knowledge, based on over 15 years with large corporations

- Experienced management strategists who have worked with the leading professional service consultancy firms

- Policy advocacy and development skills, including a previous director of a national trust organization

- Public relations and communications specialists with experience in both the EU and U.S. markets

- Experts in building partnerships and the design of collaborative projects

- Funding skills with expertise in the management of EU and nationally funded programs

- Community development and brokerage experts with over 15 years of experience with both rural and urban communities

- Early career with one or two prior jobs in business or civil society

- Masters and PhDs from a range of academic backgrounds including economics, statistics, management, anthropology, development studies and public relations as well as in sustainability and corporate responsibility-related topics[209]

Among coalition CEOs there is a rich mix of former corporate CEOs, social entrepreneurs, corporate responsibility directors, high-flying public servants, ex-corporate responsibility directors and individuals with backgrounds in civil society and foundations. See Box 9.1 for some examples.

Box 9.1 **Backgrounds of some coalition CEOs**

- Peter Bakker, WBCSD: former CEO of global logistics firm TNT
- Aron Cramer, BSR: former journalist with ABC and a lawyer
- Stefan Crets, CSR Europe: former Corporate Responsibility director, Toyota Europe
- Stephen Howard, BITC: former CEO of Cookson Group plc and Chief Executive of Novar plc
- Yanina Kowszyk, Forum Empresa: sociologist
- Raphael Lopa, PBSP: former CEO of a charity foundation
- Clare Melford, IBLF: former business executive, MTV Scandinavia and NGO Open Europe
- Thomas Koenen, econsense: lawyer
- Jane Wood, Scottish Business in the Community: former external affairs and marketing director with international retailing firm
- Joanne Yawitch, NBI: former Director-General of South African Government's Department of the Environment

Table 9.3 shows the length of exposure to the sustainable development/corporate social responsibility field of those coalition CEOs who responded to the GlobeScan Coalitions Survey (Appendix 3, Question 2dd) as at June 2012.

Table 9.3 **GlobeScan Coalitions Survey: average length of time spent in corporate responsibility field by coalition CEOs**

1–2 years	3–4 years	5–10 years	Over 10 years	No prior experience in field
6%	6%	38%	48%	2%

9.3 **Funding models and membership**

The various business-led corporate responsibility coalitions around the world have chosen different funding models, reflecting national possibilities, traditions and business preferences. Some coalitions rely on membership subscriptions. Some are partly financed by grants from public or philanthropic sources. Others rely on consulting fees, project grants or sponsorship. Some have hybrid funding models. Some also benefit from considerable help-in-kind including premises provided free or at minimal rent by member companies; secondees (executives on loan from both companies and the public sector); and *pro bono* help from professional firms for a variety of services such as communications, strategy and legal advice and auditing.

Again, these funding models have changed over time for individual coalitions. BSR, for example, now generates a substantial amount of its income from consultancy. This more than doubled from financial years 2006 to 2010. BITC grew its public-sector income dramatically in the late 1990s and early 2000s, only to see this decline again just as dramatically, especially after a change of government in 2010 led to deep cuts in government spending overall. Some of the coalitions, especially those that started in the 1990s or subsequently as part of the transition from planned to market economies in Eastern and Central Europe, and those in developing countries or countries recovering from recent conflicts, have received financial support from national and international donor agencies such as the U.S. Agency for International Development (USAID), German development agency GIZ (previously GTZ) and the UK Department for International Development (DFID) or from internationally focused philanthropic foundations such as the Soros Open Society, Avina, Ford and Rockefeller foundations.

Table 9.4 shows budgets for 2011 for international coalitions and some national coalitions.

Table 9.4 **Budgets for 2011 for international coalitions and some national corporate responsibility coalitions (rounded to nearest US$1 million)**

Source: Annual reports, interviews and authors' correspondence with coalitions, June 2012.

BITC	BSR	CECP	CSR Europe	Forum Empresa	Instituto Ethos	NBI	PBSP	UNGC	WBCSD	WEC
35	19	2	2	0.2	6*	3	48**	11	15***	2

* Including UniEthos

** Core or unrestricted budget was US$2.3 million while the program or restricted was US$45.46 million

*** WBCSD: this is core budget only and excludes project funding; it is therefore not directly comparable to the other budgets shown as WBCSD runs a number of well-funded and extensive projects

Among the coalitions responding to the GlobeScan Coalitions Survey, 77% say a significant proportion of their funding comes from membership fees; 54% get some funding from consulting fees, which is a significant or very significant proportion for 14% of respondents. Some 8% get a significant or very significant proportion of their income from governments, with 43% getting some government funding. Around 4% get a significant or very significant proportion of their income from multinational donor agencies with 40% getting some income from this source. Other sources include individuals and philanthropic foundations, entrance fees from running events and, in one case, fees from national member coalitions (see Fig. 9.1).

Around 56% of coalitions say their funding is currently increasing; 21% say funding is static, 17% report declining funding and 6% did not know or did not answer. The main competition they see for funding comes from other corporate responsibility coalitions (63%) and, interestingly, from consulting firms (27%) and government initiatives (15%) (Question 4C). Coalition CEOs are generally very confident of their budget increasing over the next 5–10 years: 81% expect it do so, with just 4% forecasting a decline (13% expect it to remain static) (Question 5C).

Like the size of their staff teams and budgets, the numbers of companies in membership of coalitions also varies dramatically. Refrigerants, Naturally has just four corporate members: The Coca-Cola Company, McDonald's, PepsiCo and Unilever. The Liberian Corporate Responsibility Forum has 14 member companies so far. By contrast, BITC boasts 850

Figure 9.1 **GlobeScan Coalitions Survey: funding sources**

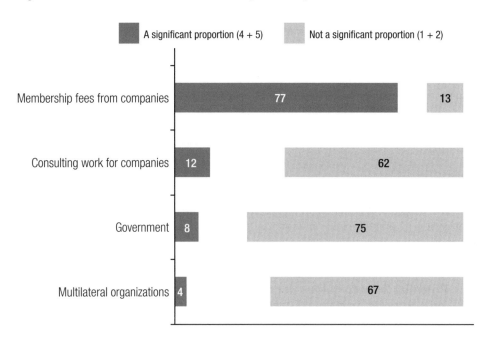

member companies and a further 10,700 involved in BITC programs globally, and Instituto Ethos has over 1,500 member companies (Question 6Ab).

Table 9.5 shows the split in membership among the GlobeScan Coalition Survey respondents, where response rates were skewed to the larger coalitions with almost all the significant coalitions responding to Question 4DD.

Table 9.5 **GlobeScan Coalitions Survey 2012: size of membership of coalitions**

1–49 members	50–99 members	100–149 members	150–199 members	200+ members
34%	22%	17%	7%	20%

In the survey, 65% of the CEOs say their membership is increasing, with 22% reporting membership static, 9% declining and 4% not knowing/answering (Question 4A). In answer to Question 4B, half of the respondents said the seniority of their main regular contacts in member companies was increasing, while slightly fewer than half said seniority was static. A full 89% of respondents generally anticipate an increase in membership numbers over the next 5–10 years (Question 6Ac).

9.4 **Tools used by coalitions**

In helping to raise awareness and create the enabling environment for corporate responsibility, the business-led corporate responsibility coalitions use a variety of tools including awards for excellence; case studies; indexes to benchmark business performance (either on corporate responsibility overall or on particular aspects such as environmental impacts or community engagement); media partnerships; "blue-ribbon" commissions of top business leaders to examine new responsible business challenges; and mentoring by more experienced corporate responsibility member companies for corporate newcomers.

In identifying and codifying good practice in corporate responsibility, the coalitions also employ various approaches. These include commissioning outside experts from academia or consultancies; borrowing and adapting work already done by other corporate responsibility coalitions; supporting groups of business leaders to tease out emerging good practice from their general business experience and what their own companies are doing; establishing working groups of practitioners; and sharing of good practice material identified through awards, indexes and case studies. There is clearly potential for further identification and dissemination of best practices and "how-to" experience between the coalitions (see Box 9.2).

Box 9.2 **Potential 'how-to guides' for transferring expertise among business-led corporate responsibility coalitions**

How to run . . .

- Awards for excellence
- Media partnerships
- Business leadership teams – on particular topics or generally on how to engage business leaders
- Corporate membership engagement teams
- Corporate Responsibility Index or other benchmarking initiatives
- Marketplace campaigns
- Workplace campaigns
- Environment campaigns
- Guidance to companies on better corporate community investment strategies
- Employee volunteering promotion
- Local brokerage for business–community involvement
- Campaigns to involve business in education, enterprise, etc.
- Capacity-building of businesses, public and third sector to work together
- Member-company account management
- Thought-leadership and public-policy inputs
- Working with public sector and government
- Effective collaboration with business schools and schools of public policy
- Membership recruitment
- Social media campaigns e.g., around responsible business and sustainable consumption

---

Some sharing of experience and good practice is taking place among the coalitions through increasing networking – the subject of the next chapter.

10

Networking among the coalitions

Within each of the global field-builders networks, in particular, there has been some sharing of expertise, models and best-practice guidance. Some of this networking occurs as a by-product of staff from other coalitions attending the major annual coalition conferences such as those of BSR, BITC, CSR Europe and Instituto Ethos. Regular electronic newsletters, both about their own initiatives and on corporate responsibility-related news and external reports and initiatives, such as CSR Europe's *News-bundle* and the WBCSD's monthly *Business and Development News*, provide more real-time information dissemination.

Thought leadership and guidance on how to embed responsible business practice is made available to affiliated coalitions by the umbrella coalitions such as CSR Europe and the WBCSD, which also profile their affiliates and provide hot-links to their websites. CSR Europe's *Enterprise 2020* initiative has also inspired similar enquiries in Forum Empresa, China and Turkey.

WBCSD's regional network consists of more than 60 national BCSDs – two-thirds of which are in developing countries. Their membership comprises leading local companies and subsidiaries of foreign enterprises, many of them WBCSD members.[210] WBCSD's *Vision 2050* was developed with the national affiliates and has also been a significant resource for them:

> More than 25 regional dialogues and workshops, most of them organized with our Regional Network partners, provided input into the preparation of Vision 2050. The global launch of Vision 2050 was organized in cooperation with TERI BCSD India at the Delhi Sustainable Development Summit in February 2010. Other Regional Network partners have also responded enthusiastically to Vision 2050. The report has been translated into 11 languages, and various partners are using the Vision as a tool for sparking dialogue with opinion leaders, with the aim of designing pathways to a sustainable future in their own countries and regions. Regional Network partners in Austria, Argentina, Brazil, Hungary, Poland, New Zealand, South Africa, and the United Kingdom, among others, are in the process of developing their own Visions.[211]

Box 10.1 **The development of CSR360 Global Partner Network**

In 1997 BITC responded to a request from the UK-headquartered retailer Marks & Spencer to help them initiate an employee community involvement program, Development Assignments (already successfully implemented in its UK stores) in its operations in Paris. Contact was made with another coalition, IMS in France, founded by the then chairman and founder of AXA Assurances, Claude Bébéar (see Section 3.1). The program was implemented successfully, followed by a similar identification of partners in Madrid (Fundación Empresa y Sociedad) and Brussels (Link Inc).

In a sense, this set the model, as we could not implement the employee-involvement program outside the UK without a proper local partner, and there was no point in having a partner if we had nothing to share with them or programs to run jointly with them. We could then potentially offer to BITC member companies an additional service by being able to support their operations outside the UK.

With limited funding from the European Commission, we were able to expand the network in Europe, still concentrating on employee involvement and focused on identifying partners whom we could train, share tools and case studies with, and provide support at their own promotional events.

This EU funding was matched by additional funding from the founding companies of the network, which included IBM, KPMG, Freshfields, and Allen and Overy. These companies continued to support generously, being joined regularly by other firms with similar interests outside the UK.

Inevitably, some of the partners we worked with, being by and large the key organizations in their country in this area of work, also became partners with CSR Europe. For a number of years the network was known as the Cecile Network – Coordinating Employee Community Links in Europe.

The first major growth in the network was into Central and Eastern Europe, always with a focus on employee involvement. Then in the early 2000s organizations outside Europe became partners, either because we approached known entities such as Instituto Ethos in Brazil or PBSP in the Philippines or because organizations made contact with us about partnership. The network grew, thanks in part to the program of more than 30 seminars and conferences we ran together with British Embassies and High Commissions between 1998 and 2009, which, funded by them, enabled us to meet and support new partners in specific countries. This was the case with many of our partners in Asia and in the Americas.

The growth of the network into a global one has reflected the growth of understanding and interest in the principles of responsible business practice, and so has seen a widening of partner competences beyond employee engagement.

In order to reflect this, and to continue to provide relevant support both to member companies and to partners, we were able to secure separate funding first from BHP Billiton in 2006 and then from KPMG in 2007 to address the building of a website. This work culminated in the renaming of the Cecile Network as the CSR360 Global Partner Network.[212]

Similarly, the national affiliates benefit *from* and also promote wider use *of* WBCSD tools such as the Global Water Tool and the Measuring Impact Framework. BCSDs in Mexico, China, India, Brazil, the Philippines and elsewhere worked with their respective national governments to make the WBCSD Greenhouse Gas Protocol (GHG Protocol) the official tool to measure industry's greenhouse gas emissions. The WBCSD believes "this greatly helped to ensure that the International Standards Organization now recognizes the protocol as the most important GHG measurement standard for business."[213] (See WBCSD in the Profiles for more detail.)

One of the umbrella initiatives seeking to share expertise among the corporate responsibility coalitions is the CSR360 Global Partner Network (CSR360 GPN). This is described as a "global network of not-for-profit organizations working with businesses to improve their positive impact on society. It involves over 124 independent organizations in 64 different countries, covering every continent, and working in total with more than 6000 companies around the world."[214] An analysis of the partner profiles on the CSR360 website suggests that just under one-third of these are business-led corporate responsibility membership coalitions, as defined in this book.

CSR360 GPN now pools resources including toolkits and handbooks and expertise across the corporate social responsibility spectrum. Given the global reach and the difficulties of organizing physical meetings, CSR360 GPN has championed virtual meetings through an expanding webinar program. In 2011 webinar topics included how to get the Board on board; "the risks and opportunities of hosting international sporting events in your country" (involving coalitions in Brazil, Canada, India, South Africa and the UK); and how BITC campaigns around women and race could be adapted for use in developing countries in support of the Millennium Development Goals. Typically, these webinars have attracted from 5 to 70 partner coalitions.[215]

The creation of the network was the inspiration of Henk Kinds (Community Partnership Consultants [CPC] Netherlands), Michael Tuffrey (Corporate Citizenship) and David Halley (Business in the Community) at the turn of the millennium. It is coordinated by Business in the Community. One of the founders, David Halley – now retired from BITC – describes the evolution of this network in Box 10.1.

Another "umbrella" network is Forum Empresa (discussed briefly in Chapter 3), which was created in 1997 and made up of corporate responsibility coalitions throughout the Americas from Canada to Chile (see Box 10.2).

Box 10.2 **Forum Empresa**

Forum Empresa was formed in 1997 following a conference in Miami convened by Peggy Dulany (founder and chair of Synergos – a USA-based non-profit organization promoting sustainable and systems-changing collaboration to address poverty, equity and social justice: www.synergos.org) and Bob Dunn (then CEO of BSR and now CEO of Synergos), among others from Social Venture Network (www.svn.org). Dulany and Dunn had invited a group of what were considered the most progressive business people in Latin America at the time, such as Oded Grajew from Brazil, Miguel Arango from Mexico and Javier Cox from Chile. At this Miami meeting, they discussed how they could strengthen the social entrepreneurship movement in Latin America and decided to create an umbrella organization. They decided on a "forum of companies," thus Forum Empresa. The Forum was created by Dan Gertsacov (CEO 1997–2003) as part of his Fulbright Scholarship; 15 years later, there are 22 member organizations in the Forum Empresa network, which is now based in Chile.

Since 1997, Empresa has been an umbrella organization for Latin American CSR organizations to help expand learning about CSR. It supported the creation of national organizations across Central and South America and has subsequently facilitated the cross-fertilization of programs and initiatives among Empresa members. Empresa has managed the creation of CSR indicators for Latin American companies. From 2003–2008, Empresa ran a joint project with four members (Brazil, Chile, El Salvador and Peru), the Inter-American Development Bank and the Organization of American States. This was worth around US$2 million and allowed Empresa to create the products and services that the Empresa network provides until today. From 2008 the services were transferred to the other 18 countries in the network.

Empresa's work involved more than just conversing with senior corporate leadership; it also involved creating sustainability/CSR departments and champions within network member companies. Services also included looking at how member-companies could better manage their supply chains. This exercise helped Empresa to define the most material aspects of CSR for Latin America. This led to the publication of the Forum Empresa CSR manual, which for each CSR dimension gives details of what tools exist in the market, and highlights the most successful company cases for implementation.

Empresa then created a manual advising network coalitions on how to sensitize senior management teams of member companies to corporate responsibility. Further how-to manuals followed on conducting workshops about CSR for the general public. It also ran train-the-trainers courses for CSR experts/consultants. Empresa has implemented this program in more than 18 countries and in numerous companies. Further Empresa workshops target SMEs; there is also a toolkit for SMEs and a methodology for consultants to deliver this material to them.

Additional Empresa work has focused on influencing Latin American journalists. Empresa has also worked on poverty eradication with members in several Latin American countries in partnership with Instituto Ethos, AVINA Foundation and ICCO (Interchurch Organisation for Development Cooperation);[216] and on anti-corruption programs with Transparency International.

The most significant impacts of Empresa and its members are seen as the broad dissemination and promotion of the subject of corporate responsibility, and the increased capacity-building of people who can deal with CSR in companies.[217]

Forum Empresa's then Director, Yanina Kowszyk, sees major challenges still facing Empresa and its member organizations, including greenwashing. "Some companies," she says, "believe any isolated action of a company counts as CSR and try to gain publicity for this. They should take more care. CSR is not so easy to do, and it's not just a program." She also sees a tension between creating tools for small changes in individual companies and creating public policy for deep systemic change:

> We need to create a new form of economy. However, within our network of member organizations we have very different positions and respective

challenges. For some countries we need to continue creating tools and instruments to be used by executives; whereas in other countries we can – with other actors – be more ambitious and try to create new business models that allow you to show how to create a new economy.

The Forum Empresa member coalitions, between them, represent more than 3,500 companies. In recent years, Empresa has focused on sustainability, poverty, climate change, public–private partnerships, sustainability through the value chain, and public policies to enhance sustainable development. It has done this through webinars, a monthly newsletter, working groups, publicizing member coalitions' events and activities across the network, staff exchanges, research and publications.[218]

Overall, however, the distances involved, costs of travel, different stages of development and levels of organizational capacity have generally militated against extensive sharing and networking among the coalitions except on a largely ad hoc basis and often rely on personal relationships and individual circumstances.

In the GlobeScan Coalition CEOs Survey, respondents were asked which, if any, other corporate responsibility coalitions their own coalition looked to for ideas, insights, help and advice. Unsurprisingly, Latin American coalitions referred to Forum Empresa and some of the European coalitions referred to CSR Europe. There were a number of respondents who referred to BITC (11) and BSR (10) and fewer to CSR360 and the IBLF. But by far the most frequent source of ideas, insights, help and advice for coalitions among the other coalitions is the WBCSD, mentioned 21 times. This is not solely explained by an especially high response rate to the survey from national BCSDs (around 10% of BCSDs responded). It would seem that the range and business-friendly tone of the WBCSD materials currently makes it the premier coalition for the other coalitions seeking inspiration, tools and guidance.

Given the uncharted territory that the coalitions have traversed, it is not surprising that it has not all been "plain sailing" – not all the new coalitions or attempts at networking have prospered. In 2000, a small group of corporate responsibility thought leaders in South Africa created the African Institute for Corporate Citizenship (AICC) and in April 2002 held an inaugural African Corporate Citizenship conference in Johannesburg. Whatever the reasons – the distances involved, lack of finance, insufficient ongoing corporate support, limited awareness of corporate responsibility or disparity in business sophistication around the continent – the AICC did not develop as its founders had hoped and key figures dispersed to other roles. With the more buoyant economic conditions now developing in parts of Africa, the AICC and other African-focused business-led coalitions such as the NEPAD Business Foundation,[219] Business Action for Africa, the Frontier 100 program of the Initiative for Global Development, and the Grow Africa initiative in agriculture should have better prospects for networking and sharing good practices within and among African countries and on a global basis. Indeed, some of the world's fastest growing and most innovative economies are now in Africa, as the continent benefits from rising commodity prices, a growing middle class and widespread governance reforms. The World Bank said in a report in 2011 that "Africa could be on the brink of an economic take-off, much like China was 30 years ago and India 20 years ago."[220] *The Economist* newspaper, which a decade ago labeled Africa as "the hopeless continent," now predicts: "The sun shines bright: the continent's impressive growth looks likely to continue."[221] The time could, therefore, be ripe for a concerted drive to strengthen the "architecture" for corporate governance, corporate responsibility and sustainability across Africa, and to develop more national coalitions either as independent entities such as South Africa's National Business Initiative, or as units within broader business organizations.

Similarly, if the early promise of the Arab Spring is to be realized and the massive challenge and opportunity of ensuring youth employment and enterprise is to be met in the region, there is a need to support the development of business-led coalitions promoting responsible business practices and workforce development across the Middle East. A growing number of Arab institutions, governments and corporations are working with each other and with donor agencies and global corporations to explore such approaches and networking opportunities.

There is potential to learn from the effective networking that has taken place between business-led corporate responsibility coalitions in Asia, Latin America and Europe. In Asia, for example, the annual Asian Forum on CSR (AFCSR) organized by the Asian Institute of Management has flourished since it began in 2001 and has become an important annual focus for regional debate on corporate responsibility and an opportunity for dialogue on responsible business issues with other parts of the world. The tenth anniversary of AFCSR in Manila in October 2011 attracted a record 545 delegates, with an address from the President of the Philippines, Benigno Aquino III, and lively debates around the Porter and Kramer model of "shared value"[222] and whether corporate responsibility needed more regulation – particularly for the heavy footprint industries such as mining, energy and infrastructure. The 2012 conference in Bangkok focused on social innovation.

Similarly, in Latin America the annual corporate responsibility conferences organized by the Inter-American Development Bank and the annual Instituto Ethos conference in Brazil have become important meeting places for intra-regional debates in South and Central America.

In the late 1990s and early 2000s, there were annual informal meetings of the CEOs of a number of the larger coalitions, together with a few other key "multipliers" such as WEF and the NGO AccountAbility. However, the tyranny of the "in-box" and immediate work pressures when attendees returned home, and the lack of any additional resources to support networking activities, meant that the good intentions to collaborate were rarely translated into sustained action; and the meetings ceased altogether after the 2006 get-together.[223] The conclusions of the final (2006) meeting of this group, in terms of common organizational challenges and key operational concerns, look eerily topical today. The informal CEOs group identified some common organizational challenges and strategies shown in Table 10.1.

Table 10.1 **Common organizational challenges and strategies in 2006**

Broaden	• Managing growth and new expectations • Going into new markets, especially China • Expanding focus from firm-level internal corporate responsibility issues to systemic-level governance issues • How/if to engage SMEs
Deepen	• Need to better understand companies worked with – business models, internal incentive structures, internal change processes and competitiveness issues • Working with more functional and operational areas and business units within companies – no longer only corporate responsibility professionals • Being able to engage with CEOs and Boards of Directors
Anticipate	• Need to allocate time and effort away from short-term operational issues to make time for "horizon scanning" – identifying new issues and understanding and shaping the way corporate responsibility and public policy agendas are moving • Need to think creatively about fundamentally new business models, ownership structures and accountability and organizational models

The group also identified some key common operational concerns:

- **Capacity constraints.** Not enough qualified people who really understand business or public-policy agendas plus corporate responsibility; often lose best people to member companies; constant need to fundraise; and need to set priorities in the face of massive increase in the demands, issues and opportunities

- **Competition.** Emerging competition from non-mission-driven organizations; questions of how much we can afford to continue to be "open source" in terms of intellectual capital

- **Cooperation.** Recognize need for greater cooperation between mission-driven organizations in order to achieve greater leverage, influence and impact; and to avoid wasteful replication and inefficiency, but time-consuming, high transition costs in doing so, plus lack of clarity in terms of our core differences and most effective sharing of competencies[224]

The same meeting went on to identify a number of areas for potential collaboration such as China, management education (integrating into business schools and schools of public policy), anti-corruption, corporate responsibility and corporate governance, financial markets, climate change, supporting what was called "the big bet" (harmonization of the Global Compact Principles, Global Reporting Initiative and AA1000 Assurance framework), spreading corporate responsibility indexes particularly via regional networks to emerging markets, and mobilizing business support for the Millennium Development Goals.

A few of these proposed joint efforts developed further, but what the CEOs had identified as their common challenge, the "short-term operational issues" and "massive increase in demands" on them, got in the way of following up on more regular collaboration between this core group of corporate responsibility coalitions. We return to these ideas for coalitions working more collaboratively together in Part III.

11
Assessing the impact of coalitions

Previous sections have mapped the emergence and current status of business-led corporate responsibility coalitions, from the social activist pioneers to the global field-builders and more recently the industry and issue specialists. Their growth, and presumably their impact, has been cumulative. Most of the pioneers continue to operate today although they have generally reframed their roles and adapted their areas of focus over time. It seems as if almost every week there is news of another new coalition being established that is primarily business governed, funded and led and that is dedicated to improving business sustainability performance or increasing business engagement in addressing socioeconomic and environmental challenges.

In an era of constrained resources, it is increasingly necessary to focus on results and impact, and to ask the following questions: Have the high levels of financial and managerial resources and the large amounts of time and energy expended by thousands of individual champions and companies over the past four decades of coalition-building been worth the effort? Have these business-led coalitions made the private sector more responsible and responsive? Have they made business more sustainable and successful in finding solutions to complex societal challenges while also contributing to profitability and competitiveness? Have they made companies better performers? Have they made the world a better place?

These questions – while valid and important – are extremely difficult to answer with any degree of analytical rigor or empirical credibility. Given the different histories, strategies, sizes, areas of focus and longevity of business-led corporate responsibility coalitions, it is difficult to generalize about their impacts. Despite our own attempt at providing a definition at the beginning of Chapter 2, there is no commonly agreed definition or categorization of these coalitions, let alone a common set of baseline data or universally accepted metrics for evaluating their success and impact. Moving beyond anecdotal stories to evidence-based results has been a challenge in assessing ESG performance as well as ESG links to financial performance. This is the case at the level of individual companies as well as in the more complex area of collective corporate action and business-led corporate responsibility coalitions.

Causality is also notoriously hard to establish, especially as these coalitions are now part of what is a rich and complex ecosystem for more responsible and sustainable business practice. As outlined in Chapter 7, the ecosystem not only includes companies, business leadership coalitions and representative business organizations, but also a wide variety of governments, investors, consultants, foundations, NGOs, consumers, think-tanks and academic institutions. Their impact is both individual and cumulative, and it is almost impossible to directly ascribe success or failure to a particular institution or even group of institutions.

Despite these challenges, and the clear need to develop better performance metrics in future, we believe it is both possible and useful to evaluate the performance and impact of business-led coalitions against the following three questions:

- **Have coalitions been effective at raising awareness** of the societal need and the business case for responsible business practices and sustainability – within the business sector and beyond?

- **Have coalitions helped individual companies to embed responsible business practices and sustainability into their core business strategies**, operations, governance and accountability?

- **Have coalitions helped to scale responsible business practices and sustainability** by reaching more companies and geographies or by covering more issues than would have occurred otherwise, through a combination of business-led voluntary actions and by enabling greater engagement of governments, investors, the media, educators and other stakeholders?

Each individual coalition should assess its own performance against these three criteria. In Table 11.1, we offer our own overall assessment of whether corporate responsibility coalitions have had a positive impact. Our assessment is clearly subjective, based on our own experiences with the coalitions and our biases as coalition-builders. We are both optimists. While we also provide some of the common criticisms of coalitions in Section 11.2, most of which we agree with, we believe that overall many of the business-led coalitions have made a positive difference to the ESG performance and engagement of their member companies, and through this to the broader socioeconomic and environmental contexts in which these companies and coalitions operate, in particular, in terms of embedding and scaling of corporate responsibility (see Fig. 11.1).

Having said that, as we outline clearly in Part III, progress to date has been positive but not nearly sufficient. Many key socioeconomic and environmental indicators are still moving in a negative direction at the global level and within the majority of countries. Equally, many individual companies still have a long way to go in aligning ESG performance with their core business strategies and financial objectives, and in aligning short-term financial performance with long-term economic performance. We believe the situation would be even more problematic without four decades of coalition-building, but that is not an excuse to protect or to justify the status quo. It is clear that in an era of constrained resources, growing competition and increased complexity and uncertainty, most business-led corporate responsibility coalitions will need to "up their game" in order to remain relevant and forward-looking. They will need to be able to respond to and challenge their business members in order to keep improving.

11.1 **The positive impact of business-led corporate responsibility coalitions**

Table 11.1 and Figure 11.1 summarize our assessment of the positive role that corporate responsibility coalitions have played in raising awareness of, embedding and scaling responsible business practices through their member companies and networks.

Figure 11.1 **Business-led corporate responsibility coalitions**

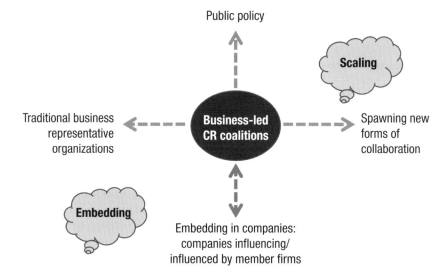

Table 11.1 **Assessing the impacts of coalitions**

RAISING AWARENESS	Have coalitions been effective at raising awareness of the business case and the societal need for corporate responsibility and sustainability – within the business sector and beyond?
Supporting widespread communications activities	Coalitions have been at the forefront of making the business case for corporate responsibility through publications, conferences, presentations, case studies, dialogues, media coverage, "seeing is believing" project visits, and increasingly through social media and cause-related or social marketing and advertising. Examples include: the annual conferences of BSR and Instituto Ethos that both attract over 1,000 participants; several thousand different publications that have been produced by the leading business coalitions; and the hosting of many first-ever dialogues between companies, governments and civil-society organizations on a range of challenging social and environmental issues. The terms corporate social responsibility and corporate responsibility, rarely used in the 1970s, have entered the mainstream business lexicon and garner respectively more than 86,000,000 and 26,000,000 million mentions on a 2012 Google search

Producing empirical evidence and independent research, indices and awards	Coalitions have commissioned academic research and analysis by financial institutions to provide better data and empirical evidence on the links between corporate financial performance and ESG performance. Several have supported the creation of indices and independently-judged awards programs, such as the Maala Index for corporate responsibility in Israel; the Johannesburg Stock Exchange Index for corporate responsibility in South Africa; the BITC Corporate Responsibility Index and annual Awards in the UK; the World Business and Development Awards led by IBLF, the International Chamber of Commerce and the UN; and annual award programs supported by the Global Business Coalition on Health and the Committee to Encourage Corporate Philanthropy
Working with CEOs and senior executives as champions	A number of coalitions have been effective at providing platforms for corporate CEOs, senior executives and political leaders to act as vocal champions and advocates for corporate responsibility, not only within their own companies and industry sectors, but also more broadly. WEF and WBCSD are two examples that have developed both written statements signed by leading CEOs and opportunities for individual executives and politicians to speak publicly to widespread audiences about the business case and the societal need for voluntary corporate responsibility and sustainability. Some of these speeches have reached tens of thousands of people, such as the 1998 WEF speeches by former UN Secretary-General, Kofi Annan, calling on business to support universal principles in the areas of human rights, labor and the environment (which led to the creation of the UN Global Compact) and the WEF speech by Bill Gates in 2008 on creative capitalism. WBCSD's 1992 book *Changing Course* outlined a new vision for corporate sustainability that has been adopted by thousands of companies since then
EMBEDDING	**Have coalitions helped individual companies to embed responsible business practices and sustainability into their core business strategies, operations, governance and accountability?**
Developing strategic visions and roadmaps for action	Some coalitions have developed strategic blueprints or roadmaps for action on corporate responsibility and sustainability that have subsequently been used by thousands of companies and in some cases by governments and other stakeholders to inform their strategic direction on these issues. Examples include WBCSD's Vision 2050 project; BITC's Visioning the Future; CSR Europe's 2020; NBI's National Energy Efficiency vision; and Instituto Ethos' Platform for an Inclusive, Green and Responsible Economy
Providing practical guidance, frameworks and tools for action	Coalitions have developed a wide variety of practical guides, frameworks and tools to help corporate executives develop corporate responsibility policies, management systems, incentives, metrics and measurement processes, and public disclosure and reporting practices. They have also codified and disseminated good practices through a variety of benchmarking tools, case studies and award programs. In some cases they have provided hands-on advisory services and technical assistance in helping companies find solutions to difficult social issues. Examples include The Ethos Indicators for corporate responsibility; WBCSD's management tools such as the Greenhouse Gas Protocol, Business Ecosystems Training; and Global Water Tool; CECP's corporate philanthropy benchmarking tool; IBLF's Guide to Human Rights Impact Assessment and Management and toolkits for cross-sector partnering; and BSR's extensive advisory services to member companies that cover a range of both functional advice and advice on tackling specific corporate responsibility issues and dilemmas

Building skills and capabilities	Linked closely to the guidance and tools above, many coalitions engage and train specific individuals or teams within companies, ranging from strategic leadership programs for senior management teams to practitioner-focused training for sustainability or corporate responsibility professionals to employee volunteering and engagement support for mainstream employees Examples include: • Instituto Ethos, which has run its own corporate university, UniEthos, for several years as a free-standing management development institute focused on corporate responsibility and sustainability • An online training program called Chronos, offered by WBCSD in cooperation with the University of Cambridge Programme for Sustainability Leadership; there have been almost 40,000 users of the license • WBCSD's Future Leaders program for high-potential young executives in member companies; a range of certifications and courses for cross-sector partnership building developed by IBLF in partnership with other organizations • BITC's Seeing is Believing program, which offers peer-to-peer experiential learning opportunities for senior executives • Maala's CSR Management Training Program in Israel It is difficult to estimate how many people have been trained by coalitions over the past few decades, but on a conservative estimate would run into several tens of thousands of senior and middle-ranking business leaders In addition to running specific training and certification programs, some coalitions have also played a key role – often in partnership with academic institutions – in undertaking research on defining the critical leadership skills needed for business executives in the 21st century. Examples include a BITC business leaders taskforce in 2010 that defined the critical skills for sustainability at different levels of the company from the boardroom to the shop floor and a 2012 study by IBLF and Ashridge Business School on leadership skills in a rapidly changing world
SCALING	**Have coalitions helped to scale up responsible business practices and sustainability by reaching more companies and geographies or by covering more issues than would have occurred otherwise?**
Leveraging private resources	Coalitions have had an important and arguably growing impact, in supporting more systemic and transformative solutions by providing platforms for companies to work collectively on a specific issue or set of issues, and in some cases also enabling companies, governments and civil-society organizations to work together. Such collective action platforms are able to leverage more resources, skills, influence and political attention focused on addressing particular social, economic and environmental priorities Some of the coalitions that have been particularly effective at convening collective action platforms are BSR and IBLF with their industry and public–private partnership initiatives; NBI in South Africa convening companies around programs such as the Business Trust, the Education Quality Improvement Program, and the National Energy Efficiency Strategy; WBCSD's industry-sector initiatives; and BITC's task forces to tackle specific social challenges in the UK

Facilitating collective self-regulation within business	Some coalitions have also facilitated new forms of collaborative governance and collective self-regulation, in addition to leveraging business resources through collective action. This has enabled the scaling of corporate accountability and transparency through creating a more level playing field and encouraging leaders in a particular country or industry sector to set a bar for self-regulation above legal compliance, in the hope that their competitors and suppliers will follow suit. Industry or issue-specific coalitions and multi-stakeholder platforms have been especially effective in this area, with examples including the Equator Principles for project finance banks; the Extractive Industries Transparency Initiative; the International Council on Mining and Metals; the Partnership for Responsible Medical Donations; and the Fair Labor Association. Some of the more generalist corporate responsibility coalitions require their member companies to sign up to particular principles or codes of conduct, but most do not require such a level of commitment or have sanctions against members that don't adhere to these criteria (see criticisms in Section 2.7). UNGC offers one example of a generalist coalition that is built on the foundation of its participant companies adhering to ten voluntary principles and in recent years has added reporting requirements and expelled companies that do not meet the criteria
Using traditional business associations as platforms to scale	Some corporate responsibility coalitions have influenced the thinking and practice of traditional business and small business representative organizations such as chambers of commerce, institutes of directors, sector trade associations and employers federations. Many of these bodies are starting to support specific corporate responsibility and sustainability initiatives; given that their members often number in the thousands or hundreds of thousands, they offer high potential for scaling up impact. The lessons from Responsible Care in the chemical sector and the ICTI CARE foundation in the toy industry (Box 6.1, page 82), both of which are implemented through membership of representative trade and industry associations illustrate this potential
Replicating across companies and countries	The field-building coalitions and networks have been particularly effective in engaging many more companies around the work in more countries. It is estimated that some 9,500 companies are members of the different affiliates of the CSR360 Global Partners Network. About 8,000 companies are signatories to the UNGC, while more than 3,000 companies operating in Latin America are members of the affiliates of Forum Empresa. Coalitions such as IBLF contributed to the transformation of many companies in the former Soviet Union and Central and Eastern Europe to market economies and helped in particular to improve environmental performance and business standards in some of these economies in transition. Through its national affiliates in over 60 countries, WBCSD has also played a key role in spreading sustainable business practices to a wide variety of both industry sectors and national contexts

Influencing government policies and practices	In many cases, business-led coalitions have helped to shape the policies and programs of governments, both nationally and regionally. NBI in South Africa has influenced government policy in areas ranging from education and housing to skills development, tertiary education and energy efficiency. Philippine Business for Social Progress has also worked closely with national government on health and education policies. CSR Europe and its national affiliates have played a central role in influencing the corporate responsibility strategies and policy guidelines of the European Union, and IBLF and WBCSD can both point to large-scale programs and initiatives that they have played a direct role in helping to develop at inter-governmental institutions such as the UN and World Bank Group. In all these cases, government policies and programs can be a crucial platform for scaling impact
Engaging investors and the financial sector	Another important platform for scaling impact in improving ESG performance is the investment community and the financial sector more broadly. Some coalitions have been effective in engaging with financial actors to create a multiplier or scaling effect. In Israel, South Africa and Brazil, the coalitions have helped to develop stock exchange indexes to drive and scale more responsible business practices. In these countries, any company now wishing to list on the national stock exchange has to meet certain ESG criteria, which helps to spread good practice even to companies that are not members of corporate responsibility coalitions. UNGC has played a vital scaling role in this sector by helping to establish the Principles for Responsible Investment (profiled in Box 6.2, pages 85f.), which now bring together over 1,000 asset owners, fund managers and professional service firms with billions of dollars under management
Engaging other key stakeholders	Coalitions have also increased the awareness, capacity and, in some cases, influence of civil-society organizations, academic institutions and intermediaries that are able to scale impact through their own channels and communities. WBCSD, for example, has worked with the International Union for the Conservation of Nature (IUCN) on developing ecosystem and biodiversity tools and platforms for business, harnessing the IUCN's platform of more than 1,200 member organizations (including over 200 governments and some 900 NGOs and about 11,000 environmental scientists and experts). CSR Europe and some of its corporate members were the driving force behind the creation of EABIS, which today has a network of over 100 business schools and companies promoting responsible management education. In turn, with the support of UNGC, EABIS has helped to drive the Principles for Responsible Management Education, which reach almost 500 academic institutions around the world
Achieving wider political and societal impacts	The multiplier impacts of the coalitions have extended beyond responsible business behavior. In several countries, these business-led coalitions have also contributed directly to national reconciliation or nation-building. In South Africa, the Consultative Business Movement (one of the forerunners to NBI) played a central role in providing secretariat support for the constitutional negotiations between the ruling apartheid National Party and the African National Congress that led to the peaceful transition to democracy in that country (see Profile). In Northern Ireland, BITC Northern Ireland helped to create a climate in which centuries-old enmities between Protestant loyalists and predominantly Catholic nationalists could be overcome.[225]

We discuss the specific impacts of ten of the leading corporate responsibility coalitions and two *sui generis* organizations in the individual profiles at the end of the book.

Overall, coalition leaders who responded to the GlobeScan Survey were bullish about the impact of their coalition, with 63% describing the impact of their coalition on their member companies as being significant or highly significant and only 2% assessing that they have had little or no impact (Appendix 3, Question 3D).

11.2 **Criticisms of the business-led corporate responsibility coalitions**

Business-led corporate responsibility coalitions have been criticized on a number of counts, both individually and generally. Among the criticisms leveled against coalitions, it is claimed:

They have not been sufficiently "critical friends" to business:

- Many coalitions refuse to "bite the hand that feeds them" – they do not generally criticize corporate members or individual leaders of member companies for poor behavior: for example, the role of their banking members during the global financial crisis in 2008. "Why," asks one academic critic, "if these Corporate Responsibility coalitions have been so successful, is the *Financial Times* running a series on 'Capitalism in Crisis'?"[226]

- They give spurious legitimacy to some company members who are only paying lip-service to corporate responsibility. How many corporate responsibility coalitions have expelled or even suspended a member for dubious behavior?

- They generally shy away from raising difficult issues for their member companies, such as corporate tax policies of multinationals, executive pay, corporate lobbying or inconsistencies between espoused progressive positions on, for example, climate change and companies' membership of representative business and trade associations that lobby for radically different positions on climate change

- They thus sometimes seem to represent the lowest-common-denominator thinking of what corporate responsibility means – and as they grow and establish more complex membership structures and decision-making criteria, it becomes ever harder to persuade members of the need for tougher standards

- Furthermore, some argue that the practice of responsible business and corporate sustainability is now becoming much more sophisticated and industry- and issue-specific. As a result, it becomes much harder for generalist coalitions to be able to offer leading-edge advice or challenges to the top-performing companies among their members

- The proliferation both of corporate responsibility coalitions but also of voluntary performance standards and other initiatives creates duplication, and even the leading global companies lack the resources, including personnel, to work with all these different organizations. A number of experienced and thoughtful corporate responsibility directors from international companies have told us privately that there are now just too many initiatives and coalitions. They recognize this may be less a criticism of the coalitions themselves than of companies, including sometimes their own, and other stakeholders, who have chosen to establish yet more new initiatives and business organizations. Nevertheless, the proliferation is seen by representatives of a number of the leading companies in corporate sustainability as distracting from the positive impacts of the coalitions because companies like theirs cannot do full justice to all the coalitions and initiatives that might be relevant to them. In this case, it is argued, the "coalition whole is less than the sum of the parts"

They have diverted energies and resources from the public sector and civic leadership:

- They have diverted political attention and energies away from effective regulation – Professor Robert Reich, Labor Secretary in the first Clinton administration, for example, argues that CSR is a distraction and that policy-makers and those seeking to achieve significant change, would do better to concentrate on establishing and effectively enforcing regulations[227]

- They have confused the public (as consumers, citizens, employees, voters, ultimate beneficial owners via institutional investors, etc.) about what corporate responsibility standards should be expected by championing corporate members' efforts and, therefore, implicitly suggesting that companies are doing enough. Thus critics of business such as the NGO Corporate Watch argue: "CSR was, is and always will be about avoiding regulation [and] covering up the damage corporations cause to society and the environment"[228]

- They may be diverting resources away from front-line delivery organizations to pay for the coalitions' own infrastructures

- The campaigning NGO Greenpeace has explicitly named one coalition, the WBCSD, as being heavily influenced by the extractive industries and what Greenpeace calls "carbon-intensive industry" and as being part of the strategy of such firms to prevent effective global action on climate change. Kumi Naidoo, Executive Director, Greenpeace International, states that "Our research shows beyond a doubt that there are a handful of powerful polluting corporations who are exerting undue influence on the political process to protect their vested interests."[229] Greenpeace claims that "the WBCSD executive committee is a 'Who's Who' of the world's largest carbon-intensive companies who continue to profit from continued inaction on climate change" and that the WBCSD is spearheading a private-sector drive to "institutionalize a direct and privileged private-sector input into the UN Framework Convention on Climate Change agenda"[230] – a charge vigorously denied by the WBCSD

- Some have criticized CSR Europe and the UN Global Compact for making it too easy for companies to get additional access to the EU institutions and the UN and to benefit from implied association with these institutions

They have been too timid in their goals regarding both the standards of corporate responsibility that they promote and their own impact targets:

- As the coalitions grow, they may become more bureaucratic and slower to spot and raise new issues because a larger part of their energies and personnel are focused on, and have a vested interest in, keeping members happy and maintaining existing programs, irrespective of whether the need for these programs remains or whether the coalition is still the best host for the particular programs. Some have become rooted in their original objectives and context, thereby missing the opportunity of adopting a continuous-improvement or even transformational approach that responds dynamically to their changing environment and context and enables them to be more demanding of their members and participants

- While headline membership numbers might superficially look impressive, many companies are still not engaged. It is estimated that perhaps 10,000 to 12,000 companies are engaged in some type of corporate responsibility coalition or set of activities around the world; yet the UN estimates that there are some 80,000 multinational companies. Even some companies that are nominally members of these coalitions are not always embedding responsible business practices into their core operations, as some recent corporate scandals have demonstrated

- Few of the coalitions have successfully engaged SMEs, which represent between 65 and 90% of the formal private sector in many countries

- There has also been a tendency for some leading companies to use their participation in collective action initiatives as a means of avoiding direct and public engagement on key sustainability issues; as a result the voice of their business leaders is not heard directly or loudly enough on these issues. Furthermore, although business leaders are often actively engaged at the formation of collective action initiatives, it has often proved difficult to sustain their engagement in the longer term – leading to the delegation of participation to more junior colleagues and thereby a weakening of impact on both their organization and the coalition

- Some coalitions have been criticized for having lofty ideals and aspirations but lack of clarity on specific actions and achievable and measurable goals, making it difficult to demonstrate their added value in practical ways

- A number of interviewees for this book and expert panelists criticize the coalitions for insufficient reflection and self-examination, and not being sufficiently open to criticism. Although this is a perception, it should be noted that at least some of the coalitions carry out regular membership satisfaction surveys. Perhaps, sometimes, these are too much like the proforma "happy sheets" beloved of conference organizers, in which participants are asked to give instant evaluations on speakers, venue, quality of conference catering etc. There are certainly coalitions that have surveys showing membership satisfaction at greater than 90% but still worry about companies whose continued membership is deemed to be at risk. Regular and robust self-evaluation should be an automatic part of a coalition's life – something we return to in Part III

11.3 **Conclusions on criticisms**

The expert panel was asked if the authors had made a fair summary of the criticisms leveled at the corporate responsibility coalitions. As one replied,

> It does seem a fair reflection, but that does not make the criticisms all fair. Most of these criticisms contain unexplained assumptions. Their main assumption seems to be that markets and economies on their own allocate "resources" to the right places and that when these go to the "wrong" places there is something wrong. That is nonsense. Markets and economies do not contain intrinsic intelligence that is not first provided to them by people and these people make value judgments, including whether or not to do things responsibly.

The same respondent also pointed out, and the authors concur, that the critics:

> Fail to distinguish between compliance and adherence. As voluntary outfits, these organizations are not compliance-based but are adherence-based. They are thus persuasion not forced-behavior models and choose not to be compliance-based. This is more in the nature of a social movement than a legal one, and social movements often precede new legal and social norms, but do not themselves frame them.

The criticism that advocates of corporate responsibility divert attention from ensuring effective regulation and better public policy may be somewhat, but not entirely, rejected. While some companies and lobbyists have undoubtedly promoted a version of corporate responsibility to avoid regulation, we see corporate responsibility (individual and collective *self*-regulation) and smart regulation that is fairly and effectively enforced as being largely mutually reinforcing. Advances in companies reporting on their significant environmental, social and economic impacts, for example, demonstrate an interesting transition from purely voluntary, to a requirement of membership in certain trade associations in some industries, to a requirement for listing on certain stock exchanges, to being mandated by regulation in certain countries. Having said that, there are clearly examples where voluntary standards and self-regulation can substitute for or undermine effective regulation rather than complement or help to shape and inform it. All efforts at collective self-regulation need to be carefully and constantly reviewed for their interaction with the design, implementation, monitoring and enforcement of effective regulations.

Some of the other criticisms are also valid at least to *some* extent and for *some* coalitions. In practice, for the boards and senior management of the coalitions, it is a constant tension and challenge to know how far to push the boundaries. What today may look, in retrospect, like baby-steps in terms of lifting the bar on expectations of business, may, at the time, have been a difficult, risky and brave decision for a coalition to take. BITC (UK), for example, faced threats of corporate resignations when it first launched an annual Business in the Environment Index and the IBLF faced similar threats when it first focused attention in the mid-1990s on the need to address business complicity in human rights abuses and the need for business to tackle HIV/AIDS.

Nor are all the critics of the coalitions entirely disinterested. Some critics, for example, are also critical of the concept of corporate responsibility *per se*, dismissing it as diverting attention from what, they argue, should be a focus on strengthening regulation of business.

Nevertheless, the coalitions now face increasing challenges in relevance, competition and capacity, not least from multi-stakeholder initiatives, industry- or issue-specific corporate responsibility coalitions and sustainability consultancies; and questions as to whether they can respond effectively to the scale and speed of global problems that now effect business and society more broadly.

11.4 **Lessons learned and critical success factors**

There appear to have been a series of critical success factors behind the establishment of the first coalitions:

- Credible champions with convening power such as Stefan Schmidheiny (WBCSD), Viscount Davignon (CSR Europe), HRH The Prince of Wales (IBLF), and Oded Grajew and Ricardo Young (Instituto Ethos)

- Talented social entrepreneurs able to act as brokers to create the coalitions such as Stephen O'Brien (BITC), John Heaslip (BITC Northern Ireland), Robert Davies (IBLF), Bob Dunn (BSR), Talia Aharoni (Maala), Ricardo Young Silva (Instituto Ethos), Jan Noterdaeme (CSR Europe) and Malini Mehra (Centre for Social Markets, India)

- Critical mass of credible companies as core members whose presence effectively provided "due diligence" for other companies that it was safe to join and become active

- A collective sense of a "burning platform" among core member companies: an urgent societal need that needed to be addressed, such as social and economic inequalities or environmental degradation

- Relevant "agenda for action" for business, with mechanisms that ensure that this agenda is periodically refreshed and updated

- Usually, a relatively sympathetic government, although in some cases (e.g., Venezuela, Philippines, South Africa) it was the opposite that provided the initial stimulus to create a coalition[231]

- Absence of powerful business representative organizations wanting to operate in the responsible business space

Based on these critical success factors, and on our own experiences as campaigners and leaders in corporate responsibility coalitions, there are a number of lessons learned that might serve as practical tips for any social entrepreneurs considering themselves as new coalition-builders:

- Find some top business leaders who:
  - Understand the business and the ethical cases for corporate responsibility
  - Are credible with their peers
  - Are prepared to give their time and leadership to engage other business leaders (typically these latter will be a mix of "elder statesmen" and "rising stars")

- Use the first businesses engaged to recruit others

- Have a mixture of recruiting devices that can appeal to heart and head: some business leaders respond to a cerebral, data-driven and evidence-based pitch, others to more experiential and emotional approaches

- Include various thought-leadership activities to demonstrate expertise and credibility

- Recruit executive staff who are energetic, enthusiastic and credible with businesses; and who are able to broker effectively between business and its stakeholders

- Keep refreshing the agenda and the arguments

- Work with the public sector – but avoid becoming associated with one political party

- Create the platforms for dialogue among businesses themselves, and between business and other parts of society, in order to explore difficult issues, test solutions and spot future questions

In practice, a young generalist corporate responsibility coalition is likely to be operating in a society in transition and it will need a mix of experience from the early years of the older coalitions and some "new technologies" that it can leapfrog straight to without the painful learning of the early coalitions. And, of course, there will still be some things that it will have to customize for its own national circumstances.

11.5 **Strategic questions for corporate responsibility coalitions**

Those responsible for creating, funding or running a business-led coalition in today's world now face a very changed context.

Corporate social responsibility today is much more widely discussed and practiced; however, there are great disparities in how it is interpreted and implemented. The global financial crisis has led to renewed questioning of the legitimacy of business and the global social contract is widely seen to have broken down: there is a **trust deficit.** There is growing concern about a global **sustainability crisis** alongside the global trust crisis and the global financial crisis, and intense debate about what the business response to this sustainability crisis needs to be. There is also a global **governance deficit**. In the face of criticisms, competitors and the sheer complexity of the issues now confronting business, we would argue that the business-led corporate responsibility coalitions now face a number of hard questions:

- How do the coalitions respond to multiple, complex and interlocking global crises: a global financial crisis, an emerging global sustainability crisis, a global trust crisis and a global governance crisis?

- How do generalist coalitions transform themselves as the agenda and territory becomes much more complex and sophisticated, and demands much deeper knowledge to stay relevant? Leading companies now need much more specialist and technical expertise. This is expensive, time-consuming and manpower-intensive for general membership organizations to provide compared to industry- and issue-specific coalitions and for-profit consultancies. Is a core coalition skill around convening businesses to discuss business and society-critical issues going to be sufficient in the future?

- How will coalitions keep momentum and their cutting-edge when a generation of charismatic founders and influential CEOs move on? These social entrepreneurs – "larger than life" personalities such as Oded Grajew and Ricardo Young (Instituto Ethos), Talia Aharoni (Maala), Robert Davies (IBLF) or Julia Cleverdon (BITC) – can be hard acts to follow

- How do coalitions maintain institutional memory when they have the mind-set of campaigning organizations and so do not typically codify their learning?

- How do coalitions retain "air-time" with top business leaders when competition and pressures for CEOs' attention both within and outside their companies is increasing?

- Can coalitions reinvent themselves when their initial tasks to promote the idea of corporate responsibility and to provide basic how-to advice is seen to have been largely achieved, and, therefore, there is less funding for this basic awareness-raising activity?

- How do coalitions respond to the increasing competition from think-tanks, business schools, consultancies and NGOs working with business, and from rival coalitions, in what is increasingly an international marketplace for air-time with companies?

- Companies will increasingly see that membership of a coalition is not an insurance policy against criticism if there are any inconsistencies in their corporate behavior, so will some be less prepared to pay for membership, especially if they are not really committed to responsible business practices anyway?

- Are more multinationals going to look for organizations that can help them internationally rather than those confined to one national market, and if so, how do national coalitions respond?

- How do coalitions across the world engage with Chinese and other emerging-market-headquartered[232] companies as these companies internationalize?

- Will business-led coalitions become more or less influential versus multi-stakeholder alliances and networks such as national chapters of the UNGC or can they complement each other?

- Will general, business-led corporate responsibility coalitions become more or less influential versus single-issue initiatives (which are either business-only or multi-stakeholder)?

Part III looks at the possible and desired futures for the business-led corporate responsibility coalitions.

Part III
The future
The leadership challenge for corporate responsibility coalitions

Part III looks to the future of business-led corporate responsibility coalitions. It is argued in Chapter 12 that, despite the progress made by these coalitions over the past four decades, the impact of voluntary collective action has often been too superficial, too shallow, too narrow, too small-scale and not systemic enough to tackle complex ethical, social and environmental challenges. In the face of increasingly complex and inter-dependent global challenges, the need for corporate responsibility and collective action by business and other actors to promote inclusive, green growth is greater than ever. Chapter 13 outlines an "Agenda for Action," highlighting ten areas where corporate responsibility coalitions could play an increasingly valuable and important role in helping to achieve this goal. The crucial question is whether today's voluntary business-led corporate responsibility coalitions are able to rise to this leadership challenge. Are they fit for the future? To explore this question, Chapter 14 reviews the survey results of the leaders of over 50 business-led corporate responsibility coalitions and feedback from more than 20 international corporate responsibility experts. It outlines some potential scenarios for the future and proposes a "Fit for the Future" diagnostic that coalition leaders can use to assess their strategic capability. Chapter 15 concludes with recommendations for companies, governments, funders and coalitions themselves on how they might become more effective in driving sustainable capitalism.

12

The need for greater corporate responsibility and collective action

Over the past 30 years, measurable progress has been made by thousands of individual companies to embed more responsible and sustainable practices into their core business operations and value chains. An estimated 4,000 companies now produce annual sustainability or corporate responsibility reports, providing public disclosure of their non-financial performance. Individual companies are spending billions of dollars on the development of new technologies, products, services and even business models to drive more environmentally sustainable, economically inclusive and socially responsible competitiveness and growth. There are thousands of project-based partnerships between companies within and across industry sectors and among individual companies, NGOs, governments and research institutes aimed at achieving the same goals. Hundreds of multi-stakeholder alliances and platforms are emerging, aimed at tackling social and environmental challenges at a more systemic and large-scale level. In many cases, the business-led corporate responsibility coalitions profiled in this book have helped to inspire, drive or convene these efforts.

Despite such progress, there is growing evidence that voluntary leadership by the private sector has been too superficial, too shallow, too narrow, too small-scale and too "siloed" to have the impact that is needed to drive more responsible, sustainable and inclusive growth. Consider the following:

- **Progress has been too superficial.** Almost every week, a new corporate scandal is exposed, where so-called leadership companies or groups of companies within a particular industry are found to have operated unethically or irresponsibly in terms of their broader economic, social, environmental or governance performance. The global financial crisis has been underpinned by numerous such cases, from sub-prime mortgages sold to millions of homeowners who didn't fully understand what they were buying, to the manipulation of the London Interbank Offered Rate (LIBOR), which is used by some of the world's largest banks to value about US$360 trillion in loans and financial contracts. During 2011–12, five of the world's largest and most respected pharmaceutical companies faced fines ranging from several hundred million to several billion dollars for fraudulent marketing practices. Leading companies in the mining and energy sector face NGO campaigns and lawsuits on several continents for complicity in human rights abuses or environmental crises. Several of the world's largest corporations in industries from retailing to infrastructure have been embroiled in systematic multimillion-dollar bribery and corruption cases. Nearly all of these companies are members of the corporate responsibility coalitions we have profiled. Most of them have corporate codes of conduct and sustainability policies in place. Many have been, and continue to be, social and environmental innovators. Their CEOs and senior executives have often been outspoken proponents for corporate social responsibility. Yet their publicly stated commitments to responsible business practices have clearly not been deeply embedded in their day-to-day operations. The scandals these companies have created, and the high economic and human costs that these scandals have wrought, undermine public trust in the private sector more broadly and result in strong skepticism that business leaders can self-regulate, or even respect the rule of law.

- **Progress has been too shallow.** In the vast majority of cases, companies that are members of corporate responsibility coalitions have not faced major ethical or corporate responsibility scandals, but they still demonstrate a gap between their public commitment to sustainability and their actual performance on environmental, social and governance issues. Peter Lacy at Accenture and others have called this an "execution gap" or "strategy–performance gap."[233] In other words, these companies are demonstrating their commitment to embedding sustainability polices and practices, but that commitment is still relatively shallow in terms of actually transforming the business practices or business models of individual companies. As Lacy comments:

  > With a closer lens, real progress on sustainable business looks questionable. The extent of the challenge appears not to have fully penetrated mainstream [business] discussions, and objective performance assessments reveal a mixed bag. A recent study by CERES on U.S. companies' progress on sustainability makes for a stark reality check. Despite good examples, few of the 600 companies assessed against sustainability leadership criteria had made anything more than minimal progress against their 4-tier performance measures.[234] Furthermore, a cold hard look at the numbers in many industries on issues like carbon and natural resource use shows that while efficiency is improving and there are real pioneers, in most sectors growth continues to mean absolute emissions levels continue to rise. Social issues, such as human rights and labor standards, come up against even more obvious tensions against prevailing economic incentives (lacking the obvious direct "efficiency" benefits of natural resource management), and show a similar questionable trend of improvement at an aggregate level.[235]

- **Progress has been too narrow.** As stated previously, an estimated 4,000 companies now produce public reports on their sustainability performance. The UN Global Compact (UNGC), the world's largest corporate citizenship coalition, has about 8,000 corporate signatories. An estimated 10,000 to 12,000 companies are members of business-led corporate responsibility coalitions. It is likely that most of the FT Global 500 or Fortune 500 largest corporations in the world are members of at least one of the coalitions profiled in this book, including growing numbers from emerging markets. Yet this is still a fraction of the estimated 80,000 multinational companies in the world, let alone the millions of small and medium companies.[236] Even if the leading companies were not facing an execution or performance gap, the voluntary actions they are taking are necessary but not sufficient to engage the majority of private-sector enterprises in the world, which in turn employ and serve most of the world's population.

- **Progress has been too small-scale.** In the vast majority of cases, voluntary action by individual companies, either within their own business operations and value chains or in partnership with others, has failed to achieve impact at scale. There are successful examples to be sure. These include the impact of information technology helping to reach millions of low-income consumers in areas such as mobile banking, microfinance and mobile health in developing countries, and certain clean technologies in areas such as wastewater treatment and energy. Yet in far too many cases an inclusive business model or new clean technology fails to spread at the speed and scale needed even within the global subsidiaries of a single multinational corporation, let alone across entire value chains, industries or markets. As a result, neither governments nor the private sector are making a sufficient impact on alleviating poverty or reversing the decline in environmental systems. As Lacy comments:

  > Stripping it down to the brutal reality of the facts and figures of the business impact on sustainability, although there is much to be optimistic about, the numbers tell us that inequality and poverty persist almost unabated around the world (excepting the incredible impact of China's economic growth since the 1980s on global poverty statistics). Since 2005, according to the World Bank, the food crisis and the global financial crisis have sent at least another 100 million people under the poverty line. So if business is the way we organize our economy to provide prosperity, and if we are serious about sustainable business, much remains to be done. In parallel, our environmental systems are declining at an alarming rate . . . So many of the social and environmental costs of doing business remain economic externalities – a cost or benefit that is not included in the market price of a product or service because it is not included in the supply price or the demand price (e.g., pollution, carbon emissions etc.) – so incentives and market signals remain too weak to create an imperative for business action at scale.[237]

- **Progress has been too siloed.** Linked to the point above, in addition to the failure to achieve impact at scale, voluntary progress by business has often not been systemic enough. There are growing interdependences and "feedback" loops between the economic, political, and ESG risks and challenges faced by the business community and the world in general. One example is growing recognition of the nexus between food, water and energy security; another, the link between ecosystem services and public health; yet another, the linkages between governance failure and political, financial and environmental crises. In its *Global Risks 2012* Survey, the World Economic

Figure 12.1 World Economic Forum Global Risks Map: growing interdependence and systemic impact of global risks

Source: World Economic Forum, *Global Risks 2012: An Initiative of the Risk Response Network* (Geneva: World Economic Forum, 7th edn, 2012)

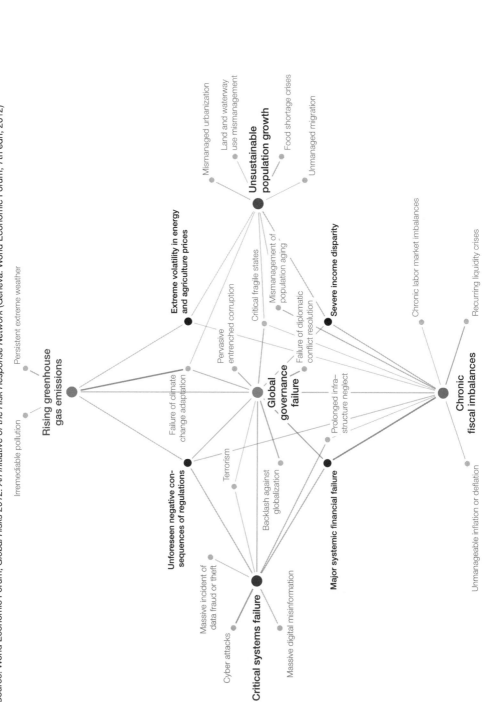

Forum illustrated some of these linkages as shown in Figure 12.1.[238] Such complex and systemic challenges require systemic solutions, and these can only be achieved through more collaborative action between business, governments and civil-society organizations.

In short, while corporate responsibility today is widely discussed and practiced, there are great disparities in how it is interpreted and implemented. In far too many cases, even the leading companies are failing to embed responsible and sustainable business practices into the core of their corporate strategy and operations. This execution or performance gap within individual companies is illustrated by some of the responses to a global survey of corporate CEOs undertaken by the UNGC and Accenture in 2010. These are illustrated in Figure 12.2.

Figure 12.2 **The 'performance gap' in embedding corporate responsibility into core business strategy, operations and governance**

Source: P. Lacy, T. Cooper, R. Hayward and L. Neuberger, *A New Era of Sustainability: Global Compact–Accenture CEO Survey 2010* (New York: UN Global Compact/Accenture, 2010)

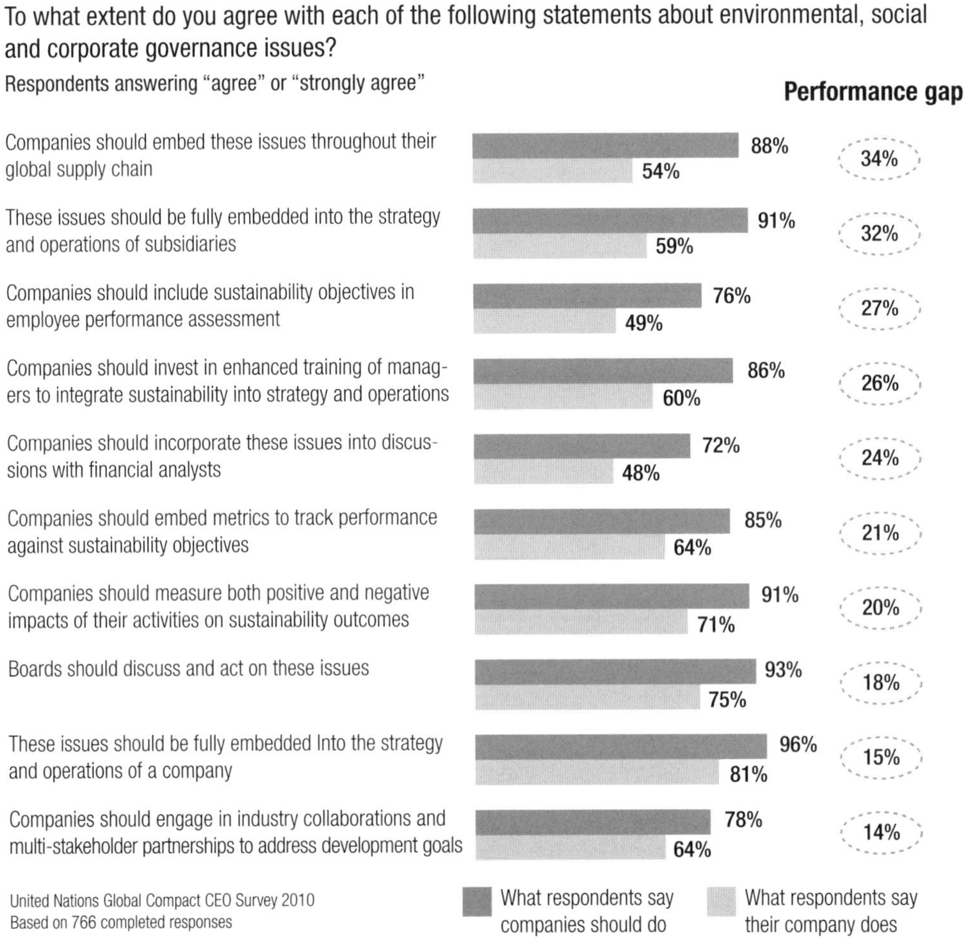

To what extent do you agree with each of the following statements about environmental, social and corporate governance issues?

Respondents answering "agree" or "strongly agree"   **Performance gap**

Statement	What respondents say companies should do	What respondents say their company does	Performance gap
Companies should embed these issues throughout their global supply chain	88%	54%	34%
These issues should be fully embedded into the strategy and operations of subsidiaries	91%	59%	32%
Companies should include sustainability objectives in employee performance assessment	76%	49%	27%
Companies should invest in enhanced training of managers to integrate sustainability into strategy and operations	86%	60%	26%
Companies should incorporate these issues into discussions with financial analysts	72%	48%	24%
Companies should embed metrics to track performance against sustainability objectives	85%	64%	21%
Companies should measure both positive and negative impacts of their activities on sustainability outcomes	91%	71%	20%
Boards should discuss and act on these issues	93%	75%	18%
These issues should be fully embedded Into the strategy and operations of a company	96%	81%	15%
Companies should engage in industry collaborations and multi-stakeholder partnerships to address development goals	78%	64%	14%

United Nations Global Compact CEO Survey 2010
Based on 766 completed responses

■ What respondents say companies should do   ▨ What respondents say their company does

In addition to the corporate responsibility performance gap that exists at the level of individual companies, there is also a failure to achieve scale and systemic impact across value chains, industries, and markets more broadly in the transition to sustainability. This is due to a variety of factors, ranging from the short-term pressures of the financial markets to the lack of enabling public policies. Some of the key barriers to embedding and scaling sustainable business practices are summarized in Figure 12.3, showing the results of a global survey of sustainability leaders carried out in 2012 by GlobeScan and SustainAbility.

Figure 12.3 **Barriers to business's transition to sustainability**
Source: GlobeScan and Sustainability, *The Regeneration Roadmap Unfinished Business: Perspectives from the Sustainable Development Frontier*

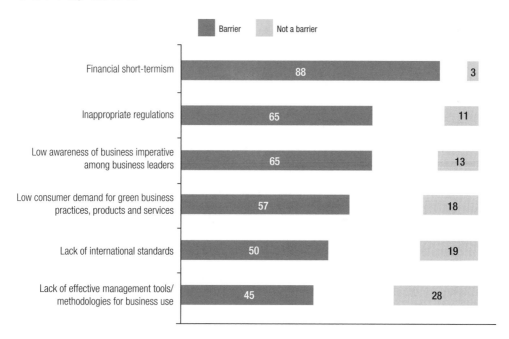

As a result of the failures to embed, scale and achieve more systemic transformation through voluntary corporate responsibility initiatives, there is a growing crisis of public trust in business. Public trust in business leaders continues to decline in many countries in the face of corporate scandals, high levels of inequality and unemployment, and severe environmental degradation. There is renewed questioning of the legitimacy of business. Many people view the global social contract as having broken down. There is growing concern about a global ecological crisis alongside the global financial crisis, and debate on the appropriate business response to these interrelated crises. Declining public-sector resources and political paralysis in many governments serve to simultaneously raise expectations that the private sector will play a greater role in solving complex public problems and concerns about the legitimacy of this role. There are growing concerns that voluntary self-regulation and collective action by business is becoming a substitute for, or even an impediment to, progressive public policy and regulation rather than a complement or driver of more progressive public-sector approaches.

At the same time, corporate chief executives face ever-shorter tenures as they juggle pressures to successfully compete and deliver short-term results to shareholders in an increasingly competitive global economy, while also trying to invest in long-term business strategy and addressing complex sustainability challenges. There is increased competition for their time and attention both within and outside their companies. As a result, the business case for corporate responsibility has to be argued in an even more compelling and clear manner by both its internal and external champions.

Business-led corporate responsibility coalitions are themselves facing growing competition from well-resourced strategy consulting firms, boutique sustainability consultancies, business schools and think-tanks. The generalist coalitions have to renew efforts to demonstrate their value to members as the corporate responsibility agenda becomes more complex and sophisticated, and member companies require more specialist and technical expertise. Industry- and issue-specific coalitions are on the rise, alongside multi-stakeholder initiatives that bring NGOs and governments to the table in addition to companies. These two emerging models of collective action offer alternatives to companies that wish simultaneously to go "deeper" on the specific issues that are most material to their business and their industry, and at the same time achieve greater scale and leverage through also working with governments and civil society.

So what needs to be done by business leaders and business-led corporate responsibility coalitions in the face of increasingly complex and interdependent economic, social and environmental risks and opportunities, and in an era of increasing public distrust of the private sector? More than ever before, we believe that corporate responsibility coalitions need to play a leadership role in some or all of the following areas:

- Supporting individual companies to overcome the "performance gap" and to embed responsible business policies and practices into the core of their corporate strategy, operations and value chains

- Promoting pre-competitive collective action within specific industry sectors, geographies and value chains to drive scale and systemic impact

- Convening companies to be part of more systemic and large-scale multi-sector collaboration between business, government and civil-society organizations

- Spreading innovation from key emerging markets

- Engaging with small and medium enterprises

- Working with governments and advocating for progressive public policies and regulation

- Improving the financial enabling environment

- Partnering with business schools and universities

- Raising public awareness and spreading the practice of sustainable consumption

- Promoting more broadly a new vision for sustainable capitalism

The following chapter outlines an "Agenda for Action" in each of these areas.

13
An Agenda for Action for corporate responsibility coalitions

In this chapter, we outline a ten-point Agenda for Action that we believe is crucial for business-led coalitions around the world to succeed in the next stage of helping individual companies embed sustainability into their core business operations and to scale up the leadership role of the private sector. Probably no corporate responsibility coalition can, or should, play all the ten roles outlined in the Agenda for Action. Some actions will be more important in certain industry sectors or in certain countries; there is no "one size fits all" solution. It is clear, however, that failure to make progress in these ten areas of action will mean that the private sector will increasingly become an impediment rather than part of the solution to achieving new models of more inclusive and sustainable growth.

There is still a need for coalitions in almost every country to play their more traditional role of promoting the business case for corporate responsibility, identifying and sharing best practices, and building the capacity of companies and their stakeholders so that individual companies are able to overcome the performance gap in embedding sustainable business practices into their core business operations. This remains an ongoing leadership challenge even for many major multinational corporations, let alone the millions of small and medium companies operating around the world, or larger companies based in developing economies, especially in those societies where public governance is weak. Corporate responsibility coalitions can be a global conduit for relevant best practices between different countries and can help their member companies to work together in overcoming common obstacles to embedding sustainability. They can also help member firms to address difficult and complex issues collectively, such as climate change or anti-corruption efforts, where individual companies are at risk of being isolated or of losing competitive advantage if they try to act unilaterally.

At the same time, many leading companies are looking for much more specialized, sophisticated and deeper understanding of critical sustainability issues and how they can have a more systemic impact beyond their own individual business operations and value chains.

As more multinational companies evolve from "compliers" to "risk mitigators" and "opportunity maximizers," they need interlocutors able to give them more advanced advice. This is one of the drivers underpinning the ongoing proliferation of industry- and issue-specific coalitions, whether comprised of businesses alone or of companies working together with civil society or with governments and international institutions. The leading companies also increasingly recognize the need for more transformative and systemic change that can only be achieved by large-scale collaborative action supported by some of the actions outlined in this section.

In short, in the face of new competitors and the sheer complexity of the issues now confronting corporations, the generalist business-led corporate responsibility coalitions can, and must, continue to play a vital role in some or all of the following ten areas.

13.1 **Support individual companies to overcome the performance gap**

Coalitions can support member companies to overcome the performance gap that persists between strategic commitments to sustainability made at the corporate level and embedding these commitments into business unit operations and global supply chains. Many businesses today acknowledge a performance gap between corporate-level *intent* to embrace sustainability and *implementation* at the level of strategic business units. As outlined in Figure 12.2, in a 2010 Accenture survey of CEOs of corporate signatories to the UNGC, 91% of respondents said that sustainability needed to be embedded in strategy and operations of business subsidiaries yet only 59% thought their own companies were achieving this.[239] There is an obvious role here for properly equipped corporate responsibility coalitions to help companies overcome this performance gap. Some of the core elements to address this strategy–performance gap are summarized in "the responsible business manifesto" (Box 13.1).

Many members of the experts panel and interviewees for this book have stressed that corporate responsibility coalitions are generally "coaches," inspiring member companies with corporate responsibility principles and supporting them with practical tools, rather than "cops" policing standards and monitoring performance. The coalitions have neither the manpower to police nor the wish to do so. We respect this and suggest these recommendations are presented as opportunities for companies rather than as obligations. We also recognize, however, that over time some coalitions *may* choose to make this putative responsible business manifesto a condition of continuing membership of the coalition.

Box 13.1 **The responsible business manifesto**

Companies should be encouraged to:

- Build corporate responsibility into their **business purpose and strategy**, in a way that makes sense to the particular business, ending adherence to the notion that the purpose of business is to maximize shareholder value – when optimizing shareholder value for the long term should be the *consequence*, not the purpose
- Ensure there is **effective board oversight and governance** of the company's commitment to corporate responsibility – with whatever structure (dedicated board committee, extended remit for existing board committee, mixed board/ executive or executive committee reporting to board, or otherwise) that suits the culture and governance philosophy and requirements of that business and its business circumstances
- Review the **management skills and perspectives** the company needs going forward. Ensure that if the company's leadership believes sustainability, stakeholder-engagement and partnership-building skills are critical areas of competence, these are evaluated as part of talent-management and succession-planning, rewarded in performance and compensation reviews, and specified in the executive education commissioned by the company from business schools and other providers. And ensure that recruiters from the company understand these requirements – there is little evidence that they do today
- Ensure that **investor relations** departments are capable and confident in explaining how improving ESG performance is integral to overall corporate strategy and contributes to long-term value-creation, and that they are proactive in explaining this, especially to their institutional investors
- Build sustainability into **R&D, innovation and new business development** strategies so that the commitment to corporate responsibility is leading to new products and services, access to new or under-served markets or new business models on a regular basis, and collectively leads to business transformation
- Scope regularly their most **material ESG risks, opportunities and impacts** and prioritize action to minimize negative impacts and maximize positive impacts
- **Report publicly** on the company's performance against these ESG priorities, ideally with independent, third-party verification
- Ensure close **functional and operational alignment** between any dedicated corporate responsibility or corporate sustainability function and other business units and support functions rather than operating in isolation. Companies should create senior-level cross-functional committees that include senior business unit leaders and other key corporate functions as well as the sustainability and corporate responsibility leaders to drive the company's strategy and priorities in this area

13.2 **Promote pre-competitive collective action within specific industry sectors and value chains**

As outlined in Part II, there has been a marked growth of industry- and issue-specific organizations either as business-led coalitions or as multi-stakeholder initiatives. Once the core "good housekeeping" of embedding sustainability policies, management systems and performance metrics is tackled, many of the tough issues remaining are more industry-specific or issue-specific. While some of these tough issues may lead to competitive advantage from disruptive innovations and the development and deployment of breakthrough technologies, many of the issues are unlikely to confer such competitive edge and are better tackled by industry pooling its expertise and resources.

Business for Social Responsibility (BSR) and the World Business Council for Sustainable Development (WBCSD) are two of the international coalitions that have developed industry-specific sectoral specializations. Both are committed to expanding their sectoral specialization. A number of significant business sectors, however, remain uncovered or under-covered by any corporate responsibility coalitions. While one or more coalition might seek to develop a sectoral initiative independently, there is also the option to partner with other organizations (other coalitions, trade associations, business representative organizations, specialized academic centers of expertise etc.) to run an industry-specific initiative.

13.3 **Convene business engagement in broader multi-stakeholder platforms**

Coalitions can convene and facilitate the engagement of companies in multi-stakeholder platforms that also include government and civil society to come together to tackle complex sustainability challenges either within a particular city, country or region or on an international basis; or they can convene the collective business participation in existing multi-stakeholder initiatives.

In some instances, these multi-stakeholder initiatives are seen as more focused alternatives to the more generic business-led corporate responsibility coalitions. While they may sometimes be competitors for business time and resources, they can also be complementary to, and expand the impact of, the coalitions. Earlier writers, such as former World Bank Vice President Jean-François Rischard and academic Steve Waddell, have developed the concept of what Rischard calls "global issues networks"[240] and Waddell "global action networks,"[241] where different actors with an interest, resources and expertise to contribute work together to analyze a complex global problem and develop systemic solutions. We envisage more of these global action networks emerging.

As a refinement and elaboration of multi-stakeholder initiatives, some national governments are experimenting with the concept of collaborative "responsibility deals" (see the United Kingdom's experience in Box 7.1 in Section 7.1). The idea is at an exploratory stage and the early evidence is mixed as to their efficacy. Other examples of a national government working with the business associations and corporate responsibility coalitions in its country to scale voluntary business action for sustainability include Denmark's Action Plan for Corporate Responsibility, South Africa's Industry Charters, which support the country's Black Economic Empowerment Act, Colombia's Green Markets program, and the Energy Star program in the United States (see brief profiles in Box 7.1, pages 95ff.). These examples and others like them could be adapted by business-led corporate responsibility coalitions and governments in many other countries.

Common to collaborative public–private commitments, responsibility deals and charters is the idea that government sets an overall goal or objective, and then groups of businesses voluntarily accept more responsibility as part of a series of interlocking commitments and actions by different players. Each player is willing *and able* to do more because of what other players do. Such sophisticated partnerships across the sectors need capable and experienced honest brokers to facilitate and choreograph the often-intricate sequencing of commitments and concessions. Here again is an important potential role for corporate responsibility coalitions. Just as in the past, they created the safe space for businesses to explore their responsibilities for ESG impacts, and how those responsibilities could best be discharged by commercial entities, so in the future, the coalitions could help to take collective business action to a much greater scale by facilitating business input to the management of the global commons, and coordinating that with other sectors of society.

There is a skill to identifying a group of companies, sometimes including fierce competitors, and showing them the value of collaboration while not falling foul of anti-trust or competition laws designed for other purposes. There is a skill too in building the trust of other players: civil society, governments and international institutions. This would be a further very complementary role for corporate responsibility coalitions.

Supporting such transformational cross-sector partnerships will require a critical mass of professional staff from corporate responsibility coalitions to be trained and confident in working across traditional boundaries at the most senior levels with business, civil society and the public sector. The expertise has already been developed in the Partnering Initiative,[242] started by the International Business Leaders Forum. This expertise needs pump-priming from one or more foundations, corporations or high-net-worth individuals prepared to make a significant social investment in capacity-building the corporate responsibility coalitions.

13.4 **Spread innovation from key emerging markets**

As outlined in other chapters, some of the most interesting and large-scale advances in corporate sustainability and new models of business and government cooperation are coming from emerging markets. These markets, especially Brazil, Russia, India, China plus South Africa (the BRICS) and other middle-income economies, such as South Korea, Indonesia, Mexico, Colombia and Turkey, are an increasingly important source of new business opportunity and innovation. Almost half the world's population (46.8%) live in just seven so-called emerging economies, according to the International Monetary Fund.[243] Many of these economies are rich in natural resources, and over the past decade these seven countries have started to account for a growing percentage of the world economy – an estimated 29.3%[244]

adjusting for purchasing power parity, with an associated increase in large-scale infrastructure development and widespread consumption. These countries offer companies the opportunity to reach new customer segments and to develop new technologies, products, services and business models that profitably serve both an emerging middle class and previously under-served or unserved low-income or base-of-the-pyramid consumers. Above all, they offer the potential for a different path to prosperity: a path that is not only more inclusive of low-income producers and consumers but also less resource intensive and more sustainable. They offer the potential for a path that also supports more resilient and inclusive models of urbanization and rural development.

It is fair to say that the ability of the international community to achieve more inclusive, green growth in the 21st century will be determined in large part by what models of economic growth and capitalism emerge in these markets. Yet to date most of the debate and practice on corporate responsibility and sustainability has been Western-led. As BSR and the UNGC state in a report published in June 2012:

> International debate on corporate sustainability – the private sector's contribution to sustainable development – has largely been dominated by viewpoints and institutions in North America and Europe. [There is] a critical need to look beyond the usual places and highlight business contributions to sustainable development from emerging and high-growth markets – the new "geographies."[245]

Their research, supported by local consultations in Brazil, China and India, concludes:

> Emerging markets are 21st century laboratories where the future is being shaped . . . they should not be seen as recipients of solutions created elsewhere. Indeed, they are laboratories for innovation and breakthrough solutions that develop locally, and which can be applied elsewhere. For example, in China, solutions may develop in relation to clean-tech, in India in relation to market-access for those at the lowest socio-economic strata, and in Brazil in relation to payments for ecosystem services which go beyond a pure subsidy model. As companies from these regions increasingly go global, their perspectives and innovations will increasingly shape the global practice of corporate sustainability.[246]

By extension, the business-led corporate responsibility coalitions that want to help shape the global agenda for the next few decades need to be able to learn from, partner with and spread innovations from emerging markets, as well as from more established economies. Indeed, there is great potential for what General Electric and others have called "reverse innovation" *from* emerging markets *to* the OECD economies. This is already happening at the level of individual firms and in some cases industry sectors and is likely to also hold for at least some of the major corporate responsibility coalitions. More than ever before, they will need to be learning organizations and open to taking ideas from non-traditional sources. International networks with well-established local networks or platforms in emerging markets, such as the WBCSD and the UNGC, are well positioned to harness this opportunity and spread innovation.

13.5 **Engage small and medium enterprises**

Coalitions can also play an important role in the engagement of small and medium enterprises (SMEs), which account for the majority of job creation in most countries. In particular, they can support the provision of practical guidance and help to owner-managers and SMEs generally. All too often, the language, examples and recommendations for action to embed responsible business practices are targeted at large national and international companies. Research and practice, however, indicate that SMEs need something tailored to their circumstances with examples of best practice and business benefits based on "businesses like us." "Businesses like us" typically means of similar size, in the same business sector, from the same area or facing similar challenges.[247] Many of the general corporate responsibility coalitions have tried to engage SMEs. CSR Europe and most if not all of its 33 national partner organizations have at some stage run initiatives with SMEs. Some of these been with funding from the European Commission Directorate General for Enterprise and have been run in partnership with organizations representing small business, such as chambers of commerce and national members of the European Association of Craft, Small and Medium-Sized Enterprises (UAPME), the pan-Europe small business lobby, or with small business development organizations.[248]

CSR Europe's Dutch national partner, MVO Netherlands, a multi-sectoral initiative, has played a leading role in SME engagement, providing advice and training. Sodalitas in Italy, UPJ (affiliated to CSR360) in Germany, and Business in the Community (BITC) in the UK and Scottish Business in the Community have also been active. Scottish Business in the Community and BITC, for example, led the Small Business Consortium (also involving Accountability, Arts & Business, British chambers of commerce, CSR Europe, the Federation of Small Businesses, the Forum of Private Business and the Institute of Directors with Lloyds Bank), which operated from 2002 to 2010 and ran small-business adviser training and a website offering advice, news, good practice examples and signposting targeted at SMEs. This was called The Small Business Journey and was modeled on a subway map with subway "stations" representing plus-points in terms of how small businesses could improve their profitability while becoming more sustainable (see Fig. 13.1). Scottish Business in the Community is now building on this experience in designing a new program in close consultation with SMEs themselves.

Developing an online toolkit that could be adapted with local examples by different coalitions could enable more coalitions to engage SMEs, both directly and by supporting their own national small business representative organizations such as chambers of commerce and federations of small businesses, and small business development organizations in their efforts to support sustainability with profitability among SMEs. The coalitions could bring another essential ingredient to the mix, besides their convening power and sustainability subject expertise: the ability to work with national and international member companies to rationalize sustainability data requirements for their suppliers. Models already exist to build on, such as Sedex, the Supplier Ethical Data Exchange. Historically, some large companies have also opened up their unwanted R&D ideas and patents libraries to entrepreneurs from within and outside their organization. Coalitions could leverage this process by developing a further "killer application" for the "small business journey to sustainability" that shares this R&D and new business development expertise of their member companies with SMEs that have the aspiration and the potential to grow. Advances in ICT might make such schemes

Figure 13.1 **The Small Business Journey: a toolkit for small businesses and business advisers**

more successful in future, especially if there was a critical mass of corporate responsibility coalitions involved.

13.6 **Work with government and advocate for progressive public policies and regulation**

Corporate responsibility coalitions could play a more proactive role in working directly with governments and, where appropriate, publicly advocating for more progressive public policies and regulation to drive sustainable business practices at the local, national and international levels. Such policies are going to be essential to create clearer market signals and incentives for private-sector leadership on social and environmental issues. Corporate responsibility coalitions can also work directly with governments and civil-society organizations where relevant to strengthen public institutional capacity to make these policies more effective. This role can be particularly important in countries with weak governance systems, low-income countries or those emerging from periods of conflict.

Companies at more advanced stages of corporate responsibility maturity have recognized that, however successful their own efforts are to embed sustainability, they will not be able to become truly sustainable or help to achieve more systemic impact at scale without public-policy and regulatory changes. These companies are starting to cooperate with each other and with non-governmental organizations to take a more proactive stance on public-policy reform. Helping groups of businesses to be effective advocates for sustainability-friendly regulations, laws and policies is an important potential role for some coalitions to play. In recent years, the WBCSD has adopted a more proactive stance on calling for greater leadership by government. In the run-up to the Rio + 20 conference, for example, it published the *Changing Pace* report, which calls on governments to take action in a number of core areas, from regulations and fiscal incentives to putting a price on carbon and other natural resources and leveraging more innovative public-sector financing mechanisms.[249]

Coalitions also have the potential to play a more substantial role in building public-sector capacity in countries with weak governance institutions and under-developed infrastructure to enable markets to operate more effectively. Such a public-policy advocacy and capacity-building role could, of course, put business-led coalitions on a collision course with traditional business representative organizations such as chambers of commerce, employers' federations and trade associations. On the other hand, handled intelligently by the leading companies, this could be more akin to "co-opetition" (sometimes collaboration and cooperation and sometimes competition) with the business representative organizations. The distinctive contribution of coalitions in preference to traditional representative organizations is that they could be more open to and credible with other stakeholders, and potentially better placed to mobilize collective business contributions in multi-stakeholder initiatives.

13.7 **Improve the financial enabling environment**

Coalitions can work with investor networks, stock exchanges and accounting firms to improve the capital markets and the financial enabling environment necessary to drive better social and environmental risk management and innovation. This can include efforts to develop stock exchange and investor sustainability indexes; clearer financial incentives to encourage long-term investments as well as short-term performance, and to reward better environmental and social performance; support for public reporting on sustainability and integrated reporting[250] models; and the creation of new financing mechanisms that combine hybrids of both commercial finance and donor or philanthropic funds (so-called "blended value" or impact investing models).

Over the past decade there has been growing momentum both within the financial sector itself and also engagement between leading sustainability corporations, corporate responsibility coalitions, financial-sector organizations, and increasingly regulators and policy-makers. A few of the most interesting and high potential multi-stakeholder networks aimed at improving the financial environment for sustainable business were profiled in Box 6.2 in Chapter 6, page 85. All of them have demonstrated increased activity and reach in recent years and they offer valuable platforms for corporate responsibility coalitions to help their members embed and scale sustainable business practices.

13.8 **Partner with business schools and universities**

Coalitions could partner with business schools and universities to research best practices and case studies, and to develop the necessary awareness, leadership and partnership skills needed for a more sustainable model of capitalism in future. Coalitions often have considerable raw data on business efforts to embed sustainability but lack the time or inclination to analyze it. The up-to-date material from the coalitions would provide researchers, who often lack timely access to companies, with good contemporary material. While the world's more than 13,000 business schools are an obvious target, schools of law, engineering and public policy could also benefit from such partnerships. The 50 + 20 report from a group of business school professors and faculty across the world, coordinated by the UN Principles for Responsible Management Education, the Global Responsible Leadership Initiative and the World Council of Business Schools for Sustainable Development (see Section 7.4), offers a framework for how business schools need to change. Coalitions could work with their member companies to assist business schools that want to embed sustainability with a number of practical steps.

Coalitions could also help to persuade member companies to open themselves up to universities and professional schools to research and write teaching cases about their challenges in embedding corporate responsibility and sustainability. The world's largest mobile phone business, China Mobile, has done this with professors from Harvard Business School, Ross School of Business at the University of Michigan, and Cranfield School of Management. Coalitions could form collaborations of member companies to offer mentoring and privileged research access to bright younger faculty wanting to make their academic names with relevant and rigorous research around corporate responsibility and sustainability.

Coalitions could also encourage their member companies to make it clear to business school career services and MBA/MSc course directors that companies expect graduate recruits to have a good understanding of how to manage environmental, social and governance factors in the business (both as risk mitigation and opportunity maximization). At present, all too often the signals that corporate recruiters are sending to business schools are just the opposite. Member companies need to ensure their heads of talent development and executive learning are specifying learning outcomes about sustainability and corporate responsibility when commissioning executive education from business schools. Executive education directors in schools say this is not currently the general message. Company staff who are business school alumni and interested in corporate responsibility and sustainability could be encouraged to become active in their alumni associations and to agitate for their schools to take these issues more seriously, if for no other reason than because not to do so may devalue their own qualifications from that school in the years to come.

Coalitions might also run speaker bureaus providing senior leaders from member companies to speak on business school campuses, who can weave in ideas about ESG performance as an integral part of their narratives. But they should make it clear to the schools that, if CEOs or senior executive directors are speaking on campus, faculty as well as students are expected to attend. Experts from coalitions can also teach in business and other schools as visiting or part-time faculty, as a few are already doing.

13.9 **Raise public awareness and spread the practice of sustainable consumption**

Coalitions could engage proactively with traditional media, social media platforms and advertising agencies to raise public awareness and spread the practice of sustainable consumption. A number of leadership companies are now attempting to engage their consumers in sustainability initiatives but admit they are struggling. Some of the major coalitions working together and with leading companies and marketing professionals could support these consumer-focused efforts.

There has also been increasing interest in recent years in redesign, re-use and recycling as part of advancing eco-efficiency and sustainable value chains from production to end-use consumption and disposal. Some companies are committing to "zero waste" or Cradle-to-Cradle© manufacturing.[251] The challenge remains, however, how to address exponential increases in consumer demands for more "stuff" as an additional 100–150 million middle-class consumers join the global economy *every year* between now and 2030.[252]

Coalitions typically include many of the world's leading business to consumer (B2C) and fast-moving consumer goods (FMCG) companies and often also have many of the leading advertising agencies in their membership. Through these members, the coalitions should be able to access the best branding and communications experts and those specializing in behavioral economics, social media and "nudge" theories of behavior change.[253] Working with such experts, some coalitions could help to design and execute campaigns to make sustainable consumption aspirational and fashionable.

The Joint U.S. China Collaboration on Clean Energy (JUCCCE; www.juccce.org), an innovative Chinese NGO coalition started by Chinese-American social entrepreneur Peggy Liu, provides an interesting work-in-progress model of what might be done. Working with leading advertising agencies such as Saatchi & Saatchi, Chinese social media experts and bloggers, and international business schools, JUCCCE is developing the "China Dream." The concept is that for the last 30 years, China has been modernizing with an implicit pursuit of the "American Dream" of material affluence and consumption. American brands such as Coca-Cola, KFC, McDonald's and Levi's have become popular in China. The vision of the China Dream (in Mandarin, the "harmonious, happy dream") is to promote a new lifestyle with less emphasis on consuming more and more focus on living more. In parallel, JUCCCE is also running high-level training programs for city mayors and other key officials, under the auspices of the Ministry of Housing and Urban Development, which gives the NGO access to senior policy-makers across the country who can "nudge" consumers towards more sustainable behaviors and lifestyles. Columnist Tom Friedman commented in an op-ed in the *New York Times* that praised the work of JUCCCE:

> On Nov. 8 [2012], China is set to hold the 18th National Congress of the Communist Party. We already know who will be the next party leader: Vice President Xi Jinping. What we don't know is what matters: Does Xi have a "Chinese Dream" that is different from the "American Dream?" Because if Xi's dream for China's emerging middle class – 300 million people expected to grow to 800 million by 2025 – is just like the American Dream (a big car, a big house and Big Macs for all) then we need another planet.

> . . . Juccce has been working with Chinese mayors and social networks, sus-
> tainability experts and Western advertising agencies to catalyze sustainable hab-
> its in the emergent consuming class by redefining personal prosperity – which
> so many more Chinese are gaining access to for the first time – as "more access
> to better products and services, not necessarily by owning them, but also by
> sharing – so everyone gets a piece of a better pie." That means, among other
> things, better public transportation, better public spaces and better housing that
> encourages dense vertical buildings, which are more energy efficient and make
> shared services easier to deliver, and more e-learning and e-commerce opportu-
> nities that reduce commuting. Emphasizing access versus ownership isn't just
> more sustainable, it helps ease friction from the differences between rich and
> poor.[254]

Clearly, sustainable consumption is not only a challenge for China and the other big
emerging markets; it is also a challenge for consumers and the companies that serve them
everywhere. Corporate responsibility coalitions can play a role in helping to raise awareness
and mobilize action on this next crucial challenge for corporate responsibility. It is an issue
that several coalitions such as BSR and WBCSD and organizations like WEF have publicly
recognized and started to address. WEF, for example, has launched an initiative on sustainable consumption with some of the world's leading consumer brands.[255]

13.10 **Promote a new vision for sustainable capitalism**

Coalitions could contribute to the growing public debate on the future of capitalism by helping to promote a new vision for sustainable capitalism,[256] incorporating more inclusive and
green growth economic models, and being advocates for this vision.

In seeking to pull together the strands of the argument that the *Financial Times* had
initiated with its "Capitalism in Crisis" series, in January 2012 a *Financial Times* editorial
combined a resolute defense of market capitalism with stringent criticism of the failure to
regulate:

> The excesses that drove the bubble and the breakdown that followed happened
> because leaders forgot that free enterprise requires rules . . . Good ground rules
> are a public good; as such they are the responsibility of states. Capitalism needs
> the state: not to run the economy but to regulate how individuals run it and have
> them face the consequences of their actions. Governments did not tend to this
> essential function – least of all in financial markets.[257]

However, the editorial went on to argue that:

> . . . laws and regulations are not all. Since Adam Smith, intelligent defenders of
> free markets have known that capitalism works best when people's free choices
> are also governed by moral values. The cardinal virtue for capitalists is to sup-
> port rules that make capitalism a success.

Those of us with long memories (and old-fashioned filing systems) recall another *Financial Times* editorial from a decade earlier in the aftermath of the collapse of the global pharmaceutical companies' court case against the South African government over patent protection. On that occasion, the *Financial Times* had opined: "If businesses want to make good profits and to protect their good names, they must stand up and argue their case – for globalization, for free trade, and for responsible corporate behavior."[258]

A few of the business-led coalitions have assumed thought-leadership roles in the debates about the future of capitalism: for example, the IBLF through the launch of its *Redefining Growth* agenda, CSR Europe with *Enterprise 2020* and the WBCSD's *Vision 2050*. BITC's *Visioning the Future – Transforming Business* aims to help member companies contribute to the "pursuit of a quality, modern and sustainable life for all." Instituto Ethos has similarly launched a new platform for sustainable and inclusive growth. The National Business Initiative, the South Africa affiliate of the WBCSD, has explicitly endorsed and promoted *Vision 2050*. In other words, without conscious coordination or any formal decision to collaborate, the leading coalitions are coalescing in practice around an agenda for green, responsible, inclusive growth – what may be defined as "sustainable capitalism." This emergent consensus of coalitions needs to be expanded and made more explicit.

Some of the established coalitions could play a more central role in making the case for responsible business being one of the building blocks for sustainable capitalism. The Occupy movement may have dissipated and disappeared from the headlines, but the fears and anger that inspired the protestors remain. While individual CEOs and others are articulating the case that corporate responsibility is good for their individual businesses, the case for corporate responsibility as being essential for capitalism is less frequently heard above the general hubbub of social and political discourse. Yet markets need morals. Even if influential individual media such as the *Financial Times* or *Business Week* discuss corporate responsibility intelligently, there are still many skeptical or even hostile media. The influential *Economist*, for example, has modified its previous hostility to corporate social responsibility but remains cautiously skeptical.[259] More generally, as new media in emerging markets and social media platforms grow in reach and influence, making the case for corporate social responsibility becomes even more important. There is a specific role to promote the concept of responsible business as integral to sustainable capitalism. Here potentially is the "big picture" context for the work of the coalitions: ethical (responsible) business is an essential pillar of sustainable capitalism.

This list of additional tasks is illustrative rather than exhaustive. As we have already mentioned, there are embryonic examples for each of these tasks already taking place somewhere in the network of the coalitions. The question now is whether for each of these suggested additional roles there will be a critical mass of what, in a related context, Peter Bakker of the WBCSD has called "coalitions of the willing," which will be energized and capable of taking each additional proposed role forward.

Only some coalitions will have the aspiration and the potential to take on these roles, and it is not suggested that any coalition should take on *all* of them.

14

Are corporate responsibility coalitions fit for the future?

14.1 The views of coalition leaders, companies and other stakeholders

The GlobeScan CEOs Survey (Appendix 3) suggests coalitions want to play an expanded role and are confident that they can do so. According to the survey, CEOs of the coalitions expect that there will be increased staff numbers, budget and corporate membership in the next five to ten years. More consulting for members is also expected. A large majority of the CEOs (80%) also expect that coalitions will be more active in challenging member companies to become leaders in tackling ESG issues. A similar number expect that coalitions will be more effective in influencing corporate behavior on ESG issues.

The CEOs recognize the external context and global challenges summarized earlier in Chapter 12 as drivers of the greater role they expect to play. In answer to why they expect that coalitions will be more active in challenging their member companies to become leaders in tackling ESG issues, coalition CEOs told us, in response to both the global situation and to national imperatives:

> "More and more CEOs in our country realize that their businesses can either be part of the problem or part of the solution that affects the society they are operating in. Today, there is a growing desire to be part of the latter."

> "We need to change the pace if we want to make the economy green, inclusive and responsible."

> "There is increasing acceptance that CSR is important, especially among brand name companies. Increasing media and social media coverage creates reputation risks."

> "Corporate members are more confident and open about dialogue. We must have an honest but tough attitude to constructively challenge our members. However there is a suspicion towards open dialogue. Government and NGOs are late starters."

> "Due to recent economic disorder people have lost their trust to businesses. The time of just showing good practices has past. Companies should change patterns of behavior and culture. They should become more and more responsible. Stakeholders are seeking to hold companies accountable for social and environmental issues. As CSR is a source of social progress we need to challenge our members to integrate social considerations more effectively into core business operations and strategies."

> "Stakeholders, governments and civil society have ever-increasing expectations in this area."

There is also recognition that the business case for corporate responsibility is much stronger nowadays and that companies can get competitive advantage from embedding responsible business practices – and, therefore, that companies are more receptive to challenge and being pushed further:

> "A larger number of global companies will become more aggressive in using sustainability to differentiate themselves in the marketplace. Organizations like mine will play an important role as transmission agents to disseminate leadership concepts and practices across a broader array of companies as markets evolve to reflect sustainability criteria and practices."

> "Sustainability and corporate responsibility are considered more and more important for the competitiveness of a company."

> "Sustainability will be a must-have business strategy. Member companies need us to help them walk the talk."

Some coalition CEOs also explicitly refer to their own organization's growing expertise and confidence:

> "We have gained credibility over the last decades so that we can now move to the next level."

> "With sustainability having reached the mainstream, it is crucial that dedicated coalitions continue to push forward for greater impact. The basic work can be done by others."

> "Our engagement with international business is on a long-term increasing trend."

> "Our own expertise is providing us with a confidence to bring together business leaders and engage them in tackling issues. I also think the recession has made leaders stop and think about the issues that are obvious and what they can do about it. The zeitgeist seems right."

"The time for advocacy will be over. We will be suppliers of solutions and implementation, and not precisely to convince that sustainable development and CSR
are the right way. Time for action!"

Most of the coalitions expect their organizations to be more effective at influencing corporate behavior on ESG issues over the next 5–10 years (Appendix 3, Question 6D) because
they believe their organizations are becoming more professional and better able to work
with companies:

"We would like to think that we will do our work extremely well and we will
do just that!"

"Our success comes from understanding the corporate mind frame and challenges in implementing any kind of change."

"We learn and we get better and get braver. I hope."

"Collaboration is key as is reputation over the next while. Companies are struggling to find meaning and purpose. I think it is still going to be a hard slog but I
think we are becoming more effective."

"Need to demonstrate value for money and build on the leading role that has
already been established."

"Global challenges will drive low carbon and green economy. Coalitions will
play an important role in raising the bar."

In particular, the coalition leaders talk about their greater focus:

"More focus in subjects, more selective in membership, looking for impact."

Coalitions' survey respondents also suggest that a stronger business case means they can
be more effective:

"Because companies are becoming more aware of the positive impact of social
and environmental behaviors on their overall strategy."

"Continued demonstration of successful Sustainable Development solutions that
produce triple-bottom-line results."

"As companies are more convinced of the value added."

"Companies are the only force powerful enough to make the transformational
changes required to make the world sustainable. It is imperative that we do all
we can to support and challenge companies to do that."

However, there are caveats:

"Those that do not become more effective will fade in relevance."

"We need to be more effective in order to deliver the role that we have been
entrusted with."

"I think the picture is diverse, more in the emerging world, less in the developed
world."

> "Same level, but different methodology. Currently providing orientation and the state of the art, we are moving to providing solutions and practical tools, BUT within a safe place where to exchange experiences in a suitable manner."

Although some coalition leaders also emphasize again that businesses need to be challenged:

> "Most companies don't want to be leaders. They will do what's required to manage business risk, protect their relationships with customers and preserve their cultures."

> "More cohesion; more practical action (time for best practice sharing only is over). Business will need platforms to really collaborate and work together to make and implement solutions."

In contrast to the generally bullish responses of the coalition leaders in the GlobeScan Survey, in interviews with businesses and with other stakeholders of the coalitions in civil society, international institutions and the media and among corporate responsibility experts, there was some skepticism and questioning about the generalist corporate responsibility coalitions and whether individually and collectively they are fit for purpose.

To be fair, many of the coalition CEOs recognize that they face major challenges in playing the greater role they aspire to, and acknowledge the barriers to achieving the greater impact and effectiveness that they believe possible. The most common challenge by far is seen as funding, which is frequently linked to the increasing number of competitors, within the context of a tough economy:

> "The greatest challenge is the economy. How to get the money to do all the good work."

> "Providing 'value' to corporate members in tight economic conditions."

> "Balancing between joint initiatives and institutional profit margins and business expansion."

> "Lack of resources to deep-dive into technical issues."

> "Over-competition between coalitions and industry associations."

> "Many similar international initiatives in same space (Global Compact, WBCSD, Carbon Disclosure Project, ISO 26000)."

> "Business talks with us and develops projects with us, but during the implementation they go to PR agencies, so PR companies make money not us."

The coalitions' own capacity and expertise are considered to be another major set of challenges:

> "Staying relevant to the evolving needs of member companies in steering their companies and businesses to be more effectively engaged with other stakeholders in fast-changing social, economic and environmental landscape."

"Lack of clarity regarding value proposition, and lack of differentiation from other sustainability-related business organizations. This translates into insufficient brand identity and recognition."

"Staying ahead of the curve in terms of expertise, and maintaining business relevance while not losing a sense of mission."

"Having the internal expertise to match the appetite for leadership in business."

"Achieving meaningful impact."

"Unwillingness to start a tough dialogue with members."

"Skepticism of stakeholders regarding motivation."

"Staying relevant to all members, despite big differences across the member organizations. The 'media' spectrum is very wide and the Forum is made up of a very diverse set of media companies."

"Increasing the impact of current activities and make business work together."

"Satisfying an increasing members demand, in a tailor-made way. To maintain 'member care' activities with a high level of members."

"Dealing with organizational growth issues. Willingness and actual adherence from members for change."

This is often linked to the ability of companies to stay the course and to engage in a truly strategic manner. GlobeScan Survey respondents spoke of:

"The short term perspective of many business leaders."

"Breaking through corporate boundaries."

"Fragmentation of CSR work into non-cooperating initiatives on the national and international level."

"CEO support and commitment."

"Transparency, anti-corruption, disclosure, review, innovation and other issues are challenges to be spread to businesses and value chains."

"Legislation which will make (companies) take the lowest common denominator approach."

"To make corporate responsibility fully integrated in the strategy, core business and governance of the company."

"Involve CEOs in taking the lead."

"To make the companies understand that CSR is not marketing."

"Recognition of the value possible through collaborative, multi-industry projects that address sustainable development challenges like water, energy, materials."

Although based on perceptions, we chose not to under-play this apparent gap between the ambitions of the coalitions to achieve more impact, and particularly to be able to operate at scale, and some stakeholders' views of their lack of capacity to do so. Instead we want to suggest how it can be closed. To be clear, a number of the coalition leaders also recognized the gap and that it will have to be closed if the coalitions, or at least those with the aspiration to change and grow, are to optimize their future impact. Another study by GlobeScan – this time with over 1,600 sustainability experts across the world on the state of sustainable development, produced with the consultancy SustainAbility and presented at business meetings around Rio + 20 – emphasized the leadership role of multi-sectoral collaborations and partnership, and, by implication, an opportunity for coalitions able to galvanize collective business inputs to such collaborations (see Fig. 14.1).[260] This will, however, require new approaches, new collaborations and new competencies for coalitions.

Figure 14.1 **Who should lead versus performance on sustainable development progress**

Source: GlobeScan and Sustainability

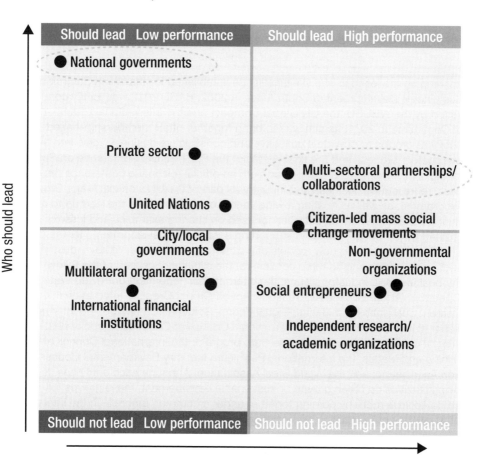

14.2 **The role of collaboration among the coalitions**

If there is a single word that summarizes the most frequent responses both from the experts panel and from the GlobeScan CEOs Survey, when both groups were asked about how corporate responsibility coalitions should operate in the future, it is "collaboration": collaboration with other national and international coalitions, with industry- and issue-specific coalitions, with multi-stakeholder initiatives, with business representative organizations, with organizations representing and helping SMEs, with NGOs, and with governments and international institutions. Yet there was also acknowledgment that collaboration is neither easy nor risk-free.

More collaboration among the major coalitions will occur if their boards and senior executive teams believe that there is added value from doing so. The ad hoc Business Action for Sustainable Development coalition built around the WBCSD, the UNGC and the International Chamber of Commerce and others for the Rio + 20 conference is one such example (see Box 14.1).[261]

Box 14.1 **Business Action for Sustainable Development (BASD) 2012**

Building on the lessons of a similar alliance established for the World Summit on Sustainable Development in South Africa in 2002, BASD 2012 was jointly convened by the WBCSD, the UN Global Compact and the International Chamber of Commerce in 2011. Its aim was to bring together other membership-based business groups to provide a collective and constructive business voice into the preparatory process and the final events of the Rio + 20 UN Conference on Sustainable Development. BASD played both an official role in the conference process, representing business and industry as part of the UN's official Major Groups Programme, as well as hosting a wide variety of side events in the lead up to and during the conference. Its activities focused on sharing examples and lessons learned by the private sector in supporting sustainable development over the past 20 years and exploring new models of partnership in a number of key industry sectors. In addition to its three conveners, the alliance consisted of the following business and industry groups: the International Federation of Private Water Operators (AquaFed); the Air Transport Action Group; CropLife International; the Cement Sustainability Initiative; Digital Energy Solutions Campaign; the International Aluminium Institute; the International Council of Chemical Associations, which coordinates the Responsible Care program; the International Council on Mining and Metals; the International Petroleum Industry Environmental Conservation Association; and the World Steel Association. Although each entity has its own initiatives on green growth or sustainable development, these groups felt they could achieve more by coming together under a common umbrella in the interests of accelerating and scaling up business impact.

It is possible to conceive of other opportunities for companies to collaborate around specific events or international negotiations, such as the Conference of Parties (COP) to the UN Framework Convention on Climate Change to establish a post-Kyoto Protocol for tackling climate change, and efforts to support the UN in defining the next stage of global development goals after the focus on the Millennium Development Goals ends in 2015. In September 2012, UN Secretary-General Ban Ki-moon established a High-Level Panel to advise him on the post-2015 global development agenda, co-chaired by President Yudhoyono of Indonesia, President Johnson Sirleaf of Liberia, and the Prime Minister of the UK, David Cameron. Unusually for a high-level UN panel, the group also includes Paul Polman, the CEO of Unilever, and Betty Mania, CEO of Kenya's Association of Manufacturers, to provide a direct business perspective to the panel's deliberations and proposals. Some of the other tasks identified in the "Agenda for Action" in the previous section also lend themselves to collaborative action by several coalitions: for example, to influence management education reform or to help shape new thinking and practice around sustainable consumption.

Another area that shows high potential for greater collaboration and coordination is between accountability and compliance mechanisms that have been established within specific industry sectors and as multi-stakeholder initiatives to ensure greater corporate respect for human rights and improved working conditions along global supply chains. Initiatives such as Business Social Compliance International, the Fair Labor Association, the International Council of Toy Industries ICTI CARE Process, Worldwide Accredited Responsible Production (WRAP), SA8000, the Electronic Industry Citizenship Coalition, the Responsible Jewellery Council, and a growing variety of agricultural, mining, fishery and forestry commodity initiatives, to name a few, all aim towards a common goal of improving the working conditions and livelihoods of people working in these industries. Yet they all have their own specific codes, monitoring, auditing and capacity-building programs and activities. For the manufacturers, factories and farms trying to comply, this can often be a costly, time-consuming and even confusing process, especially in countries where national regulation and governance is weak.

Over the past decade there have been a growing number of efforts to ensure greater coordination and shared learning between some of these corporate responsibility coalitions and multi-stakeholder initiatives. There is an opportunity to take this collaborative action further. International intergovernmental organizations such as the International Labour Organization and the OECD, along with donor agencies and some of the global business-led coalitions, (such as BSR) and organizations like the UN Global Compact have already played a valuable role in providing platforms for dialogue on this challenge and also supporting joint capacity-building activities.

Another development, which offers great potential, has been for different accountability coalitions to cross-recognize each others' standards and processes.

One recent example has been in the area of conflict minerals, where both BSR and the UNGC have played a leadership role for some years, alongside some of industry- and issue-specific coalitions. In September 2012, for example, an announcement was made by the Responsible Jewellery Council, the London Bullion Market Association, the Electronic

Industry Citizenship Coalition and the Global e-Sustainability Initiative to cross-recognize three different auditing and compliance programs they had separately developed to tackle the challenge of gold mining and refining being a potential cause of conflict and human rights abuses in developing countries. The three initiatives have also publicly recognized a new standard developed by the World Gold Council in 2012, which also aims to prevent armed conflict and associated human rights abuses. All of these voluntary business-led coalitions (which together account for most of the major miners, refiners and retailers in the industry) are working closely with the OECD, donor agencies, NGOs and governments in developing countries to tackle this complex challenge, while at the same time exploring ways to address the needs of small-scale and artisanal miners (estimated to number at least 30 million) so that they do not lose their livelihoods.

Indeed, each of the potential additional tasks for coalitions outlined in Chapter 13 lends itself to collaboration among a number of the coalitions. For national coalitions, increasing collaboration will depend on their ability, and that of their respective "umbrellas" such as Forum Empresa, the WBCSD, CSR360 Global Partner Network and CSR Europe, to make a case to external funders for more common services and joint initiatives.

To enhance collaboration between national coalitions and industry- and issue-specific coalitions, coalitions need practical evidence of just how such collaborations could add value to both parties, as BSR and the WBCSD have demonstrated with their industry-focused initiatives.

In contrast, for smaller national coalitions with fewer resources, is there an option to become part of an international alliance that provides thought leadership, best-practice guidance and a menu of potential programs from which individual coalitions, based on their experience and understanding of their country's needs and possibilities, can decide which elements to "franchise"? Analogies might be international airline alliances such as One World, SkyTeam or the Star Alliance, or the joint marketing groups of independent hotels that band together loosely to compete more cost effectively with the big chains. One example of such an alliance is Business Action for Sustainable Development 2012, profiled briefly above (Box 14.1).

Pursuing the analogy of the "back-room" services for the international airline alliance and boutique hotels group, some better-resourced coalitions could potentially offer thought leadership and training for national coalitions staff in how to develop and deploy cross-sector brokers and partnerships and how to operate as credible and well-qualified account managers to work in depth with senior-level executives in companies. They could help emerging coalitions to build a basic coalition "package" in societies where governance is weak, and work with business, governments, civil society and business representative organizations in-country to tailor market-friendly and culturally appropriate support for those countries' own efforts to promote responsible and civically engaged business.

To do this properly would be resource-intensive and put a considerable strain on even the longer-established and better-resourced of the corporate responsibility coalitions. While a certain amount of ad hoc activity in several of the categories above is already taking place, in some cases informally and in some instances more formally (notably CSR Europe, Forum Empresa, the WBCSD), it will always be constrained – and probably not a high priority for many of the coalitions on their own. In order to optimize a global sharing of expertise among business-led corporate responsibility coalitions, a number of preconditions will need to be met:

- Recognition that there are legitimate competitive pressures between the leading corporate responsibility coalitions

- Net extra resources found to fund this capacity-building

- The creation of an accepted global "convening" vehicle for collaboration – whether this is an individual or an institution with sufficient convening power

- Serious discourse between the main existing players about the purposes and required *quid pro quos* of any capacity-building

- Agreement among participating coalitions about "the rules of the game" – criteria for involvement, responsibilities of all participants, etc.

- Skill in the local coalitions to be the "transformer": able to assess different corporate responsibility programs and tools from around the world and work out which would be most relevant in their own countries (with or without adaptation to local circumstances)[262]

- Ability to harness Web 2.0 and its manifestations such as social networking, webcasts, member-only online discussion forums and resource libraries, which can help coalition-building to leap-frog existing barriers to cooperation such as distances, costs and difficulties of regular international travel, and other barriers to developing corporate responsibility coalitions across cultures and across stages of market development

- In turn, this should lead to some standardization of practice globally among corporate responsibility coalitions, not by fiat but by following, particularly because global businesses cannot afford to repeat their involvement in capacity-building of corporate responsibility coalitions from scratch in each national market

Alternatively, some of the smaller national coalitions may choose to expand their multi-stakeholder links and perhaps transform into a multi-stakeholder initiative or become a specialized division of a well-established and progressive business representative organization – for example, as Vietnam Business Links has done (previously independent, it is now part of the Chamber of Commerce). Another approach would be to develop more industry- or issue-specific competences, perhaps by developing a close link to a sector- or issue-specific international coalition.

14.3 **Fit for the future**

A key message is that coalitions need to review and, if necessary, renew their purpose and strategy as a number of those included in the Profiles section of this book (e.g., BSR, BITC, CSR Europe, Instituto Ethos and the NBI), have done in the past few years. A good example of this renewal process is Maala–Business for Social Responsibility in Israel. A wave of social protests against business in 2010 led to an intense debate with member companies that has resulted in the reframing of its mission to promote business with social purpose and taking it to a broader canvas to help promote sustainable development internationally.

Apart from a crisis such as Israel's social protests, how might other coalitions initiate such a reframing? One analogy might be found in the business school world where teams of deans and immediate past deans of business schools visit another school. In their case, the visit is to accredit or re-accredit the business school on behalf of one of the three internationally recognized accreditation bodies. For coalitions, it does not need to be for accreditation, just a willingness on the part of some coalition leaders to devote some time to examine the strategy of another coalition and to give constructive feedback.

A number of coalitions over the years have managed to persuade one of their consulting member companies to undertake a strategic review for them. Where that possibility is either not available or not considered appropriate, a coalition board and senior management team might do the job themselves with some external facilitation or with help from some strategists from non-consultancy member companies or business school students. Whatever the mechanism, the key is to be willing to ask searching questions and then to reframe.

We propose a "Fit for the Future" diagnostic audit that would provide these searching questions (see Box 14.2).

Box 14.2 'Fit for the Future' diagnostic

1. **Organizational purpose.** Is the aim to promote responsible business or a particular aspect, e.g., business action on climate change? To organize collective business action for commercial *and* social benefit? Is the organizational purpose fit for the future?

2. **Governance.** Is the board predominantly CEO-level or corporate responsibility/sustainability practitioner-level? Is the board setting strategy and holding the executive to account for effective implementation of the strategy? Are critical relationships – chair and CEO, chair and board, among the board collectively, and between the board and senior management team – working well? Is overall governance fit for the future?

3. **Strategy and operating plan: quality and range of activities.** Is the coalition a campaigner or deliverer – or both (and if both, in what proportions)? Is the focus on encouraging individual companies to behave better or a collective business action model, mobilizing business to tackle pressing societal problems – or some mix of the two? Are there distinctive niches that a critical mass of companies will pay for and use, and which the organization is capable of delivering to sufficient quality? Does the internal allocation of resources reflect the strategic priorities? Is the strategy and operating plan fit for the future?

4. **Business model and financing.** What proportion of the budget comes from membership fees, sponsorship, consultancy fees and charges for services, and public and charitable grants? Is the current funding model sustainable? If not, what is the transition strategy, over what time-horizon and is it attainable? Going forward, is the organization capable of providing specialized in-house expertise to member companies? Or is it a clearing-house to signpost to external expertise? If the latter, on what basis will members continue to pay for the coalition? Will the coalition remain business-only or evolve into a multi-stakeholder forum? Are the business model and finances fit for the future?

→

5. **Senior management team and staff.** Does the coalition have employees with the skills, competences, breadth of experience and expertise to deliver the strategy? Is there a robust succession-planning and continuous professional development? Are these fit for the future?

6. **Membership and standards.** What is the range and number of companies, seniority of main contacts, breadth and depth of engagement with members, robustness of account-management system? Does the coalition aspire to be operating at CEO or corporate responsibility professional level in terms of main contact with member companies? What is the quality of knowledge-management systems? Quality of new business development? Membership and services? Ability to spot new needs and issues? Does the coalition already have, or wish to establish, any minimum standards of business behavior required in order to join/stay in membership? And if such membership standards are established, how will they be policed and what sanctions will there be for non-conformers? Is the organization sufficiently independent politically and financially to contemplate expelling or rejecting non-performers? Are membership and membership requirements and servicing fit for the future?

7. **Communications and stakeholder engagement.** Internal and external. What is the core philosophy or "house style" of the organization: to inspire, to bludgeon or to cajole corporates? In other words, what is the tone of voice with which it speaks to its member companies and the business community generally? In future, how will the coalition generate what venture capitalists call the "deal-flow" of good-practice examples with which to inspire and advise member companies? Through awards, research (its own or by accessing that of others?), benchmarking indexes, best practice visits, etc.? Are these fit for the future?

8. **Authenticity.** Does the coalition "walk the talk" when it comes to its own sustainability and reporting practices? Does it have goals and practices to improve its own environmental and social performance? How transparent is it about its sources of funding, annual budgets and results? How are employees engaged and consulted on major strategic developments? Are the coalition's own sustainability and reporting practices fit for the future?

9. **Impact measurement and new business development**. How does the coalition assess and benchmark its impact? What are the key performance indicators? Who determines these and are all staff focused on them? How are performance metrics used to assess progress against the coalition's strategy, to support "course corrections" when needed, and to communicate the coalition's value proposition to its member companies? Are these metrics fit for the future?

10. **Thought leadership.** Does the coalition aspire to thought leadership on business in society, responsible business and sustainability issues? Or will it rely on others to fulfill that role? And for either option, how will it do so? Is the capacity for thought leadership fit for the future?

14.4 **Possible futures for individual business-led corporate responsibility coalitions**

Looking ahead, and depending on their ability to collaborate and make themselves fit for the future, there are five broad scenarios for the future for individual business-led corporate responsibility coalitions:

- **Scenario 1: Consolidation/absorption.** Particular coalitions merge, integrate with business representative organizations or with a global coalition, or metamorphose into becoming the national representative for one or more of the global standard-setters and effectively become a multi-stakeholder body

- **Scenario 2: Becoming a niche player.** The coalition effectively becomes a boutique consultancy focused on certain issues or sectors

- **Scenario 3: Closure.** The coalition closes, either "forced" because of lack of financial resources to continue or "voluntarily" because the board and members conclude that the job of the coalition has been achieved

- **Scenario 4: Maintaining the status quo.** The coalition retains enough critical mass to continue as an independent business-led corporate responsibility coalition

- **Scenario 5: Transformational change.** A critical mass of coalitions and their stakeholders – business, governments, international institutions, civil society, multi-stakeholder initiatives – work to develop their capacity to achieve transformational change, as outlined in Chapter 13

The coalition leaders responding to the GlobeScan Survey are bullish! Asked to say which scenario was most likely for their coalition in ten years' time (Appendix 3, Question 6F), 85% thought their coalition would have evolved into something bigger with other partners, while 8% thought there would be little or no change and only 4% thought their coalition would have ceased to operate because its job will be done (4% were don't knows).

Which scenario becomes the reality for a particular coalition will depend on its track record, current resources (human and financial), social capital, quality and connectivity of leadership, perceived ongoing need in that society for the coalition's services, scale of ambition, and future organizational capacity. The future scenario will also depend on the decisions of the coalitions themselves and their stakeholders. Some of the interviewees for this book have asked if there are too many coalitions. With all the specialist initiatives now operating, this may be the case for the leading global companies. There remains, however, a significant number of the 80,000 multinational companies still to engage, let alone vast numbers of national firms, family-owned businesses and small and medium enterprises.

15
Recommendations and conclusion

Our initial motivation in writing this book was to look back over four decades to capture some of the experiences and knowledge of a generation of remarkable individuals and institutions that have helped to build the corporate responsibility and sustainability movement through collective business leadership. We had played an active part in this process ourselves and we knew at the outset that each business-led corporate responsibility coalition that we planned to review not only had a rich and varied history, but also an ongoing strategy and range of activities. We soon realized that an equally important part of our story was looking to the future to explore how these business-led coalitions will remain relevant and vibrant in increasingly complex and challenging circumstances.

As we have outlined in Chapter 12, we believe that the need for collective business action and more large-scale systemic collaboration between business, government and civil society is more urgent now than ever. The system of market-based capitalism within a framework of good governance and an active civil society has been one of the greatest inventions of humankind. It has served to lift hundreds of millions of people out of poverty around the globe. Even in China, where state-ownership and government controls still dominate, more market-based approaches to production, consumption and wealth creation have improved the quality of life for millions of people over a relatively short period of time. Yet capitalism has come at growing cost to the natural ecosystem that sustains life. Equally, after decades of being a driving force in creating more equal opportunity based on merit and in building a middle class in numerous nations, some of the more unbridled "free-market" approaches of capitalism in recent years have started to undermine the very social benefits and economic gains that the system has created.

We both believe passionately that capitalism and economic growth remain more essential than ever for creating opportunity, alleviating poverty and addressing the environmental challenges that the world faces. It is clear, however, that the *quality* of capitalism and economic growth needs to change. As we have argued throughout this book, capitalism and economic growth need to become even more inclusive of lower-income producers, workers and consumers. They need to become even more responsible in terms of ethics, transparency, good governance, anti-corruption and accountability for respecting human rights, labor rights and the environment. And they need to become even greener or smarter in terms of innovation and the development of new technologies, products, services and business models that are able to produce more or better products and services for larger numbers of people with fewer natural resources and less waste. In short, we need economic growth that is inclusive, responsible and green. As our colleagues at the WBCSD have argued so succinctly in their *Vision 2050*, one of the central leadership challenges of our time is to build "a pathway to a world in which 9 billion people live well, within the limits of one planet by mid-century. This presents the biggest economic opportunity ever. However not one that can be achieved under current mainstream business, consumption and policy conditions."[263] As we have outlined in the book, their vision is shared by other business-led corporate responsibility coalitions – BSR, CSR Europe, IBLF, Instituto Ethos, BITC, NBI and others – all of which have developed similar frameworks over the past few years to explicitly promote more inclusive, responsible and green growth.

We also passionately believe that the private sector and the power of private enterprise and innovation is one of the main hopes for achieving this vision, albeit within the context of more effective government leadership and public policies. And we believe that business-led corporate responsibility coalitions have a central leadership role to play in driving collective business action and in providing platforms for companies to collaborate more with governments and civil-society organizations. Our view is that both the generalist coalitions, on which we have focused primarily in this book, and the more industry- and issue-specific coalitions that are becoming increasingly common have differing but important roles to play. If this potential is to be met over the next few critical decades, it will be essential for individual corporate champions and companies to work together with the leaders of the coalitions, and with relevant leaders in governments; intergovernmental agencies, such as the United Nations, the European Commission, the World Bank and regional development banks; in philanthropic grant-making foundations; and in think-tanks, business schools and universities to develop the capacity of corporate responsibility coalitions across the world so that they can consistently embed and scale more responsible and sustainable business practices.

In Table 15.1 we provide our recommendations for each of these groups of actors on how they can help to increase the scale and impact of business-led corporate responsibility coalitions.

Table 15.1 **Recommendations for key stakeholders to increase the scale and impact of corporate responsibility coalitions**

Stakeholder	Recommendations
Individual business champions	• Corporate CEOs and chairs can be vital spokespeople for the role of collective business action and corporate responsibility coalitions and can play an important governance and leadership role in selected coalitions most relevant to their company and industry sector. Among other things, they should challenge the coalitions to be as ambitious as possible in embedding and scaling responsible business practices, not simply "exercises in 'ticking the box' " • Senior sustainability and corporate citizenship executives should play an active leadership role in key coalitions most relevant to their company and industry sector • Chairs and CEOs should keep their senior executive teams and their boards of directors informed about the work of the business-led corporate responsibility coalitions in which they are involved
Individual companies	• Companies should incentivize the coalitions they are involved with to collaborate with others – using a mixture of carrot and stick incentives • They should provide contact details of all relevant company representatives who are active in different coalitions and encourage the exchange of ideas and information among them • They can offer their future leaders the potential to participate in training programs, experiential learning, and other platforms offered by corporate responsibility coalitions and encourage the coalitions they are working with to establish such leadership development programs and internships with coalition leaders for young corporate managers on fast-track programs
Governments	• Governments should encourage the creation of national-level business-led corporate responsibility coalitions where these do not exist – either dedicated coalitions or the establishment of corporate responsibility or sustainability units within national and local chambers of commerce and industry and trade associations • Governments should invite leaders of corporate responsibility coalitions to participate in relevant policy dialogues and the co-creation of national green growth and sustainable development plans and public policies (while making clear they expect corporate representatives to be sustainability leaders rather than companies seeking access to influence governments) • Presidents and prime ministers can establish a business advisory group to inform and engage with senior officials on corporate responsibility and sustainability issues • Government ministers can create incentives for responsible business practices by partnering with business-led coalitions to support award programs, joint financing mechanisms and other platforms to identify and spread best practices; and by including genuine and stringent sustainability criteria in public procurement requirements

Stakeholder	Recommendations
Intergovern-mental insti-tutions and development agencies	• Organizations such as the UN, World Bank, regional development banks and bilateral development agencies can provide valuable funds and political support for the creation, funding and capacity-building of business-led corporate responsibility coalitions in developing countries. Their role can be especially valuable in fragile states and countries with weak governance and public institutions or with small or less-developed private sectors • They can help to build the capacity of national and local governments to work more effectively with companies and with business-led coalitions in achieving national development and green growth goals • They can commission best-practice studies and fund capacity-building and exchanges among the coalitions within the same region, industry sectors and issue areas and globally • They can push coalitions to be more rigorous in challenging their member companies to perform and set criteria or principles for only working with companies that publicly report on their corporate responsibility or sustainability performance • They can work with coalitions to develop and fund independent indexes to track corporate performance, such as the Access to Medicines Index and national stock exchange sustainability indexes and they can support programs to improve national data collection on such performance and build the capacity of local media and NGOs to hold companies and business-led coalitions accountable
Grant-making philanthropic foundations	• Foundations can support many of the above activities in addition to other field-building, capacity-building, and information collection and dissemination activities • They can support enhanced capacity for faster codification and dissemination between the coalitions of effective corporate engagement mechanisms • They can fund opportunities for high-flyers from coalitions to have exchange programs with other coalitions to enhance skills and speed up dissemination of best practice • They can take a lead in sponsoring the development of rigorous metrics and impact-assessment methodology for assessing coalitions, and pilot studies to test and refine this methodology with volunteer coalitions
Think-tanks, universities and business schools	• Academic institutions and scholars have a role to play in supporting the spread, scale and impact of coalitions by undertaking research, supporting education and training, and informing policy and practice through evidence-based data and analysis • More academic institutions could establish dedicated research centers and courses and executive education programs (along the lines of some profiled in this book) focused on corporate responsibility and sustainability, in collaboration with coalitions or independently; and on supporting the learning and capacity-building of corporate responsibility coalitions themselves • At a national, local or industry level, they can develop memoranda of understanding with relevant coalitions, establishing access to their data and members in return for sharing research findings and outcomes • Policy think-tanks can also establish more dedicated research programs to inform government policy-makers of the role of business in supporting more inclusive, responsible and green growth and of the role of business-led coalitions in working with governments to achieve change at the scale and systemic level that is needed

Stakeholder	Recommendations
Well-established corporate responsibility coalitions	• The established coalitions have a key role to play in continuing to build the field for corporate responsibility and sustainability coalitions • They need to be more prepared to address two "elephants in the room": how to challenge and, if necessary, sanction the laggards in their membership; and how to address some of the most difficult corporate responsibility issues such as corporate tax policies, executive compensation, corporate lobbying and unethical behavior • They can use their well-established networks to support faster transfer of expertise in how to engage companies between coalitions in different countries, sectors and subject areas • They can experiment with new forms of collaboration with strategic and boutique consultancies and with social enterprises specializing in particular issues and aspects of corporate responsibility • They should consider "franchising" their most effective corporate engagement tools, perhaps with *pro bono* assistance from international franchise experts (academics and practitioners) • They can encourage their high-flyers to have exchange programs with other coalitions to enhance skills and speed up dissemination of best practice • They can promote board exposure programs to make it easier for board members of coalitions, when traveling internationally, to be "twinned" with board members of the host country to exchange ideas and experiences
Corporate responsibility coalitions generally	• Coalitions, especially new ones, should be open to sub-contracting to/from other coalitions • They should be rigorous and demanding on their member companies in terms of the obligations of membership and the sanctions for poor corporate responsibility • They can encourage faster take-up of standardized measurement and reporting metrics, e.g., the GHG Protocol, CECP's philanthropy measurements, integrated reporting standards etc. • They should periodically review their purpose, performance, projects, prospects and possibilities to determine future strategy and operational plans using the "fit for the future" audit outlined in Box 14.2. Good governance and effective management suggests this should be based on stakeholder wants and needs of the organization and the organization's wants and needs of stakeholders, and a determination of whether these marry sufficiently to ensure a viable and effective organization • They should apply rigorous social-impact measurement methodology and be transparent and accountable in their sources and uses of funds, the impacts they have achieved, and the challenges they have faced and lessons learned

If individual champions, companies and coalitions, and their key stakeholders, are able to succeed in the years ahead, we believe they will achieve even greater impact than in the previous 30 years in helping to meet the following challenges:

- **Raising awareness** of the societal need and the business case for responsible business practices and sustainability – within the business sector and beyond

- **Helping individual companies to embed responsible business practices and sustainability into their core business strategies**, operations, governance and accountability

- **Helping to scale responsible business practices and sustainability** by reaching more companies and geographies or by solving more issues than would have been addressed otherwise, through a combination of business-led voluntary actions and by enabling greater engagement of governments, investors, the media, educators and other stakeholders. Such an approach will be essential for having the type of systemic impact that is needed to overcome the governance gaps and the market failures that still undermine a more inclusive and sustainable future

If the coalitions are to realize this possible future, they will need to enhance their individual capacity to do so and their willingness and ability to work in collaboration with others. This will require leadership action from coalitions themselves as well as from their stakeholders.

15.1 **Conclusion**

Creating, building and sustaining business-led corporate responsibility coalitions are neither easy nor quick tasks to undertake. They take long-term commitment and persistence on the part of individual champions and companies. They require supportive governments, intergovernmental institutions, foundations and non-governmental and academic organizations. Above all, they need outstanding leadership from the men and women in the coalitions themselves; both the ability to envision and articulate a different future for capitalism and the role of business in society, and the ability to mobilize their staff, their member companies and their other partners to execute and deliver on this vision. This requires the ability to identify and track emerging trends and to adapt to constantly changing and often challenging circumstances. And above all, real success in leading corporate responsibility coalitions and their members requires the courage to question the status quo and the imagination to come up with new, but feasible, ideas and innovations for the way forward.

We are often asked by our students whether we are optimistic or pessimistic about the future of the planet and of humankind. Our shared view is captured well by the words of David Landes, Economics Professor Emeritus at Harvard:

> In this world, the optimists have it, not because they are always right but because they are positive. Even when wrong, they are positive, and that is the way of achievement, correction, improvement, and success. Educated, eyes-open optimism pays; pessimism can only offer the empty consolation of being

right. The one lesson that emerges is the need to keep trying. No miracles. No perfection. No millennium. No apocalypse. We must cultivate a skeptical faith, avoid dogma, listen and watch well, try to clarify and define ends, the better to chose means.[264]

The views of this respected economist and academic are echoed by those of respected environmentalist and activist Paul Hawken:

> When asked if I am pessimistic or optimistic about the future, my answer is always the same: If you look at the science about what is happening on earth and aren't pessimistic, you don't understand the data. But if you meet the people who are working to restore this earth and the lives of the poor, and you aren't optimistic, you haven't got a pulse. What I see everywhere in the world are ordinary people willing to confront despair, power, and incalculable odds in order to restore some semblance of grace, justice, and beauty to this world.[265]

We agree. We hope we have done justice to the remarkable vision and hard work of some of those "ordinary people": the hundreds of men and women around the world who have conceived, created and built the corporate responsibility coalitions profiled in this book. Some of them were already famous and successful business, civic or political leaders. A few of them have achieved a degree of international or national recognition through their work in the coalitions. Most of them have worked tirelessly and quietly without public recognition. We are proud and humbled to have worked with and known many of them.

In the face of injustice, inequality, social exclusion, environmental decline and the many other challenges impacting all parts of society, the people who built corporate responsibility coalitions chose to act. They used their reputation, their status, their influence, their skills, their relationships and their convening power to convince other business and civic leaders to come together and take practical action. They inspired collective action and they lit the fires, many of which have spread around the globe.

Today, the challenges to the planet and to humankind are more pressing than ever. Businesses alone cannot, and should not, attempt to solve them. At the same time, the private sector has a vital role to play and must harness its resources, capabilities, networks, influence and global reach to ensure that it is part of the solution. This requires many more companies to understand the business case for embedding responsible and sustainable business practices into their corporate strategy, governance and operations than are actually doing so in practice. It also demands collective action by companies, and it requires the business sector to advocate for and support progressive public-policy reforms to bring about the necessary policy changes to achieve more inclusive, responsible and green growth.

We believe that business-led corporate responsibility coalitions continue to have a vital role to play in helping to achieve this progress. Every coalition must lead and inspire its members and partners on an individual basis. At the same time, more than ever before coalitions need to look for opportunities to collaborate with their peers and with governments and civil-society organizations to achieve greater scale and systemic impact than has been possible to date. Only then can we be confident of a world where economic growth and capitalism both drive and are underpinned by social inclusion and environmental sustainability; a world where private enterprise and innovation are a source of solutions to complex challenges and where they create a solid foundation of opportunity and hope for the next generation.

PROFILES

The following section of the book provides in-depth profiles of ten of the most established and long-standing independent, business-led corporate responsibility coalitions (selected on the basis that all of them have been in existence for over a decade) and two *sui generis* organizations (the UN Global Compact and the World Economic Forum) that have also played a significant role in embedding and spreading responsible business practices and corporate sustainability around the globe over the past few decades. The 12 profiles are:

Profile 1: Business for Social Responsibility

Profile 2: Business in the Community

Profile 3: CSR Europe

Profile 4: Instituto Ethos

Profile 5: International Business Leaders Forum

Profile 6: Maala–Business for Social Responsibility

Profile 7: National Business Initiative for Growth, Development and Democracy

Profile 8: Philippine Business for Social Progress

Profile 9: World Business Council for Sustainable Development

Profile 10: World Environment Center

Profile 11: United Nations Global Compact

Profile 12: World Economic Forum

Profile 1
Business for Social Responsibility

David Grayson and Jane Nelson*

BSR in its own words

BSR works with its global network of nearly 300 member companies to build a just and sustainable world. From its offices in Asia, Europe, and North and South America, BSR develops sustainable business strategies and solutions through consulting, research, and cross-sector collaboration.

We see new possibilities. BSR shows companies how to create opportunities from global challenges, derive value from sustainability, and maintain competitive advantage while benefiting the world.

We keep good company. When your company joins BSR, you'll gain access to a powerful network of companies, as well as our other partners – all focused on creating viable sustainability solutions.

We take solutions to scale. BSR leads member companies in working groups and grant-supported initiatives that enable collective action, resulting in comprehensive, lasting solutions that make a global impact.

---

* This profile is based on interviews with Aron Cramer, background discussions with members of the BSR management team, and a discussion with staff from BSR's Beijing office who met David Grayson in Beijing (June 2012). It draws on BSR publications, notably its 2010 report to stakeholders, and an article by Mallen Baker published in the magazine *Ethical Corporation*: M. Baker, "Business for Social Responsibility: Concentrate on the Core," *Ethical Corporation*, December 2010. Our thanks to Toby Webb of Ethical Corporation and to Mallen Baker for permission to use material from this article.

We deliver results. For nearly two decades, BSR has been working in board-rooms, communities, and factories in more than 70 countries to achieve results that go beyond traditional business outcomes.

www.bsr.org   June 2012

Background context and history

The story of Business for Social Responsibility (BSR) has been one of constant reinvention, both responding to and influencing the evolving priorities of its membership and their oper-ating context.

BSR was founded in 1992 in Washington DC by, among others, Josh Mailman, Laury Hammel and Mal Warwick and originally focused on activist mid-sized companies such as Tom's of Maine, Patagonia and Ben & Jerry's, which sought to combine business with a social mission. It was essentially a lobby group for progressive policies and supported a number of local chapters.

Two years later, the board changed BSR's mission to provide resources to help companies to implement more responsible practices, and moved the headquarters to San Francisco, where they remain to this day. The agent for change at this point was Bob Dunn, who had argued against the organization's political lobbying role because he thought it would be a barrier to getting greater business involvement. He was appointed as chief executive in 1994, previously having been a vice president at Levi Strauss. His former company had been one of the corporate pioneers in recognizing the link between its core business operations and social and environmental issues, and in publicly addressing some of the most challenging of these issues such as workplace and civil rights, HIV/AIDS, and the need for voluntary codes of conduct to more responsibly manage global supply chains. Drawing on this experience, Dunn brought with him a corporate mind-set, credibility in tackling challenging corporate responsibility issues and a wealth of corporate contacts – as well as a broader perspective, from also having worked in government and the NGO world before coming to BSR.

Dunn had previously served briefly as co-chair of BSR (along with Arnold Hiatt of Stride Rite and Helen Mills, the first franchisee of The Body Shop in the USA). He initially turned down an invitation to take on the executive leadership after the previous director left BSR, having signed on to do public-policy work, not to focus on internal company operations and impacts. Dunn retold the story of how Arnold Hiatt persuaded him to change his mind, in *The Difference Makers*. Hiatt told him:

> ". . . just go back to San Francisco and write me a letter and say, 'You know, Arnold, I would really love to do this, and here's the set of problems for me that would have to be overcome.' " So I went back to San Francisco, wrote this letter and said, "I'm not willing to move to Washington and I wouldn't want to take this on and spend the whole year just trying to raise my own salary. There would have to be an assurance of pledges from board members, and it would be imperative for me that the organization would be an open organization and that we not set ourselves up to sit in judgment as to who's virtuous and who's not.

I'd rather just say we're going to make everyone more virtuous and not worry about it." I knew that was a very contentious thing in the organization. I wrote probably seven or eight things, and said that again I appreciated the offer and I was sorry that it would not work . . . I think two days later Arnold called and said, 'You know, Bob, I have wonderful news for you. The board's been talking and we've agreed to all of your conditions.' "[266]

Some of the smaller companies were opposed to the influx of the big corporations as members, whose presence they saw as betraying the values of the original concept. The shift in strategic focus was confirmed when BSR later moved to shut down its local chapters in favor of focusing on developing relationships with the big companies. One of the founders, Laury Hammel, went on to create the Business Alliance for Local Living Economies as an alternative.

Under Bob Dunn, BSR quickly grew to become a serious force as a network of major corporations committed to social responsibility. Its reputation as an influential thought leader and convenor has developed further under the leadership of Aron Cramer since 2004. As BSR marks its 20th anniversary in 2012, it can point to having played an increasingly pivotal leadership role in influencing the global corporate responsibility movement. In the 2012 GlobeScan survey of over 50 corporate responsibility coalitions around the globe, other coalition directors cited BSR, along with the World Business Council for Sustainable Development (WBCSD), as the two corporate responsibility coalitions that they looked to most often for learning and benchmarking purposes.[267]

Key activities and phases of development

The following summarizes some of the key activities and roles that BSR has played over the past two decades as it has evolved from a small U.S.-focused organization to establishing a global presence. Over this period it has developed an increasingly strategic approach to raising awareness about corporate responsibility as a material driver of corporate risks and competitiveness, to advising companies on how to embed responsible business practices into their core business operations, and to convening collective business action and multi-stakeholder platforms to address complex global challenges that no one company can address on their own.

Popularizing and legitimizing corporate responsibility

In its initial years BSR focused mainly on "making the case" for responsible business practices and introducing its member companies to key evolving issues such as global supply-chain management and human rights.

Almost from the outset, starting in 1993, it used an annual conference to serve as its foundational platform for raising awareness, making the case, highlighting new issues and trends, and sharing good practices in corporate responsibility. As the keynote speaker for its inaugural conference, BSR was able to attract no less a luminary than the newly elected President Clinton, and used this example to attract influential corporate CEOs, political and civic leaders, and socially active celebrities as keynote speakers at all its subsequent annual conferences. Over the past two decades the BSR Conference has become a key event on the United States and, increasingly, the global corporate responsibility calendar, and today it attracts over 1,000 participants from around the world.

Alongside its annual conference, BSR also started to raise awareness of specific corporate responsibility challenges that U.S.-based companies were facing in the mid-1990s as their operations and supply chains became more global and complex. It established one of the most useful web-based information platforms that identified key corporate responsibility issues, explained why they were important for business to address, provided action steps for what companies could to in practice, and shared brief examples of other corporate good practices for that specific issue. The aim was to help corporate responsibility professionals to access both information and effective arguments to make the case for corporate responsibility within their own companies.

At the same time, BSR started to develop a few targeted programs to help companies manage corporate responsibility issues along their global supply chains. In 1995, for example, a decision was made to establish a human rights and business program. Bob Dunn hired Aron Cramer, a lawyer by training, to lead this new program. Working from the United States and then from Europe, Cramer established a reputation as a good strategic thinker with a global world-view and as someone who was respected and trusted by both the corporate and the non-governmental organization (NGO) community. Together with other equally experienced and internationally minded colleagues, such as Mark Lee, who went on to serve as CEO of the consultancy SustainAbility, the BSR executive team recognized the need to move beyond providing useful information and case studies on key corporate responsibility issues to more proactively advising companies on how to mainstream corporate responsibility into their core business operations and how to engage effectively with increasingly vocal NGOs.

BSR continues to raise awareness and provide thought leadership. Its 2011 conference, for example, was built around the theme of "Redefining Leadership," which was also the title for its annual report to stakeholders for 2010 activities. Through a range of personal reflections, leaders' insights and studies, it sought to explore what leadership for sustainability means. Much of this is presented through BSR's extensive social media presence, connecting its Facebook, YouTube, LinkedIn, Twitter, blog and website activities. Arguably, BSR has become the coalition most adept and "joined up" in its use of social media.

While the organization continues to raise awareness on current and evolving corporate responsibility issues through its annual conference, research program, website and increasingly effective social media platform, it has also developed a substantial program of hands-on advisory and consulting services for member companies.

Advising companies on how to embed corporate responsibility along global supply chains

The growth in activism by NGOs and media campaigns against multinational companies from the mid-1990s, and the high profile anti-globalization protests around the World Trade Organization negotiations in Seattle in late 1999, provided an important impetus to BSR's growing focus on corporate responsibility issues along global supply chains. As globalization became a flash-point for many critics of business, the organization found itself starting to directly advise member companies on the complexities of social risk management in the global economy, as well as on corporate responsibility in terms of being ethical and the "right thing to do." During this phase, according to Aron Cramer, BSR started to mature and itself become more global. The organization undertook a number of pioneering and challenging corporate engagements around the globe:

- BSR was one of the first business-led coalitions to bring in NGOs to help member companies monitor labor conditions, when it facilitated cooperation between the clothing retailer Gap and the Interfaith Center for Corporate Responsibility (ICCR) and other NGOs to monitor labor conditions in Guatemala and subsequently other countries in South and Central America

- BSR was also one of the first to run significant corporate training programs for businesses with a presence in China, with a strong focus on improving working conditions in apparel factories and other light manufacturing plants. At a time when many NGOs and activists were calling on multinational companies to stop operating in China, BSR took a more pragmatic approach, looking at ways to help companies improve local working conditions while at the same time creating local jobs and benefiting from lower labor costs. This period marked the beginning of what is now a substantial consulting, auditing and capacity-building "ecosystem" to improve working conditions not only in China, but also in many other emerging economies. Cramer reminisces: "It was so long ago that we were using overhead transparencies not PowerPoint!"

- BSR was also one of the interlocutors for Shell as it struggled to make sense of the high-profile corporate responsibility and subsequent reputation crises it had endured in 1995. The first was over Brent Spar, when an attempt by Shell to dispose of a redundant North Sea Oil installation by deep-sea sinking caused international uproar after a dramatic and effective media campaign was carried out by Greenpeace against the disposal. The second crisis resulted from Shell's operations in Nigeria and accusations of the company's complicity in the executions of Ken Saro-Wiwa and seven other Ogoni community leaders who were protesting against Shell's activities in their region. The company recognized the need to implement more rigorous and credible human rights and environmental standards throughout its global operations and to engage more effectively with its NGO stakeholders. It started to work more strategically with BSR, the IBLF, the WBCSD and other corporate responsibility coalitions and consultants to develop a new sustainability strategy

- BSR also helped Ford Motor Company with a major stakeholder-engagement dialogue around the Millennium, which helped to shape the company's growing commitment to sustainability, not only through its products but also as an active participant in wider debates on sustainable mobility

From 2002 to the collapse of Lehman Brothers and the start of the global financial crisis in 2008, BSR was focused on widespread mainstreaming of corporate responsibility as it helped companies to conduct stakeholder dialogues, map their most material environmental, social and economic impacts, and produce corporate responsibility and sustainability reports. As Aron Cramer recalls, "Companies were not asking so much about 'what is corporate responsibility?' or 'why corporate responsibility?' but much more 'how do we manage corporate responsibility effectively?' " During this era, BSR grew significantly, became more global and provided much more direct assistance to member companies through consultancy, on top of the more traditional membership services and research collaborations.

This was a conscious and strategic decision by the BSR board and executive leadership. In late 2002, Bob Dunn had told the board that he planned to step down as CEO in 2004. Rather immediately moving to recruit a new CEO, the board, still chaired by Arnold Hiatt, decided first to review the organization's strategy and then, in the light of that review, recruit someone suited to implement the chosen strategy. This led to an intense year-long strategy review, culminating at the end of 2003 with a decision to become more global and to maintain the membership base, but also to develop more one-to-one consultancy with companies The mantle was handed to Aron Cramer, and his leadership has helped to reinforce the evolution of BSR towards being an organization that achieves significant impact as well as income through consultancy. He is also directly engaged in the content of the issues, and has become an active thought leader in the corporate responsibility field. He is, for example, a member of the global advisory group helping the UK-headquartered retailer Marks & Spencer to identify what they have to do in order to become the world's most sustainable major retailer by 2015, and a member of Barrick Gold's external sustainability advisory group.

Today, BSR offers an extensive range of operational and strategy services to help companies embed responsible business practices. These include help to embed sustainability into core strategy, advice on appropriate governance structures, reviewing supply-chain risks and opportunities, as well as helping companies to develop and implement supply-chain sustainability strategies, stakeholder-engagement services, environmental improvements in areas like water, energy, or biodiversity; and more effective and credible reporting and communications materials. BSR also provides specialist help for companies on implementing climate change and human rights policies and management systems. In order to meet the increasingly specific and sophisticated needs of large corporations, BSR has not only recruited more staff with consulting skills and with specific industry and issue experience, but also organized itself more along industry specialist teams.

Achieving scale through industry groups and collaborative platforms

BSR increasingly recognized that working with individual companies to improve their global supply-chain management and stakeholder engagement strategies was a necessary but not sufficient step in achieving its mission to work with member companies to "build a just and sustainable world." Alongside its ongoing efforts to raise awareness and make the business case for corporate responsibility, and its advisory support to individual companies, the organization started to focus increased attention on facilitating collective action. Over the past decade in particular, it has built an impressive array of industry- or issue-specific working groups and multi-stakeholder partnership platforms.

BSR leads or participates in a range of about 16 working groups. These are essentially precompetitive forums where competing companies in the same industry can come together, often with other key stakeholders, to work jointly on identifying challenging and complex issues that no one company can resolve on its own and co-creating leading-edge and industry-wide solutions to addressing this issue or set of issues. Two diverse examples of these working groups are as follows:

- **Ecosystem Services.** Leading companies are recognizing the need to address environmental issues not only on a discrete issue-by-issue basis, but also in a manner that allows for a more integrated approach that looks at the entire ecosystem of environmental services. Whether it is exploring ways to effectively manage the risks and opportunities of the water–food–energy nexus, or developing comprehensive biodiversity strategies, most companies are realizing the benefits of working with each other, including competitors. A growing interest in "natural capital accounting" is also driving the need for companies to collaborate on developing principles, guidelines, metrics, standards and reporting requirements. This working group enables participating companies to keep up with and influence the evolving debate, corporate practices and policy implications of ecosystem services. Members range from major extractive companies such as ExxonMobil, BP, Chevron and Shell to the Dow Chemical Company and Walt Disney.

- **Beyond Monitoring.** This working group was convened between 2006 and 2011 to help companies define and develop tools for supply-chain management that goes beyond basic code compliance, monitoring and auditing to developing more holistic solutions for high-performance, high-quality supply chains that improve commercial performance as a result of improving social and environment performance. Achieving this requires greater internal alignment between the incentives and practices of a company's supply-chain managers and auditors and their buyers, marketing and product designers. It also requires programs that support worker empowerment at the factory level and in many cases public-policy reforms and incentives. Building on its 15 years of experience on advising individual companies on how to embed responsible business practices in their global supply chains, BSR convened a working group of companies from diverse sectors and geographies to define what this next-generation of approach would entail in practice. The working group consisted of AP Møller-Maersk, Burberry, Dell, Electrolux, Ford Motor Company, Gap, H&M Hennes & Mauritz, Hallmark Cards, Li & Fung, Marks & Spencer, Nordstrom, Novo Nordisk, Starbucks Coffee Company and the Varner Group. The group developed a set of guidelines and best practices around four main areas of action: internal alignment, supplier ownership, empowering workers, and public-policy frameworks. In addition to being publicly available via BSR's websites, the lessons learned from the working group are also informing the evolving supply-chain management practices of its participating companies and BSR's own advisory services to other companies.

In addition to these working groups, BSR has also convened other groups focused on improving global supply-chain management in specific sectors, such as the Pharmaceutical Supply Chain Initiative (which convenes over 10 of the world's leading pharmaceutical companies), the Clean Cargo Initiative, and the Better Coal Initiative, to name a few of its 14 working groups

Another way that BSR is trying to help its members achieve greater scale and systemic impact is through building a set of grant-funded multi-sector partnership platforms that aim to address particularly complex issues that the private sector – even working collectively in industry groups – cannot solve alone. Two diverse examples of such partnership programs, which BSR has developed with grant funding from philanthropic foundations and bilateral government development agencies, are:

- **HERproject**. This is a factory-based women's health education project. The factories in global supply chains employ millions of people, many of them young women, and they provide a valuable platform for reaching and serving these factory workers. There is an opportunity to move beyond efforts to protect human rights and improve labor standards in factories (i.e., avoid the risk of running "sweatshops") to proactively empower factory workers and deliver a range of services that will directly enhance not only their working conditions but potentially also their quality of life more broadly. Such efforts often require companies to work with partners who have skills in areas that the company may lack, such as education, health and financial literacy, and who can bring additional technical or financial resources to share the costs of running these more inclusive business models and worker-empowerment programs. The HERproject is an example of such a collaborative approach. It was originally established by BSR in 2007 in China and has had ongoing grant-funded support from the Levi Strauss Foundation and the Swedish International Development Cooperation Agency. The project brings together multinational companies and their local factories with local NGOs to create workplace programs that explicitly and proactively increase women's health awareness. Working with its network of partners, BSR also seeks to demonstrate the return on investment for factory-based women's health programs, making a "business case" for moving beyond compliance. In addition to its growth in China, the HERproject is now also active in Bangladesh, Egypt, Kenya, India, Indonesia, Pakistan and Vietnam.

- **Conflict minerals.** Another complex, challenging and often controversial issue that no single company, or even the metals and mining sector and its major customers can address alone, is the issue of so-called "conflict minerals." These are minerals that are mined in failed states or zones of conflict or very weak governance, where their extraction often supports armed groups and leads directly or indirectly to dangerous working conditions and, in many cases, human rights abuses. Numerous activist campaigns have been aimed at stopping the trade in these minerals. And yet they often represent vital livelihood opportunities to some of the world's poorest communities. The challenge is to find ways for governments, NGOs, producers and major customers for such minerals to work together in order to mitigate these risks as much as possible, while at the same time trying to create decent work and economic opportunities for the low-income producers along these supply chains. The challenge has been further complicated in recent years by the passing of the Dodd-Frank Bill in the United States, which focused primarily on financial-sector reform following the 2008 financial crisis, but has also made requirements for the U.S.-based users of certain minerals that are mined in the Democratic Republic of the Congo, such as tungsten, tantalum, tin and gold, to provide evidence that they are not using "conflict minerals." This requirement has challenging implications for supply-chain management, stakeholder engagement and reporting for companies that sell or use these minerals, especially in the electronics and automotive sectors. BSR is working with a group of these companies and with industry groups, NGOs, investors and the U.S. State Department to help companies better understand and address the risks involved and to take practical steps in integrating risk-management efforts into their broader supply-chain programs.

Building a global network and local presence

BSR has long aspired to be global in reach and scope, rather than limited to the United States. Although its membership base remains predominantly comprised of a majority of American corporations, the organization's board and employees are increasingly globally diversified, as are its operations. Its globalization strategy has been built through a combination of, first, supporting the development of and partnering with other corporate responsibility coalitions, and, second, building BSR's own global on-the-ground presence by establishing local offices and undertaking local consulting projects and collaborative programs in key geographies of operation.

BSR'S "partnership network" approach to growing its global presence was spearheaded in 1997 by its active engagement as one of the founding members of Forum Empresa, which is aimed at helping to spread awareness and practice of corporate responsibility throughout Latin America. BSR also played an influential role in helping with the establishment and strategic focus of Maala in Israel and provided guidance and input to other emergent national corporate responsibility coalitions. This global field-building role is described in Part I (Section 3.2). Details of Forum Empresa's activities can also be found in Part II (Box 10.2, page 131).

Another way in which BSR has globalized its influence and impact has been through undertaking joint research and outreach projects with other established global corporate responsibility coalitions. For example it has pooled staff time and resources with other organizations such as the UN Global Compact and the World Economic Forum to identify and publish best-practice guidance and thought leadership. Recent examples have included working with the WEF on sustainable consumption; and with the Global Compact on "The New Geographies of Sustainability" workshop series and research initiative, which identified the perspectives of key opinion-formers in Brazil, China and India on sustainability. BSR lists over 60 organizations that it partners or collaborates with around the world. These include other corporate responsibility coalitions, business councils and trade associations, as well as UN agencies and academic institutions and think-tanks.

BSR's "local presence" approach to building its global operations is based on a combination of local offices and on-the-ground consulting and partnership projects. The organization's international presence has historically involved a few outpost offices, but in recent years that has begun to change, with a major build-up of its presence in Asia, and particularly China and the recent addition of an office in Brazil.

Four years ago, Cramer says, 95% of the organization's staff were based in San Francisco. Today, it is about 45%, with most of the rest in Asia; but getting close to having as many people in Europe (~ 20) as in Asia (~ 30). Thus the weekly management team conference call starts for the California headquarters at 06.30 to accommodate the international time zones in which different members of the team are based.

The greater number of people on the ground in Europe, China and, more recently, Brazil is reflective of the fact that BSR is now doing more projects in the field. BSR has undertaken projects in more than 75 countries, including direct work in factories and plant sites in China, Mongolia and Peru. In 2010 alone, it worked on projects in 50 countries. In particular, it is now working much more not only outside the United States but also outside OECD states generally. Many of the organization's most recent assignments – whether collective action or individual advisory services – have been in the Middle East, sub-Saharan Africa,

Latin America, China and the rest of Asia. Some collective and individual examples are as follows:

- The China Training Institute. This was established in 2004 with grant-funded support . It provides training on better factory management to managers in China from factories in the apparel, footwear, high-tech and toy sectors, which together employ more than 3.6 million workers. As of 2012, the institute had trained more than 8,000 managers, providing them with access to world-class experts in technical issues, labor, lean manufacturing and environmental, health and safety management. The program is described further in Part II, Section 6.1.1

- In Saudi Arabia, BSR has established close working relationships with Jeddah-based companies, the Jeddah Chamber of Commerce, civil-society partners and human rights organizations to develop and deliver company workshops and improve corporate responsibility. In particular, BSR has been helping companies explore the role of Saudi business in protecting migrant labor and human rights. Funding has come from the U.S. Department of State, Bureau of Democracy, Human Rights and Labor

- In Papua New Guinea, BSR has worked with ExxonMobil, which is constructing a Liquefied Natural Gas Project (PNG LNG) – a large-scale integrated development project that includes gas production and processing facilities in the highlands, as well as onshore and offshore pipelines and liquefaction facilities in the Port Moresby region. The project finance for PNG LNG amounted to over US$15 billion, and once operational the project could double the country's GDP. BSR's work included research into existing workforce, supplier and civil-society capacities and needs; and engagement with potential suppliers, helping ExxonMobil to develop a robust National Content Plan to ensure local businesses and community organizations share the benefits of this major infrastructure and energy development project

- BSR worked with Starbucks on a comprehensive stakeholder engagement strategy to learn more about the potential social and environmental impacts of sourcing cocoa from West Africa for a new product line. BSR identified 20 to 30 key stakeholders – including suppliers, government agencies and NGOs from around the world – and then facilitated a stakeholder dialogue process to help the company identify high-risk issues and explore opportunities for collaboration that would enable it to sustain a reliable and high-quality source of cocoa supply while also investing in rural and community development, providing smallholder farmers with incentives for adopting eco-friendly farming practices and raising awareness of hazards of child labor. This engagement helped the company develop its respected Cocoa Code of Conduct and implement a supply-chain management process that aims to promote more equitable relationships with farmers, workers and local communities, and provides Starbucks with the data it needs to report publicly on its progress

As BSR undertakes a growing number of global assignments – either advising individual companies or convening working groups and partnerships around specific global supply chains and issues – is there a danger, as some contend, that the organization might be simply exporting a U.S. world-view of social responsibility that will not fit the local context? Cramer says that this is not the case:

> As I go around the world, the issues that I see people talking about are the same issues. The local context shapes how people see those issues, and the priority they give to them, but something like climate change is relevant wherever you go.

Impact and lessons learned

Established in 1992, during the same year as the original Rio Earth Summit, BSR's evolution and impact in many ways track the progress that has been made more broadly by the business sector during this 20-year period. BSR has had a significant impact on professionalizing corporate responsibility both in the USA and internationally – particularly through its industry-specific initiatives and pioneering work on global supply-chain management from its early days. It can claim considerable credit for changing global supply-chain practices – especially of U.S.-headquartered firms.

Through its inspiration of and continuing involvement in Forum Empresa, BSR has also played a significant role in spreading responsible business practices to South and Central America. It has also inspired the creation of Maala in Israel (Profile 6).

BSR's early emphasis on corporate responsibility as businesses taking responsibility for their impacts in the marketplace, workplace, environment and community has been a way of thinking about corporate responsibility copied by Business in the Community, CSR Europe and others.

In short, the organization can claim to have played a particularly influential role in:

- **Raising awareness and making the business case for corporate responsibility**, especially in the United States, but also in many other countries through its thought-leadership and partnership networks with organizations such as Forum Empresa, Maala, the UN Global Compact and the World Economic Forum

- **Advising companies on how to embed corporate responsibility into their core business operations**, through a combination of consultancy services, stakeholder engagement activities, working groups, workshops and conferences

- **Helping member companies to achieve scale** in addressing complex sustainability issues through convening and participating in collective action working groups and multi-sector partnership platforms.

Some of the success factors that have underpinned this impact and challenges that BSR has faced are as follows:

Effective platforms to disseminate thought leadership

As outlined in the previous section, BSR has been very effective in spreading best practice and thought leadership through a combination of its annual conference, its partnership networks and its growing social media presence. The annual conference built its reputation in the early years by providing a safe space for companies to discuss the issues. It actively limited non-profit attendance at the start. This was before most companies became more relaxed about dealing with NGOs. One long-standing corporate member says of the conference:

> I was able to take a team member who is relatively new. She was immediately able to go to a range of different content sessions and to access this huge network of people from different companies. It was like drinking from the fire hose.

The conference routinely attracts more than a 1,000 delegates. Cramer says the event has been evolving in three important ways in recent years. First, he says, the audience has become more global in scope. BSR's expanding activities in different parts of the world have served to bring more diverse people to the conference. Second, the parallel sessions cover content in greater depth, and the focus on different topics has identified where companies can be shaping the agenda. Third, the web is being used to change the way people interact. This has helped BSR to offer its delegates enhanced ways of making the most of the event's networking potential. For instance, BSR was one of the first organizations to enable delegates to contact each other via its website to set up meetings in advance of the event.

Such moves have probably been supported by the changing nature of the delegate list. The rise of the CSR professional has resulted in higher expectations of attendees. Regular attendees report that they also see more communications professionals, lawyers and other

Figure P1.2 **Level of engagement with CSR/Sustainability function**
Source: GlobeScan

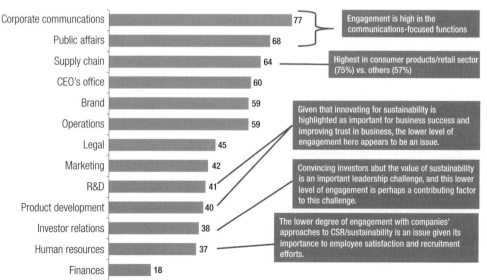

Q: Please rate the level of engagement that each of the following functions within your company has with your company's CSR/sustainability function.

"Engaged" (4 + 5), 2011*

Corporate communcations	77
Public affairs	68
Supply chain	64
CEO's office	60
Brand	59
Operations	59
Legal	45
Marketing	42
R&D	41
Product development	40
Investor relations	38
Human resources	37
Finances	18

Engagement is high in the communications-focused functions

Highest in consumer products/retail sector (75%) vs. others (57%)

Given that innovating for sustainability is highlighted as important for business success and improving trust in business, the lower level of engagement here appears to be an issue.

Convincing investors abut the value of sustainability is an important leadership challenge, and this lower level of engagement is perhaps a contributing factor to this challenge.

The lower degree of engagement with companies' approaches to CSR/sustainability is an issue given its importance to employee satisfaction and recruitment efforts.

*Percentage of respondents who selected (5) plus (4) on a 5-point scale, where 1 is "not at all engaged with CSR/sustainability," and 5 is "very engaged with CSR/sustainability."

key business functions present who are now much more knowledgeable about how the social agenda affects their company. Nevertheless, as a GlobeScan survey of 2011 attendees at the BSR conference found, there remains a lot of work to do to ensure corporate responsibility and sustainability professionals inside large companies are working closely across the company with different business functions – see Fig. P1.2.

BSR has also been effective in making use of emerging social media platforms to share research findings and to position its staff as experts on a wide variety of global corporate responsibility issues.

A diversified funding base

In common with most corporate responsibility membership organizations, BSR does not get sufficient income from member subscriptions alone to run its operations. Initially, its membership subscriptions were supplemented primarily by the revenue generated from participant fees and sponsorship from its successful annual conference. It also grew its global activities using income from a number of private and corporate philanthropic foundations and a few government development agencies, which were interested in supporting projects that raised the overall standard of corporate responsibility or spread corporate responsibility to countries where it was in a much earlier stage in formation. Such projects are still a major feature of BSR's activity and include the HERproject and Conflict Minerals platforms described earlier in this profile. In 2012, the organization was receiving grant funding from a variety of donors to support its collaborative project work. These included the British Consulate in Guangzhou, China, The MacArthur Foundation, the Levi Strauss Foundation, the Rockefeller Foundation, the Rockefeller Brothers Fund, the Swedish International Development Cooperation Agency (SIDA), the U.S. Agency for International Development (USAID), and the U.S. State Department.

In recent years, BSR has become more focused on growing its income through consultancy services. These services are offered at a significant discount for members and, as outlined earlier in this profile, have developed over time to cover a range of industry sectors and a number of practices, such as stakeholder engagement, supply-chain management and reporting.

This multi-pronged approach to revenue generation has enabled BSR to successfully develop a diversified funding base drawn from membership subscriptions, a profitable annual conference, consulting fees, and grant income from charitable foundations and government entities. In its 2010 annual review, BSR reported a 21% increase in its annual revenue to US$15.1 million, with growth experienced from all four categories of funding. The 2011 accounts showed a further 24% increase to $18.8m.

Up-skilling staff and delivery capacity

BSR's increasingly global focus and issue and industry specific activities have meant a continuing process of up-skilling the organization's staff. Cramer acknowledges that:

> We can only succeed if BSR has staff competent in, and excited about, crossing borders. This includes geographic as well as sectoral and intra-company borders. We can't have staff who are U.S.-centric. We need staff who instinctively know how to help companies cross borders.

BSR's employees also need to be able to operate at and gain respect from more senior levels of executives. As corporate responsibility has become a more business-critical issue, the seniority of the people inside companies and government departments who are dealing with these issues has risen to higher levels. BSR now finds that its employees are dealing more with chairpersons, CEOs and boards than in its early years. In order to handle this greater sophistication, BSR has not only had to hire better qualified and more experienced staff, but has also had to organize differently internally. Instead of generalists, BSR is now structured increasingly along industry-sector lines to ensure greater specificity and depth of experience. There are now 11 industry-specific teams at different stages of maturity and development, covering industries such as healthcare, media and entertainment, and travel and tourism. Information and communications technology (ICT) and extractives are the two most established industry-sector teams with strong links to leading companies, NGOs and public-sector figures relevant to and familiar with those sectors. In addition to their domain expertise, however, staff members are also expected to have a good working knowledge of general industry issues and trends and not just of the corporate responsibility and sustainability issues in their particular sector. In addition to recruiting staff with cross-border experience and skills, BSR has also launched a new employee-development initiative, with the objectives of increasing staff training in areas such as facilitation, public speaking, writing and coaching, and also establishing clearer and better-supported career paths for employees.

Managing the balance between membership and consultancy services

Some members and observers of BSR have questioned whether the organization's membership proposition is robust enough, especially for companies with established and well-integrated corporate responsibility programs and increasingly sophisticated and in-depth needs. One long-standing member firm that opted to allow its membership to lapse said the company continued to value the conference and its presence on some of the working groups, but these benefits were available for non-members. The cost differential did not equal the cost of actually being a member, according to an employee of the lapsed member. The same interviewee added: "I do feel that BSR gives great value for those just getting started. For companies like us that already have a sophisticated and forward-looking program it's less obvious."

Cramer acknowledges that the membership proposition has changed over time. When BSR was first created, almost none of its members had a dedicated corporate responsibility function, and basic information was scarce. Now, he says, the organization has tried to go much further towards analysis and insight that adds real value, as well as the excellent growing network that it supports of corporate responsibility practitioners. Despite the views of certain critics, the organization's membership base has stayed remarkably stable during a difficult economic period for most companies and corporate responsibility coalitions.

Other observers have questioned the long-term viability of BSR's dual strategy of membership subscriptions and consulting fees. As the world's major consulting firms become more active in providing strategic advice to global and national companies on social and environmental issues, and are able to draw on substantial existing networks of consultants and shared cost structures, will BSR be able to "compete"? To date it has been able to more than demonstrate its ability to do so, as its consulting fees and services continue to grow.

BSR can also make a strong case for the mutually reinforcing linkages between its research work and the lessons learned and the practical guidelines developed from its working groups and partnership platforms, which are then shared more widely through focused sessions at its annual conference and its website and expanding social media platforms, while at the same time informing its ability to offer competitively priced and well-informed consulting services in its core industries and issues of focus. Cramer is robust in defending the dual strategy of consultancy and membership:

> We have maintained a membership structure because we believe that networked solutions have huge potential . . . Yes we are a hybrid. I think the world needs more hybrids. I think it is good that Human Rights Watch criticizes businesses but also engages with them. I think it is good that McKinsey and other global consulting firms have growing sustainability practices. I think it is good that there are more social enterprises. The world needs more hybrids not less.

This hybrid model appears to be working well for BSR. In its 2010 financial reporting, the organization could point to an increase in revenues of 15% from its consulting and 12% from its membership fees. In terms of the number of members, membership has remained stable over the past decade, and even grew slightly over the past four years of economic recession, to the current number of almost 300 companies.

Authenticity

Another factor that underpins BSR's success in sustaining and gaining members, consulting projects and partners has been its own reputation as an organization that aims to "walk the talk" in terms of emulating the responsible practices that it calls on companies to follow and reporting transparently on its progress and challenges.

For a relatively small global non-profit organization of around 100 people, BSR can point to a good record in its efforts to improve the environmental footprint of its operations, especially at its head-quarters in San Francisco, and its employee value proposition. In terms of the latter, as described earlier in this profile, BSR has launched an employee-development program, and it also undertakes an annual employee-engagement survey to identify key areas where it can improve employee experiences. The organization also sets diversity targets and reports publicly on its performance against them, not only among employees but also at the board level.

In terms of reporting and transparency, BSR is probably the most transparent of the corporate responsibility coalitions studied in depth for this book. In its annual performance review, it explicitly covers not only the areas where it has a successful story to tell but also where it has internal challenges and what it considers to be its major external challenges in its current operating environment. In its 2010 annual review it publicly recognized some of the internal operational challenges associated with operating a hybrid organization, giving a specific example where trade-offs had occurred, and it also highlighted some of the management risks and challenges of managing growth and knowledge.

The future

BSR's strategy has been periodically reviewed and refined since the board's extensive strategy review in 2003–04, but the essence has remained the same. In the summer of 2012, a fresh strategic review process was initiated.

BSR will continue to evolve and adapt as global circumstances for business change. New challenges and opportunities lie ahead, particularly if the value of open markets begins to be more seriously questioned. Clearly, since the global financial crisis of 2008, there has been renewed questioning of the legitimacy of market capitalism, and a ferment of new ideas for how to improve capitalism at a more systemic level. In its report *Redefining Leadership*, BSR argued:

> Leadership in business looks very different in today's global, integrated, digital, and transparent world. Business aims to deliver more than just rising share prices and faces a more diverse array of questions than ever before. Meeting these challenges requires finding the right balance of flexibility and commitment, listening and communicating, and a global view that respects diversity. What's more, leadership today must be earned and renewed daily; it is no longer bestowed by self-perpetuating hierarchies. At its best, business can lead the way toward prosperity for 9 billion people, create groundbreaking technologies for social benefit, and find ways to help us radically reduce our use of natural resources. Achieving this is no small feat.[268]

In order to meet the leadership challenge, Cramer sees that there will be a growing need for more networked solutions where groups of companies work together and with civil-society and public institutions. He believes that:

> This should be a great moment for the coalitions – if they get ahead of the curve. BSR will continue to engage and become more global. Throughout our history our mission has stayed the same, but our methods have changed. That is how we have stayed relevant.

One approach to achieving more systemic change and networked solutions will be large-scale issue and industry-specific efforts. BSR, along with the WBCSD, has been at the forefront of the generalist coalitions that are expanding their specialization on specific issues and industry sectors, both by running their own industry-sector initiatives and by servicing sector initiatives put together by other groups. Greater specialization around specific industry sectors, issues and geographic locations is a key element of BSR's likely future strategy, along with increasing consultancy, thought leadership and collaborative action.

In October 2012, BSR marked its 20th anniversary with the publication of *BSR at 20: Accelerating Progress*. In this report, the organization provides a valuable overview of the key trends shaping the future and identifies four building blocks of change that it believes are central to accelerating progress in meeting BSR's mission of "working with business to build a just and sustainable world":

- **Integrated business models.** Businesses that integrate sustainability fully have a competitive advantage. Achieving that requires vision, innovation, and the right metrics and incentives

- **Financial markets that promote long-term value.** As important as integration is within individual companies, large-scale and durable change also requires significant market reforms to focus on long-term value. Business has an essential role in making this happen

- **New frontiers of collaboration – upgrade your networks.** Collaboration – between and among companies, investors, NGOs, governments, consumers and beyond – has become widespread. Now it is time to scale up our partnerships to accelerate systemic change

- **Empowered individuals, connected communities**. The dramatic increase in technology and access to information is upending traditional notions of commerce and community, enabling individuals to chose and connect in unforeseen ways. What will this mean for sustainability?[269]

These building blocks will underpin the organization's strategic direction as it continues to work with its members and other partners to: raise awareness of emerging trends and solutions; catalyze change within companies; and build systemic solutions. And to achieve this, BSR recognizes the need to be increasingly networked, agile and collaborative:

> It is our core belief that hybrid organizations are best suited to meet the global, cross-disciplinary challenges that define the 21st century. So we are single-minded in our purpose but multifaceted in our approach. Traditional organizations – content to operate within clearly defined boundaries – just won't get the job done.[270]

This statement offers a useful summary of the type of business-led corporate responsibility coalition that is needed for the future. Dedicated to working with and through business to drive sustainable capitalism, but open to new approaches and alliances in order to achieve this goal.

Profile 2

Business in the Community (BITC)

David Grayson*

BITC in its own words

Business in the Community stands for responsible business. We are a business-led charity, have a growing membership and work locally, nationally and internationally through a network of partners worldwide. Our vision is for every business to act responsibly.

We do two things.

We ask our members to work together to transform communities by tackling social issues where business can make a real difference.

We offer our members practical support to help them to integrate responsible business practices wherever they operate.

www.bitc.org.uk

June 2012

---

* This profile is abridged and updated from D. Grayson, *Business-Led Corporate Responsibility Coalitions: Learning from the Example of Business in the Community in the UK – An Insider's Perspective* (London: Business in the Community; Bedford, UK: Doughty Centre for Corporate Responsibility; Cambridge, MA: Kennedy School of Management, Harvard, 2007). A full list of interviews and sources is included there.

Particular thanks for contributions to the update go to Sue Adkins, Catherine Carruthers, Gail Greengross, Stephen Howard, Peter Lambert and Patrick Mallon.

Background context and history

Established in 1982, Business in the Community (BITC) is one of the oldest and largest of the national business-led corporate responsibility coalitions. It began as a broker (principally from businesses to local enterprise agencies and trusts). Over time it has evolved to the point where it now fulfills all of the key roles of coalitions described in Part II, Chapter 8 except, arguably, that of standards-setter. Today, it has over 850 member companies; a further 10,700 are engaged in its campaigns globally. It is a business-led charity. The President of BITC (since 1985) is HRH The Prince of Wales. The Chairman is Mark Price, Managing Director of the retailer Waitrose. He succeeded another retailer, Sir Stuart Rose of Marks & Spencer, in 2011. An Annual General Meeting of member companies elects a board of business leaders[271] elected on rotation for three-year terms, including the chairs of Campaign and Regional Business leadership teams. Overall strategy is approved by the Board, although in practice there has always been considerable discretion devolved to the individual campaign leadership teams and to the CEO and the senior management team. BITC employs 370 staff (down from 450 in 2007). The organization is based in a head office in London or in one of ten offices around the UK. Today, the organization's annual budget is c. £20 million of which approximately 20% now comes from the public sector (down from over 40% in 2005–06).

In 2011, 7,500 individuals attended BITC conferences, workshops and seminars; 50,000 participated in BITC-brokered employee volunteering; and more than 800 companies were supported and challenged to improve their responsible business practice through involvement in one or more of the BITC indexes. 637 business leaders went on The Prince's Seeing is Believing visits in 2011. Almost 300 business leaders currently sit on one of the BITC leadership teams, which provide the top-level business engagement and direction of the organization and its campaigns.[272]

The context for BITC's emergence and growth over the past more than 30 years has been that business has become a much bigger part of British society. The UK, of course, was the first country to privatize significantly in the 1980s as BA (British Airways), British Gas, BT (British Telecom), the water companies, the railways, electricity and many other state-owned enterprises came under private control. Many of the most prominent and influential business leaders of the time, such as Allen Sheppard (the then CEO of Grand Metropolitan),[273] were clear that the *quid pro quo* for a smaller state was a more activist business community.

In retrospect, BITC has benefited from a British business culture somewhere between the continental European social model and U.S. free-market voluntarism. Arguably, globalization is now producing a convergence in these very different models of capitalism, but the UK's early adoption of responsible business ideas reflects the prevailing UK business culture. Many business leaders felt both a moral duty and a business imperative to act. In the words of one early BITC board member, Sir David Sieff of Marks & Spencer, "you cannot have prosperous High Streets without prosperous back streets." Geography has also helped: corporate UK remains heavily concentrated in London and the south-east.. Engaging a critical mass of business leaders based in close proximity is easier in the UK than in the United States or Australia where corporate headquarters are more dispersed across the country.

BITC has not operated in isolation. It has been part of a rich, if sometimes confusing and overlapping, tapestry of national and local organizations such as: Arts & Business (formerly the Association for Business Sponsorship of the Arts, created in 1976 to encourage arts–business partnerships and now part of BITC); Common Purpose, created in 1990 to encourage the development of active citizens through joint leadership development of people from business, the public and the voluntary and community sectors; the Media Trust, formed in 1994; the Centre for Tomorrow's Company, created in 1994 out of the Tomorrow's Company Inquiry run by the RSA; and Forum for the Future, established by three prominent environmental campaigners (Paul Ekins, Sara Parkin and Jonathon Porritt) in 1996.

Key activities and phases of development

There have been three phases of BITC so far. During phase one in the 1980s, it predominantly championed business support for local enterprise agencies (cash, secondees [i.e., executives on loan], premises, equipment, expertise and employee volunteering) as a way of business helping to regenerate local economies depressed by large-scale corporate factory closures, through encouraging small business development and re-skilling. This quickly extended to other forms of local community regeneration, including early support for urban regeneration, community entrepreneurs and business–education links. The predominant driver for business in this phase was social cohesion and a recognition of the social costs of just walking away from the human consequences of massive corporate restructuring. This was described as corporate community involvement – later amended to corporate community investment – to signify that business might gain benefits (such as enhanced reputation or improved staff morale) that would not necessarily accrue from ad hoc corporate philanthropy. Phase two, during the 1990s, involved BITC promoting a wider agenda of corporate community involvement, including how businesses should better organize their involvement for business and social benefit – an early form of what today Porter and Kramer have described as "shared value."[274] The business driver in this phase shifted more to the international competitiveness agenda – the need to address the UK's decline in the international competitiveness league tables and to improve basic skills in literacy and numeracy; and the war for talent that drove more companies to embrace diversity in their workforce – while simultaneously addressing social cohesion. In the words of one prominent British politician of the day: "international competitiveness and social cohesion: two sides of the same coin."[275]

Phase three has seen BITC embrace corporate responsibility – or as the organization has called it from 2007 onwards, "responsible business." The business driver has shifted more to competitive advantage for individual companies and the pressures of sustainability as a business challenge. Throughout, BITC has been concerned with encouraging more companies to get involved individually and also with encouraging collective business action.

BITC's first decade coincided with a rapid and wholesale restructuring of the British economy, promoted by the then Thatcher Government. It was a time of bitter domestic politics, a divisive year-long coal-miners' strike and dramatic decline of the traditional manufacturing base. The government promoted an enterprise culture and supported a range of programs to help small businesses and urban regeneration. While careful to work with local authorities controlled by different political parties, BITC also worked with the government of the day to mobilize business engagement in small business development and regeneration – initially through replicating early examples of local enterprise agencies, such as the Community of St. Helen's Trust and London Enterprise Agency (LEntA), and subsequently also through

One-Town Partnerships and local business leadership teams, notably through the Calderdale Partnership based in the Yorkshire mill town of Halifax, which was championed by the Prince of Wales, later replicated in Blackburn and elsewhere. After Margaret Thatcher's third election victory in 1987, BITC's CEO Stephen O'Brien was quick to exploit Mrs. Thatcher's election-night remarks about inner cities[276] to organize additional BITC campaigns around urban revitalization. New campaigns focused not just on enterprise and education but also included partnership sourcing, pre-recruitment customized skills training and small-business expansion finance, which led to a network of commercially funded regional enterprise funds led by Midland Bank (now part of HSBC).

In early 1992, Julia Cleverdon – previously one of the joint managing directors of BITC (with David Grayson) – took over from Stephen O'Brien as CEO. By now the organization was working with its member companies on a number of issues, such as diversity in the workplace, business–education links and early environmental initiatives by business. Tony Cleaver, then chairman of IBM UK, had become the first chair of BITC's Business in the Environment (BiE) initiative in 1987. One of BiE's early successes was to persuade the Prince of Wales to revive his Cambridge Footlights days as a comic actor. The Prince co-starred with the veteran British comedian John Cleese in *Grime Goes Green*. *Grime* was a light-hearted BiE film made by the highly successful management-training company Video Arts to get serious messages about improving environmental performance across to business.

A significant boost to the scale of BITC operations and capacity around the country came with BITC's merger with the Action Resource Centre (ARC) in 1995.[277] ARC pre-dated BITC; it was formed in 1973 as a charity to mobilize business resources for community organizations. Whereas BITC came more from a business tradition, ARC had more of a community culture. Mergers of this sort are rarely easy, and this one was no exception. Following the merger, however, BITC was able to strengthen its regional offices[278] and offer a more comprehensive local brokerage service for businesses, especially to support more employee volunteering in the community. Before the merger, few of the FTSE 100 largest companies had formal employee-volunteering programs; today, there are few who don't. The merged organization's vehicle for volunteering was Cares.

The strengthening of BITC's regional teams in 1995–96 was to prove prescient, as an incoming Labour Government in 1997 was to move quickly to implement its devolution agenda. This involved the establishment of the Scottish Parliament in Edinburgh and the Welsh Assembly Government in Cardiff. In England, it involved the establishment of nine Regional Development Agencies (RDAs). The RDAs were to become partners and outlets for program delivery at some times and at other times funders and target audiences for BITC to influence. In Yorkshire and Humberside, BITC was to sign a multimillion pound, three-year contract (later extended) with Yorkshire Forward (the RDA) to increase the quality and extent of corporate responsibility.[279]

In Northern Ireland, under the entrepreneurial leadership of John Heaslip (BITC's Northern Ireland Director since 1989, when the organization was re-established in the province), the organization has been able over the years to bridge the sectarian divide with extensive education–business links and partnerships between businesses and community organizations from the different traditions.[280]

Several of BITC's ten chairs to date have had a distinctive theme for their term. For Peter Davis, then CEO of Prudential, it was to push business to measure its impact on society. A leadership team led by Bill Cockburn, then managing director at BT, was asked to do this and specifically to investigate tools for measuring business impacts. Cockburn's Business Impact Task Force helped to generate a common understanding among several of the world's business-led coalitions promoting corporate responsibility such as BITC, BSR and CSR Europe that business impacts should be measured with respect to four dimensions: marketplace, workplace, environment and community. BITC's work also pointed to the need to link responsible business to purpose and values and guiding principles for business and human rights.

The Business Impact Task Force reported in November 2000 under the banner of *Winning with Integrity*.[281] By 2012, most of the Fortune Global 500 companies report their societal impacts. It is easy to forget how quickly this trend for companies to measure and report their non-financial impacts has occurred. It has been the result of pressure from a wide variety of sources, and the Business Impact Task Force was undoubtedly one of them. Its suggestions for how to measure impacts was a unique selling point for BITC, at a time when, for example, the Global Reporting Initiative had only just started.

Following *Winning with Integrity*, BITC established the Business Impact Review Group (BIRG) under the chairmanship of Phil Hodkinson. BIRG brought together 20 leading companies that agreed to try out the indicators proposed in the Cockburn team's report and to report on their experience of doing so after two years. The result was *Indicators that Count*, published in July 2003.[282] Asking companies to produce a sustainability/corporate responsibility report represented a significant new request from BITC of its member companies.

The Business Impact Review Group was one of the major drivers of greater corporate responsibility reporting in the UK. Many critics of business argue that voluntary disclosure by some companies is at best only partial progress and dilutes the arguments of those seeking mandatory reporting by business of its environmental and social impacts. So far, campaigns in the British and European Parliaments for mandatory reporting have been largely unsuccessful. In a relatively rare policy stance,[283] BITC has opposed mandatory measurement and reporting, believing that a mix of marketplace, employee and investor pressures, combined with companies' spirit of volunteerism, will produce superior results.[284] Subsequently, Hodkinson led a consultation exercise with BITC member companies to produce recommendations for a UK Government review of reporting requirements. In 2006, a group of leading corporate responsibility practitioners who meet under BITC coordination as the Integration Peer Group advised on BITC's submission to the Global Reporting Initiative (GRI) for their consultation on the G3 (third generation) GRI.

After the original work on *Winning with Integrity* and the Business Impact Review Group, BITC subsequently published a *Director's Guide to Corporate Responsibility Reporting* (with Arthur D. Little, Camelot and HBOS) in 2005,[285] and *Taking Shape: The Future of Corporate Responsibility Communications* (with Radley Yeldar) in 2007.[286]

Implicit to *Winning with Integrity* was the idea of a Corporate Responsibility Index (CRI). In 1996, BITC's Business in the Environment campaign had launched the BiE Index. Today, BITC's membership surveys show that the opportunity to benchmark is one of the most valued aspects of BITC. At the time of the launch of the BiE Index though, many thought that its publication could lead to mass resignations. It was an act of leadership on the part of CEO Julia Cleverdon, the BITC Board and the BiE Leadership Team to press ahead. As with so many of BITC's innovations, it was championed by a senior business figure, in this case the then BiE Chair Tony Cleaver,[287] who provided much-needed protective "air cover" for BITC with his industry peers.

Nevertheless, the publication of the first BiE Index,[288] was controversial, particularly as newspaper headlines emphasized "pollution." One key member company implied that its share price had been negatively impacted by the Index. There was even talk of FTSE 100 chairmen closing ranks against BiE and boycotting any future surveys. With perseverance and improvements to its methodology, and with the appointment of KPMG as independent auditors for the process, member companies came to accept that the Index was a useful management tool and that publication of the BiE Index as an effective league table of corporate environmental performance had sounded a much-needed and timely wake-up call in the UK's boardrooms. It was to provide the basis for the BitC *Corporate Responsibility Index* launched in 2002.

Winning with Integrity and the Indexes are two examples of the way BITC has tried to keep the agenda fresh for member companies and other businesses. Earlier thought-leadership exercises included *Directions for the Nineties* and, during 1993–94, *Work in Society*.

In 2002, the then BITC Chairman David Varney talked about "The Perfect Storm" in a number of speeches using the title of a popular film of the time.[289] Varney warned his fellow business leaders that in the aftermath of WorldCom, Enron and other international business scandals, expectations of business were growing massively around the world, while perceptions of performance were declining dramatically – a point subsequently confirmed by the polling organization GlobeScan in their annual surveys of international public opinion.[290] For BITC's 20th anniversary, the former editor of the *Financial Times*, Richard Lambert, attended a series of Anniversary Dialogues and then produced *The Lambert Commentary*, summarizing what he believed that BITC and the corporate responsibility agenda had achieved. Lambert had memorably advised BITC at the Awards for Excellence 2000 dinner that it was time to "kick the tires," in other words, to check on the substance of companies' commitments.[291] In part, his *Commentary* reviewed how robust the tires had become.

All too often, businesses have treated corporate responsibility as a *bolt-on* to business operations rather than as *built in* to business purpose and strategy.[292] The development of the Corporate Responsibility Index and the detailed CRI questionnaire that participating companies have to complete each year effectively summarized those steps that BITC considers to be essential elements for a business that wants to integrate corporate responsibility. Through a somewhat ad hoc mixture of awards, CRI results, conferences and how-to guides on individual aspects of responsible business, BITC has tried in recent years to flesh out the guidance it gives to member companies.

In turn, BITC guidance has led to a professionalizing of the corporate responsibility and sustainability function in many companies, which has also been supported by organizations such as the Corporate Responsibility Group, an association of individual corporate responsibility directors of leading companies, formed in 1987.

In his *Commentary*, Richard Lambert identified the impact of globalization for BITC and its member companies. BITC had never been immune from overseas influences, dating back to the original Anglo-American Sunningdale Conference in 1980 that had inspired BITC's creation. Social innovations BITC has imported to the UK from abroad include:

- Lowell One-Town Partnership, in Massachusetts, USA, inspiring Halifax One-Town Partnership

- Boston Compact – also in Massachusetts – as the model for the East London Education Business Partnership and the other EBPs and the Training and Enterprise Councils

- New York CARES inspiring BITC's UK Cares movement

- Gifts in Kind – also from the United States (the UK organization is now known as In Kind Direct)[293]

There were to be (abortive) attempts to start a Business in the Community in each of the Australian states in the late 1980s (largely focusing on the enterprise agency and Information Technology Centre models from the UK).[294] Weeks after the fall of the Berlin Wall, and against the advice of the British Foreign Office, which feared failure, BITC, led by The Prince of Wales, hosted a gathering of international business leaders in Charleston, South Carolina. This Charleston meeting gave birth to the International Business Leaders Forum (IBLF) (see Profile 5).

BITC was less enthusiastic when the then President of the European Commission, Jacques Delors, called on European business leaders in 1993 to play a more prominent role in tackling social exclusion across the EU. The resulting organization, the European Business Network for Social Inclusion, now known as CSR Europe (see Profiles), included many of BITC's core member companies. The original UK partner, however, was not BITC but the London Enterprise Agency, LEntA. Only in 1999 did BITC take over as UK national partner. One might argue, as some continental European colleagues have done, that BITC's early attitudes and engagement with CSR Europe rather mirrored the UK's broader ambiguity to relations with continental Europe![295]

In fact, the BITC Board had been clear back in 1990 that, while it recognized the relevance and importance of promoting responsible business engagement internationally, it did not want to distract the organization from the continuing challenges of doing this well in the UK; hence the decision to create a separate organization: the IBLF. Often unknown to BITC, however, its publications popped up in translation around the world: the BiE *Environment DIY Guide* was published in Mandarin, for example.

As privatization, liberalization and globalization gathered pace through the 1990s and beyond, more and more of BITC's member companies spread their operations internationally and began to expect that BITC could advise on corporate responsibility issues elsewhere – or at least would be able to make introductions to similar organizations in other parts of the world. In response, in recent years, the ambivalence with which BITC had previously approached international work has now been replaced with a clarity that to remain relevant to a corporate membership with global focus, BITC itself needs global partners and links. As well as enthusiastically developing the ENGAGE network with IBLF to facilitate international employee volunteering, and coordinating the CSR360 Global Partner Network (see Chapter 10, Box 10.1, page 130), where partners can exchange good practice and "franchise" successful corporate engagement models, the BITC board has agreed an international strategy. This focuses on six priority countries – India, China, Ghana, South Africa, Brazil and Mexico – where BITC will work with interested member companies and local partners to help support the development of responsible business practices.

The period 2007–12 has been a time of consolidation and some organizational down-sizing as first the global financial crisis and consequent recession hit, and then public expenditure was cut back in the UK in the aftermath of the change of government in 2010. Significantly, however, BITC retained membership numbers during this time. Despite the financial pressures, the organization developed a number of new programs including its first ever campaign aimed at consumers, *Start*, to promote sustainable living.[296]

Like CSR Europe and the WBCSD, BITC has also worked with a group of member companies to develop *Visioning the Future – Transforming Business* to help boards and senior management teams of member companies to envision their future business models and strategies in a resource-constrained world. This is led by the CEO of Kingfisher, Ian Cheshire.[297]

The change of UK government in 2010 showed, as in the previous transition of power from Conservative to New Labour in 1997, that BITC could work effectively with governments of different political persuasions. Like senior civil servants, BITC staff shifted seamlessly from advising and working with the Labour administration to a similar role with the Conservative–Liberal Democrat coalition. It was noticeable, however, that a new government-inspired "localism" agenda, which echoed many of the themes of the 1980s with efforts to secure big-business support for regeneration initiatives, now had to engage a business community and BITC membership whose operations are far more global than a quarter of a century ago, and for whom "local" could just as easily be Ghana or India as Bourneville or Cowley.

Domestic critics and critical friends still question the organization's capacity for (as opposed to in-principle commitment to) working in partnership. In its defense, BITC points to initiatives such as Mosaic to engage the Muslim community, and a new generation of One-Town Partnerships, starting with Burnley in the North-West of England and extending next to Stoke-on-Trent in the Midlands. These One-Town Partnerships are run with the Prince's charities and public authorities to mobilize corporate support for economic and social regeneration.

Since 1990, BITC's work with community regeneration has benefited greatly from the interest and contacts generated through The Prince's Seeing is Believing program (SiB). Like so many of the most successful and enduring of the BITC programs, SiB began as a single project in 1990. Leading firms of headhunters (executive search) were asked to open up to BITC their "little black books" of contacts of rising-star business leaders they were tracking for future work appointments. The combined list produced the invitation list for the original SiB visits. Each visit was led by a prominent business leader already committed to BITC and personally engaged in the particular topic of the visit, such as how businesses could help schools or projects to tackle homelessness. Groups, usually of six to ten people, of senior business figures and rising stars were taken on the SiB visits to look at a particular social problem in a specific part of the country and then report back as a whole group to the Prince of Wales.[298]

There are now three broad dimensions to BITC's work:

- **Leadership,** built around a series of campaigns focused on different aspects of responsible business or on mobilizing business energy and expertise to tackle social problems

- **Account management,** with individual member companies to support their continuous improvement in responsible business and sustainability, using the products and services that have been developed to help integrate responsible business practices such as the Corporate Responsibility Index and the annual Awards for Excellence

- **The ability to scale engagement,** both domestically, through the regional offices supporting member companies and campaigns and brokering business support in the community, and also increasingly on an international basis, initially through employee volunteering (ENGAGE) but also now on corporate responsibility broadly – especially through the CSR360 Global Partner Network

Impact and lessons learned

BITC has reached not only the boardrooms of most leading British businesses but also some of the most deprived communities around the UK. To read the lists of BITC Board, leadership teams, conference speakers and Seeing is Believing visits is to study a "corporate Who's Who" of the past 30 years. Most leading politicians of the era, from all the major parties, have also been involved, alongside thousands of voluntary and community organizations.

While it is possible to provide hard numbers (companies in membership, budgets, participants in Indexes are a few of the measures commonly used), it is much harder to assess impact accurately. Perhaps it is best summed up in two interviewees' comments, one an influential adviser to the Blair/Brown Labour Government, and the other a key adviser to the Conservative leader and current Prime Minister, David Cameron. Both these people have known BITC for a decade or more. One said BITC "has made it socially acceptable for business leaders to admit corporate responsibility is important . . . allowing private belief to become public . . . without BITC it is unlikely that the agenda would have been taken up so broadly by so many companies." The other said of BITC that it is "the largest and most influential and visible of all the corporate responsibility groups . . . its strengths are the relentlessness of the agenda-setting . . . BITC has helped to institutionalize and mainstream the practice of corporate responsibility and created a consensus or expectation for it."[299] Many share the view that BITC's great success has been in making responsible business mainstream; getting influential business leaders personally involved, and keeping them involved. In doing so, it has created a range of campaigning techniques for engaging business and a practical menu of things for businesses (and individual business people) to do, whether they are experienced or just starting out.

BITC has been the catalyst in create or taking to a broad-scale a whole range of organizations and corporate responsibility activities such as the Employers' Forum on Disability; the International Business Leaders Forum; employee volunteering; the idea of businesses voluntarily benchmarking their performance through the Corporate Responsibility Index; and encouraging companies to regularly measure and report on their environmental and social impacts.

Inevitably, in 30 years, BITC has not always gotten it right: sometimes it was the right idea but the wrong time, sometimes the right idea but insufficiently resourced, and sometimes BITC just did not grab the opportunity. Some things that BITC is now criticized for having not done are clearly comments made with the benefit of hindsight. Some are items that campaigners wish *some* organization might have picked up and, in this case, the criticism is directed at the responsible business movement generally rather than BITC in particular.

While BITC is now well resourced by the standards of many community and voluntary organizations, its resources have always been very limited compared to the scale of its operations and the scale of resources available to the senior figures in business, politics and society that the organization is seeking to influence and work with. Through sheer hard work, dedication and entrepreneurialism, it continues to pull off events on often short lead-times that would defy many far larger organizations. Furthermore, many of the issues for which it is criticized for not tackling are deeply intractable social issues that continue to challenge governments and civil society. As one candid friend of the organization put it, "I recognize that when I criticize BITC for not doing things, I really mean that I wish someone, anyone, would do them, and BITC is a convenient focal point for my impatience!"[300]

Table P2.1 **Illustrative BITC impacts**

Impact on	Example
Individual business leaders	More than 9,000 have participated in The Prince's Seeing is Believing program visits and report-backs; 7,000 business leaders were twinned for two-way mentoring with school head teachers; at any one time, more than 300 top business leaders are providing strategic direction through membership of BITC boards, leadership teams and as speakers at BITC events
Individual businesses	A number of BITC brands, such as the Mayday Network to mobilize action on climate change and the National Business Travel Initiative, reach many more companies than are in membership of BITC. Thus, while earlier ideas of a movement of 10,000 members has not materialized, BITC is reaching many more companies through member firms' supply chains and the BITC subsidiary brands Many hundreds of companies now have the BITC Big Tick Award for excellence in Responsible Business[301] and have developed their corporate responsibility from participation in the benchmarking Corporate Responsibility Index
Business world in UK and internationally	Institutionalized the concept of corporate responsibility; promoted corporate responsibility reporting by companies as a management and communications exercise
NGOs/voluntary and community sector	Started In Kind Direct, supported the creation and subsequent re-formation of Employers' Forum on Disability and of Teach First to place the best and brightest of young graduates in teaching for 1–2 years prior to starting high-flyer careers with investment banks, management consultancies etc.; established concept of "community and social entrepreneurs" and helped build all-party support for them. At one stage, nearly a quarter of all UK head teachers had a business mentor through the BITC-led Partners in Leadership program
Government/ government policy/ delivery of public services (e.g., convening power to get business collectively involved, influencing thinking of civil servants)	Created the expectation of cross-sectoral partnerships as integral to delivery of social policy and worked with local, regional, and successive national governments irrespective of political persuasion. For example, during the Brown Government BITC played a prominent role in the Government's Talent and Enterprise Taskforce
Management education (thinking about role of business in society and how it operates *vis-à-vis* other aspects of society)	Report for BP in 1995 on how to introduce corporate responsibility into Business Schools which led to BP-supported Centre for Corporate Citizenship at Warwick Business School and to early work that led to the creation of the Academy for Business in Society (EABIS), profiled in Chapter 7, Box 7.5, page 103).

Impact on	Example
Specific localities	Halifax One-Town Partnership for the regeneration of the former mill-town – a model subsequently replicated in a dozen other locations and which encouraged the then British government to engage business leaders in local regeneration through Training & Enterprise Councils, Business Links and Regional Development Agencies. The locality focus has been recently revived with a new generation of One-Town Partnerships Bridge-building cross-communities Northern Ireland: vehicle for younger generation of business people to participate in civic life in the 1990s in a non-political way
Specific social and environmental issues	Affordable housing in rural areas; support for community entrepreneurs; Opportunity Now (from late 1980s) and Race for Opportunity (from mid-1990s) campaigns enabled organizations to benchmark and improve their performance on gender and racial diversity respectively
Corporate responsibility coalitions elsewhere	Inspiration for Federación Española de Seguridad (FES – Spanish Security Federation) Spain, BITC Ireland. Support for employee volunteering around the world through ENGAGE; created the IBLF

Another experienced corporate responsibility practitioner likens the relationship with BITC to that of any long-term partnership between people: "There are highs and lows; there are arguments and differences of opinion. The relationship has to be worked at so that it can be successful with one's eyes continuously on the horizon of what together people are trying to achieve."

Critical success factors: lessons learned

Arguably, BITC has been most successful when it has applied **five critical success factors.** These are:

- **Leadership.** BITC has relentlessly pursued the current top business leaders. CEOs and main board directors of FTSE 100 companies head its board and all its campaign leadership teams

- **Apprenticeship.** Developing a series of tools based on effective brokerage to engage business. Even some of BITC's critics acknowledge its intense, eclectic networking

- **Showmanship.** In the style and content of BITC events, but also its formal and informal media partnerships

- **Entrepreneurship.** Like the businesses it is seeking to inspire, BITC has always been opportunistic in spotting and filling gaps, pulling together resources from many disparate places, and being prepared to experiment and take successful examples such as the benchmarking Indexes and spread them quickly

- **Partnership.** Working variously with national charities, local community and voluntary organizations, governments at local and national level, and international institutions such as the European Union

By far the most significant of these has been **leadership.**

Leadership

BITC has always enjoyed the active engagement of top current business leaders. It has been a "club everyone wants to belong to." Each area of BITC work, region and campaign has a business leadership team in charge. Membership of the BITC Board and of leadership teams has been at the level of company chairmen, CEOs and main board members of the FTSE 100. Strategic direction has come from the top of companies rather than been confined to the CSR function. The continuing ability to attract and retain the most senior levels of business leadership has been crucial.

One aspect continuing to engage top current business leaders has been leadership to set the agenda and move the debate about business and society forward. This has included a series of ground-breaking initiatives such as the previously mentioned Business Impact Review Group, which encouraged more companies to measure and report on their environmental and social impacts, and the subsequent work to launch the Corporate Responsibility Index; and more recent campaigns around homelessness and business action on health and well-being.

The engagement of top current business leaders has also enabled BITC to take a leadership role as an authoritative, independent third-party endorser of good practice in responsible business, for example, through the annual Awards for Excellence.

BITC has also benefited from strong executive leadership, with just three CEOs in 30 years: Stephen O'Brien (1982–92), Julia Cleverdon (1992–2008) and Stephen Howard (since 2008). The charisma and convening power of these CEOs and specifically their phenomenal "people-tracking" and networking skills have complemented the skills and experience of the chairmen who have led the organization. BITC has also benefited from the personal drawing power and reputation of BITC's only president (from 1985 until the present): HRH The Prince of Wales.

The future

Does the new corporate responsibility agenda imply the need for organizational change? If the enduring unique selling point of BITC is the capacity to inspire and engage top business leaders with the most relevant and important aspects of responsible business, should BITC focus more on this campaigning role? Does this imply fewer "own labels" and a greater capacity to signpost to a range of strategic partners? These strategic partners might be a mix of specialist NGOs and campaigns, boutique corporate responsibility consultancies and business schools, as well as different organizations expert in particular aspects of responsible business such as human rights, business ethics, sustainable production and consumption, and responsible sourcing. These organizations might deliver more services to companies, brokered perhaps through BITC and leaving BITC free to focus on its core competency as a convener of business.

In one sense, BITC's future role is a continuation of earlier debates. In a major study of the growth of corporate community involvement in the UK published in 1991, Michael Fogarty and Ian Christie noted that "a number of our own informants fastened particularly on what they saw as confusion over the division of responsibilities between BITC and other more specialized agencies . . . BITC's principal responsibility should be to start things off and back them up."[302]

In practice, the issue is not campaigning versus *any* delivery. Without some delivery experience, it would be hard for the organization to understand the campaign issues or the practical obstacles to be overcome. The real question, therefore, is likely to be the *scale* of delivery and *how* BITC finds partners to deliver on a broad scale.

One significantly expanding area of delivery is likely to be in on-the-ground brokerage. In summer 2012, BITC received confirmation of a grant of £5 million from the UK National Lottery to finance a three-year roll-out of a brokering program that should enhance capacity to engage small and medium-sized enterprises in community partnership. This takes BITC full circle to the 1980s, when its newly established network of regional directors brokered business engagement.

A new challenge for the organization is how to use social media effectively. Younger, more technically savvy junior staff are using social media constantly themselves and pushing the senior management and board to be more proactive in social media. This, however, sits uncomfortably with the need to avoid political controversy – especially given the hands-on presidency of the heir to the throne and the close relationships with senior politicians across the spectrum.

Another challenge is that of articulating public statements that will carry the corporate membership – especially as the corporate responsibility agenda becomes ever more mainstream and confronts what have previously been "elephants in the room" such as executive compensation, corporate tax strategies and responsible lobbying by business. Plenty to keep BITC occupied as it enters its fourth decade.

Profile 3
CSR Europe

David Grayson and Jane Nelson
from original research by Amelio Portfilio and Zi Jia
MBA students, Doughty Centre for Corporate Responsibility*

CSR Europe in its own words

CSR Europe is the leading European business network for corporate social responsibility with around 71 multinational corporations and 34 national partner organisations as members. The organisation was founded in 1995 by senior European business leaders in response to an appeal by the European Commission President Jacques Delors. It has since grown to become an inspiring network of business people working at the forefront of CSR across Europe and globally. In total, the network reaches out to approximately 4,500 companies throughout Europe.

CSR Europe's main function is to provide its members with the expertise and help they require in addressing the issue of CSR. In this sense, CSR Europe's agenda is defined by the needs of its membership network. Their needs in turn come from an internal desire to change their business strategies, as well as from external pressures and expectations from government, international institutions, stakeholders and civil society.

* The authors of the profile are grateful for interviews in 2011 with Peter Davies, Managing Director, Business in the Community; Harry Goldman, Jobs and Society Sweden; Marianne Bogle, manager at CSR Sweden; Karen Davidson, Scottish Business in the Community and CSR Europe board; and Jan Noterdaeme, CSR Europe Senior Advisor on External Relations; and in 2012 with Stefan Crets, Executive Director, CRS; Celia Moore, Chair of CSR Europe; and Jan Noterdaeme (and subsequent emails). The authors thank James Celor, Stefan Crets, Jan Noterdaeme and Christine Stewart of CSR Europe for their inputs to the text.

CSR Europe responds to these needs by connecting practitioners to share best practice within a peer to peer setting, innovating new types of partnerships between businesses and between businesses and stakeholders for cooperative projects and by providing practical and inspiring input into the European policy developments.

www.csreurope.org   June 2012

Background context and history

Originally called the European Business Network for Social Cohesion (EBNSC), CSR Europe was founded in January 1995. The organization was born as a response to a call made in 1993 by the then President of the European Commission, Jacques Delors, who invited businesses to address the problem of structural unemployment by tackling social exclusion and discrimination.

Two officials of the European Commission, Patrick Venturini, a member of the Delors cabinet, and Jan Noterdaeme, an official at Directorate General for Employment, Industrial Relations and Social Affairs, with the assistance of Annick Loise, brought together a group of companies and business associations willing to respond to that appeal. Business leaders from a group of 20 companies and business associations, including Levi Strauss, BP, Accor, Glaverbel, Philips, Bayer, BT, the London Enterprise Agency, the Manifeste Français des Entreprises contre l'Exclusion and the International Christian Union of Business Executives (UNIAPAC) signed up to the European Business Declaration against Social Exclusion,[303] which defined the principles and actions needed to fight social exclusion. The same companies and associations entrusted the young commissioners Jan Noterdaeme and Ann Vandenhende with the task of forming and coordinating the European Business Network for Social Cohesion. The King Baudouin Foundation, (a Belgian charity established to create greater justice, democracy and diversity in society), provided initial support and facilities in Brussels to the newly born network. The European Commission also provided financial support.

From the outset, the EBNSC was built around a network of member companies. Membership was open to interested companies fulfilling three main criteria: companies having their main activities in the European Union; readiness to share best practices and experiences with each other; and willingness to support the expansion of the network across Europe. EBNSC's initial mission was to facilitate the exchange of experience and best practices on social exclusion between its members, in order to promote the integration of under-privileged people in the labor market and preventing exclusion in the workplace.

The businessman and politician Viscount Étienne Davignon[304] played a central role in the foundation of the EBNSC. He was appointed chairman in 1998. Previously, he had contributed to the European integration cause as the foreign minister of Belgium in the 1960s, as chair of a committee of experts that drafted the Davignon Report on European Foreign Policy in 1970, and as vice president of the European Commission from 1981 until 1985. Under his chairmanship, the EBNSC promoted the cause of ethnic diversity at work not only as a principle in itself but also as a business practice that adds value to the workforce.

With the support of the European Commission, the EBNSC initiated the report *Gaining from Diversity*, which was published in 1997, the European Year Against Racism.[305] In the same year, the EBNSC encouraged an increasing number of companies across Europe to share best practices and acquire new knowledge; and produced tools to address discrimination at work and in the community.

At the same time, multinational companies interested in CSR more generally joined the organization. The growing number of member companies provided the EBNSC with additional resources and influence and with a growing mandate. Having been established initially as a response to a specific initiative from the European Commission, the EBNSC began to develop a life of its own and to evolve as a truly business-led organization. Members took the driving seat and began to set the agenda for the organization. Different companies from many diverse industries began putting new issues on the table for discussion, such as the depletion of natural resources, climate change and human rights. At that time, multinationals were also under increasing pressure for greater transparency in their corporate communications. The organization was called on to help European companies build a culture of reporting on their economic, environmental and social performance and impact on society.

In November 2000, the EBNSC held a major conference in Brussels, was renamed CSR Europe and broadened its mission to encompass all the economic, social and environmental issues pertaining to corporate social responsibility. Having gained momentum from members representing a significant share of the European business community, CSR Europe was poised to raise awareness and to promote the philosophy and practice of corporate social responsibility not only among companies but also with European Union institutions, national governments, academia, and other stakeholders.

Key activities and phases of development

Building a network of national partner organizations

An important evolution in the nature of the organization occurred in January 2001, when CSR Europe made a decision to extend its reach at the national level. CSR Europe sealed a protocol of cooperation with national partner organizations established in 12 European States: Belgian Business Network for Social Cohesion (BENSC; Belgium), Business in the Community (BITC; UK), Irish BITC (Ireland), CIME (France), Fundación Empresa y Sociedad (Spain), Finnish Business & Society (Finland), Hellenic Network for Corporate Social Responsibility (HBNSC; Greece), IMS–Entreprendre pour la Cité (France), Philias (Switzerland), Samenleving & Bedrijf (the Netherlands), Sodalitas (Italy), Swedish Jobs and Society (Sweden) and Talentum (Portugal). The goal was to build closer collaboration with organizations at the national level in order to leverage impact and to involve local companies.

Partner organizations were required to be associations operating in one of the EU member states and to represent either national businesses or stakeholders of business. Some of them were existing organizations while others, such as the HBNSC and Business and Society Belgium (formerly BENSC), were set up with the help of, and under the aegis of, CSR Europe. Partner organizations also became involved in the governance of CSR Europe. Along with corporate members, they gathered once a year in an assembly held in Brussels in order to review CSR Europe's annual progress, approve the budget and financial results, and set future strategy. The assembly elected the board of directors, which was given responsibility for evaluating key societal challenges and trends for companies with regard to corporate responsibility and working with the CSR Europe staff to set out a strategy for the organization.

Establishing a dialogue on CSR between business and European Union Institutions

First and foremost, CSR Europe became the platform through which member companies tried to establish a permanent dialogue with the EU institutions on CSR. Businesses acknowledged the semantic and cultural gap existing between them and the EU institutions on CSR and sought to close it by performing a "pedagogic role."

In 1999, the incoming Portuguese Presidency of the EU asked Viscount Davignon together with 15 business leaders (CEOs) to engage the members of CSR Europe with the European Summit on Employment, Economic Reform and Social Cohesion to be held in Lisbon in March 2000. Viscount Davignon addressed the EU governments and the European Commission, asking them to recognize that businesses could successfully combine economic competitiveness and social responsibility. Viscount Davignon and the CEOs proposed to the Portuguese Prime Minister, leading the EU Presidency at that time, to enrich the conclusions of the Lisbon Summit with a high-level appeal on CSR and offered concrete actions to build an entrepreneurial and inclusive knowledge society, develop a culture of communication and multiplication of best practices, expand teaching of corporate social responsibility and invest in public–private partnerships. As a result, the EU governments placed corporate social responsibility at the heart of the Lisbon Strategy launched at the summit. In turn, this helped to shape the objective of making "Europe the most competitive and dynamic knowledge-based economy in the world capable of sustainable economic growth with more and better jobs and greater social cohesion by 2010."[306] By asking for such an appeal on CSR at the level of EU Heads of State, CSR Europe knew that this would be the catalyst for the European Commission to reflect and develop a European Strategy on CSR.

In July 2001, the European Commission presented its Green Paper on Corporate Social Responsibility.[307] This policy document launched a wide debate on how the European Union could promote corporate social responsibility at both the European and international level. The Green Paper aimed to underpin a consultation process on how to combine profitability with sustainability and accountability. The paper generated about 25 written responses from various kinds of stakeholder, including businesses, employer federations, trade unions, NGOs and academics. Following the consultation, the European Commission issued its first "Communication on Corporate Social Responsibility" where corporate social responsibility was defined as "a concept whereby companies integrate social and environmental concerns in their business operations and in their interaction with stakeholders on a voluntary basis."[308]

By means of that declaration, the Commission indicated that CSR should primarily be driven by the voluntary initiative of businesses rather than by binding regulations. CSR Europe was intimately involved in the consultation process leading up to this Communication, setting a pattern to be repeated in what one participant, using a table-tennis analysis, has described as the European Commission and CSR Europe playing "ping-pong" on the evolution of EU policy on CSR and the development of corporate practice.

In 2001, CSR Europe co-hosted the first European Presidency Conference on CSR organized by the Belgian government. In the closing session, Viscount Davignon was challenged by Jean Lapeyre from the European Trade Union Confederation to negotiate on putative European legislation on CSR reporting. Explaining that the public, private and civil-society partners in Europe were not yet knowledgeable, nor experienced enough in the field of CSR, Viscount Davignon instead proposed the creation of a European stakeholder platform on CSR. One year later, CSR Europe played a leading role in defining the objectives, methodology and initial scope of, and became part of the coordination for, the European Multi-Stakeholder Forum on CSR,[309] which is still active today. The main parties involved in the Forum, apart from the Commission itself, were: the European Trade Union Confederation; the employers' representative body, UNICE (now Business Europe); and the Platform of European Social NGOs, which brought together European non-governmental organizations, federations and networks interested in promoting a European social dimension.[310]

The Forum met at two levels. A high-level gathering of the Forum's participants took place once a year to agree on its guidelines and rules of procedures, set the agenda and assess progress, while a series of theme-based discussion roundtables took place regularly, bringing together Forum representatives, observers and experts in the specific field of CSR under discussion.[311]

The main conclusions of the Forum were collected in a report in 2004.[312] The first part of that document contains widely recognized principles, standards and conventions relating to CSR. The second part analyzes the internal and external factors driving CSR initiatives and the obstacles to achieving these initiatives. The third part offers recommendations to all stakeholders for building future capacity in CSR. The fundamental message of the report is that CSR success depends on raising awareness of core values and principles and developing the capacities and the tools to mainstream it as part of core management practice. The report also made a strong recommendation for governments to play a more active role in ensuring "an enabling environment" for CSR. The Forum was appealing to the EU and national governments to take a leading role on the issue of sustainable development.

Engaging the academic community

CSR Europe also played a pivotal role in involving the European academic community on CSR issues. On the occasion of the Belgian EU Presidency Conference on CSR in 2001, Viscount Davignon illustrated CSR Europe's new European campaign. He referred to the preparation of tomorrow's managers through academic education as one of CSR Europe's priorities.

In 2002, at INSEAD in France, CSR Europe launched EABIS, originally the European Academy of Business in Society (since 2010 known as the Academy of Business in Society while retaining the same acronym).[313] INSEAD, Ashridge, Bocconi, Copenhagen Business School, Cranfield University, IESE, IMD, London Business School, Vlerick School of Management and Warwick Business School on the academic side, and IBM, Johnson & Johnson, Microsoft, Shell and Unilever on the business side, joined forces to support the foundation of EABIS.

EABIS's mission was to become a respected reference point for the integration of CSR into the mainstream of business theory, research and education, and to enhance models for sustainable business success. To that end, EABIS set itself three main objectives:

- To encourage Europe's top universities and business schools to integrate the changing role of business in society into the core of business education

- To build Europe's largest network of excellence and deliver interdisciplinary research on CSR

- To promote innovative training practices and develop new teaching methods and materials

Since its foundation, more than 120 academic institutions and business corporations have joined EABIS (see Chapter 7, Box 7.5, page 103).

Promoting CSR as a mainstream business practice

In 2003, two of Europe's leading CSR practitioners were appointed to senior management and governance positions at CSR Europe. On the initiative of Noterdaeme and Vandenhende, who had been co-managers of the organization up to this point, CSR Europe decided to appoint an executive director. Bernard Giraud from Danone was appointed by the Board as the first Executive Director. Meanwhile, Frank Welvaert from Johnson & Johnson was appointed as Chairman of the Board, in succession to Alan Christie from Levi Strauss. This allowed Noterdaeme and Vandenhende to continue as senior managers of the organization and to focus on building relationships with the EU institutions, member companies and national partner organizations. With this shift in leadership, CSR Europe geared up for a new challenge: to set out a vision for embedding CSR in business practice.

In 2005, on the occasion of CSR Europe's tenth anniversary, Welvaert presented *A European Roadmap for Business: Towards a Sustainable and Competitive Enterprise*.[314] This paper, written by CSR Europe in collaboration with its national partner organizations, argued that voluntary commitments on the part of European businesses helped them to achieve substantial progress in CSR. The document concluded that CSR should remain a voluntary initiative beyond legal compliance.

As part of an effort to promote a mainstream approach to CSR, CSR Europe organized the first European MarketPlace on CSR in 2005. Rather than a conventional conference with many speeches, participants were free to wander from stall to stall to learn about successful initiatives. It was a market-based platform where up to 500 businesses and CSR practitioners could share practical CSR solutions to business challenges; 600 of these solutions were subsequently made public on the CSR Europe website. The success was such that the initiative was repeated in each of the following two years and this instigated the creation of national-led CSR Marketplace events in Portugal, Spain, Turkey, Hungary, Italy and the Czech Republic.

The philosophy that businesses should voluntarily initiate the changes necessary for achieving socially responsible practices was placed at the heart of CSR Europe's message to EU institutions. The organization felt that it was, at the time, too early for any regulatory frameworks on CSR, which it feared could have jeopardized the innovation and learning process required to achieve necessary consistency and credibility. The European

Commission responded to the challenge and through the then European Commissioners Verheugen (Enterprise and Industry) and Spidla (Employment and Social Affairs) invited Viscount Davignon, with a group of business leaders, as the representative of CSR Europe, to elaborate on a business partnership for sustainable business. In their meetings with the European Commissioners, CSR Europe made the need for the European Commissioners to have similar meetings with NGOs and trade unions very clear. Soon after, the European Commission formally endorsed the method of a business-led initiative, which then became the European Alliance for CSR. For the first time, this initiative provided a platform for companies and stakeholders to cooperate practically through thematic laboratories.

In March 2006, the European Commission published a further communication entitled *Implementing the Partnership for Growth and Jobs*.[315] The document placed particular emphasis on the integration of CSR into business practices through voluntary initiatives. In that communication, the European Commission acknowledged that enterprises should be the primary actors in CSR and no compulsory legislation should constrain their ability to implement CSR principles. In fact, the Commission scrapped its original plan to propose binding legislation on CSR practices, including the idea of (a) publishing a naming-and-shaming list of companies not complying with CSR, and (b) creating a monitoring system for the implementation of the CSR principles. In the same policy document, the European Commission launched the idea of a business-led, pro-business "European alliance for CSR," an open coalition between large companies and SMEs that intended to promote CSR initiatives.

Establishment of the European Alliance for CSR

In response to the European Commission communication, CSR Europe set up the European Alliance for CSR along with Business Europe, representing big companies, and the European Association of Craft, Small and Medium-sized Enterprises (UEAPME). This event was followed by a string of protests from NGOs and trade unions that saw the Alliance as a threat to the multi-stakeholder dialogue and hence decided to step out of the Multi-Stakeholder Forum. As a result, the 2006 session of the Multi-Stakeholder Forum on Social Responsibility broke up.

While the Multi-Stakeholder Forum entered a period of crisis, and did not resume until a high-level plenary session in February 2009,[316] the business-led European Alliance of CSR gained momentum. CSR Europe remained focused on the needs of business and conducted a survey of over 500 business solutions and 140 business networking activities. As a result of this survey, CSR Europe drew up *The European Cartography on CSR Innovations, Gaps and Future Trends*, which provided useful evidence of the connections between innovation and CSR. In particular, the cartography illustrated why CSR mattered to businesses and their stakeholders, verified the impact of CSR on the bottom line of business and identified different types of constraints that companies faced when implementing CSR.[317]

In 2007, business leaders of the European Alliance of CSR Europe had a high-level meeting with EU Commissioners Verheugen and Spidla to review the progress of the Alliance and to discuss how CSR practices could boost the EU Strategy for Growth and Jobs. This opened the way for business leaders to convey their ideas to representatives of the Commission and national officials.

One of the immediate initiatives taken by CSR Europe under the umbrella of the European Alliance for CSR was the institution of CSR Laboratories. Companies, business organizations and stakeholders across Europe and beyond set up a number of CSR "laboratories" (task forces advised by corporate and other experts on the topic of the particular laboratory) to tackle some of the most pressing issues related to CSR, and, since the beginning of 2007, a total of 20 laboratories have been launched.[318] Over the years, these laboratories have involved around 200 companies and stakeholder organizations, working together to tackle issues ranging from eco-efficiency to diversity, demographic change, responsible supply-chain management, basic social services, employability, entrepreneurship, CSR reporting and well-being in the workplace. Each CSR Laboratory is led by companies and coordinated by CSR Europe and its partner organizations. The first results of the laboratories were collected in the *European Toolbox for a Competitive and Responsible Europe*.[319] In 2009, CSR Europe, along with its national partners, organized a road show around Europe to disseminate these results.

Enterprise 2020

In October 2010, CSR Europe launched *Enterprise 2020*. At first, this initiative had a twofold purpose. First, it served as a platform for companies to partner on innovative CSR practices and to collaborate with other stakeholders. Second, it was designed to engage EU institutions to provide the business contribution to the EU's 2020 Strategy for smart, sustainable and inclusive growth. Since its launch, *Enterprise 2020* has become the reference initiative for the ideal company of the future and now forms the umbrella for all CSR Europe activities.

One example of the projects now sitting under the umbrella of *Enterprise 2020* is how CSR Europe has contributed to promoting best practices of active aging within human resource departments of companies. In 2011 it produced, jointly with Age Platform Europe, the report *2012: Everyone Has a Role to Play*.[320] In the same year, it launched *The Business Contribution to Active Ageing: In Line With the European Year of Active Ageing*, a study led by some of its members, such as Intel and GDF Suez. This is an initiative that aimed at celebrating the 2012 European Year for Active Ageing and Solidarity Between Generations, by analyzing current trends in aging and intergenerational solidarity within companies, putting forward best practices and explaining their business case. CSR Europe led work with member companies and others to develop this. It is now expanding this collaborative project, "The Business Contribution to Active Ageing," and project participants will look to produce tangible outcomes that can guide business in two areas:

- **Active aging in employment.** Tendencies, best practices and methodologies with regard to HR practices on retention/capacity building/recruitment, work–life balance, skills transfer and entrepreneurship

- **Product and service development.** Identifying the gap between the current product and services offer by companies and the actual needs of aging customers[321]

Expansion and decentralization

Over the years, there have been two significant shifts in CSR Europe's membership and reach: the organization progressively expanded its geographical scope and decentralized part of its administration and activities. Although originally an organization rooted in the

Figure P3.1 **Enterprise 2020 put into practice**

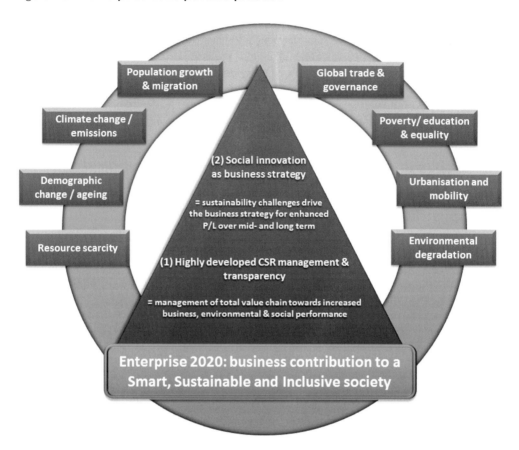

Population growth & migration

Global trade & governance

Climate change / emissions

Poverty/ education & equality

(2) Social innovation as business strategy

Demographic change / ageing

Urbanisation and mobility

= sustainability challenges drive the business strategy for enhanced P/L over mid- and long term

Resource scarcity

Environmental degradation

(1) Highly developed CSR management & transparency

= management of total value chain towards increased business, environmental & social performance

Enterprise 2020: business contribution to a Smart, Sustainable and Inclusive society

European Union both in membership and in scope of action, CSR Europe has stretched its geographic borders. As economic globalization evolved, CSR issues started to cut across geographical borders, especially through large multinationals such as CSR Europe's members. Against this background, CSR Europe accepted companies with headquarters outside Europe as members, starting with IBM, Johnson & Johnson, Coca-Cola, HP, Intel, Microsoft, Bank of America, Citigroup and Western Union. CSR Europe had a similar expansion with Japanese-parented companies, such as Canon, Toyota, Sony, Panasonic and Hitachi.

In parallel, the geographic criteria for becoming a partner business-led organization were relaxed with a view to including European business associations established in countries not belonging to the EU, such as Croatia, Switzerland and Norway (see Chapter 3, Section 3.2.4 for a list of all the current partners). The idea was that the EU as a political entity did not necessarily correspond with Europe as an area of free trade and commercial partnerships. CSR Europe's borders stretched further with the admission of partners from Turkey (in 2008) and Ukraine (in 2011). This move happened at around the same time as the acceptance of DTEK, a Ukrainian company, and TTNET, a Turkish company, as members of CSR Europe.

At the same time, as European companies shifted more of their manufacturing activities to China, CSR Europe also started to share intelligence on CSR in that market. In 2005, CSR

Europe co-organized with WTO Tribune Magazine a Sino-European International Forum on CSR in Beijing. The outcome of the forum was a joint publication on CSR in China,[322] aimed at supporting investors in China who were looking to combine performance requirements and sustainable development priorities (see Chapter 6, Section 6.1.1). Having been a success, the conference took place in subsequent years; with CSR Europe and the Japanese Council for Better Corporate Citizenship. On the occasion of the Sixth Conference in 2011, a new platform for Chinese companies to enhance their responsible competitiveness and contribute to global sustainable development was launched. In a move that validated the profound CSR implications of the stronger economic ties between Europe and China, in August 2011, CSR Europe accepted the first Chinese company among its members: Huawei, a telecom company with substantial operations in Europe.

Another significant trend in the way CSR Europe has operated in recent years has been the decentralization of its management and activities. Since its foundation, CSR Europe's network has relied on the backing of two main actors: multinational companies as members and national organizations as partners. The exercise of power inside CSR Europe initially rested mainly with its members, the multinational companies. They were the main interlocutors in the dialogue with the EU institutions and they were the members of the executive board that set out the strategy for the whole organization.

As partners grew in number, some of them established by CSR Europe itself, they became more influential within CSR Europe. Partners liaised with their own national members, in particular with SMEs, and became more proactive inside CSR Europe. For instance, national partners were sometimes involved in informing CSR Europe about companies applying for membership to ensure that they have an acceptable CSR record in their countries of origin. The major change occurred in 2008, when the partners started to elect their representatives to CSR Europe's Board. As of 2012, the governance and management of CSR Europe is built around its two categories of associates: members and partners. In 2012 the Board of Directors was composed of 12 individuals representing 75 corporate members and 3 individuals representing 31 national partner organizations. The current Executive Director, Stefan Crets, has the task of steering the course of a more sophisticated organization towards new achievements in corporate responsibility.

Impact and lessons learned

CSR Europe has been a significant external organization helping to shape European Commission thinking and policy about corporate responsibility and how this relates to EU policies such as social inclusion, international competitiveness and sustainable development. Significantly, the Multi-Stakeholder Forum coordinating group charged with monitoring progress on the 2011 Commission on CSR Communication is now working with officials across health, external relations, trade, development, research etc., as well as traditional interlocutors in the Commission's Directorates-General of Employment and Enterprise, showing how embedded CSR is becoming in the Commission's thinking.

At the same time, CSR Europe has played an important role in helping to identify and disseminate good practice in various aspects of embedding responsible business practices across the EU and beyond, through its business-led "laboratories," Marketplaces, publications and portal. Through the establishment of EABIS, it has also helped to promote research and teaching in business schools about the role of business in society, corporate sustainability and corporate responsibility.

Critical success factors for CSR Europe's existence to date have included the close relationship with the EU Commission (CSR Europe has a semi-official recognition from both the EU Commission and the stakeholders), the leadership of Viscount Davignon, and the ability to engage member companies.

The future

In terms of focus, content and groundwork, CSR Europe will continue to provide a platform for connecting members to share best practices, fostering learning, exchanging information and providing the opportunity to jointly work on practical and collaborative solutions. The organization will aim to help companies find the balance between **minimizing risks** through accountability and transparency and **maximizing opportunities** through social innovation that lies at the heart of the *Enterprise 2020* initiative. In this respect, CSR Europe will continue supporting members in their progress towards *Enterprise 2020* through:

- **Highly developed CSR management and transparency.** Guiding companies in their integration of CSR into global supply chains and ensuring that their business contributes to sustainable development worldwide. This builds on the *Enterprise 2020* work and includes topics such as measurement and reporting of extra-financial performance (including integrated reporting); and business and human rights

- **Social innovation as business strategy.** Supporting companies in their efforts to develop smart, sustainable, inclusive and growth, through innovative business models, products and services. This will build on existing *Enterprise 2020* projects, such as Active Ageing or Inclusive Business models at the Base of the Pyramid

Such *Enterprise 2020* collaborative projects will take the organization beyond best-practice sharing through more focus on practical collaboration and innovation with peers and expert stakeholders on projects to produce tangible results and models that can be shared externally across industries.

In terms of its continuous dialogue and partnership with the EU institutions, CSR Europe welcomes the fact that the European Commission recognized *Enterprise 2020* in its European Strategy on CSR (2011–14) as an example of business leadership that is particularly relevant to EU policy objectives and that it will help to review and define next steps of the initiative. It will be through the *Enterprise 2020* activities that CSR Europe will expand and accelerate synergies between business innovation and EU policies and programs on: employment, environment, industry, education, consumers, health, development, trade and external relations.[323] In the face of the economic crisis in the EU and high levels of unemployment especially among European youth, the role of CSR Europe and its member companies and national partners has arguably never been more challenging or more important.

Profile 4
Instituto Ethos

Heiko Spitzeck, extended and updated by Jane Nelson[*]

Instituto Ethos in its own words

The Ethos Institute for Business and Social Responsibility is a non-profit organization. Its mission is to mobilize, sensitize and help companies manage their business in a socially responsible manner, making them partners in building a just and sustainable society.

Created in 1998 by a group of entrepreneurs and executives from the private sector, the Ethos Institute is a center for organization of knowledge, exchange of experiences and development of tools to help companies analyze their management practices and deepen their commitment to social responsibility and sustainable development. It is also an international reference in these matters, developing projects in partnership with several organizations around the world.[324]

www.ethos.org.br   June 2012

---

[*] The original profile was written by Heiko Spitzeck, while a member of the Doughty Centre for Corporate Responsibility faculty in 2010.

The authors are grateful for interviews with João Gilberto Azevedo and Tabata Marchetti Villares, Instituto Ethos, São Paulo, Brazil, January 28, 2010..

Background context and history

Instituto Ethos was founded in 1998 by a group of "activist businessmen"[325] and is as such a private initiative. However, the roots of Brazilian businesses discussing corporate responsibility issues and playing an activist social role date back much further.[326] As far back as 1987, a group of business leaders discussed the roles and responsibilities of business in society and formed the PNBE (Pensamento Nacional das Bases Empresariais – National Thinking of the Entrepreneurial Class). The PNBE summoned about 1,000 business leaders primarily from SMEs, and they played a major role in the impeachment process of former President Collor de Mello in 1992.

Oded Grajew, one of the founders of Instituto Ethos, was president of the PNBE in the 1980s. He was a successful entrepreneur in the toy industry and in 1990 created the Fundação Abrinq (Brazilian Association of Toy Manufacturers), which brought together companies in the toy industry and other partners to actively promote and protect the rights of children and adolescents.

In 1998 Oded Grajew visited the Business for Social Responsibility (BSR) conference in Florida together with some Brazilian colleagues. On returning to Brazil they adapted the BSR template and created Instituto Ethos. Starting with 12 member companies, and the transfer of BSR evaluation tools and questionnaires into Brazil, the group hosted its first conference in the same year in which about 100 delegates participated.

From the outset the aim was to engage with and motivate Brazilian companies to improve their corporate responsibility performance. Over the past decade, Ethos has been successful in attracting members and its membership has grown from the 12 founding companies in 1998 to 700 in 2003 to over 1,300 a decade later.

It is important to note that like the other corporate responsibility coalitions, Ethos does not represent its member companies. As it is not a representative body, it is able to retain flexibility to challenge member companies to improve their corporate responsibility performance. In some cases Ethos has done so in a public fashion. A particularly high profile example was a case with Brazil's major energy company, Petrobras, when senior Ethos directors publicly challenged the company to improve certain aspects of its environmental performance and criticized it for not taking a more proactive leadership role on particular sustainability issues.

By 2012, the membership of Instituto Ethos had expanded to over 1,300 companies, and its mandate had expanded substantially in terms of both issues of strategic focus and influence.

Key activities and phases of development

Instituto Ethos perceives its key roles as:[327]

- **Broadening the corporate responsibility movement:** Sensitizing and engaging companies in the concept of corporate responsibility

- **Establishing and integrating corporate responsibility practices:** Through tools such as the Ethos Indicators for corporate responsibility, workshops, research, case studies and good practices

- **Creating an enabling environment for corporate responsibility**: Through influencing the market and its most important actors Ethos aims to create an environment that is favorable to corporate responsibility

- **Influencing public policy:** Formulating policies to support corporate responsibility and supporting companies' involvement in public policy processes. Dissemination of corporate responsibility in the public domain and assisting in stakeholder engagement

- **Knowledge creation:** Production and dissemination of corporate responsibility related information, such as corporate responsibility data, case studies and international best practices. Fostering the international dialogue between corporate responsibility leaders

The implementation of these activities has evolved over the first decade of Instituto Ethos, and they have become increasingly strategic. Three key stages of development can be identified:

Stage one: CSR – get management to act

The founders believed that "companies are able to push social change"[328] and the challenge was how to move companies to do that.[329] The leverage for change in companies was seen to be located with the company's senior management team. Recognizing that most senior executives in companies are driven by numbers, the first focus of Instituto Ethos was on developing a strong business case for corporate responsibility. It did this by developing the Ethos Indicators for responsible management and evaluating company performance against those indicators. The indicators also exemplified Ethos principles of ethical conduct and transparency.

A conscious decision was made to develop the Ethos Indicators as a self-assessment tool rather than a public index. The fear was that an index would lead companies to focus on better evaluations in the index instead of on the responsibility of their conduct. As João Gilberto Azevedo, manager of International Relations for Ethos, explained in an interview with the author: "[What is] important is the process and education, not the final grade/assessment in any kind of index." In order to have an educational impact the self-assessment challenges companies to reflect on their practices. As there is no perfect formula for success, each company is encouraged to come up with its own way of responsible management, within the broad framework of the indicators.

Another important factor in not launching a public index is Ethos's goal of inclusiveness. For Ethos it does not matter at which stage a company starts to address corporate responsibility – as long as it does so genuinely.

Stage two: Value-chain responsibility – leverage the value chain

In 2006 Ethos started to realize that "CSR is necessary but not sufficient for social transformation."[330] The scope of activities that until then concentrated on management teams within member companies was perceived to be too limited, and Ethos pushed for an extension to include the whole value chain. A company's competence to drive CSR through the whole value chain was then perceived as great leverage for social transformation. Accordingly, Ethos developed indicators and a number of projects that focused on management and measurement issues related to responsible supply-chain management. It also developed indicators for individual companies to assess what they were doing to support the Millennium Development Goals. Although the scope had broadened from internal management processes and metrics to value chain management, driving better performance through individual companies and their activities remained the central focus.

Stage three: Responsible competitiveness – towards an inclusive, green and responsible market

The year 2008 marked the tenth anniversary of Instituto Ethos. This triggered a thorough evaluation of where the organization had gotten to in mobilizing the business community around better social and environmental performance. A broad consultation process was initiated with the board, the international advisory council, internal and external members and other stakeholders to reflect on the achievements so far and the challenges ahead. There was key recognition that, in addition to ongoing efforts to embed responsible business practices within individual companies and spread responsible business practices along broader corporate value chains, there was also a need for much more systemic change to make markets and public policy more conducive to sustainable and responsible business practices. The organization recognized that such action needed effective business leadership but could only have a systemic impact if it was undertaken in partnership with governments, civil society and other organizations. The importance of public policy was also strongly acknowledged. Among the 342 proposals received during the consultation phase in 2008, 114 were in the area of regulation and 107 in government action. This led to a new era of engagement by Instituto Ethos. In addition to developing a multi-stakeholder platform to drive a more inclusive, green and responsible economy, which is described in the next section, Ethos has also embarked on some ambitious multi-stakeholder alliances to tackle key systemic challenges in specific geographic or issue areas.

One example is the initiative **"Sustainable Connections: São Paulo–Amazonia."** This program aims to develop multi-stakeholder pacts between companies, public officials and activists to improve the sustainability of livestock, wood and soy value chains between the Amazon and the mega-city of São Paulo, with the aim of preserving the Amazon rainforest and its people. The signatories to each commodity pact agree to support the financing, distribution and marketing of products that have been certified or are in the process of being certified. The signatories also commit to raise awareness among their customers and suppliers. The pacts have a Monitoring Committee, which monitors compliance against the commitments made, and all signatories are required to provide regular progress reports. Signatories include global retailers such as Walmart and Carrefour, as well as local companies such as Grupo Pão de Açúcar, Friboi and Grupo Orsa, and the city of São Paulo. The Monitoring

Committee consists of corporate signatories; Instituto Ethos and several civil-society organizations, such as Amigos da Terra (Friends of the Earth Brazil), Movimento Nossa São Paulo (Our São Paulo Movement) and Instituto Socioambiental (Socioenvironmental Institute); and the media, represented by Reporter Brasil. In addition to the major companies making specific and measurable commitments for more sustainable sourcing, the city government has also passed a law regulating the purchase of beef for the city in ways that aim to address the preservation of the rainforest and promote good working practices, including efforts to combat child labor and forced labor.

Another example of the greater strategic focus that Instituto Ethos has placed on convening and supporting more systemic and transformative multi-stakeholder platforms is the **Clean Games (Jogos Limpos)** initiative. In 2014, Brazil will be hosting the World Cup and in 2016 the Olympic Games and Paralympics. Billions of dollars will be spent on infrastructure and procurement. In order to promote greater transparency and integrity of public spending during this period, Instituto Ethos is serving as the Secretariat for a large-scale partnership platform called the Clean Games. Working with the United Nations Global Compact and the UN Office on Drugs and Crime (UNODC), and with financial support from the Siemens Integrity Initiative, Instituto Ethos is developing a series of voluntary integrity pacts between companies and public officials, a set of transparency indicators, and a public awareness platform that will enable citizens, civil society and other interested organizations to monitor ethical conduct of the games. Other supporting partners include Alcoa, CPFI Energia, Natura, Suzano, Vale, Walmart and Roland Berger. Companies and government bodies involved in the multi-billion-dollar process of preparing for the games are being called on to make public commitments aimed at taking preventative measures against fraud and corruption. At the same time, civil society will have access to the indicators and tools to support social control of public spending and investment in these major sporting events. This unprecedented public–private partnership platform could serve as a model not only for major events, but also for greater transparency and integrity of large-scale infrastructure projects more broadly.

As of 2012, Instituto Ethos continues to engage its members at all three levels: embedding corporate responsibility into internal management processes; driving corporate responsibility along external value chains; and promoting responsible competitiveness more broadly at the systemic level. Figure P4.1 illustrates the three stages of the coalition's evolution and Table P4.1 gives examples of the key products of Instituto Ethos and illustrates how these have evolved to meet member company needs and priorities in these three stages.

Increasingly, however, Instituto Ethos is focused on the third stage of helping to drive systemic change towards a more inclusive, green and responsible economy.

Impact and lessons learned

The objective of Instituto Ethos is the construction of a sustainable and just society.[331] CSR is one strategy to achieve this objective, given that companies have cultural, moral, social, environmental, economic and political influence on the functioning of society. In the first ten years of its operation, Ethos concentrated on promoting this new corporate vision and

Figure P4.1 **The three development stages of Instituto Ethos**

Table P4.1 **Examples of key 'products' developed by Instituto Ethos**

'Product'	1998–2006	2006–2008	2008–2015
Ethos Indicators	Stimulating executives and management to become more responsible within their own company	Extension of indicators to include supply-chain issues in order to broaden impact	Evaluation of how far companies contribute to the Millennium Development Goals and now a more inclusive, green and responsible economy more broadly
Ethos Annual Summit	Sharing vanguard ideas and spreading knowledge and best practices		Co-creating a shared vision of the future and negotiating relative roles, responsibilities and public commitments
UniEthos			Spread of knowledge, increasing skills, incubating social enterprises

providing knowledge, practices, methodologies and tools for change towards responsible business. It was also considered necessary to recognize corporate engagement publicly.

During its first ten years, Instituto Ethos and the Brazilian corporate responsibility "movement" achieved the following:

- It sensitized executives to the risks and reputation issues related to responsible business. Businesses extended their societal responsibilities and started reporting more extensively. More Brazilian businesses affiliated with the UN Global Compact and with policies on anti-corruption, slave labor and organized dialogues

- There was a clear shift from a defensive to a more proactive stance among Brazilian businesses

- Other actors such as media, academia, unions, NGOs, public administration and social movements integrated corporate responsibility in their deliberations and activities

- Society in general became more aware of sustainability issues

- Brazilian academics became more interested in the topic and started to offer more courses and undertake more research on corporate responsibility

However, despite the progress it had made, research by Akatu (the Institute for Conscious Consumption that was established by Ethos in 2001) indicated that the corporate responsibility movement had lost credibility in general and that options for system-level progress were running out. This demonstrates the limitations of a voluntary corporate responsibility approach by companies. Major shortcomings were seen in the following areas:

- Responsible business did not yet reach core business operations in most companies

- The financial crisis led to a cut in initiatives and many companies refocused on purely financial indicators – damaging the credibility and the seriousness of the corporate responsibility movement

- Of the 56 corporate responsibility practices that are considered basic by Ethos, on average, 20% of member companies implemented 35, 50% of the companies 22, and 70% of members only 13. Ethos found four groups of companies:
  1. Companies that understand corporate responsibility and try to balance their financial performance with societal considerations
  2. Companies that understand corporate responsibility but still focus on financial profitability and do corporate responsibility in a bolt-on fashion
  3. Companies that do not understand corporate responsibility in a strategic sense and execute a fragmented corporate responsibility approach
  4. Companies that do not understand corporate responsibility and do nothing

In this sense *more* (member companies) does not equal *better* (impact). Ethos itself writes, "the increase in member companies did not yet translate into a significant change in corporate practices."[332]

Furthermore Ethos observed:

- There is still a predominant consumption culture in Brazil

- Social exclusion still continuously nourishes a circle of poverty

- Employment relationships are mostly of low quality and highly informal (without contracts)

- There is an increasing income gap separating rich and poor

- Corruption is still well-rooted in Brazilian business, government and society

- Access to justice and law is distributed unevenly in the population

- Politics still focus on economic development as the only means of development

- Civil-society organizations lack funding and support

- There are fragmented societal initiatives with low impact

At the same time, as part of its analysis, Ethos noted that Brazil is embedded in and is an increasingly influential player driving a global economy that is facing the following trends and characteristics:

- Increased urgency to act in terms of climate change

- Growth of a "green economy" – some major governments investing in green jobs and infrastructure to stimulate the economy in order to fight the economic crisis

- Increasing attention to regulatory systems and impacts – this is even more so in the aftermath of the financial crisis

- Lost trust in the market mechanisms, which increases the demand for more responsible corporate actors and greater corporate transparency

- Social problems that were increasing even before the financial crisis, such as unemployment, food insecurity and poor health, are now increasing even more

- In general there is a new focus on the importance of governments and good politics

The general conclusion was that, after a decade of business action on corporate responsibility in Brazil, there were "a lot of advances but with little impact." Ethos concluded that there is a danger that while the corporate responsibility movement might have a positive impact on improving certain products and services it could do so without revising the market's fundamentally unsustainable characteristics in modes of production and consumption, as well as the unequal distribution of wealth.

It was this analysis that emphasized the need to be more systemic and ambitious and to focus not only on improving performance in individual companies and value chains, but also on working collectively and systemically to shift the market in driving greater inclusiveness, sustainability and responsible conduct beyond voluntary approaches. This requires more strategic engagement with government to be effective. In its first ten years, Ethos concentrated on changing corporate culture, improving corporate management practices and propagating voluntary corporate action. The reflections and consultations from 2008 to 2010, however, highlighted the need for a more comprehensive and systemic way forward.

The future

In the next ten years, Ethos aims to concentrate on uniting social forces to create a market system that inspires responsible products and services as well as new processes of production and consumption. The central focus for Ethos will be on working strategically with others towards the creation of an inclusive, green and responsible economy in Brazil.

In 2010, Ethos partnered with the strategic consultants Roland Berger, along with a core group of six leading companies, to develop an action-oriented platform defining what an inclusive, green and responsible economy would look like and what would be required to get there. The six companies were: Alcoa, CPFL Energia, Natura, Suzano Papel e Celulose, Vale and Walmart Brasil. As Roland Berger noted, "For years, Brazil has been establishing itself as a major player in the global economy. But people in the booming country have come to feel that standards of corporate responsibility have not kept up with the country's economic leap forward."[333]

In February 2011, the platform was presented to CEOs and senior representatives of almost 200 of the largest companies in Brazil, as well as media and government officials. Instituto Ethos, its core partners and others have now embarked on the next phase to design management structures, strategies and strategic alliances to support this new platform for change (see Table P4.3).

Table P4.3 **Platform for an inclusive, green and responsible economy**

Source: Adapted from Roland Berger and Instituto Ethos, *Plataforma por uma Economia Inclusiva, Verde e Responsável* (Platform for an inclusive, green and responsible economy) (São Paulo, Brazil: Instituto Ethos/Roland Berger, 2011)

Inclusive economy	• Level of participation of people at the base of the economic pyramid as producers, workers and consumers • Eradication of poverty • Increasing equality in access to income, basic products and services and to legal rights • Increasing quality of life for the different segments of society
Green economy	• Continuous improvement of production processes • High level of eco-efficiency and reduced consumption of natural resources • Reduced greenhouse gas emissions • Transformation of process waste into input in other processes • Incurring the costs of externalities in the prices of products • Protection of springs, effective use of water and universal basic sanitation • Increased energy efficiency and share of clean and renewable sources in the energy and transportation matrices • Greater mobility and effectiveness of the means of transportation • Recovery and preservation of ecosystems • Mitigation of climate change effects
Responsible economy	• Countering corruption and impunity • Valuing integrity and transparency • Encouraging fair competition • Encouraging cooperation • Respect for business laws and rules • Respect of the rights of different communities, ethnic and social groups to adopt the contemporary lifestyle in their own pace

The central strategy aims at creating a core circle of companies to push for this new form of economy. This changes the Ethos current strategy in two important ways: by focusing on a new economy the scope of activities is broadened, and the voluntary approach to responsible business needs to be complemented with new legislative requirements and public-policy reforms.

The following activities are considered central to achieving progress:

- Create partnerships between companies, unions, NGOs, universities and public organizations for the formulation and implementation of "public and private compromises" for a new economy

- Provoke, propose and collaborate with leading Ethos companies towards a social mobilization for a new economy

- Create a forum of permanent dialogue as a space for debate and collaborative construction of a model of development

- Develop mechanisms of mobilization with companies to broaden the social base of the movement. What is necessary is a change in the political system and the general culture towards a culture of sustainability and democracy

- Direct an agenda for public and private compromises for a new economy with rules, objectives, policies and instruments of support, programs of implementation in general and in sectors towards the development of an inclusive, green and responsible economy

Some examples of collective business and, in some cases, government action might be:

- Introduction of a carbon tax system and other ways to internalize social and environmental externalities into public-sector and corporate accounting, reporting and decision-making

- Increased research and investment in innovation for sustainability, including public investment in corporate activities to develop sustainable products and services

- Introduction of programs of education for sustainability as a qualification for certain types of employment

- Production and dissemination of indicators to evaluate the market and to select companies, technologies and products related to sustainability

- Public recognition mechanisms that value initiatives and practices of inclusivity, and a green and responsible economy

Ethos is aware that this ambitious new agenda requires a deep shift in how it is organized currently in terms of projects and how it is governed and financed. Ethos needs to be:

- More agile and with greater impact

- More demanding in relation to its associates

- More concentrated on a broader vision for Brazil

- The hub and instructor for change towards sustainability of the country

- Able to motivate others in joining the movement and pushing for change

With regard to member companies, Ethos wants to see them act more as promoters, articulators, mediators and advocates for the new more inclusive, green and responsible economy. It also wants to create an index that can evaluate the level of adherence of a member company to the agenda of the new economy. In addition, members will be asked to report on progress as a condition of membership.

As the Platform for an Inclusive, Green and Responsible Economy stated:

> Brazil – which is the owner of a large social diversity and of the greatest bio-logical diversity in the planet, and had increasingly positioned itself as a major protagonist in global business – needs to quickly move towards new paradigms. Just as it presents itself as a candidate for playing a key role among emerging countries in the new world order, it needs to offer itself as a key part of solutions for the major challenges of mankind.[334]

As Instituto Ethos moves towards its 20th anniversary, it aims to play a central role in this process. At the Rio + 20 Summit in June 2012, for example, it mobilized an unprecedented commitment by the CEOs of over 200 Brazilian companies to endorse a public vision entitled "Business Contributions to the Green and Inclusive Economy." The vision lays out ten prac-tical commitments to be achieved by each company. More than ever before, its goal is to be a leading actor in mobilizing Brazilian businesses in cooperation with government, civil soci-ety and workers towards the achievement of an inclusive, green and responsible economy at home, and to serve as a partner and role model abroad.[335]

Profile 5
International Business Leaders Forum (IBLF)

Profile written by Jane Nelson and David Grayson
from initial input by Ros Tennyson*

International Business Leaders Forum in its own words

The International Business Leaders Forum (IBLF) is an independent, global members organisation of over 150 leading multinational companies. We work across the sectors of business, government and civil society, focusing on critical sustainability, growth and leadership issues.

Since 1990, IBLF has focused on the themes of business leadership and corporate responsibility, working directly with CEO and Board-level executives to drive change across their companies and networks. Today our mission is to help leaders redefine growth in ways that are smart, inclusive and responsible. Our approach is to:

- Challenge and change current assumptions through original research and ideas
- Capacity-build to deliver sustainable solutions by developing "next generation" leadership and partnerships

* Ros Tennyson is the founder of The Partnering Initiative of the International Business Leaders' Forum and a former member of the IBLF senior management team. She is a visiting fellow of the Doughty Centre for Corporate Responsibility.

The authors would also like to thank Brook Horwitz, Peter Brew, Stephen Farrant, Adrian Hodges, Clare Melford and Darian Stibbe for their contributions to this profile.

- Catalyse collective action projects and new responsible business standards that put policy into practice

www.iblf.org   June 2012

Background context and history

The International Business Leaders Forum was created in February 1990, following a conference convened by HRH The Prince of Wales in Charleston, in the United States. At this event, business leaders from 15 countries debated the role of business in a world being transformed by the upheavals in the Soviet Union and political change in South Africa, with the release of Nelson Mandela that same month after 27 years in jail.

The IBLF owes its establishment to three people: Robert Davies, Stephen O'Brien and HRH The Prince of Wales. Davies was the charismatic founding CEO of the IBLF who led the organization from its inception in 1990 until his early death in 2007, having previously been Deputy CEO of Business in the Community (BITC). O'Brien was the CEO of BITC who encouraged Davies to spread his wings and create an international coalition to promote responsible business. HRH The Prince of Wales, as President of BITC, recognized in 1989 that there was much in BITC's work that could have resonance and value in other parts of the world. His enthusiasm in promoting the new organization (initially called International Business in the Community and after 1992, The Prince of Wales Business Leaders Forum, and finally in 2007, the International Business Leaders Forum) was fundamental to attracting business leaders and the heads of international institutions such as the UN and the World Bank in the early days. For the purpose of this profile, we use the organization's current name IBLF throughout.

Key activities and phases of development

The IBLF began life emphasizing its BITC heritage. The two organizations shared offices – first provided by National Westminster Bank, and subsequently in the corporate headquarters of Grand Metropolitan (which later merged with Guinness to form Diageo). Grand Metropolitan's CEO Allen Sheppard (later Lord Sheppard of Didgemere) chaired both BITC and IBLF. Initially, events and follow-up projects were built around the official visits overseas of HRH The Prince of Wales (to Brazil, India, Mexico and Hong Kong) – and especially to the former Communist countries of Central and Eastern Europe as their regimes transformed to democratic, market economies.

Relatively quickly after its establishment as an independently governed and funded entity in 1991, the IBLF developed its own path forward, working closely with local partners in the countries in which it operated. It gained a reputation for its approach to building trust and partnership between business, civil-society organizations and government bodies, and for its thought leadership on the role that mainstream business operations could play moving beyond corporate philanthropy in supporting progress in transitional and developing economies.

The following summarizes some of the key activities the IBLF has undertaken as it has evolved over the past two decades, and the role that these have played in building cross-sector partnerships and corporate responsibility institutions in over 40 countries around the world.

Supporting economic transition in Central and Eastern Europe

IBLF's pioneering early work in the Central and Eastern Europe region was based on The Prince of Wales's instinct that just as business had contributed to economic and social regeneration in the United Kingdom after the wholesale industrial restructuring of the 1980s, so it might similarly contribute to reconstruction of societies transitioning from communism to democracy and market economies.

Over the next decade, IBLF's Susan Simpson was instrumental in working closely with local partners to establish local business coalitions in Hungary, the Czech Republic, Slovakia, Poland and Bulgaria. These new entities each developed a range of business-led programs to support development activities tailored for the local market and led by local business leaders and staff. All five of these local business-led coalitions continue to exist today. A number of independent projects were also established in the region under the IBLF and the Prince of Wales's personal leadership. In most cases, these programs were based on shared learning between experts from the region and their counterparts from the UK. These included:

- **The establishment of programs to support youth enterprise** in the region, building on the models and experience of The Prince's Trust in the UK. Initiatives included the Hungarian Youth Enterprise Scheme and Autokreacja in Poland, aimed at building local human capital, skills and job creation among young people in these countries. Today, the IBLF still supports a youth enterprise program in partnership with Youth Business International in Russia

- **The development of small business incubators and business development services.** For example, with support from the corporate sector, the European Union and the United States government, the IBLF worked with local partners in Hungary to establish a small business incubator in the former Red Army barracks in Kecskemét. In Poland, the Krakow Development Forum was established as a result of an IBLF partnership workshop, providing a hub for the promotion of enterprising approaches to the economic, social and environmental development of the city

- **The St. Petersburg Partnership Initiative**, which started a 20-year commitment of the IBLF to working with Russian companies and social entrepreneurs. Initially the IBLF's work in Russia focused on projects supporting the arts and their contribution to job creation and economic regeneration. Projects included work with the Hermitage Museum and the publication of the Pushkin Notebooks facsimile. These were designed to develop management and marketing capabilities and attract investment in the area of heritage and the live arts where Russia's rich culture made it competitive worldwide. Showing sensitivity to and respect for Russia's cultural heritage helped the

IBLF to build credibility and goodwill for its wider programs. In due course, the focus of IBLF's work moved to Moscow and Russia remains one of IBLF's most successful programs in terms of its leading role in challenging and shaping business practice in this country. Box P5.1 provides an overview of IBLF's ongoing work in Russia.

Box P5.1 **IBLF Russia**

IBLF's work in Russia started in 1992 and focused on building capacity of NGOs, especially in the creative industries in St. Petersburg. Soon the business community began to show interest in creating a local organization that would promote sustainable development and social responsibility, and in 2004, the Russia Partnership for Responsible Business Practices was set up in Moscow. In 2007, the Moscow branch office of the IBLF was registered as IBLF Russia.

The mission of IBLF Russia is to enable the responsible conduct of business with the aim of ensuring the stable and sustainable social and economic development of Russia. Corporate partners include a number of global multinationals, Russian companies, and international professional services companies. IBLF Russia has a number of other stakeholders and donors who support its programs, including: the Moscow City government, the city councils of major regional centers such as Rostov, Kaluga, Novosibirsk, Vladivostok and Voronezh; international development organizations such as USAID, UK Department for International Development (DFID), EU-TACIS, CIPE, the World Bank and Oxfam; and local and global business associations and multi-stakeholder networks such as the Russian Union of Entrepreneurs (RSPP), World Economic Forum, AmCham, Association of European Businesses, Association of Independent Directors. The CEOs of corporate partners are members of the International Advisory Council, which meets biannually and oversees IBLF's work in Russia.

Over the years, IBLF Russia has addressed some of the key social issues confronting the country and impacting business. Its early programs with business involvement focused on the economic and social cost of health and safety risks and high mortality rates. Through roundtables and workshops, IBLF brought together chief medical officers and health and safety executives from major companies to exchange best practices on how to promote healthy life styles and a management culture where safety was a top priority. Other programs followed. A series on business and the environment, and training programs for young business leaders proved especially popular with executives from multinational and Russian companies alike. Currently the most successful programs led by IBLF Russia are Youth Business Russia and a Business Standards program:

Youth Business Russia establishes regional foundations that provide small loans and mentoring to young entrepreneurs wanting to set up their own businesses and who would not be able to obtain funding from commercial sources. The program recently celebrated the 100th young person receiving a loan from Youth Business Russia.

The Business Standards program works with business leaders to create a culture of good corporate governance, both within individual companies and more broadly in specific market sectors. IBLF Russia holds roundtables and workshops that encourage the exchange of best practices, for example an annual

Forum for non-executive directors. Beyond this, companies have supported the effort by participating in the development of a new compliance web-site, www. business-standards.ru, a course for business school students on business ethics, and occasional publications on how companies operating in Russia can manage corruption risk. The aim is to have significant impact in the market, and IBLF Russia's latest initiative aims to achieve such scale through a business–government dialogue on improving the efficiency, integrity and transparency of public procurement processes in Russian city administration.

Building cross-sector partnerships and partnership skills

Early in its evolution, the IBLF developed a reputation for its commitment and ability to bring together business and community leaders and entrepreneurs – often in unusual settings – to learn at first hand about each others' realities and capabilities. Based on the principle of a two-way exchange, these experiential and often intense interactions were aimed at giving decision-makers in different sectors both inspiration and practical ideas by seeing at first hand a combination of community-based and business-led solutions to tackling often intractable social, environmental and development challenges. At the same time, there was a focus on exploring the potential for new models of partnership between the sectors and, over time, testing such models in practice.

In 1991, for example, the IBLF took a group of British community innovators from business, civil society and the public sector to meet their counterparts in Brazil, bringing together people across not only cultural and national boundaries but also sector boundaries. For some of the Brazilian business leaders it was the first time they had met community leaders working in the city's shanty towns, the favelas. Likewise in India a few years later, the IBLF took local community leaders to visit the Tata Steel works in Jamshedpur and Indian business leaders to meet self-help women's groups.

In 1994, with active engagement and support from British Airways and other corporate partners, the IBLF launched its international **Insight Programme**. Over the years, business and community leaders from different countries visited partnership initiatives in the United States (the Atlanta Partnership, the New York City Partnership and ReBuild Los Angeles), Budapest, Krakow, Prague, Cairo, Johannesburg, Rio de Janeiro, Mumbai and Dhaka as part of this program.

From 1996 to 1997, the IBLF led the **Learning from Experience** program, which enabled some 100 leaders from different sectors and from 6 countries in Central and Eastern Europe to complete an intensive skills training as "partnership intermediaries" followed by a secondment in a UK organization where they could experience cross-sector partnerships in practice.

Between 1997 and 2000, the IBLF cooperated with the United Nations staff training college and other UN agencies to co-host a series of business–UN dialogues and capacity-building activities aimed at building partnership skills and identifying specific partnership project opportunities between the United Nations and business sector.

IBLF's first published guide to building cross-sector partnerships, entitled *The Partnering Toolbook*, was written by Ros Tennyson in 1998 and has been translated into 20 languages. This was the first in a series of practical guides to building partnerships, which are available free from the Internet and according to The Partnering Initiative (see below) have been downloaded an estimated 25,000 times.

These cross-sector dialogues, experiential learning programs, action research activities, case studies and practical guides were the first of numerous subsequent engagements and learning opportunities that the IBLF facilitated between business, civil society and public-sector leaders that became a hallmark of the organization's philosophy and strategic approach. Building mutual respect and, where relevant, partnerships between different sectors is an idea that underpins much of IBLF's work to this day and all its staff are encouraged to gain such experience and to think about its implications for their programs. In addition to underpinning the organization's core strategy, this approach has also led to the establishment of some of IBLF's most enduring and high-impact programs.

Most notably, in 2002, building on a decade of experience in cross-sector partnership building led by Ros Tennyson, IBLF launched **The Partnering Initiative** (TPI). Over the past decade TPI has spearheaded a variety of world-first training, capacity building and certification programs in building cross-sector partnerships. During this period TPI has trained over 2,000 people from an estimated 200 companies, governments, international agencies and NGOs and operated in over 30 countries to help them develop their cross-sector partnership strategies and skills. Today, TPI continues to work with organizations in all sectors and has achieved a strong reputation with the multilateral and bilateral development agencies. The work includes: action research and publication of a number of partnering tool books (used

Box P5.2 **Creation of a professional association for partnership brokers**

Source: www.partnershipbrokers.org, accessed March 23, 2012

The Partnership Brokers Association is the international professional association for partnership brokers and operates as a membership-driven, non-profit company. As such, any surplus income is reinvested for the ongoing development of its education and vocational training objectives. It was created to promote good partnership brokering in advancing effective cross-sector collaboration for an equitable and sustainable world by:

- **Developing education and training** courses for those operating as partnership brokers worldwide
- **Setting high professional standards** for those operating as partnership brokers
- **Advancing knowledge** in the field of partnership brokering through action enquiry and participative research
- **Providing a public voice** to communicate the benefits of professional partnership brokering for sustainable development
- **Connecting partnership brokers across the globe** so that they can m.ore confidently transform the partnering environment

From 2003 to 2011, the IBLF served as a supportive host for the partnership broking work, making it possible to grow and adapt the work to ensure quality and relevance to partnership brokers worldwide. Other supporters during this period include GIZ (the German Government's development agancy), the Overseas Development Institute, Microsoft, Nike, Rio Tinto, and Royal Dutch Shell.

by donor agencies, NGOs, business and public sector); codifying good practice in conceiving, creating, continuing and closing partnerships; and building a wide range of partnering skills training (including the new professional skill of partnership brokering) as well as facilitating and advising on specific partnership developments.[336]

Among other projects, The Partnering Initiative played a leadership role in the launch of the world's first post-graduate Certificate in Cross-Sector Partnerships in collaboration with the University of Cambridge Programme for Industry (now the Cambridge Programme for Sustainability Leadership), and in 2003, the first Partnership Brokers Accreditation Scheme (PBAS) in collaboration with the UK's Overseas Development Institute – an initiative aimed at building the skills and capacities of people from all sectors who act as intermediaries in partnership brokering and process management skills. In 2010, PBAS was incorporated into a New Partnership Brokers Project, and, in January 2012, the project scaled up and became the independently governed and funded Partnership Brokers Association (see Box P5.2).

Placing business at the heart of the international development agenda

Over the past two decades, the IBLF has also been a pioneer in raising awareness of the crucial role that the private sector plays in supporting international development and in developing practical frameworks and tools to enable companies, governments and international development agencies to work more effectively together in achieving key development goals.

In the mid 1990s, led by Jane Nelson and Ros Tennyson, the IBLF created the **Business as Partners in Development** program with support from the World Bank Group and the United Nations Development Programme (UNDP). In addition to leading senior business delegations to meet former World Bank President James Wolfensohn and former UN Secretary-General Kofi Annan and some of their key staff, the IBLF facilitated dialogues and workshops between corporate executives and international development experts. It worked with the International Labour Organization (ILO) and UN Staff Training College in Turin to host a number of cross-sector training programs focused on addressing specific development challenges. The IBLF was also instrumental in supporting the UN Secretariat in the initial phases of conceiving and establishing the United Nations Global Compact (UNGC). Subsequently, it has worked closely with UNGC and the UN Fund for International Partnerships to moderate annual training workshops of the UN private-sector network and it serves as the Secretariat for the UK network of the UN Global Compact.

In addition to convening business and development leaders, the IBLF has also produced a series of seminal publications on business as a partner in development and poverty alleviation over the past two decades. Its 1995 report, *Business as Partners in Development*, published with the World Bank and UNDP, introduced a framework to help companies and their stakeholders to understand and manage the three levels of corporate engagement in development: core business activities and value chains; community investment and philanthropy; and public-policy dialogue. This framework is still used by parts of the UN system and a number of companies today.[337]

In 1998, the IBLF led a consortium of nine academic and research partners that was selected by DFID to establish the **Centre for Responsible Business**, which produced some of the first publications and case studies on the direct links between business and poverty alleviation. Between 2000 and 2006, the IBLF also partnered with the World Economic Forum, co-authoring five seminal reports on global corporate citizenship. In 2003, working with the UNDP, the IBLF co-authored the first report focused on the role of the private sector in supporting the Millennium Development Goals. In recent years it has produced some of the seminal research on inclusive business models and served as a partner in the creation of initiatives such as the **Business Call to Action** and the **Business Innovation Facility**, supported by DFID and UNDP among others to promote commercially viable business models aimed at including low-income producers and consumers in developing countries.

The IBLF also partnered with other organizations to launch and manage several global award programs that have served to raise awareness and share good practice examples of companies and social entrepreneurs that are supporting sustainable development. In 2003, it launched the Alcan Sustainability Prize (later renamed the Rio Tinto Sustainability Prize) for NGOs demonstrating innovation and excellence in new ideas for sustainability. Managed by the IBLF between 2003 and 2011, this annual prize of $1million attracted some 600 NGOs from around the globe. In 2004, in collaboration with the UNDP and the International Chamber of Commerce, the IBLF launched the first World Business and Development Awards – a program that now runs biannually and has attracted several thousand nominations from international and national companies. The focus is on business contribution to sustainable development as part of core business rather than charitable donation.

Mainstreaming sustainability in the hotel and tourism sector

The IBLF has played a key role in promoting sustainability in one of the world's largest industry sectors, travel and tourism. Actively supported by The Prince of Wales and a small group of leading hotels, the International Hotels Environment Initiative (IHEI) was launched in 1992 at the time of the original Rio Earth Summit. In 2004 it expanded its remit and changed its name to the International Tourism Partnership (ITP), working with the hotel, travel and tourism industry to develop responsible practices in environmental issues, employment and building practices. ITP's member companies (which have included all the major global hotel chains) recognized that their long-term business interests were fundamentally and inextricably linked to environmental, social and economic stability, and that these challenges can only be addressed through collaboration, collective action and industry leadership.

Over two decades, the IHEI and now the ITP have addressed issues such as environmental management in day-to-day hotel operations, hotel design and siting, and improving labor standards in hotels. The combined reach of the membership now extends to over 22,000 hotel properties, over 3.2 million rooms and 1.5 million employees in more than 100 countries worldwide. ITP's current programs include the Youth Career Initiative, the *Green Hotelier* online magazine, the Human Trafficking Working Group, the Hotel Carbon Measurement Initiative, the *Environmental Management for Hotels* handbook, and the Sustainable Performance Operational Tool (SPOT).

Mobilizing business to tackle complex global health challenges

Robert Davies and his team pioneered a number of collaborative business efforts in tackling complex and controversial public health issues. In the mid to late 1990s they worked with the United Nations to produce the first publicly available reports on the need for greater business engagement in tackling HIV/AIDS and co-hosted some of the early dialogues and secretariat support that led to the creation of what is now the highly successful Global Business Coalition on Health (formerly the Global Business Coalition on HIV/AIDS, TB and Malaria). For a number of years, prior to the development of a global World Health Organization (WHO) strategy on physical activity and diet, Davies quietly and effectively convened a series of private meetings between leading food and drinks companies and the WHO. This was no mean feat when some in the WHO appeared to think they were dealing with the next "big tobacco," and some in the food and drinks sector saw the WHO as "anti-business." Davies was able to create the safe space for dialogue, by being trusted as a "critical friend" both by both the WHO and by the industry.

Key to Davies's success was that organizations such as the WHO and NGOs and the development community knew that, behind closed doors, he was "speaking truth to power" and urging business to assume more responsibility. Equally, his business members understood that privately Davies was similarly delivering home truths about the critical importance of business to the NGOs and public-sector agencies. In 2005, the IBLF launched the Healthy Eating Active Living (HEAL) initiative in collaboration with the food and beverage sector and international health agencies including the WHO. The IBLF has also worked for over a decade with the Global Alliance for Improved Nutrition, producing joint reports and supporting an award program recognizing corporate leaders in the field of food fortification, and in 2011 it was appointed to provide the secretariat support for the Roll Back Malaria Campaign.

Pioneering work on the role of business in respecting human rights, operating in zones of conflict and tackling corruption

The IBLF convened some of the initial business-led efforts to address challenging questions related to the role of business in respecting human rights, operating responsibly in zones of conflict and tackling corruption. From the mid-1990s, the organization worked closely with several of its long-standing members such as Shell, British Petroleum (now BP) and the Coca-Cola Company to explore in-depth case studies and to convene other business leaders on these topics. It collaborated with International Alert and the Council on Economic Priorities to establish the **Business of Peace** project, which produced a series of publications, convened workshops and field visits, and partnered with local partners in Colombia and the Philippines to implement on-the-ground collective action aimed at building peace. In Colombia, for example, the IBLF organized in-depth consultations with a wide variety of stakeholders that led to a major Coca-Cola funded report, *Development, Peace and Human Rights in Colombia: A Business Agenda*.[338] Neville Isdell, at his first AGM as Coca-Cola Chairman, quoted this Colombian work as an example of how he wanted to engage stakeholders in the future. In the Philippines, the IBLF and Philippine Business for Social Progress collaborated on a project to support peace-building between different religious communities in the conflict-affected region of Mindanao.

The IBLF was one of the corporate responsibility coalitions that provided substantive input and convened meetings for the UN Secretary-General's Special Representative on Business and Human Rights, Professor John Ruggie. The organization also worked with the International Finance Corporation to develop a practical toolkit for helping companies assess their human rights risks and to implement human rights policies and practices in their core business operations. In recent years, working with Siemens, the World Bank and others, the IBLF has been supporting a program focused on tackling corruption in high growth markets such as Russia, China and India.

Incubating and providing secretariat services for new business-led coalitions

In addition to its long-standing roles of identifying and promoting emerging corporate responsibility issues and their importance to core business, convening cross-sector dialogues, supporting collective action on the ground and building partnership skills, the IBLF has also incubated and spun off about eight independently governed and funded business-led corporate responsibility coalitions over the past few decades. Some of these have been focused on specific countries or regions. Examples include: Business Leaders Forums in Hungary, the Czech Republic, Bulgaria, Slovakia and Poland; the Vietnam Business Links Initiative; and the Indonesia Business Links Initiative (see Box P5.3). Others have focused on a specific issue or target population such as Youth Business International, and the predecessor to what is now the Global Business Coalition on Health. The IBLF has also provided secretariat services for a number of independent coalitions such as the Voluntary Principles on Security and Human Rights (in cooperation with Business for Social Responsibility), Business Action for Africa, the UK network of the UN Global Compact and the Roll Back Malaria campaign.

Facing a challenging leadership transition

By the time of the IBLF's tenth anniversary in 2000, which was marked by a day-long conference in the Royal Opera House in London and a gala dinner hosted by the Prince of Wales in Windsor Castle, the organization was able to claim work in almost 70 countries around the world.[339] As the IBLF entered its second decade, it could point to a proven ability to identify and define emerging business and development trends and to convene top-level business leaders and build effective cross-sector partnerships in order to better address these trends. Then, in August 2007, IBLF's CEO Robert Davies died after a battle with cancer. His early death at 56 deprived the organization of its visionary founder and directing spirit. In reality, like many social and traditional entrepreneurs, he had found it hard to hand his "baby" on, even if a more managerial approach might have helped it to consolidate and build on its achievements.

As is often the case with organizations that experience long leadership reigns, Davies proved a hard act to follow. The interim troika of three Managing Directors (Adrian Hodges, Ros Tennyson and the CFO Mike Patterson), who had been running the organization as Davies declined during early 2007, held the organization together for more than a year after his death, with strong support and leadership from IBLF's chairman Neville Isdell, at the time the Chairman and CEO of the Coca-Cola Company and a long-standing supporter of the IBLF. Adam Leach, from the development NGO Oxfam, was appointed CEO and led the IBLF from September 2008 to March 2010. Leach was succeeded on a temporary basis by Graham Baxter (who had joined the IBLF from BP in 2007 as director of Global Programs), prior to the appointment of Clare Melford who had worked previously at MTV and the European Council on Foreign Relations, and who served as CEO of IBLF from 2010 to 2012.

Box P5.3 Indonesia Business Links

The Asia–Pacific economic and banking crisis of 1998 brought into sharp relief the need for reform in regional financial and corporate governance systems if stability and sustainability were to be achieved. In the case of Indonesia, a multi-stakeholder discussion was convened at the October 1998 World Bank Annual Meeting in Washington, DC, attended by, among others, representatives of the World Bank, the Asia Development Bank, United Nations Development Programme, the Indonesian Finance Minister and the Governor of the Central Bank of Indonesia. An important component of the discussion was the need to transform the ethical climate for business and improve corporate governance. It was argued that the crisis provided an opportunity for change. The International Business Leaders Forum was invited to participate in this aspect of the meeting because of its experience in mobilizing international companies to address issues of corporate responsibility and sustainability. The Washington meeting led to an agreement to convene a meeting of leading companies operating in Indonesia. The IBLF was invited to visit Jakarta to begin the process of building support from the local business community and developing an agenda for action. This eventually led to the establishment of Indonesia Business Links (IBL) in 1999 as a national business-led initiative with the objective of providing practical support to companies in improving the climate for business. The IBLF was invited to be an international partner and adviser to the initiative and has continued in this role for over a decade.

The initial funding and in-kind support for IBL's activities was provided by member companies, the UN Development Programme, the UK Government's Department for International Development and the Ford Foundation. The central themes of IBL's work have been to address corruption and promote ethical business practices in Indonesia; and, recognizing the growing strategic challenge of youth unemployment in Indonesia, to promote youth entrepreneurship and build the capacity of SMEs through training, workshops, publications and other activities.

Over time, in response to the increasing awareness of the importance of CSR and demand within the local Indonesian business community for guidance on good corporate governance, IBL has expanded its activities to cover a wider sphere of corporate citizenship. This includes key environmental challenges such as clean water, sanitation, waste disposal and recycling. In 2004, supported by the Ford Foundation, IBL launched its CSR for a Better Life program to promote sound environmental practices between companies and to educate young people. Its most recent initiative is engagement in a national campaign to promote responsible packaging and waste management through the well-recognized 3R framework (reduce, re-use, recycle). IBL has also become a key participant in the growing development of Asia–Pacific regional CSR activities.

Meanwhile, at the beginning of 2009, the Prince of Wales stepped down as President after almost 20 years. At the time, his spokesman was officially quoted as saying: "The environmental challenges we face are such that it is vital the Prince of Wales's efforts are as targeted as possible. It was decided that HRH's involvement in the area of corporate responsibility should be focused on fewer organizations to better help him achieve his aims." The Prince had played a highly significant role in convening leaders from business and different parts of global society, through the IBLF platform. In turn, his presidency had given him a highly valued additional perspective on global development challenges.

As the IBLF marked its 20th anniversary in 2010, it recognized the need for a fundamental review and refining of its vision and strategy in a rapidly changing and competitive environment.

The new chairman Mark Foster, recently retired as a Senior Executive from Accenture, worked with Clare McIford and the management team to refocus IBLF's core mission: "to help business leaders "Redefine Growth" in ways that are Smart, Inclusive and Responsible":[340]

- IBLF's **Smart Growth** programs aim to engage business leaders and drive collaboration in areas such as technical innovation, efficient resource use and a supportive regulatory environment

- IBLF's **Inclusive Growth** programs aim to engage business leaders and drive collaboration in areas such as creating more jobs, frugal innovation, and building inclusion business models that commercially include low-income producers and consumers in developing countries

- IBLF's **Responsible Growth** programs aim to engage business leaders and drive collaboration in areas such as responsible consumption, reducing obsolescence, and valuing longer-term incentives[341]

In parallel, the organization is now focusing it activities on fewer countries, with a strong concentration on Russia, India and China. It has also established a Leaders Council chaired by Mark Foster, which brings together about 30 leaders from business and public policy to debate and explore some of the big ideas for responsible business in the 21st century.

Impact and lessons learned

Over the past two decades the IBLF can claim to have had substantial impact in engaging senior business executives, government officials, social entrepreneurs and community leaders at three key levels:

- **Thought leadership.** Identifying emerging trends and raising awareness and understanding of the role of core business activities in sustainable development, especially in developing countries

- **Dialogue and trust-building.** Convening leaders from different sectors and often different viewpoints to better understand each others' positions and to build trust around challenging and complex development issues

- **Collaboration and collective action.** Helping to build capacity and skills for more effective cross-sector partnerships and co-creating practical solutions on the ground, often with local partners

One of IBLF's key areas of impact has been to build greater understanding and trust between leaders in the business and the development communities. The organization can legitimately claim to be one of the coalitions that has had most impact on the thinking and practice of several key international institutions in their relationship to business, and to partnering with business. From its early years, the IBLF prioritized work with the World Bank and its private-sector arm the International Finance Corporation, the UN and several of the specialist UN agencies and programs such as the United Nations Environment Programme, the United Nations Development Programme, the International Labour Organization and the World Health Organization. In particular, the IBLF popularized the concept of partnering with business through its core commercial activities, not only its philanthropic programs, and cooperating with business to strengthen the "enabling environment" in which more responsible business behavior could flourish.

The IBLF has also impacted individual business behavior by challenging some of the world's leading companies to address emerging social, environmental and development issues that the private sector has traditionally not focused on or had been uncomfortable with, such as human rights, HIV/AIDS, the negative health impact of certain food and beverage products, and doing responsible business in zones of conflict and weak governance. It has also championed tackling corruption for almost 20 years and was one of the early pioneers arguing that bribery and corruption were critical impediments to the functioning of effective market economies and impeded economic and social progress. The IBLF was also one of the first business organizations to recognize the proactive contribution that business could make to peace building – and why such engagement was good for business. In short, the IBLF has leveraged its access to senior executives to put new issues on the business agenda that were not previously seen as matters for the senior executive suite or boardroom.

As well as raising new issues, the IBLF has also impacted business by creating vehicles for collective business action that could enable businesses to work more effectively with each other and with civil-society organizations, governments and international institutions. The IBLF was heavily involved in the creation not only of Indonesia Business Links (see Box P5.3) but of several other local and national partnerships to mobilize collective business action and to promote responsible business. These have included partnerships in Krakow, St. Petersburg and Shanghai, national Business Leaders Forums in Bulgaria, the Czech Republic, Hungary and Vietnam, and the regionally focused Business Action for Africa. They have also included international forums to engage with businesses on particular issues or in specific sectors, such as the International Tourism Partnership, the Global Business Council on HIV/AIDS, and the Digital Partnership.

Many individuals and groups can claim some responsibility for the creation and growth of the UN Global Compact. IBLF certainly played an important role, especially in the early stages. Georg Kell, the founding Executive Director of the UNGC, says of the IBLF:

The Business Leaders Forum has been an invaluable partner in helping bring the Compact to life. It has worked closely with the Secretary-General's office in conceptualising and communicating the importance of the Compact to media and to business leaders around the world.[342]

Interviews with current and former IBLF directors and corporate partners point to a number of success factors, which are outlined in Table P5.1.

Table P5.1 **IBLF strategies and critical success factors**

Critical success factors	Challenges of this approach	Innovation and impact
Starting things – identifying emerging social, environmental and development trends, demonstrating why they matter to business and what companies can do to address them – being seen to be "ahead of the evidence"	Risk of being seen as spread too thin, moving on too quickly, not having a single or clear identity	The list of what IBLF has inspired, incubated or launched is impressive. If IBLF had chosen a more conventional path it would never have had the influence or broken new ground in the way that it has (it has often been referred to as "punching above its weight")
Focus on the role of business in development and poverty: the first global business coalition to take this topic head-on as a core business rather than a philanthropic issue	Not on the face of it an "easy sell" to business, especially in the early days when mistrust between business and the development community was high	Positioned IBLF as leading edge, keen to tackle tough challenges, willing to push/challenge its corporate members to address an unpopular theme
Keeping small, not "empire-building," working through local partner organizations (often ones that IBLF helped to create as stand-alone entities rather than IBLF local offices)	Maintaining an ongoing "relationship of equals" with local partners based on sharing lessons and creating a mechanism for national/local organizations to contribute systematically to the global agenda	Focus always on locally appropriate models rather than importing/parachuting in a UK model. IBLF respected as a peer not a parent
Widely recognized/valued partnership work: when asked, business people (and others) frequently cite IBLF's partnership work	Challenging in the early days to explain to corporate partners why it was essential for the partnership work to be "sector-neutral" (i.e., building capacity and the case for partnering for all three sectors) Creating The Partnering Initiative brand met with some opposition as not being "business focused" enough for IBLF	• Some argue that no other business coalition has understood how much serious investment of people, time and resources is needed if the buzz concept of "partnering" is to be effective, innovative, taken to scale and sustainable • For two decades IBLF has led the field in this work, combining standard-setting with a capacity-building agenda →

Critical success factors	Challenges of this approach	Innovation and impact
		• As well as on some specific companies, IBLF has had significant influence on a number of UN agencies, international NGOs and bilateral donor agencies • Over time the need for the sector-neutral branding has become more acceptable and has attracted a number of significant global corporations to IBLF that may not have become IBLF "members" otherwise
Choice of countries in three phases: • Initially determined by HRH's official visits abroad (Brazil, Mexico, Poland, Hungary, Bulgaria, Czech Rep., Russia, India, Korea, Hong Kong) • Then determined by corporate partner new investment priorities (Vietnam, South Africa, China) • Now determined by issue of growth, i.e., the countries that will become the dominant corporate forces in the 21st century • Current focus on RIC (Russia, India, China) countries	Each of these approaches has brought different challenges: • In the case of Russia and India, the regular trips of HRH opened doors in the early 1990s (his personal passion for the culture of St.. Petersburg or his perceived leadership in the field of responsible business with Indian business leaders etc.) • This was obviously an important "way in" though had to be managed carefully for IBLF not to get stuck with a reputation for "selling UK Inc" • The focus of the country partnerships (CPs) has shifted frequently: IBLF would start a program (e.g., the footwear industry in Vietnam) and then CPs interest would shift elsewhere! • The major challenge has been finding the personnel in-country who could carry the agenda (with little previous exposure) • IBLF could be seen as having a quirky collection of friends/associates and local partners that have a strong sense of family and affection for IBLF but where the sum is not quite more than the parts	• IBLF has high status/reputation in Russia, stronger than other comparable organizations • On the way towards that in China (because IBLF have been there for some time although its "behind the scenes" approach means it is less visible) • Less focused results in India but a significant number of "friends" including the Confederation of Indian Industries (CII), Federation of Indian Chambers of Commerce and Industry (FICCI), the Planning Commission, and a small group of Indian corporate partner companies

→

Critical success factors	Challenges of this approach	Innovation and impact
Mission-driven with cross-sector skills and experiences in the senior leadership team	Under Robert Davies's leadership, IBLF was always "mission-driven," with a tendency to appoint front-line staff who wanted to change the world rather than staff with a strong business bias and belief in CSR per se	Davies used to work hard to keep corporate CEOs happy (enough) while doing a myriad of unrelated/radical things they didn't really know about and probably wouldn't have sanctioned if they had been asked to!
	This has always been a tension. Is IBLF a "development organization working with business" or a "business organization working on development." At its best it is a creative tension, but it can be perceived quite often as being neither one strongly or effectively enough	This kind of "boundary-spanning" is subtle and not always appreciated and requires a mix of experiences and skills from different sectors and mutual respect among senior managers
Focus on business leaders more than projects – as the name "International Business Leaders Forum" implies	Hard to maintain as business leaders change/lose interest or IBLF takes on issues that are not of primary concern to them Ambivalence as to whether IBLF corporate partner CEOs are de facto "thought-leaders" who can influence others or rather individuals in leadership positions whom IBLF seeks to influence. Another creative tension that needs to managed	At its best (and currently being revived with the newly established Leaders Council) a "safe space" for business leaders for meet (physically or, more recently, virtually)

The future

As a result of a series of leadership transitions and growing competition over the past five years, the IBLF has faced a challenge to retain its generalist thought-leadership and convening role as one of the original field-builders throughout the 1990s and early 2000s, although it continues to have an international reputation in specific issues and industry sectors. Like a number of its peer generalist corporate responsibility coalitions, the organization has recently undertaken a strategic review of its mission, strategic direction and programs, and of its current and potential competitors and partners. Building on its long-standing commitment to partnership and collective action, IBLF will continue to explore areas for greater collaboration with other corporate responsibility coalitions, while also focusing its geographic and thematic activities in a smaller number of areas where it can build on the strong foundations and relationships created over the past two decades.

Profile 6

Maala–Business for Social Responsibility

Talia Aharonii* with update by David Grayson

Maala in its own words

Maala–Business for Social Responsibility is Israel's leading advocate for corporate social responsibility (CSR) and good corporate citizenship. An umbrella organization of some 130 of Israel's largest companies, our goal since our founding in 1998 has been to promote corporate social and environmental responsibility (CSR) in Israel.

We provide a forum for sharing practical knowledge and experience, as well as training CSR managers and helping businesses set local and international benchmarks and promote innovation in the field.

Maala is part of a global network of organizations that promote corporate responsibility, including: BSR, CSR360 and the UN Global Compact.

Since 2003, Maala has produced the annual *Maala Index*, which ranks publicly traded and privately held Israeli companies on the basis of CSR criteria.

In 2012, Maala will emphasize the challenges involved in promoting fair business practices alongside development of new business models, which integrate greater social utility.

www.maala.org.il   June 2012

---

* Talia Aharoni is the founder of Maala and served as CEO from its inception until 2009. She is currently studying for a PhD at the Sorbonne, while remaining active in a range of Israeli organizations linking business and society.

Background context and history

The movement for greater corporate social responsibility predated Maala and sowed the seeds for its creation. The foundation of Maala in 1998 was initially inspired by the vision and long-term commitment of the Kahanoff Foundation[343] and the personal involvement of its President, Shira Herzog, and that of Aaron Back of the Ford Foundation. Inspired by the growing social involvement of the global business community, both Shira and Aaron aimed to motivate the Israeli business community to take on a more proactive social role. As such, they invested in the establishment of Maala–Business for Social Responsibility in Israel, which was based on the successful American model designed by Business for Social Responsibility (BSR). Maala was established as a non-profit organization determined to promote CSR in Israel.

Unlike BSR and other leading CSR organizations such as Business in the Community and Instituto Ethos, Maala did not initially evolve as a business network. It started as a concept that was imported to Israel by a social entrepreneur and a visionary social-venture foundation, was planted as a social-business venture and started developing and creating a market for its own ideas. Over time it has evolved into a business-led organization.

While building on the experience of international examples, the creation and evolution of Maala has reflected the challenges and context of Israel's political, economic and social scene. One of the most striking features of Israel towards the end of the last century was the dichotomy between its Westernized market, with a fairly modern and sophisticated business culture, and the reality of a young Middle Eastern country, with characteristics similar to those of developing markets. As such, businesses in Israel have always had to operate in a taxing environment. Since the establishment of the state of Israel over 60 years ago, the Middle East conflict has consumed Israel's public agenda. Pressing social and environmental issues have been marginalized in the public discourse and have, therefore, not been given high priority by budget and decision-makers.

The Oslo Peace Accords in 1993 created a new scene. With the vision of "a new Middle East" and the lifting of the Arab Boycott, multinational corporations that were exploring new emerging markets started looking at Israel as a hub for that new Middle East. This international business interest was coupled with the success of the emergent and promising Israeli technology industry. Major mergers and acquisitions drew funds as well as new business cultures to Israel. At the same time, the fear of a "brain drain" (would the acquisition of Israeli high-tech companies by foreigners lead to the emigration from Israel of some of its most highly talented IT professionals?) and a guilty conscience on the part of Israelis selling these companies (should they have "sold out" their know-how and expertise to foreign companies? Did this hurt national pride?) were integrated into the business culture and the public awareness.

The euphoria of the "new Middle East" that the Oslo Accords heralded has evaporated as the hope for a lasting peace quickly changed into continuous rounds of political and security battles. Successive economic global downturns and local recessions served as a catalyst to growing social tension, reflected in the increasing gap between highly compensated executives and those at the lower end of the pay scale, between orthodox and secular Jews, between the native Israelis and new immigrants etc. Over the past 20 years, Israel has developed one of the largest gaps in the Western world between the "haves" and "have-nots."[344]

The first decade of the 21st century brought about an unstable political situation in Israel. That, combined with the 2008–09 global economic downturn, has created a very difficult environment for the business community.

As of 2011–12, Israel is once again facing major challenges. They include the threat of Iranian nuclear weapons, the dead-end of the peace negotiations, internal and external political instability, the lack of political leadership, and a frightening wave of undemocratic regulation and actions that have all served to worsen the threats of global economic crisis for Israel. The country has also faced a series of unprecedented social demonstrations enabled by social media and a new generation of young protestors. These have been directed both at the government and at the business community, accusing the latter of greed, over-priced products, excessive executive compensation, business ignorance of the private sector's negative social and environmental impacts, and unfairness within society.

In the face of these challenges Maala has continued to evolve and adapt in order to meet the needs of its corporate members, and at the same time to challenge them and the Israeli business community at large to take a more ambitious approach to tackling systemic social, economic and political challenges. Following the social unrest in 2011, Maala convened a series of small, private round-table discussions, supported by the strategic consultancy Praxis, to reframe and rethink its role and that of the private sector. This has led to a further evolution in the organization's activities.

Key activities and phases of development

The adoption of CSR in Israel almost 14 years ago changed the way Israeli companies operate. It also put CSR on the national agenda, drawing the attention of the public sector, civic society and academics, and pushing forward the mainstreaming of CSR by promoting standards and regulation.

However, the transition to fully implemented CSR has not been an easy or a minor one. As indicated, the regional political and security realities meant that executives managed businesses in crisis mode, making short-term decisions directed at maximizing profits. Such decision-making can contradict the very essence of CSR – a long-term strategic approach to building sustainable companies and risk management.

It was for that reason that the concept of CSR was not fully understood in the Israeli business community at the start and, consequently, was only partially implemented. With time and education, these companies gained a better understanding of CSR and realized that it creates an advanced business culture. Israeli business leaders have navigated their companies from a basic approach of community investment and corporate philanthropy to the fully integrated approach of CSR – addressing such issues as improved environmental strategies, a diversified workplace, strategic community empowerment and voluntary embedding of corporate governance and accountability. Today, Maala's members are committed to reporting on their CSR performance against the Maala Ranking, within three years from their joining the organization (see Box P6.1).

Maala's evolution was a gradual one, as the following highlights illustrate:

Phase one: Strategic corporate community investment

In 1998, the year of Maala's launch, community investment was a prominent element of CSR. Companies wanted to respond to the growing income gap, which was partially caused by the boom in the hi-tech sector. Maala seized this opportunity to enter the market and showed companies that the money they were giving was not having sufficient impact. They were encouraged to look at their donations as investments rather than as charitable contributions. In order to achieve this view, the contributions needed to demonstrate a fiscal and communal return – an idea that companies found appealing.

It was at that time that two Israeli business leaders initiated new social initiatives. Shari Arrison[345] brought the American-headquartered charity United Way to Israel and Ronny Douek initiated Aleh – a branch of his new social movement Zionism 2000.[346] While at times these efforts overlapped with Maala, together they paved the way to greater awareness in the Israeli business community of its social role.

Phase two: Widening the scope of issues and topics

In response to this growing awareness, Maala widened the scope of CSR issues and topics presented to the business community. This expanded model followed the approach adopted by the USA-based Business for Social Responsibility and focused on the workplace, the environment, human rights, the marketplace, business ethics, supply chain and, later, corporate governance. Along with the expanded agenda, focus was put on the business benefits and the return on investment of CSR: risk management, employee morale, competitive advantage, brand awareness etc.

To embed and materialize the wider agenda of CSR and sustainability, Maala introduced in 2003 the Maala Ranking and in 2005 listed the Maala Index as a daily traded index on the Tel Aviv Stock Exchange (see Box P6.1).[347] The Maala Ranking publicly scrutinizes those companies that volunteer to participate. These companies must report on almost every aspect of the impact they have in terms of corporate governance, environmental policies, employment strategies and community involvement. The criteria are difficult to fulfill, yet many major companies have demonstrated willingness to engage in the reporting.

Enlarging Maala's agenda was accompanied by the need to diversify sources of funding. Furthermore, the Kahanoff Foundation's decision to scale down its participation in the project made it evident to Maala that the time was right to involve Israel's leading companies in sustaining the organization. As a result, the strategic plan was introduced to turn Maala into a business-led and membership-based organization.

Today Maala's membership includes around 140 of Israel's most significant companies; together they employ 258,000 employees representing almost a quarter of the country's workforce. Their total revenues accumulate to around NIS250 billion (US$67 billion) accounting for almost 50% of Israel's economic product.

Heading the members is the organization's **leadership group.** This group of 30 companies donates a substantial annual amount ranging from NIS50,000 (US$13,400) to NIS150,000 (US$42,000) annually. In total, membership fees and donations account for 80% of Maala's NIS4 million annual budgets (estimated budget 2012).

Box P6.1 **The Maala Ranking and Index: raising the bar for CSR performance**

Every year, Maala ranks dozens of companies according to their commitment to CSR principles. Companies are evaluated based on their performance in six major areas: environment, business ethics, human rights and work environment, community involvement, corporate governance and social and environmental reporting. Reports are signed by their CEO and cross-referenced with financial reports and additional quantitative assessments.

The leading traded companies that participate in the Ranking are listed on the Maala Index at the Tel-Aviv Stock Exchange. The Ranking, which has been produced annually since 2003, is prepared in partnership with McKinsey & Company, Ernst & Young, S&P Maalot, the Tel Aviv Stock Exchange and Greeneye (representative of Eiris in Israel). A public experts committee of about 30 professional leaders from academia, government, business and civic society is responsible for outlining and updating the Ranking Indicators.

The companies participating in the Ranking are public and private firms with an annual turnover above NIS320 million, and which are included in D&B Israel, BDI Ranking Company or Tel Aviv Stock Exchange (TASE) lists. Companies are ranked and given one of three possible ratings: Platinum, Gold or Silver. The Maala Ranking is completely voluntary. Participating companies choose to report their activities and expose their data without being required to do so by law.

The 2011 Ranking included 85 participating companies that together employ 205,000 employees and represent accumulated revenue of NIS332 billion, accounting for almost 60% of Israel's economic product.[348]

Phase three: Becoming an active citizen – supporting Israel's national development goals

Maala's high-profile and documented achievements led it to become the source of CSR knowledge in Israel and a facilitator for cross-sector dialogue and partnerships. To mark Maala's tenth anniversary in 2008, its team and members assessed the challenges they forecast the field of CSR and the organization would face over the following decade. The assessment included different stages of debate involving the Maala team, leading CSR directors representing companies composing the Maala leadership group, and finally the Maala Board of Directors and top executives of the Maala leadership group.

The conclusions outlined a roadmap for Maala, presenting five fields of action:

- Developing and widening a national **"responsible economy"** network around Maala's database of members

- Creating **public awareness and understanding** of CSR as a motivating power for companies and as a basis for cross-sectoral cooperation

- Expanding Maala's agenda by adding a **new business model** that defines the organization as a hub for innovative business models based on social and environmental entrepreneurship

- Promoting CSR as a major component in Israel's ability to compete in the **global marketplace**. Importing best practice and market requirements from the global scene will serve the interest of Israeli companies in their global operations and aspirations

- Using Maala members who are at the forefront of writing the business sector's agenda to promote wide **multi-sector partnerships** to address national, social and environmental challenges

These goals have been further strengthened as a response to the social unrest of 2011, with a strong focus on promoting fair business practices alongside development of new business models, which integrate greater social utility.

Impact and lessons learned

Maala can claim a number of achievements in the years of serving Israel's business community. Those include:

- The launching of the Corporate Social Responsibility Ranking and the Maala Index on the Tel-Aviv Stock Exchange

- Publishing the Israeli CSR Management Guidelines

- The positioning of CSR as a distinct managerial position by launching the first and still only Corporate Social Responsibility Management Course, which has trained nearly 400 graduates serving in key positions

- Organizing and positioning the Annual Maala Conference on Business and Society giving it a prominent reputation by making it a focal point for CSR in Israel

- Developing a market for CSR where consulting professionals strive to work with companies on different issues and different aspects of implementing CSR

- Participation as an active member in the global network of CSR organizations and CSR leaders, including BITC, BSR, the GRI, Instituto Ethos and the UNGC

- Serving as the official focal point of the UNGC, the WBCSD, and CSR360 in Israel

As indicated, Maala is largely responsible both for introducing CSR into Israel's business community and for its increasing foothold in these companies. In a special report published on Maala's tenth anniversary, the *Jerusalem Post* referred to the changes in the business sector as: "The seemingly impossible entrance of Maala into the heart of Israeli capitalism."[349]

The growing interest in CSR in Israel is not only demonstrated in the way Israeli companies manage their businesses, but also in the mainstreaming of CSR on the public agenda in Israel. This is reflected in growing coverage in the media of CSR issues, the growing number of local community partnerships, and the dialogue and meeting points between the three sectors of society – private, public and civic. Representatives from both the non-profit sector and the government agree that changing business approaches was a major catalyst for a new socioenvironmental public agenda and partnership. The launch of the Prime Minister's Roundtable in 2009[350] as a framework for a cross-sector dialogue was additional proof of this overall change. In the words of Zvi Ziv, then President and CEO of Bank Hapoalim and then Chairman of the Board of Directors of Maala, during his opening remarks at Maala's 2008 Annual Conference on Business and Society, "of all of the organization's achievements over the past ten years, above everything is that we placed the concept of CSR at the forefront of both public and business agendas in Israel."

Comparing Maala's roles to those listed in Chapter 8 it seems that Maala has fulfilled most of the roles identified:

- The organization was the number one **agenda-setter** for CSR in Israel, raising issues, creating know-how, mainstreaming CSR and putting it on the public agenda in Israel

- Maala served as a **best practice identifier and disseminator**. Its conferences, seminars and workshops portrayed a full display of best practice both from Israel and globally. Global experts were regularly invited to address these events, give media interviews and expand the coverage and understanding of CSR

- At certain periods, Maala acted as a direct **consultant to businesses** by actually giving consulting services. This gave way at a later point to admitting and enabling the emerging professional CSR consulting sector in Israel. However, Maala has always retained its position in benchmarking and being the "home" for CSR executives

- Maala acted and still does act as a **broker facilitating dialogue** and mutual learning across the sectors. It does not offer brokerage in community investments

- Maala definitely served as a **standard-setter** by setting the Maala ranking as well as participating or leading major initiatives such as the Israeli Standard 10000 for CSR;[351] the launch of the GRI, the UNGC and other global standards in Israel

At the same time Maala, like other business-led organizations, has faced criticisms and challenges. These have included the following:

- Maala addresses and subsequently includes as members mainly large corporations while small and medium enterprises do not get any attention

- Maala is criticized for accepting any company into its ranks, for being "too soft" with its members, for acting with a conflict of interest by ranking its paying members and for not denouncing malpractices of companies. Maala does not criticize its members

- Maala did not let its voice be heard during the current global financial crisis or criticize irresponsible business practices among some of its members

The organization has also faced the following organizational challenges:

- **Building an effective management team.** During its first 13 years of development, a special effort was invested in developing the Maala team. The challenge here was to recruit capable young executives, highly qualified and appreciated within the private sector, attract them to a mission-driven organization that could not offer the competitive salaries of the private sector and train them to promote and consult on CSR

- **Transitioning from a founder's leadership to a new generation of management.** Such a transition is usually a major challenge on the one hand and a great opportunity for renewal on the other. Maala developed a well-planned, carefully orchestrated process of transition in which its board was closely involved. On January 1, 2009, Momo Mahadav, who joined Maala three years earlier as a deputy, assumed the role of CEO of Maala. Mr. Mahadav brought with him a wealth of knowledge and experience in the non-profit sector. The fact that he came from the organization's own team is a sign of Maala's strength. The newly appointed CEO enjoyed the founder's advice and support for another couple of years through the founder serving as a consultant before leaving the organization

Throughout these changes a major asset of Maala has been the organization's governing board of directors. The board consists of leading top managers of Maala's members, as well as civic-society leaders and academic figures.

The future

Like the rest of the Western world, Israel's business community is facing tough challenges. Israel is not immune to the global market meltdown. The uniquely intimate structure and size of the Israeli market means that although the country's business community may not be as severely hit by the financial earthquake as its American and European counterparts it certainly feels the tremors.

However, a stronger impact on the Israeli business sector comes from the social uprising that began in the summer of 2011. Raising a call of "The people demand social justice!" a series of ongoing demonstrations began in July 2011 involving hundreds of thousands of protesters from a variety of backgrounds opposing the continuing rise in the cost of living and the deterioration of public services such as health and education.

The housing protests that sparked the first demonstrations gained momentum and media attention and they began a public discourse in Israel regarding the high cost of housing and living expenses. As the protests expanded, the demonstrations began to also focus on other related issues relating to the social order and power structure in Israel. It quickly developed into consumer activism with the "cottage cheese boycott" – a massive consumer boycott in protest against the spike in food prices. The immediate response was a significant price reduction especially of the basic food products. This did not stop the public criticism of the business sector which was accused of ignorance, greed, excessive executive compensation and abuse of consumers. Today, it seems that the Israeli business sector feels threatened and needs to figure new ways to gain the public's trust.

Any discussion pertaining to Maala's future must address the impact of the current social justice and financial crisis on Israeli businesses and Maala's subsequent response. (See Box P6.2.)

Box P6.2 **Maala: using the social crisis to reframe the organization**

In November 2010, Maala had celebrated its most successful annual conference yet with more than one thousand delegates. Maala CEO Momo Mahadav takes up the story:[352]

We were exhilarated. There was a great buzz. We had a particularly memorable diversity panel with four young Israelis – all successfully employed by Israeli companies: an Israeli Arab, a blind and half deaf investment banker working for one of the Israeli banks, an Israeli lady of Ethiopian origin, and an ultra-Orthodox Jew. They had all faced many difficulties in finding a job. Many unexplained rejections. No one in the audience moved during the session. The panelists' interventions were so powerful, and forced us all to think about whether each of us sub-consciously shuffled certain job applications to the bottom of the pile for non-valid reasons. Overall, Maala was doing very well at that stage. We were putting on new members.

A few months later, we launched our 2011 Tel Aviv Stock Exchange Index. Again, with a record number of CEOs in attendance. Everything was going very well. Then just a few days later, an incredible social movement erupted. The immediate cause was the cost of living but I think the deeper reasons were the squeeze of the middle class which is an international phenomenon not just Israel; Gen Y-ers who are really angry and really articulate – and have control of social media to express themselves; and maybe the broader sense of economic and political power shifting from West to East. Anyway, the social protests erupted. Our Board's Chair's company was targeted as part of that.

As the social protests erupted, we debated what Maala should say and do. The protestors didn't think Israeli business was being socially responsible. Businesses hunkered down. CEOs wanted to take a lower profile. In the end, we canceled our 2011 conference because I didn't think it was appropriate. Big, open conferences are for showcasing successes and good practice. You can't have soul-searching debate with a thousand people under the eyes of the media. Instead we ran a series of private, round-table discussions each with 8–10 CEOs and chairmen. No agenda. No presentations. I said very little. Just listened. It was very candid. Very cathartic.

Of course, Maala was uniquely placed to run these roundtables. No politician, NGO or media outlet would have had the convening power *and* been trusted by senior business leaders sufficiently to convene such gatherings or to get people talking so freely. Maala was able to use its heritage and track record and corporate membership to bring people together quickly and effectively. "Our role," says Momo, "is not to criticize business publicly; our role is to provide a safe, secure environment where business can explore."

Momo was already working with a small Tel Aviv strategic consultancy, Praxis, which specializes in reframing issues and organizations and disruptive change.[353] The combination of the post-protest roundtables and the work with Praxis has led Maala to develop a new strategy for the next phase of its life. Central to the strategy is an emphasis on fairness in business, asking member firms about the fairness of their core business practices: how they treat customers, employees, suppliers, etc.

Maala, however, is also now developing a major new focus on helping Israeli companies to reframe their core products and services to address the development needs of the developing countries – sustainably: sustainable base-of-the pyramid strategies. Israel has significant competitive advantages in solar power desalination, clean water, innovative crop-irrigation techniques and high tech. This is something recognized by the UN Under-Secretary-General Sha Zukang, the Chinese diplomat who was Secretary-General for the Rio + 20 conference on sustainable development. Sha Zukang said on a visit to Israel:

> Israel has proven to be a leader in agricultural technology for development, practising innovation and implementing sustainable solutions for agricultural development, food security, and climate change adaptation and mitigation. They have informed and advised the Commission on Sustainable Development on matters related to integrated water management, drylands, and sustainable crop production. We have much to learn from the Israeli agricultural experience.[354]

Maala's approach is to bring new business development and R&D specialists from member companies together, looking for unusual and unexpected but potentially positive synergies. Such as the head of R&D from one member firm in the defense sector with world-class sensor technology introduced to an agricultural business to discuss the application of sensor technologies to improve agricultural yields. Maala sees a powerful role here, again building on the trust of member companies, its brokerage skills, a change-agent mission and a growing ability to anticipate unexpected synergies. Potentially, it is a powerful combination – helping to fulfill the ancient Jewish admonition to help *tikkun olam* (repair the world).[355] It is a powerful reframing of Maala's historic mission to promote business with social purpose and takes this to a broader canvas to help promote sustainable development internationally.

A personal conclusion from Talia Aharoni

Maala, like its global peers, will be tested on its ability to produce renewed relevance that sufficiently answers the deep crisis of trust and confidence in the global and local business sectors. This relevancy cannot be achieved by the past "issue-management" approach. From a gloomy perspective, perhaps the business-led networks have completed their purpose and should give way to a new form of capitalist thinking and networking. From an optimistic perspective, Maala and its peers can act as the designers and motivators of a new business essence. This may require a very brave and dangerous decision of working "against" the immediate consensus of their own members. It may require a restart mode and a new beginning: defining a new organizational vision, mission and strategic plan. It may require a new business model for the organization. It may require a new generation of business-social entrepreneurs who will be ready to step forward rather than the new managements that more or less continue along the same path. It is risky, but in my opinion – it is the only way.[356]

Profile 7

National Business Initiative for Growth, Development and Democracy, South Africa (NBI)

David Grayson and Jane Nelson[*]

The National Business Initiative in its own words

The National Business Initiative (NBI) is a voluntary group of leading national and multinational companies, working together towards sustainable growth and development in South Africa through partnerships, practical programmes and policy engagement. This is achieved through evidence-based experience and research in key areas and thus effects systems change.

The axiom that business cannot succeed in a society that fails is particularly relevant in a developing country like South Africa. The role of business in sustainable development is becoming increasingly important especially if they want to strengthen their competitive edge for the future. Through constructive engagement and strategic collective action business can shape the economic and social environments within which they operate.

---

[*] This profile is an abridged and updated version of "The National Business Initiative Story" and of "Building a South African Future: A Review of the First Ten Years of the National Business Initiative" www.nbi.org.za/About NBI/Pages/Our History.aspx, accessed June 28, 2012, supplemented with further desk research, and an interview with Gillian Hutchings of the NBI, August 2012. The authors thank André Fourie (now of SAB Miller) and Gillian Hutchings of NBI for their comments on this profile. Unless otherwise stated, quotes and statistics are from the publications above.

- We advocate corporate citizenship and business leadership for sustainable growth and development
- We mobilize business leadership and resources to make a difference
- We facilitate collective business action and critical social dialogue
- We implement strategic projects backed by rigorous policy analysis and research
- We build relationships and trust with government, business and key stakeholders

www.nbi.org.za   June 2012

Background context and history

The origins of the National Business Initiative (NBI) date back to the 1970s. As the tempo of internal and external political challenges to apartheid South Africa increased, the idea that the South African business community could isolate itself from the political forces of the day became increasingly unviable. A small vanguard of South African business leaders recognized the need to become proactive players in finding solutions and quietly started taking initiatives towards inclusive dialogue as well as the introduction of tangible projects. A watershed came in 1976, with the Soweto student uprisings and the escalation of the struggle for full political rights for all South Africans. A key business response was to establish the Urban Foundation.

The Urban Foundation

The original intention of the Urban Foundation (UF), according to the businessmen who founded it, such as Harry Oppenheimer of the Anglo American and Anton Rupert of Rembrandt, had been "to promote and coordinate involvement by the private sector in the improvement of the quality of life of urban communities." From the start, the politicization of the organization was inevitable, as this approach explicitly aimed for the recognition of black Africans in urban areas, which was diametrically opposed to the government policy of apartheid. Therefore, at both practical and policy levels, the work of the UF immediately came into conflict with the core contention of the state's apartheid urban planning: that black people had no permanent place in South Africa's cities. At the same time, for many involved in the political struggle to topple the apartheid system, the UF represented an attempt by business to blunt the impact of the struggle on those "quality of life" issues – housing and education in particular – that fueled popular discontent. In other words, the organization was seen as frustrating the revolution and thereby perpetuating the apartheid status quo.

Throughout its life, the UF campaigned for and won changes to what was increasingly seen as an unworkable urban housing system. The business-funded UF was successful in extending land-tenure rights of urban blacks first to 99-year leasehold and finally to full ownership. Millions of black South Africans became legitimate urban citizens in their own country due to this effort. Once this process of reform had been set in motion, the next target became the apparatus of "influx control," code for the government trying to keep rural Africans away from the cities. UF personnel were responsible for the wording of the government's White Paper on urbanization, as well as for the amendments to the legislation that finally ended this destructive system in the late 1980s.

While the UF worked in this way for a more sensible policy response to urbanization, they also paid significant attention to the practical provision of housing and other urban improvements. Over 100,000 houses in urban areas were built during the 18-year life of the UF, and the organization finally made important inputs into the new housing subsidy policy that came into effect after 1994. It also focused on the physical and institutional capacity of education for marginalized black communities. Through its work, more than 2,000 classrooms were built, as well as 12 complete schools and 14 community resource centers. In addition to nearly ZAR2 billion (US$237 million) generated for infrastructure projects, the UF was also responsible for training of over 1,000 pre-school educators, with more than 20,000 school educators participating in UF-sponsored development and upgrading programs by the time the UF became part of the National Business Initiative late in 1994.

The Consultative Business Movement

At about the same time as the UF was helping to dismantle influx control and beginning to speak to many non-governmental organizations about the formulation of housing and urbanization policy for the post-apartheid era, another group of business leaders and thinkers was contemplating more direct involvement with the changing political process that was beginning to unfold. Leaders such as Christo Nel, Leon Cohen and Mike Saunders were keen to see business actively involved in dialogue between the apartheid government, beleaguered by a devaluing rand, high levels of inflation, internal violence and international sanctions, and the increasingly visible United Democratic Front (followed by the Mass Democratic Movement) as the internal arm of the banned African National Congress (ANC).

Some members of the business sector had already begun to hold meetings with progressive political leaders and had joined a group of prominent South Africans who traveled to Dakar in Senegal in 1987 to make contact with leaders of the ANC. However much the government resisted, the course was set. The foundations of the apartheid status quo had cracked beyond repair. In anticipation of the intense process of social dialogue and transformation that would inevitably follow and to accelerate the process of dialogue, the Consultative Business Movement (CBM) was established.

The initial brochure describes the CBM as "a voluntary and independent group of senior business leaders and corporations who, from a business perspective, acknowledge and support the need for constructive transformation of South Africa's political economy." Within a short time, the CBM had nearly 100 member corporations, a number of which were also members of the UF. The CBM busied itself with building networks and relationships across the political spectrum. Business leaders met with all known political groups to gain an understanding of their respective views. Inside the country, the CBM facilitated numerous workshops that provided a first-time forum for people from opposite ends of the political and economic spectrum to exchange views. The CBM also arranged further trips to see the Pan-African Congress in Tanzania and the ANC in Zimbabwe.

After the watershed end-of-apartheid announcement by President F.W. de Klerk and Nelson Mandela's release from gaol in February 1990, the pace of the CBM's work increased substantially. This period was also characterized by soaring levels of political violence in many areas across South Africa. Meanwhile, there was broad consensus among leaders that a high-level peace process was essential. However, both the National Party Government and the ANC blamed each other as being the main instigators of the violence, and neither would accept the legitimacy of the other to convene a national peace conference. It was the joint efforts of the CBM and the South African Council of Churches that initiated the course that eventually culminated in a comprehensive peace process. The first meeting was co-chaired by John Hall (Barlow Rand executive and Chairman of the Chamber of Commerce) and Archbishop Desmond Tutu.

The credibility and legitimacy of the CBM, which later became its most valuable currency during times of intense distrust in the country, was established during the peace process. This provided the rationale for the request that the CBM serve as the secretariat and administrative support for the national negotiation processes, including the Convention for a Democratic South Africa (CODESA) process and Multi Party Negotiation Process (MPNP). When CODESA deadlocked in 1992 over regional and central powers, it was the CBM that brought together academics and experts from around the world to work out an acceptable way forward. It also supported nationwide efforts to provide voter education, as the previously excluded majority of South Africans prepared to vote in the country's first democratic election.

In this way, South African business found itself at the crux of the complex and often stormy process of negotiating a new constitution and finding the pathway that the country would need to take towards those historic democratic elections in 1994. There are probably few, if any, precedents in the world where the business sector has been entrusted with such a sensitive role at the heart of such a highly contested political transition.[357]

The emergence of the National Business Initiative

Theuns Eloff, a theologian who had left the ministry to become CEO of the CBM, recalls that following the dramatic years of negotiation and first democratic elections the organization felt its work was done and that it should disband. Sources within the new government had other ideas and maintained that the expertise assembled within the CBM was too valuable to lose. The same was true of the UF. By 1994 this pioneering business organization had also started to query what its future would be and how it should be structured. The question that emerged was: should the business sector continue to support both organizations? The answer was not difficult to find: the role of business in the affairs of the country was far from over, so it was decided that the strengths of the two organizations should be combined in a new organization, the National Business Initiative for Growth, Development and Democracy (NBI).

A working document dated February 1995 asserts:

> The South African business community represents a resource that is not usually available to countries at South Africa's stage of development. It has played an important part in the country's unfolding transition by, for example, responding to the living conditions of black South Africans in the 1970s; by brokering the first contacts between liberation movements in exile in the 1980s; by facilitating

the National Peace Accord and the CODESA negotiations and the MPNP in the early 1990s; and by initiating and supporting a wide range of development programs. Drawing on the skills developed in the UF and the CBM, the NBI will seek to build consensus, generate ideas and develop institutions, policies and practices that will go into the making of a new society.

The combination of the older Urban Foundation and the younger Consultative Business Movement was a strategic and timely intervention. Establishing a single organization from very different theoretical bases was obviously not without its difficulties. The UF was essentially seen as reformist in nature, while the efforts of the CBM were concerned with transformation. The CBM's great strength and achievements lay in networking, brokering and negotiation. The UF's focus had concentrated on specialist research – notably in housing, urbanization and education – in addition to policy formulation and the delivery of often large practical projects.

Negotiating these waters required vision, skilled leadership and commitment. With the CBM's Theuns Eloff as CEO and the UF's Mike Rosholt as Chairman of the Board, the newly formed NBI faced the complex and turbulent post-1994 realities with an avowed determination to promote increased economic growth, reduce poverty and inequality, and support effective and efficient governance.

The NBI was launched on March 9, 1995. National and provincial government ministers attended the occasion, as did senior business and community leaders, along with diplomats from many countries around the world. The most significant presence, however, was that of Nelson Mandela, South Africa's new President, who had been inaugurated after the country's first democratic elections barely a year before.

The NBI's proposed role was defined in the context of a think-tank cum problem-solver, while simultaneously serving a facilitative function. Finance for the organization would stem from voluntary, self-determined annual membership fees from individual private-sector companies. The rationale was clear: business had – and still does have – a real stake in helping to make the new South Africa work; and the private sector was willing to demonstrate its commitment to the future with practical action. Mandela was generous in his approval of this approach: "There are many ways in which the special skills and know-how of the business community can help Government to achieve its development objectives," he told guests at the NBI's inaugural function. "The original thinking which has gone into the launch of the NBI is very much appreciated and I give it my unqualified support."

So the NBI started life as an organization with significant backing from the business sector, with substantial acceptance from other actors within civil society, and with the blessing of the President of a democratic South Africa and his Government of National Unity.

The NBI had been careful to explain itself within the business sector. Its original prospectus stressed that it was not "a mandated body that can (or would want to) speak or act on behalf of its members." Organizations such as the South African Chamber of Business, the National African Chamber of Commerce and Business South Africa already existed to fulfill this role. The NBI, on the other hand, was "tasked by its members to identify obstacles to and/or opportunities for socio-economic and democratic development, do research, formulate policy proposals, and facilitate partnerships and through them the delivery of concrete initiatives." In short, from the outset its specific focus was on engaging the private sector to directly help address socioeconomic challenges. As enunciated by the NBI's founding chairman, Mike Rosholt: "The NBI aimed to be an effective and accountable organization involved in solutions to the many socio-economic problems facing the country."

The need for such a business-led initiative dedicated to social and economic progress in post-1994 South Africa was obvious. Severe problems existed in most social fields, exacerbated by decades of apartheid ideology and neglect, and most particularly in education and housing. Equally daunting were the challenges in the public governance and criminal justice arenas. Straddling these areas was the stark reality of millions of people whom apartheid had excluded from the mainstream economy, and the many more who would lose their jobs as the country shook itself free from the false protection of the apartheid era and rushed into the rigors of a harshly competitive global economy.

Assertions that socioeconomic change was the responsibility of the democratically elected government, and not a concern of business, were soon silenced by the sheer magnitude of many of the challenges facing the country. The business sector was becoming convinced that sustainable business was dependent on a stable social environment. Ten months after the NBI was established, its membership had grown from a founding group of 80 to 118 of South Africa's largest and most significant companies.

Key activities and phases of development

Over almost two decades, the NBI has evolved to keep business at the forefront of the public-policy dialogue and practical implementation of efforts to promote socioeconomic development, good governance and increasingly more sustainable, inclusive and green models of growth.

André Fourie (NBI's CEO 2001–10) explains: "In the beginning, companies gave the NBI money to help the government with some of the more intractable socio-economic problems it faced. However, the challenge now has more to do with method as opposed to wherewithal." As a result, he goes on to say, "The NBI is increasingly working within partnerships with government, as well as with individual companies. Today the emphasis has shifted from support to more complex relationships and involvement." Fourie argues that this is more than enlightened self-interest and that it is driven by a sense of well-entrenched responsibility to the wider society and recognition of the need to collaborate to drive more systemic change.

Prior to looking at its key activities and two main phases of development, here is a quick overview of NBI's governance and organizational structure. Over almost two decades its corporate membership has remained remarkably stable. From the original 80 participating companies in 1995, membership settled at around 140 member companies a decade later and that remains the number in 2012.

The Board of Directors is drawn from the corporate membership base. The Executive Committee comprises the chairman of the board (Mike Rosholt from inception to 2007, now Cas Coovadia of the Banking Association) and external directors, plus the chief executive (Theuns Eloff until 2001, followed by André Fourie until 2010 and now Joanne Yawitch who was previously Deputy Director-General, Department of Environmental Affairs and Tourism). In addition, the NBI operates Provincial Boards as well as specialist or advisory committees relating to the NBI's fields of specific interest.

The number of staff employed has also changed little and illustrates the great leverage potential that is possible by also harnessing the managerial and technical capabilities of member companies. By the end of its first year of operation, the NBI had a staff of just over 50. In 2004, the staff complement was no bulkier. Indeed, after the Business Trust was spun off, total staff numbers at the NBI fell to just below 40.[358]

Phase one: Mobilizing business resources to help government address its socioeconomic priorities

Two of the largest contributions from the NBI during the first years of its existence came from activities imported directly from the UF. The first was in the field of education policy and the second in housing delivery. At the same time the CBM's work on the role of the private sector in financing public services and infrastructure for reconstruction and development helped the NBI to play a lead role in brokering public–private partnerships. Other significant inputs during this time were made into the areas of public-sector governance, local economic development and criminal justice.

The NBI's method of operation was to add value to the contributions of its small staff by involving its member companies in collective initiatives within the key intervention areas. It was not unusual for these areas to have been the subject of intensive business-sponsored research and hands-on experience before the actual interventions were planned. The following examples illustrate how this approach of collective business action was implemented in practice in education, housing, local economic development and support for public governance.

Education

In 1991, the Urban Foundation had established Edupol, a special "education policy and system change unit," which was transferred intact into the NBI. The research and policy work undertaken by Edupol had some far-reaching policy impacts in critical areas such as education financing, educator supply, utilization and demand, and school governance. Edupol research and participation in government committees and task teams contributed to the shaping of the South African Schools Act, the key legislation that laid the foundation for post-apartheid schooling. It also provided critical (and cautionary) data and analysis on current and future trends in educator supply and demand, at a time when government was beginning a major shake-up of the entire system of educator training in South Africa. From 1996 onwards, the unit began to break new ground in the vital but neglected area of further education and training. Through Edupol (later renamed the Education and Enterprise Unit), the NBI contributed significantly to the 1998 Green and White Papers on further education and training. This was followed by the provision of vital private-sector support to the Department of Education in its restructuring of the colleges sector.

Policy inputs were not the only interventions made by the NBI into education during the 1990s. The NBI Board insisted on hands-on projects to complement the high-level policy work that business was underwriting. The idea was for the NBI not so much to operate as a delivery agency but rather to identify areas of special need that state funding could not reach, and to provide specialist input and interventions, which could demonstrate the changes that business was advocating. This approach was used by Edupol to establish a project called

EQUIP, a neat acronym for the NBI's Education Quality Improvement Programme. Research in other parts of the world had established that learner achievement (obviously the most important educational output) was related less to per capita spending and educator/learner ratios than it was to basic school facilities, school governance and administrative systems, as well as educator education and motivation. EQUIP took these realities into account as it set about providing tools, resources, advice and mentoring for individual schools and their administrators to take responsibility for their own development and quality standards.

Housing

As with the NBI contribution to education, so the contribution to the crisis area of housing had its roots in the work undertaken by the UF. From the late 1970s, the UF had been directly involved in the provision of housing. So when the UF disbanded, important skills in the management of large housing projects were transferred to the NBI through experts such as Brian Whittaker and Henry Jeffreys. These skills were supported by cutting-edge UF research into the area of urbanization, the dynamics of informal settlements and the invaluable UF contribution to the new policy on capital subsidies for every first-time homeowner in the country – an initiative that was championed by South Africa's first Housing Minister, Joe Slovo.

While this policy had the potential to release large volumes of capital into the low end of the housing market, it did not follow automatically that large numbers of houses could immediately be built. Although politicians had promised in 1994 that one million new houses would be made available before the next general election, actual delivery languished. By the time the NBI became involved in 1996, it was calculated that the country would need to deliver more than 300,000 housing units a year for the political targets to be realized. This translated as over 800 houses a day for the remaining three years in that particular parliamentary term.

To start with, the NBI's involvement was restricted to commenting on the Housing White Paper to encourage private-sector participation in the task of housing provision. It then released an assessment of informal settlements and incremental housing schemes. This played an important role in persuading government not to attempt to replace such settlements and schemes with box-type housing rows, but rather to allow first-time-homeowner housing subsidies to be used to upgrade existing informal and incremental units. However, the pace of delivery remained disappointingly slow, and tensions emerged between politicians and administrators, national and provincial departments, and also between the public and private sectors.

Eventually, at the request of the Ministerial Task Team on Housing Delivery, the NBI established a Housing Development Support Team, staffed from the private sector, and steadily the housing situation began to improve. The Ministerial Task Team included prominent business leaders from various sectors whose interest in the housing crisis was broad and not based on the narrow interests of any specific housing company. A key factor in the ultimate improvements that ensued in housing delivery was that a senior project manager from one of the NBI's member companies (Brian Monteith from Murray and Roberts) was seconded into the National Department of Housing.

The NBI's Housing Development Support Team worked with member companies and applied business skills and methodologies to help in a number of practical ways, namely:

- The development and installation of a computer-based management information system that linked national and provincial housing departments to up-to-date figures on subsidy granting and house construction in every locality, region and province in the country

- An analysis of the process of subsidy application and house construction, which charted a critical path through a previously complicated process, by breaking it down into 180 related steps. As a result of this undertaking, the time needed for the development of subsidy-based housing was reduced from 24 to 7 months

- It set up teams with rapid access to technical, legal and social development expertise in eight of the nine provinces. They were given the responsibility of identifying and clearing blockages in the delivery process, while at the same time building organizational capacity within the provincial departments in which they worked

- It produced a comprehensive "housing delivery guide" for developers and housing authorities that created an integrated framework for the management of housing projects and established the time necessary for each activity in the process

- It also produced a guide for employers on how they could assist their employees to gain access to housing. The guide was based on the best practice of selected NBI member companies and described the best approaches to company housing support, in addition to identifying the resources available to companies wishing to introduce or improve housing-support schemes for employees

By the 1999 elections, promised delivery dates for a million houses had been issued and more than 940,000 subsidies had been awarded. Furthermore, 640,000 houses had either been built or were under construction. An independent evaluation by the Monitor Group stated:

> The NBI's Housing Delivery Support Team has been unwavering in its commitment to transforming project-linked subsidy delivery from a cumbersome process into a streamlined efficient system capable of producing exponential growth in the rate of delivery. That is no small achievement.

Brian Whittaker, the NBI's Chief Operating Officer, remarks that a comparison with housing projects in other countries had shown that the South African housing effort in the second half of the 1990s was one of the world's most successful in terms of the high rates of delivery and the low levels of corruption.

Local economic development

With one of its aims being to promote economic growth, the NBI lost little time in establishing an Economics Reference Group early in 1996. The country's aim at that point was to achieve a 6% growth rate by the year 2000, and the NBI lent its weight to achieving this crucial national goal. From the outset the main thrust of the NBI's concern lay at the low end of economic activity. The problems and challenges surrounding small, micro and medium enterprises (SMMEs) received considerable attention, with the NBI providing an active focus in the following areas:

- Unblocking the SMMEs funding flow

- Improving SMMEs service and procurement

- Assisting with the establishment of local business service centers

- Training for stimulating local economic development

Public-sector governance

The advent of democracy in South Africa brought extensive changes to every tier of government and the civil service. In particular, government at municipal or local level was asked to do much more than it had ever done before. President Thabo Mbeki described it as "a radically new system of local government" that was thrust on politicians and civil servants alike.

The demands of the new democratic dispensation pushed the responsibilities of local governments far beyond merely that of service providers for the largely white towns and cities. New local authority areas were geographically more logical and inclusive; the responsibility for balancing the municipal books weighed heavily on those charged with equalizing services across areas that were at widely differing stages of development; and local authorities were increasingly expected to perform a development facilitation role, not only with regard to infrastructure but also in relation to sustainable economic development among their constituents.

The NBI saw these challenges as being central to its overall aims of enhancing the business contribution to growth, development and democracy. Encouraging effective governance at the local level therefore became an initial and enduring focus area.

As early as 1996, the NBI, in partnership with the Institute for Local Governance and Development, produced a comprehensive local government training framework for the National Department of Provincial Affairs and Constitutional Development. At the same time, it also established a Local Government Facilitation Unit "to promote the development of effective local government throughout South Africa."

The unit's core focus was "to develop the strategic management and service delivery capacity of local authorities." As such, the work it undertook encompassed the following fields: policy research and dialogue; training and production of manuals; and helping to build public–private partnerships (PPPs). Given overwhelming interest in PPPs, the NBI established a PPP Resource Centre to provide key information – case studies, draft contracts and best-practice models – to both the private and public sectors. As a result of the NBI's training and awareness-raising efforts, several major partnerships were brokered, representing a transaction value of more than ZAR13 billion. (US$1.54 billion). NBI successes in PPPs resulted in the establishment of a special PPP unit within the National Treasury to advise all state departments on the whys and hows of establishing win–win partnerships with the private sector.

In addition to the examples above, where companies provided funding, technical and managerial support to enable the NBI to help build the capacity of education and housing systems, SMME support services and local governments the NBI also became actively engaged in efforts to improve the criminal justice system and to tackle high levels of crime. One of its greatest achievements was the creation of the *Business Against Crime* initiative, which was spun off as an independent entity. In addition, in 1996, it supported the creation of another independent, business-supported entity, the *Business Trust*. These two bodies are profiled in a later section.

Phase two: Building systemic partnerships to drive sustainable growth and development

As it has evolved and as public-sector capacity has strengthened, the NBI has moved beyond mobilizing business social-investment funds aimed at directly assisting the government to developing more complex, systemic-level partnerships between groups of companies and other actors, including government. It has also become active in working directly with companies to embed corporate responsibility and sustainability strategies into their core business operations and competitive goals.

Education remains a pivotal focus for the NBI, at both school level and further education and technical training college level. Likewise in the case of economic development, with the NBI focusing on specific interventions in support of small enterprise development and efforts to build more inclusive business linkages between small enterprises and large companies. An important new emphasis on sustainable development has been added since the early 2000s, with a strong emphasis on climate and energy. Today, the NBI lists three focus areas – human capital, economic linkages, and climate and energy – in addition to its role as the national partner of the UN Global Compact and the World Business Council for Sustainable Development (WBCSD) in South Africa.

Human capital

Education has been one of the NBI's strongest focus areas since inception. Particularly long-lived has been the Education Quality Improvement Programme (EQUIP) that deals with quality improvements in schools, and the work done within the further education and training colleges sector. In 2006, NBI was asked by government to lead the Joint Initiative on Priority Skills Acquisition program. This was officially handed over to the newly created Human Resource Development Council of South Africa in 2010.

Economic linkages

Through running a national business competition, the NBI realized that one of its key strengths was the expertise that emanated from its member companies and business in general. It was through this recognition that the idea of mobilizing groups of mentors for SMMEs was born. In early 2004, the NBI introduced its Youth Mentorship Programme in partnership with the Nations Trust, which tapped into existing business expertise. Significantly, most SMME business opportunities are a result of private-sector unbundling of non-core activities and of private-sector need along supply and distribution chains. As a result, the NBI increasingly focused on building linkages between its member companies and emerging SMMEs, and in 2010 it helped to create the South African Supplier Diversity Council.

Sustainable futures

In 2002, the NBI began talking about a "formal corporate citizen focus." Given its membership base, access to business leaders and relationships with government, the NBI was well positioned to move in this direction. A series of seminars and publications followed, concentrating on topics such as "triple-bottom-line reporting," "global corporate citizenship" and "socially responsible investment." Leadership initiatives that the NBI supported included the University of KwaZulu-Natal's Master's program in Corporate Citizenship and Cambridge University's Business and the Environment program.

The result of these activities was the establishment of the Sustainable Futures Unit in 2003 (now renamed Climate and Energy) to meet the growing need for NBI members to align themselves with the strategic imperatives of sustainable development, particularly in the environmental arena. The Sustainable Futures Unit defined its role as being: "to create a platform for partnerships, relationships and trust between business, government and other stakeholders, which lead to impacts on national and international objectives around sustainable development."

The NBI has worked closely with international business-led organizations to implement this new strand of work. In 2003 it became a regional partner of the WBCSD. It partnered with Incite Sustainability to bring the Carbon Disclosure Project to South Africa. More recently, it took over as Focal Point to the South African Local Network of the UN Global Compact.[359] The NBI was also the secretariat to the Big Business Working Group, a group of business leaders who met with the then President Thabo Mbeki to discuss issues affecting the country and its investment climate. It works closely with the main business representative organizations, Business Unity South Africa and Business Leadership South Africa, where there are policy implications for business related to socioeconomic and sustainability issues.

Two of the great sustainability successes to date have been the facilitation of a voluntary national Energy Efficiency Accord between government and the business community, and getting almost 70% of the top 100 companies listed on the Johannesburg Stock Exchange to measure and report their carbon footprint. As a result, in 2009 South Africa was ranked by the Carbon Disclosure Project as having the world's fifth highest response rate internationally. Efforts are now underway to develop a similar approach for water using the Carbon Disclosure Project Water Disclosure as the mechanism. This has been piloted and is now in its second year, with 40 companies participating. Feedback from these companies is that once they have disclosure, they want to work together on finding solutions.

In an emerging market like South Africa, the focus is all too often on "development or bust." The NBI's view is that economic development, and particularly the drawing into the economic mainstream of the previously excluded, is an essential ingredient for sustaining South Africa's young democracy. Some observers have, however, questioned whether this is contradicted by the NBI's newer interest in sustainable development, which, with its focus on environmental protection, often serves as a rein on unbridled development and wealth creation.

As Glen Fisher, the NBI's former Senior Policy Executive, observed:

> Our primary concerns are with poverty and the economy on one hand and with human development on the other. But you can't address these issues in the long-term unless you do so in a sustainable way. Therefore our focus on sustainable development is central. It is also strengthened by some very specific

environmental issues confronting South Africa, such as energy, water, and the serious impact that climate change will have on economic sectors such as agriculture and tourism.

Impact and lessons learned

Over almost two decades the NBI has played a vital role in driving collective business leadership, facilitating dialogue and partnerships between the public and private sectors, implementing large-scale projects, and helping to build institutional and physical infrastructure in areas crucial to the country's future. Its wide-ranging achievements can be summarized under the headings of:

- Building new institutions targeted at specific socio-economic issues

- Serving as facilitator and secretariat for strategic dialogue structures between government and business

- Leveraging private-sector resources to address public challenges

- Transferring international best business practices to South African companies

Building new institutions

Since its creation in 1995, the NBI has set up a number of new, and now independent, institutions, either directly or in support of government efforts. These include:

- **Business Against Crime.** Now an independent organization as a unique private-sector contribution to enhanced criminal justice and crime prevention, which was established in response to the high levels of crime and violence that were prevalent in the latter half of the 1990s

- **The Business Trust.** This combined the resources of the public and private sectors to support programs that accelerate the achievement of agreed national objectives. (See Box P7.1)

- **The Human Resource Development Council.** Although the NBI did not set this up, it coordinated the Joint Initiative on Priority Skills Acquisition program at the request of the government, and this formed a key foundation for the new Council's strategic agenda

- **The South African Supplier Diversity Council.** The work that the NBI undertook on promoting business linkages between its large member companies and SMMEs, alongside similar work by other organizations and industry trade associations, helped to form the basis for the creation of this new Council. Some ten leading corporations joined the Council's steering committee, which is chaired by a business leader

Box P7.1 **The Business Trust**

In 1998, after three years of successful activity, the NBI began to think in terms of increasing the business contribution to the broader socioeconomic transformation of South Africa, and cementing the partnerships already achieved with government. In concert with the South Africa Foundation and the Black Business Council, the NBI developed the concept of the Business Trust.

Although the Trust and the NBI have been closely interlinked, it is important at the outset to understand the difference between the two organizations. The latter continues to operate as a catalyst for change and a problem-solver in policy design and implementation, rather than as a delivery agency. The Business Trust, on the other hand, was envisaged as a one-off structured partnership between business and government. It was focused on combining the resources of both sectors to accelerate and scale the achievement of a small number of mutually agreed national development objectives through a limited number of joint interventions and for a limited period of time (initially five years and later extended to 12 years). The full name of the term-limited and structured-partnership mechanism became the Business Trust for Job Creation and Human Capacity Development. Importantly, and almost uniquely, the trustees of the Business Trust were drawn from senior leadership from both business and government at the CEO and Cabinet ministerial level. The NBI had provided pivotal input into the planning of the Business Trust and in March 1999 was assigned the job of managing it on a strict cost-recovery basis. The NBI's Brian Whittaker was appointed as the Trust's chief operating officer.

The public and private trustees agreed to focus on two program areas:

- **Catalyzing market-based solutions to development.** This area aimed to attract investment, develop enterprises and make markets more inclusive in a few sectors with high potential for job creation and growth. The tourism sector received the bulk of support with business process outsourcing (BPO) added as a second target sector in 2004. The Trust also supported a community investment program aimed at piloting market-based approaches to poverty alleviation, including inclusive business models and innovative financing and advisory services for low-income producers in 21 poverty nodes, including some of the country's poorest rural communities
- **Improving public services.** This area aimed to harness private-sector resources to improve the provision of public services, primarily in the area of education, but also in supporting infrastructure and public works projects

Over the course of the Business Trust's 12 years of operation from 1999 to 2011, the initiative raised almost ZAR2 billion from 140 companies. The money was provided in two funding cycles and the amounts from each company were based on company size. In addition to these funds, plus the interest earned on them, grants were also received from government departments for the oversight and management of designated projects. Specialists were contracted for the actual delivery of projects and their contracts were renewable annually, based on the results of independent audits and evaluations, and any revisions made to plans based on this evidence. Tourism and education projects received over 60% of the funds. The professional management and tight cost-control procedures of the Trust ensured that administrative costs amounted to no more than 5.5% of the funds managed.

➜

In summing up its achievements at the end of the 12 years, the Business Trust concluded:

> R1.8 billion was mobilized and managed by the Business Trust in support of government resources considerably greater than that sum. By working together, business and government were able to improve the lives of four million people. That included 600,000 work seekers who found income and work, 1.5 million learners who improved their performance, and close to 8,000 entrepreneurs who were assisted to expand their businesses.[360]

Several catalytic, and ongoing, financing and advisory funds were established. These ranged from mechanisms to support small, medium and micro-enterprises in tourism and poor communities, to a fund providing preparation advice for infrastructure projects worth over ZAR500 million. Education improvement programs were initiated in over 900 primary schools and 500 secondary schools, and independent evaluations found examples of children gaining a year in reading and writing ability in primary schools and a nine-fold improvement in math results in many of the secondary schools. A business process outsourcing industry was established, which now has seven of the world's top ten outsourcing companies operating and creating local jobs in South Africa.[361]

Serving as facilitator and secretariat for strategic dialogue

Building on the pioneering work of the Urban Foundation and the Consultative Business Movement, the NBI has continued to play a valuable role as a trusted intermediary in complex dialogues between the business community and government. As stated earlier, it has never claimed to represent its members or be an official voice of business (a role that is undertaken by other business associations in South Africa), but it has helped to facilitate dialogue and, more importantly, the development of new policies, platforms and initiatives between government and business in key areas related to socioeconomic prosperity and sustainability. Examples include:

- Serving as secretariat to the Human Resource Development Strategy for South Africa, under the leadership of Deputy President Kgalema Motlanthe, and mobilizing business resources for human capital development

- Serving as secretariat to former President Mbeki's Big Business Working Group, thus promoting dialogue and trust between business and government leaders

- Facilitating the signing and implementation of the Energy Efficiency Accord, as a tangible contribution of the private sector to environmental protection and enhanced competitiveness, and subsequently creating a Leadership Network to take the Accord forward

Leveraging private-sector resources to address public challenges

Almost every program and project undertaken by the NBI has leveraged private-sector funds, management capabilities and other in-kind resources to help meet government priorities in areas ranging from education and housing to building public-sector management capacity and including previously marginalized people in the formal economy. In addition to mobilizing private resources for particular projects, the NBI has also help to set up several financing vehicles. One example is the Colleges Collaboration Fund. This was conceptualized and managed by the NBI and has made a major contribution to the transformation of the further education and training sector through a network of technical colleges. The NBI's work on strengthening the capacity of local and provincial governments through programs that have combined advice, mentoring and efforts to improve administrative and service delivery is illustrated through examples such as the Eastern Cape Provincial Government/Business Partnership and the long-standing Education Quality Improvement Programme.

Two-way transfer of international best business practices

The NBI has become an increasingly important participant in a variety of international corporate responsibility networks and initiatives. In doing so, it is playing a valuable intermediary role in transferring international best practices in corporate sustainability and citizenship between South African companies and their international counterparts. Post-apartheid South Africa has been an incubator for some of the most interesting and progressive business-led corporate responsibility and public–private-sector cooperation in the world and has much to share internationally, especially with other emerging markets where economic growth and wealth creation is occurring alongside high levels of poverty and environmental degradation. At the same time, the NBI has brought international best practices to South Africa through its role as the local partner of the UN Global Compact and the WBCSD, among others. It has also played a key role in introducing and launching the Carbon Disclosure Project in South Africa to address the business implications of climate change.

The future

Throughout its existence, the NBI has evidenced the foresight to see ahead. At the outset it was intended as a problem-solver, serving as a think-tank and playing a facilitative role. It was envisaged that, through its independence and mobility, the organization would help to achieve consensus between the various actors, thereby driving the move towards common goals and sustained business involvement in the task of developing South Africa. It was additionally entrusted with the task of identifying obstacles to and opportunities for socioeconomic and democratic development, through research, the formulation of policy proposals and the facilitation of partnerships that would result in the delivery of concrete initiatives. "The NBI is a leading example of the unprecedented contribution that the business sector made to democracy, peace and socio-economic development in South Africa," says former NBI CEO, André Fourie. At the same time, Fourie and his successor Joanne Yawitch see the need for further evolution in the role of the private sector.

It is essential for the NBI to help business develop responses to new and increased stakeholder expectations, the growing sophistication and power of civil society, the implications of the recognition of an increase in the relative power of the private sector and the challenges to corporate reputation. Growing demands relating to the roles and responsibilities of companies in society are a major driving force of the changed global business landscape, together with increased understanding of the implications of environmental challenges. Glen Fisher explains:

> There are concerns confronting business today, in the middle of the first decade of the 21st century, which were hardly on the agenda ten years ago. Issues such as the environment, human rights, and sustainable socio-economic development that go far beyond the idea of philanthropy. It is becoming imperative that these issues are not neatly shelved in corporate social investment departments but are brought fully into the boardroom.
>
> The NBI is well equipped to assist with this crucially important process, not least because the organization recognizes the position of South Africa in a rapidly changing world.[362]

In the light of these comments, it is revealing to look more closely at the market position that the NBI currently holds. It has shifted from primarily project delivery based on responding to immediate government priorities and business concerns, although it still undertakes projects, to address a set of broader and more systemic concerns. This is illustrated in its public commitment to support WBCSD's ambitious *Vision 2050: A New Agenda for Business*, which envisages a world well on its way to sustainability by 2050. NBI intends to explore what sustainability means in the South African context, and, therefore, what is a sustainable business.

As Cas Coovadia, NBI's new chairman (only the second in almost two decades) states:

> The NBI has traditionally focused on working with business and government, but Vision 2050 challenges us to engage with broader society to develop a common vision for sustainable development. We need, for example, to engage with poor communities and define what sustainability means to citizens who are fighting merely to survive, who are forced to cut down trees just to keep warm or to cook their food. We need to interact with stakeholders ranging from labor unions to civil society groups in order to take the debate on sustainability to a higher level, and to place African issues squarely on the table. The NBI is well positioned to stimulate this dialogue and, in doing so, to add greater value for its members by enabling them to embrace a more encompassing vision of sustainable development.[363]

At the same time, the NBI's agenda remains aligned to working with and supporting the ambitious goals of the South African government to build a competitive but inclusive and sustainable national economy. According to the NBI's current CEO, Joanne Yawitch:

> The South African government and business understand the need for an integrated approach to sustainable development that acknowledges social justice, economic prosperity and environmental sustainability. Building on the work of the government's National Planning Commission's Vision 2030, Vision 2050 provides a conceptual framework that can help enrich the national dialogue and establish a basis for joint action.

To deliver this more systemic agenda, NBI has repositioned its vision, mission and goals as follows:

- Its overarching vision is to contribute to South Africa as a thriving society in which a market economy functions to the benefit of all

- Its mission is to enhance the business contribution to sustainable growth and development in the country

- Its goal is to ensure that South Africa is acclaimed as one of the great places in the world in which to live, to learn, to work and to do business

The NBI remains an independent, voluntary business coalition of leading South African businesses. This coalition is concerned with mobilizing business leadership and corporate support, by facilitating critical social dialogue, and through the implementation of strategic projects backed by independent policy analysis and research to reach its goals.

In practice, this means a careful focus of business resources into those areas that business is best equipped to influence. With this principle in mind, the NBI has identified the following priorities among the key challenges that South Africa faces:

- Poverty and inequality reduction, employment creation, economic growth

- Human capital development through education and skills training

- Ecological balance, so that the scarce resources available to the present generation are also available to the next

It is the continued existence of stark socioeconomic disparities that lends most urgency to the logic of business involvement. South Africans need to keep reminding themselves that they live in a society that can appropriately be likened to a double-edged sword. On one hand, there is unbelievable opportunity, not only in South Africa itself but also from using the country as a stepping-stone into the rest of the continent. Conversely, there are also a number of harsh and inescapable realities, which South African business leaders cannot selectively ignore. They need to remember that half of their compatriots go to bed hungry, three out of ten are unemployed, and one in ten is dying of AIDS. For custodians of capital the obligation from a purely business point of view must be to ask, what are the risks and opportunities? What is going to happen in South Africa in the decades to come? If business people take their custodianship seriously, if they wish to secure an environment in which companies can continue to do business, and business is accepted as a positive force in society, more than simply taking cognizance of the darker side of the double-edged sword, they have to actively demonstrate the commitment to take the required constructive action.

In South Africa today it is appropriate to say that collective business action is more than the sum of its parts. Most companies practice corporate citizenship through individual social investment programs. Added to this is substantial evidence to show that collective action – which lies at the heart of the history of the NBI – has contributed to real change by promoting democracy and sustainable development in South Africa. Furthermore, success in these spheres has strengthened the influence of business in public policy and governance. It would be accurate to say that this has created both opportunities that have already been actualized and challenges that have yet to be overcome. While business has certainly shown that it can have a far-reaching impact on influencing and shaping the environments in which it operates, it also needs to develop a strategic response to the complex sustainability challenges facing the country – and the world – in the 21st century.

Profile 8

Philippine Business For Social Progress (PBSP)

David Grayson with input from Jane Nelson, Rafael Lopa and Peter Brew*

Philippine Business For Social Progress in its own words

Philippine Business For Social Progress is committed to poverty reduction by promoting business sector leadership in, and commitment to programs that lead to self-reliance. It implements development projects on behalf of the private sector, and promotes the practice of corporate citizenship as a model for poverty reduction.

PBSP has proven to be a sustained and reliable vehicle for chief executives of some of the largest companies to express their social responsibility in a strategic way. With its ability to synergize and initiate partnerships from different sectors, manage projects prudently, and leverage funds, PBSP will rally the business sector towards a collectively defined development goal.

As we move beyond our 40th year, PBSP will continue to promote corporate citizenship as a model for poverty reduction. It will continue to devote expert resources towards helping opportunity-poor Filipinos create better lives for themselves.

www.pbsp.org.ph   June 2012

---

*   Sources: Interviews with Rafael Lopa, current PBSP Executive Director, Manila, October 21, 2011 and Bangkok, October 25, 2012, and subsequent email exchanges; PBSP website and annual reports; V.E. Tan and M.P. Bolante, *Philippine Business for Social Progress: A Case Study* (New York: Synergos Institute, 1997); C. Nuguid-Anden, "Enhancing Business–Community Relations: Philippine Business for Social Progress Case Study," UN Volunteers and New Academy of Business, September 1, 2003.

Background context and history

Philippine Business for Social Progress (PBSP) was established in 1970 by leaders from 50 Philippine corporations, including the heads of San Miguel Brewery and Atlas Consolidated Mining and Development Corporation who were looking for a response to the worsening political and social situation in their country. The business leaders were all active in one of three business associations: the Council for Economic Development, the Philippine Business Council and the Association for Social Action. At the time, the business community was regarded as one of the causes of the lopsided distribution of wealth. The business leaders' primary motivation was fear and their goal was self-preservation and risk management. There was also a strong influence from Catholic social justice teaching. Indeed, the animator behind, and first Executive Director of, PBSP was a Jesuit priest, Fr. Horacio de la Costa. The PBSP founders aimed to engage business in efforts to alleviate poverty and build self- reliance among disadvantaged communities throughout the country.

SyCip, Gorres, Velayo and Co., one of the leading accounting and auditing firms in the country, was asked to prepare a concept paper for a mechanism to respond to the situation. The ensuing paper, which became the basis for PBSP's founding and organization, proposed setting up a social venture capital organization composed of business corporations, which would start and support small-scale social development projects until these could become self-sustaining.

PBSP's mission was: "to make [a] significant contribution to the development and delivery of solutions to poverty by promoting business sector commitment to social development, harnessing resources for programs that promote self-reliance, and advocating sustainable development fundamental to overall growth."[364]

A series of corporate social responsibility workshops followed PBSP's founding in 1970. When the question of how to fund the organization arose, Luzio Mazzei, a Venezuelan and the President of Shell Philippines, introduced the idea used by Dividendo Voluntario para la Comunidad, a development foundation organized by Venezuelan industrialists in 1963. Corporate members of Dividendo contributed 1% of pre-tax income for the foundation's operations. The Executive Director of Dividendo was invited to present the Venezuelan experience to the Philippine business groups. As a result of this meeting a proposal was made that corporate members would contribute 1% of before-tax income to PBSP. The Economic Development Foundation was tapped to give PBSP a start-up push by carrying the initial overhead costs and seconding staff members. Despite the hostility of the Marcos regime, which was deeply suspicious of any NGO or civil-society activity that might become a vehicle for opposition, PBSP recruited companies run by families known to support Marcos as well as those run by families opposed to the dictatorship.

This initial progress was threatened when the national economy nose-dived after the assassination in 1983 of Benigno Aquino, the opposition leader, as he returned from exile to challenge the Marcos dictatorship that had ruled the country since 1965. As corporate profits tumbled, funds to PBSP also fell precipitately. Confidence only returned when Aquino's widow Corazon swept to power on a wave of "people power" in 1986 and Ferdinand Marcos fled. Thereafter, international donors were anxious to support the fledgling democracy and the building of civil society. PBSP was a credible vehicle for many of these donors because of its business leadership, existing track record and professionalism. As a result, over the years, PBSP has become a major recipient of international donor funds, in addition to its corporate support and leadership. By late 2011, the current PBSP Executive Director, Rafael (Rapa) C. Lopa was referring to PBSP as "an outsourced service provider."

Key activities and phases of development

Every five years, PBSP charts its development agenda in a strategic plan that is the result of a process in which both the PBSP Board and staff participate. SyCip, Gorres, Velayo and Co., a PBSP member company since the outset, has been commissioned to conduct regular external program reviews.

In the 1980s, PBSP focused its efforts on the 15 poorest provinces in the country, where at least 40% of the families lived below the poverty line, and where there were partner organizations PBSP could work with.

In the 1990s, the organization redefined its strategy to focus on "impact areas." It implemented the Area Resource Management (ARM) program for environmental conservation and economic development.

In the early 2000s, PBSP added workforce development as a core strategy, asserted its role in the Mindanao region (specifically basic services such as health and education), and spearheaded the business sector's support of the United Nations Millennium Development Goals.

In the last half decade, the focus has been refined into four key aspects: education, health, sustainable livelihood and enterprise development, and the environment.

In 2012, PBSP launched a platform of collective effort among the corporate sector, government and other investors and stakeholders as an innovative business solution to eradicate poverty in the country. Known as "Platforms for Collective Engagements," or PlaCEs, the new initiative aims at scaling up successful private–public partnership models primarily in the areas of health, education, sustainable livelihood and the environment.

Rafael C. Lopa sees a concrete translation of the PlaCEs strategy already in the launch of the Bayanihang Pampaaralan (BP) campaign, a collaboration of PBSP, the League of Corporate Foundations (LCF), the Philippine Business for Education (PBEd), and other advocates of education reform in the country.[365]

Table P8.1 summarizes how PBSP's programmatic focus has evolved over the years

Activities today include the following:

Education

Education has become an increasingly strategic focus for PBSP and it is working with the current government and a number of civil-society organizations to improve the country's under-performing education system. In 2006, some of the board members of PBSP formed a parallel organization, Philippines Business for Education, focused on improving teacher training. Now PBSP has added education to its work program and strongly aligned its education program with the thrust of the current government. In particular it has joined with the 57–75 movement to contribute to President Aquino's goal to build 66,800 new classrooms. This target is designed to ensure that all Filipino schoolchildren can be accommodated

Table P8.1 **Evolution of PBSP's strategy**

Source: *PBSP as a Learning Organization: Building Blocks Approach to Development, 2001* – quoted in C. Nuguid-Anden, *Enhancing Business Community Relations: Philippine Business for Social Progress Case Study* (Manila: Philippine Business for Social Progress/Makati City, Philippines: UN Volunteers/Bath, UK: New Academy of Business, September 1, 2003) and updated by authors

Period	PBSP strategies and program directions
1975–81	Prototype developer: integrated community development
1976–80	Small projects funder (many project areas): proponent-led
1981–85	Projects rationalized in four program areas: local resource management
1986–90	Program further focused by poverty group and geography: provincial development strategy and institution building
1991–99	Programs rationalized with area resource management and global concerns – in high-growth areas (HGA-ARM)
2000–05	Added workforce development – leadership in corporate citizenship – comprehensive membership and non-membership Involvement
2006–11	Greater focus on education, health, sustainable livelihood and enterprise development, and the environment; and on empowering local communities
2012–	Platforms for Collective Engagements (PlaCEs)

in classes of no more than 45 in their own classroom – albeit that this will still require two shifts a day. The 57–75 movement[366] is a consortium of NGOs that aims to reverse the education crisis through focused interventions and school–community action, towards system-wide performance improvements. The consortium is concentrating on the 40 most challenged school divisions (as measured by national achievement test results). The target is to build 10,000 classrooms at an average cost of PHP700,000 per classroom.[367] AusAID (the Australian Agency for International Development – the Australian Government agency responsible for managing Australia's overseas aid program) has recently announced a A$20 million grant to PBSP for classroom construction, which with existing corporate commitments will guarantee 3,000 of the 10,000 target.[368]

PBSP hopes to re-ignite "people power" by working with the League of Corporate Foundations (a co-convenor of the 57–75 movement) in persuading large numbers of ordinary people to contribute to the classroom-building program through TEN Moves! The Entire Nation Moves. TEN Moves! invites individual citizens to donate 10 pesos (around £0.17) per day for ten months. As part of the campaign, the Philippine-born pop-star Allan Pineda Lindo, more popularly known as Apl.de.Ap of the Black Eyed Peas, has recorded a "We Can Be Anything" song and music video in partnership with the Ninoy and Cory Aquino Foundation (NCAF). Together with Apl.de.Ap and NCAF, a group of second-generation Filipino-Americans has agreed to help spread the campaign globally through Google and YouTube products and services. Apl.de.Ap's original goal was to raise US$1 million from this one initiative alone. He has since adjusted this and now intends to adopt 15 schools across the country. He is mobilizing not only funding for new classrooms but also partnerships with various companies who seek his endorsement to provide computer labs and other needs that will be needed by these 15 schools.[369] In turn, Philippines Airlines has spotted the opportunity to use Apl.de.ap to promote "mission tourism" to encourage second-generation Filipino emigrants to return home as tourists and to make a positive social contribution as well as seeing their homeland. Lopa quotes this as an example of PBSP bringing together business and other interests and then facilitating business to spot business opportunities as well as societal gain.

Health

PBSP also manages significant global health funds through its health programs. It has become a national leader in tackling tuberculosis (TB), for example. Around 80 people die of TB each day in the Philippines (including from a multi-drug resistant strain of the disease), affecting the most productive age group of the population. PBSP has received a grant of EUR73.9 million from 2010 to 2014 from the Global Fund to Fight AIDS, Tuberculosis and Malaria[370] and US$19.5 million from USAID to fight TB. Today, PBSP manages around 40% of all TB budgets in the Philippines. Further grants of €48 million (US$$62 million) from the Global Fund for 2012–15, and from USAID for $28 million were announced during 2012.[371] TB programs currently account for around 60% of the PBSP budget, and about half of PBSP's staff of 300 are employed in implementing its TB programs. There are also initial discussions on how PBSP can help in the enhancement of Public Health Financing, especially in the treatment of TB beyond the grant assistance from multilateral and international aid agencies. PBSP has started to work with health management organizations and pharmaceutical companies on this.

Sustainable livelihood and enterprise development

PBSP's Livelihood and Enterprise Development Program aims to generate gainful employment and income opportunities for men and women. PBSP delivers business development services particularly in the areas of market facilitation, business advisory and agricultural technology development. PBSP also provides financing services, including investment matching where SMEs are matched with private investors or financial institutions for additional working capital. PBSP also works on strengthening the capacity of community-based organizations to participate in livelihood activities.

Among PBSP's individual programs is the provision of Small and Medium Enterprise Credit, to SMEs outside Metropolitan Manila. PBSP manages a US$12 million revolving fund provided to the Philippine Government by USAID and a DM14.75 million loan (around US$9 million) from a German development agency, the Kreditanstalt fur Wiederaufbau (KfW).

The STEP-UP, building on previous programs on socialized housing, helps informal settlers to acquire land using the government's Community Mortgage scheme.

The environment

The goal of PBSP's environment program is to contribute to environmental sustainability and reversal of loss of critical environmental resources. It is also aimed at reducing the vulnerability of poor Filipino households to disaster and climate change risks through the rehabilitation of critical watersheds.

On-going projects and initiatives include the adoption of critical watershed and mangrove areas and implementing activities that promote conservation, protection and sustainable use. Activities include reforestation and rehabilitation efforts as well as providing alternative livelihood activities to communities within and near these areas. PBSP had been active in the protection of Cebu Hillylands Watershed for the past 20 years and in the rehabilitation of Maqueda Bay. Recently, PBSP adopted the Montalban and Wawa sub-watersheds in the Marikina Watershed to replicate the Cebu Hillylands model.

Centre for Corporate Citizenship

PBSP's Centre for Corporate Citizenship (CCC) serves as a forum for business CEOs to engage in dialogue with their counterparts in government and civil society on the critical issues facing the country. In 1999, the CCC was reconstituted and became a fully fledged unit within PBSP. The CCC was tasked to be PBSP's Research and Product Development arm for CSR, thus making it a knowledge hub and a developer and tester of innovative CSR approaches.

Impact and lessons learned

Since its inception, PBSP has directly benefited over 5 million Filipinos and assisted over 6,400 social development projects through more than PHP7.6 billion (£0.11 billion/US$0.18 billion) in grants and development loans, as well as the indirect beneficiaries, such as family members and downstream enterprises that have started as a result of increased economic activity.

The organization has been able to combine resources from the private sector and assistance from the donor community, both public donors and private foundations, to leverage financial assets, extend its reach in the communities and expand its impact. Although it is primarily a business-led and business-funded organization, it has adopted a participatory community development model in many of its programs to reach disadvantaged Filipinos. At the same time, it has drawn on the corporate responsibility resources and skills of its corporate members to promote more responsible business practices in the Philippines and to mobilize the corporate sector around supporting key development objectives.

For example, PBSP was one of the first business-led organizations in the world to identify the specific areas where business had a crucial role to play in helping to deliver the UN Millennium Development Goals (MDGs). Building on a framework developed by the International Business Leaders Forum (IBLF), it produced a how-to guide for business on supporting the MDGs. Since 2006, PBSP has acted as Filipino Secretariat for the business contribution to the MDGs.

In recent years, PBSP has also become *de facto* the United Way agency in the Philippines. Lopa has attended a number of Asian and international meetings of United Way and has expressed surprise that PBSP is seen as more advanced in many of its programs than other United Ways around the world due to the very active involvement of companies in PBSP and its programs. More than 40 years' experience means that PBSP is now adept at absorbing philanthropic funds, corporate community investment and international aid, and scaling up the reach of its programs. Some groups have also recognized PBSP's ability to engage proactively with various stakeholders (e.g., national and local governments, NGOs and people's organizations) involved in their projects.

PBSP, together with WWF-Philippines, has been asked by the Chamber of Mines (a coalition of large mining companies) to assist in the development of a Mining Scorecard to determine the social and environmental impact of mining operations.

Box P8.1 **PBSP's Business of Peace program**

The IBLF partnered with PBSP in the Business of Peace program between 2000 and 2006. This targeted the Autonomous Region of Muslim Mindanao, which was (and still is to some extent) suffering from community conflict. At its heart was the principle that economic development was the key to addressing poverty and exclusion, which in turn was the breeding ground of conflict. It was also a pioneering initiative to bring together the largely Christian business community in Manila with the largely Muslim business community in Mindanao. The program was originally built around the work of Datu Ibrahim Paglas III (know to his friends as "Toto") who had set up a major banana plantation with international investors that employed workers from both Christian and Muslim communities and technology from Israel. Toto died of meningitis in 2006 but his son is taking his work forward with Toto's second in command, Ed Bullicer.

Particular legacies of the Business of Peace program are:

- **The Young Muslim Professionals for Business and Peace (YuPPeace) Internship.** It is a component of the Business and Peace Program, which provided young Muslim professionals from Mindanao opportunities to learn from the corporate practices in Manila and other major cities such as Cebu and Davao. These young professionals were given three to six months internships program with multinational and large scale local companies to learn up-to-date business methods which they took back to Mindanao. In turn, the host companies noted changes in the way the employees perceived their Muslim counterparts and embraced diversity in the workplace
- **The "Planning Development–Harvesting Peace" initiative.** This brought together a group of leading Mindanao business leaders to work together on the promotion of Mindanao's economic development
- **Promoting Religious Diversity in the Workplace.** A Religious Diversity in the Workplace Learning program was developed to facilitate the installation of programs that aim to create a harmonious and peaceful working environment among Christian and Muslim employees. For instance, the modules facilitates the development of policies that promote equal employment opportunity regardless of race and religion; provision of prayer room for Muslim employees, etc.

This work was largely funded by the British Embassy in Manila and the significant results of the program were captured in a number of publications, reports and CDs prepared by PBSP.[372]

Over the years, PBSP has also played an important role in providing a business voice to public-policy discussions and in some situations helping in the facilitation of peace-building activities. One example was a peace-building program it implemented in partnership with the International Business Leaders Forum in Mindanao for a number of years (see Box P7.2).

Critical success factors

Critical success factors for PBSP have included:

- **The personal involvement of some of the leading Filipino business figures.** From the early days, PBSP emphasized to prospective members that being a foundation member did not mean simply writing a check but required them to get actively involved in the work of the organization

- **Continuity of executive leadership.** There have been just eight executive directors during the 41 years of existence. Several of these had previously served within the staff team, for example, Aurora (Rory) Tolentino worked for PBSP for 15 years before her appointment as executive director when Ernesto Garilao was appointed by the then Philippine President Fidel Ramos to a Cabinet position

- **Board engagement.** Another critical success factor has been the calibre and engagement of business leadership specifically in the governance work of PBSP. There have been regular interactions between the Board and the staff team, with efforts to sensitize new board members to the realities of development in the Philippines

- **Requirements for regular member company participation.** Corporate membership of PBSP has oscillated over the years at around 250 companies. It currently stands at 240, after a peak of 263 in 2010. Any member company that is not active in PBSP for two years automatically forfeits membership. This is how what was becoming an increasingly controversial membership of Philip Morris, the tobacco company, lapsed after it had objected to a PBSP/Pfizer campaign to discourage workplace smoking. PBSP has also lost some members over the years because of poor client-relationship management or projects being unsuccessful. Generally members leave either because of business losses or a change in the company's CEO without the commitment being passed on to the successor

- **Commitment to a learning culture**. Another critical success factor from the outset has been a learning culture. PBSP developed its planning discipline, rigorous project appraisal and monitoring systems from the business backgrounds of the founders and the technical expertise of early staffers seconded from one of the founding organizations: the Filipino Economic Development Foundation

- **Improving relationships with government.** During its early years, which coincided with the final years of the Marcos dictatorship, PBSP was treated with suspicion by the regime. Once democracy was established, PBSP benefited from its political connections. When President Corazon Aquino took over the government in 1986, seven PBSP Board members were asked to serve in government posts. Although these appointments demonstrated the high regard the new government had for PBSP's

Board members the exodus almost decimated the Board. Periodically, over the years since, PBSP has been tapped for Board and staff members to serve in government. In 2010, Benigno S. Aquino III was elected as President of the Philippines. In addition to being the son of Benigno and Corazon Aquino, he had also started his first job with PBSP in 1983–85 when he served as an assistant to the executive director.[373]

The future

Under the current Executive Director, Rafael Lopa, PBSP is looking increasingly at core business behavior, recognizing, as one of the PBSP founders said many years ago:

> PBSP's relationship with its members should not be based only on the 1% allocation for social development. What happens to the 99% of the company's earnings? If the 99% is spent on business practices, which are inconsistent with development like wanton cutting of trees, polluting the environment, or selling the *uncontrolled* consumption of alcohol, then the 1% becomes "conscience money." PBSP's social development philosophy must permeate the whole company. This is the only way true development can be achieved in the Philippines.[374]

As an example, PBSP is looking at ways to harness the core business capabilities of its member companies to drive development impact, not only their foundations and philanthropic contributions. It is exploring the potential of social enterprises and helping member companies to optimize their positive core business contribution to base-of-the-pyramid (BoP) strategies – through their own supply chain management and distribution processes and, where relevant, through better promotion of BOP products and services (even if, or rather especially if, these are not currently conceived as BOP by the companies involved). One new area of focus is social housing for the large numbers of migrant workers moving into the greater Manila area. This switch in focus is not without challenges, as PBSP's unrestricted budget for membership services innovation has remained static in recent years (despite the impressive restricted budget for specified programs).

PBSP believe there are already attempts towards more socially and environmentally oriented business strategies being undertaken by some companies in the Philippines that simultaneously enhance their financial bottom-lines. PBSP is, therefore, now taking the advocacy of Shared Value Creation[375] to companies in the Philippines. This advocacy is also linked to the need to make companies realize that by innovating their products and services to benefit the huge base-of-the-pyramid market that constitutes easily 50 to 60 million Filipinos, can be a growth prospect.

Moreover, PBSP is also re-engineering its organization to fully maximize the leverage of collective corporate contributions. The organization is also working to define a common agenda for corporate action and to agree on impact measurements that companies can use. PBSP's Board formally agreed this greater emphasis on core responsible business behavior during 2012.

Influenced by the Collective Impact strategy developed by Mark Kramer and John Kania,[376] PBSP is now building its capacity to play a role that coordinates complementary and mutually reinforcing initiatives towards common development goals in the areas of health, education, environment, sustainable livelihood and employment development. It is also becoming more involved in national debates about the mining industry with the NGOs WWF and IDEA. Thus, in its fifth decade of operations, PBSP continues to innovate and re-invent itself to respond to societal and business needs, and to build on the accumulated institutional memory and expertise of the past.

Profile 9

World Business Council for Sustainable Development (WBCSD)

Jane Nelson and David Grayson*

The WBCSD in its own words

The WBCSD is a CEO-led organization of forward-thinking companies that galvanizes the global business community to create a sustainable future for business, society and the environment.

From its starting point in 1992 to the present day, the Council has created respected thought leadership on business and sustainability.

The Council plays the leading advocacy role for business. Leveraging strong relationships with stakeholders, it helps drive debate and policy change in favor of sustainable development solutions.

The Council provides a forum for its 200 member companies – who represent all business sectors, all continents and combined revenue of over US$7 trillion

---

* This profile has been drawn from L. Timberlake, *Catalyzing Change: A Short History of the WBCSD* (Geneva: WBCSD, 2006); WBCSD, *Vision 2050* (2010); WBCSD, *Changing Pace: Public Policy Options to Scale and Accelerate Action Towards Vision 2050* (Geneva: WBCSD, 2012); WBCSD, *The WBCSD's Regional Network: Rio + 20 and Beyond* (Geneva: WBCSD: 2012, www.wbcsd.org/regional-network.aspx, accessed July 30, 2012); and an interview with Peter Paul Van de Wijs, then WBCSD head of communications, Geneva, July 2012. Other materials are from the WBCSD website: www.wbcsd.org.

The authors are grateful to Vanessa Whittall and Kija Kummer of WBCSD who have patiently responded to our further queries and commented on the draft.

– to share best practices on sustainable development issues and to develop innovative tools that change the status quo. The Council also benefits from a network of 60 national and regional business councils and partner organizations, a majority of which are based in developing countries.

By thinking ahead, advocating for progress and delivering results, the WBCSD both increases the impact of our members' individual actions and catalyzes collective action that can change the future of our society for the better.

www.wbcsd.org   June 2012

Background context and history

The origins of business engagement in the global agenda on sustainable development are commonly traced back to the United Nations Conference on the Human Environment that took place in Stockholm in 1972. Attended by a small handful of business people among mostly environmental experts, the conference led to the creation of the United Nations Environment Programme (UNEP) and was followed by the appointment of former Norwegian Prime Minister, Gro Harlem Brundtland, to lead the World Commission on Environment and Development. In 1987, after extensive consultations around the globe, the Brundtland Commission issued its seminal report: *Our Common Future*.[377] The report coined the term "sustainable development," which it defined as "development that meets the needs of the present without compromising the needs of future generations." This inter-generational definition of sustainable development remains valid today, while the concept has increasingly been accepted as one that rests on three core pillars of economic prosperity, social justice and environmental sustainability. The Brundtland Commission also called for the United Nations to host an international conference on environment and development.

The United Nations Conference on Environment and Development (UNCED), which became commonly known as the Rio Earth Summit, was subsequently held in Rio de Janeiro in June 1992. Among other achievements, it led to the creation of what is today the World Business Council for Sustainable Development.

An invitation to bring the 'business voice' to the Rio Earth Summit

Maurice Strong, a Canadian businessman and diplomat, was appointed to be Secretary-General of the conference. In 1990 he invited the Swiss entrepreneur and business leader Stephan Schmidheiny to be his business and industry adviser, to lead the representation of the business voice at the summit, and to help spread the concept of sustainable development in the wider business community.

After initially rejecting the invitation, Schmidheiny relented and decided to engage a small group of other corporate leaders to help shape the "business perspective" (see Box P9.1). So began a globetrotting effort to recruit CEOs to be part of a not-yet-invited delegation to present a then-undetermined agenda at a conference two years down the road. Slowly, Schmidheiny built his network across Europe, Latin America and Asia. Gradually, the commitments

Box P9.1 **The pioneering business leaders who formed the original Business Council for Sustainable Development with Stephan Schmidheiny**

Kenneth T. Derr	Chevron Corporation
Maurice R. Greenberg	American International Group, Inc.
Carl H. Hahn	Volkswagen AG
Charles M. Harper	ConAgra, Inc
Kazuo Inamori	Kyocera Corp.
Allen F. Jacobson	3M Company
Antonia Ax:son Johnson	Johnson AB
Samuel C. Johnson	S.C. Johnson & Son, Inc.
Saburo Kawai	Keizai Doyukai
Jiro Kawake	Oji Paper Co., Ltd.
Alex Krauer	Ciba-Geigy AG
H.H.The Otunba Ayora (Mrs.) Bola Kuforiji-Olubi (M.O.N.)	BEWAC plc
Yutaka Kume	Nissan Motor Co. Ltd.
J.M.K. Martin Laing	John Laing plc
Erling S. Lorentzen	Aracruz Celulose S.A
Ken F. McCready	TransAlta Utilities Corp.
Akira Miki	Nippon Steel Corporation
Jérôme Monod	Lyonnaise des Eaux-Dumez
Shinroku Morohashi	Mitsubishi Corporation J
Y.A.M. Tunku Naquiyuddin ibni Tuanku Ja'afar	Antah Holdings Berhad
Philip Ndegwa	First Chartered Securities Ltd.
Paul H. O'Neill	ALCOA
James Onobiono	Compagnie Financière et Industrielle CFI (S.A.)
Anand Panyarachun	Former Chairman of Saha-Union Corp. Ltd.
Frank Popoff	The Dow Chemical Company
Fernando Romero	Inversiones Bolivianas S.A.
William D. Ruckelshaus	Browning-Ferris Industries
Anthony Salim	Salim Group
Elisabeth Salina Amorini	Société Générale de Surveillance Holding S.A.
Helmut Sihler	HENKEL KgaA
Paul G. Stern	Northern Telecom Ltd.
Ratan N. Tata	TATA Industires Ltd.
Lodewijk C. van Wachem	The Royal Dutch Shell Group
Sir Bruce Watson	Mount Isa Mines Pty Ltd.
Edgar S. Woolard	E.I. du Pont de Nemours and Company
Toshiaki Yamaguchi	Tosoh Corporation
Federico Zorraquin	S.A. Garovaglio y Zorraquin

trickled in. Schmidheiny promised prospective members that he would pay all the project's expenses and that the group would disband after Rio, as he had no intention of creating a permanent organization.

By the first meeting in the spring of 1991 in The Hague, there were 48 members of what had been dubbed the Business Council for Sustainable Development (BCSD). That meeting followed hard on the heels of the second World Industry Conference on Environmental Management, organized by the International Chamber of Commerce (ICC). At this conference the ICC, although maintaining its own UN status as a delegate to Rio, essentially turned business representation at the Earth Summit over to Stephan Schmidheiny and his council. Not all of the companies on the BCSD list had perfect track records with respect to the environment. That was never the point. As Frank Bosshardt, one of the executives Schmidheiny recruited from his own company to organize BCSD, put it: "The aim of this membership collection was to have people who were committed, or who were open to becoming committed."[378]

Schmidheiny had assembled a small, capable BCSD staff in a secretariat headquarters in Geneva, Switzerland. By the end of the first BCSD meeting, there was consensus on a framework that would become the basis of the council's first book, *Changing Course*.[379]

A global consultation process leading to publication of *Changing Course*

At the outset of the process, Schmidheiny produced a ground-breaking treatise on issues including clean production techniques, energy use, pricing instruments, capital markets and managing agriculture and forestry. Various BCSD members divided up the chapter topics, according to their company's experience and interest. By this point, all of the CEOs had picked "liaison delegates" who would execute the bulk of the research and participation of each company – and who remain a vital component of the organization's ability to engage with corporate leaders to this day.

The multiple task forces worked furiously over the next year (with strong support from independent and academic partners) to prepare their submissions for the book. Even in this early stage of the history of companies grappling with the complexities of sustainable development, the members were able to produce 28 case studies showing that many companies were already taking these issues seriously within their core business operations.

Schmidheiny's mandate from Strong had been twofold: to bring a business voice to Rio and to spread the concept of sustainable development among the world's business leaders and companies. To accomplish the second goal, the council organized some 50 conferences, symposia and issue workshops in 20 countries between spring 1991 and summer 1992.

Early into the work, Schmidheiny realized that getting consensus from all 50 members of the BCSD on the content of the entire book would be impossible. The differences across companies, not to mention across cultures, were vast. One of the biggest controversies was over the topic of consumption – an issue that remains a challenging point of debate today. The BCSD had a vocal Japanese contingent, for whom sustainable consumption was part of the culture. They favoured patent regulation that would support products such as more fuel-efficient auto engines. At the other extreme, the U.S. members felt that if reduced fuel consumption were recommended by the book, they wanted no part of the project. They argued that consumer choice and market democracy should be allowed free reign. The Europeans were somewhere in the middle. Schmidheiny admitted: "In the end, we found a common denominator which wasn't very convincing, but at least we addressed the relevance of the issues."

Ultimately, the book team realized that sending the project up for editing by committee would be a nightmare. So Schmidheiny came up with the idea of creating a summary declaration that the entire council could endorse as a preface for the book. And he would take editorial responsibility for the rest of the chapters. Authorial credit would read: "Stephan Schmidheiny with the Business Council for Sustainable Development." At a meeting in late 1991 in Wilmington, Delaware, the BCSD gathered to approve the document. A simple three-page statement, the "**Declaration of the Business Council for Sustainable Development**," was nonetheless controversial. The principles had to be broad enough that every company could endorse them, but not so vague as to be utterly meaningless. Schmidheiny recalls: "It was no small challenge to negotiate that consensus." He was pleased that when the book was published the declaration in the front of the book carried all the members' names, giving at least the appearance that they had signed on to the entire book. The day ended with a standing ovation for Schmidheiny, who had worked almost full time for 18 months and spent close to US$10 million of his own money to reach this moment with the council.

The manuscript was sent to the publisher, MIT Press, which published it as *Changing Course* about a month before the Earth Summit in early June 1992, where the BCSD, represented by Schmidheiny and about 28 council members, presented its findings. The book covered a wide range of issues from the need to place a price on environmental goods and services, to energy and the marketplace, the role of capital markets in financing sustainable development, trade, technology and innovation, food, agriculture and forestry. Two decades later, most of the key themes outlined in the book, and many of its recommendations, remain relevant, and the extent of its vision and pioneering contribution is even clearer today than it was at the time.

The merger of the Business Council for Sustainable Development and the World Industry Council on the Environment

The BCSD contribution at the Rio Earth Summit received media and global attention, as this was the first time a business contingent had presented so publicly and officially at a UN conference. By this time, the book was already published and had received positive reviews as a landmark step and comprehensive attempt at crafting a progressive business point of view. It would go on to be published in some 20 languages.

For Schmidheiny, for whom the experience had surpassed all expectations, the Rio Summit was a capstone to a very rewarding process. He said:

> In many ways it was really a success beyond anything I could have imagined when I first accepted the mandate. It was much bigger. It had grown much more than anyone had expected. And a deep bond had developed between an interesting and diverse group of people with influence in the world.[380]

From the beginning of the recruitment process Schmidheiny had assured the CEOs that the project would end after Rio. He had no intention of turning the council into a permanent body. But council members had other ideas, arguing to keep it going as there was so much more to do.

Schmidheiny agreed, with the caveat that he would no longer head the effort (a move to prevent the perception that the endeavor was merely his pet project) and that members pay dues to support the council on an ongoing basis. Thus, a new organization without a charter but with a commitment to make a difference was founded. While a cadre of enthusiastic CEOs wanted to continue their participation, not all of the original BCSD members who had signed the *Changing Course* declaration were eager to pay membership dues or extend the life of what they had seen as a limited commitment. Schmidheiny told those who wanted to leave that, while he hated to see them go, they had more than honourably lived up to their commitment and should leave with a sense of pride and accomplishment. The membership fell, and the staff's efforts were diffused across the difficult tasks of defining a mission, recruiting new companies and inventing a new structure to support those twin goals. But, according to Schmidheiny, the biggest challenge was the loss of a galvanizing deadline and focal point that the Rio Summit had necessitated.

Meanwhile the World Industry Council on the Environment (WICE) was created after Rio as part of the ICC based in Paris. WICE grew to 100 companies and recruited a significant number of Japanese members. The WICE model differed from the BCSD in that it was based on a corporate commitment, rather than a CEO commitment. It spent a lot of its time drafting statements on various aspects of sustainable development for the ICC. Conferences were frequent, attended by mid-level managers, and WICE was efficient with resources.

In 1994, the BCSD's first executive director, Hugh Faulkner, left the organization forcing the council leadership to seek a new director for the organization. Schmidheiny approached Björn Stigson, who for seven years had been chief executive of a Swedish multinational, Fläkt, the world's biggest environmental control technology group, who had been a part of the establishment of WICE, as well as a participant in the first BCSD gathering.

After hearing the offer, Stigson agreed in principle but noted that it did not make sense for the business community to have two competing organizations, WICE and the BCSD, representing its interests. He suggested that his first task as executive director of the BCSD should be to approach WICE to discuss a merger. In this he had especial support from ABB, a conglomerate in power and automation products and Norsk Hydro, a Fortune 500 energy and aluminum supplier in 40 countries, which both argued that splitting the business community into two groups would blunt the impact of private-sector efforts around sustainable development. The members of the BCSD and WICE were by no means all in agreement.

Rodney Chase, then Managing Director and Deputy Group Chief Executive of BP and Chairman of WICE, played a key role in uniting the two organizations. He diplomatically persuaded the ICC, which did not want to "lose" its own sustainability organization, that joining in with the BCSD was right for business and that the merger would not dilute their CEO-led approach. Chase went on to chair the newly merged organization during its first crucial year. Both the BCSD and WICE agreed internally to the merger in late 1994. The combined secretariat would be in Geneva, and staff based in Paris would relocate, with Stigson as President and the WICE head Jan Olaf Willums as Senior Director. At the time of the merger there were about 120 companies in what would be known from the official date of the merger, January 1, 1995, as the World Business Council for Sustainable Development (WBCSD).

Nearly two decades later, supported by some 200 member companies (with combined revenue of over US$7 trillion), and many hundreds more companies participating through a regional network of 60 CEO-led business organizations around the world, the WBCSD has become a major force in collective business leadership for a more sustainable world. In 2011, Björn Stigson retired as President, and was replaced by Peter Bakker, the Dutch former CEO of multinational logistics company TNT. Chad Holliday, former Chairman and CEO of DuPont, whose predecessor at DuPont was one of the founder members of the original BCSD, became WBCSD's chairman in 2012 – the tenth in a line of distinguished international business leaders to chair the organization: see Table P9.1.

Table P9.1 **Chairmen of the WBCSD**[381]

Rodney F. Chase, BP (1995)
Livio D. DeSimone, 3M (1996–97)
Egil Myklebust, Norsk Hydro (1998–99)
Charles O. Holliday Jr., DuPont (2000–01)
Sir Philip Watts KCMG, Royal Dutch Shell (2002–03)
Bertrand Collomb, Lafarge (2004–05)
Travis Engen, Alcan (2006–07)
Sam DiPiazza, PwC (2008–09)
Jorma Ollila, Nokia and Shell (2010–2011)
Charles O. Holliday Jr., Bank of America (2012)

Given its large reach and influence, the organization maintains a remarkably small core staff at its Geneva headquarters (60 people as of August 2012). This team is supplemented by the strong and experienced network of liaison delegates (mostly chief sustainability or corporate responsibility officers) through which member companies and their CEOs support the day-to-day work and task forces of the WBCSD. It is further leveraged through the regional network of 60 local BCSDs or affiliates that stretches around the globe.

Key activities and phases of development

In a 2012 publication about its regional network,[382] the WBCSD outlined what it describes as three phases of its development:

- The first Rio decade: from Rio to Johannesburg (The World Summit on Sustainable Development was hosted in Johannesburg in June 2002)

- The second Rio decade: from Johannesburg to Rio + 20 (The Rio + 20 Conference was hosted in Rio de Janeiro in June 2012)

- The third Rio decade: from Rio + 20 and beyond

These three stages offer a useful framework for the WBCSD's own phases of development. Like many of the other business-led corporate responsibility and sustainability coalitions, the WBCSD has evolved from a focus on raising awareness and developing the business case for sustainable development during the early days; to convening and promoting action on the ground around specific issues, geographies, industry sectors and value chains; to engaging in advocacy activities and broader multi-stakeholder platforms and partnerships aimed at achieved large-scale systemic change in markets, public policy and governance at global and national levels.

It is important to note that these three stages and types of activity are not mutually exclusive. Rather they build on each other. For example, the need for raising awareness, making the business case, and developing and sharing tools and best practices to help companies implement basic frameworks for sustainable development into their core business operations remains as relevant as ever, as more large companies enter the global economy and more small and medium-sized enterprises engage with the sustainability agenda. At the same time, companies further along the spectrum in terms of implementation and sophistication still face the daily challenge of managing and mitigating sustainability risks and growing opportunities to innovate and build new markets around key sustainability trends. For these companies, management tools and frameworks also need to keep evolving. Equally, new issues (such as climate change, water scarcity and ecosystems services) have become increasingly important over the two decades since Rio – and new management tools and frameworks are needed to address these at the level of individual companies and value chains.

In short, awareness-raising and company-level integration remain necessary. But they are not sufficient. The WBCSD, like other business-led networks, is recognizing the need to work more systemically and strategically with its most progressive and influential members and with other business-led groups, governments, intergovernmental agencies, non-governmental organizations and academic institutions to shift entire markets and governance systems towards more sustainable models. Since its outset, the WBCSD has recognized the crucial role of governments and public policy, and the role of the financial sector and capital markets. Both these topics were covered in *Changing Course* and re-addressed in many subsequent WBCSD thought-leadership initiatives and publications, most notably *Global Scenarios* and the *Vision 2050* project.

Yet, today more than ever, the organization is emphasizing the need to focus on advocacy and on building platforms around these more system-level interventions and more complex systemic interactions between issues such as energy, climate, water and food security. While continuing to build on and deliver the approaches that it has been developing for the past two decades, the WBCSD is likely to focus increasingly on the large-scale system-change agenda as it embarks on the third Rio decade.

The following sets of activities illustrate some of the ways the WBCSD has delivered on its vision and continues to build its engagement with business and other sectors to meet evolving member needs and to respond to and influence an evolving global agenda.

Delivering evidence-based thought leadership to set the agenda on business and sustainability

From its earliest days, the WBCSD has undertaken activities aimed at agenda-setting around key issues or system-level challenges. Its seminal book *Changing Course* was the first of a number of examples. Over the course of the past two decades the WBCSD has produced over 200 publications[383] at head-office level, many of which have been translated, adapted and disseminated around the world. Probably more important than the publications *per se*, are the processes by which many of them have been developed. In almost all cases a core group of members have led the process – so that any findings and examples are rooted in "real world" business realities. In the case of management tools and frameworks, many go through an exhaustive process of testing by pilot member companies before being published more widely. In some cases, publications have also been based on extensive global dialogues and consultations reaching far beyond WBCSD's own members and beyond the business community.

While such consultative processes are time-consuming and complex, they can add substantially to the credibility, relevance and richness of the resulting frameworks, recommendations and new ideas. The following two seminal examples, among a number of influential consultation processes and reports that the WBCSD and its members and partners have produced, illustrate what this approach involves in practice:

WBCSD Global Scenarios 2000–2050 project

About a year after the merger between the BCSD and WICE, the WBCSD and 35 of its member companies partnered with Shell in leading and co-funding the WBCSD Global Scenarios 2000–2050 project. The project envisioned three potential scenarios of where the world of business and sustainability might head, each of them archetypes or extreme versions of the outcomes likely from the single-minded pursuit of one particular path.

The first scenario, called **FROG!** ("First Raise Our Growth"), envisions a world in which business decides to meet economic challenges first and worry about the environment later, if at all. The FROG! scenario leads to a wrecked global ecosystem and a wrecked global society as well.

In the other two scenarios, environmental sustainability is successfully pursued, but the approaches differ starkly.

In the **GEOpolity** (Global Ecosystem Organization) scenario, governments force the market to respond to environmental and social issues through global treaties. It is the scenario of international environmental law and regulation.

The **Jazz** scenario is shaped by voluntary, cross-sector initiatives that are decentralized, responsive and improvised – like jazz itself. In this vision, information about business behavior is readily available, and responsible behavior is enforced by consumer choice and public opinion. Environmental and consumer groups are very active, governments facilitate more than regulate, and businesses see strategic and bottom-line advantage in acting on behalf of the environment.

Jed Davis, head of Scenario Planning at Shell at the time, presented these three scenarios at a WBCSD conference in Prague. The response was electric. Over the following year, the WBCSD presented the scenarios all over the world to groups of companies, intergovernmental groups and the World Bank. Stigson recalls that the scenarios elevated the perception of the WBCSD on the global stage from being merely an advocate of the business voice to being a thoughtful commentator on the myriad, complex roles of all of the players in the sustainable development arena.

Ultimately, the scenario planning articulated a vision in which the WBCSD had a clear role as a promoter of voluntary action, a supporter of the development of measures to drive greater transparency and a launcher of project-driven explorations of business actions in the realm of sustainability. While the specific topics the WBCSD has tackled have evolved over time, the focus on encouraging responsive, free-form collaboration is a constant, which continually harks back to that early pioneering work. The scenarios developed with Shell are still widely used today and still serve as a discussion framework for a better understanding of potential roles for all players.

The *Vision 2050* project

In 2010, the WBCSD published *Vision 2050*, another cornerstone report based on an equally ambitious process of member company engagement and consultation with hundreds of business leaders, sustainability experts and stakeholders in different countries. The WBCSD states:

> the report calls for a new agenda for business laying out a pathway to a world in which nine billion people can live well, and within the planet's resources, by mid-century. The report is a consensus piece that was compiled by 29 leading global companies from 14 industries and is the result of an 18 month long combined effort between CEOs and experts, and dialogues with more than 200 companies and external stakeholders in some 20 countries.[384]

The WBCSD sees *Vision 2050* as a "tool for thought leadership and a platform for beginning the dialogue that must take place to navigate the challenging years to come. "The report focuses on what it considers to be the nine crucial pathways to "9 billion people living well, and within the limits of the planet by 2050." These are:

- People's values
- Human development
- Economy
- Agriculture
- Forests
- Energy and power
- Buildings
- Mobility
- Materials

It documents what it describes as a set of about 40 "must haves" – developments that the stakeholders involved in consultation process believe must be put in place by 2020 to set a course towards sustainability. These include:

- Incorporating the costs of externalities, starting with carbon, ecosystem services and water, into the structure of the marketplace
- Doubling agricultural output without increasing the amount of land or water used
- Halting deforestation and increasing yields from planted forests
- Halving carbon emissions worldwide (based on 2005 levels) by 2050 through a shift to low-carbon energy systems

- Improved demand-side energy efficiency, and providing universal access to low-carbon mobility

The *Vision 2050* consultation process and report shares many common themes and recommendations with similar exercises developed by other business-led networks such as CSR Europe, Instituto Ethos in Brazil, Business for Social Responsibility (BSR) and the National Business Initiative (NBI) in South Africa, as well as frameworks developed by the G20 and the UN for a more inclusive, green and responsible global economy. Within two years, *Vision 2050* had been translated into ten major languages and used for different purposes by companies, other business-led networks, governments, NGOs and academic institutions around the world.

Building a global network for local business-led action

Thought leadership and recommendations, no matter how inspiring and hard-hitting, are only worth the paper (or iPads) they are written on unless they are actually implemented in practice. The WBCSD has developed several action-oriented platforms to facilitate such implementation among its members and other partners. In addition to the creation of member-led task forces focused on specific issues and publications and hosting regular liaison delegate meetings and sharing of good practices with its member companies, the WBCSD has adhered to a highly effective strategy of engaging with and building business-led platforms both within specific countries and regions and across crucial industry sectors and issue areas.

As of 2012, the WBCSD's Regional Network consisted of an alliance of more than 60 CEO-led business organizations, independently governed and funded separately from the WBCSD but united by a shared focus on providing business leadership for sustainable development in their respective countries or regions. Over half of them have been created as Business Councils for Sustainable Development (BCSDs). Others are existing business-led organizations either with a dedicated commitment to corporate responsibility and sustainability (such as the NBI in South Africa and Maala in Israel), or broader business associations that have a strong strategic program or unit focused on sustainability, such as Nippon Keidanren (the Japanese Business Federation), the Confederation of Norwegian Enterprises (Næringslivets Hovedorganisasjon, NHO) and the Confederation of Indian Industry.

The first local BCSD affiliates were established in 1992. As of 2012, there were 3 affiliates in North America, 17 in Latin America, 17 in Europe, 5 in Africa, and 20 in Asia, the Middle East and Oceania (see Table 3.1 in Chapter 3, page 32). In most cases they are composed of both locally based corporations and local subsidiaries of multinational companies. Although each local or regional affiliate selects its own priorities and issues and is not directed by the WBCSD, each jointly signs a formal agreement of cooperation with the WBCSD.

Marcel Engel, WBCSD's long-standing Managing Director of the Regional Network, comments:

> The Regional Network is one of WBCSD's most precious assets. It gives us legitimacy as a truly global organization and creates a bridge between global and local sustainability agendas. Our partner organizations around the world help spread our messages and tools, add valuable perspectives to our work, and provide a conduit to implement local initiatives.[385]

Partnering within and across sectors

The WBCSD started out as, and remains, a CEO-led, business-governed and funded organization. Almost from the outset, however, one of its hallmarks has been convening discussions, partnerships and gatherings of unlikely or unexpected players. As Lloyd Timberlake comments:

> In rising above the agenda of any one company, the WBCSD has found a way to navigate across sector lines and boundaries, reaching out to NGOs, governments and civil society to spark conversations and collaborations that were previously unthinkable. Certainly the opportunity to cross sector lines was created by an unprecedented openness among the various sector players. But the WBCSD has aggressively turned that opportunity into projects and conversations with groundbreaking results ... The principle of shifting polarized, dogma-driven debates into thoughtful, though difficult conversations that acknowledge all perspectives has been a constant for the WBCSD. In 1999, as negotiations following the 1997 adoption of the Kyoto Protocol were breaking down, the WBCSD organized informal conversations among some of the elite decision-makers in that convention. It has played a part in convening the various constituencies in the controversial topics of forestry certification and management, and has helped its members use this approach with their own varied stakeholders. The WBCSD did not invent the notion of multi-party dialogues, or the idea of a safe space where avowed enemies can transcend entrenched positions to exchange ideas and viewpoints. But its commitment to these ideals, and deep experience in successfully executing them, has led to its recognized leadership in this area.[386]

Examples of some of the platforms or partnerships that it has created within industry sectors and between business and other sectors include the following:

Sector projects

The WBCSD's sector projects are voluntary, industry-specific initiatives that demonstrate the commitment of companies, often fierce competitors, to come together in a "pre-competitive alliance" to address some of the most difficult and complex dilemmas within their own industry and along their value chains. In most cases, although the companies fund the work of the project, an external third party is usually engaged to conduct research and make recommendations. The projects also set up independent advisory or assurance groups to engage in consultations and review results and recommendations. These groups are usually made up of experts from UN agencies, NGOs or academic institutions whose reputations would suffer if the companies engaged in "greenwashing."

The first sector projects undertaken by the WBCSD in the 1990s focused on the global mining sector and on the pulp, paper and forestry sector. The Global Mining Initiative provided much of the foundation, and CEO-level support, for the establishment of the highly effective International Council on Mining and Metals in 2001. The Pulp, Paper and Forestry Initiative provided input to a number of global forestry initiatives, and the WBCSD continues to support a "Forest Solutions" sector project to this day. As of 2012, other sector projects include water, buildings, cement, electricity utilities, tires and mobility.

As Lloyd Timberlake notes: "At a bare minimum, these sector projects are a valuable investigation of the challenges facing various industries. Optimally, the projects are a powerful form of collaborative goal-setting, accountability and self-policing."[387]

Strategic NGO–WBCSD partnerships

In addition to convening cross-sector dialogues and consultations, and inviting NGOs and academic partners to serve as advisers or provide third-party reviews and assurance on specific WBCSD initiatives, the organization has also developed strategic partnerships with some NGOs to implement specific research or implementation projects. Just two examples of many include:

- Partnering with the **World Conservation Union (IUCN)** on making a business case and developing management and measurement tools to value ecosystems services and biodiversity. In 1997, the WBCSD and IUCN cooperated on a research project to argue that biodiversity is central to business, whether its products directly affect biodiversity (in the cases of the agriculture, mining and petroleum industries) or not. Since then, the two organizations continue to collaborate – and in some cases disagree – on the extent and nature of corporate responsibility to address these issues. They have developed joint guidelines and toolkits for business to improve its performance in this area and participate in joint advocacy and policy dialogue efforts to encourage governments to value ecosystem services more effectively

- Partnering with the **World Resources Institute (WRI)** on developing the Greenhouse Gas Protocol (GHG Protocol). In 1998, the WRI and the WBCSD convened a multi-stakeholder partnership of businesses, NGOs, governments and others with the ambitious (at that time) goal of developing internationally accepted greenhouse gas accounting and reporting standards for business and to promote their broad adoption. The initiative has created a framework and accounting system that individual companies can use to understand their own greenhouse gas emissions. Today, that GHG Protocol is used by hundreds of companies for their own internal measurement. It is used by the Chicago Climate Exchange and is also the basis for the European emissions trading system

Developing tools and capacity-building to improve business performance and accountability

Over the past few decades the WBCSD has developed a wide variety of management tools and frameworks to support its member companies and others in improving their business performance and reporting around key sustainability issues. Many of these tools are in the public domain providing a good example of the wider multiplier contribution that the WBCSD offers beyond its own members. Tools currently available include:

- **The GHG Protocol.** A set of practices and methods to help companies measure and report on their greenhouse gas emissions, developed in partnership with the WRI (see previous section)

- **The Global Water Tool.** A free and easy-to-use tool to enable companies and other organizations to map their water use and assess risks relative to their global operations and value chains

- **Business Ecosystems Training and** *Guide To Corporate Ecosystem Evaluation.* Guidelines and a framework to help companies understand their direct and indirect impact and dependence on ecosystems services and improve decision-making by having a better understanding of the risks, costs and values associated with these impacts

- **Sustainable Forest Finance Toolkit.** Aimed at supporting banks in developing effective screens and safeguards to cover their financing of forestry and forestry-related projects

- **Measuring Impact Framework.** A framework to help companies understand and measure their socioeconomic impacts on development. This was developed with 20 member companies and 15 external reviewers and co-branded with the International Finance Corporation

- **Chronos.** An e-learning tutorial on sustainable development developed as a joint project between the WBCSD and the University of Cambridge Programme for Sustainability Leadership and aimed at a general non-specialist business audience. Users have access to a mixture of information, video clips and interactive sessions such as role plays and quizzes to see how they would handle a variety of business sustainable-development dilemmas, ranging from addressing labor standards to improving energy efficiency. As a practical and cost-effective approach to engaging and educating employees, Chronos has garnered more than 150 corporate users and some universities, typically with licences for thousands of users apiece

Developing Future Leaders

Every year, member companies are invited to nominate outstanding young managers to participate in the WBCSD's *Future Leaders Team.* Some 30 managers are selected and spend up to 25 days over a nine-month period participating in a hands-on action learning initiative through workshop participation, involvement in the WBCSD and the management of individual and group projects. Each year the team focuses on a project linked to one of the WBCSD's core areas of focus or strategic priorities. In 2012, the team is addressing opportunities and challenges associated with business, biodiversity and ecosystems. In previous years they have focused on issues such as water, inclusive business models and market-based solutions to development, and the role of the investment community in driving more sustainable models of development.

Advocating and mobilizing for large-scale systemic change

Since undertaking its Global Scenarios 2005–2050 project, the WBCSD has increasingly recognized the need for more systemic-level approaches and solutions to transform society towards a more sustainable path. Such approaches were a key theme emerging from the

Vision 2050 project and are reinforced further with WBCSD's *Changing Pace* report in 2012, which calls on governments to play a more proactive and urgent role in the following seven areas: set goals, communicate and educate, regulate, adapt budgets, invest, monitor and coordinate.

As the new President of the WBCSD, Peter Bakker, and Chairman, Chad Holliday, state in the Foreword to *Changing Pace*:

> As a world society, we have not started the deep transformation that, we all know, is required. Progress is no more than sporadic. And every year, it becomes harder to catch up. The WBCSD believes that the need for action is more pressing than ever. Vision alone is not sufficient. The role of business is to innovate and provide sustainable solutions; there is no shortage of innovation and capacity to do more. But sustainable business solutions can only create an impact at the speed and scale required by the transformation, if the right mix of policy initiatives provides the right incentives to break the lock of business-as-usual.[388]

As discussed in Chapter 14 (Box 14.1, page 178), for the Rio + 20 meetings, the WBCSD joined forces with the International Chamber of Commerce and the United Nations Global Compact to form the Business Action for Sustainable Development (BASD) platform. BASD emphasized that progress towards sustainability will be limited without better enabling policies and incentives from governments and more concerted efforts on the part of businesses to work collectively to drive systemic solutions, in addition to embedding sustainable practices in their own operations and value chains.

Impact and lessons learned

Now 20 years old, the WBCSD continues to work closely with its members and regional network on pursuing an ambitious work program and growing advocacy activities and systemic-change platforms. The organization's current work program consists of the following initiatives:

- **Focus areas.** The WBCSD has focus areas that are each supported by a Focus Area Core Team (FACT) led by at least two corporate CEO co-chairs and supported by practitioner-level working groups and workstreams. Current focus areas are: the **Business Role**, which explores actions needed by companies to realize the transformation that is needed in achieving sustainable development; **Development**, which focuses on market-based solutions to supporting poverty alleviation and development; **Energy and Climate**, which gives WBCSD members a platform to engage with their peers and stakeholders in energy and climate, to address critical industry issues, share ways to solutions, and deliver business input to the design and implementation of the post-Kyoto climate architecture; and **Ecosystems**, which helps build capacity and develop tools to assess risks and opportunities related to business impacts and dependencies on ecosystems, and also engages in the global biodiversity and ecosystem policy debate

- **Sector projects.** The WBCSD currently manages industry-sector projects in the following areas, each one supported by external and independent partners in addition to companies in the relevant industry: water, buildings, cement, electricity utilities, tires, mobility and forest solutions (see also section on "Partnering within and across sectors" above)

- **Capacity-building.** The WBCSD's capacity-building workstream offers a variety of education, training and experiential learning initiatives from a variety of issue-specific tools to the online Chronos management training

- **Systems solutions.** In recent years, the organization has launched a new workstream focused on addressing more systemic challenges that require a more integrated and holistic approach, with current areas of working being urban infrastructure and sustainable consumption and value chains

The organization can look back on the past 20 years with some satisfaction. From its seminal publication *Changing Course* in 1992 to its recent call to action, *Changing Pace*, in 2012, the WBCSD has played a constantly evolving thought-leadership role in setting the agenda for the role of business in sustainable development, while also calling on governments and others to play their role more effectively. It has mobilized practical action by thousands of companies, both WBCSD members and others, and helped many of them to embed more sustainable business practices into their corporate strategies, operations and value chains. It has helped to seed new organizations and initiatives, from the International Emissions Trading Association and the International Council on Mining and Metals, to providing input into the early days of the creation of the Global Reporting Initiative. And on occasion it has partnered with other business-led coalitions to amplify the voice of progressive business for sustainable development, such as the Business Action for Sustainable Development platform, in cooperation with the International Chamber of Commerce and United Nations Global Compact.

As a membership-driven organization, the WBCSD, like others, inevitably faces the tension of expanding its projects, partnerships and publications to respond to the voices and needs of its members – while also trying to respond to global trends and dilemmas that some of its members may not wish to address. With a core membership of some 200 major corporations, there is what Lloyd Timberlake describes as:

> an innate tension between prodding member companies to move along on the continuum of sustainability efforts, while also recognizing that the legitimacy of the organization is derived from a member-driven agenda. Inevitably the line between driving a trend and being swept up in its wake is blurred. Most changes in course are the result of a multitude of actions from a multitude of actors, not the singular action of one organization. That said the WBCSD has long been recognized as one among the group of "jazz players" improvising change . . . Though the specific trends and topics explored have changed over time, the WBCSD has consistently engaged in activities that pioneer collaboration among unlikely partners and cultivate a voice for business.[389]

Achim Steiner, the visionary Director of the United Nations Environment Programme has challenged the WBCSD as follows:

> The World Business Council will need to think carefully where its future lies. Is it a club of progressively-thinking members, or is it a leader in transformational thinking and approaches to sustainable development? It has managed to keep a foot in both worlds of being a business voice and a catalyst for innovative thinking. To keep a sharp focus on these dual roles will be very important as it gains in public profile, and as the risks, responsibilities, and opportunities for business increase.[390]

The WBCSD had long debated the issue of membership numbers: how many members would make the council so large that it would no longer be "member-led, member-driven," but would instead become a bureaucratic organization with the lowest-common-denominator approach of some of the larger business organizations, held back by the concerns of their least progressive members? At the WBCSD's tenth anniversary annual meeting, former President Stigson acknowledged this challenge and promised to cap the membership at 200.

Stigson also presented the WBCSD's 2005–2015 strategy, representing a departure from the council's previous approach, which had focused on engagement: with other players, with other organizations, and other sectors besides business, but mainly with issues. The goal of issue engagement had been to get a business voice into debates and meetings about concerns such as climate change or biodiversity. In offering a business voice, the council rarely if ever advocated any particular stand. The new 2005–2015 strategy focuses on advocacy, actually trying to move societies towards more sustainable forms of progress. Stigson stated at the time:

> To us, these changes add up to a shift from merely engaging to a form of more active, intentional advocacy, not the advocacy of big budgets and bureaucracy and lobbyists, but the advocacy of a persuasive argument and a well-chosen team, the advocacy of a mission with an end in mind: a more sustainable world for all. We look forward to seeing how this new direction will evolve over our next 10 years.[391]

In January 2012, Stigson retired as CEO of the WBCSD after 17 years. He was succeeded by Peter Bakker, the former CEO of the logistics multinational TNT. In one of his first blogs as President in January 2012 Bakker reinforced this commitment to driving more systemic large-scale solutions:

> I believe that businesses – now more than ever – will play a critical role in helping to resolve the world's most pressing challenges. However, we need to look at the solutions businesses have developed and scale them up quickly. It is only then that we can truly begin to make a dent in the world's problems – to create a sustainable future for business, society and the environment.[392]

The future

In an interview at the Rio + 20 summit Bakker started to spell out key elements of what he sees as an expanded WBCSD role.[393]

First, he plans to extend the WBCSD's industry-sector-led coalitions to the tire and chemicals industries, building on success that has already been achieved in the cement and forestry sectors. Second, Bakker wants to create cross-sector working groups that can create more systemic change at city-wide level:

> With the majority of the world's population living in cities, this is where we need to concentrate on creating change . . . We need to take a systems point of view as a car company cannot make a city sustainable. We need to include every other sector such as public transport, construction and utilities.[394]

Third, the WBCSD is throwing its backing behind the Integrated Reporting Initiative that has grown out of the Prince of Wales Accounting for Sustainability Initiative. And fourth, Bakker is proposing to challenge institutional investors on how they value the companies they invest in. Interestingly, CSR Europe is also working on extra-financial performance measurement and valuing environmental, social and governance performance of companies.[395] The two organizations have looked at synergies here.

It is also intended that there will be a major update and refinement of WBCSD's widely disseminated *Vision 2050*, starting in January 2013, in order to identify more concretely what needs to be done to ensure "a world in which 9 billion people live well, within the limits of one planet by mid-century" (WBCSD's own new working definition of sustainable development). It is already understood that this updating of *Vision 2050* will, *inter alia*, give far more attention to water issues, and more to sustainable consumption and public-policy changes required to implement *Vision 2050*. The objective, says Peter Paul Van de Wijs, at the time of interview WBCSD's head of communications, is to move the WBCSD "from think-tank to do-tank," and to change the emphasis "from output to impact."

Strengthening the WBCSD regional network is also on the agenda – the national BCSDs are demanding more from the WBCSD but the central secretariat is also very clear that the BCSDs are independent organizations and that anything that comes across as "top-down Geneva orders" would be counter-productive. Nevertheless, it is understood that with more than 60 national BCSDs, much of the hoped-for increase in overall impact will need to be delivered in partnership with them, as well as through increasing collaboration with other coalitions and NGOs. WBCSD also has numerous other formal partnerships including partnerships with the Global Reporting Initiative, the International Integrated Reporting Council, Ceres, UNWater, the UN Framework Convention on Climate Change, the Global Environmental Management Initiative, the World Bank, The Economics of Ecosystems and Biodiversity, Meridian Institute, and the UN Environment Programme–World Conservation Monitoring Center. As one precedent to build on, Van de Wijs points to the successful collaboration between the WBCSD and the World Resources Institute and then with national BCSDs to develop and implement the GHG Protocol. This initiative, which represents a decade-long partnership between the two organizations, has helped to develop what is now the most widely used international accounting tool for government and business leaders to understand, quantify and manage greenhouse gas emissions. It illustrates the high potential for developing similar strategic alliances between business-led coalitions, non-governmental organizations and governments to achieve greater scale and systemic impact.

Profile 10

World Environment Center (WEC)

Terry F. Yosie with Jane Nelson

World Environment Center

World Environment Center in its own words

The World Environment Center is an independent, global, non-profit, non-advocacy organization that advances sustainable development through the business practices of member companies and in partnership with governments, multilateral organizations, non-governmental organizations, universities and other stakeholders.

WEC creates sustainable business solutions through capacity building projects in emerging markets; convenes leadership roundtables to shape strategic thinking across a range of sustainability topics; and honors business excellence through its annual Gold Medal Award for International Corporate Achievement in Sustainable Development.

www.wec.org   October 2012

Background context and history

Since the emergence of the modern age of environmentalism in the early 1970s, there has been a steady evolution of philosophical principles, values, policy initiatives, organizational structures and collaborative relationships that have culminated in the transforming concept of sustainable development.

The articulation of sustainable development by the World Commission on Environment and Development (Brundtland Commission) in 1987 has itself been increasingly transformed into:

- A framework for innovation and value creation by the private sector that can also address significant societal challenges

- A guide for public-sector policy decisions that integrate economic with environmental and social factors

- A source of new knowledge and operating practices that can be implemented to improve performance by both state and non-state institutions

One organization that embodies this evolution is the World Environment Center (WEC), established in 1974. WEC provides a lens through which to observe the evolution from the "compliance" and "command and control" decision-making of an earlier era to today's market-driven innovations and practices at the global, regional and local levels.

WEC was created through the United Nations Environment Programme in the wake of the 1972 United Nations Conference on the Human Environment in Stockholm. Known originally as the Center for International Environmental Information, WEC was constituted as a non-advocacy, non-profit organization whose early mission was to catalyze high-level dialogue and collaboration between business and government institutions to advance environmental solutions.

Its initial programs focused on the preparation of the *World Environment Report*, a publication on the status of environmental developments around the world, as well as the organization of high-level discussions on the status of environmental issues and trends. Participants in these dialogues included environmental professionals from government and industry, academia and the international community, including NGOs.

In 1977, WEC established its International Environmental Forum, with an initial group of 13 corporations, which provided a non-advocacy forum for environmental leaders of business and government to discuss issues of common concern.

In 1981, WEC became an independent non-profit, non-advocacy body that continued its original programmatic focus supplemented by two additional initiatives:

- The establishment in 1985 of the Gold Medal Award for International Corporate Achievement. This award, now initiating its 30th cycle, continues to honor business excellence in advancing environmental protection and, subsequently, sustainable development

- The creation of a technical assistance and training program available to industry in developing nations funded by the USAID (United States Agency for International Development)

With these historical antecedents, the World Environment Center has continued to adapt to the changing needs of contemporary business and society. Today WEC has become a business-led organization, with its primary core funding coming from the private sector although it frequently partners with governments to fund specific programs. Its mission is to assist its member companies to implement sustainable development in their business strategies and operations in collaboration with government, NGOs, academia and other stakeholders.

Large global companies are members of the World Environment Center. New member candidates are reviewed and elected by the Board of Directors based on three membership criteria:

- Business operations that are global in scale

- Commitment to implementing sustainability across global operations

- Willingness to share practices and other experiences by participating in WEC-organized roundtables and other events

Membership is by invitation only.

WEC's funding is provided by income from: its various capacity-building projects that are supported by government agencies, member companies and foundations; membership dues; revenue from companies that host roundtables; and funds from the Gold Medal Award celebration. WEC is incorporated in the United States and has a non-profit, non-advocacy tax status.

WEC is headquartered in Washington, DC, and maintains regional offices in Beijing, China; Munich, Germany; and San Salvador, El Salvador. Regional offices provide project management and organization of roundtables in Asia–Pacific, European and Latin American geographies. In 2012, an independent nonprofit entity was registered in Europe to support and scale WEC's work in this region.

The governance structure of WEC is led by its Board of Directors, a group of senior private-sector sustainability executives, leading academicians and senior representatives of NGOs. Dr. Terry Yosie has served as President and CEO since 2006. He was formerly at the American Chemical Council where he played a leadership role in developing the global Responsible Care® program. Recent chairs of the Board of Directors have been Wayne Balta from IBM and Jeff Seabright from the Coca-Cola Company. In 2013, Mike Barry of Marks & Spencer will become chair, representing the first non-American-headquartered company to chair the Board.

Key activities and phases of development

Three strategic premises guide WEC's mission to work with companies to implement sustainable development goals into their core business strategies and operations. These are:

- Innovation must play a central role in the future advancement of sustainable development

- WEC's programs and initiatives should advance business solutions to global sustainability challenges

- WEC's business model should be implemented through an "on-the-ground" approach to project implementation with technical assistance, project management and other sources of expertise provided by experts largely indigenous to countries where projects are implemented

WEC's strategic plan (see Figure P10.1), updated by its Board of Directors in December 2011, consists of three major focus areas that are designed to achieve differentiated value for its members and their stakeholders. These focus areas include:

Capacity-building

An outgrowth of WEC's previous technical assistance initiatives, capacity-building has been formalized through a number of interlinked projects to improve the sustainability performance of global companies and their suppliers. Over the past decade, for example, these projects (funded by both private companies and government agencies) have included suppliers to automotive companies (Australia and China), chemical manufacturers (Brazil and Mexico), beverage companies (Costa Rica), food providers (Chile, Egypt, Honduras, Morocco and Nicaragua), the hospitality sector (Costa Rica), pharmaceutical companies (Brazil), and retailers (El Salvador and Guatemala). Beginning in 2010, WEC's capacity-building focus has expanded to include improvements in the teaching of sustainability in Europe, Latin America and the United States in business and engineering schools, and the development of curricula that focuses on innovative best practices in sustainability. WEC plans a major expansion of its capacity-building program by building significant new partnerships with leading companies and universities to better prepare business school students to implement sustainable development in their roles as future business leaders.

Thought leadership

WEC, which has historically created a forum for leading environmental and sustainability professionals, has formalized a series of six to eight yearly Roundtables that focus on many of the leading sustainability topics. Roundtables are invitation-only discussions involving approximately 40 senior-level executives of government, business and NGOs supplemented by additional experts from academia.

Recent Roundtables have focused on such issues as: increasing the market demand for energy efficiency (Brussels); expectations for Chinese and foreign companies for implementation of China's 12th Five Year Plan (Beijing); innovative energy strategies for existing buildings (Washington, DC); shared value as a sustainable business model (Washington, DC); and systemic solutions for social innovation (Lausanne). In 2012, IBM and WEC co-created a new strategic initiative – the "Innovations for Environmental Sustainability Council" – which included nine additional global companies to examine new opportunities for innovations in technology, business processes and strategic collaboration. Topics addressed in 2012 include: traceability of materials across the value chain; sustainable buildings and infrastructure; innovations in water resource management; and sustainable logistics.

Figure P10.1 **WEC strategic plan**
Source: World Environment Center

Senior executives of leading companies . . . advance sustainable solutions
. . . to achieve business, environmental and societal value

In 2013, WEC also plans to implement a "Forum for Next Generation Sustainability Practices." This will focus on identifying and sharing leading-edge practices that companies are developing to: ensure greater internal alignment and governance for sustainability; shift from issues management to systems management; and create shared value and scale through increased business-to-business (B2B) collaboration.

Promoting business excellence

WEC awards its Gold Medal for corporate excellence in sustainable development in which global companies compete for this annual recognition with the recipient selected by an independent jury. An annual CEO-level event creates the opportunity to examine the business strategy and practices of the recipient company. Recent award winners have included Unilever (2013), IBM (2012), Nestlé (2011), Walmart (2010), the Coca-Cola Company (2009) and Marks & Spencer (2008). A companion Gold Medal Colloquium enables senior sustainability executives to conduct an in-depth examination of a specific sustainability topic. Recent Colloquia have addressed such issues as: the climate–water–energy–food nexus; sustainable development as a driver of business-model innovation; sustainable consumption; and collaboration strategies of global NGOs.

To implement these elements of its strategic plan, WEC has developed a number of strategic partnerships and relationships that include collaborative initiatives with the Center for Sustainability Management at IMD International, Environmental Law Institute, Forum for the Future, Net Impact, Rainforest Alliance, The Energy and Resources Institute, The Nature Conservancy, Volans, World Resources Institute, the World Business Council on Sustainable Development and WWF.

Impact and lessons learned

WEC's strategic focus has evolved since its inception in 1974, and an evaluation of its results has changed during this time. In its initial years, WEC's principal results were to develop information on environmental conditions around the world and to identify emerging issues and trends to better inform environmental professionals in business, government, the NGO community and academia.

A more recent evaluation of WEC's results would include the following:

- Developing a model green supply-chain program that integrates improvements in sustainability performance with business process innovation and economic savings

- Providing a continuing platform for the world's leading sustainability thinkers to discuss their concepts and analyses with senior company executives as a means to stimulate innovation and problem-solving

- Creating innovative partnerships that assist national governments in implementing environmental and economic development objectives that are part of free-trade agreements

- Establishing a "business solutions" approach to sustainability that increasingly links private-sector outcomes to economic, environmental/energy and social needs

- Adopting a value-chain approach to business planning for the purpose of advancing alignment among supply chains and customers on key sustainability challenges

- Integrating the growing knowledge around sustainability with private-sector-generated best practices to prepare students to become more effective future sustainability leaders in business

The future

Over the course of almost 40 years of operation WEC has evolved from a primarily govern-ment-supported center to a business-funded and -led coalition working with its corporate members and others to advance the agenda for sustainable development. At the same time, its member companies have become increasingly strategic in their sustainability activities and the organization is evolving to both influence and respond to this evolution.

In 2009 a survey and assessment was undertaken of the 25 Gold Award winners to-date. Their experiences in driving sustainability goals through their core business operations and some of the trends they identified are summarized in Box P10.1. As WEC looks to the next decade its member companies and Board of Directors are calling for more systemic-level strategic programs that will enable sustainability initiatives to be implemented at a global scale across a variety of value chains to deliver more transformative benefits for business and society.

Box P10.1 **Business and sustainability lessons from 25 years of Gold Medal Awards**

Terry Yosie and Jane Nelson, 2009

The 25th anniversary year of the Gold Medal Award provides the opportunity to examine how the winners' past achievements have advanced sustainability and raised the bar for future value creation for business and society. The companies spotlighted here have helped guide some of the most significant innovations and can still be considered leaders today, even though they may have won the award years ago.

Changing priorities

Yesterday's sustainability agenda focused primarily on operational-level policy and technical problems in specific geographic areas. Today's sustainability agenda is dominated by major systemic challenges that no one company, government agency or even group of actors can successfully resolve alone.

The most notable challenges include: climate change; energy efficiency and the demand for low-carbon technologies; water access and quality; ecosystem protection and services; urbanization and demographic shifts; and the need to integrate social and economic impacts into every aspect of the marketplace.

The ability to achieve success in these areas will build on the ideas and initia-tives of many of the Gold Medal Award companies over the past 25 years as evi-denced through the following evolution of priorities:

From compliance to prevention and global footprint reduction

Early Gold Medal awardees such as 3M (the first awardee in 1985) and Procter & Gamble (1992 awardee) were at the forefront of applying new ways of thinking to advance environmental protection.

3M's pioneering Pollution Prevention Pays (3P) program was an industry first in systematizing the concept of pollution prevention on a company-wide basis and documenting the results. Procter & Gamble was an early proponent of using life-cycle analysis to identify and quantify environmental and other impacts associated with all phases of product development and use.

Today, most of the awardees play a leadership role in efforts to measure and decrease their overall footprint, including collective efforts to develop frameworks and tools to manage global carbon and water footprints.

From assertion to accountability and transparency

Sustainability metrics, public reporting, increased transparency, stakeholder-engagement mechanisms and their relationship to broader changes in corporate governance represent critical elements for demonstrating sustainability leadership.

The BP Group (1988 awardee) played a key role in developing the Public Environmental Reporting Initiative, one of the first examples of voluntary sustainability reporting. The Dow Chemical Company (1989 awardee) established its Corporate Environmental Advisory Council in 1992 to advise senior company executives on major issues and strategies impacting its business. Other awardees now have formal mechanisms for stakeholder consultation at the operational and corporate levels.

From pilot projects to scale along global supply chains

Every significant product, technology and process innovation begins with an experiment or demonstration project that can subsequently be scaled. Philips Electronics (1998 awardee) initiated its Supplier Sustainability Involvement program in 2003 to raise performance levels of suppliers through training and audits. This broadened into the Philips Supplier Declaration on Sustainability to encompass environmental and social issues, thus providing a sustainability platform to unify the company's value-chain management process.

The 1994 awardee, S.C. Johnson, continues to differentiate itself at both ends of the global supply chain through innovative processes for sourcing raw materials for its products around the world and growing the marketplace for greener products.

From the 'backroom' to the 'boardroom'

WEC awardees have been pioneers in getting sustainable development onto the agendas of corporate "C-suites," boards of directors and major shareholders. While more still needs to be done to embed environmental, social and governance issues into financial markets and pricing signals, these issues are now no doubt part of the boardroom agenda in leading companies.

DuPont (1987 awardee) has, for several decades, institutionalized environmental and sustainability leadership at the very top of the company. Its CEO chairs its Sustainable Growth Steering Team, which helps the company make strategic level decisions. Shell (2001 awardee) has maintained a Corporate and Social Responsibility Committee of its board of directors for a number of years. The CEO also chairs the Sustainable Development and HSSE Executive Committee that reviews performance and sets priorities and targets.

From individual action to strategic alliances and systems change

Nearly all WEC awardees are engaged in industry-wide alliances to level the global playing field and achieve scale and systemic impact. CEMEX (2002 awardee), for example, has been a leader in mobilizing its business to provide housing for lower-income citizens and in creating the Cement Sustainability Initiative within the World Business Council for Sustainable Development.

Many have also established global strategic partnerships with environmental and development NGOs to better achieve their sustainability goals. The Coca-Cola Company (2009 awardee) works with both Greenpeace to introduce climate-friendly refrigerant gases and with WWF to protect critical watersheds to preserve access for current and future users.

Johnson Controls (2004 awardee) is working with the Clinton Climate Initiative, the U.S. Conference of Mayors and other city governments to improve energy efficiency, reduce greenhouse gases and lower costs in municipal and private-sector buildings around the world through its "Smart Environments" strategy.

From short-term targets to long-term strategic vision

Some of the best-managed global companies build their business strategy around an ambitious "big vision" that is supported by interim targets and building blocks.

To fulfill its public vision of a low-carbon society, Ricoh (2003 awardee) is applying its experience gained over many years of technological innovation to develop product, process and systems designs that embody energy and resource conservation and recycling.

Marks & Spencer's (2008 awardee) "Plan A" led the company to rethink and redefine its product value chain by integrating Oxfam into a business process for recycling clothing to lower-income families. This gets consumers directly involved in driving sustainability results and creates the opportunity to rethink the role of external stakeholders in creating business and societal value.

From product innovation to redesigning business models and markets

A number of the awardees have developed internal programs and external alliances aimed at fundamentally re-imagining and transforming their business models and, in some cases, even the markets in which they operate, while continuing to innovate existing products, services and clean technologies.

IBM (1990 and 2012 awardee), through its "Smarter Planet" strategic initiative, recognizes that the inter-connectedness of individual and global communications can provide a platform for smarter business solutions to address global problems. While this and other developments are at a relatively early stage, they are potentially the most revolutionary aspect of sustainable development and hold the greatest opportunities for addressing the myriad of global scale problems related to climate change, natural resource utilization, economic development and future wealth creation.

Future agenda for action

Actions of these and other WEC Gold Medal Awardees presage the future sustainability agenda and will result in a continuing redefinition of roles and responsibilities for global companies, governments, multilateral institutions, NGOs, universities and individual consumers, investors and citizens.

New leadership and business models, new technological, institutional and societal innovations, and new levels of understanding and commitment will be required to advance this agenda for action.[396]

→

Gold medal award winners (1985–2013)

2013	Unilever	1998	Philips Electronics NV
2012	IBM	1997	Compaq Computer Corporation
2011	Nestlé		
2010	Wal-Mart Stores, Inc.	1996	Alcoa
2009	The Coca-Cola Company	1995	Ciba-Geigy Limited
2008	Marks & Spencer	1994	S.C. Johnson & Son, Inc.
2007	Alcan	1993	Xerox Corporation
2006	ABN AMRO	1992	Procter & Gamble
2005	Starbucks Coffee Company	1991	Rohm and Haas Company
2004	Johnson Controls Inc.	1990	IBM Corporation
2003	Ricoh	1989	The Dow Chemical Company
2002	CEMEX	1988	The BP Group
2001	Royal Dutch Shell Group of Companies	1987	E.I. du Ponte de Nemours & Co.
2000	International Paper	1986	Exxon Corporation
1999	Eastman Kodak Company	1985	3M

Profile 11

United Nations Global Compact (UNGC)

Jane Nelson, Mattia Anesa* and David Grayson

The United Nations Global Compact in its own words

The UN Global Compact is a strategic policy initiative for businesses that are committed to aligning their operations and strategies with ten universally accepted principles in the areas of human rights, labour, environment and anti-corruption. By doing so, business, as a primary driver of globalization, can help ensure that markets, commerce, technology and finance advance in ways that benefit economies and societies everywhere.

As social, political and economic challenges (and opportunities) – whether occurring at home or in other regions – affect business more than ever before, many companies recognize the need to collaborate and partner with governments, civil society, labour and the United Nations. This ever-increasing understanding is reflected in the Global Compact's rapid growth. With over 10,000 corporate participants and other stakeholders from over 130 countries, it is the largest voluntary corporate responsibility initiative in the world.

Endorsed by chief executives, the Global Compact is a practical framework for the development, implementation, and disclosure of sustainability policies and practices, offering participants a wide spectrum of workstreams, management tools and resources – all designed to help advance sustainable business models and markets.

---

* Mattia Anesa is a researcher with the Doughty Centre for Corporate Responsibility, Cranfield School of Management.

Overall, the Global Compact pursues two complementary objectives: Mainstream the ten principles in business activities around the world; and catalyse actions in support of broader UN goals, including the Millennium Development Goals (MDGs). With these objectives in mind, the Global Compact has shaped an initiative that provides collaborative solutions to the most fundamental challenges facing both business and society. The initiative seeks to combine the best properties of the UN, such as moral authority and convening power, with the private sector's solution-finding strengths, and the expertise and capacities of a range of key stakeholders. The Global Compact is global and local; private and public; voluntary yet accountable.

www.unglobalcompact.org   October 2012

Background context and history

One of the most important developments in the field of corporate responsibility over the past two decades has been the growth in formal engagement and cooperation between business-led corporate responsibility coalitions and global governance institutions such as the United Nations, G8 and G20, as well as development finance institutions such as the World Bank, regional development banks and bilateral donor agencies. Although the United Nations has worked with the private sector in a variety of ways for over 50 years, the nature of this engagement has grown dramatically in scale, strategic intent and transformational impact over the past 20 years. The establishment and growth of the United Nations Global Compact (UNGC) has both reflected and driven this increasingly important trend.

Given its base within the United Nations and multi-stakeholder governance model, the UNGC is not strictly an independent business-led corporate responsibility coalition as defined in Part I of this book (i.e., one that is primarily governed and funded by business), but its entire strategic focus is dedicated to identifying, embedding and spreading responsible business practices and new models of partnership to help achieve international goals, and all of its workstreams are demand-driven by its signatory companies and have business-led steering committees or other forms of active business engagement. As such, we have included it as one of the key profiles in the book due to the crucial leadership role it has played, and continues to play, in shaping the emergence of voluntary collective action by the private sector at a global, national and sector or issue-based level.

Kofi Annan became the UN's seventh Secretary-General on January 1, 1997. From the outset he recognized the increasingly important role that non-State actors, including business, were playing in either helping or undermining the UN and its member governments in their efforts to achieve progress in the inter-related areas of peace and security, development, human rights and humanitarian affairs. In March 1997 he appointed Professor John Ruggie, then Dean of Columbia University's School of International and Public Affairs, to serve as his Assistant Secretary-General and chief advisor for strategic planning. Alongside other strategic initiatives, they started a more systematic process of engagement not only with civil-society organizations, but also with representative business associations, corporate responsibility coalitions and senior business executives.

Some of these efforts built on long-standing relationships between the UN and representative business bodies, others on more recent models of engagement that had been developed to engage the business community in a series of global conferences hosted by the United Nations in the early to mid-1990s.[397] They also drew on lessons from the experience of the United Nations Centre on Transnational Corporations, which had operated from 1974 to 1992, before being transferred first to the UN Department of Economic and Social Development, and then in 1993 to the United Nations Conference on Trade and Development (UNCTAD).

Georg Kell, an officer in the Executive Office of the Secretary-General, worked with John Ruggie and others to develop practical ideas for engaging the private sector more effectively in supporting the mission of the UN. They recognized the need to reflect the diversity of private-sector actors and industry sectors, to engage companies from developing as well as developed economies, to provide a platform for engagement that did not unfairly favor one company over others, and to ensure that the UN's brand and reputation wasn't misused for commercial gain. Above all, they also understood the imperative to address ongoing issues of mistrust and misunderstanding between many in the business and UN community, especially relating to questions of corporate responsibility, accountability and transparency, and to keep official representatives of UN member governments well-briefed and engaged in the process.

Dialogues between senior UN officials and business leaders were held in a number of locations ranging from World Economic Forum sessions in Davos to speeches and discussions hosted by different UN funds and agencies around the world. In 1998, for the first time, the UN Staff Training College in Turin hosted two high-level capacity-building workshops between senior business and UN leaders, co-facilitated by the UN Secretariat, the International Labour Organization and the Prince of Wales International Business Leaders Forum.

In January 1999, Kofi Annan and his team traveled again to the World Economic Forum's annual meeting in Davos where he made a seminal keynote speech calling for a new global compact between the United Nations and business leaders.[398] Over a decade later the challenge he made to the assembled business leaders remains more relevant and urgent than ever. As he recalls in his memoir published in 2012:[399]

> I went there to launch a "Global Compact" between the private sector and the United Nations that aimed to build a broader foundation for globalization based on shared values and principles. From past meetings with leaders there, I had developed a relationship of mutual respect that I believed could be the basis for something more ambitious. I warned of the fragility of globalization and its vulnerability to a backlash from all the "-isms" of our post-Cold War world: protectionism, populism, nationalism, ethnic chauvinism, fanaticism, and terrorism. To safeguard the benefits of a global trade system and the spread of technology, however, corporations had to do more than just engage with global policymakers.
>
> There was – and is – a great deal that they could do on their own, proactively. I didn't want them to think they could use the excuse of dysfunctional governments and trading regimes to delay action. "Don't wait for every country to introduce laws protecting freedom of association and the right to collective bargaining," I urged them. "You can at least make sure your own employees,

and those of your subcontractors, enjoy those rights. You can at least make sure that you yourselves are not employing underage children or forced labor, either directly or indirectly. And you can make sure that, in your own hiring and firing policies, you do not discriminate on grounds of race, creed, gender or ethnic origin." This would have to be a two-way street: we at the United Nations would abandon our past prejudices against private enterprise, but in return I believed that global business would have to rethink its role as well as its obligations if we were to put global markets on a fair and sustainable footing.

Annan's Davos speech focused on what business leaders could do both individually and collectively to embrace, support and enact a set of core values in the areas of human rights, labor standards and environmental practices. These three areas of focus were selected on the basis of first, having operational and strategic relevance to the private sector; second, as areas where universal values had already been defined by international intergovernmental agreements; and third, as areas that may pose a threat to the open global market and multi-lateral trade regime, if not acted on.

A number of business leaders responded positively to the Secretary-General's call to action. Following further UN–business engagement and support from several key UN agencies, notably, the International Labour Organization, the United Nations High Commissioner for Human Rights, the United Nations Environment Programme, and the United Nations Development Programme, the Global Compact was formally launched in July 2000. It was launched as a program within the Executive Office of the UN Secretary-General and Georg Kell was appointed as its Executive Director. There were 40 initial signatory companies from a variety of countries and industry sectors.

Over the past decade, the UNGC has become the world's largest corporate citizenship initiative in terms of the number of companies signed up. As of October 2012, there were nearly 8,000 business signatories from 140 countries and over 60 local or regional networks. Almost two-thirds of its participating companies are headquartered in developing countries. The UNGC also has non-business signatories ranging from academic institutions to civil society organizations and trade unions, alongside active and ongoing support from a number of UN funds and agencies and from member governments.

From the outset the Global Compact required its signatory companies to embrace and implement nine broad principles of business behavior in the areas human rights, labor and the environment. A tenth principle was added in 2004, addressing anti-corruption. The ten principles are summarized in Box P11.1. Subsequently, it has also worked proactively with participating companies and other partners to catalyze individual and collective business action in support of broader UN goals, most notably the Millennium Development Goals (MDGs).

The UNGC can claim to have had a significant impact in helping companies around the world to embed and spread responsible business practices and in building platforms for collective action between business, governments, intergovernmental agencies and civil-society organizations to support global development goals. A small central team, still based within the UN Secretariat and led by Georg Kell, coordinates a wide-ranging network of self-directed coalitions covering a variety of issues, sectors and geographies, many of them with their own outreach efforts and multiplier effect. The Global Compact has succeeded by being highly networked, and by being entrepreneurial and adaptive to the changing global environment,

Box P11.1 **The UN Global Compact Principles**
Source: UN Global Compact

Human rights

Principle 1: **Business** should support and respect the protection of international human rights within their sphere of influence

Principle 2: make sure they are not complicit in human rights abuses

Labour

Principle 3: **Business** should uphold the freedom of association and the effective recognition of the right to collective bargaining

Principle 4: the elimination of all forms of forced and compulsory labour

Principle 5: the effective abolition of child labour

Principle 6: the elimination of discrimination in respect of employment and occupation

Environment

Principle 7: **Business** should support a precautionary approach to environmental challenges

Principle 8: undertake initiatives to promote greater environmental responsibility

Principle 9: encourage the development and diffusion of environmentally friendly technologies

Anti-corruption

Principle 10: **Business** should work against all forms of corruption, including extortion and bribery

---

while still having the benefit of being part of the UN system and being able to work with UN agencies and national governments as a global platform for progressive change.

The initiative has not been without its critics. The Global Compact was established as, and remains, a voluntary and principle-based approach to addressing corporate sustainability. It has neither the mandate nor the resources to undertake detailed monitoring of the performance of its participating companies and networks. This commitment to voluntarism has often been a cause of contention with the initiative's critics, both within and beyond the UN system. There have been ongoing calls for legally binding international agreements to hold private firms, especially global corporations, to greater account for their human rights, labor, environmental and governance performance. There has also been criticism that the Global Compact facilitates "bluewash," enabling companies to benefit from their association with the UN's respected blue logo without having to demonstrate sufficient accountability and transparency for their activities.

The UNGC robustly defends its commitment to voluntarism and has responded to its critics with a combination of measures. These include:

- **Implementation of a series of "integrity measures,"** which include guidelines on the use of the UN name and logo by participating companies, a requirement for companies to publicly disclose their progress against the Ten Principles through an annual "Communication on Progress" report and a process for de-listing companies that fail to do so, and a system for responding to allegations of systematic and egregious abuses by participating companies

- **Regular feedback to UN member governments** through a biannual report to the UN General Assembly and active engagement with a donor group of governments that supports the work of the UNGC

- **A multi-dimensional governance framework**, which was implemented in 2005 to reflect the different roles and responsibilities of the UNGC's participants, while also allowing for a system of "checks and balances" to address concerns by some critics that the business sector had undue influence over the Global Compact's governance and decision-making processes. This framework has been a useful model for building trust and accountability, while also remaining inclusive and non-bureaucratic. It is illustrated in Figure P11.1

It should be noted, that the Global Compact has never aimed or claimed to be a substitute for regulation or legal compliance, but rather aims to be a complement. A memorandum prepared by the legal firm Latham & Watkins, describes the complementary relationship between voluntary initiatives and regulation:[400]

> voluntary initiatives – which by definition are not legally binding – should never be a substitute for effective regulation. Rather, they can be its powerful complement. Companies must, of course, comply with the law, whether or not it can be enforced. But voluntary initiatives have the unique potential to become corporate drivers. They can lead companies to strive to be better than the law requires and, in this way, move beyond lowest-common-denominator standards or rules.

The memorandum outlines how effectively governed voluntary initiatives can instill a greater culture of innovation, transparency and accountability by companies and also create a platform through which their stakeholders, including critics, can engage in dialogue to further drive better performance. While this does not always happen, there can be no doubt that large-scale voluntary corporate responsibility initiatives such as the Global Compact have helped to increase the scale and reach of responsible business practices far beyond what it would have been in their absence. Some of the many specific activities that the UNGC had undertaken to achieve this impact are summarized in the following section.

Figure P11.1 **The UN Global Compact's governance framework**

The Global Compact Board – a multi-stakeholder advisory body that meets annually to provide ongoing strategic and policy advice and play a role in implementation of the integrity measures. Chaired by the UN Secretary-General, the Vice-Chair is a former business leader, and the board has some 20 business leaders, 4 leaders from representative business associations and trade union organizations, and 4 civil society leaders

The Global Compact Leaders Summit – a tri-annual event involving senior executives of UNGC participants and other stakeholders, where participants produce strategic recommendations and propose new initiatives

Local Networks – coalitions that adva the Global Compact within a particular country or geographic region. Their role to facilitate local implementation of the Ten Principles and to encourage on-the ground collective action

Annual Local Networks Forum – Local Networks from around the world meet to share experiences, review and compare progress, identify best practices, and adopt recommendations to enhance their effectiveness

The Global Compact Office – the UN entity formally entrusted to manage the initiative. It has UN system-wide responsibilities for sharing best practices, advocacy and issue leadership, fostering network development, maintaining a communications infrastructure, implementing the integrity measures, brand management, and plays a key role in advancing the partnership agenda across the UN system

Donor Group – The Global Compact Office is funded by voluntary contributions from governments to a UN Trust Fund. Contributions from any government are welcome. Current donors are China, Colombia, Denmark, Finland, France, Germany, Italy, Republic of Korea, Norway, Spain, Sweden, Switzerland, and the United Kingdom. The Donor Group meets twice annually to review progress and ensure the effective and efficient use of the contributions that Donor Governments have provided to the Global Compact Trust Fund

The Inter-Agency Team – Seven UN agencies are represented: the Office of the UN High Commissioner for Human Rights the International Labour Organization (ILO), the United Nations Environment Programme (UNEP), the United Nations Office on Drugs and Crime (UNODC), the United Nations Development Programme (UNDP), the United Nations Industrial Development Organization (UNIDO) and the United Nations Entity for Gender Equality and the Empowerment of Women (UN Women). The team is responsible for supporting internalization of the Ten Principles within the UN and UN specialist agencies, and where relevant plays an advisory role in managing the integrity measures complaints procedure

Key activities and phases of development

Helping companies embed universal principles into core business operations and supply chains

One of the most important roles that the UNGC has played has been improving corporate performance in the areas of human rights, labor, the environment and anti-corruption by helping companies to embed and spread the ten principles. This role remains at the core of the UNGC's mission and operational activities. It undertakes the following mutually reinforcing activities in an ongoing effort to enable companies around the globe to more effectively integrate the principles into their core business activities and global supply chains: raising awareness and making the business case; identifying, publishing and disseminating good practices; convening working groups and policy dialogues; and requiring annual reporting on progress.

Raising awareness and making the business case

When the UNGC was first created in 2000, human rights, labor standards and the environment were not areas of focus for most corporate chief executives and boards of directors, despite long-standing work by the UN and a history of corporate scandals related to each of these areas. The UNGC has played an important role in making business leaders more aware of why they matter and how they apply not only to governments, but also to business. The former and current UN Secretary-Generals, along with the heads of the other UN agencies engaged in the UNGC, have committed extensive time and effort in reaching out to the business community to make the case for greater corporate responsibility in the areas of human rights, labor and the environment, and more recently anti-corruption. The UNGC has also been effective in gaining the support of high-profile business leaders to endorse the ten principles on thousands of public platforms around the globe. In addition to the business leaders on its board, the UNGC has been able to attract CEOs and chairmen of major corporations to chair various events and working committees.

For example, an Environmental Stewardship Working Group was established in 2009, co-chaired by Chad Holliday, (former Chairman and CEO of DuPont, current Chairman of the Board of Bank of America and Chairman of the World Business Council for Sustainable Development) and Habiba Al-Marashi, Chair of the Emirates Environmental Group. Sir Mark Moody-Stuart (former Chairman of Anglo American Corporation and CEO of Royal Dutch Shell) co-chairs a Human Rights Working Group with Pierre Sané (former Secretary-General of Amnesty International), which was originally chaired by Mary Robinson (former President of Ireland and former UN High Commissioner for Human Rights). Huguette Labelle, Chair of the NGO Transparency International, chairs a UNGC anti-corruption working group. The voices of these respected leaders have helped to raise awareness of the corporate responsibility to respect human rights, implement labor standards, improve environmental performance, and tackle corruption.

Identifying, publishing and disseminating good practices

Awareness is clearly only the start. Most companies, even the largest, lack the skills, management systems, tools and incentives to actually embed better practices in each of these areas. To help mobilize direct business action, the UNGC has produced a wide range of publications explaining the issues behind the ten principles, making the business case for engagement, providing practical examples of what companies can do to put the principles into practice, and giving guidance on good practice. Typically these publications and guidance tools are the product of business-led UNGC working groups and involve close collaboration with relevant UN specialist agencies and external independent experts. Over the course of a decade the small UNGC team and its growing network of local chapters has worked with *pro bono* consultants, companies and universities to produce and locally adapt hundreds of practical guidance notes and management tools. They are usually supplemented with meetings and online learning resources to facilitate greater adoption and more effective implementation.

In 2009, for example, a *Human Rights and Business Dilemmas Forum* was created as an interactive online tool for companies and their stakeholders to explore complex human rights dilemmas. It was developed by the UNGC and the risk management consultancy Maplecroft, with support from the GE Foundation. The UNGC has also developed an *Environmental Stewardship Model* with Duke University and a cohort of business participants. This explains how to develop a more comprehensive and holistic environmental strategy.[401] These are just two among many examples of practical tools that have been developed through a global network of expert partners to help drive better business performance.

Convening working groups and policy dialogues

The UNGC has also established a variety of working groups and hosted probably over 1,000 dialogues aimed at addressing specific challenges within the pillars of human rights, labor standards, the environment and anti-corruption. Executive Director Georg Kell notes:[402]

> All our work streams are demand-driven . . . Working groups are primarily concerned with the codification of what it means to do no harm and how best to support solutions. The legitimacy of this codification is defined by the process and who takes part in it. Once basic frameworks are defined a phase of learning and sharing tends to follow (tools, workshops etc). Projects and initiatives may emerge at which point a new governance structure may be developed where business tends to take the front seat.

In the area of human rights, for example, UNGC has facilitated ongoing dialogues and working groups to make the business case and to provide business guidance on implementing respect for human rights as well as initiatives focused on specific challenges such as doing business responsibly in zones of conflict, indigenous peoples' rights, children's rights, and business principles. From 2005 to 2011, the UNGC also worked with a number of other business-led corporate responsibility coalitions and the UN's Special Representative on Business and Human Rights, Professor John Ruggie, to support the extensive research and multi-stakeholder consultations that underpinned the development of the UN *Guiding Principles on Business and Human Rights*. These have established for the first time, a common framework and set of normative standards with regard to business and human rights, and have quickly become an authoritative global standard referenced by numerous other inter-governmental institutions, business associations and corporate responsibility coalitions.[403]

In the area of labor standards, the UNGC has focused on: human trafficking; HIV/AIDS; child labour; discrimination; forced labour; and efforts to support unionization and collective bargaining. The main focus of UNGC's research, working groups and policy dialogues in the environmental area are: climate change and carbon management; climate change and development; water stewardship; sustainable consumption; biodiversity; and natural capital measurement and reporting. The anti-corruption work has been implemented in close cooperation with Transparency International, the International Chamber of Commerce and the World Economic Forum, and has focused primarily on bribery, extortion, solicitation, embezzlement and public reporting.

Requiring annual reporting on progress

The UNGC requires all signatory companies to report annually on their progress in implementing the ten principles through the "Communication on Progress" mechanism. This requirement was initiated largely in response to criticisms from civil-society organizations and from within the UN system itself that the UNGC was not doing enough to ensure the accountability and transparency of participating companies. At the same time, some of the most advanced companies also recognized the importance of a more rigorous reporting framework, not only to build trust and legitimacy in relation to their own performance and to the credibility of the UNGC as a voluntary platform, but also to improve opportunities for learning and benchmarking good practice.

The annual Communication on Progress (COP) must include a description of practical actions taken, measurement of outcomes achieved and a statement by the company's CEO expressing his or her continued support. In order to accommodate different levels of business capability and maturity in embedding responsible business practices, and to also encourage companies to constantly improve their performance, the UNGC has established what it terms as the Differentiation Programme. This enables business participants that have submitted a COP to be classified in one of three categories, based on a self-assessment of the COP's content:[404]

- The **Learner Platform** is for companies who submitted a timely COP but did not meet all minimum content requirements. Companies in this category will be given a one-time, 12-month "Learner" period to submit a new COP that meets minimum requirements. The Global Compact office provides these companies with support and assistance

- The **UNGC Active level** is for business participants that fulfill all minimum COP content requirements, which includes addressing all UNGC issue areas and communicating directly with stakeholders

- The **UNGC Advanced level** is for companies that strive to be top performers and declare that they have adopted and report on a range of best practices in sustainability governance and management, based on the *Blueprint for Corporate Sustainability Leadership*, the *UNGC Management Model* and other core UN and Global Compact documents (e.g., the *Guiding Principles on Business and Human Rights* and the *Anti-*

Corruption Reporting Guidance). At the Advanced level, the Global Compact and the Global Reporting Initiative (GRI) are currently exploring synergies between the Differentiation Programme and the GRI Application Level system, to maximize the complementarities of both initiatives

Companies that fail to submit COPs within the 12-month deadline are deemed to have "Non Communicating Status" and can be expelled if they fail to report for two consecutive years. The willingness to enforce this rule and expel non-communicators has grown in recent years: by the end of 2009, nearly 900 had been expelled but this increased to nearly 3,700 by June 2012. In this way, UNGC aims to ensure that participating companies are publicly committed to sustaining good performance and adherence to the ten principles.

Mobilizing business as a strategic partner in international development

While UNGC's foundational goal is to spread implementation of the ten principles through core business operations around the world, it has also provided a valuable platform for companies to learn about and actively support achievement of the MDGs and other UN initiatives aimed at improving the quality of life and well-being of millions of people around the world. Over the course of the past decade, the UNGC has helped to broker and support literally thousands of partnerships between individual companies and UN agencies and programs, often working through its local networks at the country level.

It has also worked closely with some of its most innovative signatory companies, the United Nations Development Programme and other development agencies and corporate responsibility coalitions to explore, promote and implement more inclusive business models. These are core business models that proactively and profitably aim to alleviate poverty by including low-income producers and consumers in key value chains such as agriculture and natural resource development, financial services, healthcare, education and housing. In this area, the UNGC has co-hosted workshops and supported efforts to spread best practice with other business-led coalitions such as the International Business Leaders Forum, World Business Council for Sustainable Development, Business Action for Africa and Business Call to Action.

In addition to supporting project-based partnerships, the UNGC has also helped to engage the business community more broadly in a variety of UN-wide initiatives such as Sustainable Energy for All, Scaling Up Nutrition, Every Woman Every Child, and Education First.[405] It has started to convene an annual Private Sector Forum to coincide with the annual United Nations General Assembly in New York, thus providing a platform for business leaders to come together with heads of state, UN ambassadors, UN agency heads and leaders from civil society to address themes relevant to the General Assembly.

In 2011, the UNGC supported an unprecedented working group co-chaired by UN Secretary-General, Ban Ki-moon, and the CEO of Unilever, Paul Polman, and supported by key UN agencies and programs and some of the world's leading multinational companies to develop a framework to support more large-scale transformative partnerships between the UN and the private sector. The working group undertook research on different models of partnership, identified some of the key obstacles to more effective UN–business alliances, and proposed practical solutions for achieving greater scale and impact in future.[406] Work continues to develop a mechanism for proactively supporting and scaling such partnerships. In 2012, the UN Secretary-General appointed Paul Polman as one of two business leaders, the other being Betty Kania of the Kenya Manufacturers Association, to serve on his High-Level Panel to advise on the UN's post-2015 global development agenda and how to continue to further the MDGs.

In the lead-up to the Rio + 20 Conference, the UNGC played a key role in partnership with the World Business Council for Sustainable Development and the International Chamber of Commerce to create Business Action for Sustainable Development and to host the Rio + 20 Sustainability Forum. These two initiatives convened a wide variety of other corporate responsibility coalitions, trade and industry associations, governments, intergovernmental institutions and NGOs.[407] Over 200 commitments to action were made, together with new initiatives launched through a variety of collective action platforms focused on specific industries and issues.

Driving transformative change through industry- and issue-specific platforms

The UNGC has played a role in helping to achieve greater scale at an industry-wide or issue level through the creation of a number of dedicated leadership platforms. These platforms include the Principles for Responsible Investment initiative, the Principles for Responsible Management Education initiative, the CEO Water Mandate, the Climate Leaders Group, and the Women's Empowerment Principles. Together they convene hundreds of the world's largest companies and business schools, together with UN agencies and in some cases NGOs, around achieving and reporting on a specific set of goals in a specific industry sector or issue area.

The mission of the investor-led **Principles for Responsible Investment initiative** (PRI) is to help investors integrate the risks and opportunities that environmental, social and governance (ESG) issues bring to the investment process. The principles were launched by a small group of investors in 2006 with support from the UNGC in partnership with the United Nations Environment Programme (UNEP) Finance Initiative. As of 2012, over 1,000 investment institutions had become signatories, with assets under management of US$30 trillion.[408] Among other activities, PRI has recently partnered with the Sustainable Stock Exchanges Initiative to embed ESG issues into stock exchange listing requirements, with potential to influence the behavior of thousands of major companies around the globe.

Launched in 2007, the mission of the **Principles for Responsible Management Education initiative** (PRME) is to inspire and champion responsible management education, research and thought leadership globally. As of 2012, some 480 business schools, universities, and academic associations had become signatories to the principles and established several active working groups.[409]

The **CEO Water Mandate** was launched in 2007 and has become a public-private platform to assist companies in the development, implementation, and disclosure of water sustainability policies and practices. As of 2012, it was endorsed by over 80 major corporations from a variety of countries and industry sectors, many of them with an extensive global "water footprint" and part of a vanguard looking at innovative technologies and alliances to enable them to produce more products and services with less water.[410]

The **Caring for Climate initiative** was also launched in 2007 and is jointly convened by UNGC, UNEP and the United Nations Convention on Climate Change (UNCCC), with strategic support from the Carbon Disclosure Project and the Climate Project. It aims to mobilize companies with a track record on energy efficiency and managing carbon emissions to help them improve performance and disclosure within their own operations and value chains, in addition to supporting collective action within specific areas and advocating for effective public policies. Over 300 companies have signed up to the initiative, all at the CEO-level, and are supporting work programs addressing the links between climate change and development, developing low carbon technologies, products, services and business models, improving transparency and disclosure, and supporting the UN's Sustainable Energy for All initiative.[411]

In 2010, the UNGC launched the **Women's Empowerment Principles** to encourage companies to be more explicit and transparent in addressing gender issues in their workplaces, marketplaces and communities. Launched in collaboration with the UN Development Fund for Women (UNIFEM), by 2012 these principles had been endorsed by over 400 CEOs around the world.[412]

It is clear that a CEO signing a commitment is not enough on its own, even if he or she does so publicly. As it does with its ongoing efforts to embed and spread the ten principles in human rights, labor, the environment and anti-corruption, the UNGC and its partners are using these industry- and issue-specific coalitions not only to mobilize corporate signatories, but also: to raise awareness and make the business case; to provide specific guidance, tools and learning mechanisms to help companies embed the relevant principles; to support working groups aimed at tackling particular dilemmas and opportunities on a collective basis; and to encourage greater public disclosure and transparency on corporate performance. While certainly not a panacea to addressing extremely complex and systemic global challenges, these industry- and issue-specific platforms offer a useful model for scaling impact by supporting both individual and collective action through some of the world's largest corporations.

Spreading good practice globally through local networks

The UNGC realized early on that global platforms are necessary but not sufficient for embedding and spreading responsible business practices and new business models to support development goals. Ultimately, action has to happen "on the ground" in the factories, farms, mines and other workplaces, marketplaces and communities where companies operate. Individual multinational companies can embed and spread good practices and innovative new approaches through their own global operations and supply chains. At the same time, in many countries there are great opportunities for companies to learn from each other and to pursue the same type of collective action model described in the previous section in a specific geographic context or cluster. Achieving such on-the-ground action is the core purpose of the UNGC's evolving Local Network platform.

Since its establishment in 2000, the UNGC has been one of the most effective global field-builders described in Chapter 3. The first Local Network was launched in India in 2000 and as of 2012 there were around 100 national or regional networks either established or in development: 76 active networks, of which two are "group" networks (Scandinavian Countries and Gulf States), and 20 networks in development, each from a single country. A study from the Bertelsmann Foundation and UNGC, *A Strategy for the Commons*, launched during the Rio + 20 meetings in 2012 states:

> The Global Compact Local Networks are examples of an interesting new breed of governance structure: business-driven networks for sustainability . . . Most of the nearly 100 Local Networks in countries around the globe have established solid implementation capacities as well as funding sources for basic resources . . . Local Networks in all parts of the world are increasingly becoming forums for collective action and policy dialogue.[413]

The Bertelsmann study argues that the local networks provide five "enablers" for collective action in that they can:

- Establish common ground

- Increase legitimacy

- Ensure implementation capacity

- Organize basic resources

- Connect the local and global levels

In some cases the local network is coordinated by an existing business-led corporate responsibility coalition such as in Austria (respACT), Bolivia (COBORSE), Brazil (Instituto Ethos), Ecuador (CERES), Israel (Maala), South Africa (NBI) and the UK (IBLF). In others, new institutions have been created with support and guidance from the Global Compact, and in some countries new coalitions are just emerging. Over 20 of the local network partners participated in the Rio + 20 Corporate Sustainability Forum, and many of them have made strategic, collective action commitments to implement a range of programs at the country-level.

Harnessing the power of leadership companies

As the UNGC's global reach has grown and it has become the world's largest corporate citizenship initiative, one of the strategic challenges and opportunities it has faced is how to most effectively keep the most advanced companies actively engaged in its activities and in driving the agenda forward. In January 2011, the UNGC launched a new platform for corporate sustainability leadership called **Global Compact LEAD** to offer added-value to these companies. The approximately 50 companies that participate in Global Compact LEAD are challenged to implement a *Blueprint for Corporate Sustainability Leadership*, which was developed in consultation with a number of corporate participants and stakeholders and endorsed by business, governments and civil society at the Leaders Summit in New York in June 2010. The participants in LEAD have been invited to join because they have a history of engagement with the UNGC, locally or globally. They make an additional commitment to share their lessons and results with the broader universe of UNGC participants and are offered: CEO visibility and voice with policy makers; specialized workstreams; engagement opportunities for collective action with governments, UN agencies and NGOs; access to leading intelligence; individualized assistance from the UNGC office; and leadership recognition through profiling.[414]

Figure P11.2 **The UN Global Compact 'Blueprint'**

Source: UN Global Compact

Strengthening capacity of the UN system to partner with the private sector

Another ongoing challenge that the Global Compact is helping to address is how to make it easier for the UN to partner with business, but in a way that respects the UN's intergovernmental governance structure and protects the UN's brand while also respecting the motives and *modus operandi* of the private sector. Over the past decade UNGC has worked with other UN entities to develop common guidelines on working with the private sector and to build management capacity and promote practical steps to achieve this goal. These steps have included:

- One-stop access for business to the UN system through creation of the UN business website (www.business.un.org)

- Creation and secretariat support for the UN Private Sector Focal Points Network (a learning network of people in over 20 UN funds, programs and agencies who are working with the private sector)

- Work between 2010 and 2012 with Unilever, Dalberg, Accenture Development Partnerships and a taskforce of LEAD companies and UN agencies to help develop a dedicated partnership accelerator to help develop more transformative and large-scale systemic alliances with the private sector

Experts who know the UN system well and company representatives with experience of dealing with the UN and its specialist agencies say privately that there remain significant challenges in getting the UN and specialist agencies to partner with the private sector. It is suggested by many that the commitment is there at leadership levels, but the skill and will to engage the private sector or the UN is patchy further down within these organizations given lack of incentives, technical support and time. This partnership challenge is one that requires ongoing focus and engagement.

Impact and lessons learned

In a 2012 article reflecting on the growth of the UNGC, its Executive Director, Georg Kell, identifies and explores four key factors that have contributed to the Global Compact's growth. These can be summarized as:[415]

- **Continued relevance for the initiative's underlying idea.** The basic proposition of the UN Global Compact, which invites businesses to internalize UN values and take action in support of broader UN goals for greater market sustainability, remains as relevant today as it was 12 years ago. Over the last 12 years, the initiative has enjoyed sustained political and institutional support and responded innovatively to a swiftly changing international political, economic and social context

- **Sustained institutional leadership support**. Continued leadership support from two UN Secretary-Generals, Kofi Annan and Ban Ki-moon, and their Assistant Secretary-Generals for Strategic Planning, John Ruggie and Robert Orr, respectively, has been essential to gaining and sustaining the necessary institutional support within the UN system from various UN offices. At the same time, influential figures from academia, business, the media, trade unions and civil society also helped to secure attention and support within the organization

- **Governmental support (political back-up)**. Governments have not only given the UN Global Compact intergovernmental legitimacy, but they have also provided critical financial support to operationalize the underlying concept. Through their soft powers, governments played an instrumental role in creating awareness of the UN Global

Compact at a country level as well as institutionalizing the annual Global Compact Local Network Forums

- **Operational viability**. Ongoing institutional capacity-building has been essential in translating the underlying idea, institutional leadership support and political backing of UN member States into an effective organizational structure that has been able to create space for the interests of the UN and business to overlap while also ensuring a high level of accountability and transparency. As Kell and others note, this continues to be a challenge, but the UNGC has demonstrated the ability to facilitate and experiment with innovative new organizational structures and multi-stakeholder platforms

From the perspective of the UNGC's business participants, there is broad agreement that is has played a valuable role in helping to embed and spread responsible business practices and new models of UN–business partnerships. A McKinsey impact assessment study for the UNGC in 2004 found that:[416]

- Approximately 67% of survey respondents said they had changed their corporate policies in relation to the human rights, labor and environmental principles since joining the Compact, with 40% reporting that the Global Compact was a significant driver of these changes

- The Global Compact has helped to put corporate responsibility on the agenda in the developing world: nearly 67% of survey respondents in the developing world said they joined the Global Compact to become more familiar with corporate responsibility issues

- More than 50% of NGO survey respondents reported that since signing up to the Global Compact they were more engaged in helping companies to solve problems or make decisions in the implementation of the Compact's principles

- The Global Compact has helped to spread the acceptance of business collaboration throughout the UN network and to promote innovative intra-UN partnerships

But the report also noted that "inconsistent participation and divergent and unmet expectations limit the impact on companies" and hinder the Global Compact's credibility. Various concerns have also been raised by academics,[417] civil society[418] and other UN agencies[419] over the years with regard to the UNGC's structure, accountability and scope. These have been summarized by Andreas Rasche, co-author with Georg Kell of a book to mark the Global Compact's tenth anniversary,[420] and by an academic sounding board for the UNGC, in the following three points:

- There are dangers of cooption of the UN by the private sector

- The ten principles are vague and hard to implement

- The UNGC is not accountable because of the lack of verification mechanism for signatories' performance[421]

As outlined earlier in this profile, the UNGC has worked to address these challenges of governance, legitimacy and accountability through: a revision of its governance structure, adding additional checks and balances to ensure the multi-stakeholder nature of the initiative, while continuing to focus on the role of business; the biannual report of the Secretary-General on the work of the UNGC to the UN General Assembly; and the revision of the UNGC's "integrity measures," including expulsion for companies that do not comply with them. In responding to the criticisms of the UNGC contained in a report from the UN's Joint Inspection Unit in 2011, the Vice Chairman of the UNGC Board, Sir Mark Moody Stuart, stated:

> The reports from over six thousand companies cannot be evaluated in detail by a small office. The strength is that they are available in public to be evaluated and checked by society at large, including investors. Such measures allow corporations to be held to account by all their stakeholders, including the major investors who are signatories to the Principles of Responsible Investment, another initiative of the UN Global Compact.[422]

Professors Malcolm McIntosh and Sandra Waddock, long-standing observers of the Global Compact, have also argued:

> The Global Compact has explicitly adopted a learning approach to inducing corporate change, as opposed to a regulatory approach; and it comprises a network form of organization, as opposed to the traditional hierarchic/bureaucratic form. These distinctive (and, for the UN, unusual) features lead the Compact's critics seriously to underestimate its potential, while its supporters may hold excessive expectations of what it can deliver . . . In complex adaptive systems, such as the Global Compact, paradox, ambiguity and surprise are inherent characteristics.[423]

Dr. Steve Waddell concurs with this assessment:

> In 2000, the United Nations launched the UN Global Compact to promote the alignment of business action with the UN's universal principles. In doing so, the UN was at the vanguard, creating a new form of network-based organization. Such organizations are called Global Action Networks (GANs). GANs are multi-stakeholder change networks that are addressing critical global issues. Understanding and supporting the distinctiveness of the UN Global Compact is critical to realizing its full potential.
>
> . . . One of the top priorities for the UNGC is further development of local networks, which are essential to the future of the Global Compact: system-wide change requires transformative activities on the local level. Involving local actors in the governance framework allows integrating contextualized actions on the ground into a coherent framework for institutional change. And another top priority is to continue to develop strategies for the way the UNGC works with others in the UN family. With increased understanding of their comparative strengths and capacities, they will be able to work together to even more effectively develop a new business model and a world more broadly that reflects the UN Principles. [424]

The future

In summary, the UN Global Compact, while not strictly a business-led corporate responsibility coalition due to its location within the United Nations and its multi-stakeholder governance and implementation framework, has been of the most important and far-reaching networks over the past decade in the field of corporate responsibility. It has supported individual companies to embed more responsible business practices within their own operations and supply chains, while also seeding country-based local networks and launching some large scale industry- and issue-specific platforms. In assessing the Global Compact's growth since its launch in 2000, its founding Executive Director, Georg Kell, concludes:

> During the first twelve years of its existence, the UN Global Compact has proven to be a dynamic initiative. Many of its underlying features, such as its network-based nature, which connects global markets with local realities, have significantly shaped the corporate responsibility agenda. In particular, the initiative has helped to successfully integrate the UN system into the global corporate responsibility movement. With the recent introduction of the Differentiation Framework and the Blueprint for Corporate Sustainability Leadership, the UN Global Compact entered into its next phase in which it experiments with managing both quantitative and qualitative growth. Yet, when it comes to accountability based upon a multi-stakeholder framework, the basic assumption remains unchanged: All efforts are shared publicly to stimulate mutual learning and encourage dialogue on corporate practices. To this end, the UN Global Compact will continue to focus on its core objectives – integrating UN values into business operations and mobilizing business action around UN goals for a sustainable and inclusive global economy – while being continuously open to operational innovation emerging from its interaction with the United Nations, governments, the business community, and surrounding contexts.[425]

The UN Global Compact, together with its growing community of Local Network partners, is likely to continue to play an important role in embedding and spreading responsible business practices on-the-ground in numerous countries around the world, including in some of the key emerging markets. At the same time, the industry- and issue-specific coalitions that it has launched offer an innovative model for bringing diverse groups of companies, governments, academic institutions and NGOs together in mutually reinforcing and often self-organizing networks, with light-touch support and coordination from a small central team. While challenges remain in terms of building the individual capacities of diplomats, activists, academics and business people to work together, and the institutional capacities of UN agencies and corporations to form effective and mutually beneficial alliances, the UN Global Compact and its partners illustrate the enormous potential of such collaboration when it comes to tackling complex and systemic global challenges.

Profile 12
World Economic Forum

Jane Nelson and David Grayson[*]

WEF in its own words

The World Economic Forum is an independent international organization committed to improving the state of the world by engaging business, political, academic and other leaders of society to shape global, regional and industry agendas.

www.weforum.org   August 2012

Over the past four decades the World Economic Forum (WEF) has played a strategic leadership role in influencing public- and private-sector agendas on a wide range of socio-economic and political issues. It has done so by identifying emerging trends, providing rigorous analysis and thought-leadership, creating a space for both formal exchanges and informal dialogue, spearheading the introduction of innovative new ideas and technologies, developing platforms for collaborative action both within industry sectors and across business, government and civil society, and supporting the development of outstanding young leaders.

WEF is a multi-stakeholder organization in terms of its mission, governance, funding and membership. The scope of its activities and the topics on which it focuses go far beyond corporate responsibility. As such, it is not strictly a business-led corporate responsibility coalition as defined in Chapter 1 of the book. Yet, from its initial origins as the European Management Forum, WEF has always had a central focus on convening and mobilizing

---

[*] This profile draws extensively on: M. Zwick, A. Reyes and K. Schwab, *The World Economic Forum: A Partner in Shaping History – The First 40 Years 1971–2010* (Geneva: World Economic Forum, 2009, www3.weforum.org/docs/WEF_First40Years_Book_2010.pdf, accessed July 31, 2012). The profile also draws on information from other reports and website materials, and personal engagement with the Forum.

business leaders, and its current 1,000 corporate members play an essential role in shaping and funding the organization's strategic direction and activities in collaboration with leaders from other sectors. From its earliest years, and especially since the anti-globalization protests at the World Trade Organization conference in Seattle in 1999, WEF has also played a crucial role in driving the global corporate responsibility, corporate citizenship, social entrepreneurship and public–private partnership agendas. Its ability to convene and mobilize senior executives and board members of the world's largest corporations, alongside political, academic, media and civil-society leaders, means that WEF has had a profound impact on business leadership and on the work of other corporate responsibility coalitions. As a result, no story about the role of business-led coalitions in promoting corporate responsibility and sustainable capitalism would be complete without exploring the important role of the World Economic Forum.

After briefly outlining the organization's history and its current governance and membership structure, this profile focuses specifically on its leadership role in global corporate citizenship and responsibility. A more detailed year-by-year summary of the first 40 years of WEF is available in the book *The World Economic Forum: A Partner in Shaping History*.[426]

Background context and history

In January 1971, the first European Management Symposium was convened in Davos, Switzerland, by Klaus Schwab, with engagement from the European Commission and several European industrial associations. From the outset, Schwab, then a professor at the University of Geneva, had envisioned a platform that would enable business and political leaders to come together to exchange views, knowledge and ideas in an informal and collegial setting. The European Management Forum was created later that year as a non-profit organization based in Geneva using the surplus funds from the first symposium.

Schwab believed that the managers of a modern enterprise must serve all stakeholders (*die interessenten*), acting as their trustees and charged with achieving the long-term sustained growth and prosperity of the company. He outlined his stakeholder-thinking in a book *Moderne Unternehmensführung im Maschinenbau* (*Modern Enterprise Management in Mechanical Engineering*), which was published in Frankfurt in 1971, making him one of the earliest proponents of stakeholder theory. In 1973, at the third meeting of the European Management Symposium, this stakeholder concept became the cornerstone of a code of ethics that was developed by some of the participants and endorsed in the final session of the meeting. It became known as the *Davos Manifesto* and was one of the first collective articulations by business leaders of the fundamental principles of a corporation's broader economic, social and environmental responsibility to its stakeholders. The Manifesto is outlined in Box P12.1.[427]

The Forum's agenda grew quickly from an initial focus on business strategies and management practices to addressing broader economic, social and political issues of relevance to corporate leaders and their political counterparts. In 1979, with the publication of the first *Report on the Competitiveness of European Industry*, which later became the annual *Global Competitiveness Report*, the Forum established itself as an influential source of strategic

Box P12.1 **Code of Ethics: The Davos Manifesto**

A. The purpose of professional management is to serve clients, shareholders, workers and employees, as well as societies, and to harmonize the different interests of the stakeholders.

B. 1. The management has to serve its clients. It has to satisfy its clients' needs and give them the best value. Competition among companies is the usual and accepted way of ensuring that clients receive the best value choice. The management's aim is to translate new ideas and technological progress into commercial products and services.

B. 2. The management has to serve its investors by providing a return on its investments, higher than the return on government bonds. This higher return is necessary to integrate a risk premium into capital costs. The management is the shareholders' trustee.

B. 3. The management has to serve its employees because in a free society leadership must integrate the interests of those who are led. In particular, the management has to ensure the continuity of employees, the improvement of real income and the humanization of the work place.

B. 4. The management has to serve society. It must assume the role of a trustee of the material universe for future generations. It has to use the immaterial and material resources at its disposal in an optimal way. It has to continuously expand the frontiers of knowledge in management and technology. It has to guarantee that its enterprise pays appropriate taxes to the community in order to allow the community to fulfill its objectives. The management also has to make its own knowledge and experience available to the community.

C. The management can achieve the above objectives through the economic enterprise for which it is responsible. For this reason, it is important to ensure the long-term existence of the enterprise. The long-term existence cannot be ensured without sufficient profitability. Thus, profitability is the necessary means to enable the management to serve its clients, shareholders, employees and society.[428]

insight and analysis. Over time this role has evolved, both in terms of the range and depth of analytical reports produced and the use of innovative technology platforms and more recently social media to disseminate them. This evolution has ensured that WEF's website has become a widely accessed and referenced global knowledge hub.

The geographic reach of the Forum's participants also expanded rapidly from a European-only focus to attendance by business and political leaders from more than 50 countries in the Forum's seventh symposium in 1977. In 1979, the Forum welcomed the first Chinese delegation to Davos. A long-term relationship was initiated with Indian business and political leaders in 1984. As such, WEF has been at the forefront of building relationships between leaders in the OECD countries and in key emerging markets for well over three decades, long before the economic and geo-political significance of the big emerging markets was fully appreciated by most business and political leaders. Every year, the annual meeting in Davos provides a platform for new leaders from both developed and emerging markets, thereby giving them a high-profile and often emotionally charged opportunity to share their vision for the future with a global audience.

In 1987, the European Management Forum changed its name to the World Economic Forum. In the opening session of the annual meeting that year, Professor Schwab captured what continues to be the essence of WEF's mission and influence today, "We must finally behave as what we are – a global community."[429]

In addition to its ongoing mission as a platform for dialogue between leaders from different sectors, the Forum has also provided a space for informal diplomacy to support peace and reconciliation in specific conflict situations. Among the conflicts where WEF has played a bridge-building and brokering role are the Greek-Turkish dispute over Cyprus in the 1980s; facilitating some of the first encounters between leaders of West and East Germany and helping to support the process of German reunification; convening a series of meetings between leaders from Israel and the Palestinian Liberation Organization (PLO) during the 1990s; and hosting the first joint appearance outside South Africa between the newly released Nelson Mandela and then South African President F.W. De Klerk in 1992.

Over the years, WEF has convened an increasing number of high-level meetings around the world beyond the Annual Meeting, which continues to be held each January in Davos (the only exception to date being in 2002, when it was held in New York as a demonstration of solidarity in the aftermath of the 9/11 terrorist attacks). In addition, the Forum hosts annual regional meetings in Latin America, Africa, Europe, East Asia and the Middle East, and regular meetings in the United States, India and Russia, enabling business, political and civil-society leaders at the regional and national levels to delve into the issues and form alliances most relevant to their own location. Since 2007, WEF has also convened an Annual Meeting of the New Champions in China, which has become known as the Summer Davos, and in 2008 it launched the Summit on the Global Agenda, which has been hosted each year since by the United Arab Emirates. The summit is a gathering for over 80 of WEF's Global Agenda Councils, small multi-stakeholder groups consisting of some of the world's leading experts in key issues, industries and geographies, which are described in more detail later in the profile.

In addition to these annual global and regional events, the Forum hosts a variety of industry specific activities, convenes task forces on priority issues and supports practical partnerships for putting ideas into operation on the ground. During its first 40 years of operation, WEF organized over one thousand meetings and convened thousands of task forces and working groups.[430]

WEF's operational model is based on a membership structure. The Forum first introduced a system of membership in 1977 for companies that participated regularly in its activities. In the first year it had just over 70 corporate members. Since then, membership has expanded to over 1,000 Foundation Members drawn from the world's most influential and global corporations. These enterprises rank among the top companies in their industry sector or country in terms of turnover, assets and influence; most have more than US$5 billion in turnover. A select group of 100 of these companies serves as Strategic Partners to WEF, playing a proactive role in identifying priorities, providing financial and in-kind support, and supporting multi-stakeholder partnerships. A larger group of over 300 member companies also serves as Industry Partners, supporting industry-specific leadership agendas in about 20 different industry groups.[431]

In 2007, WEF created a new category of business membership called Global Growth Companies in recognition of the increasingly important role of new start-up firms and companies from emerging markets with the potential to become global industry leaders. These companies demonstrate high growth rates and potential and usually have annual revenues between US$100 million and US$5 billion. In addition, the Forum has a long-standing Technology Pioneers community, comprised of companies that develop transformational technologies with the potential to create business value and social benefit. Recently WEF has worked with the Boston Consulting Group to develop a community of New Sustainability Champions, companies from emerging markets that are developing unconventional solutions to driving more inclusive and sustainable models of economic growth.

In addition to the leading companies that provide the foundational support for all of the Forum's work, WEF has also established dedicated communities for young leaders, social entrepreneurs, women leaders, faith leaders, artists, academics and the media, all of which interact closely with member companies.

The governance of WEF is overseen by three governing bodies: a Foundation Board, an International Business Council (IBC), and an internal Managing Board. The Foundation Board consists of about 30 global business, political, academic and civic leaders and ensures oversight of the Forum's statutes, member selection, financing, strategic direction and activities. The IBC was established in 2002 to serve as an advisory body providing intellectual guidance to WEF and consists of 100 CEOs from a range of industry sectors. The Forum's Managing Board is led by Klaus Schwab as Executive Chairman, supported by a group of eight Managing Directors, who manage several hundred staff from over 50 different countries.

Over the past decade the Forum has also increased its commitment to including more women in its meetings, membership, communities and working groups. In 2006, it launched a seminal annual index entitled the *Global Gender Gap Report*. This benchmarks countries against each other using a set of comparative economic, political, education and health-related criteria to assess gender-based disparities. As of 2012, some 135 countries were included, with 111 countries having been tracked since the outset. Strategic Partners are also strongly encouraged to include senior women executives in their delegations to the annual and regional meetings, and the Forum has established several task forces to improve gender parity, as well as a Global Agenda Council on Women's Empowerment.

Samuel Huntington, the late Harvard political scientist, is credited with having coined the term "Davos Man" to refer to what he regarded as a global elite who, "have little need for national loyalty, view national boundaries as obstacles that thankfully are vanishing, and see national governments as residues from the past whose only useful function is to facilitate the elite's global operations."[432] While Huntington intended the phrase to be derogative, the term has stuck. It is gradually extending to encompass "Davos Man *and* Woman," and to describe an internationalist, activist, multi-sector mind-set; one that has a pre-disposition to sustainable development and recognizes the need for a combination of effective government, responsible and innovative business and an active civil society.

Professor Schwab's vision from the start of the forum in 1971 was focused on the concept of multi-stakeholder participation, collaboration and congenial exchange. Over time this vision has continued to strengthen and has become known and cherished by regular participants as the "Davos Spirit." WEF has been variously described as a meeting-place for deals and ideals, and a catalyst for brokering ground-breaking agreements and initiating on-the-ground collective action. As Kofi Annan, the former UN Secretary-General and member of WEF's Foundation Board wrote in *Time* magazine in 2007:

> A German-born economist, Klaus, turned his meetings at an initially obscure and still hard-to-reach ski resort into an annual event that nurtures understanding and spurs collective action on global issues. With great single-mindedness, he built Davos into a meeting place of business leaders, politicians, religious figures, policy-makers and, more recently, activists, celebrities and younger leaders. Davos entered the global lexicon as a place you went to try out new ideas, confirm trends or launch initiatives. That's why, in 1999, I felt it was the right place to begin my campaign for a voluntary global compact between the UN and world business leaders on respect for human rights, the environment and labor standards. Davos filled a need that was widely felt in a newly globalized world, but it also aroused suspicion among activists and demonstrators. Klaus deftly overcame much of that by inviting the protesters inside the tent. With the help of his wife Hilde, Klaus has kept Davos at the front of things.[433]

The strategic approach of the World Economic Forum is summarized in Figure P12.1. The following section focuses more specifically on some of the leadership roles that WEF has played in directly mainstreaming and scaling the concepts of corporate responsibility and sustainability.

Figure P12.1 **The strategic concept of the World Economic Forum**

Source: Adapted from M. Zwick, A. Reyes and K. Schwab, *The World Economic Forum: A Partner in Shaping History – The First 40 Years 1971–2010* (Geneva: World Economic Forum, 2009): 258

I.   Be the foremost **global multi-stakeholder organization** integrating distinct communities into partnerships

→ Partners/Members *(business)*
(International Business Council, Strategic Partners, Industry Partners, Foundation Members, Global Growth Companies, Technology Pioneers)

→ Constituents *(non-business)*
(Governments and Political Leaders, Labor and NGO Leaders, Global Agenda Councils, Global Issues Group, Media Leaders, Young Global Leaders, Social Entrepreneurs, Global Shapers, Cultural and Spiritual Leaders, Gender Parity Group)

II. Be the foremost global, regional and industry-related **convening place** for our communities.

→ Annual meetings
→ Regional meetings
→ Industry meetings
→ Roundtables

III. Be the catalyst for **knowledge-generating interaction** related to the global, regional and industry agendas

→ Global Agenda Councils
→ Global University Leaders Forum
→ Global Risk Response Network
→ Global Benchmarking Networks

IV. Be committed to **improving the state of the world** by shared problem definition, shared search for solutions and cooperative action.

→ e.g. Projects, initiatives, taskforces

Key activities and phases of development

Professor Schwab has addressed corporate responsibility and citizenship as an integral element of the WEF agenda from the outset, with his emphasis on stakeholder theory and commitment to bringing together business leaders with their counterparts in other sectors to address societal challenges. In 1997, he explained his views in an article in the *International Herald Tribune*, co-written with former WEF Managing Director Claude Smadja:

> Corporations need to give new meaning to the old notion of corporate responsibility. Business leaders will have to strike a new balance between the imperative of anticipating fast changes and the need for a long-term view, even if it sometimes means resisting the pressure for instant shareholder gratification. Managing the shareholder–stakeholder equation is more than ever a critical priority.[434]

WEF has given practical effect to this vision in a number of ways. The following examples of activities illustrate only a fraction of the work that WEF and its members have undertaken on issues that have directly or indirectly addressed the role of business in society and aimed to promote more responsible and sustainable business practices.

Creating a space for formal and informal cross-sector dialogue

WEF has developed a highly effective model for enabling business leaders to engage with their counterparts in both formal and informal settings. The official agenda for the annual meeting, regional meetings and other events usually consists of a combination of keynote speeches, panels and creative working sessions and implementation design discussions. As social media have become an important communication tool around the world and as WEF has aimed to become more inclusive, while retaining exclusiveness in the physical number of people attending its meetings, the Forum has started to partner with a wide range of traditional and social media platforms to provide print and broadcast coverage, webcasts, video blogs, Twitter feeds and other forms of online access to selected speeches and panels throughout its meetings. It also provides written summaries of many of the sessions on the official event agenda.

A small selection of the seminal speeches made at Davos over the past two decades that have directly addressed the topic of corporate responsibility and new models of partnership between business and other sectors are profiled in Box P12.2.

In addition to the wide-ranging official agenda at WEF meetings, there is also an extensive agenda of private meetings and working breakfasts, lunches and dinners. Some of these are hosted by WEF and many of them by its Strategic and Industry Partners. Most of these sessions bring together business, government, academic and civil-society leaders to tackle specific issues, and many of them have led to ongoing practical multi-stakeholder partnerships that have an impact on the ground. Some examples of recent multi-stakeholder partnerships over the past decade are illustrated later in this profile.

The Forum also hosts Governors Meetings, which bring together corporate chairmen, CEOs and presidents within specific industry groups in a private setting where they can discuss key trends and strategic issues most relevant to their own industry. The agendas for these meetings are set by the CEOs themselves, who take turns chairing the group for an agreed

Box P12.2 **Examples of speeches at Davos focused on corporate responsibility and new models of partnership**

In 1992, HRH The Prince of Wales used his speech to WEF to promote the concept of public-private partnerships, drawing on his experience as President of Business in the Community and of the International Business Leaders Forum:

> Business is uniquely well placed to take a lead and to get things done, but in partnership with local communities, governments, non-governmental organizations and other representatives of the voluntary sector.[435]

In 1998, Hillary Clinton challenged the business community to meet its social responsibilities:

> There are many large problems that confront us as a world. It is impossible to think of any corporation, no matter how large, or any government, no matter how powerful, addressing these alone. Whether we like it or not, we are more interdependent today than we have ever been. I believe that interdependence is a good development. And it should be respected by governments and businesses alike. Because through it we can meet mutual challenges of environmental degradation or security threats, and we can also work together to help build up strong, functioning markets, governments and civil societies.[436]

In 1999, Kofi Annan issued his call to action that led to the creation of the UN Global Compact:

> I want to challenge you to join me in taking our relationship to a still higher level. I propose that you, the business leaders gathered in Davos, and we, the United Nations, initiate a global compact of shared values and principles, which will give a human face to the global market.[437]

In 2008, Microsoft founder and global philanthropist, Bill Gates, outlined his vision of Creative Capitalism:

> it's the interaction between a company's principles and its commercial competence that shape the kind of business it will be. The challenge here is to design a system where market incentives, including profits and recognition, drive those principles to do more for the poor. I like to call this idea creative capitalism, an approach where governments, businesses, and nonprofits work together to stretch the reach of market forces so that more people can make a profit, or gain recognition, doing work that eases the world's inequalities.[438]

period of time. External experts are also invited to participate in certain sessions. Over the years, the corporate responsibility and sustainability focus of the forum's Governors Groups has been strengthened. Most of them now address strategic corporate responsibility risks and opportunities for their industry. In several cases they have not only put sustainability issues at the heart of the agenda for discussion in Davos, but also started multi-stakeholder projects on the ground and engaged in public-policy dialogue at major international events such as the G8, G20 and global climate change negotiations hosted by the UN Framework Convention on Climate Change (UNFCCC). Some examples of these alliances are outlined later in the profile.

Several hundred official and private sessions that are hosted at a typical WEF meeting are supplemented by thousands of scheduled one-to-one meetings between participating individuals and institutions. Of equal importance, the physical layout of the main conference center and numerous hotels where meetings are hosted, along with the regular shuttle bus service between locations, and a wide array of both official and private social events means that there is a high opportunity for random, "chance encounters" between CEOs and senior executives of major corporations, political and intergovernmental leaders, social entrepreneurs, non-governmental leaders and activists, academics, artists and faith leaders. In many ways, it is these random encounters between leaders from very different sectors and with differing world views that creates and sustains the "Spirit of Davos."

While there is no available data on the outcomes of such encounters, it is likely that a significant number of new partnerships and constructive relationships between companies, governments, UN agencies, and civil-society organizations have emerged as a result. The structure of WEF meetings and their multi-stakeholder nature, where all invited participants are there on a equal footing, allows for "unusual dialogues" between leaders from different sectors whose paths may not often cross, and these in turn often lead to "unusual alliances," given that the people who are meeting all have decision-making power to make things happen when they return home.

It was at Davos, for example, that the former CEO of Unilever, Niall Fitzgerald, agreed with the CEO of Oxfam Great Britain, Barbara Stocking, that they would work together to understand the impact that a multinational company such as Unilever has on poverty alleviation in a specific country. This led to a pioneering impact assessment of Unilever's operations in Indonesia, and subsequent country assessments for South Africa and Vietnam.[439] Likewise, the former Director of the World Food Programme, Josette Sheeran, inspired a number of food and beverage companies to get more engaged in partnerships to support food security and nutrition. Bill Gates and the pop singer Bono challenged companies in the health sector and beyond to get more engaged in advocating for and providing resources to support the global health agenda. Many similar anecdotal examples of specific cross-sector encounters and resulting partnerships exist. A number of these have led to strategic alliances and networks of cooperation that have developed far beyond the WEF event and dialogue that initiated them.

Analyzing trends and shaping the global agenda

From its early years, the World Economic Forum has focused on being not only a convener for dialogue between business and other sectors, but also a thought leader and agenda setter. It has played this role by identifying and promoting a variety of global issues and trends, and producing hundreds of research reports that are widely disseminated by the Forum itself and its member companies and research partners. A growing number of these reports are related directly to the role of business in driving more inclusive and sustainable models of growth. In addition, Professor Schwab and many of the Forum's directors are regular contributors to the media and to high-level commissions on the changing role of business in society.

In almost all its analysis and research activities, the Forum has worked with leading academics, consultants, policy think-tanks and other business-led coalitions and associations. It has also tapped into the research and strategy departments of its member companies, thereby accessing some of the world's best resourced and most innovative thinking and analysis. Every year WEF also invites a wide range of individual academics and people in its various communities to respond to surveys on global trends, risks and issues. This highly leveraged approach has enabled the Forum to demonstrate the enormous potential of collaborative research platforms and trend assessment. WEF has been particularly successful in harnessing considerable *pro bono* research support from major global consulting firms such as McKinsey & Co., the Boston Consulting Group, Accenture, KPMG, PwC, Deloitte and Ernst & Young.

The best example of this strategic approach to accessing and then sharing the ideas and intellectual capital of the world's leading experts is demonstrated by WEF's Network of the Global Agenda Councils (GACs), which was created in 2008. The Forum's vision in creating the network was to engage the very best minds from various stakeholder and geographic perspectives to allow the best knowledge to emerge and enable the exploration of cross-cutting themes. In an environment marked by short-term views and "thinking in silos," the network is intended to foster long-range interdisciplinary approaches to shaping viable solutions. Each GAC consists of 12 to 30 of the most innovative thinkers on a specific issue, industry or region. They confer every quarter, with three of the meetings conducted virtually through the Forum's online WELCOM (World Economic Leaders Community) system. The fourth meeting is held in person in Dubai at the Global Agenda Summit and the Chair of each GAC attends the Annual Meeting in Davos. There are now over 80 GACs that serve as an active "brains trust" for WEF's activities.

Numerous reports published by the Forum in partnership with its network of research and corporate partners look at specific aspects of corporate responsibility, global citizenship, creating shared value, public–private partnerships and sustainability. In addition to hundreds of issue, industry and country specific reports, the Forum produces three seminal annual reports, the *Global Competitiveness Report,* the *Global Risks Report*, and the *Global Gender Gap Report*. Over the years, all three of these have tracked the growing materiality and strategic importance of social and environmental issues to business, in addition to economic and political trends. WEF has also established a specific competence in scenario planning, and again has been able to tap into its multi-stakeholder membership base to produce scenarios for a variety of countries, regions and industry sectors.

Specifically in terms of corporate responsibility and citizenship, WEF ran a workstream from 2000 to 2010 in partnership with a core group of its member companies and with the International Business Leaders Forum (IBLF) (and later AccountAbility, Business for Social Responsibility and the Corporate Social Responsibility Initiative at Harvard Kennedy School). This Corporate Citizenship work program played a valuable thought-leadership role by adding the credibility of WEF's brand and influence and the CEO-level engagement of some of its leading member companies to support growing efforts around the world to mainstream the concept of corporate responsibility from traditional philanthropy into core business strategy and operations.

In 2002, for example, over 40 prominent CEOs endorsed the statement *Global Corporate Citizenship: The Leadership Challenge for CEOs and Boards*, which was written in cooperation with the IBLF.[440] The statement emphasized that a company's impact on society and its relationships with stakeholders are fundamental to core business operations and should be directly addressed by CEOs and Boards of Directors. In 2004, the Global Corporate Citizenship Initiative published *Values and Value: Communicating the Strategic Importance of Corporate Citizenship to Investors*, also written in cooperation with the IBLF.[441] Based on extensive interviews, the report explored how CEOs, chief financial officers and investor relations officers are starting to communicate the strategic importance of the social and environmental aspects of their firm's performance to investors. In total, a series of about eight reports were produced by the broadly focused Global Corporate Citizenship Initiative before its work was mainstreamed into more issue and industry specific activities after 2010.

Building multi-stakeholder partnership platforms to take action

While WEF's membership model (foundation members, strategic partners, industry partners and global growth companies) means that the business sector has been, and remains, the solid foundation on which everything else has been built, the Forum always emphasizes that it is a multi-stakeholder community. Partnership both within and among sectors has been at the heart of the WEF agenda since the early years. For a period of almost a decade, WEF also had a Centre for Public–Private Partnerships, which engaged businesses, civil society and political authorities in specific initiatives ranging from health in India to alliances combating chronic hunger in Africa. Today, public–private partnerships have become mainstreamed into most aspects of the Forum's work. The following examples illustrate a few of the Forum's most strategic ongoing multi-stakeholder partnership platforms.

The New Vision for Agriculture (NVA)

One of the most significant and comprehensive global, regional and national partnership platforms that WEF has developed to-date has been in the area of agriculture and food security. Launched in 2009, the New Vision for Agriculture (NVA) built on several years of research, dialogue, and some pilot projects, with an initial brainstorming in Davos in January 2006 between Kofi Annan and corporate CEOs exploring how business could address hunger. Led by WEF's Consumer Industries community, the NVA works to develop a shared agenda for action and to foster multi-stakeholder collaboration and new investment at the country level aimed at achieving more sustainable agricultural growth through market-based solutions. The initiative has defined a vision that highlights agriculture's potential as a positive driver of food security, environmental sustainability and economic opportunity. Led personally by the CEOs of major food and beverage companies and the Heads of State and Ministers of Agriculture in participating countries, and supported by a variety of donor agencies, research partners and non-profit organizations, the NVA has mobilized country-level alliances in Tanzania, Vietnam, Mexico, Indonesia, and India, and a regional partnership in sub-Saharan Africa called Grow Africa. It has also provided substantial policy input to food security initiatives launched by the G20 and G8. As of mid-2012, the NVA was supported by 28 global corporate champions, 14 government partners, and well over 30 other partners, as well as a growing number of domestic companies in the countries where it operates.

The NVA is playing a crucial leadership role at several levels. First, it has worked with McKinsey and participating companies to create a shared vision and develop a clear six-part roadmap for taking practical action.[442] It has used applied examples to raise awareness of the potential of market-based approaches to sustainable agriculture. It has made sure its goals are aligned with national public policies and has highlighted the vital leadership role of national governments. It has started to mobilize investment dollars and develop innovative financing mechanisms. For example, the *Grow Africa* partnership worked with others to provide a platform and African leadership to help develop the US$3 billion in private-sector commitments that formed part of the G8's New Alliance for Food Security and Nutrition, launched by President Obama in May 2012. NVA has also demonstrated how companies can play a leadership role both individually through their own value chains and collectively through transformational pre-competitive partnerships focused on specific geographic corridors or agricultural commodities. While still at an early stage, NVA is illustrating the potential for achieving systemic impact across different sectors, geographies and commodities.

The Global Health Initiative (GHI)

The GHI was launched in 2002 by the former UN Secretary-General Kofi Annan. Its initial purpose was to engage companies across industries, together with governments, and international and non-governmental organizations to systematically fight infectious diseases, in particular HIV/AIDS, tuberculosis and malaria, and to strengthen health systems with a focus on Africa, India and China. The GHI has worked in partnership with leading healthcare companies, other major corporations with operations in these regions, the Bill & Melinda Gates Foundation, the World Health Organization, UNAIDS and the World Bank, among others, to implement a strategy of advocacy, dialogue and partnerships. It has developed toolkits and guidelines to assist companies in setting up workplace programs. It has commissioned research and hosted high-level advocacy events to ensure that global health stays on the international community's agenda. And it has created public–private partnerships at both the country and project level to leverage each partner's skills and resources for optimum impact on the ground.

By 2010, the GHI could claim to have worked with some 170 companies representing over 10 million workers in Africa and Asia. Its India Business Alliance to Stop TB had reached over 4 million people and its work on HIV/AIDS in Africa, which focused on engaging national business coalitions with governments, donors and non-profit organizations, focused on 15 key countries, which represented close to 47% of the burden of disease at that time.[443] WEF has also provided a valuable platform for other global health partnerships, such as the Global Alliance for Vaccines and Immunization (GAVI Alliance) and the Global Alliance for Improved Nutrition (GAIN) to raise awareness and resources from the business community. While WEF continues to provide a platform for advocating on the need to tackle infectious diseases, its health agenda has also expanded to address issues such as chronic disease and wellness, mobile health services and the impact of aging.

The Responsible Mineral Development Initiative (RMDI)

The RMDI was launched in 2010, recognizing the large-scale and economically important role that mining plays in many emerging markets, the governance challenges often associated with ensuring that the substantial benefits of mining reach local communities and citizens, and the high levels of public mistrust often associated with mining activities. The RMDI has been led by the CEOs in the Mining and Metals Governors steering board, and supported by an advisory group and WEF's Global Agenda Council on the Future of Mining and Metals, with *pro bono* support provided by the Boston Consulting Group and input from the International Council of Mining and Metals, various government bodies and mining associations. It set out to develop a clear understanding of the views, priorities and concerns of key stakeholders in mineral development and then to develop a practical framework and set of good practices for ensuring better governance and socioeconomic and environmental impacts from mining.

During the first phase in 2010, the project group carried out over 250 interviews in 13 countries and four continents and identified key issues both at the country level and globally. In the second phase, 14 practical workshops were held on six continents with more than 300 participants from all sectors. The WEF project team worked with its partners to develop a practical framework of six building blocks to advance responsible mineral development, illustrating each one with specific examples of good practice and proposals for action.[444] The initiative is now piloting a series of country and regional "RMDI platforms" which will bring together senior levels of government, executives from major extractives companies, other business coalitions, donors, and key members of civil society to discuss how value is created within mining, identify key areas of priority, develop opportunities for collaboration, and implement a process to track and measure initiatives aimed at addressing these priorities and driving shared value creation.

The three examples outlined above are only a sample of the multi-stakeholder partnership platforms that WEF has convened and catalyzed over the past few decades. Others include:

- The **Partnering Against Corruption Initiative** (PACI), which was started in 2004 by WEF members in the energy, mining and construction sectors. Today it has over 170 signatory companies across all sectors and works closely with Transparency International, the United Nations Global Compact, the OECD and the International Chamber of Commerce, among others, to make the business case, develop toolkits and guidelines to improve corporate performance, and build public–private partnerships at the country level in key sectors and markets[445]

- The **Global Education Initiative,** which has directly impacted some 1.8 million students and teachers and mobilized over US$100 million in resources for projects in Jordan, India, Egypt, Palestine and Rwanda, working in partnership with some 40 companies from the information technology and other sectors, 14 governments, seven international agencies, and 20 non-profit organizations[446]

- The **Water Initiative,** which works with the Forum's members, governments and environmental groups to develop more systemic approaches for managing future water needs for agriculture, industry, human health and the environment. Among other activities, the initiative has analyzed the complex water–energy–food–climate nexus; has helped to catalyze the innovative Water Resources Group, which is now managed by the International Finance Corporation; and has developed both analytical toolkits and public–private partnerships focused on improving the management of watersheds in India, Jordan, Mexico, South Africa and Mongolia

- The **Green Growth Action Alliance,** launched at the Business 20 Summit at the G20 in Mexico in June 2012. This aims to help address the shortfall in green infrastructure investment, estimated at up to $1 trillion per year, by leveraging public and private investment, testing new financing and business models and providing policy input into clean energy, transport, agriculture and other green growth investments. GGAA is already supported by nearly 50 leading energy companies, financial institutions, and development finance institutions.[447]

Building global leadership capacity and networks

Over the past two decades, the World Economic Forum has also established several communities and initiatives focused on identifying, developing and networking outstanding young leaders and social entrepreneurs, as well as bringing their fresh and often challenging perspectives to WEF's more established meetings and dialogues.

In 1993, the Forum launched the Global Leaders of Tomorrow (GLT) community, to bring next-generation leaders to share their views at selected WEF meetings. In 2004, building on the lessons and ideas generated by 11 classes of GLTs, WEF created the Forum of Young Global Leaders (YGL) as an independent not-for-profit foundation under Swiss law. Every year thousands of leaders under the age of 40 are nominated from diverse regions and sectors. Shortlisted nominations are evaluated by Heidrick & Struggles, a leading executive search and leadership consulting firm, and final candidates are screened by a selection committee. The process identifies young leaders who already have a record of extraordinary achievement, a demonstrated commitment to serve society, a global perspective, self-awareness and desire to learn, and high standing in their community. Between 100 and 200 people are selected each year to become part of this global network. They participate in the program for five years, after which they can join an alumni community.

Once selected, the young leaders sign the YGL Charter of rights and responsibilities and participate in an intense program of dedicated YGL events and leadership training, as well as many of WEF's own meetings, including the Annual Meeting. Among other activities, they participate in a tailored leadership development program at Harvard Kennedy School. They also engage in a variety of task forces and collective action initiatives. In recent years, projects have included a YGL Water Initiative, which aims to raise awareness among young people about the use of water, a de-worming project in Kenya, efforts to promote entrepreneurship in Africa and the Arab World, and an initiative aimed at helping to keep children in school. As one of the YGLs from the business community, Andy Wales, Head of Sustainable Development at SABMiller, comments:

> The Young Global Leaders bring a great dynamism and freshness to the wider work of the World Economic Forum. As substantial leaders in their own right, with extensive networks and established reputations, they offer expert insights to the Forum's work as well as benefiting from the contributions of the many global leaders they interact with. YGL passion and entrepreneurial spirit ensures that, in its work, the Forum is always aware of the need for action on the ground.[448]

In 1998, Klaus and Hilde Schwab created a foundation to identify and support outstanding social entrepreneurs and promote the concept of social entrepreneurship. The Schwab Foundation for Social Entrepreneurship, which started its activities in 2000, is a separate institution from the World Economic Forum, but the two organizations work closely together. At the time of its establishment, the concept of "social entrepreneurship" was little known in most of the world, although it was beginning to emerge thanks primarily to the work of Bill Drayton and Ashoka, the organization dedicated to social entrepreneurship which he founded in 1980.[449] The work of the Schwab Foundation has helped to further raise awareness of the important role of social entrepreneurship by identifying, selecting, networking and promoting the work of some of the world's leading social entrepreneurs. From 2001 to 2008, the foundation organized an annual global Social Entrepreneurs' Summit. Selected social entrepreneurs have also been integrated into the World Economic Forum's own events and initiatives since 2002, thereby connecting them with global business, political and media leaders. Between 30 and 50 social entrepreneurs participate in the Annual Meeting every year. They have taken on active roles in the official program and also participate as partners in a number of WEF's multi-stakeholder partnership platforms.

In 2005, WEF launched an innovative internal initiative for outstanding young employees, the Global Leadership Fellows Programme. Gilbert Probst, its founding Dean and Managing Director of WEF's Leadership Office and Academic Affairs, describes it as follows:

> The programme takes a step towards finding the next generation of leaders, not only to address the future of the Forum's own management and governance, but also that of the world as a whole. It is a three-year programme that combines a position at the Forum with several weeks per year of intensive training and development, one-on-one coaching and mentoring, and in-depth knowledge of industry, civil society and government. It integrates academic courses from a cluster of the world's top universities with regular study modules either at "home" in Geneva or at the Forum's meetings across the globe. The objective is to train generalists: well-rounded professionals who work easily in complex environments by bringing different perspectives to help solve common problems.[450]

Typically, about half of the young executives who complete the program stay with the Forum and are expected to assume leadership positions internally. The other half of the Fellows, having completed the program, leave the Forum to take up leadership positions in member companies, governments, or international organizations, which is one of the Forum's most direct contributions towards achieving its mission. The program works closely with five academic partners: Insead, London Business School, Columbia University, Wharton and Ceibs.

In 2011, WEF launched another innovative leadership development program called the Global Shapers Community, supported by the Coca-Cola Company, DST Global and Reliance Industries. This is a creative and largely self-organizing network of city-based Hubs, which are developed and led by selected young leaders between the ages of 20 and 30 who commit to undertake projects in their own communities. They get the opportunity to connect with WEF's other communities and events, and already total over 1,600 young leaders working through 195 Hubs around the globe, with a particularly strong presence in Africa and Latin America.

Impact and lessons learned

Over the past 40 years, WEF can claim to have had a major influence and impact, both direct and indirect, on a wide range of political and business issues, including corporate responsibility and sustainability. Throughout its history it has managed to remain at the forefront of emerging trends, new technologies, and innovative models of partnership, and thereby helped its members to identify, debate and increasingly take practical action on addressing complex global challenges.

Christine Lagarde, Managing Director of the International Monetary Fund and a long-term Davos participant, has described WEF as an "agora," referring to the "gathering place, the center of athletic, artistic, spiritual and political life of the ancient Greek city-states." Peter D. Sutherland, a former EU Commissioner, Director of what is now the World Trade Organization, and Chairman of Goldman Sachs, has stated that "The Forum is far more than a forum. It provides objective expertise, and it is in this area that its continued development is crucial in helping to shape the global, regional and industry agendas."[451]

In recent decades, the World Economic Forum has become a leading catalyst of multi-stakeholder partnerships. It now operates a portfolio of partnership initiatives aimed at achieving more systemic impact, and improving policy and governance on key global and regional challenges. As WEF's official history of its first 40 years concludes:

> There is increasing need for a place in the international system where official, private sector, academic and civil society thinkers and decision-makers can work together on common concerns in a way that transcends intellectual and professional boundaries and is free from traditional constraints of intergovernmental protocol and corporate competitive pressures. The Forum's independence, informality and convening power enable it to provide the flexible, neutral space necessary for partnership – and a sense of global citizenship – to flourish.[452]

In terms of corporate responsibility, the Forum has been a significant player championing both the concept and the practice of global corporate citizenship and influencing the actions of hundreds of companies and other business-led coalitions around the world. Professor Schwab clarified the idea of "global corporate citizenship" in an article he authored in *Foreign Affairs* magazine in 2008:

> Global corporate citizenship goes beyond the concepts of corporate philanthropy, including social investing; corporate social responsibility; and corporate social entrepreneurship in that it entails focusing on "the global space," which is increasingly shaped by forces beyond the control of nation-states. Global corporations have not only a license to operate in this arena but also a civic duty to contribute to sustaining the world's well-being in cooperation with governments and civil society. Global corporate citizenship means engagement at the macro level on issues of importance to the world: it contributes to enhancing the sustainability of the global marketplace. Global corporate citizenship refers to a company's role in addressing issues that have a dramatic impact on the future of the globe, such as climate change, water shortages, infectious diseases, and terrorism. Other challenges include providing access to food, education, and information technology; extreme poverty; trans-national crime; corruption; failed states; and disaster response and relief. Each of these problems is global in scope, even if the solutions may be locally focused.[453]

The future

The World Economic Forum has provided the intellectual case for global corporate citizenship and public–private partnerships, brought this case to the attention of business leaders and their counterparts from other sectors, worked with them to craft a practical agenda for action, and then provided vehicles for engagement both within industry sectors and across sector boundaries. It has played an important role in raising awareness of the changing expectations and role of business in society. It has helped companies to embed more responsible and sustainable business practices in their own operations and to scale their impact and achieve more systemic solutions by working in partnership with others.

As WEF looks to the future, it continues to shape the agenda on emerging issues of relevance to the long-term success of its members – topics such as the water–food–energy–climate nexus, sustainable consumption, more effective strategies for integrated risk management and resilience, development of more inclusive and reliable financial systems, youth employment, urbanization, and the impact of global aging. It remains committed to playing a role as a forum for cross-sector dialogue and as a thought leader and agenda-setter, while also becoming increasingly focused on supporting practical transformational partnerships that can point to direct impact and large-scale results on the ground. And probably most critical for the future, the World Economic Forum remains committed to working with current leaders from all sectors, while being increasingly proactive in identifying and networking young leaders below the age of 40 who are already demonstrating their ability to make a difference today and in the future.

Appendix 1
Corporate responsibility time-line

	Business-led corporate responsibility coalitions	Responsible business
1970	• Philippine Business for Social Progress (PBSP)	• Polluter Pays Principle – OECD – arguing that those companies that pollute should pay
1971	• World Economic Forum (WEF) set up as European Management Forum (EMF)	
1972		• UN Conference on Human Environment
1974	• World Environment Center (WEC) • IPIECA	
1975		• 3M Pollution Prevention Pays (3P) program
1977	• Urban Foundation, South Africa	• USA: Council on Economic Principles – rating companies on their social & environmental performance • Sullivan Principles • A.C. Pocock, Shell Managing Director, delivers Ashridge lecture on need for big business to support enterprise promotion and small business development • USA: Ethics Resource Center founded • U.S. Federal Corrupt Practices Act passed
1978	• Project on Corporate Responsibility (Minnesota)	
1980		• Anglo-American Sunningdale Conference on Business and Urban Regeneration • World Consumer Study released by IUCN
1981	• ADEC Paraguay	

	Business-led corporate responsibility coalitions	**Responsible business**
1982	• BITC, UK • Scottish Business in the Community • Project on Corporate Responsibility becomes Minnesota Center for Corporate Responsibility	• Tylenol contamination scare in USA prompts pharmaceutical companies to develop tamper-resistant packaging in response to new FDA standards for drug safety
1983		
1984	• CEDICE, Venezuela	• Bhopal chemical disaster, India
1985	• Responsible Care (chemical industry) launched, Canada • WEC Gold Medal Award • Tucumán, Argentina • Jobs and Society, Sweden • EMF becomes World Economic Forum • PNBE, Brazil (precursor of Instituto Ethos)	
1986	• IMS–Entreprendre pour la Cité, France	• Guinness insider trading scandal UK • Institute of Business Ethics launched in UK. • Caux Round Table • Markkula Center for Applied Ethics, University of Santa Clara • Boston College Center for Corporate Citizenship
1987	• Social Venture Network, USA	• Brundtland Commission report on sustainable development, *Our Common Future*, coins the term "sustainable development" • Montreal Protocol to protect ozone layer
1988	• CEMEFI, Mexico	• *The Green Consumer Guide*, John Elkington and Julia Hailes
1989	• Portman Group, UK • Council for Better Corporate Citizenship, Japan	• The Natural Step think-tank for the promotion of sustainability in core business strategy • Exxon Valdez tanker ruptures off Alaskan coast • Ceres Principles established (initially named Valdez Principles)
1990	• BITC's HRH the Prince of Wales Seeing is Believing program begins • Abrinq Foundation, Brazil • International Business Leaders Forum (IBLF) • Business Council for Sustainable Development (later becoming WBCSD)	• Professor Charles Handy's Royal Society of Arts Lecture ("What is a Company for?") sets out a vision for making companies more sustainable • Forest Stewardship Council initial scoping meeting

	Business-led corporate responsibility coalitions	**Responsible business**
1991	• First meeting of Business Council for Sustainable Development takes place in The Hague	• Café Direct is founded • Amnesty Business Group • Business decide to participate in the UN Conference on Environment and Development for the first time with NGOs and governments on a new global platform to help guide world affairs • International Chamber of Commerce launches Business Charter for Sustainable Development
1992	• The Minnesota Principles • Formation of BSR including early members such as Ben & Jerry's and Tom's of Maine • Stephan Schmidheiny and the BCSD: *Changing Course: A Global Business Perspective on Development and the Environment* • BCSDs are launched in Argentina, El Salvador and Philippines • International Hotels Environment Initiative (IHEI) • Hungarian Business Leaders Forum	• United Nations Earth Summit in Rio
1993	• Thailand Business Coalition on AIDS • Czech Business Leaders Forum • ICC forms The World Council for Environment (WICE) • St. Petersburg Initiative (IBLF)	• Canada launches the Whitehorse Mining Initiative, one of the first multi-stakeholder initiatives to officially acknowledge that companies would be compelled to deal with sustainable development issues as well as establishing a sustainable vision for the industry • Transparency International • Forest Stewardship Council formal launch
1994	• Peru 2021 • Social Venture Network Europe • Bob Dunn selected as BSR President and CEO and moves BSR HQ from Washington, DC, to San Francisco • Polish Business Leaders Forum	• SustainAbility coins phrase "triple bottom line" • *Financial Times* publishes its first report on Responsible Business in cooperation with IBLF • Minnesota Principles integrated with European and Japanese concepts to form Caux Round Table Principles of Business
1995	• Merger of BITC and Action Resource Centre • WICE merged with BCSD to form the World Business Council for Sustainable Development (WBCSD)	• Shell forced to back down on scrapping of Brent Spar oil rig through environmental pressure • Anti-Shell Nigeria Campaign by Body Shop and others • RSA *Tomorrow's Company* report

	Business-led corporate responsibility coalitions	Responsible business
1995 *(cont.)*	• 20 business leaders and Jacques Delors adopt European Business Declaration against Social Exclusion • Canadian Business for Social Responsibility Sodalitas, Italy • KÖVET, Hungary • Empresa y Sociedad • National Business Initiative formed from merger of Urban Foundation and Consultative Business Movement, South Africa	• UK Pensions Act
1996	• CSR Norway • WBCSD, UNEP and Coca-Cola launch program on financial indicators of sustainable development • CSR Europe established (initially as the European Business Network for Social Cohesion)	• AccountAbility launched as the Institute for Social and Ethical AccountAbility • Anti-Nike "sweatshops" campaign • Campaign against BP Colombia and security/human rights issues • ISO 14001 formally adopted as voluntary initiative standard for corporate environmental management systems • Global Water Partnership
1997	• Croatia BCSD • Bangladesh Business Forum • Brazilian Business Council for Sustainable Development • Forum Empresa established • Danish Government conference on social cohesion • CSR Europe's European Year against Racism • BSR website goes live • WBCSD's Rio +5 Progress Report *Signals of Change* and book *Eco-Efficiency*	• Global Reporting Initiative • Marine Stewardship Council set up by Unilever and WWF • *Cannibals with Forks*, John Elkington • BP's John Browne calls for climate change action in speech at Stanford Graduate School of Business • Kyoto Protocol adopted • Toyota unveils the Prius • Ethical Trading Initiative
1998	• Belgian Business and Society • Business Trust created, South Africa • Instituto Ethos de Empresas e Responsabilidade Social (Ethos Institute for Corporate Social Responsibility), Brazil • Copenhagen Centre for Corporate Responsibility • Launch of CSR Europe's online resource center • WBCSD Virtual University in collaboration with Copenhagen University and Norwegian School of Management • The GHG Protocol formed by the world Resources Institute and WBCSD	• Campaign against Monsanto and genetically modified organisms (GMOs): European Union establishes a moratorium on approval of GM crops as the result of public anxiety over introduction of into the food chain • ILO Declaration on Fundamental Principles and Rights at Work • Blood diamonds scandal and campaign against De Beers

	Business-led corporate responsibility coalitions	**Responsible business**
1999	• The Conference Board first annual global corporate citizenship conference • Indonesia Business Links • Youth Business International • WBCSD and UNCTAD set up the International Emissions Trading Association (IETA) • Forética, Spain • Committee Encouraging Corporate Philanthropy • 20 BCSDs now created	• Mass protests at the WTO meetings in Seattle • Global Sullivan Principles • Royal Dutch Shell International produces first Sustainability Report • UN Secretary-General Kofi Annan, in an address to WEF, implores business leaders to meet a set of universal principles in the areas of human rights, labor and the environment, leading to the UN Global Compact • Committee of Inquiry into a New Vision for Business • Dow Jones Sustainability Index begins • Conference Board Corporate Citizenship Initiative
2000	• PBSP Business and Peace Program • African Institute for Corporate Citizenship AICC • Hellenic Network for Corporate Social Responsibility • Vietnam Business Links • WBCSD starts publishing member company sustainable development best practice – now more than 350 case studies • WBCSD signs MoU with China Enterprise Confederation to cooperate towards sustainability in China • AcciónRSE, Chile • FUNDEMAS, El Salvador • Finnish Business and Society • ORSE, France • econsense, Germany • BITC Ireland • Responsible Business Forum, Poland • Grace, Portugal	• UN Global Compact • Naomi Klein's *No Logo* published • Millennium Development Goals adopted by over 200 States at UN General Assembly. • OECD CSR Conference. • Launch of the Kimberley Process • CORE coalition to promote transparency and accountability • UK appoints first CSR Minister (Kim Howells) • Mars, Cadbury's, Hershey's and child labor allegations in West Africa • Voluntary Principles on Security and Human Rights • First annual Asian CSR Forum conference organized by Asian Institute of Management
2001	• Global Business Coalition on HIV/AIDS, Tuberculosis and Malaria (building on an earlier initiative) • Forum Empresa moved to Brazil • BSR opens Hong Kong office • Vietnam Business Links • Italy's Impronta Etica • International Council on Mining & Metals • UK Media CSR Forum • CSR Europe co-organizes Conference of the Belgian Presidency of the European Union, putting CSR on the European Agenda	• Chiquita, the International Unions for Food Workers (IUF) and the Coordinating Committee of Banana Workers' Unions (COLSIBA) Agreement on Freedom of Association, Minimum Labour Standards and Employment • The International Organization for Standardization (ISO) begins investigating case for establishing CSR standard. • All Party Parliamentary CSR Group in UK • FTSE4Good Index created • Association of British Insurers Guidelines on Socially Responsible Investment • Collapse of pharmaceuticals companies' court case against South African Government

	Business-led corporate responsibility coalitions	Responsible business
2002	• IBLF Partnership Initiative • BITC Corporate Responsibility Index • Launch of ENGAGE to promote employee volunteering by IBLF and BITC • First African Institute for Corporate Citizenship Conference Johannesburg • Forum Empresa HQ moved to Acción RSE, Chile • BSR opens Paris office • WBCSD publishes *Walking the Talk: The Business Case for Sustainable Development* • CERES, Ecuador • SumaRSE, Panama • RSE, Portugal • Philias Foundation, Switzerland • CSR Europe and the Copenhagen Centre team up with universities and business schools across Europe to found the European Academy of Business in Society: EABIS	• Enron collapse • WorldCom scandal • Fuping Development Institute Beijing • Sarbanes–Oxley Act, USA • Carbon Disclosure Project • European Commission adopts formal CSR strategy and Action Framework for promoting CSR launches Multi Stakeholder Forum • WEF Global Corporate Citizenship Initiative • Spain: Club de Excelencia en Sostenibilidad • World Summit on Sustainable Development in Johannesburg re-focuses attention on achieving the UN's Agenda 21 and sustainability goals. • Extractive Industries Transparency Initiative • "Publish what you pay" • France mandates large company reporting on social and environmental performance
2003	• WBCSD releases first edition of Chronos, e-learning tutorial on sustainable development. • Chinese BCSD • IBL/YES • Empresa/IADB/OAS capacity-building project • Maala Sustainability Index • Business Social Compliance Initiative of Foreign Trade Association: FTA	• Parmalat scandal in Italy • Equator Principles launched • Roundtable on Sustainable Palm Oil • Kimberly Process for diamond certification
2004	• Coborse, Bolivia • BSR China Training Institute • FUNDAHRSE, Honduras • Slovakian BLF • CSR Sweden • Ukraine Center for Corporate Responsibility Development • Arabia CSR Forum • WBCSD releases *Doing Business with the Poor*: how business can engage with the poor	• CSR Netherlands (MVO Nederland) • Conference Board of Canada: *Managing Risks, Leveraging Opportunities*, Canada's first national CSR report • *Super Size Me* documentary explores the fast food industry • CSR Asia Consortium • *The Corporation* documentary • Campaign against Coca-Cola and water, India • EU Multi-stakeholder Forum on CSR report • Kyoto Protocol comes into effect • UN Global Compact adopts tenth principle against corruption • Revised Federal Sentencing Guidelines

	Business-led corporate responsibility coalitions	Responsible business
2005	• CSR Center at the Bangladesh Enterprise Institute (BEI) • BSR opens first office in mainland China (Guangzhou) • China Business Leaders Forum with Renmin University (established by IBLF) • Business Action on Africa • CSR Europe–WTO *Tribune* Sino-Europe International Forum on CSB Beijing • WBCSD adopts its *Strategy to 2015* • CSR Turkey • Sustainable Packaging Coalition	• Ian Davis, *The Economist* "By special invitation" essay: "Business and Society: The Biggest contract" • BP Texas City refinery disaster • Numerous feature films and documentaries focus attention on corporate misconduct including *The Constant Gardener*, *Syriana*, *Good Night, and Good Luck*, *North Country*, *Enron: The Smartest Guys in the Room*, *McLibel* and *Source* (*Zdroj*) • GE CEO Jeff Immelt delivers "Green is Green" speech in Washington • Walmart CEO Lee Scott delivers "21st Century Leadership" speech with focus on sustainability • EU Emissions Trading Scheme launches • Hurricane Katrina hits New Orleans • Millennium Ecosystem Assessment
2006	• UN Principles for Responsible Investment created • CSR Romania • UNIRSE, Nicaragua • European Alliance for CSR • International Council Toy Industries CARE	• Al Gore's *An Inconvenient Truth* • EU Commission Communication on CSR • Michael Porter and Mark Kramer, "Strategy and Society: Competitive Advantage and Corporate Social Responsibility," *Harvard Business Review* • UN Principles for Responsible Investment created • Masdar "eco-city" initiated • Muhammad Yunus Nobel Peace Prize • *Green to Gold*, Daniel Esty and Andrew Winston • UK Companies Act 2006 • Google in China controversy
2007	• BITC 25th Anniversary Jubilee Dialogues • Merger of existing Austrian organizations to create: respACT–austrian business council for sustainable development • BSR opens Beijing and New York offices • U.S. Climate Action Partnership established • DERES, Uruguay • The Copenhagen Centre closed	• *One Planet Business* published by WWF; • Report of Tomorrow's Global Company Inquiry led by BP and Infosys • CEO Water Mandate • Bali summit on Climate Change • UNGC Summit Geneva • Principles of Responsible Management Education launched at the UNGC Leaders Summit by Secretary-General Ban-Ki Moon. • UNGC/ McKinsey CEOs' Sustainability survey • Beijing Olympics merchandise and child labor scandal • *Blessed Unrest*, Paul Hawken • Inter-governmental panel on Climate Change

	Business-led corporate responsibility coalitions	Responsible business
2007 *(cont.)*		• Al Gore and IGCC share Nobel Peace Prize; and *An Inconvenient Truth* wins Academy Award • BP's Texas City Refinery, the Baker Panel Report and OSHA document over 300 safety violations, fining BP $21 million - the largest fine in OSHA history at the time.
2008	• Croatian Business Leaders Forum • Serbian Business Leaders Forum • BITC publishes Legal & General/ Ipsos MORI research documenting a statistically significant link between effective management and governance of environmental and social issues and financial performance	• *The Difference-Makers*, Sandra Waddock • *The Necessary Revolution*, Peter Senge *et al.* • SASAC Guidelines on CSR for China's State-owned enterprises • UN Human Rights Council adopts a resolution stating that "transnational corporations and other business enterprises have a responsibility to respect human rights" • Global Initiative Network formed: multi-stakeholder project to protect and advance freedom of expression and privacy in the ICT sector • Lehman Brothers collapse precipitates "Great Recession" • SANLU milk contamination scandal, China • Madoff Ponzi fraud
2009	• Rådet for Samfundsansvar (Social Responsibility Council) set up as part of the Danish Action Plan for Social Responsibility • Sustainability Consortium • Fifty national BCSDs now established • Consumer Goods Forum	• *Strategy for Sustainability*, Adam Werbach • Sustainability Consortium • *Supercorp*, Rosabeth Moss Kanter • Copenhagen Climate Change Summit • UN climate change conference Copenhagen ends without global agreement
2010	• China Center for Corporate Sustainability launched by IBLF and Renmin University • WBCSD *Vision 2050* • Liberia CSR Forum • CSR Europe *Enterprise 2020* • UNGC LEAD Initiative	• ISO 26000 voluntary corporate responsibility standard launched covering seven core subjects: organizational governance, human rights, labor practices, the environment, fair operating practices, consumer issues, community involvement and development • ISO 26000 provides guidance on social responsibility. • International Integrated Reporting Committee begins deliberations • U.S. Congress passes Dodd–Frank Act, with mandate on conflict minerals disclosure • U.S. Securities and Exchange Commission mandates corporate climate change disclosure • UNGC–Accenture CEO Study 2010 • *The Responsibility Revolution*, Jeffrey Hollender and Bill Breen • *Big Business, Big Responsibilities*, Andy Wales, Matthew Gorman and Dunstan Hope

	Business-led corporate responsibility coalitions	Responsible business
2010 *(cont.)*		• Toyota product recalls during late 2009/early 2010 • Deepwater Horizon oil spill • U.S. Benefit Corporation established as a new form of corporate entity
2011	• BSR opens office in São Paulo • Instituto Ethos Platform for Inclusive, Green and Responsible Economy • IBLF Redefining Growth platform	• *Harvard Business Review*: Porter and Kramer advocate a "creating shared value" approach to business • *The Age of Responsibility*, Wayne Visser • The Conference Board Business and Society in China • *Harvard Business Review*: Dominic Barton of McKinsey & Co., "Long-term Capitalism" • KPMG's Climate Change & Sustainability Services practice and The Economist Intelligence Unit publish *Corporate Sustainability: A Progress Report*, finding that nearly 50% of all executives surveyed believe sustainability programs will contribute to their bottom line • British lawyer Polly Higgins launches campaign for UN to accept "ecocide" as a "crime against peace" that could be tried at the International Criminal Court • Family Business Network Sustainability Pledge • GRI begins to develop G4 guidelines • UN adopts Guiding Principles on Human Rights • Earthquake and tsunami strike Japan, causing the worst nuclear emergency since Chernobyl • EU Commission Communication on CSR with new definition: CSR is "the responsibility of enterprises for their impacts on society." • Occupy Wall Street and related global protests against capitalism
2012	• BSR and WBCSD celebrate their 20th anniversaries • BITC 30th anniversary • Business Action for Sustainable Development • WBCSD publish *Changing Pace*	• *Zeronauts*, John Elkington • Rio+20 Summit in Brazil and 25th anniversary of the Brundtland Commission • 50+20 report on future of management education • *Financial Times* "Capitalism in Crisis" series

Sources: Center for Ethical Business Cultures, *Corporate Social Responsibility: The Shape of a History, 1945–2004* (Preliminary Project Planning Paper 2005, Working Paper 1; Minneapolis, MN: Center for Ethical Business Cultures, 2010); CSR Centre for Excellence, "Timeline CSR Milestones," web.cim.org/csr/MenuPage. cfm?sections=67,139&menu=140, accessed September 10, 2012; D. Grayson, *Business-Led Corporate Responsibility Coalitions: Learning From the Example of Business in the Community in the UK – An Insider's Perspective* (Bedford, UK: Doughty Centre for Corporate Responsibility, Cranfield School of Management/Cambridge, MA: Kennedy School of Government, Harvard, 2007); International Institute for Sustainable Development, "The Sustainable Development Timeline" (2006) www.iisd.org update; www.edu.gov.ms.co/K12/Cvr/socstud/France_found_sr2/tns/tn-43. pdf; www.IBLF.org; www.wbcsd.org

Appendix 2
Research methodology

This study builds on an earlier report by David Grayson, as a senior fellow for the CSR Initiative at the Kennedy School of Government, Harvard, in 2006–07 on the history of Business in the Community (BITC), one of the oldest and largest of the corporate responsibility coalitions. For that study, the author used his own knowledge, having been involved in BITC from its earliest days, supplemented by his personal archive of the organization and more than 90 one-to-one interviews with current and former board members, staff and member company representatives and partners. The draft was then reviewed by several figures familiar with the organization. Definitions and typography of business-led corporate responsibility coalitions, CEO-directed corporate responsibility coalitions and practitioner-directed corporate responsibility coalitions were developed by David Grayson with Jane Nelson.

Using this first study, desk research was undertaken to establish a time-line of the formation and expansion of the business-led corporate responsibility coalitions and of significant multi-stakeholder coalitions; and to explain the drivers and societal influencers both for the creation of the coalitions individually and for their creation collectively. The emergent literature of social impact was used to help inform the evaluation of the impacts of the coalitions; and Social Movement Theory was used to help analyze the critical success factors that allowed the coalitions to develop and grow.

In parallel, desk research and interviews with key figures in specific coalitions were used to produce profiles of some of the major coalitions. These individual profiles were written either by David Grayson or Jane Nelson; or by or in association with other authors, identified in the text as appropriate. Each coalition profiled was given the opportunity to review their draft profile, correct any factual inaccuracies and suggest amendments to interpretations and conclusions.

The sections on impacts of the coalitions collectively, criticisms of them, future scenarios and recommendations were drafted by David Grayson and Jane Nelson and then tested through a Delphi Panel process of international experts listed in the Acknowledgments, mediated by David Grayson and Jane Nelson.

Separately, the authors worked with the specialist sustainability polling organization GlobeScan to design and run an online survey exclusively with the CEOs or senior executives of more than 100 business-led corporate responsibility coalitions (see Appendix 3). The survey was conducted online during May to June 2012 and over 50 coalitions responded, including all the international generalist corporate responsibility coalitions, almost all the major national coalitions and a number of the subject- and issue-specific coalitions (Appendix 3). Respondents could complete the questionnaire in either English or Spanish and were assured of anonymity. GlobeScan processed all the data so the authors saw only the anonymous results and the summary list of who had responded.

A number of colleagues in the CSR Initiative at Harvard Kennedy School and the Doughty Centre for Corporate Responsibility read and commented on the manuscript, as did several corporate responsibility academics internationally and staff from several of the coalitions. Outstanding issues were debated with experts with long-term knowledge of the coalitions.

Appendix 3
GlobeScan coalition survey and survey respondents

The following questionnaire was developed by the authors in consultation with GlobeScan. The survey was sent to corporate responsibility coalitions around the world by GlobeScan, who independently collated and analyzed all the results.

Introduction

Thank you for participating in this survey.

To navigate through the questionnaire, please use the "Previous page" and "Next page" buttons located at the bottom of the screen.

Please do your best to answer each question. If a question does not apply to you or you cannot answer it, please just skip to the next question.

The survey should take approximately 15 minutes to complete. The accompanying progress bar will show you how far you have progressed.

Your responses will remain strictly anonymous.

1. DEFINITION

We define Business-led Corporate Responsibility coalitions or associations as:

> "independent, non-profit distributing organizations which are composed mainly or exclusively of for-profit businesses (directly or through business-membership organizations); which have a directing board composed predominantly or only of business people; which are core-funded primarily (or totally) from business; and whose sole or predominant purpose is to promote responsible business (managing environmental, social and economic impacts)"

1A. How closely does this definition describe your organization?

Please use the 5-point scale provided, where 1 is "does not describe at all" and 5 is "describes completely."

    01 – Does not describe my organization at all
    02 –
    03 –
    04 –
    05 – Describes my organization completely

THOSE THAT ANSWER 01, 02 OR 03 ABOVE
1B. Why does this definition of a coalition or association not describe your organization?

2. YOUR GOVERNANCE

The boards of some coalitions are composed mainly of the Chief Executive Officers, Presidents or Chairmen of companies or of the heads of companies' business units at the country or regional level. Other coalitions have boards mainly composed of individuals holding the Community affairs / Corporate responsibility / Corporate sustainability function.

2A. Are the members of your board mainly CEO-level, mainly function level, or a mix of both CEO and function level?

Please choose one.

01 – Mainly CEO level
02 – Mix of both CEO and function level
03 – Mainly function level
04 – Other (Please specify) _____

3. YOUR STRATEGIC [AND OPERATIONAL] FOCUS

Some coalitions focus on business involvement in the community, corporate philanthropy and employee volunteering. Others are focused on overall business behavior and core business impacts in the work-place, marketplace and the environment, as well as in the community.

3A. Please rate how much of a strategic focus your organization has in each of the following areas.

Please use the 5-point scale provided, where 1 is "not at all a focus" and 5 is "a very important focus."

a) Community
b) Philanthropy
c) Environment
d) Supply Chain
e) Responsible marketing
f) Business operations
g) Workplace practices
h) Other (Please specify) _____

3B. Do you expect the current focus of your organization to change in the next five years?

01 – Yes
02 – No
03 – Maybe

IF YES IN 3B.
3C. What is driving the shift in focus of your organization in the coming years?

3D. How much impact do you think your organization has had in shaping the positive social and environmental performance of your members?
Please use the 5-point scale provided where 1 is "marginal impact" and 5 is a "significant impact."

01 – marginal impact
02 –
03 –
04 –
05 – significant impact

4. YOUR CURRENT BUSINESS RELATIONSHIPS

4A. Is your corporate membership increasing, static or decreasing?

01 – Increasing
02 – Static
03 – Decreasing

4B. Is the seniority of company involvement in the work and meetings of your organization increasing, static or decreasing?

    01 – Increasing
    02 – Static
    03 – Decreasing

4C. Is your funding increasing, static or decreasing?

    01 – Increasing
    02 – Static
    03 – Decreasing

4D. What proportion of your funding comes from each of the following sources?
Please use the 5-point scale where 1 "none at all" and 5 is "a very significant proportion."

    a) Membership fees from companies
    b) Consulting work for companies
    c) Government
    d) Multilateral organizations
    e) Other (Please specify) _____

5. OTHER BUSINESS-LED CORPORATE RESPONSIBILITY COALITIONS

5A. Which, if any, other Corporate Responsibility coalitions does your coalition look to for ideas, insights, help and advice?

    1.   _____
    2.   _____
    3.   _____

5B. Who do you consider to be your main competitors for business engagement?
Please check all that apply.

    1   Other business-led corporate responsibility coalitions
    2   Consulting firms
    3   Government-led initiatives
    4   Other (Please specify) _____.

5C. Who do you consider to be your main competitors for funding?

Please check all that apply.

    1   Other business-led corporate responsibility coalitions
    2   Consulting firms
    3   Government-led initiatives
    4   Other (Please specify) _____.

6. LOOKING TO THE FUTURE:

6A. How do you think the following aspects of your coalition may or may not change over the next five to ten years?
Please indicate if the item will increase, stay the same or decrease.

    a)   Staff numbers in your coalition
    b)   Your coalition's budget
    c)   Corporate membership
    d)   Consulting for members

6B. Over the next five to ten years, do you think coalitions like yours will be more or less active in challenging member companies to become leaders in tackling social, economic, or environmental issues?
Please indicate if you think coalitions will be less active, stay the same, or more active.

6C. Why is that?

6D. Over the next five to ten years, do you think coalitions will be more or less effective in influencing corporate behavior on social, economic or environmental issues? Please indicate if you think coalitions will be less effective, stay the same, or more effective.

6E. Why is that?

6F. Which one of the following scenarios is most likely for your coalition in ten years from now?

    01 – Status quo / no significant change
    02 – Ceasing to operate because your job will be done
    03 – Ceasing to operate because will have run out of support
    04 – Have evolved in something bigger with other partners

6G. In your view, what are the greatest challenges facing the business-led corporate responsibility coalitions?

    1. _____
    2. _____

6H. What recommendations would you offer for business-led corporate responsibility coalitions to be more effective in embedding and scaling responsible business practice in future?

    1. _____
    2. _____

PROFILE QUESTIONS

1dd. Please select your country of residence from the following list.

[DROP DOWN LIST OF ALL COUNTRIES]

2dd. I have been working or studying in the area of sustainable development or corporate social responsibility for:

                01 – 1 to 2 years
                02 – 3 to 4 years
                03 – 5 to 10 years
                04 – Over 10 years
                05 – No work experience on SD or CSR

3dd. Please indicate the name of your organization

4dd. Please indicate the number of members in your coalition.

                01 – 1 to 49
                02 – 50 to 99
                03 – 100 to149
                04 – 150 to 199
                05 – 200+

GlobeScan Survey respondents

- Acción RSE
- BCSD-Taiwan
- Business for Social Responsibility
- Business Action for Africa
- Business and Society Belgium
- Business in the Community
- Business in the Community Ireland
- China Business Council for Sustainable Development
- Canadian Business for Social Responsibility
- CEADS / Business Council for Sustainable Development Argentina
- Committee Encouraging Corporate Philanthropy
- Consorcio Ecuatoriano para la Responsabilidad Social (CERES)
- Corporate Responsibility Forum Liberia
- CSR Europe
- CSR Norway
- CSR Sweden
- CSR Turkey
- DERES
- econsense
- Fenalco Solidario
- Finnish Business & Society
- Forética
- Forum Empresa
- FUNDAHRSE
- Hellenic Network for CSR
- Hungarian Business Leaders Forum
- International Business Leaders Forum
- International Council on Mining and Metals
- International Council of Toy Industries
- Impronta Etica
- Indonesia Business Links
- International Council of Chemical Associations/American Chemistry Council
- International Petroleum Industry Environmental Conservation Association
- Maala
- Media CSR Forum
- National Business Initiative
- Perú 2021, Una Nueva Visión
- Philias Foundation
- Philippine Business for Social Progress
- respACT–austrian business council for sustainable development
- Responsible Business Forum in Estonia
- Scottish Business in the Community
- SEV Business Council for Sustainable Development
- SumaRSE
- Sustainable Business Council
- uniRSE Union Nicaragüense para la Responsabilidad Social Empresarial
- U.S. Business Council for Sustainable Development
- VirksomhedsNetværket
- World Business Council for Sustainable Development
- World Environment Center
- Youth Business International

Endnotes

Preface

1 www.iblf.org/en/about-IBLF/who-we-are/ourpeople/RobertDavies.aspx, accessed June 30, 2012.

2 The then BITC Chairman Sir David Varney talked about "the perfect storm" in a number of speeches, see, e.g., D. Varney, "CSR: More Than a Storm in a Teacup," *Corporate Citizenship Briefing* 67 (2002, www.ccbriefing.com/CSR-Management/2002/12/01/csr-more-than-a-storm-in-a-teacup, accessed July 26, 2012).

3 P. Gilding, *The Great Disruption* (London: Bloomsbury Publishing, 2011).

4 R. Dobbs, J. Oppenheim, F. Thompson, M. Brinkman and M. Zornes, *The Resource Revolution: Meeting the World's Energy, Materials, Food and Water Needs* (New York: McKinsey Global Institute, 2011).

5 D. Wolf, *Prepared and Resolved: The Strategic Agenda for Growth, Performance and Change* (Charlotte, NC: dsb Publishing, 2007). This term was originally developed in a military context but is now used in strategic leadership sessions.

Introduction

6 www.wbcsd.org.

7 www.unglobalcompact.org.

8 For summaries of the two main business-hosted events at Rio + 20, see United Nations Global Compact, "Rio + 20 Corporate Sustainability Forum: Overview and Outcomes," June 2012, www.unglobalcompact.org; Business Action for Sustainable Development, "Scale Up: Business Day Output Document," June 2012, www.basd.org basd2012.org/project/business-day-output-document-released; and see also www.wbcsd.org.

9 The term "ESG performance" was originally popularized by Goldman Sachs with its GS Sustain research published in 2007; see www.unglobalcompact.org/docs/summit2007/S1_GOLDMAN_Ling.pdf, accessed July 20, 2012.

10 European Commission, *Communication from the Commission to the European Parliament, the Council, the European Economic and Social Committee and the Committee of the Regions: A Renewed EU Strategy 2011–14 for Corporate Social Responsibility* (COM[2011] 681 final; Brussels: Commission of the European Communities, October 25, 2011, ec.europa.eu/enterprise/newsroom/cf/_getdocument.cfm?doc_id = 7010, accessed August 1, 2012).

11 See, e.g., M.E. Porter and M.R. Kramer, "Creating Shared Value," *Harvard Business Review* 89.1/2 (January 2011): 62-77; and M.E. Porter and M.R. Kramer, "Strategy and Society: The Link

between Competitive Advantage and Corporate Social Responsibility," *Harvard Business Review* 84.12 (December 2006).

12 J. Elkington, *Cannibals with Forks* (Oxford: Capstone, 1997).

13 J. Nelson, *Building Competitiveness and Communities: How Companies are Creating Shareholder and Societal Value* ((London: International Business Leaders Forum/United Nations Development Programme/World Bank Group, 1998).

14 S.L. Hart and M.B. Milstein, "Creating Sustainable Value," *Academy of Management Executive* 17.2 (2003, e4sw.org/papers/Hart_Milstein.pdf, accessed July 19, 2012); and see also www.stuartlhart.com/sustainablevalue.html.

15 D. Grayson and A. Hodges, *Corporate Social Opportunity! Seven Steps to Make Corporate Social Responsibility Work for your Business* (Sheffield, UK: Greenleaf Publishing, 2004).

16 B. Googins, P. Mirvis with C. Kiser, "Corporate Social Innovation," Babson Social Innovation Lab Working Paper (forthcoming).

17 Sustainable capitalism is a framework that seeks to maximize long-term economic value creation by reforming markets to address real needs while considering all costs and stakeholders: see Generation Investment Management, *Sustainable Capitalism* (London: Generation Investment Management, January 2012, www.generationim.com/media/pdf-generation-sustainable-capitalism-v1.pdf, accessed July 19, 2012).

18 Meeting the needs of the present generation without compromising the ability of future generations to meet their needs: World Commission on Environment and Development, *Our Common Future* (Brundtland Report; Oxford, UK: Oxford University Press, 1987). We like the formulation now being used by World Business Council for Sustainable Development to explain sustainable development as a world in which 9 billion people live reasonably well, within the limits of one planet by mid-century.

19 International Bank for Reconstruction and Development, "Inclusive, Green Growth: The Pathway to Sustainable Development" (Washington DC: IBRD, 2012).

Chapter 1

20 Up from 72% in a similar survey in 2007. P. Lacy, T. Cooper, R. Hayward and L. Neuberger, *A New Era of Sustainability: Global Compact–Accenture CEO Survey 2010* (New York: UN Global Compact/Accenture, 2010, www.unglobalcompact.org/docs/news_events/8.1/UNGC_Accenture_CEO_Study_2010.pdf, accessed July 19, 2012). A new version of the Accenture/UNGC CEOs survey, with greater emphasis on Asia–Pacific, is expected in summer 2013.

21 S. Bonini and S. Görner, *The Business of Sustainability: Putting it Into Practice* (New York: McKinsey, 2011).

22 KPMG International Corporate Responsibility Reporting Survey 2011, www.kpmg.com/global/en/issuesandinsights/articlespublications/corporate-responsibility/pages/default.aspx, accessed July 19, 2012.

23 R. Kolodinsky, T. Madden, D. Zisk and E. Henkel, "Attitudes about Corporate Social Responsibility: Business Student Predictors," *Journal of Business Ethics* 91 (2010): 167-81.

24 D. Rothkopf, *Power, Inc.: The Epic Rivalry Between Big Business and Government – and the Reckoning That Lies Ahead* (New York: Farrar, Straus & Giroux, 2012): 295.

25 Since Rothkopf wrote his book, the Fortune Global 500 ranking for 2012 put Shell and Exxon Mobil ahead of other companies.

26 While we recognize that economists and others criticize this type of comparison, we also accept that it is widely used to show the growth in scale of multinational companies.

27 The Edelman Trust Barometer tracks trust levels in different actors – business, government, NGOs and media – in 25 countries around the world. See www.edelman.com.

28 GlobeScan surveys and additional information can be found at www.GlobeScan.com.

29 2030 Water Resources Group (Barilla Group, Coca-Cola Company, International Finance Corporation, McKinsey & Company, Nestlé S.A., New Holland Agriculture, SABMiller plc, Standard Chartered Bank and Syngenta AG), *Charting Our Water Future: Economic Frameworks to Inform Decision-making* (2009).

30   Piero Conforti (ed.), Looking Ahead in World Food and Agriculture: Perspectives to 2050 (Rome: Food and Agriculture Organization of the United Nations, 2011).

31   World Energy Council, Deciding the Future: Energy Policy Scenarios to 2050 (2007).

32   R. Dobbs, J. Oppenheim, F. Thompson, M. Brinkman and M. Zornes, Resource Revolution: Meeting the World's Energy, Materials, Food and Water Needs (New York: McKinsey Global Institute, November 2011).

33   Ibid.

34   International Labour Organization, World of Work Report 2012: Better Jobs for a Better Economy (Geneva: International Labour Organization, May 2012).

35   International Labour Organization, Global Unemployment Trends 2012: Preventing a Deeper Jobs Crisis (Geneva: International Labour Organization, January 2012).

36   www.ilo.org/global/topics/youth-employment/lang--en/index.htm, accessed July 19, 2012.

37   news.harvard.edu/gazette/story/2011/12/dealing-with-inequality, accessed July 19, 2012.

38   www.pewstates.org/news-room/press-releases/pew-finds-most-americans-have-greater-income-than-their-parents-but-little-movement-up-and-down-the-economic-ladder-85899403278, accessed July 19, 2012.

39   For detailed coverage on this global framework and on business and human rights issues see Business & Human Rights Resource Centre at www.business-humanrights.org.

40   Interview with Professor John Ruggie in The International Review of the Red Cross, Number 886 (September 2012).

41   EABIS–The Academy for Business in Society, described in Chapter 7 (Box 7.5), and Yale University, supported by the European Foundation for Management Development, have organized a series of international conferences on practical wisdom for management from the world's spiritual and philosophical traditions: www.eabis.org/projects/project-detail-view.html?uid = 16, accessed July 30, 2012.

42   I. Jackson and J. Nelson, Profit with Principles (New York: Broadway Business, 2004); D. Grayson and A. Hodges, Corporate Social Opportunity! (Sheffield, UK: Greenleaf Publishing, 2004).

43   Business in the Community and Doughty Centre for Corporate Responsibility, The Business Case for Being a Responsible Business (Bedford, UK: Cranfield School of Management, 2011, www.bitc.org.uk/resources/publications/the_business_case.html, accessed June 20, 2012). See also: D. Grayson and A. Hodges, Corporate Social Opportunity! (Sheffield, UK: Greenleaf Publishing, 2004); I. Jackson and J. Nelson, Profits with Principles (New York: Broadway Business, 2004); J. Nelson, Building Competitiveness and Communities: How Companies Are Creating Shareholder and Societal Value (London: International Business Leaders Forum/United Nations Development Programme/World Bank, 1998).

44   See Prof. Atle Midttun's description of "partnered governance" in C. Marsden and D. Grayson, The Business of Business Is . . . ? (Doughty Centre Occasional Paper; Bedford, UK: Doughty Centre for Corporate Responsibility, 2007): 11-12.

45   J. Nelson, Creating the Enabling Environment: Mechanisms to Promote Global Corporate Citizenship (London: International Business Leaders Forum, 2000); D. Grayson and A. Hodges, Everybody's Business: Managing Risks and Opportunities in Today's Global Society (London: Dorling Kindersley, 2001).

Chapter 2

46   We do not, therefore, include organizations such as the Caux Round Table, founded in 1986, which promotes ethical business practices, or the European Bahai Business Forum created in 1990; or service organizations composed of individual business people such as Rotary or Jaycees.

47   Excluding from the coalition definition organizations such as the Global Reporting Initiative established in 1997.

48   The Business Social Compliance Initiative (BSCI) was established by the Foreign Trade Associa-
     tion (FTA) in 2003. Members have to belong to the FTA: www.bsci-intl.org/about-bsci/why-bsci-
     exists, accessed August 7, 2012.
49   For further details on the work of the Consumer Goods Forum see: www.theconsumergoodsforum.
     com.

Chapter 3

50   For a history of the formation and early years of the Community of St. Helens Trust see I.H.
     Fazey, *The Pathfinder, The Origins of the Enterprise Agency in Britain* (London: Financial Training
     Publications, 1987).
51   D. Kinderman, "The Political Economy of Corporate Responsibility Across Europe and
     Beyond: 1977–2007," PhD thesis, Cornell University (2010, https://sites.google.com/site/
     danielkinderman).
52   D. Kinderman, " 'Free us up so we can be responsible!' The Co-evolution of Corporate Social
     Responsibility and Neo-liberalism in the UK, 1977–2010", *Socio-Economic Review* 10.1 (2012):
     29-57.
53   D. Kavanagh, "Thatcherism and the End of the Post-War Consensus," BBC History (March 3,
     2011, www.bbc.co.uk/history/british/modern/thatcherism_01.shtml, accessed June 21, 2012).
54   D. Kinderman, " 'Free us up so we can be responsible!' The Co-evolution of Corporate Social
     Responsibility and Neo-liberalism in the UK, 1977–2010", *Socio-Economic Review* 10.1 (2012):
     29-57.
55   To encourage British business leaders to learn from the successful engagement of American busi-
     ness leaders in inner city regeneration during the 1970s that subsequently led to the emergence
     of a number of urban business leadership teams and city-level, business-led local economic
     development partnerships such as New York City Partnership, Cleveland Tomorrow, Detroit
     Renaissance and Atlanta Partnership. See J. Austin and A. McCaffery, "Business Leadership
     Coalitions and Public–Private Partnerships in American Cities: A Business Perspective on Regime
     Theory," *Journal of Urban Affairs* 24.1 (2002): 35–54, onlinelibrary.wiley.com/doi/10.1111/1467-
     9906.00113/abstract, accessed July 20, 2012.
56   www.nyforetagarcentrum.com/Startsida/In_English/About_Swedish_Jobs_and_Society,
     accessed June 21, 2012.
57   Today IMS is an association of 230 businesses that are committed to partnerships with commu-
     nity stakeholders focused on sustainable development. Its mission involves helping businesses
     incorporate innovative community policies, based on partnerships with other community play-
     ers, into their corporate social responsibility policies.
58   www.keidanren.or.jp/CBCC/en/index.html.
59   The Plaza Accord was an agreement between the governments of France, West Germany, Japan,
     the United States and the United Kingdom to depreciate the U.S. dollar in relation to the Japa-
     nese yen and German Deutsche Mark by intervening in currency markets. The five governments
     signed the accord on September 22, 1985 at the Plaza Hotel in New York City.
60   Today CBCC organizes a dialogue series with civil-society organizations such as Amnesty Inter-
     national and Human Rights Watch; runs missions to North America, Europe and Asia to learn
     about good CSR and corporate citizenship practices; and facilitates stakeholder engagement about
     integrating CSR into core business operations, and engaging in strategic partnerships with CSR
     initiatives and organizations. While CBCC sometimes advises its members, it is not a service-
     delivery organization and does not provide consulting services. This information about CBCC is
     based on an interview with CBCC, Tokyo, July 10, 2012, conducted by Dr. Daniel Kinderman.
61   Both are now affiliated to Forum Empresa (see Chapter 10, Box 10.2).
62   M. Zwick, A. Reyes and K. Schwab, *The World Economic Forum: A Partner in Shaping History –
     The First 40 Years 1971–2010* (Geneva: World Economic Forum, 2009).

63 For a useful summary of Klaus Schwab's approach to these issues see: K. Schwab, "Global Corporate Citizenship: Working with Governments and Civil Society," *Foreign Affairs*, January/ February 2008.

64 www.weforum.org/community/global-agenda-councils, accessed July 20, 2012.

65 B.K. Googins, P.H. Mirvis and S.A. Rochlin, *Beyond Good Company: Next Generation Corporate Citizenship* (New York: Palgrave Macmillan, 2007).

66 Taken from IBLF history at www-dev.iblf.org/about_us/History.jsp, accessed June 21, 2012.

67 S. Schmidheiny and Business Council for Sustainable Development, *Changing Course: A Global Business Perspective on Development and the Environment* (Cambridge, MA: MIT, 1992).

68 svn.org/who-we-are/our-story-the-founding-of-svn, accessed July 20, 2012.

69 www.empresa.org, accessed February 24, 2012.

70 A. Cramer, "Forum EMPRESA: More Than a Decade of Achievement in the Americas," blog posted October 14, 2011, www.bsr.org/en/our-insights/blog-view/forum-empresa-more-than-a-decade-of-achievement-in-the-americas, accessed June 22, 2012.

71 Ibid.

72 Created from National Partners page of www.csreurope.org and websites of national partners.

73 UNGC now differentiates between "formal," "established" and "emerging" national networks: www.unglobalcompact.org/NetworksAroundTheWorld/network_categories.html, accessed September 4, 2012.

74 www.businessmentors.org.nz/AboutUs/Our-History.aspx, accessed July 1, 2012.

75 Another coalition that paid the price of over-identification with the government of the day was the Australian Prime Minister's Business Community Partnership. Invented by the conservative Howard federal administration in 1999, to showcase examples of effective corporate community involvement, it was quickly abandoned by the incoming Labour administration in 2007: see www.fahcsia.gov.au/sa/communities/pubs, accessed June 22, 2012.

76 www.corporatephilanthropy.org/about-cecp/history.html, accessed June 22, 2012.

77 Now called the Citizenship and Sustainability Conference since its merger with The Conference Board's annual Environment Conference.

78 www.conference-board.org/retrievefile.cfm?filename = 1289_1310036501.PDF&type = subsite, accessed June 22, 2012. This was closed down in May 2012 to be replaced by an Initiative on Sustainability, whose parameters are yet to be determined as of July 2012.

79 PBSP co-founder Howard Dee of United Laboratories quoted in V.E. Tan and M.P. Bolante, *Philippine Business for Social Progress* (New York: Synergos Institute, 1997): 17.

80 N. Klein, *No Logo: Taking Aim at the Brand Bullies* (New York: Flamingo, 2000).

81 D. Korten, *When Corporations Rule the World* (San Francisco: Berrett-Koehler, 1995).

82 The Tomorrow's Company Inquiry was repeated a decade later by the Centre for Tomorrow's Company when it ran the Tomorrow's Global Company Inquiry in 2006–07 (www.tomorrowscompany. com).

83 www.communitybusiness.org.

84 www.abcn.com.au.

85 www.arabiacsrnetwork.com.

86 www.csr.ee/forum.

87 www.ccps-africa.org/NEWSEVENTS/tabid/736/Default.aspx, accessed June 27, 2012.

88 crforumliberia.org/page_info.php?&7d5f44532cbfc489b8db9e12e44eb820 = MTgy, accessed June 27, 2012.

89 The Executive Committee of the CR Forum, which manages its affairs, initially comprised six companies and the Government of Liberia. The current chair is ArcelorMittal Liberia, which also heads the Secretariat of the Forum. In February 2012, the Executive Committee was expanded to ten. The CR Forum has now appointed a young Liberian national, Roosevelt G. Tule, as Liaison Officer to coordinate Forum activities. In addition to GIZ, the UNDP has also helped sponsor some events. Membership stands at 31 companies as of spring 2012 (www.crforumliberia.org).

90 For further information on the Initiative for Global Development and Frontier 100 see: igdleaders. org.

91 For further information on Business Action for Africa and Business Fights Poverty, see: businessactionforafrica.org and www.businessfightspoverty.org.

Chapter 4

92 "Butskellism" was an amalgam of the names of two leading post-war British politicians: R.A Butler for the Conservatives and Hugh Gaitskell for Labour. Margaret Thatcher's Conservative Government after 1979 was seen as dismantling this post-war party political consensus.

93 For an overview of the energy–food–water nexus, see H. Hoff, "Understanding the Nexus," background paper for the *Bonn 2011 Conference: The Water, Energy and Food Security Nexus*, Stockholm Environment Institute, Stockholm, 2011, www.water-energy-food.org/en/home.html.

94 D. Grayson and A. Hodges, *Everybody's Business*: *Managing Risks and Opportunities in Today's Global Society* (London: Dorling Kindersley, 2001).

95 Global integrated enterprise was coined in 2006 by Sam Palmisano, then CEO of IBM Corp, who defined it as "a company that fashions its strategy, its management, and its operations in pursuit of a new goal: the integration of production and value delivery worldwide." S.J. Palmisano, "The Globally Integrated Enterprise," *Foreign Affairs*, May/June 2006.

96 D. Tapscott and D. Ticoll, *The Naked Corporation: How the Age of Transparency Will Revolutionize Business* (New York: Free Press, 2003).

97 Reference to atomization of some societies as described in R. Putnam, *Bowling Alone: The Collapse and Revival of American Community* (New York: Simon & Schuster, 2000).

98 P. Lacy, T. Cooper, R. Hayward and L. Neuberger, *A New Era of Sustainability: Global Compact–Accenture CEO Survey 2010* (New York: UN Global Compact/Accenture, 2010).

99 B. Edwards and J.D. McCarthy, "Resources and Social Movement Mobilization," in D.A. Snow, S.A. Soule and H. Kriesi (eds.), *The Blackwell Companion to Social Movements* (Oxford: Blackwell, 2004).

Chapter 5

100 For a personal reflection on the Prince of Wales's 25 years as President of Business in the Community, see Dame Julia Cleverdon's tribute, July 2010, at www.princeofwales.gov.uk/newsandgallery/focus/hrh_celebrates_25_years_as_president_of_business_in_the_comm_2045695949.html, accessed July 20, 2012.

101 S. Waddock, *The Difference Makers: How Social and Institutional Entrepreneurs Created the Corporate Responsibility Movement* (Sheffield, UK: Greenleaf Publishing, 2008).

102 www.unglobalcompact.org/HowToParticipate/Business_Participation/index.html, accessed August 29, 2012.

103 D. Kinderman, "Re-Embedding or Dis-Embedding the Corporation? The Transnational Social Networks of Corporate Responsibility across Europe: 1990–2007," paper prepared for *2010 American Political Science Association Meeting*, Washington, DC, September 2–5, 2010.

104 Interview with Celia Moore, July 2012.

105 www.environmentalleader.com/2012/01/18/ibm-gm-coke-form-environmental-innovation-council, accessed July 23, 2012.

106 For a summary of the learning from the Corporate Community Involvement Initiative see Ford Foundation, *Part of the Solution: Leveraging Business and Markets for Low-income People. Executive Summary* (New York: Ford Foundation, 2005, bwbsolutions.com/pdf/FordFoundation-PartoftheSolution-ExecutiveSummary.pdf, accessed November 2, 2012).

107 For details on the Business and Society Program's initiatives in promoting change in corporate and investor practices; integrating sustainability issues into business school curricula; and supporting exceptional business innovators to drive social value and profitability in their companies, see: www.aspeninstitute.org/policy-work/business-society.

108 For more details on the definition and potential of Impact Investing, and on the investor-led and multi-stakeholder coalitions that are driving this new field see: www.rockefellerfoundation.org/

what-we-do/current-work/harnessing-power-impact-investing; www.thegiin.org/cgi-bin/iowa/resources/about/index.html.

Chapter 6

109 Organized by a governmental organization, Saudi Arabian General Investment Agency (SAGIA), and two NGOs, the national King Khalid Foundation and global AccountAbility (see M. Gravem, "Corporate Social Responsibility: Saudi Arabia and International Standards," Gulf Research Unit blog, January 21, 2010).

110 Ludwig Erhard was the post-war Christian Democrat politician and later Chancellor who developed Germany's Social Market Economy.

111 www.ecrc.org.eg.

112 www.abcn.com.au.

113 In September 2010, St. James Ethics Centre handed back the Australia/New Zealand license for the CRI to BITC, which relaunched the Index as a global index.

114 virginunite.screwbusinessasusual.com, accessed July 1, 2012. The ad hoc alliance has since been renamed as the Business Leaders Initiative/B-Team.

115 Internet World Stats, www.internetworldstats.com/top20.htm, accessed August 1, 2012.

116 Internet World Stats, www.internetworldstats.com/stats.htm, accessed August 1, 2012.

117 According to the 11th China Cybermedia Forum at the end of 2011: H. Lu, "Number of Weibo Users Hits 300 Million," blog, shanghaiist.com, shanghaiist.com/2011/11/23/number_of_weibo_users_hits_300mln.php, accessed August 1, 2012.

118 English language brief on SASAC's "CSR Guideline for State-Owned Enterprises" by Guo Peiyuan of the Chinese CR consultancy SynTao (2008), www.syntao.com/E_Page_Show.asp?Page_ID = 6407, accessed July 29, 2012.

119 R. Dietmar, "CSR in China: Recent Developments and Trends," in *oekom CR Review* (Munich: oekom research, 2012: 51–53, www.oekom-research.com/homepage/english/oekom_CR_Review_2012_en.pdf, accessed July 26, 2012).

120 Ibid: 52. According to *Sustainable Investment in China Newsletter*, April 2012, the number of reports went up from just 23 in 2006 to more than 700 in 2011; and according to the Chinese CSR consultancy SynTao's *A Journey to Discover Values 2011* report, there were over 1,000 reports in 2011.

121 The center is called GoldenBee because "As the biological wizard living harmoniously with environment, bees gather and make honey for themselves, and spread pollen to provide the vital catalyst for plants to grow. In doing so, they also help plants reproduce so as to get more sources of nectar for future. Like bees, enterprises that are committed to building harmonious coexistence and mutual prosperous relationships with the environment and society, constantly improving responsible competitiveness, and pursuing sustainable development, are called GoldenBee Enterprises," csr-china.net/en/ind/goldenbeeforum2020, accessed July 23, 2012.

122 csr-china.net/en/ind/goldenbeeforum2020, accessed July 23, 2012.

123 www.daonong.com/English/index.htm, accessed July 23, 2012.

124 www.daonong.com/English/2011_Press3.html, accessed July 23, 2012.

125 www.daonong.com/english/green.html, accessed July 23, 2012.

126 R. Dietmar, "CSR in China: Recent Developments and Trends," in *oekom CR Review* (Munich: oekom research, 2012): 52.

127 www.sa-intl.org/index.cfm?fuseaction = Page.ViewPage&PageID = 1208, accessed July 26, 2012.

128 www.iblf.org/en/latest-news/2010/Nov-29-2010-Launch-China_Centre-Corp-Sustainability.aspx, accessed July 26, 2012.

129 China Business Council for Sustainable Development, english.cbcsd.org.cn/cbcsd/chm/index.shtml, accessed July 23, 2012.

130 ctichina.org/v2/en.

131 UN Global Compact, *Local Partners Network Report 2010* (New York: UNGC, 2010, www.unglobalcompact.org/docs/networks_around_world_doc/Annual_Report_2010/GCLN_2010.

pdf, accessed June 23, 2012). From 2012, the China Entrepreneur Confederation (CEC) replaces Rongzhi to house the secretariat of UNGC China network.

132 Fuping Development Institute in Beijing is a registered non-profit organization established in 2002 for the purposes of alleviating poverty and promoting sustainable development. The Institute consists of a team of academics, entrepreneurs, and development practitioners; www.csr360gpn.org/partners/profile/fuping-development-institute, accessed July 23, 2012.

133 According to the economic historian Angus Maddison; see *Economist*, "Hello America: China's Economy Overtakes Japan's in Real Terms," *Economist*, August 16, 2010, www.economist.com/node/16834943, accessed August 2, 2012.

134 G. Rachman, "When Will China Become the World's Largest Economy?" *Financial Times Blog*, January 16, 2011, blogs.ft.com/the-world/2011/01/when-will-china-become-the-worlds-largest-economy, accessed September 4, 2012.

135 *Economist*, "China's Environment: A Great Wall of Waste," *Economist*, August 19, 2004, www.economist.com/node/3104453, accessed August 2, 2012.

136 Source: UNDESA, World Urbanization Prospect.

137 en.wikipedia.org/wiki/List_of_countries_by_population, citing Official Population Clock of USA as at June 26, 2012.

138 According to a report commissioned by the Asia Society and the Woodrow Wilson International Center for Scholars cited in D. Barboza, "As China Invests, U.S. Could Lose," *New York Times* May 4, 2011, www.nytimes.com/2011/05/04/business/global/04yuan.html?pagewanted = all, accessed June 22, 2012.

139 *China.org.cn*, "Ministry Predicts New Surge in ODI," *China.org.cn* (January 5, 2012, www.china.org.cn/business/2012-01/05/content_24325893.htm, accessed June 22, 2012).

140 www.cabc.org.cn/english/introduce.asp.

141 Professor David Gosset, China Europe International Business School, June 2012.

142 In the EU, Responsible Care companies cut their energy intensity by 4.6% annually between 1990 and 2006. In the same period, greenhouse gas emissions fell by almost 30%. In the United States, Responsible Care companies have reduced greenhouse gas intensity by 23% since 1992. In 2006, the Japanese chemical industry reduced its unit energy consumption to 82% of 1990 levels and Korean chemical companies saved 622,000 ton of oil equivalent in 2006 compared with 1998 levels.

143 Source: www.responsiblecare.org; www.icti-care.org, accessed July 31, 2012; discussions with managing executives in both organizations.

144 The greater emphasis on human rights considerations acknowledges the UN "Protect, Respect and Remedy" Framework for Business and Human Rights and the subsequent UN Guiding Principles on Business and Human Rights (the "Ruggie Principles").

145 Source: Institutional websites and interviews with executives in the coalitions.

146 See, for example, Eurocare, *The Beverage Alcohol Industry's Social Aspects Organizations: A Public Health Warning* (Brussels: EuroCare, 2002, www.eurocare.org).

147 For a history of Drinkwise, see R. Ainsbury and D. Grayson, "DrinkWise: Uniting an Industry," ecch, 2011, www.ecch.info/educators/search/results?s = 77ABD334EEC7DC1CA2B56750FCFAA B65, accessed August 2, 2012.

148 See www.global-actions.org.

149 responsibilitydeal.dh.gov.uk.

150 For others, sticking to the community focus has been more challenging. Empresa y Sociedad was created in 1995 in Spain by Francisco Abad and was the original partner of the European Business Network for Social Inclusion (EBNSI). However, when EBNSI changed its name to CSR Europe and broadened its remit to responsible business, the Empresa y Sociedad board and membership divided over whether to follow. Legal action and mass resignations ensued, before a rump organization left CSR Europe and continued to focus on CCI.

151 www.tbca.or.th, accessed July 1, 2012.

152 Unpublished survey conducted by CSR Global Partner Network secretariat in 2009.

153 In the GlobeScan Coalitions survey 38% of respondents said they do not anticipate change of focus whereas 31% are expecting a change and 29% are saying maybe (2% don't know). The

CEOs say that what is driving this anticipated shift in focus is predominantly member require-ments and responding to marketplace pressures.

Chapter 7

154 H. Ward, *Public Sector Roles in Strengthening Corporate Social Responsibility: Taking Stock* (Wash-ington, DC: World Bank, 2004).

155 UN Global Compact and Bertelsmann, *The Role of Governments in Promoting Corporate Respon-sibility and Private Sector Engagement in Development* (New York: UNGC; Gütersloh, Germany: Bertelsmann Stiftung, 2010).

156 World Bank, *Inclusive Green Growth: The Pathway to Sustainable Development* (Washington, DC: World Bank, 2012, siteresources.worldbank.org/EXTSDNET/Resources/Inclusive_Green_ Growth_May_2012.pdf, accessed August 5, 2012).

157 D. Grayson, "EU's new CSR report offers realistic initiatives to promote sustainability," *Guardian* Sustainable Business Blog, December 20, 2011, www.guardian.co.uk/sustainable-business/blog/ eu-corporate-sustainability-report-policy, accessed August 5, 2012.

158 Belgium 2001, Denmark 2002, Italy 2003, Netherlands 2004, UK 2005, Finland 2006, Portugal 2007, France 2008, Sweden 2009, Spain 2010, Poland 2011.

159 The 2011 EU Commission Communication is being used in Colombia and Chile, and by the Cen-tral American Development Bank with the five central American countries to help the govern-ments there design their own national policies to encourage corporate responsibility.

160 United Nations Global Compact, "Denmark Introduces Mandatory CSR Reporting for Large Companies," December 17, 2008, www.unglobalcompact.org/newsandevents/news_ archives/2008_12_17.html, accessed October 30, 2012.

161 Conservative Party Working Group On Responsible Business, *Final Report: A Light But Effective Touch,* March 2008.

162 The previous Prime Minister Gordon Brown's Council on Social Action had also explored a simi-lar concept of "Collaborative Commitments," defined as: "agreements made voluntarily between individuals and organizations from business, public sector and civil society, to achieve positive social impacts which would not be possible for one sector acting alone, to obtain."

163 S. Waddell, *Global Action Networks: Creating Our Future Together* (Basingstoke, UK: Palgrave Macmillan, 2011).

164 GreenBiz, "The Myths and the Mission Behind the Sustainability Consortium," *GreenBiz.com* (December 4, 2009, www.greenbiz.com/news/2009/12/04/sustainability-consortium-myths-mission, accessed June 23, 2012).

165 GNI is a multi-sector initiative involving ICT companies such as Google, Microsoft and Yahoo and human rights NGOs, academics and institutional investors. It seeks to address how international ICT companies operate on societies that restrict privacy and free expression. For a highly critical commentary on GNI see: www.forbes.com/sites/larrydownes/2011/03/30/why-no-one-will-join-the-global-network-initiative, accessed June 23, 2012.

166 Created in early 2010. A unique platform convened by WEF, International Finance Corporation and United Nations Foundation, in association with the Institutional Investors Group on Climate Change and the Investor Network on Climate Risk.

167 Business in the Community and Doughty Centre for Corporate Responsibility, *The Business Case for Being a Responsible Business* (Bedford, UK: Cranfield School of Management, 2011, www.bitc. org.uk/resources/publications/the_business_case.html, accessed July 1, 2012).

168 Forthcoming report with Business in the Community, 2013,

169 www.cpsl.cam.ac.uk, accessed August 29, 2012.

170 www.fsg.org/KnowledgeExchange/FSGApproach/SharedValue.aspx, accessed August 29, 2012.

171 D. Grayson, "Business Schools: Keep the Academic Community Engaged," *Ethical Corporation,* December 2011.

172 R. Martin, "MBA World Needs to Broaden Its Horizons," *Financial Times,* January 11, 2010.

173 A combined initiative of several Australian business schools with initial pump-priming funding from the Australian Government.

174 G.Yip, "The Key Steps Necessary for Creating a Relevant Business School," *Financial Times* Soapbox, September 24, 2012.

175 www.50plus20.org.

176 Boxed text on EABIS written by John Swannick, Executive Director of EABIS for Corporate Membership.

177 As of November 2012 known as Carnstone Partners LLP.

178 See Media CSR Forum website: www.mediacsrforum.org. YELL is now known as hibu.

179 The Chatham House Rule for the conduct of meetings, named after Chatham House, the headquarters of the Royal Institute for International Affairs in London, states that: "When a meeting, or part thereof, is held under the Chatham House Rule, participants are free to use the information received, but neither the identity nor the affiliation of the speaker(s), nor that of any other participant, may be revealed" www.chathamhouse.org/aout-us/chathamhouserule, accessed July 22, 2012.

180 mediacsrforum.org/forum.php, accessed August 6, 2012.

181 www.mediacsrforum.org/_media/documents/map.pdf, accessed July 1, 2012. This is being revised again Autumn 2012.

182 This analysis has been prepared from G. Guillén, J. Katan and Bin Xu, "Behind the Scenes: Media Industry Stakeholders Collaborating Towards Sustainability," thesis submitted for completion of Masters of Strategic Leadership towards Sustainability, Blekinge Institute of Technology, School of Engineering, Karlskrona, Sweden, 2010, with further input from Dr. Christian Toennesen, Ancona/Media CSR Forum.

183 www.powerbase.info/index.php/Main_Page, accessed July 1, 2012.

184 www.sourcewatch.org/index.php?title = SourceWatch:Purpose, accessed July 1, 2012.

185 For another segmentation of NGO approaches to business see B. May, *How to Make Your Company A Recognized Sustainability Champion*, www.dosustainability.com/books, accessed November 22, 2012.

186 www.cii.in?About_Us, accessed June 14, 2012.

187 www.keidanren.or.jp/english/policy/csr/tebiki6.pdf, accessed July 19, 2012.

188 www.keidanren.or.jp/english/speech/spe001/s01001/s01b.html, accessed July 19, 2012.

189 "Dubai Chamber membership rises 30 per cent in H1 2012," *Khaleej Times*, August 1, 2012, www.khaleejtimes.com/kt-article-display-1.asp?xfile = data/uaebusiness/2012/August/uaebusiness_August4.xml&section = uaebusiness, accessed August 31, 2012.

Chapter 8

190 CentraRSE has also researched and published corporate and sector ethics codes, specialized tools for the implementation of corporate responsibility specific to particular issues and economic sectors, successful business cases in Guatemala and international best practice.

191 Another well-established and widely used tool for measuring and reporting corporate community investment is the London Benchmarking Group Model first published in 1997. LBG is a specialist coalition formed in 1994 and managed by Corporate Citizenship, an international corporate responsibility consultancy based in London and New York. While the LBG Model's origins are in the UK, LBG Benchmarking groups also operate in Australia, Canada, Czech Republic, Romania and Spain and are emerging in several other markets. www.lbg-online.net/about-lbg.aspx, accessed June 15, 2012

192 www.bsr.org/en/our-work/services.

193 www.respact.at/site/english?SWS = b1328de59dbc3470c251eac3d695a5d7, accessed June 23, 2012.

194 www.bitc.org.uk/princes_programmes/the_princes_seeing_is_believing/about_sib.html, accessed September 5, 2012.

195 www.btrust.org.za.

196 www.icmm.com/our-work/sustainable-development-framework/public-reporting, accessed July 1, 2012.

197 www.csr360gpn.org/partners/profile/bulgarian-business-leaders-forum, accessed July 1, 2012.

198 M. Gladwell, *The Tipping Point: How Little Things Can Make a Big Difference* (New York: Little, Brown, 2000).

199 S. Schmidheiny and Business Council for Sustainable Development, *Changing Course: A Global Business Perspective on Development and the Environment* (Cambridge, MA: MIT, 1992); World Business Council for Sustainable Development, *Changing Pace: Public Policy Options to Scale and Accelerate Business Action Towards Vision 2050* (Geneva: World Business Council for Sustainable Development, 2012, www.wbcsd.org/Pages/EDocument/EDocumentDetails.aspx?ID = 14622&N oSearchContextKey = true, accessed August 14, 2012).

200 Business in the Community, *Directions for the Nineties* (London: BITC, 1991); J. Wybrewand and D. Grayson, "Work in Society," *RSA Journal* 142.5448 (1994): 55-69.

201 J. Nelson, *Business as Partners in Development* (London: International Business Leaders Forum/ United Nations Development Programme/World Bank, 1996).

202 P. Schwartz and B. Gibb, *When Good Companies Do Bad Things: Responsibility and Risk in an Age of Globalization* (Hoboken, NJ: Wiley, 1999): 135.

203 For a discussion of the academic models of stages of maturity see F. Maon, A. Lindgreen and V. Swaen, "Organizational Stages and Cultural Phases: A Critical Review and a Consolidated Model of Corporate Social Responsibility Development," *International Journal of Management Reviews* 12.1 (2010): 20-38.

204 S. Zadek, "Paths to Corporate Responsibility," *Harvard Business Review* (December 2004); P.H. Mirvis and B.K. Googins, *Stages of Corporate Citizenship* (Boston, MA: Boston College Center for Corporate Citizenship, 2006); J.-F. Rischard, Vice President for Europe, The World Bank, quoted in R. Davies and J. Nelson, *The Buck Stops Where?* (IBLF Policy Brief 2: London: International Business Leaders Forum, 2003); J. Porritt and C. Tuppen, *Just Values: Beyond the Business Case for Sustainable Development* (London: BT/Forum for the Future, 2003, www.btplc.com/ Responsiblebusiness/Ourstory/Literatureandezines/Publicationsandreports/Archivedreports/ index.htm, accessed July 1, 2012).

205 See D. Grayson, "Stages of Corporate Responsibility Maturity," www.som.cranfield.ac.uk/ som/p17343/Knowledge-Interchange/Management-Themes/Corporate-Responsibility-and-Sustainability/Key-Concepts/Stages-of-Corporate-Responsibility-Maturity, accessed September 5, 2012.

206 Business for Social Responsibility, *BSR at 20: Accelerating Progress* (New York: Business for Social Responsibility, November 2012).

Chapter 9

207 For discussion of how companies organize board oversight and governance of their commitment to corporate responsibility and sustainability, see forthcoming Doughty Centre/Business in the Community report, D.Grayson and A.Kakabadse (2013).

208 73% say staffing will increase, 21% say it will stay the same and only 4% say it will decrease (2% don't know).

209 Information from author's visit to BITC Ireland, Dublin, May 2012, and subsequent email exchanges with Bernadette Phelan and Tina Roche of BITC Ireland, June–July 2012.

Chapter 10

210 WBCSD, *Transformation in the Turbulent Teens: WBCSD Annual Report 2010–11* (Geneva: WBCSD, 2011): 43.

211 Ibid.

212 David Halley, personal reflections to author, January 2012.

213 WBCSD, *Transformation in the Turbulent Teens: WBCSD Annual Report 2010–11* (Geneva: WBCSD, 2011): 43.

214 www.csr360gpn.org/partners, accessed June 15, 2012.

215 Interview with Sue Adkins, CSR360 GPN Director and BITC International Director, February 2012.

216 www2.icco.nl/en/about-icco; for a description of project see: www2.icco.nl/en/projects/project&project = 30, accessed August 29, 2012.

217 Comparing the difference between companies participating in the start year of each Empresa organization and 2009, there was an increase of 586% from 385 companies to 2,643. Leading this trend is Instituto Ethos, Brazil (11 companies in 1998; 1,340 in 2009), followed by the Mexican Center for Philanthropy (CEMEFI) (28 companies in 1988; 495 in 2009) and Acción RSE, Chile (14 in 2000; 93 in 2009). Other organizations also had significant membership growth: Tucumán Foundation (Argentina) and Fundemas (El Salvador) grew by 400%; LEADERS (Uruguay) by 316%; FUNDAHRSE (Honduras) by 275%; and AED (Costa Rica) by 144%. Source: Fundación AVINA and M. Korin, *En busca de la sostenibilidad. El camino de la Responsabilidad Social Empresarial en América Latina y la contribución de la Fundación AVINA* (Buenos Aires: Fundación AVINA, 2011).

218 Sources: Interview with Yanina Kowszyk, Director Empresa, June 2012; Fundación AVINA and M. Korin, *En busca de la sostenibilidad. El camino de la Responsabilidad Social Empresarial en América Latina y la contribución de la Fundación AVINA* (Buenos Aires: Fundación AVINA, 2011); W. Visser and N. Tolhurst (eds.), *The World Guide to CSR* (Sheffield, UK: Greenleaf Publishing, 2010).

219 NEPAD is the government-led New Partnership for Africa's Development. The NEPAD Business Foundation (NBF) has evolved from its original structure as the NEPAD Business Group, which was formed at the request of the South African Presidency in June 2002. NBF was established in 2005 as a fully operational non-profit membership organization to enable South African companies to partner with their counterparts elsewhere in Africa in contributing to the economic growth and social development goals of NEPAD. NBF provides a network for its members to discuss, debate, share ideas and collaborate with government and other stakeholders.

220 World Bank, *Africa's Future and the World Bank's Support to It* (Washington, DC: World Bank, 2011).

221 *The Economist*, "Africa's Hopeful Economies," *The Economist*, December 3, 2011.

222 M.E. Porter and M.R. Kramer, "Creating Shared Value," *Harvard Business Review* 89.1/2 (January 2011): 62-77.

223 The CEOs or senior directors of the following business-led corporate responsibility coalitions were part of this informal network and attended the 2006 meeting hosted by the CSR Initiative, Harvard Kennedy School: AccountAbility; Asian Institute of Management; Business and Society Program, Aspen Institute; Business for Social Responsibility; Business in the Community; Canadian Business for Social Responsibility; Center for Business Ethics, Russia; Conference Board Center for Corporate Citizenship; Boston College; CERES; Econsense; Global Reporting Initiative; International Business Leaders Forum; Maala; Philippine Business for Social Progress; SustainAbility; Tellus Institute; UN Global Compact; and World Economic Forum.

224 From summary notes from CEOs meeting, July 24–26, 2006, with minor editing.

Chapter 11

225 Beginning in 1989, BITC Northern Ireland's local leadership successfully engaged a generation of younger business leaders from both communities, who were prepared to take personal security risks, as well as professional reputational risks, to break free of the entrenched mentality of the province at that time, and to support community entrepreneurs and development organizations across the religious divide. Through a creative mix of good timing, creativity and innovation, clever customization of relevant national BITC programs, intense networking and dogged, good-humoured persistence to wear down opposition, BITC NI helped change the image and self-image of the province and provided glimpses of an alternative, better future. This also involved organizational risk-taking. One example was when the populist *Sun* newspaper ran critical front-page stories about BITC NI's program to provide business mentors to "lifers" released from prison on license – people convicted, often as teenagers, of sectarian murders who were being

released 10–15 years later. Once the politicians had reached their ground-breaking Good Friday Agreement peace settlement, BITC NI extended its activities further. Among other activities, it quietly provided business mentors and *pro bono* assistance from businesses to help the Royal Ulster Constabulary as it transitioned to become the non-sectarian Police Service of Northern Ireland, with a new culture and mind-set.

226 Private comment to author.

227 R.B. Reich, *Supercapitalism* (New York: Knopf, 2007). To be clear, Reich is criticizing CSR and its proponents rather than corporate responsibility coalitions specifically.

228 Corporate Watch, *What's Wrong with Corporate Social Responsibility?* (Corporate Watch Report 2006; Oxford: Corporate Watch, 2006, www.corporatewatch.org/download.php?id = 55, accessed June 23, 2012).

229 Greenpeace, *Who's Holding Us Back? How Carbon-Intensive Industry is Preventing Effective Climate Legislation* (Amsterdam: Greenpeace International, 2011).

230 Ibid: 13.

231 Similarly, in Northern Ireland it could be argued that the lack of local government at the time and business alienation – particularly of younger up-and-coming business leaders – from the local, sectarian political party process helped BITC to grow so rapidly and effectively in the early 1990s in the province.

232 BRICS: Brazil, Russia, India, China plus South Africa; MIST: Mexico, Indonesia, South Korea and Turkey – terms coined by economist Jim O'Neill of Goldman Sachs.

Chapter 12

233 P. Lacy, T. Cooper, R. Hayward and L. Neuberger, *A New Era of Sustainability: Global Compact–Accenture CEO Survey 2010* (New York: UN Global Compact/Accenture, 2010).

234 Ceres and Sustainalytics, *The Road to 2020: Corporate Progress on the Ceres Roadmap for Sustainability* (Boston, MA: Ceres/Sustainalytics, 2012). The joint report evaluated the progress of 600 large publicly traded companies against their governance, stakeholder engagement, disclosure and performance on environmental and social issues. In order to illustrate progress in these areas, company performance results were categorized across four tiers: Setting the Pace (Tier 1), Making Progress (Tier 2), Getting on Track (Tier 3), and Starting Out (Tier 4).

235 P. Lacy, "Why Only 'True North' and Not 'Magnetic North' Can Ultimately Get Us to Scale at Speed on Sustainable Business," Internal Discussion Paper, Accenture, 2012.

236 J. Ruggie, *Guiding Principles on Business and Human Rights: Implementing the United Nations "Protect, Respect and Remedy" Framework* (Report of the Special Representative of the Secretary-General on the Issue of Human Rights and Transnational Corporations and Other Business Enterprises; New York: United Nations, Human Rights Council, March 2011).

237 P. Lacy, "Why Only 'True North' and Not 'Magnetic North' Can Ultimately Get Us to Scale at Speed on Sustainable Business," Internal Discussion Paper, Accenture, 2012; P. Lacy, "Where Is 'True North' for Sustainable Business?" *Ethical Corporation*, October 6, 2012.

238 World Economic Forum, *Global Risks 2012: An Initiative of the Risk Response Network* (Geneva: World Economic Forum, 2012).

Chapter 13

239 P. Lacy, T. Cooper, R. Hayward and L. Neuberger, *A New Era of Sustainability: Global Compact–Accenture CEO Survey 2010* (New York: UN Global Compact/Accenture, 2010).

240 J.F. Rischard, *High Noon: 20 Global Problems, 20 Years to Solve Them* (New York: Basic Books, 2002). One of Rischard's solutions to the global governance deficit was global issues networks, which would bring together interested individuals and organizations from governments, international institutions, civil society and business to share research, thinking and experience on critical global challenges.

241 S. Waddell, *Global Action Networks: Creating Our future Together* (New York/Basingstoke, UK: Palgrave Macmillan 2012).

242 thepartneringinitiative.org.

243 International Monetary Fund World Economic Outlook (April 2012) – extrapolating only for what the IMF analyses separately as emerging economies (Russia, China, India, Brazil, Mexico, South Africa and Nigeria).

244 Ibid. Figures for BRIC only: 42.1% population and 25.9% GDP at purchasing power parity.

245 UN Global Compact LEAD and Business for Social Responsibility, *New Geographies of Corporate Sustainability: Emerging Market Perspectives for Rio + 20* (New York: UN Global Compact LEAD and Business for Social Responsibility, 2012).

246 Ibid.

247 Ipsos MORI research for BITC and the UK Small Business Consortium, 2002.

248 For a discussion of how to engage SMEs across Europe for responsible business see D. Grayson and T. Dodd, *Small Is Sustainable (And Beautiful!) Encouraging European Smaller Enterprises To Be Sustainable* (Doughty Centre Occasional Paper; Bedford, UK: Doughty Centre, Cranfield School of Management, 2008, www.networkedcranfield.com/doughty/Document Library/ Occasional papers/Small is Sustainable.pdf, accessed July 23, 2012).

249 World Business Council for Sustainable Development, *Changing Pace: Public Policy Options to Scale and Accelerate Business Action Towards Vision 2050* (Geneva: World Business Council for Sustainable Development, 2012, /www.wbcsd.org/Pages/EDocument/EDocumentDetails.aspx?I D = 14622&NoSearchContextKey = true, accessed August 14, 2012).

250 www.theiirc.org, accessed August 31, 2012.

251 Cradle to Cradle© is a biomimetic approach to the design of systems. It models human industry on nature's processes in which materials are viewed as nutrients circulating in healthy, safe metabolisms. It is a holistic economic, industrial and social framework that seeks to create systems that are not just efficient but essentially waste free. The current model is based on a system of "lifecycle development" initiated by Michael Braungart and colleagues at the Germany-based consultancy Environmental Protection Encouragement Agency in the 1990s. In partnership with Braungart, William McDonough published *Cradle to Cradle: Remaking the Way We Make Things* (San Francisco: North Point Press, 2002), which is an effective manifesto for Cradle-to-Cradle design that gives specific details of how to achieve the model. www.mcdonough.com/cradle_to_ cradle.htm, accessed July 23, 2012.

252 Based on purchasing power parity, Goldman Sachs, quoted in WBCSD, "Vision 2050," estimates c. 100 million a year, and Accenture, "New Paths to Growth: The Age of Aggregation," *Outlook* 3 (2011), suggests c. 150 million a year extra to 2030.

253 Nudge theories contend that it is possible to design environments that make it more likely for individuals to act in their own interests, and that so-called "choice architecture" can be established to nudge individuals in beneficial directions without restricting the full menu of choices available to them. These theories were popularized in R. Thaler and C. Sunstein, *Nudge: Improving Decisions about Health, Wealth, and Happiness* (New Haven, CT: Yale, 2008).

254 T.L. Friedman, "China Needs Its Own Dream," *New York Times*, October 2, 2012.

255 www.weforum.org/issues/sustainable-consumption, accessed August 29, 2012.

256 For further discussion see D. Grayson, "Future Sustainable Growth: Capitalism That Works," *Ethical Corporation*, September 15, 2010; and D. Grayson with M. McLaren, "Re-booting Capitalism: The Action Agenda for Business," *Ethical Corporation*, March 5, 2012.

257 *Financial Times*, "Ruling Capitalism," editorial, January 26, 2012.

258 *Financial Times* editorial, April 22, 2001.

259 See, for example, *The Economist* special report on Corporate Social Responsibility, January 17, 2008, and *The Economist*, "Good Business; Nice Beaches: Corporate Social Responsibility Is Evolving, and Becoming a Little Less Flaky," Schumpeter column, *The Economist*, May 19, 2012.

Chapter 14

260 GlobeScan and Sustainability, *Global Expert Perspectives on the State of Sustainable Development: Down to Business: Leading to Rio + 20 and Beyond* (Regeneration Roadshow White Paper, www.globescan.com/commentary-and-analysis/press-releases/press-releases-2012/207-down-to-business-leading-at-rio20-and-beyond.html, accessed August 7, 2012).

261 www.basd2012.org, accessed August 30, 2012.

262 This transformer role has been played very effectively for almost 20 years by John Heaslip, CEO of BITC Northern Ireland, who has adopted some of the national BITC programs, rejected others, modified some and also taken up some developed by other organizations – in each case based on an assessment of needs and possibilities in Northern Ireland at the time.

Chapter 15

263 www.wbcsd.org/changingpace.aspx, accessed July 30, 2012.

264 D.S. Landes, *The Wealth and Poverty of Nations: Why Some Are So Rich and Some So Poor* (New York/London: W.W. Norton, 1999): 524.

265 Commencement Address by Paul Hawken to the Class of 2009, University of Portland, May 3, 2009, www.up.edu/commencement/default.aspx?cid = 9456&pid = 3144, accessed August 7, 2012.

Profile 1

266 S. Waddock, *The Difference Makers: How Social and Institutional Entrepreneurs Created the Corporate Responsibility Movement* (Sheffield, UK: Greenleaf, Publishing, 2008): 202-203.

267 GlobeScan Coalitions Survey, 2012.

268 Business for Social Responsibility, *Redefining Leadership: BSR Report 2010* (San Francisco: Business for Social Responsibility, 2011).

269 BSR, *BSR at 20: Accelerating Progress* (New York: BSR, www.bsr.org/pdfs/reports/bsr-at-20-report.pdf accessed October 28, 2012).

270 Ibid.

Profile 2

271 For the current list of Board members see: www.bitc.org.uk/about_bitc/leadership_at_bitc/our_board_and_governance/index.html, accessed June 26, 2012.

272 Figures provided by Gail Greengross, BITC Communications Director, March 2012.

273 Now Lord Sheppard of Didgemere. Grand Metropolitan subsequently merged with Guinness to form Diageo.

274 M.E. Porter and M.R. Kramer, "Creating Shared Value," *Harvard Business Review* 89.1/2 (January 2011): 62-77.

275 The phrase was first used by the late John Smith, who led the British Labour Party in opposition from 1992 until his early death in 1994. It became the mantra of the New Labour modernizers. The concept, however, had been at the heart of BITC's Work in Society project and presentation for member companies developed 1992–94.

276 The then Prime Minister's remark about "now for those inner cities" probably referred to future election strategy, but O'Brien chose to interpret that Mrs. Thatcher wanted to tackle urban deprivation.

277 The merger was designed to reduce confusion in the marketplace and duplication of activity and to achieve better value for money. In practice, the BITC business-led culture prevailed over the more community-focused ARC. By summer 2007, only one person on the UK staff team remained from the old ARC.

278 The original BITC regional directors in the mid-1980s had been senior secondees (executives on loan) from member companies such as Neville Martin (Marks & Spencer) for North-East

England, George Pragnall (ICI) for the North-West and Tony Weddle for the East Midlands. These early pioneers had had to operate with only minimal office back-up and staff support.

279 See: *What a Difference a Thousand Days Make*, a BITC publication celebrating the three-year partnership with BITC Yorkshire and in the Humber region with Yorkshire Forward (2005), www. bitc.org.uk/resources/publications/1000_days.html, accessed July 26, 2012.

280 www.bitc.org.uk/northern_ireland/what_we_do, accessed June 26, 2012. See also note 225 in Chapter 11

281 Business in the Community, *Winning with Integrity: Summary* (London: Business in the Community, 2000, www.bitc.org.uk/document.rm?id = 8, accessed September 6, 2012).

282 Business in the Community, *Indicators that Count* (London: Business in the Community, 2003, www.bitc.org.uk/document.rm?id = 2089, accessed September 6, 2012).

283 The position BITC took when responding to the CORE bill in Parliament in 2005.

284 For an account of the CORE Coalition advocating mandatory reporting see the campaign's chair: Deborah Doane. See also A. Henriques, *Corporate Truth: The Limits to Transparency* (London: Earthscan, 2007).

285 BITC, Arthur D. Little, Camelot and HBOS, *Director's Guide to Corporate Responsibility Reporting* (London: Business in the Community, 2005).

286 BITC and Radley Yeldar, *Taking Shape: The Future of Corporate Responsibility Communications* (London: Business in the Community, 2007).

287 Now Sir Anthony Cleaver.

288 Companies in the Index were ranked in five quintiles and companies in each quintile were listed in alphabetical order.

289 See, for example, D. Varney, "CSR: More Than a Storm in a Teacup," Corporate Citizenship Briefing, 67 (2002), www.ccbriefing.com/CSR-Management/2002/12/01/csr-more-than-a-storm-in-a-teacup, accessed July 26, 2012.

290 See www.globescan.com.

291 Business in the Community *This Much We Know: Impact Review* (London: Business in the Community, 2007, www.bitc.org.uk/document.rm?id = 6548, accessed September 6, 2012).

292 D. Grayson and A. Hodges, *Corporate Social Opportunity* (Sheffield, UK: Greenleaf Publishing, 2004).

293 www.inkinddirect.org.uk.

294 There was a more successful export to Australia in the 2000s of Cares, the Corporate Responsibility Index and BITC's work with schools,

295 BITC has, however, led a CSR Europe campaign to share good practice across the EU in engaging small and medium-sized enterprises and is now leading a European CSR Alliance Learning Laboratory on enhancing employability through employee volunteering: www.csreurope.org/pages/en/communityengagement.html, accessed September 6, 2012.

296 www.bitc.org.uk/princes_programmes/start, accessed March 23, 2012.

297 www.bitc.org.uk/visioning_the_future, accessed March 23, 2012.

298 www.bitc.org.uk/princes_programmes/the_princes_seeing_is_believing, accessed June 26, 2012.

299 Private interviews with the author.

300 Interviewee, February 2007.

301 Submissions for BITC's Silver Jubilee "Big Tick" Awards for longevity of company–community partnerships repeatedly refer to the trigger from a Seeing is Believing visit or BITC campaign. BITC now has an extensive video library of film clips showing regional and national Awards for Excellence winners. These provide powerful testimonies of the impacts on individuals, businesses, communities, causes and the environment. The Jubilee Commentary (December 2007) also provides many testimonies from individual business leaders; see D. Grayson, *Business-Led Corporate Responsibility Coalitions: Learning from the Example of Business in the Community in the UK – An Insider's Perspective* (London: Business in the Community; Bedford, UK: Doughty Centre for Corporate Responsibility; Cambridge, MA: Kennedy School of Management, Harvard, 2007), from which BITC produced an abridged version as the central part of their 2007 Impact

Review (Annual Report): *This Much We Know* see: www.bitc.org.uk/about_bitc/our_history/our_jubilee_year, accessed July 26, 2012.

302 M.P. Fogarty and I. Christie, *Companies and Communities: Promoting Business Involvement in the Community* (London: Policy Studies Institute, 1991): xiv.

Profile 3

303 www.csreurope.org/pages/en/declaration.html.

304 Davignon serves on a number of corporate and other boards and is, inter alia, chairman of the annual Bilderberg Conference.

305 European Business Network for Social Cohesion, *Gaining from Diversity* (Brussels: EBNSC, 1997).

306 Commission of the European Communities, Lisbon Declaration 2000: www.eu2008.fr/webdav/site/PFUE/shared/import/1205_Strategie_Lisbonne/The_Lisbon_Strategy_EN.pdf, accessed September 6, 2012.

307 Commission of the European Communities, *Promoting a European Framework for Corporate Social Responsibility* (Green Paper COM[2001] 366 final; Brussels: Commission of the European Communities, July 18, 2001, eur-lex.europa.eu/LexUriServ/site/en/com/2001/com2001_0366en01.pdf, accessed July 1, 2012).

308 Commission of the European Communities, *Communication from the Commission Concerning, Corporate Social Responsibility: A Business Contribution to Sustainable Development*, (COM[2002] 347 final; Brussels: Commission of the European Communities, July 2, 2002, eur-lex.europa.eu/LexUriServ/LexUriServ.do?uri = COM:2002:0347:FIN:EN:PDF, accessed July 1, 2012).

309 Ibid.

310 The Platform of European Social NGOs was established in 1995 in response to a Green Paper on European Social Policy. The organization aims at building an inclusive society and promoting the social dimension of the EU. Its members represent a wide spectrum of civil society, including thousands of organizations, associations and voluntary groups at local, regional, national and European level. Their goal is to develop and strengthen a civil dialogue with the institutions of the EU on issues such as human rights and social justice.

311 The roundtables were working meetings of Forum participants with subject experts, with each set of roundtables facilitated by an expert rapporteur (Full disclosure: David Grayson served as the rapporteur for the roundtables on engaging SMEs.)

312 European Multistakeholder Forum on CSR, *Final Results and Recommendations*, July 29, 2004, ec.europa.eu/enterprise/policies/sustainable-business/files/csr/documents/29062004/emsf_final_report_en.pdf, accessed July 1, 2012.

313 www.eabis.org.

314 CSR Europe, *A European Roadmap for Businesses Towards a Sustainable and Competitive Enterprise*, www.csreurope.org/data/files/european_roadmap_for_businesses_2005.pdf, accessed June 26, 2012.

315 European Commission, *Implementing the Partnership for Growth and Jobs: Making Europe a Pole of Excellence on Corporate Social Responsibility on CSR*, (COM[2006] 136 final: Brussels: Commission of the European Communities, March 22, 2006, eur-lex.europa.eu/LexUriServ/LexUriServ.do?uri = COM:2006:0136:FIN:EN:PDF, accessed June 26, 2012.

316 webcast.ec.europa.eu/eutv/portal/archive.html?viewConference = 6016, accessed June 26, 2012.

317 CSR Europe, "The European Cartography on CSR Innovations, Gaps and Future Trends," www.csreurope.org/data/files/european_cartography_2006.pdf, accessed June 26, 2012.

318 For an example of how one of the laboratories – on Market Valuation of Non-Financial Performance (www.csreurope.org/pages/en/market_valuation.html, accessed September 6, 2012) – operated, see SDA Bocconi School of Management, Doughty Centre for Corporate Responsibility at Cranfield School of Management and Vlerick Leuven Gent Management School, *Sustainable Value* (report on behalf of the Academy for Business in Society [EABIS], 2009. investorvalue.org/docs/EabisProjectFinal.pdf, accessed September 6, 2012): 22-26.

319 CSR Europe's Toolbox: Equipping Companies and Stakeholders for a Competitive and Responsible Europe, www.csreurope.org/pages/en/toolbox.html, accessed July 1, 2012.

320 Age Platform Europe, Brussels, www.csreurope.org/data/files/enterprise2020/Project_info/ AGE_solidarintergener-EN.pdf, accessed June 27, 2012.

321 www.csreurope.org/pages/en/business_contribution_ot_the_european_year_for_active_ageing. html.

322 www.csreurope.org/pages/en/csr_in_china_report.html, accessed June 26, 2012 (available to members only).

323 Additional references:
       CSR Europe History: www.csreurope.org/pages/en/history.html, accessed July 31, 2012; *CSR Europe Magazine* January 2001; October 2002; European Business Declaration against Social Exclusion, www.csreurope.org/pages/en/declaration.html, accessed July 31, 2012; D. Grayson, *Business-Led Corporate Responsibility Coalitions: Learning from the Example of Business in the Community in the UK – An Insider's Perspective* (London: Business in the Community; Bedford, UK: Doughty Centre for Corporate Responsibility; Cambridge, MA: Kennedy School of Management, Harvard, 2007); W. Visser, D. Matten, M. Pohl and N. Tolhurst, *The A to Z of Corporate Social Responsibility* (ICCA publication; Chichester, UK: Wiley, 2007); Wan Saiful Wan-Jan, "Defining Corporate Social Responsibility," *Journal of Public Affairs* 6.3/4 (2006): 171-316.

Profile 4

325 Translated from Portuguese.

325 Interview with João Gilberto Azevedo, January 28, 2010.

326 This background information on the history of the Brazilian corporate responsibility movement and the foundation of Instituto Ethos has been taken from E. Raufflet, "Creating the Context for Corporate Responsibility: The Experience of Instituto Ethos, Brazil," *Journal of Corporate Citizenship* 30.1 (2008): 95-106.

327 See Instituto Ethos, "What We Do," www1.ethos.org.br/EthosWeb/pt/1434/o_instituto_ethos/o_ que_fazemos/o_que_fazemos.aspx, accessed July 30, 2012.

328 João Gilberto Azevedo, Instituto Ethos, in interview, January 28, 2010.

329 See also G. Peirão Leal, "A responsabilidade social das empresas," *Folha de São Paulo*, August 7, 1998.

330 João Gilberto Azevedo, Instituto Ethos, in interview, January 28, 2010.

331 The following section is taken from an internal document: P. Itacarambi, "Projeto Ethos 10 anos – versão preliminar_v4," working document for the team and the board [2008].

332 P. Itacarambi, "Projeto Ethos 10 anos – versão preliminar_v4," working document for the team and the board" (2008): 15.

333 Instituto Ethos and Roland Berger, *Plataforma por uma Economia Inclusiva, Verde e Responsável* (Platform for an inclusive, green and responsible economy) (São Paulo, Brazil: Instituto Ethos/ Roland Berger, 2011).

334 Instituto Ethos and Roland Berger, *Plataforma por uma Economia Inclusiva, Verde e Responsável* (Platform for an inclusive, green and responsible economy) (São Paulo, Brazil: Instituto Ethos/ Roland Berger, 2011).

335 In addition, to the sources already quoted, other sources of information consulted by Heiko Spitzeck include: S. Biehler Mateos, "Responsabilidade Social e diferencial de empresas," *Estado de São Paulo*, November 13, 1998; A. Blanco, "Entidades viram negócio para crescer," *Folha de São Paulo*, November 25, 1998; N. Costabile, "Responsabilidade Social comenca a dar lucro," *Estado de São Paulo*, August 17, 1998; *CSR Welt*, "Interview with João Gilberto Azevedo dos Santos, Ethos Institute Brazil," *CSR Welt*, 2009, available at: www.csr-weltweit.de/fileadmin/ inhalte/Dossier/ Ecogerma_2009/Interview_JGAdosSantos_final.pdf (accessed March 2010); *Gazeta Mercantil*, "Transparência na conduta social das empresas," *Gazeta Mercantil*, July 2, 1998; *Gazeta Mercantil*, "Instituto Ethos launches guide for social balances," *Gazeta Mercantil*, June 6, 2001; O. Grajew, "Forum Social Mundial – 10 años," *Folha de São Paulo*, November 29,

2009; D. Grayson,, *Business-Led Corporate Responsibility Coalitions: Learning from the Example of Business in the Community in the UK – An Insider's Perspective* (London: Business in the Community; Bedford, UK: Doughty Centre for Corporate Responsibility; Cambridge, MA: Kennedy School of Management, Harvard, 2007); *Latin Trade*, "The Latin Trade Bravo Business Awards," *Latin Trade*, November 1, 2004; M. O'Brien, "CSR Pays Off," *Latin Finance*, May 1, 2005; T. Smith, 'In Brazil, Companies Help Poor: Da Silva Makes Battle On Poverty Popular," *International Herald Tribune*, April 11, 2003; Instituto Ethos public documents: Instituto Ethos, "Ferramentas de Gestão – Empresas e Responsabilidade Social" (2007); Instituto Ethos, "Sumario Executivo – Relatorio de Sustentabilidade – Instituto Ethos e UniEthos" (2008); Instituto Ethos *et al.*, "Metodologia Tear de Trabalho em Cadeia de Valor" (2007); FGV and Instituto Ethos, "Indicatores de Responsabilidade Social nas Empresas Varejistas" (2005).

Profile 5

336 See www.partnershipbrokers.org, accessed March 23, 2012.

337 J. Nelson, *Business as Partners in Development* (London: International Business Leaders Forum/ United Nations Development Programme/World Bank, 1996); J. Nelson and D. Prescott, *Business and the Millennium Development Goas: A Framework for Action* (London: International Business Leaders Forum/United Nations Development Programme, 2006). J. Nelson, *Building Partnerships: Cooperation between the United Nations System and the Private Sector* (United Nations, 2002).

338 L. Amis, A. Hodges and N. Jeffrey, *Development, Peace and Human Rights in Columbia: A Business Agenda* (London: International Business Leaders Forum, 2006).

339 Prince of Wales Business Leaders Forum, *A Decade of Difference: 1990–2000: Promoting Responsible Business Practices Internationally to Benefit Business And Society* (London: The Prince of Wales Business Leaders Forum, 2000).

340 International Business Leaders Forum, *Redefining Growth for a Sustainable World. IBLF Review 2010–2011*, (London: IBLF, www.iblf.org/en/about-iblf/annual-reviews.aspx).

341 Ibid.

342 Prince of Wales Business Leaders Forum, *A Decade of Difference: 1990–2000: Promoting Responsible Business Practices Internationally to Benefit Business And Society* (London: The Prince of Wales Business Leaders Forum, 2000): 26

Profile 6

343 Kahanoff Foundation, kahanoffcom.tempwebpage.com/about/intro.php, accessed July 31, 2012.

344 The UNDP ranked Israel fourth on a list of the most unequal societies in 2009 based on Gini co-efficient: finance.yahoo.com/news/pf_article_107980.html, accessed June 28, 2012.

345 Shari Arison is an Israeli-American businesswoman and Israel's wealthiest woman. She is the owner of several businesses, the largest among them Bank Hapoalim.

346 www.zionut2000.org.il/index.html, accessed June 28, 2012.

347 www.tase.co.il/TASEEng/MarketData/Indices/Additional/IndexMainDataAdditional.htm?Action = 2&subDataType = 0&IndexId = 150, accessed July 1, 2012.

348 www.maala.org.il, accessed July 31, 2012.

349 J.J. Levine, "Maala Index Indicates a Revolution in Israel's Corporate Philosophy," *Jerusalem Post*, November 19, 2008, www.jpost.com/Business/BusinessFeatures/Article.aspx?id = 121037, accessed July 31, 2012.

350 www.sheatufim.org.il/civilsociety.aspx: PMO Inter Sector Roundtable is a "new platform for effective inter-sector dialogue in Israel, initiated by the Prime Minister's Office (PMO) to create a firm framework for carrying out the policy outlined by the government for inter-sector partnership. Roundtables of Israeli government, philanthropy, business and non-profit organizations meet for the purpose of developing endeavors on a national level. This dialogue is based on the

belief that effective social policy is achieved by agreement, inclusion, and respect for each sector's role and contribution to the society as a whole. The Roundtable serves as a basis for developing ventures, such as the inter-sector emergency coordination headquarters during Operation Cast Lead and the inter-sector economic plan for dealing with the economic crisis."

351 www.sii.org.il/sip_storage/FILES/4/194.pdf, accessed July 26, 2012.

352 Interview with David Grayson, Tel Aviv, June 2, 2012, and subsequent email exchange.

353 The reframing philosophy grew out of Israel's near-death experience in the Yom Kippur War when old mind-sets prevented the Israeli military and intelligence from reading the data available to them, to show the Arab armies were about to attack.

354 "Opening Statement by Mr. Sha Zukang Under-Secretary-General For Economic And Social Affairs Secretary-General of the 2012 UN Conference On Sustainable Development," Tel Aviv, October 25, 2011, www.uncsd2012.org/rio20/content/documents/490Opening statement Mr. Sha Israel EGM rev.pdf, accessed July 1, 2012.

355 *Tikkun olam* (Hebrew: עולם ותיקון) is a Hebrew phrase that means "repairing the world" (or "healing and restoring the world") which suggests humanity's shared responsibility (with the Creator) "to heal, repair and transform the world."

356 Additional sources for this profile: Maala's annual and periodical reviews 1998 to 2010; Maala Ranking 2009, 2010; T. Aharoni, "Maala's Tenth Anniversary," a personal report to the Kahanoff Foundation; D. Grayson, *Business-Led Corporate Responsibility Coalitions: Learning from the Example of Business in the Community in the UK – An Insider's Perspective* (London: Business in the Community; Bedford, UK: Doughty Centre for Corporate Responsibility; Cambridge, MA: Kennedy School of Management, Harvard, 2007).

Profile 7

357 For a detailed insider's account of the CBM see "Address by T.N. Chapman and M.B. Hofmeyr, August 10, 1994, Business Statesman of the Year Award, Harvard Business School Club of South Africa.'

358 Numbers were reduced further with the hiving off of the Diversity Council and other changes in 2012 and stood at 18 in August 2012, prior to recruitment to support new areas of focus.

359 The new South African Companies Act 2009, which came into force in 2011, requires public companies to establish social and ethics committees that *inter alia* must review performance against the ten principles of the UNGC: xbma.org/forum/south-african-update-new-south-african-companies-act-modernizes-south-african-corporate-law, accessed September 10, 2012.

360 www.btrust.org.za, accessed March 23, 2012.

361 Business Trust, "Working Together 1999–2011," www.btrust.org.za/library/uploads/documents/Business Trust 12 Year Report.pdf, accessed September 10, 2012.

362 National Business Initiative, "Building a South African Future: The First Ten Years of the National Business Initiative," www.nbi.org.za/About%20NBI/Pages/Our%20History.aspx, accessed August 14, 2012.

363 Chairman's Review 2010: www.nbi.org.za/Lists/Publications/Attachments/1/ChairmansReview2010.pdf, accessed September 10, 2012.

Profile 8

364 V.E. Tan and M.P. Bolante, *Philippine Business for Social Progress: A Case Study* (Synergos Institute Voluntary Sector Financing Program Case Studies of Foundation-Building in Africa, Asia and Latin America; New York: Synergos Institute, 1997) .

365 PBSP Media Center, "PBSP touts 'PlaCEs' as business solution platform vs. poverty", press release, February 3, 2012, pbsp.org.ph/index.php?option = com_content&view = article&id = 203:pbsp-touts-places-as-business-solution-platform-vs-poverty&catid = 77:pbsp-latest&Itemid = 172, accessed August 14, 2012.

366 57-75.org, accessed October 25, 2012.

367 As of July 2012, pledges received have reached PHP1 billion, PHP45 million had been received and more than 1,000 schools have been constructed since the campaign started in 2011.

368 Interview with Rafael Lopa, Bangkok, October 25, 2012.

369 Exchange with PBSP, July 2012.

370 www.theglobalfund.org/en/mediacenter/pressreleases/Global_Fund_resumes_TB_grant_in_the_Philippines, accessed June 28, 2012.

371 Interview with Rafael Lopa, Bangkok, October 25, 2012.

372 Source: Peter Brew, Former Director, IBLF.

373 "The Son Also Rises: Who is Noynoy Aquino?" GMA News, September 9, 2009, www.gmanetwork.com/news/story/171863/news/nation/the-son-also-rises-who-is-noynoy-aquino, accessed June 29, 2012.

374 PBSP co-founder Howard Dee of United Laboratories quoted in V.E. Tan and M.P. Bolante, *Philippine Business for Social Progress: A Case Study* (New York: Synergos Institute, 1997): 17.

375 See M.E. Porter and M.R. Kramer, "Creating Shared Value," *Harvard Business Review* 89.1/2 (January 2011): 62-77.

376 J. Kania and M. Kramer, "Collective Impact," *Stanford Social Innovation Review*, 48 (Winter 2011, www.ssireview.org/articles/entry/collective_impact, accessed September 10, 2012).

Profile 9

377 World Commission on Environment and Development, *Our Common Future* (Brundtland Report; Oxford, UK: Oxford University Press, 1987).

378 L. Timberlake, *Catalyzing Change: A Short History of the WBCSD* (Geneva: WBCSD, 2006, www.wbcsd.ch/DocRoot/acZUEFxTAKIvTs0KOtii/catalyzing-change.pdf, accessed September 12, 2012): 11.

379 S. Schmidheiny and Business Council for Sustainable Development, *Changing Course: A Global Business Perspective on Development and the Environment* (Cambridge, MA: MIT, 1992).

380 L. Timberlake, *Catalyzing Change: A Short History of the WBCSD* (Geneva: WBCSD, 2006, www.wbcsd.ch/DocRoot/acZUEFxTAKIvTs0KOtii/catalyzing-change.pdf, accessed September 12, 2012): 18.

381 List provided by WBCSD, August 2012.

382 WBCSD, *Rio + 20 and Beyond: Business Solutions for a Sustainable World* (Geneva: WBCSD, 2012, www.wbcsd.org/Pages/EDocument/EDocumentDetails.aspx?ID = 14588&NoSearchContextKey = true, accessed September 10, 2012).

383 Email exchange with Kija Kummer, WBCSD, August 2012.

384 www.wbcsd.org/vision2050.aspx, accessed September 12, 2012.

385 WBCSD, *Rio + 20 and Beyond: Business Solutions for a Sustainable World* (Geneva: WBCSD, 2012, www.wbcsd.org/Pages/EDocument/EDocumentDetails.aspx?ID = 14588&NoSearchContextKey = true, accessed September 10, 2012): 8.

386 L. Timberlake, *Catalyzing Change: A Short History of the WBCSD* (Geneva: WBCSD, 2006, www.wbcsd.ch/DocRoot/acZUEFxTAKIvTs0KOtii/catalyzing-change.pdf, accessed September 12, 2012).

387 Ibid.

388 WBCSD, *Changing Pace: Public Policy Options to Scale and Accelerate Action Towards Vision 2050* (Geneva: WBCSD, 2012).

389 L. Timberlake, *Catalyzing Change: A Short History of the WBCSD* (Geneva: WBCSD, 2006, www.wbcsd.ch/DocRoot/acZUEFxTAKIvTs0KOtii/catalyzing-change.pdf, accessed September 12, 2012): 31.

390 Ibid: 67.

391 Ibid: 72.

392 P. Bakker, "It's time to scale up sustainable solutions," The President's blog, January 27, 2012, president.wbcsd.org/2012/01/its-time-to-scale-up-sustainable-solutions.html - more, accessed September 10, 2012.

393 J. Confino, "Rio + 20: WBCSD president says the future of the planet rests on business," Guardian Sustainable Business Blog, June 22, 2012, www.guardian.co.uk/sustainable-business/rio-20-business-sustainable-development, accessed July 30, 2012; and author interview with Peter Paul Van de Wijs, then Communications Director, WBCSD, in Geneva, July 4, 2012.

394 Ibid.

395 EABIS, *Sustainable Value : Corporate Responsibility, Market Valuation and Measuring the Financial and Non-financial Performance of the Firm: Final Research Report* (EABIS Research Project; Bedford, UK: Doughty Centre, Cranfield University of Management, on behalf of the CSR Europe Laboratory, 2009).

Profile 10

396 Source: J. Nelson and T.F. Yosie, "The Transformation of Sustainable Development," Blog (www.greenbiz.com, June 8, 2009).

Profile 11

397 Examples include: the UN Conference on Environment and Development in Rio de Janeiro, 1992; the International Conference on Population and Development in Cairo, 1994; the World Summit on Social Development in Copenhagen in 1995; the fourth World Conference on Women in Beijing, 1995; and the second UN Conference on Human Settlements in Istanbul, 1996.

398 The full text of this seminal speech can be found on the UNGC website at www.un.org/News/Press/docs/1999/19990201.sgsm6881.html, accessed November 4, 2012.

399 K. Annan, with N. Mousavizadeh. *Interventions: A Life in War and Peace* (New York: Penguin Press, 2012).

400 Latham & Watkins LLP, *The Importance of Voluntarism* (New York: Latham & Watkins LLP, 2009).

401 United Nations Global Compact, *Annual Review: Anniversary edition* (New York: UNGC, 2010).

402 Correspondence with authors, November 3, 2012.

403 For more details on the UN Guiding Principles on Business and Human Rights see: www.business-humanrights.org/SpecialRepPortal/Home, accessed July 31, 2012.

404 www.unglobalcompact.org/COP/differentiation_programme.html, accessed July 31, 2012.

405 For further details on these initiatives see: sustainableenergyforall.org; scalingupnutrition.org; everywomaneverychild.org; globaleducationfirst.org.

406 *Catalyzing Transformational Partnerships between the United Nations and Business* (United Nations).

407 For summaries of the two main business-hosted events at Rio + 20, see United Nations Global Compact, "Rio + 20 Corporate Sustainability Forum: Overview and Outcomes," June 2012, www.unglobalcompact.org; Business Action for Sustainable Development, "Scale Up: Business Day Output Document," June 2012, www.basd.org basd2012.org/project/business-day-output-document-released; and see also www.wbcsd.org.

408 For further information on the Principles for Responsible Investment initiative see www.unpri.org.

409 For further information on the Principles for Responsible Management Education initiative see: unprme.org.

410 For further information on the CEO Water Mandate see: ceowatermandate.org.

411 For further information on the Caring for Climate Initiative see: caringforclimate.org.

412 For further information on the Women's Empowerment Principles see: weprinciples.org.

413 UNGC and Bertelsmann, *Strategy for the Commons* (New York: UNGC/Bertelsmann, 2012, www.unglobalcompact.org/docs/networks_around_world_doc/A_Strategy_for_the_Commons.pdf, accessed July 26, 2012).

414 www.unglobalcompact.org/HowToParticipate/Lead/LEADactivities.html, accessed July 26, 2012.

415 G. Kell, "12 Years Later: Reflections on the Growth of the UN Global Compact," *Business & Society*, October 8, 2012, bas.sagepub.com/content/early/2012/10/28/0007650312460466, accessed December 13, 2012.

416 www.unglobalcompact.org/newsandevents/news_archives/2004_06_09.html, accessed July 26, 2012. See also: J. Nelson, *Building Partnerships: Cooperation Between the United Nations System and the Private Sector* (New York: United Nations Department of Public Information, 2002): 135-48.

417 J. Bendell, "What If We Are Failing?" *Journal of Corporate Citizenship* 38 (2010): 27-31.

418 Global Compact Critics, "Reclaim the UN from corporate culture," blog globalcompactcritics. blogspot.co.uk accessed July 26, 2012; Global Policy Forum, "Whose Partnership For Whose Development?" (Speaking notes of a Hearing at the United Nations, Geneva, July 4, 2007, sponsored by CETIM, Global Policy Forum, Berne Declaration, Greenpeace International, Misereor and Corporate Accountability International, 2007).

419 P.L. Fall and M.M. Zahran, *United Nations Corporate Partnerships: The Role and Functioning of the Global Compact"* (JIU/REP/2010/9; New York: UN Joint Inspection Unit, 2010); P. Utting and A. Zammit, *Beyond Pragmatism: Appraising UN–Business Partnerships* (United Nations Research Institute for Social Development, 2006).

420 A. Rasche and G. Kell, *The United Nations Global Compact: Achievements, Trends and Challenges* (Cambridge, UK: Cambridge University Press, 2010).

421 A. Rasche, " 'A Necessary Supplement': What the United Nations Global Compact Is and Is Not," *Business & Society* 48.4 (2009): 511-37.

422 www.unglobalcompact.org/docs/news_events/9.1_news_archives/2011_03_24/SirMark_LetterJIU110325.pdf, accessed July 26, 2012.

423 M. McIntosh, S. Waddock and G. Kell, (eds.), *Learning to Talk: Corporate Citizenship and the Development of the UN Global Compact* (Sheffield, UK: Greenleaf Publishing, 2004).

424 S. Waddell, "The Global Compact: An Organizational Innovation to Realize UN Principles," presented to the Global Compact Donor Group, October 26, 2011, posted to UNGC website, November 2011, www.unglobalcompact.org/docs/news_events/9.1_news_archives/2011_11_16/UNGC_Organizational_Innovation_Note.pdf, accessed November 4, 2012.

425 G. Kell, "12 Years Later: Reflections on the Growth of the UN Global Compact," *Business & Society*, October 8, 2012, bas.sagepub.com/content/early/2012/10/28/0007650312460466, accessed December 13, 2012.

Profile 12

426 M. Zwick, A. Reyes and K. Schwab, *The World Economic Forum: A Partner in Shaping History – The First 40 Years 1971–2010* (Geneva: World Economic Forum, 2009).

427 Ibid: 16.

428 This "Code of Ethics" was published in R. Fiedler-Winter, *Die Moral der Manager* (Stuttgart: Seewald, 1977).

429 M. Zwick, A. Reyes and K. Schwab, *The World Economic Forum: A Partner in Shaping History – The First 40 Years 1971–2010* (Geneva: World Economic Forum, 2009): 72.

430 Ibid: 2.

431 In 2012, WEF's Industry Partner Groups were as follows: Agriculture, Food and Beverage; Automotive; Aviation and Travel; Banking and Capital Markets; Chemicals; Energy – Oil and Gas; Energy – Renewable Energy Shapers; Energy – Utilities and Technology; Global Health and Healthcare; Information Technology; Infrastructure and Urban Development; Institutional Investors, Sovereign Wealth Funds and Family Offices; Insurance and Asset Management; Media, Entertainment and Information; Mining and Metals; Private Investors – Private Equity, Hedge Funds and Venture capital; Professional Services; Retail and Consumer Goods; Supply Chain and Transportation; and Telecommunications.

432 S.P. Huntington, *Who Are We?: The Challenges to America's National Identity* (Simon & Schuster, 2004), quoted by Timothy Garton Ash, "Davos Man's Death Wish," *The Guardian*, February 3,

2005, www.guardian.co.uk/world/2005/feb/03/globalisation.comment, accessed November 21, 2012.

433 Kofi Annan, "Klaus Schwab: Creating a Place That's Like the UN – Only More Fun," in "Time 100: Scientists & Thinkers," *Time*, May 14, 2007.

434 K. Schwab and C. Smadja, "Join Forces to Solve the Shareholder–Stakeholder Equation," *International Herald Tribune*, January 31, 1997.

435 HRH The Prince of Wales, Address to the Annual Meeting of the World Economic Forum, Davos, February 4, 1992.

436 Hillary Rodham Clinton, Address to the Annual Meeting of the World Economic Forum, Davos, February 2, 1998.

437 Kofi Annan, Address to the Annual Meeting of the World Economic Forum, Davos, January 31, 1999, www.unglobalcompact.org/NewsAndEvents/Speeches.html#remarks, accessed July 31, 2012.

438 Bill Gates, Address to the World Economic Forum, Davos, January 24, 2008, www.microsoft. com/en-us/news/exec/billg/speeches/2008/01-24WEFDavos.aspx, accessed July 31, 2012.

439 www.unilever.com/sustainable-living/betterlivelihoods/impact-studies/indonesia, accessed July 31, 2012.

440 World Economic Forum, *Corporate Citizenship: The Leadership Challenge for CEOs and Boards* (Geneva: World Economic Forum/The Prince of Wales International Business Leaders Forum, 2001, https://members.weforum.org/pdf/GCCI/GCC_CEOstatement.pdf, accessed July 20, 2012).

441 World Economic Forum, *Values and Value: Communicating the Strategic Importance of Corporate Citizenship to Investors* (Geneva: World Economic Forum/The Prince of Wales International Business Leaders Forum, 2004).

442 World Economic Forum with McKinsey & Company, *Realizing a New Vision for Agriculture: A Roadmap for Stakeholders* (Geneva: World Economic Forum, 2011); World Economic Forum with McKinsey & Company, *Putting the New Vision for Agriculture in Practice: A Transformation is Happening* (World Economic Forum, 2012).

443 M. Zwick, A. Reyes and K. Schwab, *The World Economic Forum: A Partner in Shaping History – The First 40 Years 1971–2010* (Geneva: World Economic Forum, 2009): 263.

444 World Economic Forum, *Stakeholder Perceptions and Suggestions: Responsible Mining Development Initiative 2010* (Geneva: World Economic Forum, 2010); World Economic Forum, *Responsible Mining Development Initiative, 2011* (Geneva: World Economic Forum, 2011).

445 World Economic Forum, *17th PACI Task Force Meeting. Executive Summary.* April 18–19, 2012, www.weforum.org/issues/partnering-against-corruption-initiative, accessed November 19, 2012.

446 M. Zwick, A. Reyes and K. Schwab, *The World Economic Forum: A Partner in Shaping History – The First 40 Years 1971–2010* (Geneva: World Economic Forum, 2009): 263.

447 World Economic Forum, "Fact Sheet: The Green Growth Action Alliance," World Economic Forum, www3.weforum.org/.../WEF_B20_GreenGrowthActionAlliance_Factsheet_2012.pdf, accessed November 19, 2012.

448 World Economic Forum, *The Forum of Young Global Leader: Shaping the Future* (Geneva: WEF, www.weforum.org/community/forum-young-global-leaders, accessed September 2012): 12.

449 www.ashoka.org, accessed November 19, 2012.

450 www.weforum.org/content/pages/deans-vision-global-leadership-fellows-programme, accessed September 2012.

451 M. Zwick, A. Reyes and K. Schwab, *The World Economic Forum: A Partner in Shaping History – The First 40 Years 1971–2010* (Geneva: World Economic Forum, 2009): 267.

452 Ibid: 262.

458 K. Schwab, "Global Corporate Citizenship: Working with Governments and Civil Society," *Foreign Affairs* 87.1 (2008).

Index